Wiley CIAexcel Exam Review 2016

Wiley CIAexcel Exam Review 2016

Part 2, Internal Audit Practice

S. Rao Vallabhaneni

WILEY

Cover image: John Wiley & Sons, Inc.
Cover design: John Wiley & Sons, Inc.

Published by John Wiley & Sons, Inc., Hoboken, New Jersey.

Published simultaneously in Canada.

For general information on our other products and services or for technical support, please contact our Customer Care Department within the United States at (800) 762-2974, outside the United States at (317) 572-3993 or fax (317) 572-4002.

Wiley publishes in a variety of print and electronic formats and by print-on-demand. Some material included with standard print versions of this book may not be included in e-books or in print-on-demand. If this book refers to media such as a CD or DVD that is not included in the version you purchased, you may download this material at http://booksupport.wiley.com. For more information about Wiley products, visit www.wiley.com.

Library of Congress Cataloging-in-Publication Data:

ISBN 978-1-119-24207-9 (Paperback)
ISBN 978-1-119-24216-1 (ebk)
ISBN 978-1-119-24214-7 (ebk)
ISBN 978-1-119-24140-9 (Part 1)
ISBN 978-1-119-24217-8 (Part 3)
ISBN 978-1-119-24206-2 (Set)

Printed in the United States of America

10 9 8 7 6 5 4 3 2

Contents

Preface   vii

CIA Exam Study Preparation Resources   xi

CIA Exam-Taking Tips and Techniques   xiii

CIA Exam Content Specifications   xv

Domain 1   Managing the Internal Audit Function   **1**

   1.1   Strategic Role of Internal Audit   1
   1.2   Operational Role of Internal Audit   25
   1.3   Risk-Based Internal Audit Plan   302
   1.4   Sample Practice Questions   316

Domain 2   Managing Individual Engagements   **323**

   2.1   Plan Engagements   323
   2.2   Supervise Engagements   347
   2.3   Communicate Engagement Results   361
   2.4   Monitor Engagement Outcomes   382
   2.5   Sample Practice Questions   385

Domain 3   Fraud Risks and Controls   **391**

   3.1   Types of Fraud   391
   3.2   Controls to Prevent or Detect Fraud   394
   3.3   Audit Tests to Detect Fraud   396
   3.4   Integrating Analytical Relationships to Detect Fraud   405
   3.5   Interrogation or Investigative Techniques   415
   3.6   Forensic Auditing   423
   3.7   Use of Computers in Analyzing Data for Fraud and Crime   427
   3.8   Sample Practice Questions   436

Sample Practice Questions, Answers, and Explanations   439

Glossary   469

Index   495

Preface

The Certified Internal Auditor (CIA) Examination is a program of The Institute of Internal Auditors (IIA), Inc. The CIA Examination certifies a person as a professional internal auditor and is intended to measure the knowledge, skills, and competency required in the field of internal auditing. The CIA designation is the mark of an expert in internal auditing. The new exam syllabus, effective from the middle of 2013, tests knowledge at two levels of comprehension—proficiency and awareness, as indicated in the IIA's content specifications outlines (www.theiia.org). These levels require allocating more preparation time to proficiency-level topics and less time to awareness-level topics. The scope of the new CIA Exam consists of three parts, which are divided into 14 domains; there are three domains in Part 1, three domains in Part 2, and eight domains in Part 3.

A series of review books has been prepared for the candidate to utilize for all three parts of the new CIA Exam. Each part's review book includes a comprehensive coverage of the subject matter (theory) based on the new exam syllabus followed by some sample practice multiple-choice (M/C) questions with answers and explanations (practice). The sample practice M/C questions included in the review book are taken from Wiley's Web-based online test software to show you the flavor of the questions. Each part's review book contains a glossary section, which is a good source for answering M/C questions on the CIA Exam.

The scope of the Part 2 review book covers internal audit practice. It has three domains: Domain 1 deals with managing the internal audit function. Domain 2 addresses managing individual engagements. Domain 3 covers fraud risks and controls. The Part 2 review book contains 104 sample practice M/C questions with answers and explanations, and a glossary section.

The objective of this review book is to provide single-source, comprehensive review materials to assist the CIA Exam candidate in successfully preparing for the exam. The major highlights are presented next.

- Easy to navigate, comprehend, learn, and apply the subject matter since it was written from a student's perspective in a textbook style and format.

- The review book contains fully developed theories and concepts with complete thoughts as opposed to mere outlines. The candidate needs to know more than outlines to pass the difficult CIA Exam.

- Each theoretical domain in the review book is shown with a range of percentages to indicate the relative weights given to that domain in the exam. Candidates are expected to plan their study time in proportion to the relative weights suggested (i.e., more time and effort to higher percentages, and vice versa).

- CIA Exam content specifications included at the beginning of the book show the level of difficulty for each topic in the CIA Exam expressed as (A) for Awareness and (P) for Proficiency. Awareness means candidates must exhibit awareness (i.e., knowledge of terminology and fundamentals) in these topic areas. Proficiency means candidates must exhibit proficiency (i.e., thorough understanding and ability to apply concepts) in these topic areas.

- Greater use of comparisons and contrasts of subject matter make the key concepts come alive by providing lasting impressions. These comparisons show interrelationships between key concepts.

- Parts 1 and 2 theory of the review books offer full coverage of all the IIA's new *International Standards,* all of the Practice Advisories, and the Code of Ethics in their entirety, effective from January 2011 (i.e., International Professional Practice Framework (IPPF)). Note that all the IIA *Standards* included in the review books contain Practice Advisories in the way they were published by the IIA.

Note: Although the IIA's *International Standards* are explicitly covered in the Part 1 exam, a conscious decision was made to include certain IIA *Standards* by repeating them in the Part 2 review book for a better understanding of the subject matter as it relates to the *Standards.* This helps CIA Exam candidates to read the subject matter and the relevant *Standards* in one convenient place because each part of the exam is tested separately. Note that the IIA *Standards* are implicitly addressed in the Part 2 Exam and that both Part 1 and 2 Exams are highly integrated from a *Standards* viewpoint.

These review books focus on the student—the candidate preparing for the CIA Exam. They provide a positive learning experience for candidates by helping them to remember what they read and recall the subject matter through the use of tree diagrams, line drawings, memory aids (key concepts to remember), tables, charts, and graphic text boxes. In other words, an attempt has been made to bring life to static words through visual aids and compare and contrast approaches (i.e., which is what). The positive learning experience system provided through visual aids and memories will enable candidates to form long-lasting study impressions of the subject matter in their minds. In short, these books are student focused and learning oriented.

The aim of these books is to make learning easier, more convenient, and more enjoyable for our customer, the student. A great deal of planning and thought went into the creation of these books with the single goal of making the student's study program (whether individual or group) more relevant and more meaningful. It is hoped that these books meet or exceed the student's expectations in terms of quality, content coverage, and presentation of the subject matter. We were excited and challenged while writing these books, and we hope that you too will be excited to study, remember, and achieve lifelong benefit from them. We believe that the knowledge gained from these books will remain with the candidate even after passing the CIA Exam, serving as on-the-job reference material as well as a training source.

Our goal is to be responsive to the CIA Exam candidate's needs and provide customer (student) satisfaction through continuous quality improvement. This goal can be met only through timely feedback from candidates. Please help us to serve you better—your input counts. You can reach us at ciatestbank@wiley.com.

Administrative Matters

We encourage the new, prospective candidate to obtain a copy of the CIA "Information for Candidates" brochure by writing directly to:

Institute of Internal Auditors

247 Maitland Avenue

Altamonte Springs, FL 32701-4201 USA

Phone: 407-937-1100, Fax: 407-937-1111

Web site: www.theiia.org

This brochure contains everything the candidate needs to know about the CIA Exam (i.e., application form, fees, dates, and sites).

Acknowledgments

The author is indebted to a number of people and organizations that helped to improve the content and quality of this book: Thanks to the Director of Certification at The Institute of Internal Auditors (IIA), Altamonte Springs, Florida, for providing great assistance during the writing of these books. Special thanks to the IIA for providing previous CIA Exam questions, answers, and explanations, IIA *Standards*, the Code of Ethics, and model exam questions. Many thanks also go to Wiley's editorial content management and marketing teams for their capable assistance in completing the CIA Exam learning system.

CIA Exam Study Preparation Resources

To succeed in the exam, we recommend the following study plan and three review products for each part of the CIA Exam:

- Read each part's review book (theory).
- Practice the Web-based online test bank software (practice).
- Reinforce the theoretical concepts by studying the Focus Notes (theory).

A series of **review books** has been prepared for the candidate to utilize for all three parts of the new CIA Exam. Each part's review book includes a comprehensive coverage of the subject matter (theory) followed by some sample practice multiple-choice (M/C) questions with answers and explanations (practice). The sample practice M/C questions included in the review book are taken from Wiley's Web-based online test software to show you the flavor of the questions. Each part's review book contains a glossary section, which is a good source for answering M/C questions on the CIA Exam.

The **Web-based online test bank software** is a robust review product that simulates the format of the actual CIA Exam in terms of look and feel, thus providing intense practice and greater confidence to the CIA Exam candidates. The thousands of sample practice questions (5,275 plus) included in the online test bank can provide greater confidence and solid assurance to CIA exam candidates in that they are preparing well for all the topics required and tested in the exam. All practice questions include explanations for the correct answer and are organized by domain topics within each part. See www.wileycia.com.

A part summary showing the number of sample practice questions included in the online test bank and the number of questions tested in the actual CIA Exam is presented next.

Part Summary	Wiley Sample Practice Questions	CIA Exam Actual Test Questions
Part 1	750+	125
Part 2	725+	100
Part 3	3,800+	100
Total Questions in Three Parts	**5,275+**	**325**

Focus Notes provide a quick review and reinforcement of the important theoretical concepts. They are presented in a summary manner taken from the details of the review books. The Focus Notes can be studied just before the exam, during travel time, or any other time.

When combined, these three review products provide a great value to CIA Exam students.

We suggest a sequential study approach in four steps for each part of the exam, as follows:

Step 1. Read the glossary section at the end of each part's review book for a better understanding of key technical terms

Step 2. Study the theory from the each part's review book

Step 3. Practice the multiple-choice questions from the online test bank for each part

Step 4. Read the Focus Notes for each part for a quick review and reinforcement of the important theoretical concepts

In addition, the CIA Exam candidates should read **Practice Guides** from IIA because these guides provide detailed guidance for conducting internal audit activities. They include detailed processes and procedures, such as tools and techniques, audit work programs, and step-by-step audit approaches as well as examples of audit deliverables. These Practice Guides are not included in the Wiley Review Books due to their size and the fact that they are available from www.theiia.org.

CIA Exam-Taking Tips and Techniques

The types of questions a candidate can expect to see in the CIA Exam are objective and scenario-based multiple-choice (M/C) questions. Answering the M/C questions requires a good amount of practice and effort.

The following tips and techniques will be helpful in answering the CIA Exam questions.

- Stay with your first impression of the correct choice.

- Know the subject area or topic. Don't read too much into the question.

- Remember that questions are independent of specific country, products, practices, vendors, hardware, software, or industry.

- Read the last sentence of the question first followed by all choices and then the body (stem) of the question.

- Read the question twice or read the bolded keywords twice, and watch for tip-off words, such as **not, except, all, every, always, never, least, or most,** which denote absolute conditions.

- Do not project the question into your organizational environment, practices, policies, procedures, standards, and guidelines. The examination is focusing on the IIA's professional *Standards* and publications and on the CIA's exam syllabus (i.e., content specifications).

- Try to eliminate wrong choices as quickly as possible. When you get down to two semifinal choices, take a big-picture approach. For example, if choice A and D are the semifinalists, and choice D could be a part of choice A, then select choice A; or if choice D could be a more complete answer, then select choice D.

- Don't spend too much time on one question. If you are not sure of an answer, move on, and go back to it if time permits. The last resort is to guess the answer. There is no penalty for guessing the wrong answer.

Remember that success in any professional examination depends on several factors required of any student, such as time management skills, preparation time and effort levels, education and experience levels, memory recall of the subject matter, state of the mind before or during the exam, and decision-making skills.

CIA Exam Content Specifications

Part 2 of the CIA Exam is called **internal audit practice** and the exam duration is 2.0 hours (120 minutes) with 100 multiple-choice questions. A breakdown of topics in Part 2 follows.

Domain I: Managing the Internal Audit Function (40–50%)*

A. Strategic Role of Internal Audit

☐ Initiate, manage, be a change catalyst, and cope with change (P)†

☐ Build and maintain networking with other organization executives and the audit committee (P)

☐ Organize and lead a team in mapping, analysis, and business process improvement (P)

☐ Assess and foster the ethical climate of the board and management (P)

☐ Educate senior management and the board on best practices in governance, risk management, control, and compliance (P)

☐ Communicate internal audit key performance indicators to senior management and the board on a regular basis (P)

☐ Coordinate internal audit efforts with external auditor, regulatory oversight bodies, and other internal assurance functions (P)

B. Operational Role of Internal Audit

☐ Formulate policies and procedures for the planning, organizing, directing, and monitoring of internal audit operations (P)

☐ Review the role of the internal audit function within the risk management framework (P)

☐ Direct administrative activities (e.g., budgeting and human resources) of the internal audit department (P)

☐ Interview candidates for internal audit positions (P)

---

* Indicates the relative range of weights assigned to this topic area for both theory and practice sections in the CIA Exam.
† Indicates the level of difficulty for each topic in the CIA Exam expressed as (A) for Awareness and (P) for Proficiency. (A) = Candidates must exhibit awareness (i.e., knowledge of terminology and fundamentals) in these topic areas. (P) = Candidates must exhibit proficiency (i.e., thorough understanding and ability to apply concepts) in these topic areas.

□ Report on the effectiveness of corporate risk management processes to senior management and the board (P)

□ Report on the effectiveness of the internal control and risk management frameworks (P)

□ Maintain an effective quality assurance improvement program (P)

C. Risk-Based Internal Audit Plan

□ Use market, product, and industry knowledge to identify new internal audit engagement opportunities (P)

□ Use a risk framework to identify sources of potential engagements (e.g., audit universe, audit cycle requirements, management requests, and regulatory mandates) (P)

□ Establish a framework for assessing risk (P)

□ Rank and validate risk priorities to prioritize engagements in the audit plan (P)

□ Identify internal audit resource requirements for annual internal audit plan (P)

□ Communicate areas of significant risk and obtain approval from the board for the annual engagement plan (P)

Domain II: Managing Individual Engagements (40–50%)
A. Plan Engagements

□ Establish engagement objectives/criteria and finalize the scope of the engagement (P)

□ Plan engagements to assure identification of key risks and controls (P)

□ Complete a detailed risk assessment of each audit area (i.e., prioritize or evaluate risk and control factors) (P)

□ Determine engagement procedures and prepare engagement work program (P)

□ Determine the level of staff and resources needed for the engagement (P)

□ Construct audit staff schedule for effective use of time (P)

B. Supervise Engagements

□ Direct or supervise individual engagements (P)

□ Nurture instrumental relations, build bonds, and work with others toward shared goals (P)

□ Coordinate work assignments among audit team members when serving as the auditor in charge of a project (P)

□ Review working papers (P)

□ Conduct exit conference (P)

□ Complete performance appraisals of engagement staff (P)

C. Communicate Engagement Results

□ Initiate preliminary communication with engagement clients (P)

□ Communicate interim progress (P)

□ Develop recommendations when appropriate (P)

□ Prepare report or other communication (P)

  □ Approve engagement report (P)

  □ Determine distribution of the report (P)

  □ Obtain management response to the report (P)

  □ Report outcomes to appropriate parties (P)

D. Monitor Engagement Outcomes

  □ Identify appropriate method to monitor engagement outcomes (P)

  □ Monitor engagement outcomes and conduct appropriate follow-up by the internal audit activity (P)

  □ Conduct follow-up and report on management's responses to internal audit recommendations (P)

  □ Periodically report significant audit issues to senior management and the board (P)

Domain III: Fraud Risks and Controls (5–15%)

A. Consider the potential for fraud risks and identify common types of fraud associated with the engagement area during the engagement planning process (P)

B. Determine if fraud risks require special consideration when conducting an engagement (P)

C. Determine if any suspected fraud merits investigation (P)

D. Complete a process review to improve controls to prevent fraud and recommend changes (P)

E. Employ audit tests to detect fraud (P)

F. Support a culture of fraud awareness and encourage the reporting of improprieties (P)

G. Interrogation or investigative techniques (A)

H. Forensic auditing (A)

Managing the Internal Audit Function (40–50%)

1.1 Strategic Role of Internal Audit   1

1.2 Operational Role of Internal Audit   25

1.3 Risk-Based Internal Audit Plan   302

1.4 Sample Practice Questions   316

1.1 Strategic Role of Internal Audit

The scope of the strategic role of internal audit focuses on the role of corporate code of ethics, conflicts of interest, factors influencing ethical standards, options for facilitating ethical behavior, monitoring compliance with the Code of Conduct of the Institute of Internal Auditors (IIA), fraud in financial reporting, and integrating ethical standards in complex situations.

(a) Role of Corporate Code of Ethics

Ethics is knowing what is right or wrong, proper or improper. Ethics forms basic ground rules for individuals to follow. It resides within a person and is a personal matter. Since people run businesses, personal ethics is business ethics, and vice versa. Also, ethics is indivisible or inseparable (i.e., it is the whole thing or nothing).

CORPORATE CULTURE VERSUS CORPORATE ETHICS

Corporate culture is identified formally in written statements of corporate vision or mission statements, or as a set of basic qualities, values, beliefs, or commitments.

Corporate culture raises the overall sense of ethical behavior in a way that is easy to understand and accept. Corporate culture needs to include the ethical element.

A good corporate culture should incorporate a substantial part of corporate ethics, explicitly or implicitly.

A person's competence, integrity, and objectivity are the roots of ethical behavior. Professionals have stricter rules and higher expectations about their ethical behavior than others do. According to Stephen Landekich, the word "professionalism" means that a person acts and is expected to act as an expert at a reliable level of conduct.[1] A professional not only acts in a manner beyond

---

[1] Stephen Landekich, *Corporate Codes of Conduct* (Montvale, NJ: Institute of Management Accountants, A Research Project, 1989).

reproach but also is careful about any related conditions and circumstances that possibly might appear improper or be so perceived by others. Consequently, a code of ethics is a distinct mark of an established profession.

(b) Conflicts of Interest

The conflict-of-interest policy often is considered a part of the overall ethics policies. Conflict-of-interest concerns sometimes constitute the main part of ethics standards. Landekich's research indicated that all major companies share the view that conflicts between an employee's activities or personal interests and the company's interests are one of the most significant causes of concern with regard to proper business conduct. The guiding principle is that the best interests of the company must motivate the employee's acts. Anything that might be inconsistent with this principle constitutes an actual or potential conflict of interest or the appearance of a conflict of interest. For example, if a fund manager puts more time and energy into managing his own personal funds at the expense of his company's funds, it is a conflict-of-interest situation.

Companies uniformly prohibit conflicts of interest, unless an employee has obtained written company approval. Such a basic clause may appear within a code of ethics or in a separately issued policy. In either case, typical conflict-of-interest situations are described in considerable detail.

Landekich gathered a concise set of standards on conflicts of interest taken from a company's corporate code of conduct. For example:

- Employees are forbidden to have direct or indirect ownership interests (excluding publicly traded securities of large companies listed on stock exchange) or profit participation in organizations selling or buying goods or services to or from the company where such relationship may reasonably lead to a conflict of interest.

- Employees or members of their families may not receive compensation, services, gifts, or entertainment from such organizations which receipt could reasonably be construed to have influenced the employee in dealing with them on behalf of the company.

> **ETHICS POLICY**
>
> The ethics policy is contained in the corporate policies, internal auditing policies, or conflict-of-interest policies.

Only 5% of ethics policies are written. Ethics and quality are interrelated (i.e., one needs the other to work more effectively).

- In accordance with the personnel policy concerning "Outside Employment," the company prohibits its employees from engaging in outside employment with a supplier, customer, competitor, or a firm that may become such in the foreseeable future where such a relationship may reasonably lead to a conflict of interest.

- Certain employees will be required to sign a "Conflict of Interest Statement" annually.

- Employees who have questions regarding what constitutes a conflict of interest should discuss the matter with their division management.

Dittenhofer and Klemm undertook a research project for the IIA to determine attitudes of internal auditors relative to 20 ethics issues.[2] These 20 situations (issues) were grouped into eight ethics classifications. General comments on the eight classifications follow.

1. **Confidentiality.** There is a definite agreement between employees' attitudes and the perceived positions of their employers. No substantial differences were noted as to staff level, location, or industry.

2. **Honesty and objectivity.** Employees seem stricter about violating these areas of ethics than their employers violate. All were consistent about action to take.

3. **Loyalty.** The answers were not clear-cut. There was little agreement between auditors' and employers' positions. Whistle-blowing appears to cause differing attitudes about loyalty ties.

4. **Conflict of interest.** Auditors and their employers agree as to the action to take. Auditors outside the United States seem to be more hard line. There were no major differences in the other categories. However, the percentages in the industrial groups varied significantly.

5. **Gifts.** Internal auditors are stricter than their organizations. Generally, there is congruity in all classifications.

6. **Professional competence.** This area dealt with evidence and disclosure. Auditors' opinions and their perceived employers' positions did not display a high degree of concern over this aspect. Attitudes were reflected in the categories of internal auditors. *Disclosure:* Auditors and their organizations (as perceived) showed more concern for these incidents. This attitude was shared by all other categories.

7. **Striving for proficiency and effectiveness.** There is less concern, and the perceived organizations' opinions are somewhat less concerned.

8. **High standards of morality and dignity.** There was general disagreement about an internal auditor going to a city from an employer-paid training session to apply for a new job. It appears that there are less firm positions and that attitudes are less comparable as to the situation given.

In conclusion, there is an apparent awareness of unethical positions among audit practitioners. They recognize unethical behavior and, on an organizational basis, are prepared to take action and impose sanctions on those who act improperly.

(c) Factors Influencing Ethical Standards

In a study, Brenner and Molander asked a group of managers to list factors that they believed influenced ethical standards.[3] The replies, in order of importance, were

Factors causing *higher* ethical standards:

- Public disclosure, publicity, media coverage, and better communication

- Increased public concern, public awareness, consciousness and security, better-informed public, and societal pressures

---

[2] Mortimer Dittenhofer and Rebecca Klemm, *Ethics and the Internal Auditor*, IIA Monograph Series (Altamonte Springs, FL: IIA, 1983).

[3] Steven N. Brenner and Earl A. Molander, "Is the Ethics of Business Changing?" in *Ethics in Practice* (Boston: Harvard Business School Press, 1989).

- Government regulation, legislation and intervention, and federal courts
- Education of business managers, increase in manager professionalism, and education
- New social expectation of the role that business is to play in society and the attitudes of young adults
- Greater sense of social responsibility on the part of organizations and greater awareness of the implications of their actions
- Business responsiveness, corporate policy changes, and top management's emphasis on ethical action

Factors causing *lower* ethical standards:

- Society's lower standards, social decay, more permissive society, growth of materialism and hedonism, loss of church and home influence, and less quality, more quantity desires
- Competition, pace of life, the stress of trying to succeed, current economic conditions, and the cost of doing business
- Political corruption, loss of confidence in government, politics, political ethics, and climate
- People being more aware of unethical acts, constant media coverage, and communications that create an atmosphere for crime
- Greed, desire for gain, worship of the dollar as a measure of success, selfishness, and a lack of personal integrity and moral fiber
- Pressure for profit from within the organization from superiors or stockholders, corporate influences on managers, and corporate policies

It is easy to rationalize unethical conduct in business because of the prevailing theory that executives must provide stockholders with the greatest possible return on their investments (i.e., profit). This leads us to believe that ethical practices are rarely rewarded when compared to profits.

KEY CONCEPTS TO REMEMBER: Corporate Code of Ethics

- The best reason for establishing a code of conduct within an organization is that such codes express standards of individual behavior for members of the organization.

- An example of unacceptable behavior that should be included in a conflict-of-interest policy is providing a mailing list of company employees to a relative who is offering training that might benefit the organization. The conflict-of-interest policy should prohibit any activity contrary to the best interests and well-being of the organization.

- A conflict-of-interest policy should include, among other things: An employee shall not accept money, gifts, or services from a customer, an employee shall not borrow from or lend money to vendors, and an employee shall not use company information for private purposes. The conflict-of-interest policy for a private firm (e.g., manufacturing company) should **not** include that the employee not participate in the management of a public agency.

- A firm's code of ethics contains the statement "Employees shall not accept gifts or gratuities over $50 in value from persons or firms with whom our organization does business." This provision is designed to prevent excessive sales allowances granted by an employee.

- Several years ago, a large financial institution developed and distributed a code of conduct to all its officers and employees. The best audit approach to provide the audit committee with the highest level of comfort about the code of conduct would be to fully evaluate the comprehensiveness of the code and compliance therewith and to report the results to the audit committee.

- A review of an organization's code of conduct revealed that it contained comprehensive guidelines designed to inspire high levels of ethical behavior. The review also revealed that employees were knowledgeable of its provisions. However, some employees still did not comply with the code. To enhance its effectiveness, the code of conduct should contain provisions for disciplinary action in the event of violations.

(d) Options for Facilitating Ethical Behavior

An organization has several options to facilitate ethical behavior. The options require careful planning and proper implementation with sincere interest and commitment. According to Moore and Dittenhofer, the presentation of the code of conduct plays an important role in how employees view its importance.[4] If the code of conduct is presented casually to a new employee along with other material related to the employment entrance process, such as insurance forms, tax deduction forms, pension information, and so forth, it will be considered a perfunctory document with minimal importance or significance. However, if the code is covered in a training program, and top management attends and participates, the code will be seen as a major element of organizational governance and a positive guide to attitude and behavior.

An alternative to distributing the code in a training program is for the chief executive officer (CEO) to transmit it with a personal letter. This tone-from-the-top message should explain that the code governs conduct at all levels of the organization. The letter may include a statement that says infractions will be dealt with seriously. It should be made clear that the excuse "I did what was best for the organization" will not be acceptable.

CONFLICT-OF-INTEREST POLICY

A conflict-of-interest policy should state that employees should not do business with family members as customers or suppliers even though no fraud appears to have been committed.

Another successful method for introducing new employees to the code of conduct is in a workshop where they see examples of ethics in practice. This is a good way to expose them to role-playing exercises relating to the most common types of infractions and to the potential disciplinary action that could be taken as a result. In addition to an initial exposure to the code of conduct just mentioned, ongoing training is also needed. This may be most effective when done by individual supervisors, usually in conjunction with employee training, orientation, or professional development courses. An effective way to impress the concept of ethics on each new employee is for supervisors to explain that ethical conduct is a core value of the organization that employees are expected to comply with throughout their careers. This subject should be discussed each time the supervisor focuses on performance issues with an individual.

---

[4] Wayne G. Moore and Mortimer A. Dittenhofer, *How to Develop a Code of Conduct*, IIA Monograph Series (Altamonte Springs, FL: IIA, 1992).

In some cases, code-of-conduct training can be done on a broader scale through a seminar or meeting. If properly designed, a session of this nature can be effective. In other cases, videotapes on the subject of ethics are used, either separately or as part of additional training. This type of presentation is most effective if the CEO or a member of top management appears on the video-tape and provides supportive comments. Also, the presentation is enhanced if a knowledgeable individual is available to answer questions.

To keep the ethics momentum going, the code-of-conduct document needs to be updated periodically. The updating team should consider such elements as infractions not originally or specifically covered in the original code of conduct, changes in the organization's policies, environmental and organizational changes with material impact on the organization and its employees, and definitions and descriptions that are not clear.

(e) Monitoring Compliance with the Code of Conduct

Compliance with the code of conduct is an ongoing responsibility of each employee and is based primarily on the honor system. Employees should be asked to certify or sign a form asserting that they have complied with the code or to list exceptions to such compliance. These surveys may be administered by operating management or a staff group, such as legal, employee relations (human resources), or internal auditing.

(f) Fraud in Financial Reporting

In 1987, the Report of the National Commission on Fraudulent Financial Reporting (Treadway Commission) made recommendations for the public company to improve the financial report-ing process.[5] In it, the commission made specific recommendations on the code of corporate conduct.

> The public company should develop and enforce written codes of corporate conduct. Codes of conduct should foster a strong ethical climate and open channels of com-munication to help protect against fraudulent financial reporting. As a part of its ongoing oversight of the effectiveness of internal controls, a company's audit com-mittee should review annually the program that management establishes to monitor compliance with the code.

A strong corporate ethical climate at all levels is vital to the well-being of the corporation, all its constituencies, and the public at large. Such a climate contributes importantly to the effective-ness of company policies and control systems and helps influence behavior that is not subject to even the most elaborate system of controls. Consequently, a strong corporate ethical climate emphasizing accountability helps to protect a company against fraudulent financial reporting.

A written code of corporate conduct strengthens the corporate ethical climate by signaling to all employees standards for conducting the company's affairs. Well-defined ethical standards and guidelines for acceptable behavior promote ethical decision making at all levels of the organiza-tion and help resolve ethical dilemmas that arise.

To succeed, a code of corporate conduct must have the full support of management and the board of directors. The most influential factors in determining the code's effectiveness are the attitude and the behavior of the top officers and directors, who set the example for the entire company.

---

[5] Report of the National Commission on Fraudulent Financial Reporting, USA (October 1987).

The CEO, in particular, has a special role; the CEO's attitude, style, behavior, and expectations of others strongly influence the actions of other upper-level managers.

ACTIVITIES TO ENSURE A STANDING LEVEL OF CONDUCT

- Proper hiring practices
- Competitive levels of compensation
- Performance incentives
- Company tradition and reputation
- Control mechanisms
- Proper organization structure

The development of a corporate code of conduct is not an overnight task. A company must invest the necessary time, energy, and resources to ensure that the code is tailored to its circumstances. Since those circumstances will evolve to meet changing demands, the company must update the code periodically.

Finally, the full support of management and the board is needed to ensure that the code receives widespread understanding and support. Employees representing all levels of the corporation should be encouraged to participate in the code's development and evolution in an appropriate fashion. Such collaboration can minimize cases of noncompliance due to lack of understanding and can promote acceptance and adherence. In addition, the code and any amendments must be publicized throughout the corporation.

A code of corporate conduct can also help establish an environment where open communication is expected, accepted, and protected. Management needs a free flow of information to assist it in directing the company's operations, especially in a large, decentralized business. This need is critical in assessing the risk of fraudulent financial reporting. An atmosphere of open communication allows an employee, when confronted with suspected fraud, to bring the problem to the attention of someone high enough in the corporation to solve it without fear of reprisal.

The code must also provide an accessible internal complaint and appeal mechanism. This mechanism should be designed to facilitate internal disclosure, particularly those involving allegations of fraudulent financial reporting or other misconduct. The mechanism could take a variety of forms, such as the use of an ombudsman.

Such internal procedures offer a number of advantages. They allow management to correct inadvertent mistakes and mistakes that may result from bad judgment or failure to recognize a problem. They also encourage employees to act in good faith and tend to ensure the validity of any complaint. In addition, effective internal action may make external disclosures to government authorities or other third parties unnecessary.

BUSINESS PRACTICES THAT CONSTITUTE AREAS OF ETHICAL DILEMMA

- Hidden defects in products
- Unfair credit practices

BUSINESS PRACTICES THAT CONSTITUTE AREAS OF ETHICAL DILEMMA *(Continued)*

- Deceptive advertising
- Overselling
- Overcharging
- Unreal delivery dates
- Products that are unhealthy

The code of corporate conduct should protect against reprisal employees who use these internal procedures. Failure to adopt guarantees against reprisal as well as to provide an effective internal complaint procedure could undermine the vitality of codes of conduct and encourage a call for antiretaliatory legislation, for which there is ample precedent at the state and the federal level.

The Treadway Commission observed a great deal of diversity in written codes of corporate conduct. Some are general; others are specific in their content and direction. Corporate management should develop a code that fits the particular circumstances of its business. Nearly all codes of conduct, however, should include a conflict-of-interest policy, to prevent actual or apparent improprieties in connection with business transactions; a corporate policy of compliance with domestic and foreign laws affecting its business, including those laws relating to financial disclosures; and a policy of confidentiality relating to the company's proprietary information.

TOOLS TO MONITOR COMPLIANCE

- Annual survey
- Periodic query
- Ethics review board
- Policy guidance
- Employee indoctrination
- Periodic review by internal audit

Adequate monitoring and enforcement mechanisms are yet another element that is indispensable to the success of a code of conduct. Management is responsible for determining how best to establish adequate monitoring and enforcement mechanisms and for implementing them. This responsibility is typically carried out through the legal department, internal audit department, or a separate ombudsman function.

The board of directors should be responsible through the audit committee for reviewing the program that management establishes to monitor compliance with the code of conduct. Employees at all levels should understand that violating the law or compromising the company's code of conduct can result in serious disciplinary actions (including dismissal and criminal or civil proceedings where appropriate) and that no employee is exempt from the code.

Written codes of corporate conduct have further advantages. Such codes foster a strong ethical climate, helping to create a work environment that appeals to company personnel at all levels. With an effective code, a company's employees may be more highly motivated, and the company may be able to attract and retain better employees. In an era when loyalty between organizations and their customers seems less enduring, a company's concern for a strong ethical climate also may generate a positive image outside the organization, which can lead to increased business opportunities.

EXAMPLE: Content of a Code of Conduct

Although each organization is different in some respects, certain types of employee behavior can be expected in all organizations. The contents of a code of conduct are divided into three groups: (1) mandatory (those items that should always appear in a code-of-conduct document), (2) strongly suggested, and (3) desirable. Factors that determine what is appropriate for each specific code are based on a complete understanding of the business and corporate culture.

Mandatory

Tone at the top. Most important, the code should convey a strong tone-at-the-top message. This is usually accomplished by including a letter from the chairperson, president, and/or managing director that expresses the organization's strong commitment to ethical business conduct.

Employee responsibilities. The list of responsibilities expected from each employee should be broad and should establish a positive approach to what follows (e.g., a shared set of common understanding setting forth the philosophy expected in the workplace).

The most common responsibilities mentioned include honesty, fairness, integrity, loyalty, due care, compliance with laws and regulations, avoiding conflicts of interest, safeguarding the organization's assets, and maintaining the confidentiality of nonpublic information.

Business courtesies. In profit-oriented organizations, the customer is number one, so that is a good place to start. How should the firm conduct itself in dealing with customers?

The practice of giving gifts, granting favors, and providing entertainment is usually acceptable, but within limits. In general, guidelines such as these apply.

The amounts:

- Must not be excessive and cannot be construed as a bribe or payoff.
- Must be consistent with customary business practices.
- Must be legal.
- Should not embarrass the organization or the employee if publicly disclosed.

On the other side of the gift, favor, and entertainment equation is the receipt of such courtesies. In some organizations, the receipt of gifts is reported and monitored closely; in others, including certain governmental units, the receipt of gifts of any kind is totally prohibited.

In most organizations, however, token gifts, favors, and entertainment are acceptable. These are usually in the form of advertising and promotional items emblazoned with the organization's logo, or they may be a business luncheon/dinner or entertainment.

Gift giving and receiving is an issue that generates considerable interest and discussion and should be clearly understood. Many organizations have a double standard. For example, marketing and salespeople may be permitted and even encouraged to entertain customers in as lavish a manner as possible to complete a sale, yet the same organization's purchasing department personnel are not permitted to accept similar gratuities from someone else's sales force.

EXAMPLE: Content of a Code of Conduct *(Continued)*

Clearly it is important to identify the reasons for this double standard because readers of the code will focus on it immediately. A clear explanation will prevent any feeling that this issue is being covered up or circumvented.

Cash gifts, either given or received, are not appropriate and should be prohibited due to the lack of an audit trail and accountability of funds. However, in some countries (e.g., Japan), cash gifts are the norm. Care should be exercised in explaining such cultural differences.

Conflicts of interest. No code of conduct would be complete without a discussion of conflicts of interest. Broadly speaking, employees should avoid any situations involving a conflict between their personal interests and those of the organization. In dealings with current or potential customers, suppliers, contractors, and competitors, employees should act in the best interest of the organization to the exclusion of any personal advantage. When potential conflicts occur, employees should make prompt, full disclosure of these issues to management.

Although conflicts of interest materialize in the eyes of the beholder, their importance can vary significantly depending on the business. Common conflicts include:

- **Financial interest.** This generally involves ownership by an employee or an employee's family member of a significant financial interest in an outside enterprise that does business with, or seeks to do business with, or is a competitor of, the organization.

- **Key outside role.** In this instance, an individual serves as a director, officer, partner, consultant, or in another key role, in any outside enterprise that does business with, or seeks to do business with, or is a competitor of, the organization.

- **Agent of a third party.** This position acts as broker, finder, or other intermediary for the benefit of a third party in transactions involving the organization.

- **Other.** This is any other arrangement or circumstance, including family or personal relationships, that might dissuade the employee from acting in the best interest of the organization.

Control and use of assets. Control and judicious use of the organization's assets, including proprietary information stored both on paper and electronically, is each employee's responsibility. Employees should safeguard physical property and other assets against unauthorized use or removal as well as any loss by criminal act or breach of trust. Data transmitted and/or stored electronically are particularly sensitive and may require unique protection.

Record keeping and reporting. All financial and operational reports, accounting records, research reports, expense accounts, sales reports, time sheets, and other documents should accurately and clearly represent the relevant facts or true nature of conditions and transactions. Improper, misleading, incomplete, or fraudulent accounting documentation or financial reporting is not permitted and may also be in violation of applicable laws. Intentional accounting misclassifications and improperly accelerating or deferring expenses or revenues would be examples of unacceptable reporting practices.

Travel and entertainment. Travel and entertainment should be consistent with the needs of the organization. An employee should neither lose nor gain financially as a result of organizational travel and/or entertainment. Employees should spend the organization's money as carefully as their own.

Inside information. Confidential information, such as business strategies, pending contracts, unannounced products, exploration or research results, financial projections, or customer lists, should not be released without proper authority to anyone not employed by the organization or to an employee who has no need for such information. Nonpublic information obtained as an employee should not be used for personal gain by the employee or by anyone as a result of association with the employee. Use for personal profit includes taking advantage of such information by trading or providing information for others to trade in securities of the organization or acquiring property of any kind.

ETHICS IMPLEMENTATION PROCEDURES

- Ethics committee
- Hotline phone
- Counsel for guidance
- Compliance review board
- Internal complaint and appeal mechanism
- Ombudsman

Political contributions. Employees should not make any contribution of organization funds, property, or services, or personal funds in the name of the organization to any political party or committee or to any candidate for or holder of any office of any government. In some cases, it is legal to participate in a political action committee or for an organization to support or oppose public referenda or similar ballot issues. No direct or indirect pressure in any form should be directed toward employees to make any political contributions or participate in the support of a political party or the political candidacy of any individual.

Equal employment opportunity. While conducting business on behalf of the organization, employees should respect the rights and cultural differences of individuals. Employees should practice the principle of equal employment opportunity without regard to race, religion, national origin, sex, age, physical handicap, or political affiliation. In addition, harassment of any type should not be tolerated.

Compliance with the code of conduct. A periodic certification of compliance with the code of conduct is one way to ensure employees focus on the document. The act of signing one's name also tends to emphasize the personal nature of the responsibilities required by the code and should encourage compliance. Providing a hotline, phone number, or ombudsman for people to call and report instances of violation of the policy is another effective method of encouraging compliance with the code. Organizations often use several of these methods.

Strongly Suggested

In most organizations, the next issues should be part of the code of conduct. In not-for-profit organizations, however, they may not be necessary.

Business inducements. In this competitive world, a myriad of sales commission, rebate, discount, credit, and allowance programs exist. These inducements deserve close scrutiny to ensure they comply, in the spirit as well as in the letter, with tax regulations and currency exchange controls. Values should be reasonable, competitively justified, properly documented, and made to the business entity to which the original sales agreement or invoice was made or issued. Payments should not be made to individuals and should be made only in the country of the entity's place of business.

Again, the mirror-image transaction should be covered. Commission payments for purchases should be made only to the seller in the country where the business is located or in the country to which the product was delivered.

The organization's policy on facilitating payments should be explained in this section. The Foreign Corrupt Practices Act of 1977 prohibited such payments, but the Omnibus Trade Act of 1988 amended this provision to a more liberal interpretation of facilitating payments. Payments are permitted if they are legal; are necessary; follow an established, well-recognized practice in the area; and are for administrative actions to which the organization is clearly entitled. Such payments should be properly approved and recorded.

EXAMPLE: Content of a Code of Conduct *(Continued)*

In some countries, the concept of facilitating payments is unheard of, and omitting their mention in the code may be advisable. In multinational organizations, care should be taken to ensure that such payments are accepted in a country before the code of conduct is assumed to permit them.

Antitrust laws. Organizations in various countries are subject to antitrust laws or laws that prohibit agreements or actions that may restrain trade or reduce competition. Violations include price fixing or agreements to control prices to boycott certain suppliers or customers or to limit the production or sale of products. Care must be taken to ensure that activities with representatives of other firms, even professional organizations, are not viewed as a violation of antitrust law. In matters involving antitrust, appropriate legal counsel should be consulted.

Antiboycott laws. Organizations in various countries also are subject to antiboycott laws. For U.S. corporations, these laws prohibit participation in or cooperation with international boycotts that are not sanctioned by the U.S. government. The mere receipt of a request to engage in any boycotting activity is a reportable event by law in some countries. Because of the complexity of antiboycott laws, any questions in this area should be referred to appropriate legal counsel.

Government business. In some organizations, doing business with foreign governments is an integral part of the operation. Sometimes standards and requirements for transactions with foreign governments differ from normal commercial practices, and a clear understanding of the rules governing such transactions is critical to staying out of trouble.

An example is the giving, offering, or accepting of business courtesies, such as meals and entertainment. This may be standard practice in a commercial enterprise yet prohibited in a governmental unit. Again, reference to legal counsel is recommended to ensure that all sensitive areas are properly considered.

Competitive intelligence. Success in the highly competitive business world demands an understanding of competitors' strategies. Collecting data on competitors, while important, should be done ethically. The use of illegitimate resources and actions that may not be illegal but are in bad taste or may cause embarrassment should not be used. If any questions arise in this area, legal counsel should be consulted.

Desirable

The list of desirable items could be endless, but included here are a few items that may be useful, depending on the type of organization or type of code is being developed.

Political activities. Relationships with potential and incumbent public officials can be very sensitive and potentially embarrassing to the organization unless guidelines specify what activities are appropriate. Particular care should be taken to ensure the organization does not make payments to political groups or members to influence sales or to induce them not to perform their duties.

Purchase and sale of real estate and natural resources. Employees should be prohibited from competing with the organization in real estate and natural resources activities, or from using the organization's information or equipment to enable them to profit either directly or indirectly in the acquisition or disposal of real estate or natural resources.

Environment. Protecting the environment requires the ongoing vigilance of all employees. All facilities should be operated in accordance with applicable environmental regulations and in a manner that conserves energy and natural resources and protects the environment.

Sexual harassment. Reinforcement in the code of conduct that the organization will not permit sexual harassment establishes this commitment to all.

Source: Wayne G. Moore and Mortimer A. Dittenhofer, *How to Develop a Code of Conduct*, IIA Monograph Series (Altamonte Springs, FL: IIA, 1992).

(g) Integrating Ethical Standards in Complex Situations

It is good to integrate ethical standards with company policies and procedures, conflict-of-interest statements, job/position descriptions, employee performance evaluations, vision/mission statements, posters and marketing/advertising materials, product packing materials, management employment contracts, legal contracts with outsiders, purchase orders and invoices, employment/job applications, and company annual reports.

Ethics-related statements should be included in so many places for reinforcement purposes and because not everyone will have access to the same ethics-related materials. For example, a consultant may not have access to job descriptions and employee performance evaluations that an employee would have. Similarly, outsiders, such as investors and creditors, would have more access to a company's annual report than to a company policy manual or job application or description.

Another way to integrate ethical standards in complex situations is to measure a manager's performance based on both quantitative and qualitative factors. Usually managers' bonuses or other rewards are based on how well they meet their quantitative goals, such as increase in revenues or decrease in costs. While these goals are good, managers should also be measured on qualitative factors, such as: quality; working relations with customers, suppliers, and employees; and productivity levels.

> **DOUBLE STANDARD FOR ETHICS**
>
> Most businesspeople hold to ethical behavior in their private lives but cease to be private persons in their organizational lives. This fact indicates that people have double standards as far as ethics are concerned: one standard for private lives and one standard for their organizational lives.

An organization's goals are interrelated. This fact should be considered during the establishment and evaluation of individual manager's goals and actual performance.

By placing emphasis on only one or a few goals, the other related goals may be in jeopardy. For example, focusing on increasing revenues or decreasing costs alone is not enough because these goals might have been achieved by jeopardizing or manipulating other related goals, such as too much inventory or too little inventory, or too much maintenance expense or too little maintenance expense, or expensing fixed asset acquisitions instead of capitalizing.

IIA *Standards* Applicable to Strategic Role of Internal Audit

1111—Direct Interaction with the Board

The chief audit executive (CAE) must communicate and interact directly with the board.

Practice Advisory 1111-1: Board Interaction

1. Direct communication occurs when the CAE regularly attends and participates in board meetings that relate to the board's oversight responsibilities for auditing, financial reporting,

organizational governance, and control. The CAE's attendance and participation at these meetings provide an opportunity to be apprised of strategic business and operational developments and to raise high-level risk, systems, procedures, or control issues at an early stage. Meeting attendance also provides an opportunity to exchange information concerning the internal audit activity's plans and activities and to keep each other informed on any other matters of mutual interest.

2. Such communication and interaction also occurs when the CAE meets privately with the board, at least annually.

2000—Managing the Internal Audit Activity

The CAE must manage the internal audit activity effectively to ensure it adds value to the organization.

Interpretation: *The internal audit activity is effectively managed when:*

- *The results of the internal audit activity's work achieve the purpose and responsibility included in the internal audit charter.*
- *The internal audit activity conforms with the definition of internal auditing and the* Standards.
- *The individuals who are part of the internal audit activity demonstrate conformance with the Code of Ethics and the* Standards.

The internal audit activity adds value to the organization (and its stakeholders) when it provides objective and relevant assurance and contributes to the effectiveness and efficiency of governance, risk management, and control processes.

> No Practice Advisory for Standard 2000

2020—Communication and Approval

The CAE must communicate the internal audit activity's plans and resource requirements, including significant interim changes, to senior management and the board for review and approval. The CAE must also communicate the impact of resource limitations.

Practice Advisory 2020-1: Communication and Approval

1. The CAE will submit annually to senior management and the board for review and approval a summary of the internal audit plan, work schedule, staffing plan, and financial budget. This summary will inform senior management and the board of the scope of internal audit work and of any limitations placed on that scope. The CAE will also submit all significant interim changes for approval and information.

2. The approved engagement work schedule, staffing plan, and financial budget, along with all significant interim changes, are to contain sufficient information to enable senior management and the board to ascertain whether the internal audit activity's objectives and plans support those of the organization and the board and are consistent with the internal audit charter.

2040—Policies and Procedures

The CAE must establish policies and procedures to guide the internal audit activity.

Interpretation: *The form and content of policies and procedures are dependent on the size and structure of the internal audit activity and the complexity of its work.*

Practice Advisory 2040-1: Policies and Procedures

1. The CAE develops policies and procedures. Formal administrative and technical audit manuals may not be needed by all internal audit activities. A small internal audit activity may be managed informally. Its audit staff may be directed and controlled through daily, close supervision and memoranda that state policies and procedures to be followed. In a large internal audit activity, more formal and comprehensive policies and procedures are essential to guide the internal audit staff in the execution of the internal audit plan.

2100—Nature of Work

The internal audit activity must evaluate and contribute to the improvement of governance, risk management, and control processes using a systematic and disciplined approach.

No Practice Advisory for Standard 2100

2110—Governance

The internal audit activity must assess and make appropriate recommendations for improving the governance process in its accomplishment of these objectives:

- Promoting appropriate ethics and values within the organization

- Ensuring effective organizational performance management and accountability

- Communicating risk and control information to appropriate areas of the organization

- Coordinating the activities of and communicating information among the board, external and internal auditors, and management

  2110.A1—The internal audit activity must evaluate the design, implementation, and effectiveness of the organization's ethics-related objectives, programs, and activities.

  2110.A2—The internal audit activity must assess whether the information technology (IT) governance of the organization supports the organization's strategies and objectives.

Practice Advisory 2110-1: Governance: Definition

1. The role of internal auditing as noted in the definition of internal auditing includes the responsibility to evaluate and improve governance processes as part of the assurance function.

2. The term "governance" has a range of definitions depending on a variety of environmental, structural, and cultural circumstances, as well as legal frameworks. The *International Standards for the Professional Practice of Internal Auditing* (*Standards*) define "governance" as "the combination of processes and structures implemented by the board to inform, direct, manage, and monitor the activities of the organization toward the achievement of its objectives." The CAE may use a different definition for audit purposes when the organization has adopted a different governance framework or model.

3. Globally, a variety of governance models that have been published by other organizations and legal and regulatory bodies. For example, the Organisation for Economic Co-operation and Development defines "governance" as "a set of relationships between a company's management, its board, its shareholders, and other stakeholders. Corporate governance provides the structure through which the objectives of the company are set and the means of attaining those objectives and monitoring performance are determined." The Australian Securities Exchange Corporate

Governance Council defines "governance" as "the system by which companies are directed and managed. It influences how the objectives of the company are set and achieved, how risk is monitored and assessed, and how performance is optimized." In most instances, there is an indication that governance is a process or system and is not static. What distinguishes the approach in the *Standards* is the specific emphasis on the board and its governance activities.

4. The frameworks and requirements for governance vary according to organization type and regulatory jurisdictions. Examples include publicly traded companies, not-for-profit organizations, associations, government or quasi-government entities, academic institutions, private companies, commissions, and stock exchanges.

5. How an organization designs and practices the principles of effective governance also vary depending on the size, complexity, and life cycle maturity of the organization, its stakeholder structure, legal and cultural requirements, and so on.

6. As a consequence of the variation in the design and structure of governance, the CAE should work with the board and the executive management team, as appropriate, to determine how governance should be defined for audit purposes.

7. Internal auditing is integral to the organization's governance framework. Their unique position within the organization enables internal auditors to observe and formally assess the governance structure, its design, and its operational effectiveness while remaining independent.

8. The relationship among governance, risk management, and internal control should be considered. This item is addressed in Practice Advisory 2110-2. Practice Advisory 2110-3 discusses assessing governance.

Practice Advisory 2110-2: Governance: Relationship with Risk and Control

1. The *Standards* define "governance" as "the combination of processes and structures implemented by the board to inform, direct, manage, and monitor the activities of the organization toward the achievement of its objectives."

2. Governance does not exist as a set of distinct and separate processes and structures. Rather, there are relationships among governance, risk management, and internal controls.

3. Effective governance activities consider risk when setting strategy. Conversely, risk management relies on effective governance (e.g., tone at the top, risk appetite and tolerance, risk culture, and the oversight of risk management).

4. Effective governance relies on internal controls and communication to the board on the effectiveness of those controls.

5. Control and risk also are related, as "control" is defined as "any action taken by management, the board, and other parties to manage risk and increase the likelihood that established goals will be achieved."

6. The CAE should consider these relationships in planning assessments of governance processes:

   ■ An audit should address those controls in governance processes that are designed to prevent or detect events that could have a negative impact on the achievement of organizational strategies, goals, and objectives; operational efficiency and effectiveness; financial reporting; or compliance with applicable laws and regulations. (See Practice Advisory 2110-3.)

   ■ Controls within governance processes are often significant in managing multiple risks across the organization. For example, controls around the code of conduct may be lied upon to manage compliance risks and fraud risks. This aggregation effect should be considered when developing the scope of an audit of governance processes.

   ■ If other audits assess controls in governance processes (e.g., audits of controls over financial reporting, risk management processes, or compliance), the auditor should consider relying on the results of those audits.

Practice Advisory 2110-3: Governance: Assessments

1. Internal auditors can act in a number of different capacities in assessing and contributing to the improvement of governance practices. Typically, internal auditors provide independent, objective assessments of the design and operating effectiveness of the organization's governance processes. They also may provide consulting services and advice on ways to improve those processes. In some cases, internal auditors may be called on to facilitate board self-assessments of governance practices.

2. As noted in Practice Advisory 2110-1: *Governance: Definition*, the definition of governance for audit purposes should be agreed on with the board and executive management, as appropriate. In addition, the internal auditor should understand the organization's governance processes and the relationships among governance, risk, and control (refer to Practice Advisory 2110-2: *Governance: Relationship with Risk and Control*).

3. The audit plan should be developed based on an assessment of risks to the organization. All governance processes should be considered in the risk assessment. The plan should include the higher risk governance processes and an assessment of processes or risk areas where the board or executive management has requested work be performed should be considered. The plan should define the nature of the work to be performed, the governance processes to be addressed, and the nature of the assessments that will be made (i.e., macro—considering the entire governance framework, or micro—considering specific risks, processes, or activities, or some combination of both).

4. When there are known control issues or the governance process is not mature, the CAE could consider different methods for improving the control or governance processes through consulting services instead of, or in addition to, formal assessments.

5. Internal audit assessments regarding governance processes are likely to be based on information obtained from numerous audit assignments over time. The internal auditor should consider:

- The results of audits of specific governance processes (e.g., the whistle-blower process, the strategy management process).

- Governance issues arising from audits that are not specifically focused on governance (e.g., audits of the risk management process, internal control over financial reporting, fraud risks).

- The results of other internal and external assurance providers' work (e.g., a firm engaged by the general counsel to review the investigation process). Refer to Practice Advisory 2050: *Coordination*.

- Other information on governance issues, such as adverse incidents indicating an opportunity to improve governance processes.

6. During the planning, evaluating, and reporting phases, the internal auditor should be sensitive to the potential nature and ramifications of the results and ensure appropriate communications with the board and executive management. The internal auditor should consider consulting legal counsel both before initiating the audit and before finalizing the report.

7. The internal audit activity is an essential part of the governance process. The board and executive management should be able to rely on the quality assurance and improvement program (QAIP) of the internal audit activity in conjunction with external quality assessments performed in accordance with the *Standards* for assurance on its effectiveness.

2050—Coordination

The CAE should share information and coordinate activities with other internal and external providers of assurance and consulting services to ensure proper coverage and minimize duplication of efforts.

Practice Advisory 2050-1: Coordination

1. Oversight of the work of external auditors, including coordination with the internal audit activity, is the responsibility of the board. Coordination of internal and external audit work is the responsibility of the CAE. The CAE obtains the support of the board to coordinate audit work effectively.

2. Organizations may use the work of external auditors to provide assurance related to activities within the scope of internal auditing. In these cases, the CAE takes the steps necessary to understand the work performed by the external auditors, including:

- The nature, extent, and timing of work planned by external auditors, to be satisfied that the external auditors' planned work, in conjunction with the internal auditors' planned work, satisfies the requirements of Standard 2100.

- The external auditor's assessment of risk and materiality.

- The external auditors' techniques, methods, and terminology to enable the CAE to:

  1. Coordinate internal and external auditing work.

  2. Evaluate, for purposes of reliance, the external auditors' work.

  3. Communicate effectively with external auditors.

- Access to the external auditors' programs and working papers, to be satisfied that the external auditors' work can be relied on for internal audit purposes. Internal auditors are responsible for respecting the confidentiality of those programs and working papers.

3. External auditors may rely on the work of the internal audit activity in performing their work. In this case, the CAE needs to provide sufficient information to enable external auditors to understand the internal auditors' techniques, methods, and terminology to facilitate reliance by external auditors on work performed. Access to the internal auditors' programs and working papers is provided to external auditors in order for external auditors to be satisfied as to the acceptability for external audit purposes of relying on the internal auditors' work.

4. It may be efficient for internal and external auditors to use similar techniques, methods, and terminology to coordinate their work effectively and to rely on the work of one another.

5. Planned audit activities of internal and external auditors need to be discussed to ensure that audit coverage is coordinated and duplicate efforts are minimized where possible. Sufficient meetings are to be scheduled during the audit process to ensure coordination of audit work and efficient and timely completion of audit activities and to determine whether observations and recommendations from work performed to date require that the scope of planned work be adjusted.

6. The internal audit activity's final communications, management's responses to those communications, and subsequent follow-up reviews are to be made available to external auditors. These communications assist external auditors in determining and adjusting the scope and timing of their work. In addition, internal auditors need access to the external auditors' presentation materials and management letters. Matters discussed in presentation materials and included in management letters need to be understood by the CAE and used as input to internal auditors in planning the areas to emphasize in future internal audit work. After review of management letters and initiation of any needed corrective action by appropriate members of senior management and the board, the CAE ensures that appropriate follow-up and corrective actions have been taken.

7. The CAE is responsible for regular evaluations of the coordination between internal and external auditors. Such evaluations may also include assessments of the overall efficiency and effectiveness of internal and external audit activities, including aggregate audit cost. The CAE communicates the results of these evaluations to senior management and the board, including relevant comments about the performance of external auditors.

Practice Advisory 2050-2: Assurance Maps

1. One of the key responsibilities of the board is to gain assurance that processes are operating within the parameters it has established to achieve the defined objectives. It is necessary to determine whether risk management processes are working effectively and whether key or business-critical risks are being managed to an acceptable level.

2. Increased focus on the roles and responsibilities of senior management and boards has prompted many organizations to place a greater emphasis on assurance activities. The *Standards* Glossary defines assurance as "an objective examination of evidence for the purpose of providing an independent assessment on governance, risk management, and control processes for the organization." The board will use multiple sources to gain reliable assurance. Assurance from management is fundamental and should be complemented by the provision of objective assurance from internal audit and other third parties. Risk managers, internal auditors, and compliance practitioners are asking: Who does what and why? Boards in particular are beginning to question who is providing assurance, where is the delineation between the functions, and if there are any overlaps.

3. There are fundamentally three classes of assurance providers, differentiated by the stakeholders they serve, their level of independence from the activities over which they provide assurance, and the robustness of that assurance.

- Those who report to management and/or are part of management (management assurance), including individuals who perform control self-assessments, quality auditors, environmental auditors, and other management-designated assurance personnel

- Those who report to the board, including internal audit

- Those who report to external stakeholders (external audit assurance), which is a role traditionally fulfilled by the independent/statutory auditor

The level of assurance desired, and who should provide that assurance, will vary depending on the risk.

4. There are many assurance providers for an organization.

- Line management and employees (management provides assurance as a first line of defense over the risks and controls for which they are responsible)

- Senior management

- Internal and external auditors

- Compliance

- Quality assurance

- Risk management

- Environmental auditors

- Workplace health and safety auditors

- Government performance auditors

- Financial reporting review teams

- Subcommittees of the board (e.g., audit, actuarial, credit, governance)

- External assurance providers, including surveys, specialist reviews (health and safety), and so on

5. The internal audit activity normally provides assurance over the entire organization, including risk management processes (both their design and operating effectiveness), management of those risks classified as key (including the effectiveness of the controls and other responses to them), verification of the reliability and appropriateness of the risk assessment, and reporting of the risk and control status.

6. With responsibility for assurance activities traditionally being shared among management, internal audit, risk management, and compliance, it is important that assurance activities be coordinated to ensure that resources are used in the most efficient and effective way. Many organizations operate with traditional (and separate) internal audit, risk, and compliance activities. It is common for organizations to have a number of separate groups performing different risk management, compliance, and assurance functions independently of one another. Without effective coordination and reporting, work can be duplicated or key risks may be missed or misjudged.

7. While many organizations monitor the activities of internal audit, risk, and compliance, not all view all their activities in a holistic way. An assurance mapping exercise involves mapping assurance coverage against the key risks in an organization. This process allows an organization to identify and address any gaps in the risk management process and gives stakeholders comfort that risks are being managed and reported on and that regulatory and legal obligations are being met. Organizations will benefit from a streamlined approach, which ensures that the information is available to management about the risks they face and how the risks are being addressed. The mapping is done across the organization to understand where the overall risk and assurance roles and accountabilities reside. The aim is to ensure that there is a comprehensive risk and assurance process with no duplicated effort or potential gaps.

8. Often an organization will have defined the significant risk categories that make up its risk management framework. In such cases, the **assurance map** would be based on the structure of this framework. For example, an assurance map could have these columns:

- Significant risk category
- Management role responsible for the risk (risk owner)
- Inherent risk rating
- Residual risk rating
- External audit coverage
- Internal audit coverage
- Other assurance provider coverage

In this example, the CAE would populate the internal audit coverage column with recent coverage. Often each significant risk has a risk owner or a person responsible for coordinating assurance activities for that risk; if so, that person would populate the other assurance provider coverage column. Each significant unit within an organization could have its own assurance map. Alternatively, the internal audit activity may play a coordinating role in developing and completing the organization's assurance map.

9. Once the assurance map for the organization has been completed, significant risks with inadequate assurance coverage, or areas of duplicated assurance coverage, can be identified. Senior management and the board need to consider changes in assurance coverage for these risks. The internal audit activity needs to consider areas of inadequate coverage when developing the internal audit plan.

10. It is the responsibility of the CAE to understand the independent assurance requirements of the board and the organization in order to clarify the role the internal audit activity fills and the level of assurance it provides. The board needs to be confident that the overall assurance process is adequate and sufficiently robust to validate that the risks of the organization are being managed and reported on effectively.

11. The board needs to receive information about assurance activities, both implemented and planned, in regard to each category of risk. The internal audit activity and other assurance providers offer the board the appropriate level of assurance for the nature and levels of risk that exist in the organization under the respective categories.

12. In organizations requiring an overall opinion from the CAE, the CAE needs to understand the nature, scope, and extent of the integrated assurance map to consider the work of other assurance providers (and rely on it as appropriate) before presenting an overall opinion on the organization's governance, risk management, and control processes. The IIA's *Practice Guide Formulating and Expressing Internal Audit Opinions* provides additional guidance.

13. In instances where the organization does not expect an overall opinion, the CAE can act as the coordinator of assurance providers to ensure there are either no gaps in assurance, or the gaps are known and accepted. The CAE reports on any lack of input/involvement/ oversight/assurance over other assurance providers. If the CAE believes that the assurance coverage is inadequate or ineffective, senior management and the board need to be advised accordingly.

14. The CAE is directed by Standard 2050 to coordinate activities with other assurance providers; the use of an assurance map will help achieve this. Assurance maps increasingly offer an effective way of communicating this coordination.

Practice Advisory 2050-3: Relying on the Work of Other Assurance Providers

1. The internal auditor may rely on or use the work of other internal or external assurance providers in providing governance, risk management, and control assurance to the board. Internal assurance providers could include company functions such as compliance, information security, quality, and labor health and safety as well as management monitoring activities. External assurance providers could include external auditors, joint venture partners, specialist reviews, or third-party audit firms, including those providing reports in accordance with International Standard on Assurance Engagements 3402: *Assurance Reports on Controls at a Service Organization*.2. The decision to rely on the work of other assurance providers can be made for a variety of reasons, including to address areas that fall outside of the competence of the internal audit activity, to gain knowledge transfer from other assurance providers, or to efficiently enhance coverage of risk beyond the internal audit plan.

3. An internal audit charter and/or engagement letter should specify that the internal audit activity have access to the work of other internal and external assurance providers.

4. Where the internal auditor is hiring the assurance provider, the auditor should document engagement expectations in a contract or agreement. Minimum expectations should be provided for the nature and ownership of deliverables, methods/techniques, the nature of procedures and data/information to be used, and progress reports/supervision to ensure the work is adequate and reporting requirements.

5. If management within the organization provides the contracting of, and direction to, a third-party assurance provider, the internal auditor should be satisfied that the instruction is appropriate, understood, and executed.

6. The internal auditor should consider the independence and objectivity of the other assurance providers when considering whether to rely on or use their work. If an assurance provider is hired by and/or is under the direction of management instead of internal auditing, the impact of this arrangement on the assurance provider's independence and objectivity should be evaluated.

7. The internal auditor should assess the competencies and qualifications of the provider performing the assurance work. Examples of competency include verifying the assurer holds appropriate professional experience and qualifications, has a current registration with the relevant professional body or institute, and has a reputation for competency and integrity in the sector.

8. The internal auditor should consider the other assurance provider's elements of practice to have reasonable assurance the findings are based on sufficient, reliable, relevant, and useful information, as required by Standard 2310: *Identifying Information*. Standard 2310 must be met by the CAE regardless of the degree to which the work of other assurance providers is used.

9. The internal auditor should ensure that the work of the other assurance provider is appropriately planned, supervised, documented, and reviewed. The auditor should consider whether the audit evidence is appropriate and sufficient to determine the extent of use and reliance on the work of the other assurance providers. Based on an assessment of the work of the other assurance provider, additional work or test procedures may be needed to gain appropriate and sufficient audit evidence. The internal auditor should be satisfied, based on knowledge of the business, environment, techniques, and information used by the assurance provider, that the findings appear to be reasonable.

10. The level of reliance that can be placed on another assurance provider will be impacted by the factors mentioned earlier: independence, objectivity, competencies, elements of practice, adequacy of execution of audit work, and sufficiency of audit evidence to support the given level of assurance. As the risk or significance of the activity reviewed by the other assurance provider increases, the internal auditor should gather more information on these factors and may need to obtain additional audit evidence to supplement the work done by the other assurance provider. To increase the level of reliance on the results, the internal audit activity may retest results of the other assurance provider.

11. The internal auditor should incorporate the assurance provider's results into the overall report of assurance that the internal auditor reports to the board or other key stakeholders. Significant issues raised by the other assurance provider can be incorporated in detail or summarized in internal audit reports. The internal auditor should include reference to other assurance providers where reports rely on such information.

12. Follow-up is a process by which internal auditors evaluate the adequacy, effectiveness, and timeliness of actions taken by management on reported observations and recommendations, including those made by other assurance providers. In reviewing actions taken to address recommendations made by other assurance providers, the internal auditor should determine whether management has implemented the recommendations or assumed the risk of not implementing them.

13. Significant findings from other assurance providers should be considered in the assurance and communications internal auditing is providing the organization. In addition, results of work performed by others may impact the internal audit risk assessment as to whether the findings impact the evaluation of risk and the level of audit work necessary in response to that risk.

14. In evaluating the effectiveness of, and contributing to the improvement of, risk management processes (Standard 2120: *Risk Management*), the internal audit activity may review the processes of these internal assurance providers, including company functions such as compliance, information security, quality, and labor health and safety as well as management monitoring activities. There should be coverage of risk areas by internal auditing, but when another assurance function exists, the internal audit activity may review the performance of that process rather than duplicate the detailed specific work of that other function.

15. Assessment from the other assurance provider on significant risks should be reported to relevant areas of the organization to be included in considerations regarding the organization's risk management framework and assurance map. See Practice Advisory 2050-2: *Assurance Maps*.

2060—Reporting to Senior Management and the Board

The CAE must report periodically to senior management and the board on the internal audit activity's purpose, authority, responsibility, and performance relative to its plan. Reporting must also include significant risk exposures and control issues, including fraud risks, governance issues, and other matters needed or requested by senior management and the board.

Interpretation: *The frequency and content of reporting are determined in discussion with senior management and the board and depend on the importance of the information to be communicated and the urgency of the related actions to be taken by senior management or the board.*

Practice Advisory 2060-1: Reporting to Senior Management and the Board

1. The purpose of reporting is to provide assurance to senior management and the board regarding governance processes (Standard 2110), risk management (Standard 2120), and control (Standard 2130). Standard 1111 states: "The CAE must communicate and interact directly with the board."

2. The CAE should agree with the board about the frequency and nature of reporting on the internal audit activity's charter (e.g., purpose, authority, and responsibility) and performance. Performance reporting should be relative to the most recently approved plan to inform senior management and the board of significant deviations from the approved audit plan, staffing plans, and financial budgets; reasons for the deviations; and action needed or taken. Standard 1320 states: "The chief audit executive must communicate the results of the quality assurance and improvement program to senior management and the board."

3. Significant risk exposures and control issues are those conditions that, according to the CAE's judgment, could adversely affect the organization and its ability to achieve its strategic, financial reporting, operational, and compliance objectives. Significant issues may carry unacceptable exposure to internal and external risks, including conditions related to control weaknesses, fraud, irregularities, illegal acts, errors, inefficiency, waste, ineffectiveness, conflicts of interest, and financial viability.

4. Senior management and the board make decisions on the appropriate action to be taken regarding significant issues. They may decide to assume the risk of not correcting the reported condition because of cost or other considerations. Senior management should inform the board of decisions about all significant issues raised by internal auditing.

5. When the CAE believes that senior management has accepted a level of risk that the organization considers unacceptable, the CAE must discuss the matter with senior management, as stated in Standard 2600. The CAE should understand management's basis for the decision, identify the cause of any disagreement, and determine whether management has the authority to accept the risk. Disagreements may relate to risk likelihood and potential exposure, understanding of risk appetite, cost, and level of control. Preferably, the CAE should resolve the disagreement with senior management.

6. If the CAE and senior management cannot reach an agreement, Standard 2600 directs the CAE to inform the board. If possible, the CAE and management should make a joint presentation about the conflicting positions. For financial reporting matters, CAEs should consider discussing these issues with the external auditors in a timely manner.

2120—Risk Management

The internal audit activity must evaluate the effectiveness and contribute to the improvement of risk management processes.

Interpretation: *Determining whether risk management processes are effective is a judgment resulting from the internal auditor's assessment that:*

- *Organizational objectives support and align with the organization's mission.*

- *Significant risks are identified and assessed.*

- *Appropriate risk responses are selected that align risks with the organization's risk appetite.*

- *Relevant risk information is captured and communicated in a timely manner across the organization, enabling staff, management, and the board to carry out their responsibilities.*

The internal audit activity may gather the information to support this assessment during multiple engagements. The results of these engagements, when viewed together, provide an understanding of the organization's risk management processes and their effectiveness.

Risk management processes are monitored through ongoing management activities, separate evaluations, or both.

2120. A1—The internal audit activity must evaluate risk exposures relating to the organization's governance, operations, and information systems regarding the:

- Reliability and integrity of financial and operational information.

- Effectiveness and efficiency of operations and programs.

- Safeguarding of assets.

- Compliance with laws, regulations, policies, procedures, and contracts.

2120. A2—The internal audit activity must evaluate the potential for the occurrence of fraud and how the organization manages fraud risk.

2120. C1—During consulting engagements, internal auditors must address risk consistent with the engagement's objectives and be alert to the existence of other significant risks.

2120. C2—Internal auditors must incorporate knowledge of risks gained from consulting engagements into their evaluation of the organization's risk management processes.

2120. C3—When assisting management in establishing or improving risk management processes, internal auditors must refrain from assuming any management responsibility by actually managing risks.

2130—Control

The internal audit activity must assist the organization in maintaining effective controls by evaluating their effectiveness and efficiency and by promoting continuous improvement.

2130. A1—The internal audit activity must evaluate the adequacy and effectiveness of controls in responding to risks within the organization's governance, operations, and information systems regarding the:

- Reliability and integrity of financial and operational information.

- Effectiveness and efficiency of operations and programs.

- Safeguarding of assets.
- Compliance with laws, regulations, policies, procedures, and contracts.

2130. C1—Internal auditors must incorporate knowledge of controls gained from consulting engagements into evaluation of the organization's control processes.

1.2 Operational Role of Internal Audit

The scope of operational role of internal audit includes conducting assurance audit engagements and performing consulting engagements. The auditor's role is different in these two engagements due to their different objectives and outcomes.

(a) Assurance Audit Engagements

Assurance auditing provides an assessment of the reliability and/or relevance of data and operations in specific areas of business functions. The scope of work includes third-party and contract audit, quality audit, due diligence audit, security audit, privacy audit, performance audit, operational audit, financial audit, IT audit, and compliance audit. With these engagements, internal auditors provide reasonable assurance whether organizational goals are being accomplished.

(i) Audits of Third Parties and Contract Auditing

(A) Audits of Third Parties There will be at least three parties to certain business transactions, such as electronic procurement, electronic payment, computer-based applications service providers, computer system outsourcing services, and computer service bureaus. Key parties include the purchaser, the third-party provider, and the supplier. The purpose of third-party auditing is to ensure that controls are adequate and that proper evidence is collected in the event of a dispute between the parties.

Individual trading partners (i.e., purchasers and suppliers) will have specific controls, such as data entry and application system controls over the business transactions, while the third-party provider will have common controls. These common controls include general, translation, transaction, access authorization, balancing, data integrity, confidentiality, and privacy controls.

The internal auditor should review general controls and transaction controls at the third-party provider's computer center. Examples of general controls include system development and program change controls; security and access control methods; backup, recovery, and business continuity controls; operating system controls; and audit trails. Examples of transaction controls include transaction authorization, accuracy, completeness, compensating, and user controls.

OVERVIEW OF THIRD PARTIES

Four major types of third parties that often work with IT and users of the client organization include system integrators, vendors, consultants/contractors, and service providers.

System Integrators

System integrators are independent organizations hired to:

- Manage the software acquisition process.
- Manage the system development process.

(continued)

OVERVIEW OF THIRD PARTIES *(Continued)*

- Manage the network development and services.

- Integrate hardware and software from different platforms.

    In this role, system integrators focus on how best to integrate the client's hardware and network configurations, applications software, and systems software acquired from different vendors operating at various locations.

Vendors

Both hardware and software vendors work with their clients (customers) from planning to installation of hardware devices and software products. Here software includes applications software and systems software. Often vendors:

- Help in software product integration and implementation.

- Help in hardware installation.

- Provide technical assistance in problem troubleshooting.

- Conduct training programs for the client.

- Provide educational materials.

- Provide maintenance and service agreements.

- Conduct hardware and software diagnosis in response to client's problems.

- Coordinate new software releases and updates.

Consultants and Contractors

Consultants or contractors are usually hired for a short time period to perform specific tasks, such as:

- Conduct special studies in computer operations, operating systems, databases, capacity planning, network services, and other areas of information systems (IS) and making recommendations to management to improve operating efficiency and system effectiveness.

- Develop computer-based application systems from planning to implementation stages.

- Maintain or enhance existing application systems from inception to completion stages.

Service Providers

Use of service providers is growing and should be based on cost/benefit analysis. Organizations outside the user/customer organization provide several types of third-party IT services, as follows:

- **Service bureau.** A private organization provides IS services to its clients for a fee, basically to process certain applications. Controls required by a service bureau systems and operations are no different from in-house systems and operations.

- **Timesharing facilities.** A private organization provides IS services to process certain applications for a fee (based on time used).

- **Outsourcing or facilities management.** A private organization takes over operating the user organization's IS computer center operations and network services based on a contract.

    "Outsourcing" means an IT organization goes outside for the knowledge and experience required to do a specific job. In simpler terms, it means subcontracting or farming out for systems and services. The scope of outsourcing includes telecommunications and network support, facilities (computer center) management, disaster recovery services, education and training, ongoing hardware maintenance, data center design and construction, equipment relocation services, systems integration, application development and maintenance, and other services. The scope is broad and could include partial and full-line services.

Organizations turn to outsourcing to improve performance (system and people) and to reduce operating costs. On a positive note, outsourcing offers solutions when there is a shortage of in-house skills, when a high-risk and high-overhead project needs to be managed, and when there is an unacceptable lead time to complete a project using company personnel.

The benefits from outsourcing usually focus on performance improvements and/or cost reduction. Another benefit is that it allows internal management's time and resources to be devoted more to the core business and the company's future. Outsourcing prevents hiring additional employees to meet temporary needs. However, outsourcing does not mean surrendering control and internal management responsibility of subcontracted functions and projects to outside vendors.

Some of the organization's IT employees could work for the outsourcing vendor. The key point here is to monitor the performance of the outsourced vendor during the contract period. Selection of an outsourcing vendor is no different from selecting other types of vendors. Selection factors, such as proximity of the vendor, attitude of the vendor's personnel, vendor's reputation and knowledge, and the vendor's financial condition and management's integrity, are important to consider.

The fixed-price-type contract is best for the user organization, although this may not be feasible in all situations. The contract should spell out vendor performance-level guarantees and the remedies for nonperformance. Usually contract periods range from five to six years.

From the economics point of view, the outsourcing approach provides an option to buy IS services from outsiders rather than from the organization's IS department. Users can perform make-or-buy analysis.

- **Third-party network services.** A private organization provides telecommunication network and data interchange services between two user organizations, or trading partners. An example is an electronic data interchange (EDI) service being provided between a buying organization (e.g., retailer) and a selling organization (e.g., manufacturer of merchandise) of goods and services.

- **Financial services.** A financial organization providing charge or credit services to its customers will arrange for the processing of charge card transaction validation and updating of its customer data files from a user organization, such as a retailer, a financial institution, or a business entity.

(B) Contract Auditing   Many opportunities exist in contract auditing in terms of cost recovery in such areas as fraud, kickbacks, overcharges, and conflict of interest. As with IT system development audits, internal auditors should participate early in contract audits, such as construction audits. Early participation is required in bidding procedures, cost estimates, contractual terms, contractors' accounting (billing) systems, cost control, and project control procedures. A provision should be provided in the contract for overall project reviews, billing reviews, progress reviews, and cost recovery audits.

Construction audits generally fall into one of the three categories: fixed price (lump sum), cost plus, and unit price. Under the fixed-price contract, contractors agree to work for a fixed amount. The auditor should review escalation clauses, progress payments, incentive provisions, adjustments for excess labor and materials costs, and change orders. Risks in fixed-price contracts include: inadequate insurance and bond coverage; charges for equipment and materials that are not received; overhead cost items included as additional charges; inadequate inspection relative to specifications; and extra costs, changes, and revisions that are already part of the original contract.

Under the cost-plus contract, the contractor is reimbursed for costs plus a fixed fee (which is encouraged) or costs plus a fee based on percentage of costs (which is discouraged). Some cost-plus contracts provide for maximum costs and sharing of any savings generated. Risks in cost-plus

Contract category	Fixed price	Cost plus	Unit price
Requires built-in hedges for unknowns	Yes	No	Not applicable
Contractor self-policing	Yes	No	Not applicable
Recordkeeping is crucial	Not applicable	Yes	Yes

EXHIBIT 1.1 Comparison of Contracts

contracts include: overhead cost items are also billed directly; duplication of costs between headquarters and field offices; poor-quality work practices; poor physical protection of materials and equipment; excessive costs incurred due to idle rented equipment; excessive manning of project; and uncontrolled overtime costs.

Unit-price contracts are useful when large amounts of similar work is required from the contractor (e.g., clearing land by the acre and surveillance of a building). A price is agreed on for each unit of work. Risks in unit-price contracts include: excessive progress payment, improper or inaccurate reporting of units completed, unauthorized escalation adjustments, and inaccurate field records. Exhibit 1.1 shows a comparison of the three categories of contracts.

(ii) Quality Audit Engagements

Quality audit engagements can take place in two areas: quality audit of a company's products and services and quality audit of internal audit function. Each area is briefly discussed next.

(A) Quality Audit of a Company's Products or Services   Most organizations view quality of a product or service as a competitive weapon. Quality can increase revenues and sales, decrease costs, and increase profits. Auditing the quality department is very important for the internal audit department since it is one of the assurance functions in the organization. Both audit and quality departments provide assurance to management that organizational resources are used efficiently and effectively.

The internal audit scope of quality function includes review of the charter, organization chart, quality policies and procedures, quality control tools, quality costs (cost of quality), quality management tools, quality standards, applicable laws and regulations, and Six Sigma metrics.

The internal auditor needs to understand a number of areas, including:

- How quality management tools (affinity diagrams, tree diagrams, process decision program charts, matrix diagrams, interrelationship digraphs, prioritization matrices, and activity network diagrams) are used, including their frequency and applicability.

- How Six Sigma metrics are implemented or planned to be implemented.

- How quality control tools (check sheets, histograms, scatter diagrams, Pareto diagrams, flowcharts, cause-and-effect diagrams, and control charts) are used, including their frequency and applicability.

- How quality costs (preventive, appraisal, internal failures, and external failures) are accumulated and reported to management and their reasonableness with the industry norms and company targets.

- How service quality characteristics (intangibility, inseparability, heterogeneity, and perishability) are measured and reported.

(B) Quality Audit of Internal Audit Function Many audit departments have installed total quality management (TQM) approaches to improve audit operations. One such approach is recommended by the U.S. Government Accountability Office, which outlined eight steps to TQM in audit operations.

1. **Initial quality assessment.** This step includes:

   a. Identifying the audit department's customers.

   b. Establishing the needs of the customers.

   c. Setting priorities so as to best meet the customers' needs.

   d. Assessing the quality of the audit products (audit reports) as perceived by the audit customers in regard to timeliness, usefulness, responsiveness, and cost.

   e. Interviewing customers so as to reveal pertinent information about the audits, audit staff performance, and the audit department as a whole.

2. **CAE awareness.** Awareness training should stress the importance of TQM as a philosophy or an approach, not a program.

3. **Formation of a quality council.** Audit managers, audit supervisors, and audit staff members should be part of the quality council, and they should acquire the knowledge of TQM principles, practices, and tools. This council should report to the CAE. It should coordinate training and participate in prototypes.

4. **Fostering teamwork in audits.** The audit department should establish a participative environment that fosters teamwork and quality work. Audit plans, audit work programs, fieldwork, working papers, and audit reports all require quality orientation and thinking.

5. **Development of prototypes.** To convince some auditors who are doubtful about the TQM philosophy, the quality council should demonstrate the practical value of new ways of organizing the audit work with highly visible prototype and productivity initiatives. When tested and proven successful, these prototypes can convince the cautious of the audit staff.

6. **Celebration of success.** The audit department should publicize the achievements of the prototype to encourage the cautious and hesitant audit staff.

7. **Organizational implementation.** All units and all locations of the audit department should implement audit quality methods, and appropriate recognition should be given for those units that are most successful. Doing this provides motivation and promotes healthy competition.

8. **Annual audit quality review.** There should be an annual audit quality review for audit departments throughout the organization. The annual review, together with a rating system, will demonstrate the success of the implementation of quality in the audit department.

INTERNAL AUDIT AND TQM

An audit assignment can go wrong at any stage. It can be ill conceived, improperly directed, poorly planned, or badly implemented, and its results can be ineffectively communicated. For a variety of reasons, it can fail to meet its customers' needs.

(continued)

INTERNAL AUDIT AND TQM *(Continued)*

An appropriate quality control system identifies or flags those factors that could jeopardize the quality of an audit and establishes processes or procedures that promptly identify and correct problems before they occur. For example, it will be more effective to correct a planning-related problem in the planning phase than in a later phase (e.g., reporting phase).

An effective quality control system needs to do more than ensure the quality with which work was performed. It also needs to determine what the work accomplished and how customers and stakeholders viewed the result. This can be done by system approaches, such as surveys of customers and stakeholders, recommendation tracking and reporting systems, and auditor performance measurements and award/reward systems.

(iii) Due Diligence Audit Engagements

Due diligence involves pre-assessment, examination, analysis, and reporting on major activities before they are finalized and approved. It's purpose is to minimize potential risks from undertaking new activities or ventures. Due diligence audits provide a safety valve to management that is planning to acquire, manage, or consolidate with other businesses. Joint ventures and environmental audits are also subject to due diligence audits. These audits are the minimum managerial requirements to ensure that all applicable laws and regulations are met and that risks and exposures are minimized. For example, due diligence audits are a risk management tool for banks, land buyers, and lending agencies when a buyer is purchasing land or accepting it as a gift. Here the buyer wants to minimize the potential legal liability resulting from the land acquisition.

Due diligence audits are team-based efforts with internal auditors, external auditors, lawyers, engineers, IT staff, and other specialists. Three phases in this audit include information gathering (phase 1), information analysis (phase 2), and information reporting (phase 3). Information gathering involves collecting information through document reviews, interviews, and meetings. Information analysis may include analytical reviews, including ratio analysis, regression analysis, and other quantitative techniques. Information reporting includes writing a balanced report based on facts with an executive summary. In addition to writing reports, oral reports can be used for immediate response and clarification of issues and findings.

(iv) Security Audit Engagements

The scope of security audits, which can be unannounced audits, includes logical security, physical security, computer storage media, and safety. Logical security focuses on determining whether a person attempting access should be allowed into a computer system and what the user can do once on the system. Specific controls in logical review include authentication controls such as composition and change of passwords and user identification codes (IDs), encryption methods and routines, and restricting transactions to particular terminals and employees. Terminal-related controls include time-out limits and displaying the last time and date a user ID was used.

The scope of physical security audits can include a review of physical access to storerooms, cash vaults, research laboratories, plants and factories, computer centers, preventive maintenance procedures, and environmental controls. Physical access controls include limiting unauthorized access using electronic cards and biometrics access devices (voice recognition, electronic signature verification), fire prevention techniques, and electric power supply and conditioning.

The scope of computer storage media audits includes review of rotation of computer files to and from off-site storage, electronic vaulting at remote locations, environmental controls off-site as well as on-site, and adequacy of storage media capacity for future computing needs.

The scope of safety audits includes review of safety policies and procedures and accident statistics and investigations. The internal auditor needs to make sure that corrective actions to safety problems are proper and timely and that all applicable labor laws are complied with.

The internal auditor needs to coordinate safety audit activities with other internal assurance functions, such as quality, health, security, and industrial engineering. Possible areas of coordination include sharing work plans and schedules, conducting periodic meetings, exchanging reports, developing work statistics, providing control training, and participating in investigations and corrective actions.

(v) Privacy Audit Engagements

Privacy is the right of an individual to limit access to information regarding that individual. The term "privacy" refers to the social balance between an individual's right to keep information confidential and the societal benefit derived from sharing information and how this balance is codified to give individuals the means to control personal information. The term "confidentiality" refers to disclosure of information only to authorized individuals and entities.

Privacy means that the rights of the accused (suspect) cannot be violated during the investigation. The accused can use protective orders if his or her privacy rights are ignored or handled improperly. If accused persons can prove that evidence brought against them would do more harm to them than good, the courts will favor the accused in suppressing such evidence from being presented.

The organization can protect itself from privacy and confidentiality problems by developing a policy statement and by showing the amount of damage done by the accused. A policy statement is a prerequisite to handling privacy issues properly and legally. An incomplete or unclear policy could result in legal action against the organization by employees (suspects) when they find out that their privacy rights are violated.

The organization must show that the perpetrator actually broke into a computer system and violated its proprietary rights to the system, and then show the extent of damage caused. Organizations should have controls such as passwords, encryption, access controls, hidden files, and warning banners to establish proprietary rights to a computer system. A policy statement should define this area.

In general, internal auditors are concerned about accidental or intentional disclosure of confidential data. They are also concerned about collection and use of such data. Legal requirements dictate the collection, disclosure, and use of data, in both public and private sectors. Internal auditors must understand that there is a trade-off between the level of protection (security) and the cost of that protection and that there is no absolute (perfect) security.

Threats to security come from individuals already having authorized access to a computer system as well as from those unauthorized to have access to a computer system. The internal auditor needs to make sure that known threats, exposures, and risks are addressed during system design, that proper controls are established, and that the established controls are working effectively on a continued basis.

Privacy laws affecting the public sector include the US Privacy Act of 1974, the Freedom of Information Act, and the Health Insurance Portability and Accountability Act of 1996. Privacy laws affecting the private sector include Securities and Exchange Commission (SEC) requirements, the Foreign Corrupt Practices Act, and others.

Most, if not all, of these privacy laws require establishing appropriate safeguards (controls) to ensure the confidentiality and integrity of personal or corporate records and protecting against anticipated threats that could result in substantial harm to individuals or corporations.

The internal auditor should be concerned not only with actual compliance with privacy laws but also with how such compliance can be proved to authorities should the question arise. Documentation, in the form of manuals, should provide such proof, as documentation contains work rules, standard operating procedures, controls, and references to laws and regulations.

(vi) Performance Audit Engagements

Any operation or function, whether it is production or service, needs to be measured in terms of its performance. To measure performance, performance standards, which are tied to the primary objectives of the operation or function, must be developed and monitored. In addition, each performance standard must be expressed in terms of efficiency and effectiveness criteria. If too many performance standards or indicators exist, employees may not be able to handle them properly, which can lead to waste of resources. Therefore, both management and employees should focus on a few meaningful, key performance indicators (KPIs).

For example, the KPIs in a production plant safety operation might include:

- Number of safety inspections conducted in a month, quarter, and year.
- Number of factory equipment tested and calibrated in a month, quarter, and year.
- Number of factory operations observed for safety conditions in a month, quarter, and year.
- Number of safety accidents investigated and reported in a month, quarter, and year.
- Number of accidents reduced from month to month, quarter to quarter, and year to year.
- Amount of machine downtime reduced resulting from reduced accidents in a month, quarter, and year.
- Amount of worker's compensation insurance premiums reduced resulting from reduced accidents.

The internal auditor needs to be aware that some employees may deceive the KPIs to survive and may distort performance results to receive larger bonuses and promotions. Therefore, the auditor should compare the KPIs with the industry norms as well as with the same company data from period to period. Also, the auditor should be careful in analyzing KPIs that look too good as well as those KPIs that do not meet standards.

(vii) Operational Audit Engagements

(A) Overview of Operational Audits The economic events and business transactions of an entity are usually classified into several cycles for convenience of grouping similar and related activities and in order to manage the audit effectively and efficiently. For example, typical cycles for a manufacturing organization are (see Exhibit 1.2):

- Revenue
- Expenditure
- Production/conversion

- Treasury (financing/investing)
- Financial reporting (external)

The production/conversion cycle is the only one that will be different between manufacturing and nonmanufacturing organizations. Regardless of the nature of the organization, an internal control structure must meet several detailed internal control objectives to prevent, detect, and correct errors, omissions, fraud, and irregularities during handling of the business transaction cycles. These objectives, which are applicable to all transaction cycles, include:

- Transactions are properly authorized.
- Existing transactions are recorded.

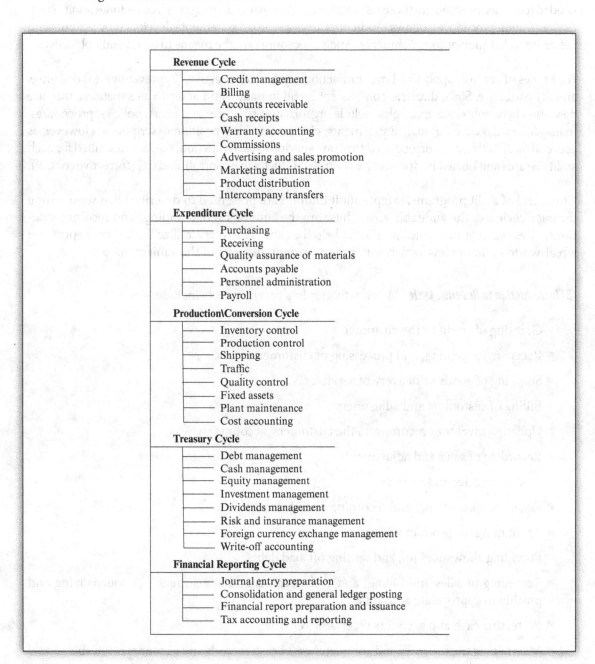

Revenue Cycle
- Credit management
- Billing
- Accounts receivable
- Cash receipts
- Warranty accounting
- Commissions
- Advertising and sales promotion
- Marketing administration
- Product distribution
- Intercompany transfers

Expenditure Cycle
- Purchasing
- Receiving
- Quality assurance of materials
- Accounts payable
- Personnel administration
- Payroll

Production\Conversion Cycle
- Inventory control
- Production control
- Shipping
- Traffic
- Quality control
- Fixed assets
- Plant maintenance
- Cost accounting

Treasury Cycle
- Debt management
- Cash management
- Equity management
- Investment management
- Dividends management
- Risk and insurance management
- Foreign currency exchange management
- Write-off accounting

Financial Reporting Cycle
- Journal entry preparation
- Consolidation and general ledger posting
- Financial report preparation and issuance
- Tax accounting and reporting

EXHIBIT 1.2 Overview Diagram for Operational Audits

- Recorded transactions are valid.

- Transactions are properly classified.

- Transactions are properly valued.

- Transactions are recorded at the proper time and are reasonable.

- Transactions are properly posted to journals, ledgers, books, and subsidiary records.

- Transactions are properly and promptly reconciled, properly summarized and reported.

For each transaction cycle and for each auditable area within a transaction cycle, we present what can go wrong—that is, potential or actual risks and exposures along with controls or control procedures needed to reduce or eliminate those risks and exposures. An audit program that includes audit objectives and audit procedures follows. Audit objectives are broad statements developed by auditors and define intended audit accomplishments. Audit procedures are the means to attain audit objectives.

Four types of controls apply to all five transactions cycles: (1) directive, (2) preventive, (3) detective, and (4) corrective. Since directive controls are broad in nature and apply to all situations, they are described here only once. Examples include organization structure and chart, policies, procedures, management directives, guidance statements, circulars, and job/position descriptions. However, as preventive, directive, and corrective controls are specific to each function, they are described for each auditable area and labeled PC (preventive control) DC (detective control), and CC (corrective control).

At the end of audit programs, sample audit findings are presented to describe what went wrong during a review of the auditable area. These are the auditor's actual findings and recommendations. These sample audit findings should help the candidate to crystallize the key concepts from a real-world point of view, which will increase comprehension of the subject matter.

(B) Introduction to Revenue Cycle   Major activities in a revenue cycle include:

- Granting of credit to the customer.

- Receiving, accepting, and processing of customer orders.

- Shipping of goods or delivery of service.

- Billing of customers and adjustments.

- Updating inventory records and the customers' accounts.

- Recording of sales and adjustments.

- Costing of sales and services.

- Receiving, processing, and recording of cash receipts.

- Accounting for product warranties.

- Providing allowances for, and writing off, bad debts.

- Recording of sales and billing, and cash receipts and adjustments, by journalizing and posting to appropriate accounts.

- Protecting cash and accounts receivable records.

- Maintaining the accuracy and completeness of cash records and accounts receivable record balances and warranty records.

Audit Cycle/Area: Revenue—Credit Management

Risks and Exposures	Controls or Control Procedures
Improper (e.g., loose or tight) credit may be granted.	Customer background verification, financial statement analysis, and segregation of duties between credit and sales functions (PC).
Loans made to fictitious borrowers.	Approval of secured collateral (PC). Test sample for properly completed loan documents (DC).
Unauthorized shipping of goods.	Segregation of duties among credit, billing, and shipping functions (PC).

Audit Objectives for Credit Management	Audit Procedures for Credit Management
To determine whether the credit management function is administered properly.	• Ensure that a thorough investigation is made of all new customers before a credit limit is established. Verify that a credit file is established for each customer with all available financial and operating background information. Verify that credit limits are reviewed, updated, and used for all customers on a continuing basis.
	• Ensure that the customer's orders are subject to review and approval by the credit department before acceptance of the sales order. Individual customer requests for credit in excess of established limits must be reviewed by authorized higher-level management. An example of attribute sampling would be to determine whether the credit department requires a credit check for credit sales when needed.
	A possible scenario is: Individual salespeople were allowed to approve credit and determine product availability and delivery increased sales. Later, write-offs of accounts receivables increased. An appropriate corrective action is an independent review and approval of credit.
	• Select a representative number of sales orders and the corresponding invoices and verify that: the terms and amounts for credit extended are within those authorized limits; and proper approval had been obtained prior to acceptance of the order when the credit limits and/or terms have been exceeded.
To determine if credit controls are inconsistently applied, preventing valid sales to creditworthy customers.	Compare credit histories for those receiving credit and for those denied credit. Evaluate the adequacy of controls.

EXAMPLES OF APPLICATION OF COMPUTER-ASSISTED AUDIT TECHNIQUES (CAATs): CREDIT MANAGEMENT

- List all shipments exceeding the customer credit limits in order to understand reasons of noncompliance.

- Compare the percentage of credit applications that were rejected with standards to determine whether the credit approval process is strict or lax.

Audit Cycle/Area: Revenue—Billing

Risks and Exposures	Controls or Control Procedures
Unauthorized persons may be accessing the order entry system via a dial-up using personal computers.	• A frequent access revalidation with logical access controls such as callback and passwords (PC).
Shipments may not be billed.	• Shipping documents, packing slips, sales order forms, credit memoranda, and customer invoices should be prenumbered and their use controlled (PC).
	• Reconciliation between shipping and billing (DC).
Improper services or goods may be billed.	• Reconcile a sample of invoices to service pickup receipts or goods receiving reports (DC).
Potential for fraud or irregularities.	• Segregation of duties among billing, credit, shipping, and marketing functions (PC).

Audit Objectives for Billing	Audit Procedures for Billing
To determine whether controls over order entry and order processing are adequate.	• Ensure that the order system does not process any customer orders when the customer order exceeds his or her credit limits. Identify exceptions and overrides.
	• Identify all preventive, detective, and corrective controls present in the system, and evaluate their adequacy.
	• Examine the order entry system manual for completeness, clarity, and currency.
	• Review system availability and computer terminal response times, and compare them with service-level objectives to ensure system performance meets operating goals.
To ascertain whether customer invoices are based only on shipments made and those invoices are mailed within the established time limits.	• To evaluate compliance with controls designed to ensure that all shipments are billed, select "prenumbered shipping documents" as the population from which to draw a sample.
	• Select a sample of customer invoices, and compare the date of invoice with the date on the relevant shipping documents. Verify that the quantity shipped and billed is the same.
To ensure that the price charged on the invoice is the approved price.	• Check that the price charged on the invoice is the same as the one found on the approved price list. Identify exceptions and reasons for them.
	• Select some missing numbers from shipping documents, sales order forms, and credit memoranda, and customer sales invoices, and check as to follow-up actions taken. Analyze the reasons given for missing documents.
To determine whether sales order backlog is properly controlled.	• To ensure prompt delivery of out-of-stock items, match the back-order file to goods received daily.
	• Analyze open sales orders for backlog and compute the number of: (1) active orders that were recently shipped but not closed; (2) orders for future delivery; orders on which delivery is past due; (3) orders that appear to be closed; and (4) inactive orders for other reasons. Ensure that additional billings are forthcoming for the orders that appeared to be closed.

To determine whether invoices and credit memoranda are handled properly and in a timely manner by the billing department.	• Review a sample of invoices to ensure that they contain invoice number, date, customer number, product identification code, price, payment terms, amount due, tax information, freight terms, etc.
	• Select a sample of credit memoranda, and trace and analyze supporting documentation. Verify the reasons for issuing the credit memoranda to customers.
	• Trace the customer Invoices to the detailed accounts receivable records. Trace totals of one month's sales summary to the sales and receivables general ledger account.

EXAMPLES OF APPLICATION OF CAATs: SALES/BILLING/INVOICING

■ Compare shipping records with sales invoices by line item for testing to determine whether all inventory shipments were billed to customers.

■ Identify discrepancies between quantities shipped and quantities billed in order to understand reasons.

■ Use controlled reprocessing techniques to identify lost or incomplete sales accounting record updates.

CREDIT MEMOS VERSUS DEBIT MEMOS

■ Credit memos are used to adjust accounts receivable balances.

■ Debit memos are used to adjust accounts payable balances.

Audit Cycle/Area: Revenue—Accounts Receivable

Risks and Exposures	Controls and Control Procedures
A division may intentionally ship unordered merchandise to customers near the end of each quarter to meet its sales goals.	Send accounts receivable confirmations to selected customers as of the end of the quarter (DC).
Allowance for bad debts may be misstated.	Perform an aging analysis of accounts receivable accounts (DC).
Potential for fraud or irregularities.	Segregation of duties among accounts receivable, credit and collection, shipping, billing, and marketing functions (PC). Receivable clerk should not have physical access to and control of cash receipts (PC).
Audit Objectives for Accounts Receivable	**Audit Procedures for Accounts Receivable**
To determine whether accounts receivable represent valid sales.	Trace a sample of accounts receivable debit entries to customer invoices and related shipping documents.

(continued)

Audit Objectives for Accounts Receivable	Audit Procedures for Accounts Receivable
To ascertain whether the total billed sales and cash receipts are accurately classified, summarized, and reported on a timely basis.	Check the timeliness of receivable postings to individual accounts receivable records. Verify that postings are made directly from customer invoices and/or credit memoranda. Establish that postings for daily cash receipts are made from remittance advices rather than from check receipts.
To ensure that all cash sales are recorded.	Observe cash sales to determine if customers are given written receipts.
To determine whether refunds granted to customers were properly approved.	Trace accounts receivable entries to credit memos. Credit memos are used to grant refunds to customers.
To determine if the allowance for doubtful accounts is accurately stated and whether trade accounts receivable are carried at net collectible amounts.	Prepare and analyze the aging schedule of trade accounts receivable, and discuss with management all potentially doubtful accounts that are material in amount.
To determine whether statements of accounts are mailed to customers on a regular basis.	Test whether statements of accounts are mailed on a designated schedule, and make sure that an employee who has no access to cash remittance or the detailed accounts receivable records does these mailings and reconciliations.
To evaluate the collectibility of past due accounts.	Review the collectibility of past-due accounts with the credit manager and ascertain that the reserve for doubtful accounts is adequate. The aged accounts receivable listing is the primary document to rely on when evaluating the collectibility of receivables and their valuation. Evaluate the reasons given for accounts written off during the period under review by examining bankruptcy, discharge notices, and other sources to make sure that accounts written off actually had not been collected (i.e., bad and doubtful).
To ensure those receivables adjustments are properly approved and controlled.	Examine whether write-off of bad debts, discounts in excess of normal credit lines, refunds, and authorized management approves allowances.
To determine whether controls over notes receivable are adequate and are being followed.	Verify that a note register is kept that includes identification of the customer, amount, maturity date, and collateral. Determine that the note register is reconciled periodically to the control account. Ascertain that a record is kept of the discount notes to reflect the contingent liability. Examination of cash receipts records to determine promptness of interest and principal payments is the audit procedure providing the best evidence about the collectibility of notes receivable.
To ensure that the aged trial balance report is prepared and confirmations are mailed on a timely basis.	Inquire whether an aged trial balance report is prepared and that positive confirmations are sent for all accounts over a certain amount and negative confirmations are sent to the remaining accounts. Test the accuracy of the aged trial balance by tracing a number of accounts to the detail records. Add the open items for a number of accounts in the ledger and trace the totals to the aging schedules and invoices.
To determine whether the receivable subledger is reconciled regularly to the general ledger.	Analyze the receivables general ledger control account for each category of receivables and trace the postings to supporting documentation, such as sales journal summaries, sales adjustment records, and other correspondence.

ACCOUNTS RECEIVABLE TURNOVER

When the accounts receivable turnover rate falls from 6.2 to 4.2 over the last two years, a more liberal credit policy would be the most likely cause of the decrease in the turnover rate. When the other variables are constant, a decrease in the turnover rate indicates a liberal credit policy while an increase indicates a tight (conservative) credit policy.

EXAMPLES OF APPLICATION OF CAATs: ACCOUNTS RECEIVABLE

- Develop a control total to verify that the dollar amounts for all debits and credits for incoming transactions are posted properly and completely to an accounts receivable master file.

- Recompute provisions for doubtful accounts and compare with management's estimates.

- List all credit balances for further analysis and interpretation because debit balances are normal.

- List all outstanding receivables balances in excess of customer credit limits for understanding reasons of noncompliance.

- Recompute customer receivables account-aging categories, and compare them with management's computations.

Audit Cycle/Area: Revenue—Cash Receipts

Risks and Exposures	Controls or Control Procedures
Inadequate physical access controls over cash.	Restricted areas, money safes, controls over night collections (PC).
Alteration of petty cash balances by petty cash custodian.	Separate responsibility for imprest fund checking account reconciliation from the petty cash custodian's duties (PC).
Misappropriation of cash receipts.	Separate the cash receipt function from the related record-keeping function (PC).
Improper handling of cash receipt transactions.	One employee issues a prenumbered cash receipt form for all cash collections; another employee reconciles daily total of prenumbered receipts to bank deposits (PC, DC).
Potential for fraud or irregularities.	Segregation of duties between cash receipts and bank reconciliation; vouching for payment, credit, opening incoming mail, and posting cash receipts to the general ledger functions (PC). Use of fidelity bonds and employee background checks (PC).

Audit Objectives for Cash Receipts	Audit Procedures for Cash Receipts
To determine whether access to cash receipts is permitted only in accordance with management's authorization.	Verify that all bank account openings and closings have been approved by the treasurer of the organization. Ensure that incoming cash is handled by the least possible number of employees while maintaining segregation of duties. Check that cash receipts are promptly deposited intact and not commingled with other cash items or petty cash funds.

(*continued*)

Audit Objectives for Cash Receipts	Audit Procedures for Cash Receipts
	Determine that employees handling cash funds are properly bonded. Based on the volume of cash receipts, analyze the need for the use of a lockbox. Ensure that when branch offices collect cash receipts, only personnel authorized by the head/home office deposit those collections in a bank account subject to withdrawal.
	Select a representative sample of checks returned by the bank as uncollectible. Ascertain that an individual not responsible for preparing the cash deposit has investigated and has taken appropriate action.
To determine whether controls over checks arriving in the mail are adequate.	Ensure that all cash receipts are deposited in the bank daily. To ensure compliance, compare cash receipt journal entries with the monthly bank statements.
To determine whether controls over petty cash are adequate.	Compare monthly balances and use change and trend analysis to detect fraud. In one situation, a remote unit's petty cash custodian had responsibility for the imprest fund checking account reconciliation. The cashier concealed a diversion of funds by altering the beginning balance on the monthly reconciliations sent to the headquarters.
To ascertain whether cash receipts are accurately summarized and reported in a timely manner.	Ensure that cash receipts are prelisted at the initial point of receipt by preprinted cash receipt forms. Verify that cash receipts are posted to detail accounts receivable records from collection advice, not the checks. Find out if an independent person promptly compares the totals with entries in the cash receipts records. *Requiring preparation of a prelist of incoming cash receipts, with copies of the prelist going to the cashier and to the accounting department, is an example of a preventive control.*
	Trace the amount received to the daily bank deposit. Note any differences.
	Ensure that no payroll or personal checks are cashed from cash receipts.
	Examine the account distribution of the cash receipt total, and compare to the detail receivables posting and the invoice as to amount and date entered. Ensure that discount and allowances taken are proper. Ensure that cash receipts regarding taxes are accurately classified and reported to the tax authorities in a timely manner. *In order to determine whether customers took undeserved cash discounts, compare cash receipt journal entries with related remittance advices and sales invoices.*
	Obtain bank statements and verify that deposits are being made on a daily basis. Investigate any unusual amounts.

EXAMPLES OF APPLICATION OF CAATs: CASH RECEIPTS

- List outstanding customer payment checks that were not applied to their account receivables records.
- Compare the accuracy of posting of cash receipts journal entries to general ledger cash accounts.

Audit Cycle/Area: Revenue—Warranty Accounting

Risks and Exposures	Controls or Control Procedures
Manipulation of warranty reserves.	Conduct trend analysis and ratio analysis (DC).
Underestimation of warranty liabilities.	Recompute and compare actual experience with accruals (DC).

Warranty costs are defined as costs incurred after passage of title to a customer in connection with defective products shipped to customers.

Audit Objectives for Warranty Accounting	Audit Procedures for Warranty Accounting
To determine whether provisions to the reserve account for warranty are made, classified, and recorded on a consistent basis.	Obtain the supporting detail or analyses of an individual warranty reserve account and reconcile the detail to the general ledger account, compare the balance at the audit date with those of the previous year, and investigate all significant changes. Check the warranty reserve calculation for consistency with the established rates, review the propriety of the contra accounts by examining entries to the reserve accounts, and verify that all significant charges are costs of the nature for which the warranty reserve was set up originally.
To ascertain whether the warranty reserve account is reviewed periodically for adequacy.	Inquire whether a detailed analysis and evaluation are made at the end of each accounting year to verify the adequacy of the reserve balance. This is to cover known and probable exposures and to ensure the compliance to local tax laws and regulations.
	Assess the basis for calculating the warranty reserves. Ensure that these items were taken into consideration for determining the base: prior experience ratings, specific sales and major contracts identified as major exposure, known past warranty claims, and known or expected quality problems uncovered in production.
	With the help of legal and marketing management, ensure that accrued warranty liabilities are properly estimated, provided for, and reported.
	Examine the justification of deductibility of warranty expenses for income tax purposes.

Audit Cycle/Area: Revenue—Commissions

Risks and Exposures	Controls or Control Procedures
Sales commissions for the year were too large.	Compute a selected sales commissions to ensure the accuracy of recorded commissions (DC).
Impropriety of sales commissions paid.	Perform a detailed commission account analysis to detect exceptions (DC).

(continued)

Audit Objectives for Commissions	Audit Procedures for Commissions
To determine whether all commission payments to dealers, brokers, distributors, and agents are based on written agreements.	Inspect all written agreements with the agents, and ensure that a master file of agreements is maintained with control numbers assigned to the agreements for tracking and controlling purposes. Inquire whether all agreements have been reviewed and approved by legal counsel. Look for any noncash considerations agreed to in the agreements (i.e., sales of merchandise at "distressed" prices), which should be discouraged and brought to senior management's attention.
To ascertain whether commission payments are made only for valid business reasons and payments are properly computed and accounted for.	Ensure that approved requests for the payment of commissions are independently verified by the accounting department before processing. This includes not only the accuracy of calculations but also the proper application of the base and rates and limits. Obtain canceled checks and review for proper endorsement. Also, compare payee's name per check with agent named in the agreement. Ensure that journal entries for commissions earned are prepared for each accounting period. Ensure that all commissions are accurately classified, summarized, and reported in the proper period. Perform an analytical review of commissions paid in relation to performance goals. Some measures include sales by product, sales by location, collections received, and individual agent's performance. Assess the reasonableness of commission expenses as a percentage of sales for several periods, and investigate any unusual variations.

EXAMPLES OF APPLICATION OF CAATs: COMMISSIONS

- Recompute sales commissions to salespersons and distributors, and compare them with management calculations and contracts.

- Verify that sales commissions were adjusted to reflect customer returns and other credits not resulting in a sale.

Audit Cycle/Area: Revenue—Advertising and Sales Promotion

Risks and Exposures	Controls or Control Procedures
Unreasonable advertising expense.	Analytical evidence developed by comparing the ratio of advertising expense to sales with historical data for the company and industry (DC).
Disputes over charges and expenses billed by an independent advertising agency.	A written agreement containing provisions as to charges and expenses billable (PC).
Informal function for advertising and sales promotion.	Plans, goals, budgets, and comparison of the actual with budgets (PC).
Potential for fraud or irregularities.	Segregation of duties among advertising, purchasing, receiving, and accounts payable functions (PC).

Audit Objectives for Advertising and Sales Promotion	**Audit Procedures for Advertising and Sales Promotion**
To determine whether approved budgets exist for advertising and sales promotion activities and that those advertising expenditures are properly classified for performance measurement.	Examine and evaluate the method of determination of approved budget amounts. Determine that the budget elements (e.g., production costs, media, and materials) are classified in a form that can be coordinated with accounting. Perform an analytical review by comparing this year's budget with prior years' budgeted levels. Inquire as to reasons for any significant variations. Examine actual expenditures by month to determine whether large expenditures are being made at year-end to use up budget balances. Conversely, determine that advertising budgets do not phase out prior to the year-end. Neither situation is desirable. Inquire whether analyses were conducted with regard to outsourcing the advertising work to an outside agency. Evaluate the advantages and disadvantages for outsourcing.
To ascertain whether a detailed budget is prepared for each advertising project and closed properly after the work is completed and that costs are documented and are reasonable.	Obtain the breakdown of the advertising and sales promotion budget by project. Study the actual expenditures against the budget, and investigate any variances. Select several projects and: (1) examine contracts with advertising agencies and determine that they include duration, cancellation, and proper approval; (2) determine the basis of allocating direct and indirect agency costs; (3) check estimation sheets showing media, estimated cost, description of advertising, date of appearance, and agency fee; (4) review billings and supporting vouchers from the agency, and determine that all items are billed in accordance with agreements and purchase orders; (5) find out if independent verification of exhibition and date of advertising is obtained from the agency or an independent service; and (6) verify that claims have been made for unsatisfactory items (e.g., wrong position in publication, poor printing, radio and television station interruptions, torn billboard, or lack of illumination at night on billboards). Verify that media billings are accompanied by evidence of appearance in such forms as: tearsheets from magazines, newspapers, and classified directories; performance affidavits from radio and television stations; and location lists for outdoor advertising. Check the calculation of the agency's commissions. Verify, by examination of published price lists, that the proper rates were used for media billings. Examine the advertising department's time sheets and vouchers for purchased materials and determine that these production charges have been properly allocated to the project.

(continued)

Audit Objectives for Advertising and Sales Promotion	Audit Procedures for Advertising and Sales Promotion
	Where agency contracts give the right to audit, visit the advertising agency and examine appropriate vouchers, time reports, overtime records, and inventory records for accuracy and completeness of work and charges. Inquire whether the agency has given due consideration to discounts and special rates and that the savings are passed to the company. Find out if the agency and the company use competitive bidding where appropriate, and understand the criteria used for agency selection. Evaluate whether existing controls are sufficient to eliminate the risk of duplicate payment of invoices to the agency.
To determine whether the quality and quantity of advertising and sales promotion materials are adequately controlled.	Review the physical controls as well as financial controls maintained over advertising and sales promotion materials, and note any significant variations with budgeted costs, levels of expenditures compared to prior years, and any write-offs. These materials include artwork, display items, tearsheets, sales brochures, and catalogs.
	Examine the charges for materials distributed to the proper budget and expense accounts, and understand the reasons for significant deviations from budget and confirm that appropriate management approvals were obtained for overexpenditures.
	Examine payment arrangements with various supply sources and determine that payments are made accordingly. Select a representative number of invoices for materials, and compare the finished advertising with the specifics of the contract as to layout, composition, and artwork to verify the work performed and that materials supplied to studios were used as intended.
	Where suppliers maintain material in their warehouses awaiting shipping instructions, examine the propriety of custody, control over access, and accountability for this inventory. Verify that proper shipping evidence is received prior to payment of charges.

Audit Cycle/Area: Revenue—Marketing Administration

Risks and Exposures	Controls or Control Procedures
Excessive sales adjustments.	Assess production quality control by evaluating the number of adjustments and ascertaining the reasons for sales adjustments (DC).
Individual sales staff approving credit for customers.	Implement independent review and approval of credit by credit department staff (PC).

Audit Objectives for Marketing Administration	Audit Procedures for Marketing Administration
To determine whether the marketing function is organized properly and that adequate documentation exists in support of the objectives, goals, and funding for each program proposal.	Review the marketing organization structure to determine the degree to which it is established along functional lines, product lines, regional and customer lines, etc., and evaluate whether the structure is logically suited to the needs of the company. Analyze the turnover of personnel to determine whether it appears excessive, and if so, ascertain the reasons.
To ascertain whether the marketing function develops long- and short-range sales forecasts and to assess their reasonableness.	Obtain copies of latest market surveys, market share analyses, new-product development plans, and long-range and short-range sales forecasts.
Evaluate the nature and reasonableness of the basis used in developing sales forecasts and the amount and degree of detail supporting the forecast development. Verify whether the sales forecast prepared by marketing is used in the development of the manufacturing forecast.
Verify whether the marketing management periodically reviews sales forecasts and revises them in accordance with changing conditions. Ascertain whether a formal program exists for the recurring analysis of variances between actual sales to budgets and forecasts. Determine that notices of revisions to sales forecasts are distributed to the same parties who received the original forecast.
Establish whether the marketing department coordinates with engineering and research and development departments to develop markets for new products.
Perform sales trend analysis by product lines, and review product lines where sales are declining. Investigate the reasons for any downward trend and recommend corrective action to reverse the trend.
To determine whether product line profitability analyses are prepared for increasing profits and decreasing losses.	Confirm whether periodic reports are prepared reflecting profitability of the various product lines and/or territories.
Investigate which lines are contributing less than budgeted profit margin and why. Review corrective actions planned or already taken. Verify whether marketing management allocates sales and whether the customer service effort is in accordance with the related product line profitability.
Determine marketing management prepares a lost-business report to reflect the extent and reasons for unsuccessful bidding.
To ascertain whether all hired sales personnel are carefully screened and provided adequate training and supervision.	Review and evaluate policies and procedures for the selection and hiring of sales personnel. Determine whether the selection process provides for formal testing techniques to verify professional qualifications and experience levels.

(continued)

Audit Objectives for Marketing Administration	Audit Procedures for Marketing Administration
	Inquire whether a formal training program is available on a continuing basis. Verify whether the training program is adequate and complete in course content and sales staff attendance. Evaluate the information provided to determine its ability to enhance sales staff knowledge of product familiarization. Verify whether the sales manager accompanies new sales personnel in the initial selling stages. Inquire whether salespeople are periodically and formally advised of changes in product features, selling techniques, prices, and payment terms and credit policy.
To determine whether the sales force is geographically allocated and adequately controlled.	Review geographical allocation of field sales force for reasonableness, taking into consideration of the size of the area and actual/potential sales volume. Review how long vacancies remain open and any corrective action taken by management. Review sales statistics of salesperson and by territory to determine whether sales staff is logically assigned to each area on the basis of sales potential. Review for timeliness, adequacy, and completeness sales call reports used by the field sales force and the use made by sales management. Verify whether an evaluation is made of calls planned versus calls accomplished. Review salespeople's expense reports for adequacy and reasonableness.
To ascertain whether sales personnel are employed on an incentive pay plan, preferably based on a written agreement.	Obtain the employment contract for a typical salesperson who is not on a straight-pay basis. Confirm that signed formal agreements covering commission rates and terms of employment are on file. Obtain a summary of total sales personnel indicating whether they are paid on a straight salary basis, an incentive basis, or a combined salary and incentive basis. Verify the type of incentive programs in effect, and review and evaluate the basis on which the incentive factor is developed. Evaluate whether the incentive factor is correlated with the gross margin contributed by the product. Determine that existing incentive compensation plans provide for penalties to be assessed for cancellations and returns by customers. Review reasons for cancellations and returns.

Audit Cycle/Area: Revenue—Product Distribution

Risks and Exposures	Controls or Control Procedures
Inefficient practices.	Product distribution policies and procedures (PC).
Nonperformance and poor-quality work.	Written agreements and contracts with agents and distributors (PC).

Audit Objectives for Product Distribution	**Audit Procedures for Product Distribution**
To determine whether the company products are distributed in an efficient and economical manner and at the same time meet customer needs and market requirements.	Document the various methods used to distribute the company's products (e.g., direct shipment from the manufacturing plant, outlying company warehouses, consignments, and commission merchants). Ask marketing management whether the distribution channels meet the current and future marketing requirements. Inquire whether studies are conducted periodically to determine the profitability of warehouse operations and distribution methods.
To ascertain whether controls over product distributors and agents are proper to facilitate timely information exchange between parties.	Obtain a list of all agents and distributors along with their written agreements. Examine a number of files containing data used for qualifying selected agents and distributors. Evaluate the adequacy of data for qualifying purposes. Test whether payments to agents and distributors comply with the written agreements, are properly authorized, and are correctly recorded. Verify and test the means by which marketing management continually updates outside agents regarding product changes. Inquire whether formal programs have been established to increase the sales competence of outside distributors.

Audit Cycle/Area: Revenue—Intercompany Transfers

Risks and Exposures	**Controls or Control Procedures**
Improper intercompany prices to show excessive profits or to avoid taxes.	Establish a transfer pricing methodology (PC).
Untimely reconciliations between intercompany accounts.	Competent staff supported by clear written policies and procedures (PC).

Audit Objectives for Intercompany Transfers	**Audit Procedures for Intercompany Transfers**
To determine whether all intercompany transactions are accurately classified and promptly recorded in the proper category of accounts.	Ensure that all financial transactions arising between company units and the originating unit through issuance of debit/credit advices reports, as follows: Select a representative number of intercompany transactions, and check whether they have been promptly and accurately recorded in the proper accounts. Select a representative number of intercompany sales invoices received during the month under review and check for evidence of having matched against the related purchase orders and receiving reports.

(*continued*)

Audit Objectives for Intercompany Transfers	Audit Procedures for Intercompany Transfers

To ascertain whether all intercompany accounts are reconciled on a monthly basis.	Check the reconciliation as of the month-end under review of statements received to the division's own records for evidence of having been reviewed by management.
	    Obtain a trial balance of the detailed intercompany accounts and reconcile to the general ledger control account.
	    Find out what measures have been taken or will be taken to clear the imbalances.
	    Scan intercompany account balances for aging or unsettled accounts or disputed items and obtain explanations for overdue accounts.
	    Review suspended intercompany items and obtain and evaluate explanations for their nonclearance.

(C) Introduction to Expenditure Cycle   Major activities in an expenditure cycle include:

- Selecting reliable, trustworthy, and competent vendors.
- Initiating and requisitioning assets, goods, services, and labor.
- Issuing purchase orders and ordering the goods requested.
- Receiving the goods or services and storing the goods received for inventory.
- Accounting for accrued expenses.
- Processing the vendor invoices and receiving reports and comparing them with the purchase order.
- Hiring employees and authorizing pay rates, deductions, and terminations.
- Preparing daily attendance and timekeeping records.
- Preparing and paying payroll.
- Paying liabilities by disbursing cash.
- Filing and paying payroll taxes.
- Recording goods and services purchased, cash, and payroll disbursements by journalizing and posting to appropriate accounts.
- Updating inventory records and employee earning records.
- Costing and reporting labor time and variances.
- Protecting physical inventory of goods and records and payroll funds and records.
- Maintaining the accuracy and completeness of inventory records, payroll bank accounts, and accounts payable records.

Audit Cycle/Area: Expenditure—Purchasing

Risks and Exposures	Controls or Control Procedures
Buyers receiving expensive gifts from a vendor in return for directing a significant amount of business to that vendor.	A policy stating that competitive bids should be solicited on purchases to the maximum extent practicable (PC).

Risks and Exposures	Controls or Control Procedures
Buyers purchasing from a vendor-relative.	Maintain an approved-vendor file for purchases (PC).
Inability to cancel a purchase order, resulting in unneeded materials and legal liabilities.	Purchase order review by legal counsel; description of conditions for cancellation; formal agreements with suppliers specifying the terms, conditions, and time intervals required (PC).
Excessive or unwanted open purchase commitments.	Rules on commitments and contracts, policies, and procedures; clear responsibilities between local purchase and central purchases, authorization levels; delegation of authority for approving purchases (PC).
Buyers favoring certain suppliers in placing orders for personal gain.	Periodic rotation of buyer assignments (PC). Implement a team approach to vendor selection (PC, DC).
Goods may not be purchased at the best price, and buyers may use their positions for personal gain.	Obtain competitive bids from approved vendors (PC).
High inventory holding costs.	Reduce purchasing lead time for materials ordered (CC).
Buyers routinely initiate, authorize, and execute both purchase requisition and purchase order forms for materials ordered for all departments.	Segregation of duties between initiating and authorizing purchase requisitions and executing purchase orders (PC).
Employees not understanding the purchasing procedures.	Develop a procedure manual for purchasing (PC).
Quantities in excess of needs may be ordered.	Have a department supervisor receive each purchase requisition prior to its being forwarded to the purchasing department (PC).
Buyers ordering materials which at that time were being disposed of as surplus.	Develop and distribute periodic reports of surplus stock (PC).
Buyer irregularities or obtaining kickbacks.	Conduct analytical techniques (e.g., change analysis and trend analysis) of buyer or vendor activity (DC).

Audit Objectives for Purchasing	Audit Procedures for Purchasing
To determine whether product demand forecasting techniques produce reliable data for purchasing decisions to be made.	Analyze the method of forecasting product demand: salesperson's projections, market surveys, economic indicators, management's input. Evaluate the method of exploding forecast demand down to component parts and that forecast is time-phased throughout the year. Test to see if purchase order firm commitments are made much earlier than established lead times.
To ascertain whether product demand forecasts are updated throughout the year to reflect actual demand patterns and changing market conditions.	Inquire about the method of updating forecasts (i.e., regeneration, net change, and exponential smoothing). Regeneration involves discarding the old forecast and substituting a new one. This technique is generally appropriate where there are widely varying forecasts and relatively few inventory levels. Net change involves updating only those items for which a forecast change is indicated, either in quantities or in timing. This technique

(continued)

Audit Objectives for Purchasing	Audit Procedures for Purchasing
	is appropriate where there are few changes and many levels in the bills of materials. Exponential smoothing technique uses the formula of New forecast = Old forecast + (Sales − Old forecast). Review techniques for tracking actual demand to the forecast, and comment on significant deviations from forecast and adequacy of tracking techniques.
To determine whether purchase transactions are authorized and are for needed materials only and that the inventory is obtained at the best price.	Review a sample of purchase orders and their related purchase requisitions for proper approval signatures. Predetermined stocking levels help ensure that unnecessary purchases of inventory are not made. Ascertain that production budgets and economic order quantities are integrated and have been used in determining quantities purchased. Purchase orders, receiving reports, and bid quotations provide evidence appropriate to determine that recorded purchase transactions were valid and at the best price.
To determine whether the company has established a formal process of appraisal for selecting vendors.	Determine whether the company has published comprehensive vendor appraisal criteria. Understand the procedures, including form layout, document flow, and authorization requirements, for the appraisal process. Confirm, for each of the A-class items in the sample, that at least two alternative suppliers have been identified. Examine the procedures to test financial and technical reliability, including obtaining credit reports, financial statements, and bank references. Inquire if the purchasing department has a formal procedure for periodic review of appraisals. Verify that the purchasing department has a mechanism for monitoring the performance of vendors and that it uses this information to update vendor appraisals. Review quality records and collect a sample of goods rejected on quality grounds. Review goods delivery records and collect a sample of significantly late deliveries. Trace these problem samples to the vendor appraisal files, and confirm they have been updated.
To ascertain whether procedures for sourcing vendors are adequate.	Verify that each production item is classified into one of these categories: make inside only, make and buy, make or buy, buy outside only. Confirm that the purchasing department head is a member of the make-or-buy committee and is active in that role. Ascertain whether the purchasing department has a reliable indication of total amount of usage for each part. Confirm that the purchasing department receives quality specifications for the goods or services to be purchased. Test for a sample of such specifications and confirm that they exist and are up to date.

Audit Objectives for Purchasing	Audit Procedures for Purchasing
	Take a sample of orders, and compare actual delivery dates with those originally requested. Find out how lead times are monitored. Ensure that regular contacts are maintained with the vendor so that purchasing is aware of problems as they develop and that they are resolved promptly.
	Review the mechanisms used to ensure that the purchasing department is aware of current prices quoted by suppliers. Confirm that for each part on the A-class item list, there are at least two suppliers with price quotations received.
	Confirm that the purchasing department documents the vendor selection process. Review the process for getting quotations, and ensure that they are considered confidential and in no case divulged to a vendor's competition. Confirm that low bids from reputable suppliers are not to be used to reduce prices from existing suppliers.
	Determine whether there is a policy about single sourcing and multiple sourcing. Prepare a schedule of the significant one-vendor purchases indicating the items, vendors, and amount purchased. Determine the dollar impact of one-vendor purchases in relation to total purchases. Investigate the reasons for significant one-vendor purchases and evaluate the risks for using only one source of supply.
	Review the policy about acceptance of gifts from vendors. Interview purchasing department staff about their views on receiving gifts. Obtain a list of visits and meetings with suppliers on the part of purchasing staff, review the expense reports for the associated periods, and confirm whether the expenses were shared each time or alternatively with the vendor.
	Inquire whether there is a program to qualify minority-owned suppliers who are capable of providing quality materials, supplies, and services. Determine whether the company is able to identify which of its suppliers are minority-owned business enterprises.
	Inquire whether the company has a program of cost reduction and cost increase avoidance integrated into its vendor relations policy. Obtain the most recent calculation of money saved through cost reduction or cost increase avoidance. Evaluate the rationale of the calculation and prove the validity of the figures.
	Confirm that all employees in the purchasing department are aware of U.S. antitrust laws. Review all correspondence files for any indication of an illicit attempt, by either the buyer or a supplier, to introduce reciprocity as a criterion for doing

(*continued*)

Audit Objectives for Purchasing	Audit Procedures for Purchasing
	business (i.e., placing orders). Identify all businesses that are both suppliers and customers. From that list of suppliers or customers, select a sample of those where the volume of business is significant and is of the same magnitude in each direction. Understand the reasons for this activity, and inform management about the possible reciprocity.
To determine whether placement of the order for purchase of goods is proper and timely.	Confirm that the purchase order cannot be processed unless there is a corresponding requisition, which can be verified by the requisition number on the order. Verify that requisitioners have been given lists of delivery lead times for major commodities and groups of commodities and that the lists are updated as significant changes occur. The listed lead times should include an adequate allowance for administrative and clerical time. Inquire whether traveling requisitions are used on repetitive items purchased—some constant information is not printed each time a request is made, and all subsequent requests will be cross-referenced to the original requisition number for convenience.
	Confirm that purchasing staff is following the rules prescribed for open purchase commitments. This is described as the maximum allowable limit of dollars that can be spent for each type of materials, such as production materials, interplant materials, subcontracted material, and installation materials. Confirm that the maximum allowable limit for total purchase commitments placed during a time period does not exceed the management-approved limits. Ask about the frequency of updating these open purchase commitments.
	Verify that all purchase orders are printed with a sequential numbering system. Identify and investigate missing numbers. Confirm that there is regular review of missing numbers by the purchasing department.
	Verify that all individual purchase orders for A-class items are written on a single-item basis only for each required production item for better tracking. Take a sample of an A-class item purchase orders, and test for the presence of this information: purchase order number and date; vendor name and address; part number and description; quantity, including correct unit or measure; unit cost; purchase and payment discounts; and freight terms, including method of shipment.
	Perform analytical reviews in the form of calculating time lags or elapsed times among identifying a need to purchase, initiating the purchasing order, and issuing the purchase order. The purpose is to make sure that the time taken to issue orders is not adding significantly

Audit Objectives for Purchasing	Audit Procedures for Purchasing
	to the need to forecast demand for material requirements planning items or to hold safety stocks for order point (OP) items. Test to see If buying practices reflect rush or emergency conditions, and determine if these practices have had any impact on price or possible quality of material accepted.
To ascertain whether the procedures for canceling the purchase order are adequate.	Verify that each major type of material has a time classification by the freedom to cancel the purchase order (e.g., not at all, up to one week before delivery, up to two weeks, etc.), and confirm that these time frames were approved by the legal department and are continually updated by the purchasing department.
	Compute the proportion of cancellations rejected by the vendor by classifying the rejections by reason, and obtain explanations for these rejections. Perform trend analysis for the number of cancellations over a certain time period.
	Identify a sample of canceled orders on which a deposit had been paid and the deposit had been repaid by the vendor.
	Confirm that the documentation canceling a purchase order is distributed to the same parties as the original order and that the cancellation notice is issued in a timely manner. Identify the communication media used: regular mail, electronic mail, or special carrier. Compute the time lags between the rising of the cancellation and issuing the cancellation, and find out how the purchasing department is planning to speed up communication for unacceptable delays.

KEY CONCEPTS TO REMEMBER: ABC Method of Inventory

- Inventory items are classified according to their value and frequency of usage expressed in dollars. "Number of items" would be least likely be used as criteria to classify inventory items. Inventory with high value and greater frequency of usage is labeled as A-class, followed by B-class and C-class. This labeling is referred to as the ABC inventory classification method. From a cycle counting perspective, A-class items could be counted monthly, B-class items quarterly, and C-class items annually. A-class items are likely to have the fewest days' supply in inventory, and C-class items will have many days' of supply. The ABC method suggests that expensive, frequently used, high-stock-out cost items with long lead times should be reviewed more frequently than others.

- The ABC method of inventory control would be appropriate to use to reduce the safety stock investment without materially increasing the probability of stock-outs in a company in which a few products account for most of its costs and a large number of products have low total cost. The ABC method can understate the potential stock-out cost of C-class parts in manufacturing companies. To compensate, some companies invest in safety stock. Note that shortage costs are excluded from classic OP formulas.

COMPUTER SIMULATION IN PURCHASING

Computer simulation can be used to evaluate a company's purchasing function with respect to the effect of alternative purchasing policies on investment in inventory and stock-out costs.

KEY CONCEPTS TO REMEMBER: Evidence in Purchasing and Accounts Payable

- Competitive bids are required on purchases exceeding $3,000 unless a waiver from executive management is obtained. The audit procedure that will result in the most competent evidence of compliance with the bid procedure would be to select a representative sample of purchase orders exceeding $3,000 and examine underlying documentation, ascertaining that requests for bids or properly signed waiver forms are on file.

- Before purchase invoices are approved for payment, an accounting clerk is supposed to compare invoice prices with purchase order prices and indicate their agreement by signing in a designated space on the payment voucher form. The audit procedure that would result in sufficient evidence that this requirement is being followed is to select a representative sample of vouchers, examine them for the signature of the accounting clerk, and compare the prices on the invoices and related purchase orders.

RISKS IN PURCHASING SYSTEMS

When a manual purchasing process is converted to an online computer system, traditional duties will be less segregated than before.

EXAMPLES OF APPLICATION OF CAATs: PURCHASING

- Produce a list of all purchase transactions processed after the cut-off date in order to determine whether all material liabilities for trade accounts payable have been recorded.

- List all new suppliers/vendors to determine whether they were properly approved with competitive bids obtained, where applicable.

- List all suppliers or vendors who exceeded certain dollar threshold limits (e.g., budgets) for further analysis and justification of doing business with them.

- List the top 10 suppliers or vendors for further analysis and identification of improprieties or irregularities, if any.

TOTAL QUALITY MANAGEMENT AND PURCHASING

The application of TQM concepts and principles to the purchasing function has many control implications that an internal auditor should be concerned about.

The TQM approach to purchasing changes the traditional role of purchasing, material acquisition strategies, buyer/supplier working relationships, and buyer/vendor performance measurements to a partnership concept. Some policy and control implications are listed next.

(continued)

- **Identify customers.** For example, suppliers are external customers, and purchase requisitioners are internal customers.

- **Implement just-in-time (JIT) purchasing principles.** The scope of JIT purchasing principles includes supplier selection and evaluation, bidding practices, incoming inspection procedures, inbound freight responsibilities, paperwork reduction, value analysis practices, and packaging needs. JIT purchasing eliminates parts stock-out situations. A formal requisition form is no longer required as the requirements are driven by materials requirements planning (MRP) system.

- **Establish policies that encourage prime contractors to establish long-term partnerships with their supplier base.** Devote more time and effort in getting suppliers involved in the design of the product. Developing a partnership with a supplier does not eliminate the need for good negotiations.

- **View the supplier as the customer.** The buyer is required to provide the supplier with the right tools and right information, such as part drawings, specifications, and delivery dates, that will allow the supplier to provide products or services as needed. The objective is to have supplier and buyer share common goals and benefits. It promotes a win-win situation. Competitive bidding is still required prior to selecting the needed suppliers.

- **Require vendor certification.** Qualify the supplier base to reduce rework and improve quality.

- **Develop single-source strategies.** Use multiple sources only when a unique technology is required or when one source cannot provide all the parts. This strategy could be a professional challenge to the internal auditor for control evaluation. The risk here is too much dependence on one supplier without a fallback.

- **Develop both quantitative and qualitative performance measurements for suppliers.** They should be rated on delivery, quality, cost, and service. Specific examples of quantitative performance measurement techniques include: on-time deliveries, quality of products, number of problems solved, and control of production processes. Some examples of qualitative performance measurements include: the degree of cooperation, technical assistance provided, responsiveness to inquiries and problems, and compliance with instructions provided.

- **Develop performance measurements for buyers.** Examples include requisition cycle time, meeting required dates, quality of products, and responsiveness to requisitioner.

Audit Cycle/Area: Expenditure—Receiving

Risks and Exposures	Controls or Control Procedures
Inadequate control over receipts.	Maintain purchase order with the units described, but both prices and quantities omitted (PC).
Not ensuring that ordered quantities are actually received (i.e., receiving department employees sign receiving documents without inspecting or counting the goods received).	For a sample of receipt: (1) Compare quantities per receiving reports to quantities per supporting purchase orders, and (2) look for authorized signatures on the receiving reports indicating that quantities had been verified (DC). Perform unobtrusive or hidden measures when goods are received (DC).
Failure to detect substandard materials received.	Establish inspection procedures for incoming materials (DC).
Unauthorized shipments are accepted.	Maintain a file of purchase orders in the receiving department for merchandise ordered but not yet received (PC).

(continued)

| Inefficient receiving operations. | Maintain a written receiving manual describing how to handle damaged materials, overshipments and undershipments, valuable items, after-hours deliveries, and materials sent directly to storage or productive facilities (PC). |

Audit Objectives for Receiving	**Audit Procedures for Receiving**
To determine whether procedures and practices of receiving materials are proper and reasonably controlled.	Establish whether receiving department employees prepare and sign a formal receiving report for all items received at each receiving point showing vendor's name, purchase order number, description of material, date received, count, and weight of the materials received. Determine whether the receiving report is based on facts in that it: shows weights of materials only if they have been actually weighed, shows numbers only if they have been counted, and describes the materials only if they have been checked. Ensure that receiving department personnel do not simply take information from documents (e.g., company's purchase order or vendor's bill of lading, packing slip, or shipping document). Determine whether guidelines have been issued on what is to be 100% counted or weighed, what is to be sampled, and when reliance will be placed on supplier information. In order to make sure whether the receiving department verifies the materials and quantities are correct, these audit tests are suggested: (1) Determine the extent to which receipts from suppliers are independently counted, weighed, or otherwise measured and identified without reference to the packing slips or purchase orders; (2) ascertain the extent to which primary verification by the receiving department is limited because of mutual confidence between the company and its vendors; (3) establish the degree of acceptance of container markings and packing slips as evidence of quantity and material identification; (4) verify the extent to which test checks are used in counting or measuring materials received; and (5) determine that quantities received are later verified by store staff or operations staff. Confirm that discrepancies in quality and quantity of materials received are promptly recorded and reported to purchasing, accounts payable, and traffic departments. Determine that goods damaged or lost in transit are properly noted on carriers' receipts and covered by loss or damage reports and that copies of these reports are forwarded to accounting and traffic departments for filing claims. Select a sample of material waiting to be returned to vendors. Confirm that this is not the material that should have been rejected by the receiving department in the first place.

Audit Objectives for Receiving	Audit Procedures for Receiving
	Select a sample of damaged materials and analyze whether the goods are (1) identifiably damaged before arrival, (2) found to be damaged when unpacked, or (3) damaged while in the company's possession. Ensure that the damage report clearly reflects the actual condition. Determine whether the material is (1) to be returned to the vendor, (2) to be reworked, (3) to be scrapped, or (4) awaiting a decision.
	Select a sample of receiving reports and look for quantities received more than preestablished guidelines (say 5% greater than the quantity ordered on the purchase order). Classify them into those where the overshipped quantity was retained or returned. For each excess quantity retained: (1) Calculate the holding cost, (2) establish who authorized retention, and (3) determine advantages from retaining and that it offsets the additional holding costs.
	Inquire whether the receiving department follows up with the purchasing department about open items in the receiving file by matching with the past-due receiving report. Take a sample of open purchase orders and classify them into: no purchase order number given, invalid purchase order number given, and purchase order number is valid but a copy of the purchase order not received. Ensure that a copy of the purchase order is used to receive only authorized purchases.
To ascertain whether goods received are physically secured from theft, loss, or damage until transferred to other areas.	Examine the labeling of all materials, whether they are stored for testing, sent in error, defective, surplus, or other. Take a sample from the receiving reports and confirm that each item is clearly labeled, physically secured and stored in the correct predesignated location, or passed to store or user.
	Match selected fields of the purchase invoice to goods received to ensure that goods received are the same as those shown on the purchase invoice.
	Identify goods received, not billed, for establishing proper liabilities.
	List discrepancies between quantities received and quantities billed for further analysis and examination.
To determine whether the receiving department dispatches goods received to users in a timely manner.	Determine whether targets are available for maximum and average time lags between delivery and receipt by store or user. Select a sample from receiving reports and prepare a schedule showing the dates of delivery and the dates received by stores or users. Investigate and obtain reasons for any time lags in excess of established standards.
	Determine the time lags between the date on which materials are received and the dates the receiving reports are received in the accounts payable department by comparing dates on receiving reports with dates received in accounts payable.

(*continued*)

Audit Objectives for Receiving	Audit Procedures for Receiving
To ascertain whether materials flow through the receiving area effectively and efficiently and that physical arrangement of the receiving area is conducive to effective operation.	Observe the physical location(s) of the receiving area(s) and the layout. Evaluate the effectiveness of material flow through the receiving area to incoming quality control and storerooms.

Review the volume and nature of materials received at various points and determine whether receiving areas could be consolidated for more efficient operation. Analyze the plant layout. Determine whether receiving areas are near points of incoming quality control, storerooms, and start of production lines rather than having to transport received material to the other end of the facility.

Observe whether work areas are adequate. Verify that scales and other mechanical or electrical measurement equipment are regularly calibrated. Review the adequacy of uncrating and counting areas. Check the receiving department storage area. Ensure that material is stored in an orderly manner and is properly identified while awaiting transfer to stores or production lines.

Review the effectiveness of protection against fire with the use of sprinklers and/or fire extinguishers. Review the effectiveness of protection against intrusion or unauthorized removal of goods with the presence of locked doors, restriction of access to essential employees, employment of security guards, use of security alarms, etc.

Determine if the receiving department was subject to a work measurement system for analyzing work flow and to enhance productivity and performance. Evaluate whether the receiving department is keeping up with its workload. Prepare a list of items of backlog and determine loss of purchase discounts resulting from delays in the receiving department.

Select a number of cases where payment was made for demurrage and trace them to determine reasons for demurrage payment and demurrage cost versus overtime pay for unloading trucks. Analyze demurrage expenditures month by month for the last 12 months and comment on the effectiveness of operation. |

KEY CONCEPTS TO REMEMBER: Receiving

- When the number of units shipped in the shipping document does not agree with the quantity shown on the receiving report, the error might be that the amounts ordered on the receiving department's copy of the purchase order or actual count was different from quantity on shipping document.

- One operating department of a company does not have adequate procedures for inspecting and verifying the quantities of goods received. To evaluate the materiality of this control deficiency, the auditor should review the department's annual inventory purchases.

- Upon receipt of purchased goods in a retail company, receiving department employees match the quantity received to the packing slip quantity and mark the retail price on the goods based on a master price list. The annotated packing slip is then forwarded to inventory control, and goods are automatically moved to the retail sales area.

TQM AND JIT RECEIVING

TQM principles and JIT receiving practices can eliminate the need for inspection of incoming materials received due to trust and reliance placed on the supplier. This practice can have a control implication and be a professional challenge for internal auditors.

Audit Cycle/Area: Expenditure—Quality Assurance of Materials

Risks and Exposures	Controls or Control Procedures
Poor-quality material supplied.	Supplying engineering specifications and drawings to the vendors (PC).
Poor inspection procedures resulting in accepting inferior-quality materials.	A written manual describing inspection and test procedures, continuous training of inspectors (PC).

Audit Objectives for Quality Assurance of Materials	Audit Procedures for Quality Assurance of Materials
To determine whether the quality control function is adequately prepared for the job of preventing the escape of defective goods into the production operations.	Confirm whether the quality assurance manual covers topics such as receiving inspection, sampling inspection, nonconforming supplies, quality control records, and corrective action. Confirm that the detailed test procedures include: sampling techniques and risk levels, specific test procedures, acceptable tolerances, and accept or reject decisions including tagging and documentation flow to purchasing, inventory control, and accounts payable departments. Review the statistical sampling techniques being used. Determine that they are the least complex possible without compromising the sample results, at least simple enough to be workable at the plant location, and being carried out according to instructions provided. Determine the extent to which vendors are required to submit actual test results with each delivery of material and whether the tests were conducted by the vendor or a reliable private testing agency. Evaluate the adequacy of training given to quality control inspectors and vendors for the purpose of preventing defects and errors. Ascertain that quality control management prepares a monthly quality status report, describing significant problems and actions planned, major actions accomplished, and the general situation of the quality program. Determine if the quality control staff has the authority to cause production to cease immediately due to nonconforming materials or operations, instead of waiting for a written report recommending such action.
To ascertain whether quality control staff members are carrying out inspection properly and that they are adequately trained and equipped to accomplish this objective.	Evaluate whether defective material reports for all nonconforming material are prepared and that they include, at a minimum: part name and number, purchase order number, date of inspection, quantity received, quantity defective, nature of discrepancy with inspector's name, further action required, and disposition suggestions.

(continued)

Audit Objectives for Quality Assurance of Materials	Audit Procedures for Quality Assurance of Materials
	Check whether the quality team has implemented a zero-defects program where applicable at the plant. Examine a sample of inspection reports covering high-usage and high-dollar items to see that instructions are properly followed.
	Conduct a plant tour and determine whether incoming quality inspection has adequate facilities, tools, and staff to perform its duties. Establish whether adequate and satisfactory equipment is provided and that the plant has its own calibrating measuring equipment. Review calibration records maintained and comment on their content and adequacy in comparison to guidelines provided.
	Determine whether targets were established for average and maximum time lags between receipt of an item by the quality control department and its dispatch to the final destination (e.g., store, user, vendor, and scrap). Evaluate the frequency of time lag measurements and monitoring of actual against targets. Age materials on hand awaiting inspection by comparing the date on receiving reports with the audit date, and label them "time lag of five working days or more," "time lag between two and five days," "time lag of less than two days," etc. Note and investigate with quality control management unusual time lags, and obtain reasons for delay.
	Ascertain whether the purchasing management initiates effective and timely actions on inspection deficiencies requiring follow-up with vendors. Calculate the average time taken by the purchasing agent in disposing of defective material, and compare actual with targets.
	Evaluate technical qualifications of the quality control staff to determine the degree to which individuals are qualified to substitute for one another.
To determine whether cost-of-quality reports are prepared accurately and promptly.	Analyze the latest month's cost-of-quality reports, tracing amounts on reports to general ledger accounts. Summarize the costs of rework expense, scrap expense, and warranty expense in each work center by responsibility for a given accounting period. In order to locate the source of a quality problem, prepare a schedule for each class of expense in detail, reflecting part name and number, date inspected, reason for defect, quantity defective, total cost, and vendor supplying the basic material. Identify those costs that relate to failure of purchased parts or material.
	Determine that a work order procedure has been established to accumulate costs of reworking vendor defective material. Ascertain that formal procedures have been established for charging rework costs back to vendors for nonconforming material resulting from vendor cause. Review the procedures and evaluate for adequacy. Take a sample of rework orders completed and determine whether costs were billed back to the vendor or absorbed by the company. Obtain reasons for deviations from established procedures.

Audit Cycle/Area: Expenditure—Accounts Payable

Risks and Exposures	Controls or Control Procedures
Merchandise billed by the vendor was not received by the company.	Compare the vendor's invoice with a copy of the receiving department's receiving report (DC).
Payment had been made for items without a purchase order and receiving report.	Have accounts payable department match the purchase order with the receiving report (PC). Purchasing department should not be performing this match due to possibility of fraud.
Duplicate requests for checks to pay vendors for specific invoices.	Cancel the paid invoices (PC). Periodic spot checks of payments by accounts payable staff (DC).
Unauthorized withdrawal of items from the goods received and unauthorized payment for goods received.	Separate the incompatible functions of access to goods received and authorization of payment of vouchers (PC).
Overpaying a vendor.	Review and cancel supporting documents when a check is issued (PC).
Payment for goods not received.	Have a departmental supervisor other than the employee ordering the goods approve vendor invoices (PC).
Alteration of employee expense report.	Verify copies of receipts from vendors to the amount submitted by the employee (DC).

Audit Objectives for Accounts Payable	Audit Procedures for Accounts Payable
To determine whether all known liabilities arising from the receipt of goods or services have been recorded in proper accounts and in a timely and accurate manner.	Check that all purchase requisitions, purchase orders, receiving reports, and vendor invoices are filed under numerical control by the accounts payable department. Select a number of missing numbers and voided numbers, and query as to the follow-up action taken. Analyze the reasons given and trace to appropriate source documents.

Review open files of receiving reports and vendor invoices in accounts payable department and conduct these audit tests: obtain an aging schedule of these documents; review for correspondence with vendor on billing differences; check for duplicate posting by verifying with vendor's statement; and inquire about actions taken to resolve "unmatched" items. Verify that unmatched receiving reports, unpaid invoices, and open purchase orders are followed up on a current basis.

- In order to determine if any substantial liabilities existed or should have been accrued as of the audit date but had not been booked, perform these audit tests: (1) Examine vouchers recorded and payments made after the audit date; (2) examine receiving reports for the last few days of the audit date; (3) examine monthly statements received from creditors having large balances; (4) examine large construction contracts; (5) examine correspondence regarding disputed items; and (6) consider confirming a randomly selected number of creditors, including regular suppliers with zero balances.

(continued)

Audit Objectives for Accounts Payable	Audit Procedures for Accounts Payable
	In order to test the year-end cutoff for unrecorded liabilities, examine shipment date and terms of shipment on vendor invoices received prior and subsequent to year-end. A possibility of understated payable exists.
	In order to ensure that all debit or credit memoranda have been properly approved and recorded in accounts, conduct these audit tests: Inspect whether debit/credit memos are prenumbered, and verify that all adjustments are approved by management outside the accounts payable department that issued the debit or credit.
	In order to test the accuracy and completeness of invoices entered into an accounts payable system, conduct these audit tests: Batch totals processed equal charges to general ledger accounts and credits reflected in the accrued accounts payable; and batch totals plus opening balance in accrued accounts payable minus payments made equal closing balance in accrued accounts payable.
	In order to verify the propriety of account distribution, compare account distributions on selected vouchers with voucher register and/or account distribution sheets. Investigate any charges to accounts that appear unusual. Make sure that standard journal entries are used to record items charged to prepaid and deferred accounts, and inquire if a single journal entry is prepared for write-offs and amortization and that management approved them.
	• In order to test whether the general ledger balance agrees with the detailed accounts payable subledger, conduct these audit tests: (1) Reconcile the total to the general ledger control account; (2) confirm that detailed records are maintained supporting the general ledger control accounts for prepaid expenses and deferred charges; (3) test if the general ledger control totals can be derived independently of the detailed vouchering function; (4) inquire if monthly reconciliations are made of unpaid vouchers with the general ledger accounts; and (5) find out the reasons for delays in payment of past due items and make sure that they are actual liabilities. Scan the trial balance of open accounts payable for significant debit balances and determine the reason for their existence.
	Verify that proper control is exercised over purchase orders and sales invoices in cases where merchandise is purchased for direct shipment to customers. These are called drop shipments.
To ascertain whether vendor statements have been reconciled properly and promptly.	Inquire who is responsible for reconciling vendor statements with the vendor's accounts in the accounts payable department, and determine the extent to which vendor's statements are checked.
	Review files of selected vendors and trace their vendor statements to appropriate documents (e.g., purchase orders, receiving reports, vendor invoices, and debit/credit memos) to determine whether transactions and liabilities appear to be normal and that they are accurately recorded. Investigate unusual items.

Audit Objectives for Accounts Payable	**Audit Procedures for Accounts Payable**
To determine whether controls over payments are proper, including taking trade discounts and refunds.	Inquire if there is an approved list of authorized signatures prescribing the scope of authority and expenditure limitation of each individual who can sign and approve the payment. Make sure this list is current.

Review the policy document explaining when to make payment to vendors and the procedures to ensure those payments can be made promptly. Select a sample of paid invoices and compute elapsed times between actual date and due date of payment.

In order to ensure whether trade discounts are being taken, conduct these audit tests: (1) Review procedures about when to take discounts and under what conditions; (2) review invoices paid for several major vendors who regularly allow trade discounts and investigate the reasons for lost discounts noted; and (3) establish the extent to which discounts are taken after the payment date authorized for the taking of the discount. To determine the cost of late payment of invoices containing trade discounts, draw a sample population from the file of paid vendor invoices.

Verify whether invoices and supporting documents have been canceled to prevent their reuse, preferably showing the date of cancellation.

For refund payment processing, make sure refund checks are issued only after proper authorization is obtained. |
| To ascertain whether controls over approved vendors are appropriate. | Examine whether the accounts payable department has a list of approved vendors and that this list is current and used as a control tool prior to processing payments to vendors.

Inquire as to who is responsible for maintaining the vendor information, including controls over vendor additions, changes, and deletions to the master vendor file. Make sure that system access privileges given to this person are in accord with his or her job duties.

Inquire whether historical files are maintained for vendors, including price history, purchase orders, part numbers, job number, and quantity ordered. Ensure that these historical files are summarized and archived for future reference. |
| To determine whether controls over advance payments to vendors and employees are proper. | Evaluate the reasons for advance payments to vendors. Verify that trade discounts are taken before making payments for materials not received at the time of payments. Identify the system in place to ensure that materials are subsequently received. Select a sample to test that materials are subsequently received by tracing receiving reports to vendor invoices.

Evaluate the reasons for advance payment to employees, whether officers or not. Identify the system in place to ensure that advance monies are recovered through offsets to business expense payments or payments received directly from employees. Select a sample to test that those tracing business expense reports or checks to the employee advance payment register subsequently receive monies. |

RISKS IN SAMPLING

An internal auditor suspects that the invoices from a small number of vendors contain serious errors and therefore limits the sample to only those vendors. A major disadvantage of selecting such a directed sample of items to examine is the inability to quantify the sampling error related to the total population of vendor invoices.

 KEY CONCEPTS TO REMEMBER: Credit Memos versus Debit Memos

- The vendor for returns and adjustments of goods or services issue credit invoices (memos) to vendor accounts. The vendor owes or gives credit to the purchaser (customer), which results in a debit balance with a supplier. Debit balances with vendors can be a result of the normal delays in recovering monies due from them under the request for credit procedure.

- Debit invoices (memos) are issued by the purchaser for vendor errors, rebates, overcharges, corrections, allowances due the company, and recovery of overpayment. The purchaser charges the vendor. Debit memos are charge backed to the vendor and applied to vendor accounts.

EXAMPLES OF APPLICATION OF CAATs: ACCOUNTS PAYABLE

- Identify unauthorized vendors in a vendor database for testing to determine existence of valid recorded liabilities. The presence of unauthorized vendors is an indication of fraud and overstates liabilities.

- Identify debit balances for further analysis and interpretation since credit balances are normal.

- Use the test data method to test the accuracy of application program controls over the purchase transactions.

- List payable balances with no scheduled payment date, which is an indication of a lapse in procedures.

- Recompute the file balance to reconcile the accounts payable balance listed in the company's month-end trial balance report to the master accounts payable file.

- Use generalized audit software to verify that all purchases were authorized, that all goods paid for were received, and that there were no duplicate payments.

Audit Cycle/Area: Expenditure—Personnel Administration

Risks and Exposures	Controls or Control Procedures
Hiring a highly qualified person with questionable background.	Perform an adequate check on prior employment background for all new employees (PC).
High employee turnover.	Competitive compensation package, including salary, benefits, and bonuses; ongoing training; employee development programs (PC).
• Employment discrimination suits.	• At least two levels of functional management conduct interviews of candidates after initial screening by personnel staff; standard interview and evaluation procedures; use of a checklist to ensure that all points

Risks and Exposures	Controls or Control Procedures
	are covered regarding job requirements, qualifications, work conditions, fringe benefits; use of standard and competency measurement tests (PC).
• Errors in payroll rates for new employees.	• Have personnel department verify the payroll changes processed in the form of an edit listing (DC).
• No career guidance to management trainees.	• Develop a plan for recruiting, selecting, training, and development (PC).
• Listing of bogus agencies as referring the candidate for recruiting.	• Verify new agency names and addresses through the telephone book or call the other agencies to see if they have heard about the new agencies (PC, DC).

Audit Objectives for Personnel Administration	Audit Procedures for Personnel Administration
• To determine whether controls over employee hiring, indoctrination, and termination procedures are proper and in accordance with policies.	• *Hiring procedures.* Examine the job/position descriptions of randomly selected positions. Establish that these are consistent with official job grade, job category, and other job classifications by analyzing job duties and responsibilities. Establish that all approved position descriptions are represented in the organization charts and that no positions in the organization charts lack a position description. Ensure that the job description indicates requirements such as education, training, experience, and special skills. Match these job descriptions to personnel requisition forms, interview forms, and performance evaluation forms. Investigate any discrepancies.
	• Make sure that the actual count of employees classified as permanent, temporary, and seasonal is within the limits of budgets or plans. If actual numbers exceed budgets or plans, find out the causes for the excess and the effectiveness of measures taken and planned toward reducing the excess.
	• Where applicable, ensure that all new employees are hired subject to their passing physical, psychological, mental, or other specific-capability examinations. Confirm that education, work experience, reference, credit, security, and background checks have been conducted prior to making a job offer.
	• Ascertain that the hiring function is adequately organized and staffed and that its employees are suitably trained and are knowledgeable concerning the company personnel policies and procedures.
	• Review the company's policy regarding hiring internal candidates versus external candidates. Establish that the employee search methods (i.e., newspaper advertisement, use of professional recruiting firm, advertisement in professional/business journal, use of employment agency) utilized are responsive to the needs of the company and are effective and economical.

(continued)

Audit Objectives for Personnel Administration	Audit Procedures for Personnel Administration
	• Select a random sample of completed application forms in the personnel files and establish the degree to which they are clearly and completely filled out. This is to ensure that all legal requirements (i.e., privacy laws, antidiscrimination laws) have been satisfied or not violated.
	• Verify that decisions on offers or rejections of job applicants and candidates are supported by properly filled-out application and interview forms and signed evaluations by the personnel and requisitioning functional department management.
	• *Employee indoctrination procedures.* Establish that the personnel department has formal procedures for the indoctrination of new employees. Indoctrination should cover topics such as pension plans, group insurance, medical service, employee loans, travel arrangements, vacation, holidays, sick pay allowances, and education reimbursement programs. Select a sample of new employees who have gone through the indoctrination process, and check their files to see if these documents are available in their personal folders: employment agreement; fidelity bond application; covenant against disclosure agreements; conflict-of-interest statements; patent agreement; payroll authorization and deduction forms; employee acknowledgment to return company assets such as keys, manuals, badges, tools, and computers at the time of termination.
	• *Termination procedures.* Take a random sample of terminated employees, obtain their personnel folders, and ensure the presence of these documents: exit interview form completely filled out first by functional department management and then by personnel department management; use of a checklist by personnel department to make sure that company property has been turned in by the terminated employee. (The checklist should include items for manuals, automobiles, instruments, tools, computers, credit cards, uniforms, identification badges, protective clothing, loans, advances, etc.)
	• Verify that the payroll department does not release the final paycheck or separation allowances without approved release forms signed by personnel management, functional department management, and general management.
	• Inquire whether information collected from an exit conference is communicated to concerned management and whether it is combined with other exit interview data to yield statistical information on the stated reason for voluntary and involuntary separation.

Audit Objectives for Personnel Administration	Audit Procedures for Personnel Administration
• To ascertain whether policies and practices over employee promotions and transfers are fair and effective.	• Review the policy document regarding employee promotions and transfers. Ensure that it is based on objective criteria and in the best interests of the company while being fair to employees concerned.
	• Establish that employee transfers and promotions are effected as a consequence of formal requests by management of the initiating department. From personnel records, randomly select a representative number of employees transferred or promoted and examine pertinent requests, memoranda, and supporting documentation. Ensure that policies and good business practices have been followed by interviewing concerned management and employees as required and that approvals were based on documented review of concerned employees' performance evaluations and qualifications against the position requirements.
• To determine whether policies and practices over employee salary/wages and bonuses are fair, equitable, and competitive.	• Establish that there is a separate group within the personnel department responsible for administering formal compensation (salary) and benefit policies and programs. Make sure that salary, wages, and benefits are related to grade levels or salary ranges that are, in turn, formally related to each position as indicated in the position description and organization chart. Ensure that the benefits provided are cost effective for the organization. A system of compensation based on a current job analysis is a good control to ensure a fair and equitable compensation program administration.
	• Examine employee records for completeness and accuracy of wage and salary rates and check that records are easily retrievable. Compare the actual grade or salary against the published grade or salary levels. Obtain explanations for apparent deviations from policy or for any evidence of inequitable treatment. Inquire about the frequency of updating salary and benefits after taking into account changing labor markets (demand and supply forces), inflation factors, budget impact, turnover of specific key positions, and labor union requests.
	Establish the actual bases utilized in selecting employees entitled to annual bonuses and for determining the amount of bonus to be paid. Ascertain, through a review of policy and interview of employees concerned and their management, that bonuses paid were not arbitrarily established through an inadequately supported decision by the employee's management but rather were the result of a properly documented and executed performance evaluation. Inquire if personnel management was fully involved in the bonus establishment and execution.

EXAMPLES OF APPLICATION OF CAATs: PERSONNEL ADMINISTRATION

- List employees who have not taken vacations, which is an indication of a fraud.
- List employees who have taken excessive sick leave, which is an indication of an abuse.
- Compare employee pay rates used in calculating payroll to official pay rates to determine discrepancies.

Audit Cycle/Area: Expenditure—Payroll

Major activities and responsibilities of a payroll department include:

- Maintenance of employee records showing authorized pay rates and payroll deductions for each employee.
- Maintenance of control totals for each class of fixed payroll deductions, such as group insurance and savings bonds or investment plans.
- Determination of total hours on which gross amounts payable for hourly wages will be calculated.
- Maintenance of record showing eligibility and payments for time not worked (i.e., vacation, holidays, sick leave, excused absences, jury duty).
- Processing employee travel advance and business expense reports.
- Maintaining timekeeping records.

Risks and Exposures	Controls or Control Procedures
Unauthorized changes to the payroll.	Have the personnel department authorize the hiring of all employees, setting pay levels and pay rate changes; ensure that there exist: management approvals, dual controls, system access controls, and supervisory reviews (PC, DC).
Misappropriation of unclaimed payroll checks.	Unclaimed payroll checks should be controlled by accounting employees who have no payroll or cash functions; unclaimed paychecks should be returned promptly to the treasury department for interim hold and subsequent redeposit; unclaimed paychecks should be voided by the treasury department after a specified period (PC, DC).
Fraudulent practices in payroll preparation.	Ensure the existence of: segregation of duties; periodic audits by internal and/or external auditors; good record keeping; periodic and surprise reviews by supervisors for unusual entries, big adjustments, unusually high payments, and checks to nonemployees (PC, DC).
Employees might be paid for hours not worked or submitting excessive hours for payment.	Have time cards approved by department supervisor, not by employee, and submit them to timekeeping department (PC).
Unauthorized alteration of computer payroll programs for fraudulent purposes.	Implement authorization, testing, and software quality assurance procedures for payroll program changes (PC, DC).

Risks and Exposures	Controls or Control Procedures
Terminated employees had not been removed from the payroll.	Reconcile payroll and timekeeping records (DC).
Payroll checks are drawn for improper amounts.	Obtain supervisory approval of employee time cards (PC).
Unauthorized alteration of hourly pay rates by payroll clerks.	Limit access to master payroll records to payroll supervisors only (PC).
Payroll clerk adding fictitious employees to the payroll.	Allow payroll changes to be authorized only by the personnel department (PC) Perform periodic floor checks of employees on the payroll (DC). Ensure that all hiring and terminating is performed by the personnel department (PC).
Payments to unauthorized recipients.	Examine procedures for proper distribution of paychecks (DC).
Payroll fraud.	Authorize payroll master-file additions and deletions by the personnel department (PC).

Audit Objectives for Payroll	Audit Procedures for Payroll
To determine whether payroll preparation procedures are effective in preventing the processing of unauthorized transactions.	Establish that: (1) there is adequate segregation of duties regarding time reporting, payroll preparation, payroll approval, check deposit/bank transfer preparation, journal entry preparation, input (data entry) to computer, and reconciliation of system output; (2) only designated, appropriate persons are authorized to input payroll information to the computer and that system access privileges are based on employee job duties; and (3) there are built-in automated program edit checks to prevent improper, erroneous, or unusual inputs to the computer. For selected payroll periods, verify that batch control totals of entered data and pay period totals of output data were maintained and compared by the payroll department and that these totals were either agreed or reconciled and exceptions were resolved in a timely manner. Some examples of control totals that can be made of include total number of hours, number of employees, number of documents, and number of transactions. In order to ensure the accuracy and completeness of the payroll calculations, conduct these audit tests: foot and cross-foot the payroll register, trace payroll totals to the general ledger, and trace the total net pay to the reimbursement of the imprest payroll account. Verify that any unusual entries, adjustments, or checks to nonemployees have been noted and investigated by the payroll department; and compare the payroll by department with that of the previous month for reasonableness.

(continued)

Audit Objectives for Payroll	Audit Procedures for Payroll
	Select a representative number of employees from one or two departments and perform these audit tests: (1) Check the name, job classification, clock card number, employee number to the employment authorization and personnel data records; (2) check the propriety of job classification with the job description; (3) check the rates of pay to the wage authorization, incentive plan, and union contract; (4) check the computation of gross and net pay and check the calculations and propriety of each deduction; (5) check the recorded shift time and premium to ensure correctness of the shift differentials applied; (6) trace gross pay, net pay, and deduction amounts to employee earnings records; (7) verify that deductions are formally authorized by the employee; (8) if the payroll is paid by check, examine paid, endorsed payroll checks for agreement with payee name, payment amount, check number, date of payment as indicated in the payroll register; (9)if the payroll is paid by direct deposit in the employee bank, check bank payment report for agreement with the payee name, payment amount, bank deposit number, date of payment as indicated in the payroll register.
	Verify that when an employee's pay rate or deduction has just been changed or when the initial pay of a new employee is being prepared, pay rates, deductions, and computations are verified and signed by a disinterested second employee or by the supervisor of the payroll department.
To determine whether payroll disbursement procedures are effective to prevent the receipt of unauthorized pay.	From an examination of the payroll run, verify that amounts actually paid for wages and salaries are readily traceable to the totals for all employees and to the pay period.
	Ensure that payroll checks are prenumbered and the numerical sequence is accounted for by the payroll department. Ensure that canceled, voided, and missing check numbers are accounted for.
	Establish that for each pay period, the computer-based payroll system lists all employee names and amounts paid even when the amount is zero. This is to ensure that all employees are accounted for, which can be easily and readily compared to other records of employee count.
	Evaluate procedures, interview employees concerned, and inspect storage facilities to verify that blank payroll checks are stored in a locked area accessible only to authorized employees and issued only in blocks, with the check number sequence monitored.
	Verify that payroll checks are distributed to employees by nonpayroll department employees, by a nonsupervisory employee of the functional department with no payroll authorization or preparation duties, or by internal auditors. Employees should wear the company identification badge during the payoff of wages.

Audit Objectives for Payroll	**Audit Procedures for Payroll**
	To determine if salaried employees are taking more paid vacation time than they have earned, observe which employees on the audit day were absent because of vacations and trace those absences through the payroll records to subtractions from accumulated vacation time.
	To ascertain that no payments to fictitious employees were made, perform a payroll payoff test.
	Payoff of cash wages should be discouraged, where possible. If cash wages are used, verify that dated payroll receipts exist or that the proper employee signs listings immediately on being paid. Verify that these receipts are subsequently compared with payroll records, that signatures are spot-checked, and that receipts are canceled to prevent reuse. Employees should wear the company identification badge during the payoff of wages.
	In order to ensure that controls over unclaimed paychecks are proper, these audit tests should be conducted: obtain all unclaimed pay envelopes and checks, trace these back to the payroll registers and signed receipts, and verify that the receipts for these unclaimed paychecks have not been signed. Verify that the liability had been correctly and promptly set up for these unclaimed wages.
	To determine whether persons on the payroll of a particular department actually work there, observe for the physical presence of properly identified employees during a surprise department floor check. This test provides the best source of evidence.
To ascertain whether accounting for payroll is adequate and proper, including bank account reconciliations.	Through an examination of bank account authorizations, deposit and transfer documents, and recent bank statements, verify that all payroll funding is controlled through separate imprest bank account(s).
	Trace the amounts deposited and/or transferred into and out of payroll bank account(s) to respective payroll registers and other related internal memoranda. Investigate any discrepancies. Ensure that there is no mixed application of funds between payroll-related expenditures and nonpayroll types of expenditures.
	Establish that payroll bank accounts are reconciled promptly by an employee independent of all payroll functions, preferably by treasury department employees. Select a sample of bank accounts and conduct these audit tests: Verify that each reconciliation has been dated and signed by the preparer, the reconciliations are correct as to format and content (i.e., descriptions, amounts, totals), and reconciling items have been promptly followed up and resolved.
	In order to ensure that good accounting practices are followed, conduct these audit tests: Verify that: the gross payroll is reconciled to the respective accrual and the accrual is reconciled to the respective

(continued)

Audit Objectives for Payroll	Audit Procedures for Payroll
	labor distribution and all employee compensation payments are promptly recorded in the accrued payroll account. Where detailed labor distributions are not prepared, ensure that: Each payroll is regularly reconciled with the previous one; vacation pay is accrued properly; bonus payments and other performance awards are accrued each month rather than recorded when paid; and general ledger control accounts for each payroll deduction are supported by subsidiary records detailed by employee. In order to ensure the accuracy of the distribution of payroll, labor charges, and payroll adjustments, these audit tests are suggested: Confirm that labor distributions and adjustments are reviewed by a responsible person other than the preparer, inquire if adjustments are signed by an authorized person, and confirm that labor distributions and adjustments are made in accordance with GAAP. Review the payroll accounting procedure manual to ensure that it describes how to compute, record, classify, summarize, and report these transactions: amounts due the employee, employer's contributions, employees' contributions, income tax and social security deductions, payroll taxes, and payroll adjustments. Verify that general ledger subaccounts are maintained in sufficient detail for all categories of taxes withheld to facilitate management analysis, investigation of erroneous entries, and timely development of tax information for reporting to tax authorities.
To determine whether payroll records are retained long enough to meet statutory requirements.	In order to ensure that all salary data and personnel and payroll records are stored securely and protected against damage, loss by fire or flood, or unauthorized access, these tests or inquiries should be conducted: verify that all sensitive records are stored in a locked, fireproof area accessible only to authorized employees, and examine whether stored documents are not exposed to excessive heat, humidity, chemical vapors, steam, water leaks, rain, etc. Ensure that sensitive records are retained in accordance with statutory period requirements and approved by the legal counsel and the taxing authorities. Establish that the controls and procedures followed in destroying or disposing of expired records are adequate.
To ascertain whether controls over employee travel advance and business expense reports and accounting procedures are accurate and timely.	Ensure that these activities are separated and performed by different employees: review of travel authorizations, vouchers, requests for advances, and approval of these documents; preparation of journal entries and approval of these entries; preparation of check requisitions for travel advances or for employee expense reimbursement and approval or check signing; and maintenance of employee advance records and preparation of related journal entries.

Audit Objectives for Payroll	Audit Procedures for Payroll
	Employee travel advances. Verify that the company does not provide any employee with an advance for business travel without a properly approved cash requisition on which the travel is stipulated. Ascertain how emergency conditions are handled. Verify that related vouchers had been submitted with a copy of a properly completed and approved travel authorization form.
	Ascertain whether the person requesting an advance is refused if the person: has a significant outstanding balance due the company or is soon to be terminated and has an unsettled balance due the company. Confirm that the personnel department is responsible for notifying, with sufficient lead time, the payroll department of any impending transfer or termination of an employee.
	Confirm that the payroll department is responsible for ascertaining the status of an employee's advance account before computing the final net pay of any employee it has been notified will be soon transferred or terminated.
	Determine if there have been any instances of any employee having been denied an advance because of unsettled, excessive balances. Ensure that this procedure is consistently followed in all departments and at all grade levels.
	Ascertain if balances due the company were either reimbursed by the employee prior to separation or deducted from the employee's final paycheck.
	Business expense reports. Ensure that expenses incurred by employees are for business travel or other specified business-related expenses. Verify that these expense reports are prepared using a standard form and submitted within a few days after returning from the business trip. Examine whether all expense reports are reviewed by the functional department management for accuracy and propriety and then by the accounting department. *Fraudulent use of corporate credit cards would be minimized by subjecting credit card charges to the same expense controls as those used on regular company expense forms.*
	Make sure that travel and related costs that are incurred but not recorded by the close of an accounting period are properly accrued and that these accruals are reversed in the following accounting month.
	Examine copies of the three most recent reconciliations of individual account balances or advances with the general ledger control accounts. Examine a sample of employee expense account statements, and verify that periodic confirmation of significant balances is actually solicited and followed up by the accounting department.

(continued)

Audit Objectives for Payroll	Audit Procedures for Payroll
To determine whether controls over timekeeping and labor utilization practices and reporting are proper.	Ensure that written policies and procedures are available describing how to account for time and attendance for all categories of positions. Establish that labor utilization objectives and performance monitoring and reporting requirements are formally defined in production control, the personnel department, and the cost accounting department policies and procedures. Determine that these policies and procedures contain guidelines regarding performance reporting, controls over direct and indirect labor, controls over overtime pay and shift premium rates, application of labor standards, and reporting of idle time and cost variances. *Timekeeping practices and reporting.* Select a sample of employees from different departments who were paid for authorized absences (e.g., vacation, holiday, illness, military service, approved leave of absence). Trace the hours or days of authorized absence back to supporting departmental or timekeeping records and ascertain that proper departmental approvals have been documented and are reasonable. Investigate major instances or patterns of deviations from policy. Examine the departmental or timekeeping records documenting lateness or early departures. For hourly employees, trace the time not worked forward to the payroll wage computation sheets and backward to the time sheets or cards. For salaried employees, trace the lateness and early departures recorded by the employees' departments or by the timekeeping function. Ensure that follow-up and corrective actions have been adequate and effective for any cases of chronic lateness or early departure. Ascertain that any manual adjustments or changes made to the hours originally entered are adequately explained, appear reasonable, and are signed by authorized persons in accordance with the company policy. Conduct spot observations of time clock punching by employees on an entirely surprise basis in an unobtrusive manner from a position not readily visible to those approaching the time clock. Observe that: no one has punched in or out for anyone but him- or herself or punched using someone else's time card and that all persons, once punching in or out, remain in or out and do not subsequently leave or enter the facility without again punching the time clock. Obtain payroll records for selected departments and verify that all the employees listed on the payroll are physically present at their place of work or otherwise accounted for (e.g., business travel, training, illness, and authorized absence). Verify, through interview of accounting and production managers, that the time actually worked on each job is being charged to the job and that the system for distributing direct and indirect labor costs

Audit Objectives for Payroll	**Audit Procedures for Payroll**
	to jobs is reliable. Select a random sample of completed time sheets or clock cards. Trace summary time and cost figures to jobs charged through the use of journal entries. Ensure that supervisors approve any modifications to these time cards.
	Labor utilization practices and reporting. To ensure that overtime and premium pay are effectively controlled, conduct these audit tests: (1) Verify that overtime hours and premium pay are regularly accumulated on a departmental basis; (2) review the procedures for deriving actual overtime hours worked and overtime pay; (3) check for prior solicitation in writing by designated supervisors; (4) compare overtime hours paid to the actual basic time cards, verify that they are the same, and investigate any differences; and (5) compare approval signatures on the time cards and on overtime requests with those approved to sign.
	To ensure that production statistics facilitate realistic evaluation of performance and the derivation of specific corrective measures, perform these audit tests: (1) Review whether proper records are maintained showing the actual and targeted production by major cost center and product line; (2) review whether proper records are maintained showing direct labor hours actually worked and indirect labor costs distributed; (3) compare standard direct labor hours against with actual hours; (4) analyze production performance indices (e.g., productivity ratios and nonproductive time by department or product line); and (5) ensure that labor efficiency variances from budget are regularly developed on a departmental basis. Ensure that performance records are maintained in sufficient detail to provide a basis for evaluating the utilization of labor by function, cost center, or department.
	To ensure that standard times are derived independent of production operations, preferably by industrial engineering time studies, conduct these audit tests: (1) Ascertain that standards are developed based on either time studies or historical data, or a combination of both; (2) review the policies and procedures for deriving standard times and for updating them to cover engineering changes, time studies of estimated standards, and the correction of errors; (3) examine the supporting documentation for time studies or historical data; (4) verify the accuracy of calculations on a sample basis and that these standards are periodically updated as needed; and (5) obtain copies of standard time process sheets covering a representative number of production operation steps, and compare them to the standards used in computing labor efficiency variances.
	To test the adequacy and effectiveness of worker incentive plans, these audit tests are suggested: (1) Understand the policies and procedures describing

(continued)

Audit Objectives for Payroll	Audit Procedures for Payroll
	how to calculate incentive pay; (2) select a random sample of employees receiving incentive pay and verify that each payment is supported by approved production counts and authorized rate schedules, correctly computed, and complies with the established policies and procedures; (3) interview a representative sample of workers and supervisors and ascertain whether incentive plans motivate them or not and whether incentive plans are administered fairly or not; and (4) for maximum reliability and effectiveness, ensure that the function administering the incentive plans is separate from the function that granted incentives. Conduct a trend analysis of incentive payments relating them to productivity and labor efficiency.

COMPATIBLE AND INCOMPATIBLE FUNCTIONS IN PAYROLL

Preparing attendance data and preparing the payroll activities are incompatible. Examples of compatible activities include: hiring employees and authorizing changes to pay rates, preparing the payroll and filing payroll tax forms, and signing and distributing payroll checks. It is a control weakness when a payroll clerk has custody of the check signature stamp machine.

SAMPLING IN PAYROLL

In testing payroll transactions, an auditor discovers that in 4 out of 100 (statistical sample), the appropriate supervisor did not sign selected time cards. To evaluate the materiality or significance of this control deficiency, the auditor should compute an upper precision limit and compare with the tolerable error.

EXAMPLES OF APPLICATION OF CAATs: PAYROLL

Use of Mainframe Computer Audit Software

- Use the test data method to test the accuracy of computations of employee withholding for tax and benefit deductions, and compare the actual results with predetermined results. Identify unusually small tax deductions.

- Use the parallel simulation technique to ensure that the payroll program is reliable and to test the accuracy of the payroll calculation.

- Use the test data method to test calculation of regular and overtime pay amounts and compare the results with predetermined or expected results.

- Produce a cross-reference list after matching individual employee payroll time card information to personnel department records and files to conclude that individuals are bona fide employees.

Use of Microcomputer Audit Software

- Compare current-period amounts with previous-period amounts for employee gross and net payroll wages. Identify employees with unusual pay amounts after performing reasonableness tests.

- Select all transactions in specified activity codes and in excess of predetermined amounts. Trace them to proper authorization in personnel files in order to determine if payroll changes are authorized.

(D) Introduction to the Production/Conversion Cycle Major activities in a production/conversion cycle include:

- Initiating production or manufacturing orders.
- Requesting withdrawal of raw materials from stores.
- Scheduling of production orders.
- Processing of raw materials according to process sheets or other specifications.
- Performing quality control inspection work.
- Accounting for costs of production and processing.
- Preparing production and cost accounting reports.
- Storing of processed goods.
- Shipping of processed goods.
- Recording of production activities by journalizing and posting of manufacturing transactions.
- Analyzing production or manufacturing variances for corrective actions.
- Updating of production and work-in-process or work-in-progress (WIP) records.
- Protecting physical inventory of raw materials, work-in-process, and finished goods.
- Maintaining the accuracy and completeness of inventory records and of property, plant, and equipment (PPE) records.

Audit Cycle/Area: Production/Conversion—Inventory Control

Risks and Exposures	Controls or Control Procedures
Defects in finished goods due to poor-quality raw materials.	Implement specifications for purchase of raw materials and parts (PC, DC).
Excessive investment in raw materials inventory.	Implement TQM and JIT principles in purchasing and receiving functions (PC).
Unsatisfactory customer service levels.	Establish service-level goals (PC) and obtain customer feedback periodically (DC).

Audit Objectives for Inventory Control	Audit Procedures for Inventory Control
To determine whether inventory levels are sufficient to achieve satisfactory customer service levels and to maintain balanced production throughput without requiring excessive investment in inventory.	Ascertain that the inventory control function is organizationally separate from the manufacturing function to ensure that inventory decisions are not overridden by production considerations. Review the overdue backlog of customer orders to determine the extent to which original promised delivery dates are not being achieved. Prepare a schedule showing total customer orders: total orders meeting on-time delivery and total orders with overdue delivery expressed as a range of delivery slippage in weeks. Determine the percentage of orders that have been delayed due to inventory problems.

(continued)

Audit Objectives for Inventory Control	Audit Procedures for Inventory Control
	Determine the extent of production line disruptions, downtime, and rescheduling due to material shortages. Review production department reports of production line downtime due to material shortages and/or out-of-specification material. Determine the frequency and the effect of multiple line setups due to material shortages.
	Ensure that inventory turnover goals are achieved and that the inventory mix is in proper balance. Select a representative sample of items in each ABC inventory and calculate the turnover rates using this formula:
	Annualized usage for the period in units / Average inventory for the period in units.
	Compare the actual turnover rates with the established goals. Discuss exceptions with management.
	Compare the actual turnover rates with the established goals for each category of inventory. Discuss exceptions with management.
To ascertain whether the inventory control techniques used are appropriate considering the composition of the products and the demand patterns.	By discussion with inventory control and marketing management, determine the demand patterns for finished goods. Also, determine the demand patterns for inventory items (both manufactured items and purchased parts) by discussion with purchasing and production control management. Determine the degree of common parts between the manufactured items and purchased parts. Based on these discussions, determine whether OP or MRP techniques are appropriate.
	These guidelines would help in this matter: An OP system is useful where the life of the product is long, demand patterns are stable, and many parts have a high degree of commonality of usage. A MRP system is useful where product life is uncertain and demand patterns are subject to significant fluctuations. For OP systems, determine that the reorder point is calculated properly using this formula:
	Reorder point = Lead time × Demand during the lead time + Safety stock
	Select representative samples of manufactured and purchased parts and calculates the reorder points. For purchased items, determine whether the lead time includes processing time for requisitions, purchase orders, receiving, inspection, stocking, and vendor lead time. For manufactured items, determine whether the lead time includes production scheduling time, sequencing time, move time, queue time, setup time, run time, inspection time, and stocking time.

Audit Objectives for Inventory Control	**Audit Procedures for Inventory Control**
	Compare actual lead times to stated lead times and comment on discrepancies. For the sample selected, verify that new orders are placed when the reorder point is reached, not before.
	Check the actual historical on-hand balances when the new orders are received. If the safety stock level is not being reached, the reorder point is probably too high. If there is never a stock-out, the reorder point and/or safety stock levels are probably too high.
	For OP systems, select a representative sample of manufactured and purchased items and calculate the economic order quantity (EOQ). Compare the calculated EOQs against the order quantities actually used. In the event of significant discrepancies, determine the management overrides that allow other than an EOQ to be ordered, and comment on the appropriateness after calculating the overall effect on inventory levels. *For MRP systems,* analyze the method of forecasting demand and determine whether forecasts represent reliable data on which accurate materials decisions can be based. Review marketing's forecasting techniques for adequacy and appropriateness, whether they are salesperson's projections, market surveys, economic indicators, or a combination of all. Evaluate the method of exploding forecasts down to component parts. Ensure the forecast is time phased throughout the year.
	Review techniques for tracking actual demand to the forecast and comment on significant deviations from the forecast and adequacy of tracking techniques. Determine the method of updating the forecast: exponential smoothing, regeneration, and net change.
	Determine whether a new components parts explosion is generated when revised finished goods or subassembly requirements are identified.
	Determine whether scrap and shrinkage are given adequate consideration in requisitioning parts. Determine basis for scrap and shrinkage factors. Test scrap factors against recent experience.
To determine whether controls over perpetual inventory records are proper.	Ensure that: (1) only inventory control staff can update perpetual inventory records and that they do not have access to the physical inventory; (2) all perpetual inventory records maintenance flows through a centralized, controlled function; (3) all changes to inventory records are properly authorized and approved; and (4) individuals charged with the custodianship of physical inventories do not have access to the perpetual records.

(continued)

Audit Objectives for Inventory Control	Audit Procedures for Inventory Control
	Determine that inventory control staff is notified of all receipts of materials and all material that fails incoming quality inspection. Determine whether satisfactory actions are taken to obtain substitute material or rework failed material.
	Verify the adequacy of paperwork controls to ensure that inventory control is assured of receiving all documentation relative to material movement. This includes relief of preprocess inventory to work-in-progress (WIP), bookings to finished goods from WIP, and relief of finished goods based on sales.
	Ensure that perpetual inventory quantity balances are periodically verified by cycle counts. Ensure that significant differences between the cycle counts and the perpetual records are verified independently prior to updating the perpetual records. Investigate reasons for negative balances in inventory. This procedure identifies inventory shortages.
	Ensure that there are general ledger control accounts for raw materials, purchased parts, manufactured parts, WIP inventory, finished goods inventory, goods at suppliers, consigned goods, shop supplies, and small tools. Ensure that individuals who maintain the perpetual records do not have access to the general ledger inventory accounts.
	In order to ensure that all inventory transactions are promptly and accurately posted to the general ledger, perform these audit tests: (1) Review accounts payable controls for properly coding the preprocess inventory; (2) review procedures that relieve preprocess inventory and charge WIP; (3) review controls that charge direct labor and overhead to WIP; (4) review controls that relieve WIP and charge finished goods; and (5) review controls that relieve finished goods inventory.
	Review controls over material sent to suppliers for processing (e.g., plating, anodizing). Ensure that controls cover: (1) authorized shipping documentation; (2) physical counts of parts shipped; (3) notification sent to accounting; (4) segregation of the inventory in a goods-at-supplier inventory account in the general ledger at standard cost; (5) verification of counts of inventory received back from the suppliers and any discrepancies are accounted for by the supplier; and (6) preparation by accounting of appropriate general ledger inventory records relieving the goods at supplier account and charging the appropriate inventory account at the new standard.
	Verify that accounting records for material stored or consigned away from the plant include: (1) proper approvals prior to shipment; (2) warehouse,

Audit Objectives for Inventory Control	Audit Procedures for Inventory Control
	consignment, or other agreements in effect to protect the company in the event of fire, theft, negligence; (3) periodic confirmation from consignee of quantities on hand; (4) reconciliation of consignee's confirmation with company records; and (5) taking of physical inventories at least once a year of quantities on consignment and reconciliation with company records.
	Verify that the accounting department maintains separate records of material owned by others but in the hands of the company (goods consigned in, materials being processed for others). Ensure that: received quantities are verified; the goods are physically safeguarded; periodic confirmations are made with the owner; quantities shipped are accurate and are reconciled to consigned quantities; and the company is adequately covered against loss in the event of fire, theft, deterioration.
	Ensure small tools and shop supplies are accurately accounted for and are controlled. Ensure that: accounting controls are appropriate to account for all receipts and issues of small tools and shop supplies; and physical controls over small tools and shop supplies are sufficient to preclude unauthorized removal.
To ascertain whether controls over excess and obsolete inventory and reserve provisions are adequate.	Obtain copies of the perpetual inventory records and identify excess and obsolete inventory items. Verify that the items identified are included in the company's excess and obsolete inventory stock listing. Understand the methods used to identify slow-moving stock: annually at physical inventory time, at the time of cycle counts, periodic reviews, and judgment. Evaluate the adequacy of method(s) used to identify slow-moving stock.
	Compare the calculated excess and obsolete reserve requirement to that actually provided in the general ledger and comment on discrepancies. Obsolete inventory may be defined as inventory that has had no movement in the last year. Excess inventory may be defined as the quantity in excess of one year's supply on hand. Scanning, recomputation, and analytical review are procedures that can be used to identify the amount of obsolete inventory and to collect audit evidence.
	Ensure that excess and obsolete inventory to be disposed of is physically segregated and securely stored and is accounted for separately and that an aggressive disposal program is in effect. Review the dollar value of inventory disposed of in light of total excess and obsolete inventory, and comment on the effectiveness of disposal activities.

(*continued*)

Audit Objectives for Inventory Control	Audit Procedures for Inventory Control
	Determine that surplus stock disposal efforts are sequenced in order to minimize loss: returning to vendors, selling to other companies or other divisions of the same company, reworking or modifying, selling to customers at a reduced price, and selling for scrap. Determine that once stock has been identified for disposal, it is physically segregated and maintained in a secured area. Ascertain that the proper management level authorizes inventory disposal. Ensure that authorized write-offs and write-downs are promptly and accurately charged against the appropriate inventory and reserve accounts.

FORMULAS IN INVENTORY

Calculate the turnover rates for raw material, WIP, and finished goods using these formulas:

Raw materials = Relief of preprocess inventory (raw material) to WIP in dollars/ Average preprocess inventory in dollars

WIP = Relief of finished goods inventory in dollars/Average WIP inventory in dollars

Finished goods = Cost of goods sold in dollars/Average finished goods inventory in dollars

GUIDELINES FOR FORECASTING TECHNIQUES

The formula for exponential smoothing is:

New forecast = Old forecast + (Sales − Old forecast)

- **Regeneration.** This technique involves discarding the old forecast and substituting a new one. This technique is generally appropriate where there are widely varying forecasts and relatively few inventory levels.

- **Net change.** This technique involves updating only those items for which a forecast change is indicated (either in quantities or timing). This technique is generally appropriate where there are few changes and many levels in the bills of materials.

KEY CONCEPTS TO REMEMBER: Inventory Control

- If controls over the perpetual inventory system are weak, a good recommendation is to schedule a physical inventory count.

- Statistical sampling would be appropriate to estimate the value of a firm's inventory because statistical sampling is reliable and objective.

- During an investigation of unexplained inventory shrinkage, the auditor is testing inventory additions as recorded in the perpetual inventory records. Because of internal control weaknesses, the information recorded on receiving reports may not be reliable. Under these conditions, vendors' invoices would provide the best evidence of additions to inventory.

- During the year-end physical inventory process, the auditor observed items staged in the shipping area and marked "Sold—Do Not Inventory." The customer had been on credit hold for three months because of bankruptcy proceedings, but the sales manager had ordered the shipping supervisor to treat the inventory as sold for physical inventory purposes. The auditor noted the terms of sale were "FOB [freight on board] warehouse." The auditor should recommend that the inventory staged in the shipping area be counted and included along with the rest of the physical inventory results. Conclusions: The inventory belongs to the company and was not sold to the customer due to FOB warehouse and the title to the goods remains with the company. Risk was not passed to the customer.

EXAMPLES OF APPLICATIONS OF CAATs: INVENTORY CONTROL

- Use tagging and tracing techniques to provide a computer trail of all relevant processing steps applied to a specific inventory transaction in an online perpetual inventory system. To accomplish this, select certain file-updating transactions for detailed testing. Inquiry-type transactions will not be useful since they are merely data lookups, with no file updating. File updating is a critical, risky activity since the file contents can be changed.

- List old or slow-moving inventory items for possible write-offs.

- List large differences between the last physical inventory and the perpetual book inventory for further analysis and review of adjustments.

- Test the numerical sequence of physical inventory count sheet numbers to account for all numbers, whether used or not.

- List inventory items with negative balances for further analysis and follow-up.

- Test the accuracy of reduction of inventory relief for cost of sales.

- Calculate inventory turnovers by product (including finished goods, raw materials, and WIP components), and compare them to targets.

- Use the control flowcharting technique to review the overall business control context of the work-in-process computer processing application system. This technique is similar to a normal flowchart except that it focuses more on controls and control points in a work-in-process flow in a manufacturing environment.

Audit Cycle/Area: Production/Conversion—Production Control

Risks and Exposures	Controls or Control Procedures
Production delays as a consequence of equipment breakdowns and repairs.	Establish a preventive maintenance program for all production equipment (PC).
Building of unnecessary finished goods inventory.	Comparison of actual inventory against production schedules by time period (DC).
Audit Objectives for Production Control	**Audit Procedures for Production Control**
To determine whether inputs to the annual production plan are proper.	Ascertain that the production control function is organizationally independent of manufacturing to ensure that production control decisions are not overridden by manufacturing considerations. Determine the inputs or basis of the annual planned production (i.e., a finished goods replenishment plan based on reorder point techniques, a plan based on forecasted demand using materials requirement planning techniques, or a combination of techniques).

(continued)

Audit Objectives for Production Control	Audit Procedures for Production Control
	Ascertain the degree of participation and involvement by the marketing, manufacturing, and inventory control staff and management in developing the production plan. This is very critical since subsequent decisions, such as acquisition of capital equipment, manpower, inventory, and facility expansion, are made based on the production plan.
To ascertain whether short-term production schedules support the overall annual production plan.	Analyze the production schedules and detail significant deviations from the production plan. Where significant deviations exist, ensure they are caused by changes in demand patterns, not bad production schedules. Evaluate the effect of deviations from the production plan on: preprocess inventory levels; production floor balancing to ensure that machines are neither overutilized nor underutilized; and finished goods inventory levels where production is focused on few items at the expense of many other items (i.e., giving unequal weight). Verify that production control staff considers existing WIP and current machine loading capacity prior to generating new production schedules. Determine whether similar products are scheduled together to minimize setups. The more frequent the setups are, the more interruption to the production schedule and the more cost. Ensure that production runs are neither excessively long nor short. Lengthening production runs excessively can result in delivery slippage or bottlenecks in other products. The ultimate goal should be a balanced production throughput that maximizes utilization of the production facilities yet meets the demand for the products.
To determine whether product-related documentation exists and whether it is complete and current.	Verify that appropriate documentation exists for each product so that only approved parts and manufacturing processes are utilized. Select a sample of parts and ensure that drawings, specifications, and manufacturing process sheets are available and that they are current. This includes routing sheets, production process sheets, material travelers, etc.. Ensure that the documentation contains, at a minimum: (1) a description of sequence of operations, (2) a description of operator motion sequence, (3) an indication of standard time allowed for each operation, (4) a description of accepted toler(ances for scrap and breakages, and (5) a description of accepted tolerance for downtime during operation.
To ascertain whether engineering changes are controlled properly.	In order to ensure that engineering change notices (ECNs) are properly approved and controlled and are processed promptly, identify the conditions leading to the ECN (e.g., quality control failures, customer complaints, product returns, and initiating product improvements).

Audit Objectives for Production Control	Audit Procedures for Production Control
	Determine whether the company has an engineering change review board composed of managers of production control, inventory control, industrial engineering, design engineering, marketing, and production operations. Inquire if approval levels have been established for each type of change. Determine that full consideration is given to on-hand and on-order material that will be scrapped or become obsolete due to change. Review procedures in effect to dispose of material obsolete by engineering changes. Confirm whether consideration is given to using the old parts prior to introducing the new parts into production, reworking the old parts, returning the old parts to the vendor, or sales to other companies and scrap sales. Ascertain whether obsolete parts are segregated into a controlled area to prevent accidental use in the production line.
To determine whether manufacturing operations adhere to specifications.	Select a sample of production orders and ensure that the packet includes an approved production order, a list of component parts that must be withdrawn from stores, routing or process sheets that list the sequence of operations from cost center to cost center, and manufacturing steps. The production order should also include time standards by labor class and by department, special machines or tools required, and setup instructions. Ensure that approved manufacturing orders are delivered to the shop floor and travel with the order, detailing customer name, part number, quantity required, start date, and completion date. Ensure that manufacturing operations adhere strictly to the route sheets, which include sequence of operations, drawings of all dimensions, tolerances, and material usage standards, including offal and production scrap. Determine the extent to which substitute material is used. Indicate and evaluate the approval of substitute material. Calculate the additional cost of substitute material. Determine the reasons why the substitute material was necessary.
To ascertain whether production reporting is accurate and timely.	Obtain copies of production reports and ensure that these items are presented: (1) material usage; (2) production direct and indirect labor used; (3) machine utilization; (4) scrap, spoilage, and rework costs; (5) downtime and idle time; (6) good production quantities; and (7) percentage of compliance with production schedules. Ensure that there are adequate controls over preprinted forms for material issuance to the production line, preprinted forms for returns to stock and production floor transfers to finished goods inventory, and method of charging labor and overhead to WIP at pay points.

(continued)

Audit Objectives for Production Control	Audit Procedures for Production Control
	Evaluate the method of recording factory direct and indirect labor to specific shop orders. Evaluate machine utilization reporting. Verify actual setup times to standards, actual run times, and machine downtime. Determine incidence of production line downtime and comment on amount of downtime. Evaluate the causes of idle time (e.g., bottlenecks, stock-outs, incorrect scheduling) and comment on shop floor throughput.
	Evaluate the reporting procedures and controls over scrap, spoilage, and rework costs. Test the accuracy of production quantity reporting. Sample test-count quantities run against reported.
	Determine whether control procedures are adequate to prevent subsequent operations reporting more pieces completed than previous operations.
	Perform production-aging schedules. Select a sample of closed production orders and determine: number of orders completed on schedule; number of orders completed early; and number of orders completed less than a week late, less than a month late, or more than a month late. Evaluate the reasons for production orders that are completed late or early. Where customer orders are to be delivered late, determine whether production control informs the sales department so that customers can be contacted regarding the delay. Quantify the financial impact of late deliveries resulting in fines, premium freight charges, and changes in shipping schedules of other products. Assess the level of loss of goodwill.

EXAMPLES OF APPLICATIONS OF CAATs: PRODUCTION CONTROL

- List production orders with no due date of production scheduling and no delivery (shipping) date.

- Compare production counts between production system records and cost accounting system records to ensure that costs are allocated based on correct production count.

- Test the accuracy of accumulation of production costs.

Audit Cycle/Area: Production/Conversion—Shipping

Risks and Exposures	Controls or Control Procedures
Unable to ship replacement parts on time.	Establish shipping time standards by part category (PC).
Unauthorized shipments.	Implement strict procedures to ship approved sales orders only (PC).

Audit Objectives for Shipping	Audit Procedures for Shipping
To determine whether all material movements into and out of the shipping department are completely and accurately documented and all shipments are promptly reported to billing function.	Determine whether copies of sales orders are forwarded to the shipping department on a timely basis by comparing the dates sales orders were prepared to the dates received in shipping. Ensure that sales orders are prenumbered and that shipping maintains a numerical control log. Investigate gaps in the numerical sequence. Determine whether shipping is responsible for reviewing sales orders and the documents authorizing the transfer of material to shipping for proper approval and for verifying that the proper material has been forwarded for shipment. If it is not, determine why not. When many rush shipments are found, determine the need for rush shipment services. Perform a substantive audit test by selecting bills of lading from the warehouse and tracing the shipments to the related invoices. Relevant facts include: Shipments are made from the warehouse based on customer purchase orders, the matched shipping documents and purchase orders are then forwarded to the billing department for sales invoice preparation, and the shipping documents are neither accounted for nor prenumbered. Evaluate the method used to notify the billing department of shipment. The sales order form should be used as a shipping advice in both shipping and billing departments. Ascertain that prenumbered bills of lading are properly approved and accounted for. Ensure that copies of bills of lading are sent to the billing function and as support documentation for prepaid freight billings.
To ascertain whether the material is physically safeguarded while in the shipping department and that the physical layout facilitates free flow of material.	Observe the physical location(s) of the shipping area(s) and the layout. Comment on the material flow to the shipping area(s) and the efficiency of operations within the shipping department. Ensure that shipping is functionally and physically separated from receiving and inventory stores. Analyze the plant layout. Observe whether shipping areas are near the point of finished goods storage or the end of the production lines so that materials need not be transported to the other end of the factory for shipment. Determine whether the physical locations and layouts of shipping areas are conducive to constant surveillance by security guards. Ensure that loading dock doors are kept closed and locked when trucks are not actually being loaded and the shipping department is physically secured when unattended. Ensure that all material movement documents and shipping papers are protected to minimize the risk of their loss or destruction.

EXAMPLES OF APPLICATION OF CAATs: SHIPPING

- List customer orders that were shipped late by comparing order due date on production records with shipped date on shipping records.

- Identify items shipped but not billed, which is an indication of lapse in procedures.

Audit Cycle/Area: Production/Conversion—Traffic

Major activities and responsibilities of the traffic department include procurement of public carrier services; analysis and study of routes, rates, and carriers; checking of bills submitted by carriers; handling of claims for loss or damage; and administration of the day-to-day operations of receipt and shipment of goods.

Risks and Exposures	Controls or Control Procedures
Vehicle theft or loss.	Maintain vehicles in a secured location with release and return subject to approval by a custodian (PC).
Movement of trailers not controlled properly.	Have security guards log the time in and time out of trailers and compare the actual elapsed time with standards (PC, DC).

Audit Objectives for Traffic	Audit Procedures for Traffic
To determine whether a written procedure manual is available to guide the traffic department.	Determine that a current and complete transportation procedure manual exists outlining the activities relative to inbound and outbound traffic procedures and assigning responsibility limits of authority. At a minimum, the manual should contain these topics for inbound traffic: scheduling carriers; signing delivery receipt; verifying freight charges; tracing and expediting shipments; and filing loss, short, damage, and overcharge claims. At a minimum, the manual should contain these topics for outbound traffic: scheduling carriers; preparing packing lists; tracing and expediting shipments; arranging for in-transit insurance; and packing to meet tariff requirements.
To ascertain whether interdepartmental coordination is in effect to minimize inbound and outbound freight expenditure.	Determine whether close coordination exists between purchasing and traffic for inbound freight; that traffic receives notice of incoming volumes of purchases from purchasing for planning purposes; and that traffic furnishes routing instructions to purchasing for inclusion on the purchase orders. Ascertain the effectiveness of procedures followed in specifying and controlling routings on inbound shipments. Select a representative sample of purchase orders, freight bills, and routing and rate guides, and perform these audit tests to determine: (1) that the procedures followed ensure that adequate shipping information is given to vendors; (2) that the routing was specified by traffic and

Audit Objectives for Traffic	Audit Procedures for Traffic
	adhered to; (3) that the basis on which the rates were based was verified; (4) the cost of items delivered by premium cost carriers, such as Express Mail, or airmail; (5) the extent to which items normally received in large quantities are delivered on a less-than-carload or less-than- truckload basis; and (6) whether freight allowances from vendors were verified and the controls existing to ensure that freight bills are not paid on freight-allowed deliveries. Where terms of the purchase orders were based on carload or truckload shipments and delivery was made on a partial basis, determine whether the vendor made an allowance for increased transportation cost. Select a representative sample of shipping department records or billings by carriers and perform tests to determine that: (1) the routing was specified by traffic and followed in shipment; (2) proper action was taken when prescribed routing was not followed; (3) routing and rate guides used are current; (4) there exist controls to ensure that additional costs resulting from using customer routing are collected or there exist approvals for waiver of such costs; and (5) the extent to which shipments were made at premium rates resulting from rush shipments to customers or shipping less-than-a-carload or less-than-a-truckload interim shipments to normal carload locations.
To determine whether the selection of carriers and routes is based on economical factors.	Evaluate the allocation of the overall freight workloads among various carriers and owned or leased vehicles. Obtain reasons for various modes of transportation and the support for the selection of individual carriers. Ascertain whether procedures exist for determining whether services of contract truckers should be used in lieu of owned or leased vehicles, railroad facilities, or a combination of transportation modes. Evaluate whether unusual preference appears to have been given to a particular carrier or mode of transportation. Review several major carriers and determine the basis on which their selection was made. Determine the extent to which commercial carriers are selected on the basis of competitive bids and the frequency with which bids are solicited. Where numerous carriers are employed, discuss with management whether benefits could be obtained from consolidating shipments using fewer carriers. Ascertain whether action has been taken to determine cost savings that might be obtained by such action. Determine whether all contracts with trucking firms are approved by traffic and legal departments and that they are for specific periods and contain provisions for periodic review and adjustment of rates.

(continued)

Audit Objectives for Traffic	Audit Procedures for Traffic
	In order to minimize freight charges, determine whether procedures provide for and adequate measures are taken to pool shipments to obtain rate benefits on incoming and outgoing shipments. Select a representative sample of carriers and determine the cost differential incurred by not pooling shipments.
	Review and evaluate procedures relative to shipments to customers from outlying warehouses, basis for selection of warehouse locations, and assignment of responsibility for control of warehouse stock. Consideration should be given to factors such as determination of routing of shipments, minimization of warehouse charges through direct shipments to large-volume customers, or a regional warehouse concept.
To ascertain whether procedures and controls are appropriate and adequate to minimize demurrage charges.	Review records covering payments for demurrage during the past few months, noting the number of occurrences and amounts involved. Determine whether they are separately identified in accounting records.
	Determine whether truckers assess a penalty for excess waiting time pending loading or unloading of trucks. Relate the penalties to total demurrage.
	In selected cases where demurrage is paid, calculate the differential between cost versus the overtime pay that might have been incurred for unloading. Determine the operating department that is primarily responsible for demurrage charges, and establish the action taken by traffic to correct operating inefficiencies to prevent future recurrences.
To determine whether procedures and controls are appropriate to collect on shipments that have been completely or partially lost or damaged during shipment.	Prepare a schedule of all unpaid claims. Establish that goods lost, short, or damaged in transit are properly noted on carrier's receipts and are covered by loss or damage reports. Ascertain whether copies of these reports are forwarded to traffic and accounting departments. Establish whether claims were filed for all items covered by these reports.
	Evaluate the adequacy of traffic department follow-up action taken with respect to outstanding or unpaid claims. Evaluate the procedures for receiving, handling, and accounting for cash received in the settlement of claims. Determine whether a floor has been established for convenience and speed below which a claim will not be submitted.
To ascertain whether freight invoices are accurately processed for payment.	Evaluate the procedures to validate, process for payment, and audit freight invoices. Conduct these audit tests: Measure the elapsed times between when the freight bill was received in the mailroom and when it was received in the traffic department; when the freight bill was received in the traffic department and when it was approved by the traffic

Audit Objectives for Traffic	Audit Procedures for Traffic
	department; and when the freight bill was received in the accounts payable department and the date the payment was actually made.
	In order to evaluate the procedures established for the in-house audit of freight bills, perform the next audit procedures on a sample of paid freight bills: (1) Determine that the carrier's charges are valid and that the services billed have been rendered; (2) ascertain whether freight bills were paid prior to the audit by traffic; if so, evaluate the controls that exist to ensure that a postaudit is made; (3) ascertain that rates and weights charged on transportation bills are in accordance with published tariffs, classifications, and agreements with private carriers; (4) determine the basis used for substantiating and approving the weights used for billing purposes; and (5) evaluate the controls in effect to prevent duplication of payment of freight bills.
	Ascertain whether the feasibility of retaining an outside agency to process and/or audit freight bills has been considered. If so, determine the advantages and disadvantages of in-house audit and outside audit of freight bills.

AUDIT APPROACH IN A TRANSPORTATION DEPARTMENT

A transportation department maintains its vehicle inventory and maintenance records in a database on a stand-alone microcomputer in the fleet supervisor's office. The audit approach that is appropriate for evaluating the accuracy of this information is to verify a sample of the records extracted from the database against the supporting documentation.

Audit Cycle/Area: Production/Conversion—Quality Control

Major activities and responsibilities of the quality control department include:

- Measuring and test equipment calibration.
- Inspection of incoming materials, production process, and completed assemblies.
- Sampling inspection.
- Identification of nonconforming materials.
- Field inspection.
- Maintaining quality control records and costs.
- Planning and implementing corrective actions to improve quality.

These activities are a continuation of those described for quality assurance of materials in the expenditure cycle.

Risks and Exposures	Controls and Control Procedures
Quality control not involving vendor selection.	Implement quality team concept among purchasing, quality control, inventory control, and production control staff (PC).
Cost-of-quality reports not prepared.	Establish procedures for tracking quality costs (PC).
No charge-back of rework costs to vendors for poor-quality work.	Implement a work order cost accounting system to accumulate costs of reworking defective vendor material (CC).

Audit Objectives for Quality Control	Audit Procedures for Quality Control
To ascertain whether quality control staff participates in qualifying new vendors and in assessing vendor quality performance.	Verify that records are maintained, by vendor, of deviations from purchase orders or receipt of out-of-specification material. Determine the disposition of such material: returned to vendor, scrapped, reworked, and used as is. Determine the manufacturing or customer service problems caused by such materials: production delays, multiple line setups, shipping delays, product failures, or additional field service expenses. Determine the extent to which the additional costs were billed back to the vendor. Determine the adequacy of procedures in effect to evaluate prospective vendors for inclusion on the approved vendor list. Ascertain whether formal checklists outlining the elements required for an acceptable quality control function at the supplier's facility are utilized in this evaluation. Review the criteria used in selecting vendors and that the available data in the vendor file supports the qualification of the vendor.
To determine whether procedures for incoming quality inspection of purchased parts and raw materials are timely and adequate.	Verify that complete engineering specifications and drawings are supplied to the vendors so that there is no misunderstanding of material requirements. Verify that the quality control department has adequate facilities, tools, and human resources to perform its duties and that inspectors measure vendor conformance to specifications on a timely basis. Determine that the quality control department receives copies of all purchase orders with complete sets of specifications and drawings attached. Compare a sample of the drawings and specifications to those maintained in the product engineering department to ensure they are current. Establish that written test procedures exist for all products purchased, including: sampling techniques and risk levels, specific test procedures, acceptable tolerances, and "pass" and "reject" material procedures. Age materials on hand awaiting inspection by comparing the date on receiving reports with the audit date, with details such as time lag 5 working days or more, time lag more than 2 working days but less than 5, time lag 2 working days or less. Find out the reasons for the delay.

Audit Objectives for Quality Control	Audit Procedures for Quality Control
	Verify the extent to which vendors are required to submit actual test results with each delivery, whether the tests were conducted by the vendor or a reliable private testing agency, and the degree of reliance that the company places on these test results.
	In the case of nonconforming purchased materials, ascertain the time required to notify the purchasing department of the defective material by comparing the date of issue of a number of defective material reports to the date received in the purchasing department. Find out the reasons for the delay. Ascertain whether the purchasing agent initiates effective and timely action on inspection deficiencies requiring follow-up with vendors. Calculate the average time utilized by purchasing in disposing of defective materials by comparing the date on which the defective material report was received in the purchasing department to the date the files reflect final disposition.
	Determine if a vendor evaluation report is prepared by either the purchasing agent or the quality control inspector for defective parts. Determine that a work order procedure has been established to accumulate costs of reworking defective vendor material and that formal procedures are in place to charge rework costs back to vendors. When a work order system is not employed for accumulating rework costs of vendor nonconforming material, understand how such work is accounted for.
To determine whether procedures for in-process and finished goods are timely and adequate.	Establish that quality control staff members have these documents to carry out in-process and finished goods inspection: inspection checklists, applicable drawings and specifications, production work orders, records of nonconformance, operating time logs, and accept or reject criteria for statistical sampling.
	Age materials on hand awaiting inspection by comparing the date on selected move tickets transferring the materials to the inspection station with the audit date with details such as time lag 5 working days or more, time lag more than 2 working days but less than 5, time lag 2 working days or less. Find out the reasons for the delay.
	Review statistical sampling techniques, establishing that they are simple, workable, and effectively used. Ensure that test results from these sampling techniques are sent to appropriate members of the engineering, production, purchasing, and inventory control departments.
To ascertain whether quality control management prepares defective material reports and distributes them to interested parties in a timely manner for corrective action and helps accounting or other departments in developing cost-of-quality reports.	Take a sample of defective material reports prepared by the quality control department for all nonconforming materials. Ensure that each report contains this information: part number and name, purchase order number, vendor identification number, date of inspection, quantity received and

(*continued*)

Audit Objectives for Quality Control	Audit Procedures for Quality Control
	checked, quantity defective, inspector's identification number, nature of discrepancy, further action required, and disposition rules. Comment on the timeliness of reporting. Ensure that the defect reports are distributed to the individuals responsible for correcting the problem. Review various control charts available to determine the quality trend at the facility and comment on unfavorable trends.
	Determine if quality control has the authority to cause production to cease due to nonconforming materials or operations rather than waiting for a written report recommending such action. It is too late by that time.
	Ascertain that cost-of-quality reports are prepared regularly and that report amounts are reconciled to general ledger accounts. Ensure that the report elements contain preventive costs, appraisal costs, and failure costs (internal and external). Understand the focus of the quality control program: defect prevention or defect detection. Prevention is better than detection.
	Inquire whether programs such as zero defect committee, quality councils, or quality teams are in place to improve quality continuously. Ensure that formal training programs for error prevention are available to all employees, including supervisors, and that quality awareness is created through the use of periodic meetings between employees and management, display of posters, articles in the company's newsletter, special recognition events, and quality awards.

Audit Cycle/Area: Production/Conversion: Fixed Assets

Risks and Exposures	Controls or Control Procedures
Potential for financial losses due to theft of fixed assets.	Establish physical access controls (PC). Obtain insurance coverage in an amount supported by periodic appraisals (PC).
Misclassification of capital acquisitions as expenditures.	Scan repair and maintenance records and investigate large dollar-value entries (DC).
Overcharge of fees on contractor billings.	Review of invoices before funds are disbursed (PC).
Contractor could be charging for the use of equipment not utilized in the construction project in a cost-plus contract.	Comparison of invoice items with the contract terms (DC).
Potential for inflated costs in the cost-plus contract.	A provision for maximum costs and sharing any savings (PC).

Audit Objectives for Fixed Assets	**Audit Procedures for Fixed Assets**
To determine whether requests for capital budgets and project appropriation for all capital projects are properly controlled.	Review the capital budget prepared for the current year and determine that adequate data supporting proposed projects have been prepared. Review rejected proposals and ascertain the reason for their rejection in light of accepted proposals.
	Review project appropriation requests and verify that complete documentation of the project exists, including analysis of available optional course of actions, and that all required approvals were obtained prior to the commitment of funds to the project. Ensure that alternatives to purchasing, such as leasing, in-house manufacture, or transfer from other divisions, have been thoroughly explored prior to commitment of funds. Ensure that adequate coordination exists with all long-term financing needs of the company.
	Verify that the specific project was included in the approved capital budget. Determine that the project appropriation request and the attached work sheets and schedules provide the necessary detail, including description and purpose of the project, anticipated benefits, estimated costs, and time schedules for starting and completion of the project. Ensure that the estimated cost figure includes cost of material, labor, overhead, and other costs as necessary. Establish that all approvals were obtained prior to commitment of funds.
To ascertain whether postcompletion audits are performed to compare the actual results with the expected.	Ensure that postcompletion audits are performed by individuals other than the original preparers of the project appropriation request. Select a representative sample of postcompletion audit reports and perform these reviews: Compare cost estimates to actual costs and investigate significant differences; trace actual expenditures to construction-in-progress (CIP) detail records; and compare actual benefits with expected benefits. Evaluate the accuracy of explanations for unfavorable variances and assess their implication on overall project planning. Where actual expenditures exceed budget due to changes in specifications, establish the justification of the changes and verify that proper approvals were obtained prior to the issuance of change orders.
	During a postcompletion audit of a warehouse expansion, the auditor noted several invoices for redecorating services from a local merchant that were account-coded and signed for payment only by the cost engineer. The auditor should compare the cost and description of the services to the account code used in the construction project and to relate estimates in the construction-project budget.

(*continued*)

Audit Objectives for Fixed Assets	Audit Procedures for Fixed Assets
To determine whether controls over CIP expenditures are proper and adequate.	In order to ensure proper accumulation of costs and accounting for capital projects, review the fixed asset accounts for both open and closed projects. Perform these audit tests: (1) Compare total expenditures to date plus estimate to complete the approved project appropriation request, including supplemental requests; (2) evaluate estimates to complete by comparison of actual costs to date with original estimate, considering percentage of completion, review of open purchase commitments, and discussion with engineers; (3) verify direct purchases by reference to construction contracts, examination of properly approved vendor invoices, and receiving reports; (4) examine material requisitions in support of materials issued from stockrooms; (5) trace labor charges to payroll distribution summary; (6) trace the burden rate used to the master standard listing; (7) for purchase of land and buildings, verify evidence of ownership by examinations of deeds, title abstracts and policies, tax bill descriptions, and real estate contracts; (8) determine the propriety of useful life and salvage value by discussion with engineers; and (9) ensure that material being used on one project is not being charged against the budgets of other projects.

Review the open work orders supporting the CIP account to ensure that they are either current items related to property that will be capitalized when the property is put into service or current expense items that will be charged against operations in the current period. Utilizing the work orders closed during the period under audit, review amounts transferred from the CIP account to determine: that transfers to property accounts are proper and comply with laws and regulations; that they exclude expense items; and that amounts written off to expense accounts do not include capital items. |
| To ascertain whether controls are adequate over outside contractors working on capital projects. | Determine that competitive bids are obtained for all outside construction-related purchases and that the same controls are exercised over these purchases as over routine purchases.

In order to ensure that appropriate controls are maintained over outside contractors with **cost-plus contracts,** these audit tests are suggested for a sample of projects: (1) Review the contracts for inclusion of specifications, estimated costs, and technical and time constraints; (2) where the right of audit is included, review the contractors' time records, vendor invoices, fee calculations (be particularly alert for materials included in fee calculations that should have been excluded, transfer of contractors' materials from their own inventory, discounts and rebates not passed on to the company); (3) where the right of audit is not |

Audit Objectives for Fixed Assets	Audit Procedures for Fixed Assets
	included, ascertain that appropriate supporting documents (e.g., vendor invoice, payroll summaries) accompany the billing from the contractor. Test vouch a representative number of such billings.
	Inquire as to why the right of audit is not included in the contract and, if feasible, suggest that an attempt be made to insert this right when contracts are negotiated in the future. Ensure that all contractors have provided certificates of insurance.
	Cost-plus construction contracts require early and constant on-site monitoring due to the inherent risk that overcharging or other irregularities can occur.
	In order to ensure that appropriate controls are maintained over outside contractors with fixed-price contracts, these audit tests are suggested for a sample of projects: (1) Review the bid file to ensure that the lowest bidder was selected (if not, why not); (2) ascertain that the finished work was inspected by company management before final payment was made; (3) where a contractor submits a claim for renegotiation or incentives due under a contract, relate the details of the claim to the contract and analyze for appropriateness; and (4) ensure that all contractors have provided certificates of insurance.
To determine whether physical controls over fixed assets are proper.	Ensure that a permanently fixed physical asset identification tag is assigned to each capital asset, that it is uniquely numbered, and that the number is included in the detailed property records.
	Review the procedures for the taking of physical inventories of fixed assets. Ensure that a count is taken periodically and reconciled to the general ledger accounts and that all adjustments are approved. Observe physical count where possible, and ensure that proper cutoff was observed between before and after the inventory date for assets received and disposed.
To ascertain whether procedures and controls over disposition of fixed assets (i.e., sales, retirements, and transfers) are proper.	Select a sample of land, buildings, and other capital assets that had been disposed of during the current fiscal year. Verify that a written procedure is available to be followed in disposing of fixed assets, and review it for adequacy. Verify that competitive bids are obtained to ensure that the best price is obtained.
	To ensure that costs and related depreciation reserves applicable to asset retirements have been properly removed from the accounts, review the fixed asset accounts for the period under review and, on a sample basis, perform these audit tests: (1) Verify sales proceeds and trace them to the cash receipts book; (2) verify the computation of depreciation against date of sale; and (3) trace to the general ledger accounts and the detailed property records the relief of the asset cost and the related accumulated depreciation reserve.

(*continued*)

Audit Objectives for Fixed Assets	Audit Procedures for Fixed Assets
	To ascertain if there have been any unrecorded sales or retirements of fixed assets, perform these audit tests: (1) Review work orders for indication of retirements related to additions of property; (2) discuss the existence of any major asset retirements or sales with production operations staff and management; (3) tour the plant facilities to determine if any major assets have been removed; (4) review changes in manufacturing processes that would necessitate replacement or retirement of existing fixed assets; and (5) review credits in nonoperating income and maintenance expense accounts to determine if they are generated by sales of assets.
To determine whether accounting controls over fixed assets are accurate and adequate.	Ensure that the accounting department receives copies of project appropriation requests, purchase orders, vendor invoices, work orders, and receiving reports pertaining to capital assets. Reporting should include all actual expenditures and commitments.
	In order to determine whether fixed assets employed in the business are properly reflected in the accounting records, inspect the fixed assets used and trace them to the asset subsidiary ledger.
	Review the PPE records and ensure that: (1) separate general ledger control accounts are established and maintained for each major category of PPE; (2) the costs of all items of PPE are recorded in the appropriate account; (3) the cost of labor directly related to overhead employed in the construction and installation of PPE is capitalized as part of the cost of the assets and that its source is the labor distribution summary; and (4) the cost of freight is capitalized as part of the cost of capital assets.
	Ensure that a written policy exists governing the distinction between expenditures to be capitalized and those to be charged to repairs, maintenance, supplies, and small tools accounts and that costs of individual items below a certain amount are expensed when purchased.
	Verify that appropriate amounts of improvement or betterment expenditures are capitalized when such expenditures increase the rate of output, lower operating costs, or extend the useful life of fixed assets. To verify that the proper value of costs are charged to real property records for improvements to the property, the best source of evidence is the original invoices and supporting entries in the accounting records.
	Ascertain that a work order system is maintained for all capital expenditures and major repair jobs whereby all charges applicable to each project are identified and accumulated and that a separate series of work orders is assigned to accumulate costs relative to additions to PPE.

Audit Objectives for Fixed Assets	Audit Procedures for Fixed Assets
	Ensure that open work orders are balanced to the CIP account each month, that all additions to PPE accounts are cleared through the CIP account, and that the CIP account is cleared each month of all charges of a noncapital nature.
	Review the repair and maintenance accounts for the period under the audit to ensure no capital additions have been expensed. Compare the repair and maintenance accounts for significant monthly variations and for variations from budget and from the same period in the prior year.
	Ensure that the detailed asset accounting record contains, at a minimum, this information: date of acquisition, total cost, asset description, asset identification number, estimated salvage value, asset life, depreciation method, and asset location. Ensure that year-end accruals are based on invoices covering work completed or goods received.
	Ensure that leased equipment is properly identified and that company maintenance staff does not attempt to repair broken leased equipment without the specific written permission of the lessor.
	Review the method(s) of depreciation utilized to ensure there is consistent application for similar categories of property. Verify the adequacy of the detail supporting the general ledger account for accumulated depreciation. Conduct these audit tests: (1) Trace the supporting detail for the separate reserve amounts relative to the various depreciation computations to the general ledger control account; (2) ensure that fully depreciated assets are excluded from the computation of depreciation; (3) verify that the cost of fully depreciated equipment is continued in the accounts and shown as gross amount (not net of depreciation) on the balance sheet until retired from service; (4) ascertain that the engineering department has furnished estimates of salvage value to be used in calculating depreciation charges; and (5) review these estimates for reasonableness.
	To test the accuracy of recorded depreciation, compare depreciation schedules with the maintenance and repair logs for the same equipment.
	Make an overall test of depreciation for the period under audit and compare to the same period for the prior year. Explain any major variations between comparable periods to ascertain changes in depreciation methods or major computation errors. Select a category of fixed assets for a detailed test of depreciation. Verify the computation of the provision to date as to adequacy and consistency with prior periods, and trace the distribution to the general ledger accounts. Where applicable, determine that depreciation rates approved by government regulatory agencies are in use.

> **EXAMPLES OF APPLICATION OF CAATs: FIXED ASSETS**
>
> - List high-dollar-value assets for physical inspection.
> - List asset additions and disposal for vouching to supporting documentation.
> - List high-dollar-value maintenance expenses for possible capitalization.
> - List fully depreciated assets.
> - Compare depreciation periods with guidelines provided by management and tax authorities for compliance, and list unusually long or short depreciation periods.
> - List assets without any depreciation charges, which would increase income.
> - Use the parallel simulation audit technique to calculate depreciation charges using the declining balance method.

Audit Cycle/Area: Production/Conversion—Plant Maintenance

Major activities and responsibilities of a plant maintenance department include:

- Maintenance of physical plant, power, light, and water systems.
- The service, repair, and maintenance of plant equipment and production machinery.
- A standard preventive maintenance program.
- Keeping maintenance cost records.
- Acquiring, storing, and controlling maintenance supplies and parts.
- Preparation of the maintenance budget.
- Preparation of formal maintenance requests and orders.
- Control of labor and material costs.

Risks and Exposures	Controls or Control Procedures
Inadequate documentation over property.	Issue guidelines for documentation, including the use of checklists (PC).
Excessive machine downtime.	Establish a preventive maintenance program (PC).
Incorrect and/or improper accounting of costs.	Implement a work order system for tracking maintenance costs (PC, DC).

Audit Objectives for Plant Maintenance	Audit Procedures for Plant Maintenance
To determine whether the plant maintenance department maintains complete records of all PPE and machinery, including drawings, specifications, and maintenance history, and that it performs a preventive maintenance program.	Ensure that the maintenance department obtains factory repair manuals and the manufacturer's maintenance schedules for all machinery and equipment at the time of acquisition or later and that the manuals are up to date and are utilized by maintenance department staff. By discussion with maintenance management and review of maintenance records, ascertain that the preventive maintenance program is operating properly and covers key production equipment

Audit Objectives for Plant Maintenance	Audit Procedures for Plant Maintenance
	and building items. Test a sample of machinery preventive maintenance records to the manufacturer's recommended maintenance routines and intervals. Ascertain whether checklists are used during periodic inspections of plant and equipment.
	Ensure that a complete maintenance history file is maintained for all property items and that this file is reviewed on a regular basis by maintenance department management to revise preventive maintenance schedules and to make replacement recommendations to plant production management.
	Review production time lost due to unplanned machine downtime and preventive maintenance routines that were not completed on schedule during the past year. Calculate the cost of time lost by unplanned downtime, and evaluate the effectiveness of the preventive maintenance program. Compute downtime for selected, critical machines and, where significant, determine what action has been taken to either replace the machine or schedule a major overhaul. Evaluate whether maintenance work can be outsourced.
To ascertain whether the maintenance department utilizes a maintenance work order system to control costs more effectively and to schedule jobs.	Review the maintenance work order system and ensure that: (1) all jobs are properly authorized and estimated; (2) actual costs are accumulated and compared; and (3) appropriate schedule control is maintained. Determine that the system for the accumulation of actual maintenance costs provides the following information: (1) A formal work order system accumulates costs by job and account number that will be charged to the department initiating the request for service; (2) a comparison of estimated cost to actual cost is done regularly; (3) blanket work orders are issued to cover routine and repetitive-type tasks; (4) allocations of costs to benefiting departments is reasonable and proper; and (5) compliance with established procedures regarding capitalization and expense is followed.
	Evaluate the control over closeout of completed work orders. When possible, physically inspect completed maintenance jobs to determine that work has been completed and is in agreement with the job order. Also, ascertain that the equipment records have been updated to reflect this work. Determine if completed jobs are inspected by maintenance department management under a quality control program.
	Analyze maintenance costs for the year and compare them to the last two years. Obtain explanations for significant increases, if any. Determine whether the preventive maintenance program is effective in reducing costs. Determine whether management has included the maintenance department in the cost reduction programs similar to other service centers.

(continued)

Audit Objectives for Plant Maintenance	Audit Procedures for Plant Maintenance
To determine whether effective controls exist over the procurement of maintenance equipment, materials, parts, and outside contract services and that the associated record-keeping procedures are adequate.	Ascertain that appropriate approvals have been obtained prior to initiating the procurement activity for maintenance material, machinery, and equipment. Determine that written bids and quotations are received for maintenance materials, spare parts, equipment, and outside contract services. Determine that purchased maintenance materials are formally received through the receiving department of the company, not straight to the maintenance department. In order to assure that control procedures are working properly over the maintenance equipment, material, and parts inventory, conduct these audit tests: (1) Determine whether there is a significant storage area for small tools, repair parts, and supplies, and that it is well protected; (2) determine whether physical access to the storage area is restricted to authorized personnel; (3) verify that issuance of supplies and parts is supported by approved withdrawal tickets and is in accordance with authorized and approved job orders; and (4) test count selected items and compare them to the perpetual inventory records. Review inventory cards to determine economics of purchases. Also determine whether there are any excess, slow-moving, or obsolete parts on hand. Evaluate the adequacy of the records.

Audit Cycle/Area: Production/Conversion—Cost Accounting

Risks and Exposures	Controls or Control Procedures
Unattainable standards affect employee performance negatively.	Request employee involvement in developing and updating standards (PC).
Standards may not reflect all cost elements.	Develop quality control procedures and use checklists (PC).
Improper use of cost classification, thus distorting cost picture.	Study cost behavior patterns (PC). Conduct data validation routines (DC).

Audit Objectives for Cost Accounting	Audit Procedures for Cost Accounting
To determine whether standard costs have been developed for each significant cost element and class of inventory, for significant operations and cost centers, and for significant products.	For a sample of the more significant products, compare standards per the frozen standard cost file to current bills of material and process sheets. Ensure that the structure of the standards is consistent with the bills of material and process sheets and that the standards are used to control shop operations. Determine the extent of materials and operations "not on standard": Evaluate the impact on proper inventory valuation and effective cost control due to items not on the standard cost system. If effects appear significant, investigate underlying causes of the problem and evaluate the adequacy of management's corrective action.

Audit Objectives for Cost Accounting	Audit Procedures for Cost Accounting
	Determine the extent of use of temporary standards: (1) Evaluate the method used in developing the temporary standards and whether it is consistently applied; (2) ensure temporary standards are approved at an appropriate level before being implemented; (3) ensure temporary standards and related costs generated are clearly identified; and (4) ensure temporary standards are replaced with engineered standards on a timely basis.
To ascertain whether direct material specifications and material usage standards are attainable and that efficient performance is achievable.	Perform a walkthrough review of the process to establish material usage standards. Select a small sample of representative items and note the basis for the standards; examine supporting documents; check approval levels; and trace to the current standards file.
	Ensure those unavoidable loss (shrinkage) allowances and scrap recovery allowances have been included in the standards where applicable: Analyze shop operations to identify processes that tend to generate significant shrinkage losses and scrap, and relate to the basis of the standards; and ensure loss factors have been developed with reasonable precision (i.e., engineered, not estimated).
	Trace a sample of items from the frozen standard cost file to supporting documents to ensure that the material usage standards in the standards file accurately reflect the detailed material usage buildup in the supporting documents.
To ascertain whether purchase price standards represent average prices expected to prevail in the marketplace.	Select a small sample of representative purchased items and determine the basis for the standards. Examine supporting documents, check approval levels, and trace to the current standards file. Ensure that standards reflect proper treatment of all cost elements (i.e., they include freight and customs charges and exclude discounts).
	Evaluate the adequacy of documentation supporting the standards: Where numerous items and significant time is involved in setting standards, determine whether an ABC inventory classification approach was followed, and ensure documentation is current in relation to the effective date of the standards. Review the basis for any overall assumptions reflected in the standards (e.g., inflation or vendor cost allocation factors).
	Trace a sample of items from the frozen standard cost file to supporting documents to ensure that the purchase price standards in the standards file accurately reflect the detailed prices in the supporting documents.
To determine whether direct labor time and work class standards represent attainable and efficient performance standards.	Perform a walkthrough review of the process to establish labor time and labor grade requirements and standards. Select a small sample of representative labor time standards and labor grades, and determine the basis for the standards. Examine supporting documents, check approval levels, and trace to current standards file.

(continued)

Audit Objectives for Cost Accounting	Audit Procedures for Cost Accounting
	Ascertain that standard hours are based on accepted time study and work measurement techniques. Determine whether a work standardization study was performed in developing the standard hours. Evaluate the assumptions made by the engineering staff with regard to operating conditions, and ensure such factors as routing of work, waiting time, and plant layout reflect actual current conditions and are properly considered in setting the standards.
	Trace a sample of labor time standards from the frozen standard cost file to supporting documents to ensure that the time standards accurately reflect the detailed time buildup in the supporting documents.
To determine whether direct labor rate standards represent average labor rates expected to be paid under efficient production levels.	Perform a walkthrough review of the process to establish labor rate standards. Select a small sample of representative labor rates, and determine the basis for the standards. Examine supporting documents, check approval levels, and trace to the current standards file.
	Evaluate the adequacy of the documentation supporting the standards: (1) Ensure that the labor rate standards are related to the planned requirements for the various labor grades per the production budget; (2) ensure that shift premiums and other associated labor benefits are treated as indirect costs and are excluded from the standards; and (3) trace labor rates and labor classes used in developing the standards to source data (e.g., current and anticipated union contracts, personnel records, manning tables, employment contracts).
	Trace a sample of labor rate schedules from the frozen standard cost file to the supporting documents to ensure that the rate standards accurately reflect the detailed rate buildup in the supporting documents.
To ascertain whether material burden standards are utilized to absorb the indirect costs of acquiring goods and services and that they are applied in a reasonable and consistent basis.	Perform a walkthrough review of the process to establish material burden standards. Select a small sample of representative departments involved in material acquisition, and review the basis for projected departmental costs. Examine supporting documents, check approval levels, and trace to the current standards file.
	Ensure that the material burden standard is used to recover all anticipated manufacturing burden related to these operations: purchasing, ordering, and expediting, receiving, and incoming inspection by quality control. Check the material burden rate calculation, and trace the cost elements to the departmental budgets or other supporting data.
	Ensure that the standard material burden is applied to purchases of these items: raw materials, packing materials, items for resale, items shipped directly

Audit Objectives for Cost Accounting	Audit Procedures for Cost Accounting
	to customers by vendors. Determine whether a single material burden rate is applied or whether multiple, varying rates are used for the different types of purchases. Evaluate the appropriateness and effectiveness of the method utilized.
	Ensure that the material burden rate is reflected in the item standards per the standard cost file for all applicable classes of material.
To determine whether standard manufacturing burden rates, excluding the direct material burden rate, are based on detailed departmental flexed budgets representing indirect manufacturing costs expected to be incurred.	Perform a walkthrough review of the standards-setting process. Using a small sample of burden applicable rates for a selected production department or cost center, note the basis for the standards. Include the basis for individual departmental fixed and variable costs and basis for costs allocated to the selected production department. Examine supporting documents, check approval levels, and trace to the current standards file.
	Review the basis for classifying indirect costs as fixed versus variable and semivariable. Perform these tests: (1) Determine whether the cost classification is based on a reasonably current study of cost behavior since cost behavior changes over time and volume; (2) review and assess the adequacy of documentation supporting the determination of fixed versus variable costs; (3) ensure the range of activity (relevant range of production level) used on the fixed versus variable cost study is consistent with current operating plans; and (4) investigate the causes of any major changes in allocation methods between years.
	Ensure that variable indirect costs included in flexed budgets are based on normal plant capacity as reflected in the production budget.
	Evaluate the measurement techniques used in developing standard indirect material and labor costs. Determine whether indirect material physical standards (both quantity and specifications) for significant cost categories are based on engineering measurement techniques.
	Evaluate the reasonableness and consistent application of the method of allocating service department costs to production departments.
To determine whether standard manufacturing burden rates, excluding direct material burden rate, are based on normal operating capacity and take into account all elements of indirect manufacturing costs.	Determine that standard manufacturing burden rates are calculated for each operating department rather than for the factory as a whole. Determine that the standard manufacturing burden rates are established using direct labor hours, machine hours, direct labor cost, or other as a burden absorption basis. Verify that anticipated production levels are derived from the master production schedule.

(continued)

Audit Objectives for Cost Accounting	Audit Procedures for Cost Accounting
To ascertain whether standard burden rates are applied on a consistent basis to ensure accurate and timely absorption of all indirect manufacturing costs.	For a sample of items, verify that the application of standard burden rates is appropriate to the particular manufacturing process being reviewed and that there is full absorption of manufacturing overhead. Select a sample of indirect manufacturing charges from each manufacturing department and ensure that the correct standard manufacturing burden rates were applied to the direct charges. Review the burden variances. Ensure that the total of the standard burden rates plus the total of the burden variances equal the total of all indirect manufacturing costs (i.e., ensure there is full burden absorption on a current basis). Ensure that extraordinary burden costs, such as equipment relocation or facility rearrangement costs, special product obsolescence costs, and catastrophe costs, are charged to income.
To determine whether standard costs are sufficiently detailed and are classified in a manner that permits a timely and meaningful comparison with actual performance and that variance accounting and reporting is proper.	Review the process for accumulating actual direct labor and direct material charges. Ensure that all direct labor charges are accumulated and are charged to the proper cost center or operation. Ensure that material price variances are accurately calculated and charged to income as period costs at the time the invoice is charged to the inventory account, as opposed to when the material is used. Ensure that material usage variances are accurately calculated. Ensure that appropriate controls, such as use of prenumbered material requisition forms, are in place to identify materials usage variances. Ensure the process for accumulating actual burden charges. Ensure that all manufacturing indirect charges are accurately accumulated, including an allocation of utility costs that are chargeable to the factory. Verify that no other charges that would normally be considered general and administrative expense are included in the manufacturing burden costs. Ensure that the cost accounting system requires the identification and analysis of causal variances by: (1) analysis of the primary variances; (2) cause; or (3) establishing specific account codes for the specific causal variances, segregating the costs at the time of original entry on the books, and reporting these variances separately. Examples of causal variances include lot size variance, rework variance, spoilage variance, scrap variance, and the standard revision variance. Examples of primary variances are direct labor, direct materials, and burden variances. Causal variances may contain elements of one or more of the primary variances (e.g., the rework variance is comprised of direct labor, direct materials, and burden variances).

Audit Objectives for Cost Accounting	Audit Procedures for Cost Accounting
To ascertain whether all inventories are physically counted, priced, and reconciled to the general ledger and that appropriate adjustments are made.	Ensure that detailed instructions are issued to each of the various groups involved in the physical inventory (i.e., count teams, ticket pullers, ticket checkers). Review the instructions for adequacy. Review the inventory checklist and ensure all items were completed. Note the impact of quantity and price adjustments. Ensure that complete reconciliations are performed and analyses are prepared detailing the causes of all significant inventory adjustments. Ensure that all inventory adjustments are passed through the "Reserve for Inventory Adjustments" account. Where **cycle counts** are utilized, review for these items: (1) the method of selecting items for cycle counts; (2) the thoroughness in locating all items; the use of recounts; (3) the reconciliation procedure; (4) booking inventory adjustments; and (5) procedure to fine-tune inventory control techniques where recurring problems are uncovered. Check the inventory valuation calculations. Ensure that the period between the physical inventory date and year-end is not excessive, considering the adequacy of the system of internal controls over the inventory and past experience relative to the accuracy of the inventory balances.
To determine whether appropriate controls and documents are in place to ensure that all material is promptly and accurately accounted for and that all material movement is properly authorized and controlled.	Perform a walkthrough of material movement from receipt into the stockroom, to material issues, to the production line, to finished goods. Include material sent to outside vendors for processing, returns to stores from production, returns to inventory from customers, and scrap controls. Ensure that material move documentation is generated at the time of issue or return of material and is recorded for inventory control purposes for each of these events: (1) issues to production from raw materials stores, subassembly stores, or directly from third parties, such as vendors or contractors; (2) returns to raw materials stores of excess or unsuitable material; (3) transfers within WIP from one pay point to another; (4) transfers to and returns from outside processors and contractors; (5) scrap or spoiled material; (6) transfers from production to finished goods or subassembly stores; (7) finished goods inventory relief to cost of sales; and (8) material returned from vendors.
To ascertain whether direct labor and overhead charges are promptly and accurately accumulated and reported and whether inventory valuations include all added labor and overhead input.	Ensure that direct labor and overhead costs are accumulated at definitive stages of production (i.e., pay points) and that these stages are logical break points in the production process. Pay points should not be so large as to preclude meaningful analyses of the production process (i.e., one pay point at the end of all production operations) or so fragmented as to require overly burdensome administrative effort (i.e., multiple pay points at one operation).

(continued)

Audit Objectives for Cost Accounting	Audit Procedures for Cost Accounting
	Ensure that work tickets are prepared by all direct labor employees and include, at a minimum: employee number, date, job number, department, operation, account (work in process, rework), start time, stop time, hourly rate, pieces worked, pieces rejected, good pieces completed. Ensure that the production foreperson or supervisor approves the work tickets. Where incentive pay is involved, review the methods of verifying production counts and hours worked.
	Ensure that the work tickets are summarized by cost accounting, the inventory records are updated for the standard direct labor and associated standard overhead expended, the variances are calculated and charged to income, and variance analysis work is conducted.
	Ensure that the correct overhead rate is being applied in those cases where there are variable overhead rates based on production and where overhead rates vary between departments. Ensure that all overhead is being fully absorbed regardless of actual production levels.

ACTUAL COSTS AND STANDARD COSTS

A comparison of actual costs to standard costs will assist management in its evaluation of effectiveness and efficiency of business operations.

EXAMPLES OF APPLICATIONS OF CAATs: COST ACCOUNTING

- Use the test data method to determine whether all overhead is completely allocated to cost centers by the computer program.

- List large cost variances (between standard and actual) for further analysis and interpretations.

- Recompute inventory valuation and compare it with actual.

- Compare cost of sales data between summary totals and aggregation of individual item totals to ensure that they are the same.

- Test the accuracy of the accumulation of production costs by cross-referencing to the production system.

VARIANCE CALCULATIONS

Ensure that the **burden expenditure variance** is calculated as

> Actual indirect manufacturing expense incurred − Allowed burden at actual
> activity level (fixed plus variable) = Burden expenditure variance

Ensure that the **burden efficiency variance** is calculated as

> Actual direct labor hours at the fixed portions of the burden rate − Standard direct labor
> hours earned at the fixed portion of the burden rate = Burden efficiency variance

Ensure that the **burden volume variance** is calculated as

> Actual direct labor hours at the fixed portions of the burden rate − Budgeted direct labor
> hours at the fixed portion of the burden rate = Burden volume variance

---

BASIC DEFINITIONS OF VARIANCES

Lot size variance. The difference between the standard number of units in a standard lot size and the actual number of units in actual lot size times the standard unit setup cost.

Rework variance. It is calculated as the cost of actual labor hours at the standard rate plus the standard labor burden plus any material required at the standard cost to correct defective production to meet engineering specifications.

Scrap variance. It is calculated as the difference between the actual weight of recovered residual material and the standard allowed weight times the standard scrap price.

Spoilage variance. It is calculated as the full standard cost through the last completed operation of spoiled production that does not meet specifications and cannot be reworked to meet specifications less the standard cost of any salvaged parts or components.

Standard revision variance. It is calculated as the difference between the old standard cost and a new standard cost in those cases when standards are revised in the period between general revisions for operating measurements, but the standard cost documents and inventory pricing are left unchanged until the next general revision.

(E) Introduction to Treasury Cycle Major activities in a treasury cycle include:

- Issuing of capital stock and debt securities.
- Paying dividends and interest.
- Paying debt at maturity.
- Repaying debt and repurchase of securities issued.
- Purchasing of capital stock and bonds.
- Receiving of periodic dividends and interest on investments.
- Selling of capital stock and bonds.
- Conducting cash flow analysis.
- Recording of financing and investing activities by journalizing and posting such transactions.
- Filing of proper tax forms.
- Protecting physical records and inventory of capital stocks, bonds, and other securities.
- Maintaining the accuracy and completeness of securities and shareholder records and financing and investment account balances.

Audit Cycle/Area: Treasury—Debt Management

Risks and Exposures	Controls or Control Procedures
Improper authorization of company transactions dealing with debt instruments.	Written company policy requiring review of major repayment of debt proposals by the board of directors (PC).
Loss or theft of debt instruments.	Install physical security controls (PC). Prenumbered debt instruments (PC). Reconciliation of physical inventory to perpetual inventory of debt instruments (DC).
Potential for fraud or irregularities.	Segregation of duties between treasury function and accounting function (PC).

Audit Objectives for Debt Management	Audit Procedures for Debt Management
To determine whether long-term and short-term debt is authorized and issued in accordance with the board of directors' resolutions.	Review debt instruments on file for approval signatures to ensure that all debt has been authorized by individuals designated to do so by the chief financial officer (CFO). If variances exist, investigate the circumstances and confirm with the CFO. Determine that debt placement is only through approved banks or brokers and then only up to amounts authorized by the board of directors' resolutions. Reconcile banks and brokers used and amounts involved to the board of directors' resolutions and credit lines authorized. Review if variance exists and that they have been specifically authorized. If not, investigate the circumstances and confirm with the CFO. Ascertain that new debts are incurred only after calculation of total costs of different banks. Ascertain that new debt incurred is reviewed against restrictions in place regarding debt to equity ratio, current ratio, and other relevant financial ratios. Review all debt agreements and determine if there have been any violations of debt restrictions. Review debt issuance to cash forecasts and debt planning objectives. Ensure that the issuance of debt is consistent with the cash forecasts and the objectives. If not, comment on the variances that exist and on the exposures, if any. Ascertain that procedures are in place that result in separation of duties in regard to authorization of debt, receipt of funds, and recording of funds and debt (i.e., separation between the treasury function and the accounting function). Review transaction registers and monthly reconciliations to ensure that all activity is reflected by a relevant category in both treasury and accounting records. Ensure that all bank debt instruments are prenumbered and kept in locked storage under a perpetual inventory system. Ensure that the system's data are reconciled daily to use record and monthly to a physical inventory. Verify that the custodian of bank debt instruments has no other responsibility in the debt issuance process. Evaluate the adequacy of the storage facilities to prevent theft and casualty loss. Check if the documents are prenumbered. Review record of daily use. Review reconciliations at month-end to physical inventory.
To ascertain whether principal payment of long- and short-term debt is repaid promptly and accurately in accordance with the contractual document.	Reconcile the debt schedule to the files of banks and brokers involved in debt issuance and the amount of debt to the board of directors' resolutions to ensure all debt is correctly included. Review the debt schedule to a sample of debt agreements and test due dates and other key items.

Audit Objectives for Debt Management	Audit Procedures for Debt Management
	Review debt payment procedures. Identify variances and analyze as to causes and if they indicate administrative problem or system control weaknesses. Verify that all required payments are included in the cash forecast. Identify variances and discuss with management.
	Review requests for voucher check or debt payment instrument. For payment of debt, test the authorization by both treasury and accounting management. Test that the payment is accurate and timely and consistent with the terms of the agreement.
	Review control reports and daily transaction registers, and test daily reconciliations to ensure all activity is recorded by relevant category. Reconcile the updated debt balance to payments in total and by specific debt paid. Review paid note documents for endorsements and cancellations. Reconcile debt payments to general ledger debt and cash accounts. Review payment confirmations received from trustees or creditor representatives.
To determine whether interest payments on short- and long-term debt are made in accordance with the requirements of the debt instrument and that they are recorded correctly.	Review schedules of interest payments due: Test that cash flow and budgeting projections have been updated to reflect payments due. If variances exist, explain them, review the reconciliation of interest calculations to the schedules and in total to general ledger records for relevant categories of debt, and verify that interest payment schedules have been reconciled to a trustee or creditor record and that, if variances exist, they have been reconciled.
	Verify interest calculations for payments made for each type of debt reviewed. Review for adequate separation of duties between authorization and recording of payments. If interest payments are confirmed, verify confirmations to payments requested and made. Trace payments made to cash accounts in the general ledger.
To ascertain whether interest is accrued for short- and long-term debt accurately and promptly.	Verify that interest accrual schedules are reviewed and reconciled to total debt outstanding as of statement date. Review and reconcile interest accrual schedules to total debt outstanding, and ensure that the total accrual appears reasonable. Compare current year's accrual to prior year's accrual and comment on the variance.
	Analyze and reconcile changes to interest accruals to interest payments made, debt payoffs, and new debt incurred. Comment on general reasonableness of the accrual. Ascertain that treasury and accounting records of interest accruals are maintained independently of one another and are reconciled.
	In order to test whether commitment fees are accrued and paid promptly and accurately, these audit tests are suggested: Test calculations of fees paid, verify that all fees have been paid as required, and review accrual balances and reconcile to the appropriate agreements. In order to determine

(*continued*)

Audit Objectives for Debt Management	Audit Procedures for Debt Management
	that banks confirm commitment fees, these audit tests are suggested: Ascertain that commitment fees recorded are compared with bank's billings, test accrual dates to agreement dates, and analyze variances between accruals and actual.

EXAMPLES OF APPLICATION OF CAATs: DEBT MANAGEMENT

- List securities for physical inspection or confirmation.

- List interest payments for vouching to supporting documentation.

- List unusual interest rates on loans after comparing them with management guidelines; unusual rates could indicate a fraudulent situation.

- Conduct a reasonableness test between interest amount paid and principal amount for each category of debt and for aggregate.

Audit Cycle/Area: Treasury—Cash Management

Risks and Exposures	Controls or Control Procedures
Making and concealing unauthorized payments.	Separation of duties between check preparation and bank reconciliation functions (PC, DC).
Fraud in electronic cash transfer system.	Dual controls, system access controls, system callbacks, and confirmation of transfer requests (PC, DC).
Loss or theft of blank checks.	Establish physical security controls over blank check stock (PC).

Audit Objectives for Cash Management	Audit Procedures for Cash Management
To determine whether cash receipts are properly secured and promptly deposited to authorized bank accounts.	Ensure that receivables due the company or divisions are mailed to lockboxes and are deposited in the company's bank accounts. Review that all cash receipts are clearly labeled as to source (e.g., lockbox and debt). Ensure that all bank accounts used have been authorized and established by the company's treasurer's department. Ensure that all banks involved have received instructions as to the correct procedures to be followed in authorizing and confirming cash receipts activity, including the names and signatures of authorized individuals. Review system logs to determine if attempts to record cash deposits to other than approved banks have occurred. Determine responses taken by management. Review data file access controls and verify that computer access is limited based on primary job duties. Verify that all access to the data files is recorded on a system log by access code or other forms of identification of the individual who accessed the system. Ensure that the cash management system generates a daily transaction register that reflects all activity processed.

Audit Objectives for Cash Management	Audit Procedures for Cash Management
To ascertain whether physical security controls, administrative controls, and system controls over cash receipts are adequate and proper.	Review separation of duties with regard to persons responsible for the application of cash. Test to ensure that they are prohibited from performing the following activities: reconciling bank accounts; opening incoming mail; preparing, recording, or approving vouchers for payment; preparing, signing, mailing, or delivering checks for payroll and other; and performing work on notes payable or any other evidence of indebtedness. For mail receipts, test to ensure that they are: opened by someone other than the cashier, accounts receivable, or billing person; and listed in detail at the time the mail is opened, and that the listing is reconciled to book entries and deposit slips by an independent person. For other than mail receipts, ensure that they are prelisted and accounted for by one of these procedures: tape is prepared by validating machine for receipt forms issued, cash register used, prenumbered receipt forms used, and test that all receipts and prelisting forms are accounted for serially as being recorded in the cash receipts journal.

Audit Objectives for Cash Management	Audit Procedures for Cash Management
	In order to ensure that all checks received are restrictively endorsed and cash is applied and deposited on a timely basis, these audit tests are suggested: (1) Review cash application and deposit procedures for adequacy and completeness; (2) ensure that cash receipts are promptly recorded and deposited; (3) ensure that access to cash receipts is restricted to those parties who have custodial responsibility at each step in the procedure; (4) ensure that cash receipts are deposited in accounts receivable accounts and are not commingled with other funds; (5) ensure that a deposit memo is prepared describing the nature of the receipt and is furnished to the accounting department for each batch of checks received; (6) ensure that payroll or personal checks are not cashed from cash receipts; (7) ensure that undeposited receipts are restrictively endorsed and are under effective physical security control (e.g., lock and key, vault) to prevent theft or loss; (8) ensure that cash receipts are posted to the detailed accounts receivable records from collection advices rather than from cash items; (9) ensure that custody of all other cash funds or securities is separated from the function responsible for applying cash; (10) ensure that there is an adequate safeguard against misappropriation of cash through the recording of fictitious discounts or allowances by persons handling cash; (11) ensure that checks returned unpaid for insufficient funds are delivered directly to a responsible employee (other

(continued)

Audit Objectives for Cash Management	Audit Procedures for Cash Management
	than cashier) for investigation; (12) ensure that branch offices or divisions making collections deposit these funds in a bank account subject to withdrawal only by the home or head office; (13) ensure that proper physical safeguards and facilities (e.g., safes, restricted areas) are employed to protect cash; and (14) ensure that persons receiving or handling cash funds are properly bonded and take annual vacation time.
To determine whether cash disbursements are made only to authorized recipients in accordance with management-specific instructions.	Review the electronic cash transfer systems; observe sign-on procedures, instructions entered, and register(s) generated. Test to documented procedures to determine if variance exists between actual processing and documented procedures. Evaluate the administrative cash transfer procedures in place. Test to ensure that all transfers have been approved in writing by both cash section management and general accounting management and confirmed by the bank to the authorizing parties. Review instructions sent to the disbursement banks for adequacy and consistency. Verify that the list of banks to which money can be transferred has been reconciled to treasury letters authorizing establishment of the bank accounts. If variances exist, research and reconcile them. Review to determine if transfers have been attempted to other than an approved bank. Discuss controls that would highlight such an attempt and comment on their adequacy. Determine that all amounts transferred are confirmed by the bank, review confirmations received, and reconcile them to accounting and cash management records. Specifically, review daily cash transfer activity registers to ensure they have been reconciled to source documentation and confirmations and that the reconciliations have been reviewed and approved by management.
To ascertain whether bank reconciliations are performed promptly and correctly.	Ensure that bank statements are received by the bank reconciliation section directly from the various authorized banks. Select a sample of bank reconciliations and conduct these audit procedures: (1) Observe that the information is supported by bank statements and the general ledger; (2) determine that the reconciliation format used is consistent with the prescribed format; (3) verify that differences are resolved; and (4) test that reconciliations are signed by the person performing the reconciliations and that they are timely. In order to test how the differences in reconciliation have been resolved, the next audit procedures are suggested: (1) Ascertain that all adjustments are adequately supported by acceptable documentation;

Audit Objectives for Cash Management	Audit Procedures for Cash Management
	(2) ensure that documentation is cross-referenced to adjustments; (3) review transmittals of correction entries to the accounting department; and (4) verify that out-of-balance conditions are promptly followed up for correction. Review bank reconciliations for management approval evidenced by signature and date. In order to ensure that the canceled checks have authorized signatures, examine a representative sample of signed checks and determine that the signatures are authorized in the corporate signature book.
To determine whether controls are adequate over petty cash disbursement and reimbursement activities.	In order to ensure that cash disbursed and received by the person handling petty cash is based on approved documentation and that it is timely and accurately recorded, perform these audit tests: (1) Review established procedures regarding processing the disbursement of funds and comment on their adequacy; (2) ensure that advances made to employees are approved as required; (3) ensure that a maximum amount for individual payments from the fund has been established; and (4) ensure that petty cash vouchers are: prepared for each disbursement; adequately supported; in ink or typewritten; dated; fully descriptive of the item paid for; clearly marked to show the amount paid; and signed by the person receiving the cash. Ensure that all documents supporting the cash disbursement are canceled to prevent reuse. Review reimbursement requests and the attached documentation for compliance to established procedures. Specifically, confirm that: all supporting documents contain authorized approvals, the sums of the individual voucher totals are accurate, and all vouchers and supporting documents are canceled at the time of reimbursement to prevent reuse. Ascertain that supervisors perform periodic audits of the petty cash funds and reconcile to the general ledger accounts. Understand how reconciliation problems are resolved. Ascertain that the size of the petty cash imprest funds is based on good business judgment consistent with usage.

AUDIT CONCERN OF A MULTINATIONAL CORPORATION

A primary audit concern of a multinational corporation's foreign branch money transfer operations located at international headquarters is ensuring compliance with foreign government money transfer regulations. Good internal control requires that the person making wire transfers should not reconcile the bank statement.

Audit Cycle/Area: Treasury—Equity Management

Risks and Exposures	Controls or Control Procedures
Improper authorization of company transactions dealing with equity instruments.	A written company policy requiring review of major funding proposals by the board of directors (PC).
Loss or theft of issued stock certificates.	Physical security controls, sequentially numbered receipts, maintain receipt logs, taking physical inventory, and periodic reconciliations (PC, DC).
Improper or incorrect conversion of instruments.	Written procedures, management reporting, and recomputations (PC, DC).

Audit Objectives for Equity Management	Audit Procedures for Equity Management
To determine whether all stock certificates received are acknowledged properly and documented as to source, number of shares, and certificate numbers to aid in ensuring that all stock certificates are transferred and accounted for.	Review stock receiving area for physical security and protection afforded the stock certificates delivered for transfer processing. Evaluate the adequacy of the protection. Observe stock certificate receipt procedures for a selected sample of activity: (1) Validate that the stock certificates received are reconciled to accompanying shipping documentation as to total number of shares, certificate numbers, and other information provided; (2) validate that receipts are assigned for stock certificates received by source (e.g., mail, stock exchange, bank, broker, personal delivery, depository trust company) with total number of shares noted; and (3) review receipt log to ensure that all sequentially numbered receipts are accounted for.

Review a sample of securities in the area for endorsements, guarantees, transfer instructions, and general appearance. Review procedures for handling incomplete stock certificates. Evaluate their adequacy and appropriateness. |
| To ascertain whether blank stock certificates are adequately protected against theft and loss. | Review blank-certificate storage facilities and access controls; determine that storage facilities adequately protect blank certificates against theft and other casualty damage. All stock certificates released should be accurately recorded and signed for by the individual physically transporting the items. Ascertain that access is restricted to individuals who are independent of the transfer function.

Review monthly physical inventory and reconciliations to daily use records and the perpetual inventory system: Determine if variances have existed, and, if so, verify that they have been researched and resolved on a prompt basis; and ascertain that a record of void certificates on hand and certificates destroyed exists. For those destroyed, ensure that destruction has been witnessed; and determine if the physical inventory reconciliation is reviewed and approved by management. |

Audit Objectives for Equity Management	**Audit Procedures for Equity Management**
To determine whether stock transfer requests are processed promptly and accurately.	Review stock certificate preparation for a sample of activity: (1) Ascertain that certificates have been prepared consistent with transfer instructions; (2) ensure that unused blank stock certificates are returned to the vault as required; (3) determine that erroneously filled out stock certificates have been voided; and (4) verify that an audit trail exists between old and new certificates. Verify that discrepancies between file information and information on the stock certificate being presented for transfer are researched and reconciled on a timely basis. Analyze errors to determine if patterns exist that indicate repetitive processing problems. Determine whether outstanding discrepancies as of the dividend payment date that are effective on the record date are properly recorded to ensure the accuracy of the dividend payment. Ensure that transaction registers are reviewed and reconciled daily. Verify that management reviews the reconciliations. Determine that all variances are resolved on a timely basis. Determine that the ability to modify and maintain the stockholder files is assigned to an individual who is independent of the transfer process.
To ascertain whether the registrar reviews all stock cancellations and reissues daily, and updates records accordingly.	In order to ensure that the registrar reviews the number of shares canceled and reissued to the number of shares authorized and outstanding, the next audit procedures are suggested: (1) Review the shipment of canceled stock and newly issued stock certificates to the registrar; (2) observe the controls that ensure all certificates are sent to the registrar; (3) verify that the transaction register is sent with the certificates and that controls are in place to ensure it accurately reflects transfer activity; (4) ensure that packaging and shipment of certificates is performed independently of the treasury department; and (5) determine that the shipping packages are securely bound and sealed prior to shipment. Review the daily file reconciliation supplied by the registrar. If variances exist, ascertain that they have been reviewed and resolved on a timely basis and approved by management. Repeat this for month-end, quarter-end, and year-end reconciliations. Observe or ensure that shipments of securities returned by the registrar are sealed, and ascertain that they are properly receipted with the receiving individual(s) clearly identified.
To determine whether newly issued stock certificates returned by the registrar are distributed to the new owner per the original instructions and that canceled stock certificates are securely stored.	Observe physical security and general safeguards. Ascertain that newly issued certificates are adequately safeguarded to ensure that only people for whom they are intended will receive them.

(continued)

Audit Objectives for Equity Management	Audit Procedures for Equity Management
	Observe techniques and procedures utilized by the stock distribution area: verify that securities are distributed per original transfer instructions; ascertain that the receipt log for securities distributed is cross-referenced to sources of original securities; and verify that the distribution log is reconciled to the receipt log. For a sample of activity, review to ensure that all canceled stock certificates are physically canceled and stored securely and in a manner consistent with the record retention guidelines.
To ascertain whether preferred stock and debentures are converted into common stock consistent with the terms of the various agreements and are accurately and promptly recorded.	Review documentation supporting the conversion of preferred stock and debentures into common stock and comment on its adequacy in regard to key operating items. Determine that the conversion calculation (amount of common shares to be issued) is performed and verified independently. Review the conversion calculation procedure and operation: Observe whether the calculation is performed twice independently to ensure accuracy and verify that controls are in place to ensure that the correct conversion rate is used and that a history file is maintained regarding rate information. For checks issued in lieu of fractional shares, verify that the amount is accurate. Review inventory controls over treasury stock and authorized but not issued shares: (1) Test that inventory records are updated daily and are reviewed and approved independently of the area responsible for maintenance; (2) verify that all activity including the issuance of treasury stock and authorized but unissued shares is transmitted to the accounting department daily; (3) ensure that issuance is confirmed independently to both the treasury and accounting departments; and (4) review month-end reconciliations and comment on the discrepancies noted. Review actual issuance of stock certificates: Verify that the number of shares issued is consistent with the rate and the amount of preferred stock and debentures presented for conversion; check that the number of shares issued has been transmitted to the accounting department; and ensure that appropriate journal entries have been made to reflect the activity.
To determine whether controls are adequate over the issuance of additional shares.	Review the board of directors' resolutions. Ensure that the actual issuance of new shares is consistent with the board's authorization. Review to ensure that the issuance of additional shares has been subjected to legal review. Review notifications to regulatory and governmental agencies (e.g., Securities and Exchange Commission) per instructions issued by legal counsel and determine that the notifications are consistent with the instructions.

Audit Objectives for Equity Management	Audit Procedures for Equity Management
	Review procedures followed in regard to actual issuance of new shares, and test to ensure consistency with the board of directors' resolutions and specific treasury department instructions. Review entries made by the accounting department to ensure that they are consistent with the board of directors' resolutions and stock transfer activity. Test that the various accounting records affected have been reconciled.
To ascertain whether common stock issued as a result of the exercise of stock options is promptly and accurately recorded consistent with all terms of the option granted.	Review approvals and documentation supporting procedures regarding the exercise of stock options and comment on their adequacy. Review the stock option plan and ensure that the plan has been approved.
	Review the list of eligible employees and the specifics of their eligibility. Test the stock option plan for a sample of individuals to ensure that options granted are consistent with the established criteria. Review the procedure followed in notifying individuals of their eligibility: Check that all properly approved individuals were notified, and establish that notification was consistent with the specifics of eligibility that were determined.
	Verify that, when options are exercised, designated individuals in the personnel department have approved the specific request and that all conditions are validated.
	Review requests to exercise the options that have been granted: Ensure that they are consistent with the authorization, and check that they contain the correct approvals. Verify that a check for the required amount of money accompanied the request and that it has been deposited on a timely basis.
	Review the stock option account file that is compiled as stock certificates are issued for options granted, and determine that it is reconciled to source documentation supporting the issuance of shares. Review accounting entries made as the result of the exercise of the options. Verify that they correctly reflect the activity that has taken place.
	Review reporting to governmental and regulatory agencies. Ascertain that it is consistent with the requirements, accurate, and reflective of actual activity. Determine that stock certificates for exercised stock options are issued, registered, and delivered consistent with normal stock transfer processing procedures.
To determine whether conversion of preferred debentures into common stock is performed properly and accurately.	Verify that documented processing procedures, controls, and management reporting requirements are in place to provide department guidance in regard to conversion activity. Verify that once it has been determined that the preferred debenture

(*continued*)

Audit Objectives for Equity Management	Audit Procedures for Equity Management
	submitted is a valid document, it is converted into common stock and the shares are issued, registered, and distributed via the processing procedures in place regarding all other types of transfer activity. Review the conversion calculation verification procedure followed. Indicate if they are adequate to ensure that calculations are made correctly. Test a sample of calculations made, and comment on their accuracy.
To ascertain whether controls over redemption of securities are proper.	Verify that the redemption of securities is in accordance with the board of directors' resolutions as to the type of securities to be redeemed, the number of shares or dollar value of securities, monies to be paid, the time period the offer is open, the restrictions as to source, and total or minimum amount from one person. Review the selection of the redemption agent; establish that the agent is licensed and that business and character references have been obtained; and verify that a contract has been signed, that it details the responsibility of respective parties and specifies payment terms. Test that the contract has been complied with; and ascertain that the payment document has been approved at the appropriate management level. Review the accounting entries made as a result of the board of directors' resolutions. Check that the expenses involved have been correctly accrued. Review the register of securities redeemed and payments made. Ensure that amounts paid are consistent with the securities surrendered and authorizing resolutions. Review accounting entries. Test that they correctly reflect the redemption activity that occurred.
To determine whether securities acquired as a result of an acquisition of a company are stored under conditions that are adequate to protect them from theft and loss.	Review practices and procedures regarding the receipt of security documents: Verify that receipt is documented and that it includes time and date, certificate number, and number of shares involved. Test that the record is maintained in duplicate and that it contains a signature or a confirmation from the individual or company delivering the security. Determine that the security is subject to adequate safeguarding to protect it from theft or casualty loss. Ensure that persons involved in the receipt and transfer of securities are at appropriate job levels and are bonded. Review monthly reconciliations between the treasury and accounting departments and, if differences exist, analyze as to causes and determine if they have been resolved. Ascertain that the reconciliations have been reviewed and approved by management.

Audit Objectives for Equity Management	Audit Procedures for Equity Management
	Review physical storage of securities and general inventory control procedures: Observe and test that storage facilities are adequate to prevent theft and casualty loss except under the most extreme conditions; ascertain that access restrictions are in conformity with requirements. Vaults should be opened for a limited time period each day with dual persons attending; check that all employees involved are bonded; verify that securities carry adequate and reasonable insurance coverage; and verify that inventory listings of the securities stored are transmitted to the insurer as required by insurance policies. Perform a count of the securities and trace the results to the treasury's physical inventory records.
To ascertain whether the divestiture of securities is accurately and timely recorded.	Confirm divestiture to the board of directors' resolutions. Review inventory records to determine they are adjusted correctly and that, if variances exist, they have been documented. Review confirmation of the receipt and transmittal of securities to the acquirer including signed receipts. Determine that all required parties have been notified. Review receipt of cash or other payment (e.g., notes receivable, alternative securities). Determine that they are accurate and consistent with the amount called for in the agreement. Review to ensure they have been correctly receipted and deposited. If variances exist, discuss with the responsible management. Determine that appropriate entries are made in the accounting department to reflect the divestiture and release of the securities.
To determine whether additional capital contributions are recorded promptly and accurately.	Review the approved request and verify that it is consistent with the board of directors' resolutions regarding approvals for additional capital contributions. Review journal entries made to record the additional contributions and ensure that they are accurate and consistent with prior entries and with accounting rules and regulations. Review the monthly settlement statement indicating receipt of the funds.

EXAMPLES OF APPLICATION OF CAATs: EQUITY MANAGEMENT

- List capital stock purchases, sales, and redemptions for vouching with supporting documentation.
- Recompute profits and losses on redemption of stock for accuracy and completeness.

Audit Cycle/Area: Treasury—Investment Management

Risks and Exposures	Controls or Control Procedures
Improper accounting of dividends.	Establish procedures for dividend declaration and payment (PC).
Improper accounting of notes receivable.	Perform positive confirmation of notes receivable (DC).
Improper use of debit/credit advices.	Issue written guidelines (PC). Conduct periodic checks to ensure proper use (DC).

Audit Objectives for Investment Management	Audit Procedures for Investment Management
To determine whether all investment acquisitions are approved by the board of directors and properly recorded.	Review initial acquisition proposals. Verify that the terms, conditions, costs, and benefits to the company are clearly stated. Examine that the proposal has been signed and approved by senior management. Review approved acquisition proposals. Verify against minutes of the board of directors' meetings. Review external auditors' involvement and check that their comments are consistent with that of the department submitting the proposal. If inconsistencies exist, determine if they have been brought to the attention of senior management. Review preliminary agreements. Determine that they are consistent with the board of directors' instructions. Determine if negative confirmations are required from the requesting division and, if so, what subsequent actions occur. Test that the acquisition agreement has been reviewed and approved by the board of directors. If differences exist, evaluate their resolution and management levels involved. Review the letters of intent to ensure that they are consistent with preliminary agreements. Review the purchase agreement and closing; test if there are differences from the letter of intent and the approved preliminary agreement. If so, review to determine if the exceptions have been noted and resolved; determine that the closing process has been documented; and inquire whether all affected parties are notified. Determine that the acquisition is established in the general ledger and that appropriate documentation is maintained in a permanent file to record the acquisition. When the internal auditor is conducting a **due diligence review,** the following audit program is suggested: (1) Review articles and bylaws for the company and subsidiaries to be acquired, including major employment contracts, bonus or stock purchase plans, management contracts, insurance policies including the board of directors' liability limits; (2) review federal and state tax returns and

Audit Objectives for Investment Management	**Audit Procedures for Investment Management**
	audited financial statements, material guaranties, contingent liabilities: class action suits, product liability claims, insider trading issues; (3) review all business activities including material litigation pending and status of tax audits, environmental problems, or any special investigations; (4) review industry regulatory requirements, if any; (5) review compliance with Securities and Exchange Commission requirements regarding issuance of financial securities; (6) perform tests in accounts receivables and long-term payables; (7) mail confirmations of significant receivables and payables to customers; (8) ensure that there were no pledged or otherwise encumbered assets; (9) review lease or purchase agreements, looking for generous arrangements, such as an option to purchase equipment for a fraction of its cost, indicating a related-party transaction; (10) review for irrevocable lease arrangements that increase the risk to the acquiring company; (11) conduct a physical count of inventory, and bring in an independent expert if necessary to value the inventory items; (12) ensure that cash is properly stated by preparing and reviewing the standard bank confirmation inquiries; and (13) review fixed asset capitalization procedures for adequacy and compliance with tax guidelines and management directives.
To determine whether all investment divestitures are approved by the board of directors and properly recorded.	Review the initial divestiture proposal: Ensure that it contains signatures of the preparer and management; establish that it clearly presents the proposed divestiture; and verify that it has been approved by senior management and the board of directors. Review distribution to prospective buyers for confidentiality of process, quality of buyers, and agents used. Review the preliminary sales agreement and ensure that it has been distributed to all relevant parties. Reconcile the final sales agreement to the minutes of the board of directors. Review board of directors' minutes to ensure that all modifications have been made. Research and obtain explanations for any differences that may exist. Ascertain that the final sales agreement is distributed to all affected parties. Review distribution controls in place and comment on their adequacy. Review accounting entries made as a result of divestiture: Verify that accounting entries are consistent with the agreement and ensure that no entries have been omitted; and ensure that accounting entries are consistent with GAAP and company policies and procedures.

(continued)

Audit Objectives for Investment Management	**Audit Procedures for Investment Management**
To ascertain whether investment escrow cash and/or securities are properly safeguarded and released to the seller in accordance with the purchase agreement.	Review the purchase agreement: (1) Verify that escrow is deposited consistent with the amount and type called for in the purchase agreement; (2) ensure that the escrow agent is a bank or other financial institution of unquestionable integrity with the technical competence to handle the responsibility and is preselected by the treasury department for this purpose; (3) check that the escrow agent has adequate insurance coverage; and (4) determine that receipt of the escrow payment has been acknowledged or confirmed by the agent and that the treasury has copies of the confirmation. Ensure that the funds, if any, involved in an escrow arrangement have been used to purchase interest-bearing instruments consistent with the terms of the agreement. Determine to whom the agreement states the interest accrues and verify that it was paid consistent with the agreement. Review escrow payment activity: Validate that the trustee has released the escrow to the seller as authorized on a timely and accurate basis. Ensure that confirmations are reviewed promptly and that problems are expeditiously resolved; ascertain that interest earnings, if due, have been paid per the agreement. If paid to the company, determine that they have been recorded as interest income.
To determine whether dividends from subsidiaries are declared and paid properly and promptly.	Reconcile dividend declaration and payment to the company by its subsidiaries. Verify that the dividend amounts to be paid are consistent with the percentages of consolidated net income. Ensure that public notice of the intention to declare a dividend has been made as required. Test that the corporate treasury has been notified promptly when a dividend has been declared. Ensure that subsidiaries prepare a monthly cash flow forecast, copies of which are sent to both the treasury and accounting departments. Evaluate the adequacy of analysis and follow-up. Review dividends received for a period of time. Verify that dividends have been received in the amounts specified and on the dates due. If the amount received differs from the planned receipt, verify that the difference has been researched, documented, and approved. Review debit/credit advices supplied by subsidiaries to ensure that dividends have been correctly reported and the advice forms are utilized correctly. If the dividend was netted or offset against balances owed by corporate, test to determine if treasury management approval was obtained prior to the reduced payment.
To ascertain whether notes received as part of the payment for divestitures are timely and accurately recorded both as to principal and interest accruals and are presented for payment when due.	Review final sales agreements for terms of notes receivable. Review notes receivable accounts in the general ledger to determine if they are established consistent with the agreements and if they are subject to control. Specifically, ensure that segregation

Audit Objectives for Investment Management	**Audit Procedures for Investment Management**
	of duties is maintained between employees who post the detail notes receivable from employees who post general ledger control accounts, have cash functions, and have voucher functions.
	Review the notes receivable schedule system for controls over payment dates. Evaluate the collectibility of questionable items and adequacy of collateral where appropriate, and review the adequacy of the allowance for uncollectible accounts. Review the cash flow forecast system to determine if notes receivable is entered correctly.
	Ensure that the duties of the custodian of notes receivable and related collateral are segregated from general ledger functions, maintaining detailed records of notes receivable and collateral, and cash functions.
	Request positive confirmation of at least a representative sample of notes held by custodians and with makers; specifically confirm the unpaid balances, interest, maturity dates, and collateral pledged with the makers of the notes, and follow up on those for which a reply was not received. Investigate differences reported as a result of the above confirmation requests by examining the underlying data (e.g., sales contracts, billing documents, and shipping documents).

EXAMPLES OF APPLICATION OF CAATs: INVESTMENT MANAGEMENT

- Recalculate amortization of discounts and premiums on investment accounts, and compare them with management calculations.

- Compare interest and dividend records with investment registers for determining relationships between accounts. Conduct reasonableness tests between the interest amount and the principal amounts of the investment.

- Recompute profits and losses on disposal of investments for accuracy and completeness.

Audit Cycle/Area: Treasury—Dividends Management

Risks and Exposures	**Controls or Control Procedures**
Inadequate controls over blank dividend checks.	Establish dual-person control (PC). Use prenumbered checks (DC).
Misappropriation of funds.	Establish controls over returned dividend checks (PC).
Violation of state escheat laws.	Implement procedures to handle undeliverable dividend checks (PC). Conduct periodic reviews for compliance (DC).

(*continued*)

Audit Objectives for Dividends Management	Audit Procedures for Dividends Management
To determine whether dividends to shareholders are paid promptly and accurately consistent with the board of directors' resolutions and in accordance with governmental and regulatory rules and regulations.	Review record date closing procedures: Determine that all record date activity up to and including the record date has been updated to the database used to run dividend files by sampling transfers occurring after the record date; ascertain that the record date database is subject to adequate access security controls to prevent accidental destruction and unauthorized modifications; and verify that all stockholder address changes have been updated to record date database between record date and payment date. Review preparations for printing of dividend checks: review procedures used in updating the dividend program for proper criteria (e.g., date, rate), and comment on their adequacy and the control procedures followed to ensure the update is accurate and properly authorized; and review preliminary testing regarding calculation accuracy and evaluate procedures followed. Review the printing of dividend checks: (1) Test that blank dividend check stock is controlled: cartons are sealed; checks are prenumbered and under dual-person control; (2) test that checks are used in sequence; (3) verify that misprints and damaged checks are voided and retained; (4) ascertain that the required calculations have been made prior to signing; (5) determine that checks are signed by facsimile signature under **dual-person control;** and (6) ascertain that the signature plate is adequately secured and is maintained by someone independent of check storage and printing. Verify that printed checks are placed in prenumbered cartons in run sequence and sealed prior to shipment to the bank for mailing. Establish that the shipment is subject to adequate physical security. Ensure that the bank confirms the number of checks mailed and that this figure is balanced to the number of checks printed. Review the accounting journal entries as a result of dividend checks presented for payment. Test and reconcile to the supporting documents provided. Review the month-end accrual for outstanding dividend payments and verify its accuracy. Review monthly bank reconciliations: Verify that the bank is being funded as checks are presented consistent with a zero-balance policy; if reconciling items exist, ensure that they have been resolved, documented, and approved by management; and establish that the reconciliations have been formally approved by management.
To ascertain whether controls over undeliverable dividends are adequate to prevent misappropriation of funds or to support eventual transfer to state government as required by the escheat laws.	Verify that all dividend checks that have been returned are reviewed and tested prior to a final determination that they are not deliverable: (1) The addresses as printed are reviewed for obvious printing mistakes; (2) the stock ownership file is

Audit Objectives for Dividends Management	Audit Procedures for Dividends Management
	checked and the addresses on the envelopes are verified to addresses in the computer database; (3) the prior dividend payment is reviewed to determine if the checks were cashed and, if so, they are reviewed to determine if information on them indicates new addresses or bank account numbers; (4) if a recent stock purchase, transfer tickets are reviewed and the organization's originating the transaction are contacted to determine if they have additional information; and (5) formal letters are sent to the addresses asking for information about the persons involved.
	Ascertain that, once a determination has been made that a check is undeliverable, these activities occur: (1) Convert the check to cash and establish the liability in a special account maintained for dividends that have been returned and determined to be undeliverable. Include all relevant information regarding dividend number, number of shares, certificate numbers, and so on; (2) code the stock transfer database so that checks are not printed during future dividend runs; (3) ensure that all nondeliverable coding entered into the database is reviewed and approved by management; (4) verify that undeliverable dividends are grouped by state and date of check; and (5) verify that undeliverable dividends are escheated to the various state governments based on their respective abandoned property laws, where applicable.
	Test the following for compliance with procedures: (1) Ascertain that the checks have been canceled and the amounts involved were set up as a liability; (2) review dividend accumulation by state; (3) ensure the record is complete and included holder name, address, dividend date, amount, number of shares of stock, dividend number; (4) review the most recent escheat payment to several states and confirm that a listing by individual and amount is included as a backup to the check; (5) determine that the age of the items included is consistent with state law; and (6) determine that appropriate accounting entries have been made to reflect the payments to the various states.

EXAMPLES OF APPLICATION OF CAATs: DIVIDENDS MANAGEMENT

- List dividend payments for vouching with supporting documentation.
- List unusual dividend rates applied to capital stock.
- List missing check numbers for making dividend payments for further analysis.
- Compare dividend records with stock registers to prove that dividends are for the valid stocks.
- Conduct a reasonableness test between total dividend amounts paid and the average number of shares and dollar aggregate.

Audit Cycle/Area: Treasury—Risk and Insurance Management

Risks and Exposures	Controls or Control Procedures
No insurance due to not reporting property to an insurance company.	Written procedures to notify additions or deletions of property to the insurance carrier (PC).
Possibility of excessive insurance coverage.	Report listing of all properties covered (PC). Periodic review for double, overlapping, or no insurance coverage (DC).
Improper handling of loss claims.	Written procedures describing the required reporting for losses experienced (PC). Computation of elapsed time between claim submission date and settlement date (DC).

Audit Objectives for Risk and Insurance Management	Audit Procedures for Risk and Insurance Management
To determine whether all insurance needs are defined accurately and on a timely basis to reduce or eliminate the exposure of an uninsured loss.	Review the list of assets and exposures whose coverage is requested. Ensure that all coverage provided by a third party (e.g., by lessors in case of leased equipment, forwarding agents for goods shipped, insurance provided by governmental institutions in the export business, legal obligations for producers of purchased goods) is properly reported to the insurance department to prevent double insurance.
	Ensure that all upgrading of security programs and improvements to buildings and equipment that could result in a better insurance rating is properly reported to the insurance department.
	Determine if the company has exposures in these areas that may require specialized local coverage: new product development, large sales contracts over a predetermined dollar amount, unusual controversies surrounding a product or market, and changing foreign or political conditions relevant to the company.
	Determine that procedures ensure that all property (e.g., company, vendors, and employees' property) is reported to the insurance department and that the department has controls to ensure it is reported to the insurance carrier where required. Ensure that the insurance carrier is notified of property additions or deletions.
To ascertain whether the company obtains insurance coverage to satisfy defined needs at the lowest cost and that the coverage is reviewed periodically for adequacy.	Review the insurance coverage in effect. Evaluate types of coverage selected so as to optimize premium expense relative to coverage provided. Ensure that the file indicates dollar limits and coverage specifics. Ascertain that the listing is reconciled to the general ledger and that variances have been analyzed. Review procedures followed in selecting insurance carriers, and ensure that the selection process was documented and indicates single sources, bidding, or negotiations.

Audit Objectives for Risk and Insurance Management	**Audit Procedures for Risk and Insurance Management**
	Determine if there are any overlaps in coverage provided. Ensure that certificates of insurance are provided by third parties performing work for the company.
	Review insurance carrier inspection reports. List the exposures pointed out, and determine if they have been corrected. Check that insurance carriers have made all required inspections or, if they have not been made, that the carrier has been contacted.
To determine whether claims are filed for losses and that a loss control program is in effect to minimize the potential for theft and casualty loss.	Review the published procedure that describes the required reporting for losses experienced. Ensure that the procedure includes such items as: (1) identifying physical losses or damages; (2) valuing the losses; (3) routines to be followed in reporting the losses; (4) methodology to determine if losses were the result of accidental circumstances, willful acts of sabotage, and frauds or theft; and (5) appropriate documentation to be completed and reporting responsibilities for each of the various types of loss.
	Review the file of loss reports to ascertain that reports have been filed promptly, are consistent with the requirements, and clearly identify and explain the incidents. Ensure that loss notification includes the following information: (1) location, date, and cause of loss; (2) description of property damaged; (3) estimated amount of loss; (4) person to be contacted by the insurance adjuster; and (5) if a manufacturer's output–type coverage, the transportation company inspector's report of damage-in-transit claims. Review emergency procedures to protect assets from further damage once loss has occurred. Review their implementation in regard to several incidents. Determine if they have protected the property from further loss or damage.
	Review the receivable that has been established to reflect the claim and perform the following audit tests: Check if it is based on the loss estimate; if not, review the support of the entry, determine if aged items are researched to determine their current status, and ensure that management is informed of claims collections problems. In the event of disputed claims, determine whether: full documentation of both parties' correspondence is maintained in a secured file, all contractual avenues of resolution are being explored, and the advice of legal counsel has been solicited.
	Review access controls to facilities and buildings. Observe that unrestricted access to the facility is limited to employees. Test the means to accomplish this. Observe that all others are directed to a reception area where the purpose of their visit is validated and recorded. Ensure that the employee being visited escorts visitors. Observe that locked

(continued)

Audit Objectives for Risk and Insurance Management	Audit Procedures for Risk and Insurance Management
	facilities are used for the storage of materials with access and inventory controls. Review access and material sign-out procedures.
	Review procedures to identify areas with a high degree of potential for fire and explosion. Ensure access to these areas is restricted to authorized employees by means of locked gates and/or security guards. Determine whether protective clothing is required for individuals entering dangerous areas. Review emergency procedures and responsibilities (e.g., fire drills, firefighting containments, and evacuation) in the event of a disaster. Be alert for conditions, such as faulty storage of hazardous material or blocked or locked emergency exits, which could contribute toward the negative effects of an emergency.
	Review reports of facilities inspection conducted. Determine if recommendations to reduce hazards to people, equipment, and property have been implemented, and, if not, that the reasons have been documented and approved by senior management.
	Verify that: firefighting equipment is inspected on a regular basis; safety showers are operative; first-aid kits are maintained; and all of these items are readily accessible for use.

EFFECTIVENESS OF INSURANCE FUNCTION

One way to assess the effectiveness of the insurance function is to know when final settlements are negotiated after claims are developed and submitted.

Audit Cycle/Area: Treasury—Foreign Currency Exchange Management

Risks and Exposures	Controls or Control Procedures
Incompatible duties.	Segregation of duties between foreign exchange function and other functions (PC).
Employees favoring certain banks or customers to do business for personal reasons.	Require all employees to take annual vacation (DC).
Incorrect use of exchange rates.	Test the procedures and verify a sample of exchange transactions (DC).

Audit Objectives for Foreign Currency Exchange Management	Audit Procedures for Foreign Currency Exchange Management
To determine whether foreign currency exchange transactions are consistent with specific policies established by treasury management and the board of directors' resolutions.	Review a sample of foreign currency exchange transactions and determine if they are consistent with stated policy. If variances exist, review documentation on file supporting the variances. If documentation is not on file, research the situation and discuss with the appropriate levels of management.

Audit Objectives for Foreign Currency Exchange Management	Audit Procedures for Foreign Currency Exchange Management
	Review activity that has taken place when procedures indicated a currency should be followed closely for revaluation or devaluation. Verify that it was complied with.
To ascertain whether the need to exchange currencies is clearly identified so that exchanges can take place in a manner benefiting the company.	Review reporting requirements and ascertain that they specify the receipts and disbursements to be included so that the reports are accurate and comprehensive. Ensure that the coverage includes trade payables and receivables, royalties, service arrangement fees, management fees, dividends, capital funds, and loans.
	Verify that actual receipts and disbursements are compared to forecasts and that the variances are analyzed. Validate that transactions that were to be netted did occur and have been confirmed and recorded correctly in the accounting records.
	To ensure proper segregation of duties, determine that individuals responsible for foreign exchange transactions are excluded from these functions: (1) preparing, validating, and mailing foreign exchange contracts; (2) recording foreign exchange transactions, maintaining position ledgers and maturity files, and preparing daily activity and position reports; (3) periodically evaluating foreign exchange positions and determining gains and losses; (4) settling transactions and other paying or receiving functions, such as issuing, receiving, and processing cable and mail instructions and foreign drafts; (5) operating and reconciling the due-to and due-from accounts in foreign currencies; and (6) preparing, approving, and posting other accounting entries.
	Ascertain that the function of evaluation, approval, and periodic review of creditworthiness of banks in foreign exchange transactions and establishment of general policy and guidelines for foreign exchange activity are performed by persons outside the foreign exchange department.
	Check that all employees are required to take an annual vacation and that their duties are assigned to others during their absence.
	Review the documentation utilized by the department and determine that it is prenumbered and numerically accounted for by both foreign exchange and accounting departments.
	In order to ensure that controls are in place to prevent or detect material errors, excessive risks, adverse trends, unreported losses, or transactions engaged in beyond authorized limits, two audit tests are suggested: (1) Ascertain if significant limit excesses are approved in advance and on an individual transaction basis; and (2) review exposure and devaluation or revaluation reports and evaluate

(continued)

Audit Objectives for Foreign Currency Exchange Management	Audit Procedures for Foreign Currency Exchange Management
	their adequacy in regard to: an independent review to ensure that all appropriate foreign currency assets, liabilities, and futures positions are included in these reports; the exchange rates used for revaluation are obtained by someone other than the employee in the area and checked to independent sources; and computations are independently checked and reviewed by appropriate management outside the area, evidenced in writing.
	In order to ensure that proper procedures were in place to review the foreign exchange settlements that were made, these audit tests are suggested: (1) Ascertain that settlements are carried out consistent with written instructions; (2) ascertain that settlements are made on a timely and accurate basis; (3) determine that daily activity or transaction registers reflect all settlement activity; and (4) test that all settlement activity is confirmed by the bank involved and the depository or disbursement bank.
To determine whether accounting controls over foreign currency exchange transactions are proper.	Compare monthly reconciliations between transaction activity as reported by the foreign exchange department to the activity listing provided by the settlement bank and records maintained in accounting department.
	Review to ensure that the rates used in converting foreign currencies to dollars are at prevailing rates and are accurately and consistently applied. Review to ensure that: gains and losses on transaction activity have been correctly calculated and recorded, that they comply with GAAP, forecasted fees are compared to actual fees charged by banks and other financial institutions involved, and differences are investigated.

Audit Cycle/Area: Treasury—Write-Off Accounting

Risks and Exposures	Controls or Control Procedures
Unauthorized write-offs of investments.	Establish write-off and recovery procedures (PC).
Improper write-off of goodwill.	Require management approvals (PC).
Improper classification of write-off.	Interview the CFO and review the board of directors' meeting minutes (DC).

Audit Objectives for Write-Off Accounting	Audit Procedures for Write-Off Accounting
To determine whether procedures to write off and remove any investment that is deemed worthless from the company's books are based on appropriate management approvals.	Review write-off requests. Test that they are properly supported and justified. Examples of justification include judicial decisions, appraisers' reports, financial newspapers, and trade journals. Evaluate the information in relationship to the write-off request.

Audit Objectives for Write-Off Accounting	Audit Procedures for Write-Off Accounting
	Review actual write-offs: Establish that they contain the required approvals and that the write-offs have been performed consistent with approvals. Review journal entries and: (1) test that they are supported by authorization letters; (2) verify that investments written off as worthless have been transferred to a separate memorandum account and are periodically reviewed for possible recovery; (3) review the type of investment written off to verify whether a change in financial statement reporting of the investment is required; and (4) review the reasons for the investment having become worthless and possibly classifying the write-offs as extraordinary items in the financial statements.
To ascertain whether a goodwill write-off is approved by management.	Verify that goodwill write-off procedures are in conformity to approved proposals. Review the accounting entries made and ensure that they are correct and conform to the approved proposals. Research and report any differences to management.
To determine whether write-offs resulting from governmental or political actions are properly recorded.	Review write-off requests resulting from governmental or political actions, such as nationalization of certain industries and economies. Ensure that they are adequately supported and contain independent information to support the write-off. Ensure that the write-off has been approved by the board of directors. Review the type of investment written off to verify whether a change in financial statement reporting of the investment is required. (The partial write-off of an investment due to expropriation may decrease the ability to exert significant influence [control] over the investee to the point where a change in financial statement reporting status is required.) Review the reason for the investment having become worthless and whether the write-off can be classified as an extraordinary item in the financial statement.

(E) Introduction to Financial Reporting Cycle Major activities in a financial reporting cycle include ensuring that:

- The financial statements are prepared and presented in conformity with GAAP.
- The GAAP have been observed consistently.
- The related financial or other informative disclosures are stated adequately.
- The audit report contains an expression of opinion regarding the financial statements.
- There exist controls over financial statement valuation processes.
- Accounting principles have been selected properly.
- Unusual or nonrecurring activities and events are handled properly.

Audit Cycle/Area: Financial Reporting—Journal Entry Preparation

Risks and Exposures	Controls or Control Procedures
Unauthorized preparation of journal entries.	Develop a list of employees authorized to prepare journal entries (PC).
Use of incorrect account codes.	Conduct a periodic comparison of journal entry codes to the chart of accounts (DC).
Possibility of management fraud or irregularities.	Segregation of duties between journal preparation and approval (PC). Conduct periodic audits (DC).

Audit Objectives for Journal Entry Preparation	Audit Procedures for Journal Entry Preparation
To determine whether journal entries are prepared, reviewed, and authorized in accordance with established procedures.	Obtain a log of individuals authorized to prepare, review, and approve specific journal entries, and compare signatures of prepared journal vouchers to the log. Ensure that all journal entries are assigned to specific individuals. Ascertain that there is an adequate segregation of duties relative to the individuals authorized to prepare or approve specific journal entries (e.g., accounts receivable may be recorded independently from sales). Also, ensure that review and approval of journal entries is by supervisors who did not actively participate in their preparation. Ascertain that individuals preparing or approving journal entries have a sufficient understanding of the entry's subject matter to ensure that their preparation or approval is meaningful. Review journal entries to ensure they are in compliance with GAAP, regulatory body requirements, and company policies and procedures. Review journal entries to ensure that where alternate accounting methods are acceptable, those used are applied on a consistent basis. Review accrual journal entries for vacation pay, dividend rates, inventory obsolescence, and depreciation methods to ensure they are in accordance with underlying union agreements or company policies.
To ascertain whether journal entries include proper documentation and that they are accurately recorded prior to the close of each fiscal period.	Review journal entries processed for proper documentation. If referenced to documentation that is available elsewhere, trace the journal entry to that documentation. Where documentation includes calculations or assumptions, test the calculations or ascertain the validity of the assumptions made. Review the chart of accounts to ensure that all changes to it have been properly approved. Review journal entries to ensure that account coding is accurate and conforms to the proper accounts listed in the chart of accounts.

Audit Objectives for Journal Entry Preparation	Audit Procedures for Journal Entry Preparation
	Review the current closing schedule to ensure that it is complete and that the journal entry due dates appear reasonable to allow for completion of the financial closing work on schedule. Review the journal entry computer processing system to ensure that it provides for adequate controls in the form of data editing and validation, limited access to data files, batch balancing routines, and transaction logging techniques to give reasonable assurance that all journal entries have been posted to master files or otherwise accounted for.

Audit Cycle/Area: Financial Reporting—Consolidation and General Ledger Posting

Risks and Exposures	Controls or Control Procedures
Erroneous data entering the financial systems.	Establish data editing and validation routines in all financial-related computer programs (PC, DC, CC).
Delays in processing journal entries.	Issue a monthly accounting closing schedule (PC).
Lack of audit trails in computer systems.	Implement "account proofing" routines into financial-related computerized application systems (DC).

Audit Objectives for Consolidation and General Ledger Posting	Audit Procedures for Consolidation and General Ledger Posting
To determine whether all consolidation journal entries have been properly prepared and approved and are accurate reflections of the consolidation worksheets and statements.	Verify that a journal entry control log is maintained. Ensure that the journal entry control log includes the assignment of each consolidating journal entry to a particular individual; and provides for prenumbered, standard, consolidating journal entries and that each consolidating journal entry processed has been logged. Verify posting of the consolidating journal entries to the consolidation working papers.
To ascertain whether consolidated reports are prepared accurately and on a consistent basis.	Review the written procedures for consolidated reports for completeness and ensure that they are consistently followed. Ensure that there are established procedures for checking consolidation working papers and consolidated statements. These procedures should be performed by individuals who did not actively participate in the consolidation and statement preparation process and should include these trace consolidating statements to underlying trial balance; review adjusting, elimination, and reclassification entries, ensuring that intercompany account balances were in agreement and have been eliminated by entries and that intercompany sales, cost of sales, and profits in inventory have been eliminated. Trace foreign exchange rates to documented sources.
To determine whether general ledger processing is performed accurately and promptly to ensure that financial statements and reports will be issued at the established due date.	Ensure that there is adequate segregation of duties between: the initiation of transactions and their summarization and recording; custody of company property; and the maintenance of subsidiary ledgers and control accounts. In particular, cash receipts and

(continued)

Audit Objectives for Consolidation and General Ledger Posting	Audit Procedures for Consolidation and General Ledger Posting
	disbursements duties should be segregated from general ledger recording duties.

Ensure that a monthly closing schedule is issued each fiscal period that indicates the due dates for: (1) the completion of journal entries by the department responsible for their entry into the general ledger system; (2) the issuance of preliminary trial balances and submission of corrections thereto; (3) the issuance and review of the final trial balance and subsidiary ledgers; and (4) the issuance of financial statements and reports.

Verify that a control point and log have been established, and review current and past logs to ensure that journal entries are being received and processed in a timely manner. Obtain explanations of significant delays in processing journal entries, and test validity of the schedule due dates. Review processed journal entries to ensure that documentation has been canceled to prevent reuse. Ensure that control totals are determined and batches are submitted to computer processing. Verify that data editing and validation is performed and that debit and credit amounts and hash totals are in agreement with predetermined totals. Ensure that errors are corrected by preparing offsetting entries using the journal entry forms in order to leave an audit trail of corrections (i.e., debit entry is used to fix the incorrect credit entry).

Ensure that preliminary general ledger trial balances are reviewed for accuracy and reasonableness by authorized individuals and that any noted discrepancies or unusual items are investigated and corrected prior to issuance of a final trial balance and general ledger. This should include a review for out-of-balance conditions, erroneous account codes, reasonableness of balances, large fluctuations, and absence of balances.

Ensure that general ledger accounts are reviewed, analyzed, and approved in accordance with a formal monthly closing schedule by authorized employees. The analyses should include these steps: (1) Verify the current month's opening balance to the prior month's closing balance; (2) review the current month's transactions, including reversal of the prior month's accruals; (3) review accounts without the current month's activity for possible omission of data; (4) verify the legitimacy of accounts with credit balances that normally carry debit balances and debit balances in accounts that normally carry credit balances; (5) verify balances of an intercompany account with comparable offsetting balances on the other company's general ledger; (6) analyze ending balances and activity in accounts to establish |

Audit Objectives for Consolidation and General Ledger Posting	Audit Procedures for Consolidation and General Ledger Posting
	propriety of balances, and investigate large fluctuations in balances from month to month; (7) verify subsidiary ledger balances against the controlling general ledger account balances; (8) verify account balances by cash counts, securities inventory, or property inspection; (9) compare recorded amounts of securities held with market values; and (10) compare account balances with budgeted amounts.
	Ensure that, for accrued liabilities and reserve accounts in particular, the stated account balances appear reasonable and reflect company policies. Review explanations and supporting documentation where account balances change significantly during the year. Examine payment of accrued amounts in subsequent periods to determine adequacy of the accrual balance, and verify that related expense or income accounts are charged to offset accrual and reserve accounts credits (i.e., salary expense should be charged to accrued payroll, tax expense is charged to accrued taxes, etc.).

Audit Cycle/Area: Financial Reporting—Financial Report Preparation and Issuance, Including Records Retention

Risks and Exposures	Controls or Control Procedures
Data errors between general ledger and financial reports.	Trace data through the system for accuracy (DC).
Errors or omissions in financial statement disclosures.	Perform quality assurance reviews by independent third parties (DC).
Inadequate or excessive records retention.	Issue written procedures describing record retention and disposition schedules (PC). Conduct periodic review to determine its compliance (DC).

Audit Objectives for Financial Report Preparation and Issuance, Including Record Retention	Audit Procedures for Financial Report Preparation and Issuance, Including Record Retention
To determine whether financial reports are prepared in accordance with various requirements.	Ensure that a monthly closing schedule is issued each fiscal period and that the due dates appear reasonable. Ensure that the responsible individuals are aware of due dates to be met. Test the actual completion dates to the corresponding due dates and obtain explanations for those that have not been met; assess the impact of not meeting critical due dates.
	In order to ensure that financial reports are based on information shown in the final general ledger or consolidating working papers, perform these audit reviews: Reconcile key data from selected financial reports to the final general ledger or consolidating

(continued)

Audit Objectives for Financial Report Preparation and Issuance, Including Record Retention	**Audit Procedures for Financial Report Preparation and Issuance, Including Record Retention**
	working papers, and ascertain that a standard approved format is used to show which general ledger accounts comprise which lines or data elements on financial reports.
	Compare the accounting methods used in the compilation and presentation of financial reports with those of prior periods to ensure that they are consistently applied. Ensure that financial reports are reviewed for reasonableness and that they are compared against forecast data.
	Verify that financial reports are issued by the required due dates, by reference to prescribed monthly closing schedules and dates included on instruction forms.
	In order to ensure that all supplementary disclosures of information affecting the financial status of the company is properly presented in the form of notes or other, these audit tests are suggested: (1) Ascertain that all relative disclosures in the financial, legal, and operation areas have been made or have been considered; (2) ensure that prospective disclosure data have been considered in the areas of lease information, tax provisions, earnings per share data, replacement cost data, stock options and purchase plan information, special debt agreements, pending legal settlements, open purchase commitments, loss contingencies, and blocked funds; and (3) ensure that the selection of disclosure data for inclusion in financial reporting has been made by senior management in legal, financial, and operating departments.
To ascertain whether financial documents and records are retained in accordance with management's and regulatory requirements.	In order to ensure that documents and records are retained for such periods of time as business needs dictate and considering legal and regulatory requirements, these audit tests are suggested: (1) Ensure that records retention and disposition schedules have been established that list, by title, each type of record maintained, retention period, and ultimate disposal date; (2) ensure that such schedules indicate approval by responsible department management; (3) ensure that the records retention facility and procedures permit the withdrawal of stored documents when necessary, under controlled conditions, and ensure their timely return; (4) observe that storage areas are fireproof, contain a sprinkler system, and are locked or alarmed to prevent unauthorized access and use; (5) ensure that tax records for a period are destroyed only after tax audits for that period are completed; and (6) ensure that the final disposition of outdated material is by incineration, shredding, pulping, secured waste basket, or other method, depending on its sensitivity.

Audit Cycle/Area: Financial Reporting—Tax Accounting and Reporting

Risks and Exposures	Controls or Control Procedures
Incorrect preparation of payroll-related taxes.	Written procedures and training of employees in the tax and payroll departments (PC). Periodic review for quality assurance (DC)
Incorrect application of sales tax and use tax rules.	Written procedures and training of employees in the tax and purchasing departments (PC). Periodic review for quality assurance (DC).

Audit Objectives for Tax Accounting and Reporting	Audit Procedures for Tax Accounting and Reporting
To determine whether tax policies are adequate, that tax effects are considered in all major decisions, and that tax adjustments are properly made.	Assess whether tax procedures provide information about how to accumulate: sales and use tax, payroll taxes, state and local income taxes, real estate property taxes, and foreign taxes. Outline tax aspects of key business transactions for tax planning purposes. Ensure that tax calendars are prepared to provide reminders to file tax returns and tax payments. Examine whether the tax calendar contains the following information: name and type of tax, taxing authority, due date for filing the tax report, payment dates, lead time to complete the report, and source of data.

Review the effects of operating loss carryforwards and offsets of other companies in a consolidated return; evaluate whether the tax policy goals will maximize tax benefits. Review opportunities for acceleration or deferral of income. Review situations that will result in minimizing taxes: moving facilities, such as sales office, warehouses, branch offices, plant, from high-tax jurisdiction area to a low-tax jurisdiction area; and verify that calculating depreciation of fixed assets for tax purposes is on a basis that will achieve the most advantageous deductions.

In order to ensure that all required tax adjustments and required analyses are promptly prepared, conduct these audit tests: (1) Establish that only accrued income legally enforceable is included for tax purposes; (2) review questionable or controversial items of income with management; (3) ascertain that adjustments recommended by tax agents are corrected; (4) review the ratio of the bad debt reserve to sales for the last fiscal year. If the ratio is materially higher than the previous five years' ratios, determine that appropriate explanations were furnished; (5) review depreciation methods to ensure compliance with tax authorities; (6) review disposition of fixed assets and ascertain that no gain or loss is recognized on a trade-in; (7) ascertain that mixed expenditures (repairs and improvements) made under a general plan for rehabilitating or improving property are capitalized in total; (8) attempt to segregate ordinary gains or losses (treated as ordinary

(continued)

Audit Objectives for Tax Accounting and Reporting	Audit Procedures for Tax Accounting and Reporting
	income or loss) and capital gains or losses (subject to capital gains treatment); (9) review inventories and ascertain that obsolete items are written down to realizable values and that there is detailed support for the write-down; (10) review leasehold amortization and ascertain that improvements are amortized over the lease period, including optional extensions, but not exceeding the useful life; and (11) investigate if property taxes and franchise taxes are being expensed for the taxable year in which they accrue, as permitted, regardless of payment date (unless in dispute).

In order to verify that all required adjustments to income tax accounts are recorded promptly and accurately, conduct these audit tests: (1) Ensure that all adjustments to tax accounts, except tax payments, are made by journal entry; (2) obtain tax accounting journal entries and verify the basis of calculations for accuracy; (3) trace the tax accounting journal entries to ensure that they are posted to the proper general ledger accounts prior to the close of the fiscal period; (4) ensure that subledgers are maintained by the taxing authority and reconciled to the relevant general ledger accounts; and (5) ascertain that tax payments are first charged to a balance sheet control account to facilitate control and audit.

Ensure that there is an account analysis for every income tax account and that the analyses indicate that they have been reviewed and approved by financial accounting management. Obtain copies of correspondence with taxing authorities, and ensure that all prior-year tax adjustments are reflected in the appropriate accounts or in a permanent adjustment schedule.

Review analyses of all prepaid and accrued tax account balances and ensure that there are no accruals for tax years that have been closed or exorbitant excess accruals for prior tax years. Physically verify the existence of tax working papers and reports in a locked, fireproof file cabinet until the tax audit for the relevant years has been completed. |
| To ascertain whether sales taxes are promptly and accurately calculated and recorded on sales invoices. | In order to ensure that sales taxes are charged and collected as appropriate, these audit tests are suggested: (1) Verify that the company is registered in all states where sales taxes are collected and that tax returns are filed in all such states; (2) test sales invoices to ensure that the proper tax is calculated and charged on sales to end-use customers; (3) determine that exemption certificates are on file for every customer claiming exemption from sales and use taxes; (4) verify the recording of sales taxes billed to customers from invoices to a copy of the sales register; and (5) test the accumulation of total sales taxes on the sales register. |

Audit Objectives for Tax Accounting and Reporting	Audit Procedures for Tax Accounting and Reporting
	In order to ensure that the company does not pay sales taxes on purchases for resale or use in finished goods, the following audit tests are suggested: (1) Review vendors' invoices for items purchased for resale. (2) Ensure that sales tax is not charged. If charged, follow up to see if an exemption certificate has been filed with the vendor. (3) Ensure that the sales tax charged is deducted from the current or a subsequent payment or that a refund has been applied for; (4) Ensure that the purchasing department has an established practice to furnish all suppliers with sales tax exemption certificates where the materials being purchased are exempt from sales taxes.
To determine whether use taxes are promptly and accurately calculated and recorded on vendor invoices.	In order to ensure that practices have been established to provide for the accurate calculation and recording of use tax, these audit tests should be conducted: (1) Ensure that controls have been established to identify vendor invoices subject to use tax and to provide for their calculation and accumulation by assigning account codes for use tax; (2) verify vendors' invoices to ensure that use taxes have been calculated; and (3) ensure that use taxes have been properly recorded to the appropriate general ledger expense and payables accounts. *Coding and accumulating use tax from vendors' invoices is better than making a separate journal entry for the total use tax.* Trace the detail of the journal entry to total sales tax from the sales register or subsidiary ledger. Trace the tax accounting journal entries to ensure that they are posted to the proper general ledger accounts prior to the close of the fiscal period. Ensure that sales and use tax returns are prepared and reviewed by authorized individuals and are paid and filed by the scheduled due date.
To ascertain whether payroll taxes are prepared accurately and filed on a timely basis.	Ensure that payroll tax data are promptly and accurately submitted to and processed by the tax department to ensure timely filing of returns. Processing should include verification of data to payroll summaries; verification of rates and calculations; and supervisory review of tax working papers, tax payments, and tax returns. Conduct these audit tests: (1) Ensure that payroll summaries are the basis for taxes paid; (2) verify data on payroll summaries to payroll registers; (3) trace data from payroll summaries through tax work sheets to the returns and/or depository receipts; (4) verify calculations of the employer's share of payroll taxes, including verification of rates through the worksheets to quarterly and annual tax returns; and (5) determine that sick pay is treated as exempt wages for unemployment and Social Security tax purposes.

(continued)

Audit Objectives for Tax Accounting and Reporting	Audit Procedures for Tax Accounting and Reporting
	Ensure that quarterly tax returns are reconciled to payroll tax account balances before they are filed. Obtain journal entries for recording payroll taxes, and verify data to payroll summaries and work sheets. Check calculations of employer payroll taxes. Verify tax calculations relative to accrued (unpaid) payrolls, and verify that general ledger account codings are proper. Verify the accuracy of taxes calculated on the accrued (earned but unpaid) payrolls by references to the actual tax calculated in the subsequent period when the payroll is actually paid.
To determine whether real estate and personal property taxes have been paid on a timely basis.	Review real estate and personal property tax accruals. Ascertain that the monthly amount is based on the most current information and calculated correctly. Research the last payment to ascertain that it was charged against the accrual, and verify that the annual accrual approximates the annual payments. Ensure that the property tax statement contains correct values of property for all pertinent assets and is properly approved before submission to the taxing authority. Obtain a copy of the most current property tax statement. Trace the statement total to general ledger property accounts.
To ascertain whether foreign taxes are paid in a timely and accurate manner.	Ensure that: (1) a schedule for foreign taxes is maintained for all tax returns and reporting dates to ensure timely submission of returns and reports; (2) tax data are promptly and accurately accumulated to facilitate the preparation of tax returns and related accounting entries; (3) adequate working papers and/or records are maintained to support tax data; (4) tax returns and reports are properly prepared, reviewed, and authorized prior to issuance and are filed along with the required payments by the scheduled due date; (5) all tax accounts are accurately summarized, classified, and reported promptly at the close of each fiscal period; and (6) all tax working papers, returns, reports, and tax data are adequately protected from unauthorized access and are secured in fireproof storage containers.

EXAMPLES OF APPLICATION OF CAATs: TAX

- In order to detect whether sales taxes are applied properly and computed correctly, sort sales orders by geographic area, compute taxes in aggregate, and compare the aggregate amount with the sum of individual taxes charged for each geographic area.

- Perform reasonableness tests between taxes actually collected and taxes that should have been collected. Identify discrepancies.

(viii) Financial Audit Engagements

"Financial auditing" is defined as determining whether financial statements present fairly the financial position and results of operations. More specifically, financial auditing provides reasonable assurance about whether the financial statements of an audited entity present fairly the financial position, results of operations, and cash flows in accordance with GAAP. Balance sheet and income statements are the focus; balance sheets provide the financial status of an entity at the end of an accounting period, while income statements report income earned during an accounting period.

During financial auditing, auditors: obtain a sufficient understanding of the entity's internal control structure to plan the nature, timing, and extent of tests to be performed; assess the control risk associated with the control environment; and assess the control risk associated with control procedures for safeguarding assets that the auditors conclude are vulnerable to loss or misappropriation.

The **purpose and scope of a financial audit** are to determine whether the overall financial statements of an entity are prepared and reported in accordance with specified criteria (standards). The audit scope is usually limited to accounting-related data. Financial audits are conducted by independent auditors who are external to the organization being audited. External auditors express an opinion on the overall fairness of the financial statements. The audit report contains the auditor's opinion. Four types of audit opinions can be included in an audit report. However, only one type of opinion can be included in any one report.

The four types of audit opinions are:

1. **Unqualified opinion.** This is a clean opinion. It is the standard and most commonly used. This condition applies when all professional standards have been followed on the audit engagement, sufficient evidence has been accumulated, financial statements are presented in accordance with GAAP, or other, and no additional explanatory paragraphs are included in the audit report.

2. **Qualified opinion.** This is rarely used. The auditor uses the term "except for" in the opinion paragraph. This implies that the auditor is satisfied that the overall financial statements are correctly stated except for a particular aspect. A qualified opinion can be issued from an audit scope limitation or failure to conform to GAAP and only when the auditor believes that the overall financial statements are fairly stated. An adverse opinion or a disclaimer must be used when the financial conditions are highly material; the qualified opinion is given for less severe types of conditions. However, a qualified report is still a departure from an unqualified report.

3. **Adverse opinion.** This is also rarely used and is suitable only when the financial condition is highly material. The auditor will issue such an opinion only when he or she believes that the overall financial statements are so materially misstated or misleading that they do not present fairly the financial position in conformity with GAAP. As a result, the auditor has determined nonconformity to GAAP.

4. **Disclaimer of opinion.** This is rarely used and is appropriate only when the condition is highly material. Auditors will issue such an opinion only when they have been unable to satisfy themselves that the overall financial statements are fairly presented. This condition arises when the audit scope is severely limited and/or when auditors are not independent from the client. The disclaimer varies from an adverse opinion in that the former can arise only from a lack of knowledge of nonconformity to GAAP by the auditor.

A suggested framework for describing the general audit and control procedures performed by external auditors for conducting **financial audits** is:

- Obtain background information about the client.
- Assess preliminary risks and exposures.
- Obtain an understanding of the client's internal control structure.
- Develop an audit plan and audit program.
- Perform compliance tests of controls.
- Perform substantive tests of transactions and account balances.
- Evaluate test results.
- Form an audit opinion.
- Issue the audit report.

External audit reports require strict compliance to professional audit standards in terms of report content, specific wording, and format. In addition to issuing financial statements, external auditors issue management letters to their clients to improve internal controls.

General audit objectives for a **financial review** are to:

- Evaluate whether the account balances appear reasonable in the financial statements.
- Determine whether the amounts included in the financial statements are valid.
- Determine whether all amounts that should be included have actually been included in the financial statements.
- Ensure that assets included in the financial statements are owned by the entity and liabilities belong to the entity.
- Determine whether the amounts included in the financial statements are properly valued.
- Determine whether correct amounts are included in the correct accounts and those accounts are properly classified in financial statements.
- Determine whether transactions near the balance sheet date are recorded in the proper accounting period.
- Determine whether details in the account balance agree with related subsidiary ledger amounts, foot to the total in the account balance, and agree with the total in the general ledger.
- Ensure that all balance sheet and income statements accounts and related information are correctly disclosed in the financial statements and properly described in the body and footnotes of the statements.

KEY CONCEPTS TO REMEMBER: Financial Auditing

- The external auditor would most likely detect an unreported disposal of a fixed asset due to the audit objective.

- Internal auditors are often requested to coordinate their work with that of external auditors. For example, external auditors would keep the work of attesting to the fairness of presentation of cash position in the balance sheet. Shared audit work between these auditors would be: evaluating the system of controls over cash collections and similar transactions, evaluating the adequacy of the organization's overall system of internal controls, and reviewing the system established to ensure compliance with policies and procedures that could have a significant impact on operations.

(ix) Information Technology Audit Engagements

Significant progress has taken place in auditing computer-based information systems (ISs) and operations. It includes new audit methodologies and new techniques, such as participating in systems development projects, getting involved in the implementation of new information technologies, and more auditing through the computer instead of auditing around the computer. More research needs to be done to improve audit methodologies.

(A) Information Systems Audit Scope   The information technology (IT) audit function is not a stand-alone activity. Rather it is an integral part of the external or internal auditing function (see Exhibit 1.3). Information system audits deal with the review of computer operations and application systems where computer equipment is located and computer-based systems are used. **The purpose and scope of IS audits** are to determine whether controls over computer systems and IT assets are adequate. These particular types of audits are conducted by IT auditors, who may be external or internal to the organization being audited.

Materiality, as it relates to IT audits, considers the issues for both financial and operational audit situations. Specifically, it deals with issues such as the impact of computer operations control weaknesses on the organization's financial and operating records; impact of system integrity and security control weaknesses on the application system's data and system usefulness to users; and impact of system errors and irregularities (e.g., computer fraud and theft, embezzlement, and abuse) on the financial statements. For example, major computer security breaches can be treated as material weaknesses of the internal control system.

(B) Information Systems Control Objectives   An internal control structure must meet several detailed IS control objectives to prevent, detect, and correct errors, omissions, irregularities, and computer intrusions (such as viruses and worms) and to recover from such activities to ensure continuity of business operations. Here the term "system" includes hardware, data, software, people, documentation, and the associated procedures, (whether manual or automated).

The next list presents IS control objectives.

- **System assets are safeguarded.** An organization's technology assets and resources, such as computer facilities, computer equipment, people, programs, and data, are to be safeguarded at all times to minimize waste and loss.

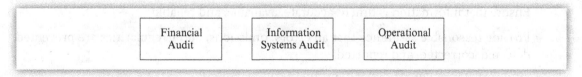

EXHIBIT 1.3 Integrated Information Systems Audits

- **System reliability is ensured.** The objective is to ensure that the hardware, software, and data are stable and that people are trustworthy to carry out the organization's mission.

- **Data integrity is maintained. Data integrity** deals with controls over how data are entered, communicated, processed, stored, and reported. The objective is to ensure that the data are authorized, complete, accurate, consistent, and timely.

- **System security is ensured.** An organization's assets and information resources are to be protected from unauthorized access and use.

- **System availability is ensured.** The objective is to ensure that the system (hardware, software, and data) and its components are available when they are needed, where they are needed, and for whom they are needed.

- **System controllability is maintained.** Adequate manual and automated controls and procedures should be available over hardware, software, data, and people.

- **System maintainability is ensured.** The system, which includes hardware and software, should be maintained with existing resources at minimum cost and time.

- **System usability is ensured.** For example, the application system is appropriately user friendly, or the system design invites the authorized user to use as opposed to inhibiting.

- **System effectiveness is ensured.** For example, system effectiveness is measured by determining that the system performs the intended functions and that users get the information they need, in the right form, and in a timely fashion.

- **System economy and efficiency are maintained.** An economical and efficient system uses the minimum number of information resources to achieve the output level the system's users require. Economy and efficiency must always be considered in the context of system effectiveness.

- **System quality is maintained.** This is an overall goal. In addition to the other objectives, the computer system should have built-in quality-related features such as testability, portability, convertability, modifiability, readability, reliability, reusability, structuredeness, consistency, understandability, and, above all, adequate documentation.

(C) Information Systems Audit Objectives   The objectives of an IS audit are to:

- Ensure that adequate audit coverage of major risks and exposures in an IS environment is available.

- Ensure that IS resources are allocated to computer hardware, peripheral equipment, software, services, and personnel in an efficient and effective manner to achieve the IS department's and the organization's goals and objectives.

- Provide reasonable assurance that computer-related assets (e.g., data, programs, facilities, equipment, and supplies) are safeguarded.

- Ensure that information is timely, accurate, available, and reliable.

- Provide reasonable assurance that all errors, omissions, and irregularities are prevented, detected, corrected, and reported.

- Obtain the most efficient usage of audit resources (staff time and money).

(D) Information Systems Audit and Control Procedures The following is a suggested framework for describing the IS audit and control procedures performed by auditors for conducting IS audits:

- Obtain background information about the IS operations and the systems.
- Conduct a preliminary evaluation of internal controls.
- Develop an audit plan and audit program.
- Perform compliance tests of controls.
- Perform substantive tests of transactions and account balances.
- Evaluate the test results and issue an audit report.

After an audit work program is developed and approved by audit management, the auditor is ready to perform compliance and substantive reviews and/or tests.

Essentially, compliance reviews and tests in an IS environment include whether policies and documentation are available and that they are followed and whether management approvals are obtained prior to acquiring technology assets and services.

Basically, substantive tests and reviews in an IS environment include analysis of information or data related to system/program/job/operations activities, service-level exception reporting, system logs, and system/data integrity. These are in addition to reconciliation of financial accounts, confirmation of amounts and account balances with external sources, and comparison of physical counts with recorded amounts. Scope includes both manual and automated systems as well as manually or system-generated logs and reports (see Exhibit 1.4).

Examples of the first five substantive reviews or tests include:

1. **System outage analysis.** Outages can occur due to:
   a. Power failures (brownouts, blackouts)
   b. Magnetic/optical disk failures
   c. Operating system–related problems and failures
2. **System storage media analysis.**
   a. Amount of allocated space by data set
   b. Amount of allocated space not used by data set
3. **System aging analysis.**
   a. Inactive data sets with 6-month, 12-month, or 24-month-old run dates
   b. Number of computer jobs run one hour or two hours late
4. **System interruption impact analysis.**
   a. Estimated revenue loss associated with a one-hour system interruption
   b. Estimated degree of external customer services lost due to a one-hour system interruption
5. **System resource utilization statistical analysis.**

EXHIBIT 1.4 Examples of Information Technology Compliance and Substantive Reviews and/or Tests

Compliance review/test description	Substantive review/test description
Whether written IT policies, procedures, and standards are available	System outage analysis
Whether written IT policies, procedures, and standards are followed	System storage media analysis
Whether errors are present	System aging analysis
Whether documentation is available	System interruption impact analysis
Is the required documentation up to date	System resource utilization statistical analysis
Whether security and other system-based logs are reviewed	Transaction activity analysis
Whether passwords are changed periodically	Program activity analysis
Whether transactions are approved	Job activity analysis
Whether disaster recovery plan is documented	Operations activity analysis
Whether disaster recovery plan is tested	System activity analysis
Whether disaster recovery plan is updated	IT financial analysis
Whether disaster recovery plan is complete	IT turnover statistics
Whether disaster recovery plan is accurate	Development of account balance or interest confirmations
Whether the disaster recovery plan meets stated objectives	System response-time analysis
Whether system development methodology is available	Comparison of book computer inventory to actual count
Whether the system development methodology is followed	Service-level exception reporting analysis
Whether program changes are approved	System trend analysis
Whether program changes are tested	System exception analysis
Whether program changes are documented	System availability analysis
Whether manual overrides are approved	System log analysis
Whether system overrides are approved	System performance analysis
Whether hardware acquisition is approved	System/manual reconciliation of accounts and transactions
Whether software acquisition is approved	System/data integrity analysis

(E) Information Systems Control Types According to the Committee of Sponsoring Organizations (COSO) of the Treadway Commission study, with widespread reliance on IS, controls are needed over all IS, whether financial, operational, large, or small. Two broad groupings of IS controls can be used. The first is **general or information technology controls,** which ensure the continued, proper operation of computer IS. General controls are designed to focus on IS or IT as a whole.

> **APPLICATION CONTROLS VERSUS GENERAL CONTROLS**
>
> The relationship between the application controls and the general controls is such that general controls are needed to support the functioning of application controls, and both are needed to ensure complete and accurate information processing.

The second category is **application controls,** which include computerized steps within the application software and related manual procedures to control the processing of various types of transactions. Together these controls serve to ensure completeness, accuracy, and validity of the financial and other information in the system. General controls and application controls are presented next along with their relationships.

General Controls General controls commonly include controls over data (computer) center operations, system software (not applications software) acquisition and maintenance, access security (both physical and logical), application system development and maintenance, and overall IS department administration. These controls apply to all systems: mainframe, minicomputer, and end user computing (EUC) environments.

Data Center Operations Controls These controls include job setup and scheduling, operator actions, backup and recovery procedures, and contingency or disaster recovery planning. In a sophisticated environment, these controls also address capacity planning and resource allocation and use.

In a high-technology environment today, the job scheduler is automatic and job control language is online. Storage management tools automatically load data files onto high-speed devices in anticipation of the next job. The shift supervisor no longer needs to initial the console log manually, because it is not printed out; the log is maintained on the system. Hundreds of messages flash by each second on a consolidated console that supports multiple mainframes. Minicomputers run all night, unattended.

System Software Controls These controls include controls over the effective acquisition, implementation, and maintenance of system software—the operating system, database management systems (DBMSs), telecommunications software, security software, and utility programs (service aids)—that run the system and allow applications to function. The master director of system activities, system software also provides the system logging, tracking, and monitoring functions. System software can report on uses of utility programs, so that if someone accesses these powerful data-altering functions, at the least the use is recorded and reported for review.

Access Security Controls These controls have assumed greater importance as telecommunications networks have grown. System users may be halfway around the world or down the hall. Effective access security controls can protect the system, preventing inappropriate access and unauthorized use of the system. If well designed, they can intercept hackers and other trespassers.

Adequate access control activities, such as changing dial-up numbers frequently or implementing dial-back—where the system calls a potential user back at an authorized phone number, rather than allowing direct access into the system—can be effective methods to prevent unauthorized access.

Access security controls restrict authorized users to only the applications or application functions that they need to do their jobs, supporting an appropriate division of duties.

There should be frequent and timely review of the user profiles that permit or restrict access. Former or disgruntled employees can be more of a threat to a system than hackers; terminated employee passwords and user IDs should be revoked immediately. By preventing unauthorized use of and changes to the system, data and program integrity are protected.

Application System Development and Maintenance Controls Development and maintenance of application systems traditionally have been high-cost areas for most organizations. Total costs for IS resources, the time needed, the skills of people to perform these tasks, and hardware and software required are all considerable. To control those costs, most entities have some form of system development methodology. It provides structure for system design and implementation, outlining specific phases, documentation requirements, approvals, and checkpoints to control the development or maintenance project. The methodology should provide appropriate control over changes to the system, which may involve required authorization of change requests, review of the changes, approvals, testing results, and implementation protocols, to ensure that changes are made properly.

An alternative to in-house development is the use of packaged software, which has grown in popularity. Vendors provide flexible, integrated systems allowing customization through the use of built-in options. Many system development methodologies address the acquisition of vendor packages as a development alternative and include the necessary steps to provide control over the selection and implementation process.

Application Controls As the name indicates, application controls are designed to control application processing, helping to ensure the completeness and accuracy of transaction processing, authorization, and validity.

The scope includes controls over inputs, processing, and output phases of a system. Particular attention should be paid to an application's interfaces, since they are often linked to other systems that in turn need control, to ensure that all inputs are received for processing and all outputs are distributed appropriately.

One of the most significant contributions computers make to control is their ability to prevent errors from entering the system as well as detecting and correcting them once they are present. To do this, many application controls depend on computerized edit checks. These consist of format, existence, reasonableness, and other checks on the data that are built into each application during its development. When these checks are designed properly, they can help provide control over the data being entered into the system.

Relationship Between General and Application Controls The COSO study went on to say that these two categories of control over computer systems are intertwined. There must be an appropriate balance of both in order for either to function. General controls are needed to ensure the function of application controls that depend on computer processes. For example, application controls such as computer matching and edit checks examine data as they are entered online. They provide immediate feedback when something does not match or is in the wrong format, so that corrections can be made. They display error messages that indicate what is wrong with the data or produce exception reports for subsequent follow-up.

If there are inadequate general controls, it may not be possible to depend on application controls, which assume the system itself will function properly, matching with the right file, or providing an error message that accurately reflects a problem, or including all exceptions in an exception report.

Another example of the required balance between application and general controls is a completeness control often used over certain types of transactions involving prenumbered documents. These are usually documents generated internally, such as purchase orders, where prenumbered forms are employed. Duplicates are flagged or rejected. To effect this as a control, depending on its design, the system will reject an inappropriate item or hold it in suspense, while users get a report that lists all missing, duplicate, and out-of-range items. Or does it? How do those who need to rely on the report content for follow-up know that all items that should be on the report are, in fact, listed?

The answer is the general controls. Controls over system development requiring thorough reviews and testing of applications ensure that the logic of the report program is sound and that it has been tested to ensure that all exceptions are reported. To provide control after implementation of the application, controls over access and maintenance ensure that applications are not accessed or changed without authorization and that required, authorized changes are made. The data center operations controls and systems software controls ensure that the right files are used and updated appropriately.

The relationship between the application controls and the general controls is such that general controls are needed to support the functioning of application controls, and both are needed to ensure complete and accurate information processing.

(F) Classification of Computer Controls Computer controls can be classified in different ways. Two basic categories are general controls and application controls, which were just described. Another way to classify controls is by their nature, such as management controls (e.g., policies, procedures, standards, separation of duties), physical controls (e.g., access to computer facilities and equipment), and technical controls (e.g., logical access controls to programs and data files, use of options and parameters). Another way is to classify controls by functional areas, such as application controls, network controls, development controls, operations controls, security controls, and user controls. Still another way is to classify controls on the basis of action or objective, such as directive, preventive, detective, corrective, and recovery (see Exhibit 1.5). The latter category is discussed in detail.

Directive controls are management actions, policies, procedures, directives, or guidelines that cause or encourage a desirable event to occur. By their nature, directive controls affect the entire system or operation. Directive controls address system usability, maintainability, auditability, controllability, and securability attributes of software as well as the integrity of data and reliability and availability of system resources.

Preventive controls include all standards, methods, practices, or tools and techniques (manual or automated) that will result in quality, reliable systems. Preventive controls also deter or minimize the occurrence of undesirable events, such as computer-related fraud, theft, or embezzlement, as well as possible errors, omissions, and irregularities. Preventive controls address the maintainability, securability, usability, and controllability features of the system. A specific example of preventive control is avoidance control, which means the separation of assets from threats

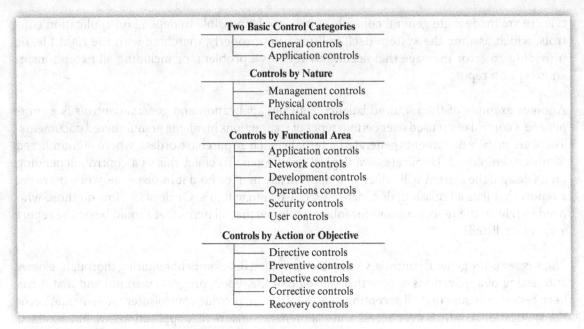

EXHIBIT 1.5 Controls by Action or Objective

or threats from assets so that potential risk is minimized. Also, resource allocation is separated from resource use. Directive controls can be grouped with preventive controls for convenience, if desired.

Detective controls give feedback as to whether the system's directive and/or preventive controls have achieved their objectives and whether standards or guidelines have been met. They detect errors, omissions, and irregularities and identify aspects of system quality, control, and security features that need management's attention. Detective controls include both manual and automated tools and techniques. Detective controls provide some information about the adequacy and completeness of audit trails, thereby addressing the auditability of the system as well as its securability and controllability.

> **CONTROL ASSESSMENT CHALLENGE**
>
> The key issues are to know how much control is needed, how to measure it, how to evaluate whether a control is deficient or sufficient, and how to balance it.

Corrective controls provide information, procedures, and instructions for correcting the errors, omissions, and irregularities that have been detected. They may simply identify the areas where corrective action is required or actually may facilitate the corrective action. Corrective controls include both manual and automated tools and techniques. These controls address the usability and auditability of the system.

Recovery controls facilitate backup, restoration, recovery, and restart of an application system after any interruption in information processing. They promote an orderly environment in which all the required resources would be readily available to ensure a reasonably smooth recovery from disaster. This permits continuation of a specific activity or of the entire operation of the organization. Recovery controls include timely backup and rotation of data and program files, checkpoints, restart/rerun procedures, record and file retention, journaling, recovery logging, and contingency plans. Recovery controls address issues of system usability, auditability, controllability, and securability. Recovery controls can be grouped with corrective controls for convenience, if desired.

During an assessment of control strengths and weaknesses, the auditor might run into situations where a business function, system, or manual/automated procedure is overcontrolled or undercontrolled. This means that there may be too many controls in one area and not enough controls in other areas. Also, there may be a duplication or overlapping of controls between two or more areas. Under these conditions, the auditor should recommend eliminating some user controls, some IT controls, some manual controls, some automated controls, or a combination of them. The same may be true of situations where a system or operation is oversecured or undersecured and where an application system is overdesigned or underdesigned.

This assessment requires differentiating between relevant and irrelevant information, considering compensating controls (which are discussed later in this section), considering interrelationships of controls (which are discussed later in this section), and judging materiality and significance of audit findings taken separately and as a whole.

Rarely will a single finding lead to the conclusion of an unacceptable audit or uncontrolled area. Usually a combination of control weaknesses is required to call an area unacceptable. For example, a finding such as "housekeeping is poor in the data center" alone or in combination with "there are no no-smoking or no-eating signs in the data center" will not qualify for giving an unacceptable or uncontrolled audit rating. The audit findings must be significant. The nature of the operation (e.g., automated or manual and sensitive or routine), criticality of the system (high risk versus low risk), costs to develop and maintain controls, and the materiality (significance) of the finding are more important criteria to consider than simple observation of control weaknesses.

ATTRIBUTES OF A CONTROL

A control should be appropriate, practical, reliable, simple, complete, operational, usable, cost effective, timely, meaningful, reasonable, and consistent.

Note that materiality is relative, not absolute. What is material to one organization may not be material to another. Audit judgment plays an important role in deciding what is material, what is a significant control weakness, what is an efficient operation, what is an effective system, and which should be considered separately and as a whole. In other words, the auditor needs to focus on the entire environment of the audited operation or system and take a big-picture approach instead of taking a finding-by-finding approach. A cost/benefit analysis might help the auditor in the process of evaluating controls.

(G) Cost/Benefit Analysis of Controls   A cost/benefit analysis is advised during the process of designing each type of control into an application system during its development and maintenance as well during its operation. Ideally, costs should never exceed benefits to be derived from installing controls. However, costs should not always be the sole determining factor because it may be difficult or impractical to quantify benefits such as timeliness, improved quality and relevance of data and information, or improved customer service and system response time. When controls are properly planned, designed, developed, tested, implemented, and followed, they should meet one or more of these 12 attributes: appropriate, practical, reliable, simple, complete, operational, usable, cost effective, timely, meaningful, reasonable, and consistent.

(H) Costs versus Controls versus Convenience Costs of controls vary with their implementation time and the complexity of the system or operation. Control implementation time is important to realize benefits from installing appropriate controls. For example, it costs significantly more to correct a design problem in the implementation phase of an application system under development than it does to address in the early planning and design phases.

There are **trade-offs** among costs, controls, and convenience factors. The same is true among system usability, maintainability, auditability, controllability, and securability attributes of systems. For example:

- High-risk systems and complex systems and operations require more controls.

- Excessive use of tight security features and control functions can be costly and may complicate procedures, degrade system performance, and impair system functionality, which could ultimately inhibit the system's usability.

- System users prefer as few integrity and security controls as possible, only those needed to make the system really usable.

- The greater the maintainability of the system, the easier it is for a programmer to modify it. Similarly, the greater the maintainability of the system, the less expensive it is to operate in the long run.

(I) Compensating Controls Normally, auditors will find more control-related problems in first-time audits of an area. Generally, the more frequently an area is audited, the less probability of many control weaknesses. Therefore, determining the nature of efficient and effective operations needs both audit instinct and business judgment. During the control evaluation process, the auditor should consider the availability of compensating controls as a way to mitigate or minimize the impact of inadequate or incomplete controls. In essence, the concept of compensating controls deals with balancing of weak internal controls in one area with strong internal controls in other areas of the organization. Here the word "area" can include a section within a user or IT department.

An example of a weak control is a situation where data control employees in the IT department are not reconciling data input control totals to data output control totals in an application system. This control weakness in the IT department can be compensated for by strong controls in the user department where end users reconcile their own control totals with those produced by the application system. Sometimes automated compensating controls and procedures are needed to shorten the lengthy manual controls and procedures (e.g., replacing a manual report balancing system with an automated report balancing system).

Compensating controls are needed whenever:

- Manual controls are weak.

  Solution: Look for strong computer or other controls.

- Computer controls are weak.

  Solution: Look for strong manual or other controls.

- Interface controls between manual and automated systems are weak.

  Solution: Look for strong controls in either the receiving or the sending system.

- Functional (system) user controls are weak.

  Solution: Look for strong IT or other controls.

- IT controls are weak.

  Solution: Look for strong controls in system user or other departments.

- Third-party manual controls are weak.

  Solution: Look for strong controls in the in-house system in either the manual or the automated part.

- Third-party computer controls are weak.

  Solution: Look for strong controls in the in-house system in either the manual or the automated part.

- Physical access security controls are weak.

  Solution: Look for strong logical access security controls.

- Logical access security controls are weak.

  Solution: Look for strong physical access security controls, supervisory reviews, or more substantive testing.

- A specific general control is weak.

  Solution: Look for a strong and related application control.

- An application system control is weak.

  Solution: Look for a strong and related general control.

- Employee performance is weak.

  Solution: Look for strong supervisory reviews and more substantive testing.

(J) Review of Compensating Controls One way to strengthen internal controls and reduce the possibility of errors, omissions, and irregularities is to build compensating controls into operations and systems and to review their adequacy. Control-related information should be produced for review by supervisors or managers so that any irregularities are noticed for further action. Some tools and techniques that facilitate a review of compensating controls are listed next.

- **Audit trails.** The audit trail is also called processing trail, management trail, information trail, or transaction trail. The audit trail provides the ability to trace a transaction from its initiation to final disposition, including all intermediate points. Similarly, it offers the ability to trace quantitative information, such as financial totals or quantity totals, to its supporting details, including source documents and vice versa. A clear and understandable audit trail is needed for business users, management, auditors, and government agents, such as tax collectors. Audit trails offer accountability, reduce fraud, show what actions were taken by people and the system, and provide the ability to reconstruct events or transactions.

  According to Davis and Olson, an audit trail should always be present. Its form may change in response to computer technology, but three requirements should be met.

  1. Any transaction can be traced from the source document through processing to outputs and to totals in which the transaction is aggregated. For example, each purchase of goods for inventory can be traced to inclusion in the inventory totals.

2. Any output or summary data can be traced back to the transaction or computation used to arrive at the output or summary figures. For example, the total amount owed by a customer can be traced to the sales and payments that were disbursed to arrive at the balance due.

3. Any triggered transaction (a transaction automatically triggered by an event or a condition) can be traced to the event or condition. An example is a purchase order triggered by a sale that reduced inventory below an order point.[6]

In general, audit trail references begin at the transaction level with one or more of these numbers:

□ Preassigned document number

□ Number assigned by document preparer at preparation

□ Batch number assigned to a batch of documents

□ Transaction number assigned by computer

The next references are used as processing references in updating master data files records and displaying on control reports and audit trail lists.

□ **Control total verifications.** Control totals, such as record counts, document counts, line item counts, financial totals, quantity totals, and hash totals of account numbers and employee numbers, can be used to verify the accuracy of data entry and data processing activities. The control total is entered with transaction data and verified by the computer system as part of its data editing and validation activity. The control totals appear on batch reports, error reports, exception reports, and other reports.

The rejected totals and accepted totals should be equal to the total input or output. These control totals can be used by both the data control section of the IT department and the functional user department to ensure that all transactions are processed properly. In online application systems, control totals can be provided by terminal, data entry operator, transaction type, or by location.

□ **Transaction logs.** In addition to acting as compensating controls, transaction logs help in recovering from a disaster, such as lost or damaged data files and hardware/software failures. These logs include application transaction, database, operating system (console), telecommunication, access control security, job accounting, problem management, change management, hardware preventive maintenance, and system management logs. Usually these logs capture pertinent system activity data that can be used for tracing, audit analysis, and substantive reviews/tests. These logs, in turn, can be used to determine whether controls have been circumvented or followed.

□ **Error logs.** Manual or automated error logs can be maintained to show errors detected and corrected by the application system. The log can indicate the type of error occurred, who corrected it, and when. Error summary reports by error type, by person, by department, by division, or by application system can be produced according to the volume of data the system collects. The error log can be maintained in either the IT department or the system user department, or in both places.

□ **Control grids/matrices.** Two-dimensional control grids/matrices can be developed to show security threats or business and audit risks and exposures on one axis and the controls or control techniques that minimize or eliminate such threats, risks,

---

[6] G. Davis and M. H. Olson, *Management Information Systems*, 2nd ed. (New York: McGraw-Hill, 1985).

and exposures on the other axis. Control grids help the auditor in understanding the relation between risks and controls and in evaluating and recommending appropriate controls.

A single control may reduce more than one type of threat. One control may well compensate or complement the other. An exposure may require several controls to provide reasonable assurance of preventing or detecting failures. Controls could be manual or automated. Control grids/matrices are best to use in a dynamic or constantly changing environment. However, control grids take longer to use since the auditor needs to set the matrix and analyze it. Also, a more complete and clear understanding of the computer center environment must be obtained to use the control grids/matrices approach effectively.

☐ **Internal control questionnaires.** Many auditors use the internal control questionnaire (ICQ) as a mechanism to obtain an initial understanding of the computer center operations or a computer system. ICQ contains many closed-ended questions requiring a "yes," "no," or "not applicable" answer. One drawback of the ICQ is that the questions are preestablished and not unique to any specific environment. Because of this, ICQ is less flexible than open-ended questions. ICQ is best when used by a new, inexperienced auditor in evaluating controls. ICQ should be supplemented by other information-gathering and control evaluation techniques, such as flowcharting and documentation review.

☐ **Bank reconciliations.** Monthly reconciliation of the general bank account on a timely basis by someone independent of the handling or recording of cash receipts and disbursements is an essential internal control over the cash balance. The reconciliation is important to make sure the books reflect the same cash balance as the actual amount of cash in the bank after consideration of reconciling items. It also provides the verification of cash receipt and disbursement transactions.

Since computer-based application systems are used to record and process cash receipt and cash disbursement transactions, an independent reconciliation of bank accounts performed by someone outside the IT department provides a strong compensating control for a possible exposure: perpetration of fraud using the computer system.

☐ **Independent reviews.** Management can conduct unannounced independent reviews when it has a suspicion about an employee, operation, or activity. Management can delegate this work to auditors or consultants to assess and evaluate the adequacy of controls over certain systems or operations. Such reviews may include the identification of preparer (i.e., verification by signature, initials, date, and system sign-on code) and evidence of approval (i.e., signature, initials, date, and approval codes).

☐ **Logical access security controls.** If manual controls and physical access controls are weak in certain areas, logical access controls can act as a compensating control device. These controls include restricting unauthorized persons accessing computer data and program files. Access rules can be defined in terms of who can do what functions (e.g., add, change, delete, inquire), when, using what devices (visual display unit/cathode ray tube [VDU/CRT] terminal), and from where. Usually both a user identification and password code, which can be combined with biometric techniques (i.e., fingerprint, signature), are required to access computer program and data files,

☐ **Exception and statistical reports.** These reports produce deviations from standards or threshold levels established. This information can then be used to analyze situations leading to such deviations. Patterns, trends, and clues may be obtained about the nature of transactions or operations.

☐ **Manual/automated reconciliations.** In the absence of manual logging of control totals between input and output operations of an application system and reconciliation of such totals for accuracy and completeness of operations, an automated reconciliation process should take place. This may include run-to-run control totals of computer records or data fields of significance, where totals from one passing or sending application program are verified by the receiving program. In this case, automated reconciliations are compensating controls for missing manual control reconciliations. This reconciliation also serves as a check against unauthorized insertions of extra records or program logic into an application system.

☐ **Report balancing.** Balancing rules for application system-generated reports would help in ensuring data integrity and program processing logic accuracy. The balancing rules can be based on physical quantities, such as the number of units sold, or on financial quantities, such as dollars received or paid. The report balancing task can be done manually or automatically by a computer program.

(K) Interrelationships Between Controls   Controls are interrelated. Lack of controls in one area may affect other interrelated areas. Similarly, what is an accepted control in one area may not be applicable to another area. This is because life cycles of a system or data are different. For example, a life cycle of an application system can take the phases shown in Exhibit 1.6.

System development requires different controls from operation and maintenance. For example, the system development process requires more project management controls, system operation requires more operational controls, and system maintenance requires strict program change and configuration controls. However, documentation is common to all these phases, and it acts as a preventive, detective, and corrective control as well. Weak controls during system development impact both operations and maintenance activities.

For example, the life cycle of a data item (or element) can take the phases shown in Exhibit 1.7.

Different controls are required in each of the phases shown in the exhibit. For example, processing of data requires more data editing and validation controls, and data disposition requires more physical security controls, such as shredding or burning the reports and degaussing the magnetic media.

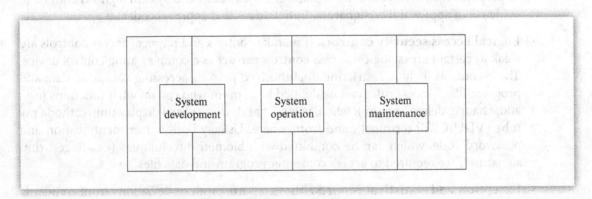

EXHIBIT 1.6 Life Cycle of an Application System

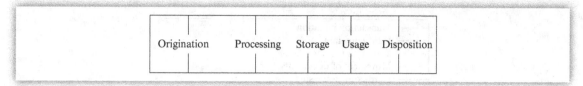

EXHIBIT 1.7 Life Cycle of a Data Item

(L) Use of Controls Implementation of controls requires money and other resources. Hence, judicious use of controls is needed. Proper use of controls depends on many factors, situations, and environments. Some major common considerations are listed next.

- Size of the IT department
- Size of the organization in which the IT department is a part
- Availability of financial and other resources
- Value of the assets and resources to be protected
- Level and complexity of computer technology in use
- Type of industry to which the organization belongs
- Risk levels of the system or operation
- Management's tolerance to risk levels
- Management's commitment to and support of controls
- Competitive position of the organization in the industry in which it operates
- Government, tax, accounting, legal, and regulatory requirements placed on the organization

(M) Information Systems Audit Evidence

Audit Evidence Types The evidence produced by automated IS, whether financial or operational, may be different from that produced by manual systems.[7] It is important for the auditor to understand these new forms of evidence because the methods used for auditing will change as the forms of evidence change. A list of **14 traditional forms of evidence** that exist when manual processing is used is presented in Exhibit 1.8. The description provides an example of how the computer can change the forms of that evidence.

1. **Transaction initiation.** Transactions are originated by people and entered into a system for processing. In computerized applications, transactions can be automatically generated. For example, the application system can automatically issue a replacement order when inventory falls below a reorder point.

2. **Hard-copy input.** The manual recording of information is needed to originate a transaction. In computerized application systems, information can be entered through a terminal that does not leave hard documents. For example, a pay rate change can be entered on a computerized payroll master file through a computer terminal.

---

[7] National Bureau of Standards (NBS) Special Publication 500-153 by Ruthberg, U.S. Department of Commerce, Gaithersburg, Maryland, April 1988. The NBS was later changed to National Institute of Standards and Technology (NIST).

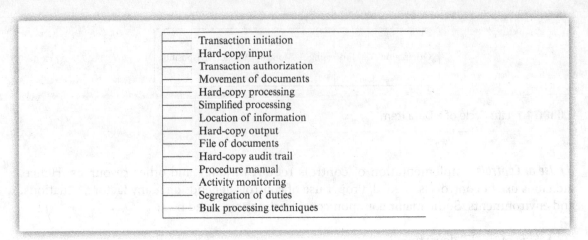

Transaction initiation
Hard-copy input
Transaction authorization
Movement of documents
Hard-copy processing
Simplified processing
Location of information
Hard-copy output
File of documents
Hard-copy audit trail
Procedure manual
Activity monitoring
Segregation of duties
Bulk processing techniques

EXHIBIT 1.8 Information Systems Audit Evidence Types

3. **Transaction authorization.** Supervisors review transactions and then affix their signatures, initials, or stamps to the document, indicating authorization for processing. In computerized application systems, authorization can be predetermined. For example, sales on credit can be automatically approved if a predetermined credit limit is not exceeded. Other methods of electronic authorization include entering a password, inserting a magnetically encoded card, turning a supervisory key in a terminal, or entering an authorization code into the application function program.

   With EDI systems, for example, employees affixing signatures, initials, and dates on purchase orders, on vendor invoices, or on vendor payments are not present because of electronic transfers of data. Authorization codes and date and time stamps can be captured and made available in a computerized environment.

4. **Movement of documents.** People carry documents from one workstation to another or move the documents by mail or equivalent service from one place of business to another. By these methods, a physical document is moved. In computerized application systems, the data can be sent electronically. The data are transcribed, coded, often condensed, and then moved electronically over telecommunication lines. Examples of electronic movement of documents and data are electronic data interchange (EDI) systems, electronic mail, and electronic fund transfer systems (EFT).

5. **Hard-copy processing.** Processing is manually performed using the transaction documents. For example, a form might show the steps performed by a procurement officer in selecting a vendor. Normally the documents contain workspace to perform the necessary processing. In computerized application systems, processing is done electronically within computer storage by computer programs following predetermined rules.

6. **Simplified processing.** The processing performed must be simplified so that people can perform the steps repetitively without a high probability of error. In computerized application systems, processing can be extremely complex due to the speed and accuracy of the computer. For example, production scheduling can be calculated hundreds of different ways in order to select the most effective schedule.

7. **Location of information.** The permanent-type information needed for processing, such as pay rates and product prices, is maintained in manuals. In computerized application

systems, this information is stored on computer media, such as tapes, cartridges, mass storage devices, optical disk, magnetic disk, USB devices such as flash, thumb and pen drives.

8. **Hard-copy output.** The results of processing are listed on hard-copy documents, such as checks and reports. Frequently these documents contain the intermediate processing results. In computerized application systems, processing may not result in the production of hard-copy documents. For example, funds (EFTS) or purchase orders (EDI) can be transferred electronically, with output reports displayed on terminals. In some systems, routine information is withheld so that the recipient receives only exception items, which require action.

9. **File of documents.** Input, processing, and output documents are stored in file cabinets or similar containers. When the data are needed, they can be manually located and retrieved from the physical storage area. In a procurement system, purchase orders might be stored in a file cabinet. In computerized application systems (e.g., EDI), most files exist on computer media, such as backup tapes, mainframe, and disks. Retrieving data from these media requires the use of data extract programs, computer-based record retrieval programs, or computer audit software.

10. **Hard-copy audit trail.** The information needed to reconstruct processing is contained in hard-copy documents. These documents contain source data, the authorization signature, methods of processing, and output results. This is normally sufficient information to reconstruct the transaction and to trace the transaction to control totals or from control totals back to the source document. For example, a payroll paper audit trail would permit the reconstruction of each employee's salary.

   In computerized application systems, the audit trail may be fragmented, as often occurs in a database environment. Also, much of the audit trail information may be stored on computer media. Computerized audit trails frequently require the auditor to understand the rules of processing because it may not be obvious which processing path was taken, especially when computer processing is complex.

11. **Procedure manual.** All of the steps needed to process transactions through a system are contained in one or more procedure manuals. These are guides for people in moving and processing transactions. For example, procedures might be developed to define the steps to follow when a transaction is outside normal processing, such as a claim for a nonreimbursed health care expense. In a computerized environment, procedures are included in help screens and online documentation facilities.

12. **Activity monitoring.** Supervisors oversee and review processing to determine its reasonableness, accuracy, completeness, and authorization. For example, a supervisor would review department purchase orders for correctness and need prior to sending them to procurement. In computerized application systems, much of this monitoring is performed automatically using predetermined program logic, such as data editing and validation routines. It is difficult to have people monitor processing as computer systems become more integrated and complex and the processing cycle is shortened.

13. **Segregation of duties.** Segregation of duties occurs by dividing tasks among people. In computerized application systems, segregation of duties involves not only the division of tasks among people but the division of tasks among automated processing steps. For example, one computer program may process one part of a transaction, while another

computer program processes a different part. Another example involves one person entering a transaction into the computer system and another person(s) changing or deleting the same transaction based on security clearances established by management and controlled by an access control security system. When the same person enters, changes, and deletes the same transaction, compensating controls, such as supervisory review, are needed to ensure that the person is discharging his or her responsibilities properly.

14. **Bulk processing techniques.** The processing of large amounts of data may involve resequencing or matching diverse data elements. This is often difficult and costly in a manual system, so it is done only when necessary. In computerized application systems, large amounts of data can be stored in a single database. The speed and processing capability of the computer makes these data available in any format desired. In a computerized environment, more complex analyses and secondary uses of data can be made. For example, large amounts of data can be sorted, matched, and reported in much less time using the computer.

Audit Evidence-Gathering Sources The IS auditor uses one or more sources or techniques to gather audit evidence during an audit (whether it is financial or operational in nature). These techniques include:

- Reviewing IS organizational structure.
- Reviewing IS documentation standards and practices.
- Reviewing systems documentation, such as flowcharts, manuals, system/program specifications.
- Interviewing appropriate personnel in both IS and functional departments.
- Observing operations and employee performance of duties in both IS and functional user departments.
- Using audit documentation techniques, such as flowcharts, questionnaires, system narratives, decision trees and tables, control grid charts, and security clearance matrices.
- Selecting and testing key controls in either the IS or the functional user department.
- Applying sampling techniques, where applicable, to select sample accounts (say for confirming accounts receivable balances with customers).
- Using CAATs to sort, extract, compare, analyze, compute, reperform, and report the required data residing on computer data files. This can be done with the use of generalized data-extraction program report writers, third-generation programming languages (e.g., COBOL), fourth-generation programming language–based software products, fifth-generation, or computer audit software products.

(N) Operating Systems

Audit Objectives The audit objectives to review operating systems include ensuring that:

- The systems software function is administered and managed properly.
- Appropriate control options, parameters, and system commands are selected in the system software products.

- Systems software is installed and used properly and that only authorized personnel have access to the systems software.

- Appropriate control features are included in the systems software being used.

- Changes to systems software are made in a controlled environment to provide an audit or management trail.

- Security over mainframe computers, workstations, and servers is adequate and effective.

Audit Procedures　The audit work programs or procedures for an operating systems software review include security over mainframes, workstations, and servers.

Systems Software Administration

- Ensure that separation of duties exists among systems programming, data security, database, computer operations, and applications programming functions. Inquire whether cross controls are established among these functions.

- Determine whether the systems programming management issues periodic status reports to management describing progress and current and potential problems with planned action.

- The auditor reviewing the systems programmer(s) activities and associated controls should conduct these audit procedures.

- Inquire whether systems programmers get dedicated test machine time for testing the installation of new releases of operating systems, databases, data communications, utility programs, and other systems software and for testing the changes to such software. Ascertain whether test members are created using systems programmer's initials embedded in them for easy identification of their source of origination.

- Ensure that all changes to systems software are documented using online documentation tools and techniques, such as text editors and word processors.

- Review the functions and uses of supervisor calls (SVCs) in systems software, whether written in-house or supplied by vendor, and determine their appropriateness. Ascertain whether program code walkthroughs are performed on the SVCs before installing them into production status, and ensure that source code for all SVCs is physically protected (i.e., locked up in a cabinet).

- Compare the production version of SVCs with its source code to ensure that the object code is derived from its corresponding source code.

- Inquire whether systems programmer access to security systems software, data sets, utility programs, and macros is limited to individuals on a need-to-know basis.

- Determine whether sensitive programs are protected by security systems software by placing them in a protected library. Inquire whether the volume table of contents (VTOC) is protected as a separate dataset.

- Change memory utility programs, which can display and alter computer memory, are powerful and should be used cautiously. Determine whether security features in these utilities are bypassed. Inquire who has "OPER" authority to access these utilities, and confirm that computer operations management properly approves them. Inquire whether automated logs are produced by the use of these utilities, and, if so, who is reviewing them.

- Ensure that systems programmers are restricted from accessing production application programs and data files and that only certain commands and parameters are allowed to access from remote areas.

- Verify whether systems programmers participate in developing contingency plans and that they monitor operating system performance considering seasonal, unexpected demand, volume mix, and other factors.

CONTROL RISK IN SYSTEMS SOFTWARE ADMINISTRATION

Systems programmers may have direct access to powerful utility programs and sensitive routines that may bypass security controls and logging facilities. They may have the ability to move operating systems software changes between test and production libraries without going through the designated program change control coordinator.

Operating Systems Software

1. **Access security features.** Interview technical services manager, systems programming manager, or the person in charge of operating system activities. Assess the following items, and note any exceptions needing improvement:

   □ Systems programmer actions should be restricted with the use of passwords, and these programmers should be allowed to access system resources on a need-to-know basis.

   □ Inquire whether modifications to the object code (resulting from source code of an application program) and operating system can be controlled through the use of a program library management system similar to the source code of an application program.

   □ Determine whether there is a need to use program comparator tools to detect unauthorized modifications to operating systems software in its object code form. Some ways it can be approached are to compare the total bit count at two different points in time.

      Any differences to this count indicate modifications to the operating system software. Similarly, security over and integrity of internal tables can be measured by reading hash totals of records or bit counts.

   □ Confirm that hardware/software vendor maintenance staff is positively verified with vendor ID card, a phone call from the vendor, and/or other means.

   □ Ensure that the operating system has a feature to erase all scratch space assigned to a sensitive and critical job after normal or abnormal termination of the job. This is to prevent unauthorized browsing or scavenging of data files on the system.

   □ Ensure that certain commands that turn off the operating system logging feature are closely controlled and that their invocation is recorded in the log, which should be protected from unauthorized modifications.

2. **Performance measurement and accounting.** Determine whether the operating system performance measurement and accounting software, do the following:

   □ Analyzes disk input/output (I/O) activity within a volume and shows where to place data sets to minimize seek contention.

   □ Analyzes disk I/O activity across volumes and shows where to place data sets across volumes to balance strings, which reduces path contention and queue time.

- Simulates the effect of recommended reorganizations and calculates the percentage improvement that would be gained if the reorganizations were implemented.

- Analyzes and simulates cache control units to evaluate how effectively the cache resource is being used. Determines the model and size of cache storage that should be acquired and identifies which volumes or data sets should be placed under cache.

- Recommends data set reorganizations based on data set member and directory access analysis.

- Generates history files that can be used to perform trend analysis.

- Generates reports showing I/O volume by job name, data set name, and unit name.

- Produces reports showing I/O volume by job for each data set.

- Generates reports showing I/O volume by data set from each job.

- Provides exception reports when user-defined thresholds are exceeded. This means indicating different job names contending for resources on the same volume.

- Generates response-time degradation analysis to examine online application program performance and to identify contention areas. This information helps fine-tune the system to meet its requirements.

- Monitors individual online system tasks and overall teleprocessing system utilization.

- Measures activity for CPU, I/O, paging, swapping, real storage, virtual storage, auxiliary storage, and workload.

3. **Buffer management.** For batch and online systems, performance is a major concern. Ascertain the need to install a buffer management system to optimize the performance of storage access methods in order to

- Reduce the number of physical I/O operations.
- Reduce the CPU usage.
- Increase system throughput.
- Reduce run times of heavily I/O intensive batch jobs.

However, be aware that there are trade-offs among these benefits and possible increases in paging rates and storage requirements.

4. **Integrity analysis.** Determine whether operating system software integrity analysis can be provided in these areas:

- Library analysis detecting inactive system libraries, duplicate modules, SuperZap activity, and authorized program facility problems
- Hardware display showing operator's consoles and tape and disk error rates
- Detecting invalid modules, zapped-off bits
- Program freezer detecting program and data file changes
- Providing online comparison of data files, source, and load program modules
- Detecting modifications to the operating system by trapdoors, logic bombs, Trojan horses, and computer viruses
- Detecting abnormal conditions and flagging entries needs additional follow-up

Control Options, Parameters, and System Commands Interview systems programmers to understand the control options, operating parameters, and system commands selected in the various operating systems software products. Review the product installation document and through online viewing and determine whether:

- Parameters used are appropriate to the needs.
- Options used are correct to the circumstances.
- System commands selected are proper to the tasks.
- Incompatible options and parameters are used.
- Circumvention of control procedures is possible.
- Duplicate system files names and procedures are used.

Assess the reasonableness and applicability of options and parameter selections. Note any exceptions.

Systems Software Changes

1. **Systems software changes.** To ensure effective controls over systems software program changes, the following audit procedures are suggested:
   - ☐ Select a sample of several systems software library changes.
   - ☐ Ensure that the change request form is complete in all respects.
   - ☐ Ensure that the change request form is approved by the appropriate individuals within the technical support or services group.
   - ☐ Verify the existence of and compliance with all deliverables as defined in the data processing program turnover checklist.
   - ☐ Document and evaluate the procedures followed by quality control coordinators when assessing individual changes before migration to the production environment.

2. **Emergency database systems software changes.** To ensure effective controls over database program changes, the following audit procedures are suggested:
   - ☐ Select a sample of several emergency database program changes.
   - ☐ Determine if the emergency ID and password were obtained according to IT standards.
   - ☐ Ensure that the emergency change request was completed according to standard and appropriate approvals were obtained.
   - ☐ Determine if a migration request was submitted to the database administration group to move the change from the emergency dictionary to production.
   - ☐ Determine if the same modifications were performed to the dialog or table residing in the test area.
   - ☐ Determine if all changes in this category fit the definition of an emergency change as defined by the IT standard.
   - ☐ Determine if the production job schedulers were contacted regarding dependent moves associated with the database change migrations.
   - ☐ Review all items currently residing in the emergency library and determine their status.

☐ Document and evaluate the procedures followed by quality control coordinators when assessing individual changes before migration to the production environment.

3. **Master catalog changes.** To ensure effective controls over catalog changes, the following audit procedures are suggested:

☐ Assess the internal procedures in place to control changes to the master catalog for high-level qualifiers. Test a small sample to determine if these procedures are adequate to provide proper control over such changes. Pay particular attention to communication existing between the data security manager or officer and the technical support/service group.

☐ Review several changes applied to cataloged procedures. Determine if change requests were completed for those changes. In addition, review the method by which the quality control coordinator communicates the successful approval of the proposed change to the technical support group. Determine if any changes are applied before appropriate approvals are obtained.

Security over Mainframes, Workstations, and Servers

- Determine whether all system activities, such as log-on and log-off, are recorded.
- Determine whether system starts and stops of sensitive processes or applications are logged and reviewed by system administrators.
- Ensure that access violations to mainframes, workstations, and servers are recorded and reviewed, including improper time of day, unauthorized directory and terminal, and communications entry mode, or failed access attempts.

(O) Application Development Timely participation of auditors in the application system development process is based on the belief that early detection and correction of inadequate and incomplete controls planned during the system design phase will save time and money in the long run. This is because of the expensive nature of bringing up inadequate controls to an acceptable level at a later stage when the system is put into operational status. Ideally, controls should be built in rather than built on.

The auditor's participation in the system development and maintenance project may take the form of continuous or intermittent reviews and tests. It is important to note that the application systems development and maintenance process should be reviewed against IT/IS standards or methodology.

ROLE OF INTERNAL AUDITOR IN SYSTEMS DEVELOPMENT

Internal auditors should refrain from designing and installing any computer systems for their organizations. However, they can review and evaluate any computer system.

The degree of auditor participation really depends on the audit staff's time availability and required skills and on the riskiness of the phase and the application system. Some phases are considered to be more critical from the standpoint of the auditor's contribution to the system development process. The auditor should participate in the early phases where critical decisions are made regarding system requirements, control/security requirements, design approaches, and software testing plans and approaches. The auditor should also participate during file/system conversion and postimplementation reviews.

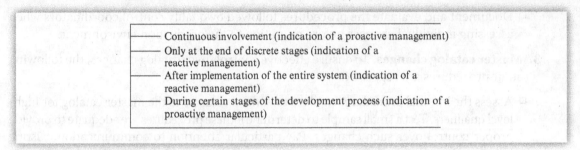

- Continuous involvement (indication of a proactive management)
- Only at the end of discrete stages (indication of a reactive management)
- After implementation of the entire system (indication of a reactive management)
- During certain stages of the development process (indication of a proactive management)

EXHIBIT 1.9 Auditor Participation in the System Development Process

How Much Auditor Participation Is Enough?   The internal auditor can participate in the review of the systems development process at varying intervals in four ways, as shown in Exhibit 1.9.

1. **Continuous involvement** requires the auditor to participate in all phases of the system development process and all the time. The advantages include: improved design and specification of controls, the opportunity to provide significant suggestions to the system design team, reduced need for subsequent rework of controls, and reflection of a proactive management thinking. The disadvantage is cost in terms of time and effort by the auditor and audit management. Auditor's time has an opportunity cost.

2. The auditor participates **only at the end of discrete stages,** such as system requirement definition, testing, or conversion. The advantages are: reassignment of audit staff to other audits and reduction in audit costs. The disadvantages include: missed opportunity in contributing to strengthening of controls, greater need for subsequent rework of controls, and reflection of reactive management thinking.

3. The auditor can participate **after implementation of the entire system**. The advantages are: reassignment of audit staff to other audits and reduction in audit costs. Disadvantages are: expensive to add controls later, missed opportunity to strengthen controls, greater need for subsequent rework of controls, and reflection of a reactive management thinking.

4. Participation **during certain stages of the development process,** such as requirements, design, testing, and conversion. The advantages include: improved design and specification of controls, the opportunity to provide significant suggestions to the system design team, reduced need for subsequent rework of controls in the phases participated, and reflection of a proactive management thinking. The disadvantages are: missed opportunities for not participating in other important phases, greater need for subsequent rework of controls in the phases not participated, and cost in terms of time and effort by the auditor and audit management.

Audit Approaches   The auditing of software development, acquisition, and maintenance process may require a two-pronged approach. In the first, the auditor reviews the standard systems development, acquisition, and maintenance methodology itself. Based on the review, the auditor suggests improvements when needed. In the second, the auditor reviews an actual application system as it is being developed, acquired, or maintained.

Approach 1: Auditing the Software Development, Acquisition, and Maintenance

Methodology. A standard software development, acquisition, and maintenance methodology should contain management's philosophy, guidelines, and direction in developing, acquiring, and maintaining an application system. The directives and guidelines included in the methodology become standards and procedures for IT/IS staff and system users to follow on a day-to-day basis. The methodology should:

- Describe the phases or stages and tasks or activities required, including project management techniques for successfully completing a software development, acquisition, and maintenance project.

- Identify each task as being either required (mandated) or optional (advisable).

- Define the responsibilities of functional department users and IT staff.

- Describe the expected deliverables (end products) from each phase of the project.

- Define guidelines for using software development, conversion, maintenance tools and techniques.

- Describe the criteria for automated and manual controls, security, and audit trails.

- Define guidelines for software quality, usability, and maintainability.

The rationale for having auditors review the methodology itself is that proper guidelines should help systems development and maintenance staff and system users carry out their duties in the system development and maintenance process, even when the auditors themselves cannot participate because of lack of adequate time and staff. Periodically, auditors should review the system development and maintenance methodology to make sure it reflects changes in:

- Software development and maintenance tools and techniques.

- Control, security, and audit requirements.

- Management's overall direction.

- Technical improvements in hardware and software.

- Business and system strategies.

The auditor's review of the methodology will ensure that it is clear, complete, understandable, consistent, practical, and achievable. Here the term "consistency" refers to compliance with the organization's policies, procedures, and management's philosophy; with generally accepted industry standards and IT/IS standards; with official directives, circulars, and pronouncements; with legal, accounting, tax, government, and regulatory requirements; and with good business and management practices. Auditors need to ascertain whether deviations from the standard system methodology are allowed, whether reasons for deviations and approvals at various levels are required, and whether these requirements are followed.

Approach 2: Auditing the Software Development, Acquisition, and Maintenance Project The auditors' review of the standard system development, acquisition, and maintenance methodology should not replace their review of the actual system development and maintenance project. There is no other way to be sure that the issued standards and guidelines will be followed uniformly and completely for all of the application systems being developed or maintained.

Therefore, auditors have a professional responsibility and an obligation to their organization to plan and schedule audits of the actual application systems development, acquisition, and maintenance projects. They can conduct risk analysis to determine which of several application systems under development should be audited.

Risk evaluations are used to rank projects as high, medium, and low risk. High-risk systems should be the first to be audited unless the risk is outweighed by other factors, such as management's judgment. Some **risk factors** to be considered for risk assessment and evaluation are listed next.

- Scope and the nature of the system
- Assets controlled by the system
- Will system results be used to make management decisions?
- Programming language used
- Total system development cost
- Total system development hours
- System impact on financial statements
- Regulatory agency requirements for the system
- Computer processing mode
- Who is participating in the system development process?
- Systems development methodology used
- Total number of programs/modules including update programs and excluding utility programs

Auditors can use the standard system development, acquisition, and maintenance methodology standards and guidelines in developing audit work programs for use during their participation in the project. The guidelines and standards give them meaningful criteria by measuring the efforts and project activities of the software development staff and system user staff in an objective manner. Without such standards, auditors' evaluations and recommendations are open to question from auditees, and there may be no basis for recommendations.

Auditors and IT quality assurance analysts have the responsibility for reviewing and testing for adherence to standards and for reporting any deficiency findings to management for corrective actions. Senior management has the ultimate responsibility for ensuring adherence to standards by both system users and IT staffs. It is up to management, not the auditor, to take corrective action in response to deficiency reports or to assume the risk resulting from inaction.

(P) Auditor's Role in Software Development, Acquisition, and Maintenance: Audit Objectives and Procedures

Auditor's Role The role of the auditor in the auditing of purchased software is similar to the auditor's role in-house application system development efforts, except for participation in the acquisition process of vendor-developed software. The objectives of the auditor in reviewing, testing, and evaluating the vendor-developed applications software packages are to:

- Participate in the software evaluation or acquisition, modification or adaptation, installation or implementation processes as a member of the project team consisting of functional users, IT staff, and others.

- Review security, audit, control, maintenance requirements, and evaluate software packages against these defined requirements.

- Express an opinion on whether the software meets these requirements.

- Review software features, functions, and capabilities to determine that they meet user needs, such as ease of use, and IT staff requirements, such as software portability, convertibility, maintainability, and testability.

- Assess vendor-supplied documentation for its adequacy and completeness.

- Participate in the testing of software to determine whether it performs according to its features as defined in the vendor-supplied documentation.

Note that the auditor does **not** make decisions with respect to project's resource allocation and use.

The auditor's role in the software acquisition process is consultative and preventive in nature. This is keeping with traditional, moderate, and participatory concepts. In this independent role, auditors may act as controls specialists and systems consultants to the software project team in determining the adequacy and completeness of software usability, maintainability, auditability, and controllability and in assessing security features, functions, and capabilities. Auditors may recommend that management should not select an unusable, unsecurable, unauditable, unmaintainable, or uncontrollable system, but they do not make the final decision to acquire a software package. Clearly, the final decision of selecting a software package is the responsibility of the functional user operating management and others.

As user organizations acquire off-the-shelf applications software packages from vendors and others as viable alternatives to in-house software development, the auditor's control review responsibility is shifted from in-house–developed systems to vendor-developed software. The auditor's role has changed because of increased computerization of IS with software packages.

A major difference between vendor-developed applications software and in-house–developed software is that the auditor's review of vendor software is postdevelopmental in nature. Where validating the system functions and controls (i.e., system features and capabilities, maintainability, securability, testability, usability, auditability, controllability) and assessing the quality and adequacy of documentation are concerned, the auditor's review responsibilities are the same.

Audit Scope The auditor needs to focus on five software attributes during software development, acquisition, and maintenance activities. These attributes are in addition to project management controls, such as milestones, planning tools, progress reports, and project structure.

1. Usability
2. Maintainability
3. Auditability
4. Controllability
5. Securability

For each of these five audit attributes, the auditor needs to ask the questions in the next sections prior to or during the software development process.

Usability   Is the software easy to use? Is the documentation easy to understand? Are automated and manual procedures flexible enough to handle unexpected business events? Are video display unit (VDU/CRT) screen menu procedures too long? What is the system response time for data inquiry and data editing purposes? In other words, how user-friendly is the software? A simple question might be: What is the purpose of developing a system that cannot be used easily?

Many application systems are developed in both public and private sectors that later are discarded because they cannot be used at all or, at most, can be used only in a limited way. This occurs because system designers did not fully consider software usability criteria. As a result, public and private organizations waste millions or even billions of dollars.

Auditors should review system design features not so much for the technical accuracy of design specifications but to ensure that the software is usable by the functional users of the system. It is possible that IT staff members might have taken for granted the usability features or not considered them at all when they were concentrating on the technical complexity of the system and its associated design features and functions.

Maintainability   Is the software easy to modify? Are the software maintainability criteria addressed during the software development process? Are structured techniques being used during the software development process? Are programs modular in nature? Is the system flexible or expandable as needed? The real question is: What is the use of developing a system that cannot be easily maintained (now or later)?

Typically, IT departments spend more than 50% of their operating budget and computer programmers and systems analysts spend 50 – 75% of their time and efforts on maintaining the existing software in an operational mode. Simply stated, maintaining business software consumes more resources than developing new software. Of course, some part of this resource consumption is due to legitimate need for new or changing requirements, which cannot be avoided. However, it has been estimated that a major portion of this resource consumption is due to the fact that the original software was developed without considering its future maintenance. Hence, more time and effort is required when the software needs to be changed, because the system is not easy to modify.

Auditors should ask the designers of the system whether software maintainability criteria (e.g., structured techniques) are addressed and built into the software during its development process (i.e., during software requirements definition, analysis, design, programming, and testing activities). Conventional programs written using nonstructured techniques are like bowls of spaghetti code; they are difficult to handle, control, understand, trace, review, modify, and maintain. When properly planned, structured techniques provide many benefits:

- Structured analysis produces usable, controllable, securable, and auditable systems.
- Structured design produces flexible and maintainable systems.
- Structured programs produce readable and understandable program code.
- Structured testing produces reliable and quality results and outputs.

Auditability   Is the system auditable? How can a user or an auditor trace transactions from initiation to completion? What kind of audit trails (paper or electronic) are planned and designed into the system? Can the system be audited in accordance with generally accepted auditing standards (GAAS) or generally accepted government auditing standards (GAGAS) or other standards? The important question is: Does the system provide enough data to the auditor to rely on the integrity of the data and the reliability of operations (computer and manual) in order to form an opinion on the financial health of the organization?

Applications software may not have adequate audit trails. Auditors should identify what audit trails are planned and designed into the system and, if necessary, recommend additional audit trails to trace transactions (on paper or electronically) from one point to another.

Controllability   How accurate are the input data? How reliable are the output data? Are the input data subject to data editing and validation rules to ensure the integrity of data? How do we correct errors? The question is: How do we control the system inputs, processes, and outputs to ensure data integrity?

Applications software may not have adequate internal program processing (automated) controls planned and designed into the system. Manual controls may not have been well thought out to supplement or complement automated controls. Controls could be bypassed or circumvented. Compensating controls (access controls and supervisory/management reviews) may not be available to balance the controls between functional user departments and the data processing department. Controls may be overlapped between departments, thus wasting organizational resources. Auditors should identify and assess what controls are available in the software and recommend additional controls necessary to assure data integrity and reliability.

Securability   How are computer resources (programs, data, and equipment) protected from undesirable events or actions, such as computer-related fraud, crime, theft, and embezzlement? The basic question is: How secure or vulnerable is the total system, including hardware, software, and data?

Applications software may not have adequate built-in security features to protect computer programs, data files, job control procedures, and VDU/CRT terminals from unauthorized access and use. Auditors should identify and assess what security features are planned and designed into the software and, if necessary, recommend additional security measures to prevent, detect, or correct unauthorized access to computer data files, programs, and terminals and other hardware devices.

AUDIT/CONTROL RISKS: RESPONSIBILITIES

- Auditors may not participate in the system development, acquisition, and maintenance activities, as doing so would limit their contribution to the organization.

- There may not be a fallback system in place when the new system does not work properly.

- One party (e.g., system users) may overrely on the other party (e.g., data processors) at the expense of self-responsibility.

Software Development

Audit Objectives   The audit objectives are to review an organization's systems development life cycle procedures to determine adherence to generally accepted system development standards.

The goal is to develop a usable, securable, auditable, maintainable, and controllable application system that produces consistent results to satisfy user requirements.

Audit Procedures The audit work program for an application system development review consists of 14 steps.

1. Review the **user service request** report in detail to determine the reason(s) for the request, user description of new system requirements, anticipated benefits to be derived, and their reasonability and attainability.

2. Review the **feasibility study** report to analyze alternative system solutions for organization problems and determine their relevancy and applicability to the organization problems and final choice. Review all cost/benefit analyses with respect to the alternative solutions to make sure that the appropriate approach has been selected. Review project scope, objectives, tasks, deliverables, work plans, and schedules to determine their reasonability and attainability.

> **BUSINESS/CONTROL RISKS IN FEASIBILITY STUDY PHASE**
>
> - The feasibility study results may not be available or be incomplete.
> - The assumptions made in the feasibility study may not be practical or relevant.
> - Cost-capabilities-benefit analysis may not be reasonable and thorough.

3. Review detail requirements definition reports or documents.

   a. Determine that during the study of the current system, its weaknesses have been identified and addressed in the new system requirements or specifications.

   b. Examine the software requirements document for completeness.

   c. Ensure that the programming language to be used is fairly common and that programming resources will be available during development and maintenance activities.

   d. Determine the extent of user participation required in developing and understanding the new system specifications.

   e. Evaluate input, processing, and output control specifications, and determine their adequacy and completeness. Identify preventive, detective, and corrective controls. Recommend additional controls, if necessary. Review and evaluate the planned audit trails, security features, and software maintenance requirements. Identify the need to build audit modules or routines into the system.

   f. Review and evaluate project organization, scope, and objectives.

   g. Determine the degree of adherence to the project work plan, budget, and work schedule.

   h. Verify that project management status reporting is available, accurate, and timely and that all due dates for tasks and deliverables are on schedule. If the project is behind schedule, determine the reasons. Identify applicable problems.

4. Review **general systems design** reports or documents for:

   a. Application systems flowchart.

   b. Application system input, processing, and output descriptions.

   c. Database schemas and subschemas.

   d. Data file characteristics.

   e. Security features, automated processing controls, and audit trails that include editing, error detection and correction procedures, batch controls, run-to-run controls, and so forth.

   f. System test and acceptance test criteria and approach.

   g. Data file conversion criteria and approach.

   h. Project management written status reports.

   i. User sign-off letters.

   j. Evaluate the need for building into the new system audit programs or modules for collecting data during production processing, to be analyzed at a later stage by the auditors and/or data processing staff. Some examples are: integrated test facility, embedded data collection, extended record, and snapshot techniques. These audit techniques would allow timely evidence collection and evaluation of required data during production processing.

5. Review the **detail systems design** reports or documents to determine the administrative procedures for controlling revisions to design and program specifications, including the recording, evaluation, implementation cost and time, and management and user approval levels.

6. Review **program(s) development** process by observing or participating in program code review walkthrough. This may include reviewing computer programs to ensure conformance with the program specifications to prevent logic errors and misinterpretation of user specifications.

CONTROL RISKS IN PROGRAM DEVELOPMENT PHASE

- Computer programs may have been developed without program or design specifications.

- Walkthroughs, independent inspections, peer reviews, and desk reviews may not have been performed or may not have been thorough, leaving many bugs or errors in the program.

- Programmers may not have made liberal use of comments in the computer application program, making it difficult to understand the purpose of the program.

- Programmers may be accepting user-requested changes over the phone, thus leading to incorrect implementation.

- Programmers may produce unmaintainable program code.

---

7. Review **program/unit test** plan, test data, expected results, and actual results for adequacy.

8. Review **systems test** plan, test data, expected results, actual results, overall systems testing approach, and user sign-off letters. Ensure that the systems testing scope includes all functions, programs, and interface systems. Ensure that all systems test discrepancies were adequately documented, reconciled, and corrected. The test data used in the system test could be actual or created data.

9. Review **manual(s) development** process to ensure those user manuals, terminal operator guides, and computer operations instruction manuals are adequately developed.

10. Review **training** plan and approach to ensure that training objectives were accomplished. Determine whether timely feedback was received from the initially trained users and that it was timely reflected in the training program for later users.

11. Review **user acceptance** of the system by verifying user sign-off letters. This is very important in determining whether users participated in testing and accepting the new system as their own. Review the acceptance test plan, test data, expected results, and actual results.

Determine whether the acceptance test plan includes system's tolerance to errors and the ability to respond to exceptional circumstances, such as a high volume of input transactions, illogical test conditions, and out-of-sequence transactions processing. Here the objective is to attempt to make the system fail. In other words, users need to identify the errors in the system. Ensure that all acceptance test discrepancies were documented, reconciled, and corrected. This is the last line of defense for the users before accepting the new system.

Determine how well the users understand their system. The difference between system testing and acceptance testing is that users may or may not participate in the system testing, whereas such participation is a requirement in acceptance testing. The data processing staff will be participating in unit and systems testing and may participate in acceptance testing activities. In some organizations, acceptance testing will be conducted by an independent testing team.

CONTROL RISKS IN USER ACCEPTANCE PHASE

- Criteria for accepting the new system may not have been defined and agreed on by system users and data processors.

- Software test data and test conditions may not be sufficiently comprehensive (including both valid and invalid conditions) to provide reasonable assurance that errors and problems (bugs) in the software are detected.

- Expected test results in the form of computer terminal screens, reports, and listings may not be prepared, making it difficult and time consuming to verify and approve test results.

- Software training processes and materials may be incomplete or ineffective. Some key system users and computer operations and production control staff may not have been trained properly.

12. Review file **conversion** plan and approach to ensure that file control totals are maintained and that problems are identified, documented, reconciled, and corrected quickly and properly. Where applicable, ensure that purchased hardware/software is installed and tested properly. Verify that the results of parallel operation of old and new system are the same, where applicable.

13. Review the **production** trouble reports. Identify the type of production problems encountered, and verify whether sufficient investigation and analysis was made to classify the problems as requiring immediate corrective action or later modification or enhancement.

CONTROL RISKS IN CONVERSION AND PRODUCTION SUPPORT PHASES

- All data, program, and job files and procedures that need to be converted may not be inventoried or known to the data processing staff and system users.

- Data editing and validation routines in conversion programs may be less complete than in normal programs.

- Operations (production) acceptance testing may not be performed by computer operations and data/production control staff and management.

14. Review the **postimplementation** report to determine the accuracy, timeliness, and completeness of anticipated and actual costs, benefits, and savings. Verify whether the users' original system objectives have been met. Ensure that any lessons learned from the current review are highlighted in the report to improve the quality of future systems development processes.

BUSINESS/CONTROL RISKS IN POSTIMPLEMENTATION PHASE

- Postimplementation reviews may not be performed at all.

- Production and operational problems may not be logged and monitored adequately.

- System development methodology procedures may not have been updated to reflect the results of postimplementation review or to learn from past mistakes.

Software Acquisition

Audit Objectives The audit objectives for the software acquisition process are the same as for in-house software development except for determining whether the software vendor selection process is thorough, that the software contractual arrangements are complete, and that the contract document is approved by legal staff to reduce business, technical, and legal risks and exposures.

Audit Procedures This list provides audit procedures for reviewing the software acquisition process.

- Review cost/benefit analysis documents and assess its completeness and relevancy.

- Assess whether software selection criteria are fair and reasonable.

- Determine whether the vendor selection process is clear and complete.

- Review the license/maintenance agreement and contract for completeness and applicability.

- Review the adequacy of system controls, audit trails, and security features within the application system.

CONTROL RISKS IN SOFTWARE ACQUISITION

- Software contracts may not have been reviewed by qualified legal counsel and auditors, thus exposing the organization to business, technical, and legal risks.

- Software vendors may not have tested the software thoroughly, leaving obvious errors (bugs). Although the software vendor may have been in business for many years with a heavy user base, the software version that an organization gets may not have been tested completely due to constant changes, enhancements, and customization. The original bad design and poor programming practices may not have been corrected due to time pressures to introduce new software releases.

Software Maintenance or Program Change Control: Audit Objectives and Procedures

Audit Objectives The audit objectives of a maintenance review or program change control are to ensure that authorized modifications, revisions, or changes to operational application systems are made in a controlled and secured environment.

Audit Procedures The audit work programs for a maintenance review consist of these steps.

- Ascertain that a standard maintenance policy is established regarding application program modifications. If a policy is not available, assess risks and exposures relevant to the situation.

- Verify whether users actively participate in program change or modification activities. Review the need for and extent of auditor and/or data processing quality assurance staff participation.

- Where the auditor could not participate in the software maintenance activities because of time and staff constraints, the auditor may wish to stratify program changes according to the number of hours required or spent (i.e., 10, 20, 40, 80, or 120) by the data processing staff (maintenance analyst, maintenance programmer, etc.) and take samples using judgmental or statistical sampling methods. Then the auditor performs three steps:

Step 1. Manually selects load/executable (object) programs whose length (indicated by the number of characters or bits) or address had changed between 1 and $1 + N$ time periods (where N = days or hours).

Step 2. Using generalized audit software or other report-writing software, lists any program library activity that had occurred against the correspondingly named source programs during the same time period as in Step 1.

Step 3. Determines whether the changes in source programs as indicated in Step 2 correspond to the authorized users' software change request forms.

The purpose of Steps 1 through 3 is to ensure that the object code in the production library is generated from the corresponding and correct version of source code; this is a major problem in the IT department and a major concern to the auditor.

- Determine whether each system/program revision or change is supported by a "request for change" form with proper management and user approvals.

- Determine whether each system/program revision or change is supported by adequate systems analysis and detailed design and/or written program specifications.

- Verify whether each system/program revision or change is supported by adequate testing and updating or system, program, user, help desk, network control, and computer operations documentation.

- Test to see whether system/program revisions or changes are made in the test library rather than in the production library. This is to prevent the destruction of production programs and data files during program changes and testing processes.

CONTROL RISK IN SOFTWARE MAINTENANCE

The applications programmer may have direct update access to the production application program and data files, although such access is logged and reviewed. The programmer may have the ability to move application program changes between test and production libraries without going through the designated program change control coordinator.

- Evaluate whether descriptions of system/program revisions or changes together with their effective dates are documented so that an accurate chronological record of the system is preserved.

- Determine whether a clearly identifiable and traceable audit trail is available for each program change or modification.

- Determine whether backup computer programs and files and documentation at off-site storage are kept current.

- Ascertain the need for the use of automated software tools to compare source code programs and/or object code programs at different points in time to detect possible unauthorized program changes or modifications.

- For critical and sensitive application systems, review computer programs manually to determine whether program changes or modifications are performed accurately and properly.

- Determine the need for the use of an automated program library system software tool to keep track of all activities (add, change, delete) to a computer program. Such a tool can facilitate detection of unauthorized program changes.

- Inquire whether a separate control group in the data center is responsible for planning and coordinating the manual procedures with the automated program library procedures in the areas of:

  - Developing and enforcing standard naming conventions to establish relationships between similar programs in different program libraries.

  - Developing formal procedures and forms explaining the authorization and approval levels required to transfer programs from test to production status and vice versa.

  - Requiring formal recording of program version numbers, effective dates, password protection levels, and name of the person making changes to provide an effective audit trail of program modifications.

  - Requiring a program turnover checklist to ensure that important steps or tasks are not omitted or forgotten

- Verify whether user sign-off or other written approvals have been obtained before moving program changes into production status.

- Evaluate whether all system/program revisions or changes are adequately handled in terms of user request, project planning, change analysis, programming, testing, documentation, and user final approvals.

- Ascertain whether it is advisable to completely redesign the application system instead of applying repeated small maintenance changes.

- Recommend developing and monitoring software metrics to increase the software development team's productivity and software quality.

Software Prototyping

Audit Objectives

- To ensure that potential risks and exposures resulting from incomplete or incorrect prototype goals, analysis, design, development, and testing are minimized, if not eliminated.

- To determine whether software usability, auditability, controllability, security, and maintainability requirements are properly addressed, either prior to or during prototype work, but prior to developing the final software product.

- To ensure that the final software product is not overcontrolled (oversecured) or undercontrolled (undersecured). A balance of controls and security is required.

- To ensure that functional users or data processors do not abuse the prototype approach to bypass certain activities (e.g., system development methodology, project management controls, documentation) that are still required, even in a prototype project environment. However, the degree of detail may vary.

Audit Procedures   The following audit work program is effective for the auditor. It should be used as a starting point and adjusted as needed. Some of the significant audit procedures are:

- Ascertain how a fourth-/fifth-generation programming language (4GL/5GL) is used and for what purpose. Do not include this system in the audit scope if: the 4GL or 5GL is used for developing a new and small application system for the benefit of a single user and/or single department or section for onetime use only, the system is not a critical or sensitive one, or the system is just an automation of a previously manual system. However, use professional skepticism because onetime-use systems often stay active a long time and continue to run in a production/operational mode. If these systems run in a production operational mode, then these system should be reviewed now or later by the auditor.

- Verify whether the programmer/analyst developing the prototype with the end user(s) is more people oriented than machine oriented and has good verbal communication skills as opposed to writing skills. Effective verbal skills are important in a prototype environment because of frequent interaction with the user. Confirm that the functional (end) user representative(s) has a comprehensive knowledge of the functions and capabilities of the department or section and can assess his or her department and system needs. Doing this is important for a successful prototype.

CONTROL/AUDIT RISKS IN SOFTWARE PROTOTYPING

- User attitudes and prototype developer attitudes may not be conducive to a good prototype development environment.

- Online system response time for the prototyped application system in the production environment may be degrading or excessive.

- Overall production system resource requirements may increase due to prototyped application system developed in programming languages that require excessive resources (e.g., CPU memory, disk space).

- Both end users and prototype developers may have mistaken or misguided preconceptions about the prototyping approach and its benefits, which could frustrate or disappoint all participants in the project.

- If end users develop prototypes and finally move them to production status without the involvement and participation of IT staff, report this to management and explain the consequences of such practices in terms of missing or inadequate audit trails, controls, and security features that the users may not have been aware of. Inquire whether computer operations or information center (IC) consultants reviewed the documentation of such systems and tested the software prior to moving it into production mode. Implementation controls and program version control are still needed for prototyping systems.

- Determine whether high-level systems analysis is conducted for prototyping systems prior to programming. Systems analysis is still needed even for prototyping systems, but the degree of detail may vary.

- Review the end user documentation manual or user's guide for the prototyped system that is being developed before it is moved into production status. Ascertain that it describes how to use the system, not what it does; that complex algorithms, calculations, tables, and codes are explained; and that the documentation is understandable and complete.

- Ascertain whether the prototype project team is considering controls (manual and/or automated), audit trails, and security features as a part of the prototype design.

- Suggest the saving of prototype programs with data files that were used to develop a model of the system. Future maintenance work can be performed more effectively using the same prototype to implement program changes and enhancements.

- Inquire whether backup and recovery procedures are included in the prototype system, regardless of who developed them (i.e., user or IT staff). This is to minimize the accidental or intentional destruction of data and program files. Inquire whether periodic backups are done and that disks that contain sensitive data and information are locked up at all times when not in use. This assumes that a personal computer (PC) is used for data entry, updating, and printing purposes. Inquire whether the PC has a security package to control users through a password and log all activities.

CONTROL/AUDIT RISKS IN SOFTWARE PROTOTYPING

- Software controls and security criteria may not have been addressed properly or were handled incompletely in the prototyped system and/or in the final system.

- System, computer operations, and user documentation may be inadequate, incorrect, incomplete, or unavailable for the prototyped system.

- Backup and recovery procedures may not have been addressed or may not be effective in the prototyped system.

- Walkthroughs, desk reviews, peer reviews, and independent inspections may have not been practiced.

- Data storage and file retention, backup, purging, archiving, and rotating procedures may not have been specified or adequate.

- System/data ownership and system usage responsibilities and accountabilities may not have been established and agreed on among multiple end users sharing the system and its results.

- Expand the audit scope when the prototype is planned to be developed exclusively by end users to fully or partly replace a production system that is a heavy-duty transaction processing application system (e.g., accounts payable, general ledger) and/or the system is sensitive from a financial and regulatory agency reporting requirements point of view. Notify management that the system is being developed by end users when it rightfully requires data processing staff expertise.

- A production application system can be developed using a 4GL/5GL, with parts in a 3GL (COBOL), or even a 2GL (BAL) programming language. If the 4GL/5GL portion of the system consumes a considerable amount of processing time and computer resources (e.g., main memory, disk and tape space) during its production runs, suggest ways to: redesign the most heavily used sections of the system, recode such sections as subroutines using COBOL or assembler programming languages, recode the entire system when the prototype does not represent all functions in the final system, or use modules of reusable code and change as needed.

End User Computing

Audit Objectives

- To ensure that end users develop application systems in a controlled and secured manner.

- To ensure those end users extract data files or download from host computer to micro-, mini-, or personal computer for further processing on a need-to-know basis.

- To ensure that EUC and processing work is performed according to the organization's EUC and processing guidelines.

Audit Procedures

- Inquire whether data processing and senior management have issued guidelines in EUC in the areas of system request, analysis, design, programming, testing, training, file conversion, documentation, backup and recovery, and program maintenance. Review these guidelines for relevancy and currency.

- Inquire whether EUC guidelines are issued regarding quality assurance standards and their enforcement. The standards should be verified by IC staff and others to certify and validate the system that is being developed. These standards include documentation guidelines: file descriptions, comments in the program code, screen formats, terminal operating procedures, error messages, error correction procedures, complex formula explanations, and use of a data dictionary (DD).

AUDIT CHALLENGES IN END USER COMPUTING: IIA STUDY RESULTS

The IIA study on EUC identified seven challenges to organizations and auditors:

1. Understand the present use or impact of EUC.
2. Link EUC activities with business objectives.
3. Coordinate potentially synergistic EUC activities.
4. Ensure connectivity and interoperability.
5. Assist end user department managers and staff to identify business risks, control points, and benefits for adopting controls.
6. Implement the application selection and development methodology.
7. Expand audit programs to include EUC when significant financial or operational issues exist.

Source: Larry Rittenberg, Ann Senn, and Martin Bariff, *Audit and Control of End User Computing* (Altamonte Springs, FL: Institute of Internal Auditors Research Foundation, 1990).

- Inquire as to what types of application systems are developed by end users and understand their functions and purposes. Ascertain whether these systems can be better developed on mainframe or minicomputers as opposed to PCs. If these systems are financial or otherwise sensitive systems, review them to determine the adequacy of controls, security, audit trails, backup and recovery, and documentation.

- Verify whether the functional user initiates a project request form describing the problem with the current system, whether it is manual and/or automated; the scope and objectives of the new system; the known requirements of the proposed system; and the projected costs and benefits of the proposed system. Confirm whether the project request is approved by the user and IT management. If there is no project request document available, assess the potential risks and exposures resulting from an uncontrolled situation, where every user develops his or her own systems without management approval and without following standards.

- Determine whether end user–developed systems use a DD for standard data definitions and that the system includes controls in the form of data editing and validation routines, audit trails, and security features. Inquire whether all probable users were trained by user department staff, that the documentation developed by the users is complete, and that the system (prototype or not) is thoroughly tested by users and IC staff. This approach must be followed whether the system being considered is a production system or not.

- Inquire whether user-developed systems handle ad hoc query or data extracting from an existing database. If the systems do not, ascertain whether the IC staff reviews and certifies user-developed systems for adherence to quality assurance standards when the systems:

  - Involve the creation of a new database.

  - Are to become an integral part of one's job.

  - Are to be used by others.

  - Supply data and information to others for decision-making purposes.

- Understand the organization's standards regarding data security, integrity, and privacy. Inquire what types of security and access control functions are available in a multiuser microcomputer environment, using multiple systems, to minimize deliberate or accidental errors, irregularities, and omissions. Review the security policies and procedures manual to determine whether it addresses penalties for security violations.

  Ascertain whether uploading of data to a host computer is allowed. If so, ensure that passwords are used for accessing the host data and program files. If the user-developed system feeds data to a central database, review the data control procedures in terms of data preparation, data input, data editing, and validation routines to ensure that the data are accurate, consistent, authorized, current, and complete.

- Take a sample of completed systems. Review the documentation (systems and user) developed by end users for the application that they created. Assess its clarity, understandability, and completeness. The systems documentation, at a minimum, should include: system flowchart, system narrative of its functions, input forms, input and output screen layouts, output reports, and explanation of complex calculations and formulas. The user documentation, at a minimum, should include computer terminal operating procedures including backup and recovery procedures; job submission procedures; data downloading and uploading procedures; and data inquiry, updating, and printing procedures.

- Understand the security and access control mechanism in place. Determine whether passwords, lockwords, or other means are used to control access to data and program files residing in a PC as well as when accessing them through a PC when they are stored on a mainframe or minicomputer. Inquire whether the data and program files are uploaded or downloaded from the PC. Where the data are uploaded to a host computer, determine whether data editing and validation routines are in place prior to accepting the data from the PC. This is to prevent or minimize data contamination or data corruption in the host computer data files. Inquire whether a dial-up and callback procedure is practiced to detect unauthorized people trying to access the host computer from their mini- or microcomputer. Confirm whether the reports and screens generated by end users indicate the program number, name of the user who developed it, and his or her department for tracing and identification purposes.

CONTROL/AUDIT RISKS IN END USER–DEVELOPED SYSTEMS

- Information (audit) trails, controls, and security features may not be available in an end user–developed application system.

- Data storage and file retention, backup, purging, archiving, and rotating procedures may not be available or adequate.

- Documentation may be inadequate or incorrect.

- Backup and recovery procedures may not be available or effective in the application systems developed by end users.

- Program change controls may not be available or effective.

- Understand how user views or user profiles are established to access corporate or division data files from employee PCs. These profiles should define the data that the user ar authorized to access and/or extract for downloading to a PC from the host computer. Understand how downloading of data is performed in terms of:

☐ Accepting a user's data request entered via a PC.

☐ Verifying the user's right to access the requested data.

☐ Receiving the desired data.

☐ Formatting, converting, and transmitting the data to the PC.

■ Most mainframe computers use EBCDIC code for data transmission; most microcomputers use ASCII code. Most data communications software packages for mainframe computers use synchronous transmission; microcomputers use asynchronous transmission. Because of lack of standards in this area, error detection and correction is a problem during data transmission. Inquire whether the micro-to-mainframe link software package has error detection, automatic correction, or automatic retransmission features when text files are transferred from mainframe to microcomputers.

■ Ascertain who owns and maintains the application system. Understand whether the software maintainer is the same person as the developer. If it is not clear, determine appropriate risks and exposures. For small systems, it is preferable that the software maintainer and the developer be the same or to have a backup user knowledgeable in the system. Review program change control procedures to determine whether someone other than the maintainer (preferably another end user) reviews program code and other documents to ensure the accuracy of program change.

■ Inquire whether there is a policy stating that an application program or system developed by an employee using a PC or minicomputer on company time belongs to the organization and not to the employee. Ensure that all such programs/systems are residing in a central software library so that a backup is available, any changes made by one person will be known to others, and the same software can be used or shared by others to eliminate reinventing of the wheel.

■ Ascertain whether the organization's policy forbids its employees from copying the organization's software for personal use at home. Where employees take the organization's software to their homes, ascertain whether management has approved it.

■ If the application system is a purchased package from vendors, determine whether the vendor license agreement restricts the use of that software to a specific machine (hardware) or location. If so, inquire whether the vendor software is copied for use on other machines at other locations. (This is illegal.) Usually vendors exempt a software copy for backup from this restriction.

Assess potential risks and exposures to the organization in terms of legal suits brought by vendors as a result of illegal copying of copyrighted software. Ascertain whether the organization's policy and applicable laws state any punishments or penalties for doing such illegal acts.

■ Confirm whether multiple vendor hardware devices and software products are available. If so, determine whether they are compatible. If not, assess the potential risks and exposures. Some exposures are: lack of coordination between users; reinventing of wheels; increased learning curves; no common body of knowledge retained among users; problems with vendor support and training; data communication problems between PCs and the host computer and operating systems; and loss of price discounts for volume purchases and maintenance contracts.

SAMPLE AUDIT FINDINGS: WHAT WENT WRONG IN SYSTEMS DEVELOPMENT?

Audit Finding No. 1. Internal audit was asked to help implement a new customer information system by ensuring that conversion programs were functioning properly. The auditors wrote and ran programs that matched the old and new files and printed exceptions. Several conversion program errors were discovered and corrected. As a result of the audit work, greater reliance was placed on the conversion programs, and implementation time was reduced by four person-weeks.

Audit Finding No. 2. During a review of the customer information system file maintenance area, auditors noted that the only documentation for the control programs consisted of the programs themselves. And these were quite complicated.

It was suggested to the IS department that a statement describing these control programs would not only be excellent documentation but would provide a training tool for computer programmers. In addition, a copy of the test file, developed by the IT audit staff, was turned over to IS department for use in conducting independent tests of the system.

Audit Finding No. 3. During an audit of a vendor-supplied and remote online computer system, the auditor noted the contract specified that user access to the computer system was guaranteed for a total number of hours per day. The auditor pointed out that this would be meaningless because the contract failed to include any performance standards, such as maximum acceptable terminal response times or the number of file accesses necessary to ensure that the required volume of work could be processed in the designated number of hours. As a result of the auditor's recommendations, tough performance standards for the vendor to meet were included in the new contract. Failure to meet the standards will result in heavy monetary penalties for the vendor, creating a great incentive to provide acceptable service.

Audit Finding No. 4. A company's sales incentive plan is complicated by the many incentive earnings determinants based on product type, product profitability, and sales volume. Incentive penalties are also provided. Using a computer program greatly facilitates the calculation of each salesperson's incentive earnings.

The IT auditors employed an audit retrieval program to test the accuracy of computer calculations under various conditions. As a consequence, the auditors found that in the process of amending the program, the company's programmers had inadvertently changed the program so that incentive penalties were no longer calculated and charged to salespeople.

Overpayments to salespeople totaling significant amounts were recovered, and procedures were strengthened to guard against unauthorized and/or improper changes in financially sensitive computer programs.

(Q) Data and Network Communications and Connections: Audit Objectives and Procedures Reviewing controls and procedures in a data and network communication environment is technical in nature and is challenging for the auditor. The auditor should take a business approach instead of a technical approach. Technical assistance should be requested where necessary to supplement the auditor's knowledge and experience in this area. The trend in telecommunications usage is growing as the demand for network interoperability is increasing.

Data Communications

Audit Objectives

- To evaluate controls over data communication messages.
- To evaluate controls over data communications software.

Audit Procedures

- Determine whether input and output messages contain sequence numbers. If not, ascertain how messages are controlled.

- Verify whether each message destination is a valid and authorized point in the network.

- Verify that the system acknowledges the successful or unsuccessful transmission and/or receipt of all messages.

- When the data communication network allows incoming dial-up connection, determine whether telephone numbers are changed regularly, kept confidential, and not posted in the computer room.

- For data entry involving network communications, determine that messages are transmitted and logged properly to reduce the risk of loss and that each message is identified as to terminal with a message sequence number and user or operator password number.

- Verify that the number of messages transmitted equals the number of messages received.

- Data communications software supporting online application systems contains control program modules. These control program modules provide the interfaces between the online application systems and the operating system. Each control program module performs a specific function, such as sending and receiving of terminal messages, obtaining working storage, and loading the application program(s) needed to process each transaction.

Some reviews and tests that can be performed for data communications systems software follow.

- Determine whether accurate and current system initialization tables are used in the production processing.

- Ascertain whether adequate and effective written procedures exist to back up vendor-supplied libraries and source libraries, and verify whether these libraries are protected by appropriate security codes using multiple-level passwords.

- Review user-created tables, such as sign-on tables, to determine whether user- or operator-entered security codes are authorized and matched with the codes established in the security tables.

- Review terminal control tables to determine whether transaction coding restricts terminals to specific transaction types, time of the day, and day of the week.

- Verify whether each user is assigned a unique sign-on system of identification code and password.

- Ascertain that an adequate audit trail in the form of a transaction history file is maintained and available for printing to review for authorized accesses and unauthorized attempts.

- Review authorization levels for table updating for tables, such as terminal control, program control, file control, sign-on, and system initialization. Assess their appropriateness.

CONTROL/AUDIT RISKS IN DATA COMMUNICATIONS

- System options and parameters (e.g., maximum sessions, maximum users, terminal time-out, terminal inactivity period, error recovery) may not be set up properly, which could affect system performance.

- Not all terminals may be defined to the session manager software, thus risking unauthorized use.

- System default values (undefined users, number of attempts to unlock a locked session, maximum concurrent applications per user) may not be set up properly in order to minimize system overhead and performance degradation problems.

- Who can override default values and parameters, who can update system option tables, and who can access system commands may not be defined clearly, or too many individuals may be defined.

Network Management Systems

Audit Objectives

- To review the adequacy of administrative procedures.
- To assess the effectiveness of the configuration management function.
- To assess the effectiveness of the network security function.
- To assess the adequacy of the terminal expansion system and performance management software.

Audit Procedures

1. **Administration.** The auditor concerned about the adequacy of controls over telecommunications and network facilities should conduct these reviews and tests:

   □ Obtain a copy of organization chart for the telecommunications and network function. Determine whether job descriptions are current and that they reflect actual practices.

   □ Inquire whether segregation of duties is available among computer operations, data security, systems programming, application programming, and network control group.

   □ Understand the type of network services being used. Basically, there are three types: (1) dial-up, which is used to connect terminals from all points; (2) leased line, which is used to connect terminals from one point to another; and (3) microwave, in which data are transmitted by satellite. Leased lines are better from a security standpoint than a dial-up approach.

   □ Take an inventory of data circuits, both incoming and outgoing, and communications equipment and software. Confirm that the organization is paying only for items that are being used.

   □ Identify physical security and controls over data circuits and communications equipment and facilities. Recommend improvements if needed.

   □ Take an inventory of terminals. Determine whether a log is maintained showing: the location of terminals and hours of use; types of transactions entered, updated, and inquired; terminal model number; whether owned or leased; and the last time the terminal was serviced. Inquire whether transactions can be limited to certain terminals and certain times of the day. Recommend improvements if needed.

☐ Inquire whether the network control group monitors terminal and network usage in terms of hours of use and unusual low- and high-usage patterns. Ascertain whether security violations are reported for corrective action.

☐ Review network traffic volumes for identifying trends. Determine whether there is a need for alternative forms of transmission (e.g., half duplex versus full duplex).

☐ Inquire whether network-balancing procedures are being practiced periodically to reduce the excessive load or stress on the system. This can be checked by reviewing the circuit usage and rerouting the traffic volumes during peak usage.

☐ Ascertain whether terminal response time is reasonable. Identify causes for low response and suggest improvements.

☐ Determine whether backup and recovery procedures for the network are included in the organization's contingency planning document and that these procedures are tested periodically.

☐ Inquire whether a telecommunications analyst participates in the application system development and maintenance processes for online and distributed processing systems. The role of the telecommunications analyst is to: review network and load requirements in terms of current and future transaction volumes, and their impact on terminal response time and network throughput rate; recommend network balancing procedures and improvements; and develop a telecommunications manual for users, computer operations, and others.

CONTROL RISK IN NETWORK ADMINISTRATION

The telecommunications analyst may have the ability to change telecommunications software and hardware without going through the designated program change control coordinator and without using the problem/change management system.

■ With the use of audit software or other means and by accessing automated system log records (e.g., telecommunications logs, job accounting logs), determine: connect time, type, and volume of transactions transmitted; and inactive and low- and high-volume users. Confirm findings and recommend improvements if needed.

2. **Network configuration management.** Determine the adequacy of network configuration management procedures for the next situations.

☐ When network components malfunction

☐ When network components are withdrawn from service for replacement, repair, or periodic maintenance

☐ When nodes are added to or removed from networks either temporarily or permanently

CONTROL/AUDIT RISKS IN NETWORK CONFIGURATION

■ Node numbers may be duplicated, which makes problem determination and isolation difficult.

■ Double cables may not be used, although they provide greater protection of critical links and nodes.

■ Network testing and network management procedures may vary from department to department.

■ Network testing facilities from remote sites may not be available.

Confirm that network management has adequate procedures to:

☐ Diagnose and remedy performance degradation problems in order to provide quality and reliable service to system users.

☐ Assist value-added network (VAN) service providers in terms of accounting capabilities to support billing for services

---

CONTROL/AUDIT RISKS IN NETWORK MANAGEMENT

- Network management may adopt a reactive approach, waiting for something to break down before taking any action. A proactive method of testing network equipment on a regular basis would be better.

- Network equipment may not have been tested end to end before it becomes operational. End-to-end testing means both the user organization and the vendor organization test the network from their respective sides.

- Monitoring of the entire network configuration would be more efficient from one console instead of several.

It is difficult to control and maintain large and varied computer networks and to diagnose network-related outages with traditional software or using manual methods. Determine whether expert system–based network problem management systems software is available to diagnose and report network-related outages across multiple and dissimilar networks. Knowledge-based modules correlate, format, prioritize, and present network problems and recommend corrective action in a standard method. Specifically, ascertain whether the knowledge-based system

☐ Produces alerts	☐ Displays alarms
☐ Indicates troubles	☐ Notifies failures
☐ Tracks problems	☐ Produces reports

3. **Network security.** Determine whether access can be restricted to a specific time of the day with automatic time zone adjustment.

☐ Confirm that access can be restricted to a specific day of the week.

☐ Ensure that terminal locking is provided for users who must leave their terminals.

☐ Ensure that terminal time-out is available to protect abandoned terminals.

☐ Ensure that a user ID and password are required to reconnect a session.

CONTROL RISKS IN NETWORK SECURITY

The network operator may be given access to sensitive and powerful network commands and parameters. Unauthorized connections to business application systems could occur. Access control security could be circumvented.

---

4. **Network terminal expansion system.** Determine whether the terminal expansion system has the ability to:

☐ Produce an audible alarm when changes occur in a hidden session.

☐ Provide duplex support, which allows concurrent access to a single session from two physical terminals.

□ Add, drop, or redefine logical terminals to the system.

□ Lock dedicated terminals into specific session profiles.

□ Initiate the first logical session automatically.

   Determine whether network performance management software:

□ Measure network component response time down to the terminal level.

□ Build log files continuously as events occur.

□ Provide threshold-driven, selective, online, and real-time network monitoring information.

□ Support network message and transaction tracing, display, and replay features.

□ Provide through network news facility the latest status for each application system.

□ Include network trend and capacity planning reports.

CONTROL/AUDIT RISKS IN NETWORK PERFORMANCE MANAGEMENT

■ Network performance management system standards may not be established to define the ability to: select the events, resources, or measures to be monitored; specify measures or resources to be polled and recorded; and specify the threshold level used to trigger the notification of a performance abnormality.

■ Simulation models may not be used to help determine the effect of network management on efficiency issues.

System Utility Programs

Audit Objective

■ To evaluate controls over system utility programs.

Audit Procedures   Interview systems programmers and application programmers to understand the controls in place to access and use powerful and critical system utility programs. A combination of control procedures is suggested prior to the use of powerful utility programs. Conduct the next audit procedures to ensure that utility programs are properly controlled:

■ Determine whether powerful utility programs are removed from disk magnetic media and copied onto a tape or cartridge for later use.

■ Inquire whether powerful utility programs are renamed so only a few authorized people know of their existence.

■ Ascertain whether a separate password is required to access and use these powerful utility programs.

■ Examine whether formal approvals with documented procedures and forms are required prior to use.

Local Area Networks

Audit Objectives

■ To determine the adequacy of security controls over local area networks (LANs).

■ To determine the adequacy of integrity controls over LANs.

Audit Procedures

- Determine who is responsible for the day-to-day operation of the LAN system.

- Verify that written procedures are available to use and operate the LAN- based application system.

- Identify who is responsible for updating the LAN system user procedures, and confirm the responsibility with that person.

- Verify that each user has his or her own log-on ID and password and that no group passwords are being used.

- Due to the added risk of shared data, determine if proper levels of security exist for that installation. Conduct these reviews or tests:

  □ Consult with management and determine if there is additional need to protect individual files and databases and also data records, data fields, and even byte level in a data field.

  □ Ascertain whether there is a need for data encryption to protect sensitive and critical data and program files.

- Determine whether the network operating system provides the security features to:

  □ Create security groups and classes.

  □ Set account expiration dates and time restrictions.

  □ Lock account after multiple failed passwords.

  □ Designate intruder detect threshold.

  □ Set log-in count retention time.

  □ Impose mandatory password changes.

  □ Limit concurrent connections.

  □ Provide an option to allow or forbid a user to set password.

  □ Set minimum password length.

  □ Disable/lock accounts.

  □ Require unique passwords.

  □ Restrict to specified workstations.

  □ Automatically disconnect after specified inactive period.

- Confirm that the LAN administrator is the only person who can add or delete server names.

- Confirm that the LAN administrator is the only person who can approve the addition or removal of a node on the network.

- Confirm that end user management approves the addition or deletion of organizations, departments, work groups, or sections authorized to use the LAN system.

- Confirm that the "write verify" switch is not turned off to make the operating system run faster. Be aware that turning off the switch could compromise the integrity of data.

> ### BUSINESS/CONTROL RISKS IN LOCAL AREA NETWORKS
>
> - There may not be a backup person for the LAN administrator
>
> - The backup person, even though designated, may not have been trained adequately to take over the LAN administrator's job duties when needed.
>
> - Changes made to the LAN network may not be transparent to end users.

- Confirm that the LAN administrator is the only person who can set up and change server parameters, such as maximum:

  - Number of simultaneous users per server (e.g., 100, 1000, or unlimited).

  - Server volume size (e.g., expressed in megabytes [MG], gigabytes [GB], terabytes [TB], or unlimited).

  - Number of volumes (e.g., 10 or 32).

  - Number of shared printers per server (e.g., 5 or 10).

  - Number of open files on one server (e.g., 1,000 or 100,000).

- Inquire whether passwords are required to be changed periodically, unique, and of a minimum length; and have a limited number of **grace log-ins** allowed after expiration. (Grace log-ins are extra sign-ons allowed beyond password expiration time.)

- Ensure that passwords are sent down the wire in an encrypted form and that encryption is not turned off at the file server console.

- Ascertain whether the vendor-provided documentation is complete, well organized, and consistent. At a minimum, it should contain system administration, network supplements with protocol information, utility program references, system concepts, external bridge supplements, and system messages with help screens.

- Determine whether the LAN operating system provides this information:

  - Full logs on important file server activities

  - Long-term file server up-time, when it was shut down, and by whom

  - Bad blocks that had been found on the magnetic media, their locations, and where data was redirected to on the media

  - Protocol anomalies like router errors

  - Transaction tracking service

  - Warnings on low disk space, excessive bad password attempts, and notices such as printer out of paper

- Verify the existence of an effective, clear audit trail and that system user staff and management regularly review it.

- Determine whether the LAN administrator measures and tracks network problems and failures. Specifically, inquire whether these items are addressed:

  - Total number of network disabilities per month and year

  - Number of disabilities by single protocol

- ☐ Number of disabilities by multiple protocols
- ☐ Number of disabilities by network segment (i.e., Ethernet, token ring)
- ☐ Average number of hours lost per each disability
- ☐ Amount of damage suffered when the network is inoperable due to downtime, expressed as the number of dollars lost per hour; the loss can be expressed in lost productivity, lost revenue, or expenses for year

- Determine whether the LAN administrator monitors network performance with the use of network monitoring software or protocol analyzers. Specifically, inquire whether these traffic counts and other items are addressed:

- ☐ Number of error packets, including cyclic redundancy check, alignment, short and long packets
- ☐ Number of workstations: total, active
- ☐ Protocol usage: average, current
- ☐ Packet size distribution
- ☐ Test results for cable breaks on a network
- ☐ Line echo tests
- ☐ Number of frames and bytes: total, current
- ☐ Frames or bytes per second
- ☐ Average frame size
- ☐ Summary statistics on network use over a period of time (filtered and unfiltered network load), displaying average, peak, and error activity

- Confirm that the LAN file management utility programs are used to provide users and supervisors with the ability to restrict files as well as directories. Examples of file attributes include archive needed, copy and delete inhibit, execute only, hidden, indexed, purge, read and write, read only/read write, and shareable. Ensure that supervisors can set up work group managers over disk volumes instead of the whole system.

- Determine whether error-checking routines are available in the wireless LANs and whether security controls can be exercised. Encryption may be necessary as well as implementation of transmission in different channels.

Value-Added Network

Audit Objective

- To ensure that VAN services are meeting business needs.

Audit Procedures

- Review VAN services, such as access to the Internet, EDI applications, and dial-in services for proper security and use.
- Review protocols used in the VAN network and determine whether they are properly configured.

Wide Area Network

Audit Objective

- To ensure that wide area network (WAN) services are meeting business needs.

Audit Procedures

- Determine whether WAN devices, such as bridges, repeaters, routers, and switches, are properly protected from logical and physical security viewpoints.
- Review protocols used in the WAN network and determine whether they are properly configured.

Network Changes

Audit Objectives

- To evaluate the network change procedures.
- To assess the adequacy of network change controls.

Audit Procedures

- Take a sample of changes implemented in the operating system, database system, network operating system, and network management system, and determine the impact of such changes on the access control security systems software. Confirm all such changes are documented, tested, and approved.

    Similarly, take a sample of all changes made to security systems software, and ensure they are recorded in a manual or automated log with request forms approved.

CONTROL/AUDIT RISKS IN NETWORK CHANGES

- Unauthorized individuals can add or delete a network node.
- Unauthorized individuals can change a node from active to inactive status and vice versa.
- Passwords may not be required to access communications control facility.

- Take a sample of network change requests. Determine the elapsed time between the change request date and the completion date. Compare the elapsed time with the stated goal. Understand the reasons for excessive delays and suggest alternatives for improvement.

SAMPLE AUDIT FINDINGS: WHAT WENT WRONG IN TELECOMMUNICAITONS AND NETWORKS?

Audit Finding No. 1. The internal audit department was reviewing expenses for transmitting data across a nationwide network to terminals at remote office. A comparison of all in-service terminals against the supplier's invoices disclosed that many of the terminals charged for having been in service had, in fact, been disconnected. After obtaining copies of requests for disconnection to substantiate the dates, the internal auditor and senior management of the company visited the supplier to discuss this discrepancy. The discussion resulted in the supplier reimbursing the company a significant amount in retroactive billing adjustments.   *(continued)*

SAMPLE AUDIT FINDINGS: WHAT WENT WRONG IN TELECOMMUNICAITONS AND NETWORKS? *(Continued)*

Audit Finding No. 2. During the audit of telephone usage, the auditors found that employees call direct instead of using wide-area telephone systems (WATS) lines because of convenience. The auditors also found that employees who required a lot of long-distance calls for their work did not have direct access to the WATS lines and had to make long-distance calls through the office switchboard operator. Other employees had direct access, but many of them did not know how to use WATS, and they also placed long-distance calls through the switchboard operator.

The auditor recommended that more WATS-access lines are installed and a WATS-training program is developed. The adoption of these recommendations resulted in a 25% decrease in long-distance telephone costs and a 29% increase in the use of the WATS lines.

Source: E. Theodore Keys, Jr., ed., *The Round Table, How to Save Millions* (Altamonte Springs, FL: IIA, 1988).

(R) Voice Communications: Audit Objectives and Procedures

Audit Objectives

- To ensure that all risks and opportunities in using voice communications are fully understood before implementation.
- To ensure that quality of service issues, such as latency, jitters, packet losses, and bandwidth congestion, are understood.
- To ensure that proper controls are in place over voice mail to prevent toll fraud.

Audit Procedures

- Determine whether all risks and opportunities in using voice communications are documented and distributed.
- Determine whether small packets, as opposed to large packets, are transmitted through the voice network to reduce latency and bandwidth congestion.
- Determine whether forward error correction and packet loss concealment schemes are implemented to reduce loss of packets.
- Determine whether header compression techniques are implemented to reduce jitters.
- Determine whether controls such as personal identification numbers (PINs) to voice mailboxes are periodically changed, that all unused or unassigned mailboxes are removed, that collect calls are restricted, and that telephone bills are reviewed.

(S) System Security
System security or logical security is divided into two categories: software security and data security. Within software security, implementation of logical access control (external) security software is discussed first. Then general audit procedures for security controls over systems software, applications software, data communications software, and computer terminals are presented. Firewalls work well with logical security. Physical access security and environmental controls are also discussed as part of the systems security.

Software Security Controls Review: Access Control Security Software Review—Audit Objectives and Procedures

Audit Objectives

- To determine whether options and parameters selected in the access control security software are relevant and useful.

- To ensure user profiles established for the IT staff and functional users for accessing program files are relevant and current.

- To ensure system libraries and user exits are controlled properly.

- To determine whether security software is adequately protected, including related tables.

- To ensure configuration management is properly handled with respect to security.

Audit Procedures

A. Implementation of logical access control security software

1. **Control options and parameters.** In order to evaluate the options and parameters selected in the access control security systems software, the next audit procedures are suggested:

   □ Obtain a printout of currently used system options and parameters. Some options control the various logging functions, access class protection functions, security modeling functions, and password functions.

   □ Review the option settings to be sure no integrity exposures exist.

   □ Determine if the password rules and options are adequate to ensure integrity and confidentiality of passwords.

   □ Verify access to tape data sets is controlled by security software. Ensure that the tape bypass label processing option is under the control of security software.

   □ Verify that control over passwords is properly exercised.

   □ Verify that all disk data sets are protected through the security software.

   □ Verify that all other required options are properly selected.

2. **Interface validations.** In order to determine if security software performs appropriate validations for interface systems, the next audit procedures are suggested.

   □ Review the table to verify that no unnecessary access is given to sensitive or critical data sets.

   □ Verify that the online teleprocessing monitor is properly controlled through security software in terms of access to sign-on tables, key parameters, files, transactions, records, and programs.

   □ Verify that the DBMS is properly controlled through security software in terms of tasks, programs, subschemas, and control areas.

   □ Verify whether security software controls online programming and development facilities to limit access to critical and sensitive commands and options.

   □ Verify that the interfaces between security software and other systems software products are properly controlled by examining the interfaces and determining if security software is called for validations of every sign-on attempt.

   □ Determine whether online programming facility users defined in the system library are also defined to the security systems software. Evaluate the reasons for any user not being defined to the security system.

AUDIT/CONTROL RISKS IN EXTERNAL SECURITY SOFTWARE

The computer operator may have the option of making the external security software inactive at the time of initial program load.

3. **Data ownership and separation of storage resources.** In order to determine who owns the data and to evaluate the separation of storage resources, the next audit procedures are suggested.

   □ Enter the critical commands from the master console and review the listings for appropriate information.

   □ Determine who owns all system disk volumes. Assess whether the ownership is authorized.

   □ Determine ownership of all disk/tape data sets by data set name prefix. Assess whether the ownership is authorized.

   □ Review the list of all volume profiles and determine that adequate separation of data volumes exist among the various storage media.

4. **Access security rules.** In order to ensure the design and structure of access security rules and user profiles are proper, the next audit procedures are suggested.

   □ Verify that the log-on IDs used for production jobs are properly defined.

   □ Verify that the security database is efficiently and effectively organized from most general to most specific levels of hierarchy.

5. **System and user exits.** To ensure that all operating system and user exits in the security software are properly documented and controlled, the next audit procedures are suggested.

   □ Identify all active operating system and user exits.

   □ Determine what security software exits are used. These exits can control data set naming corrections and password duplication.

   □ Request and examine source code for each active exit for the presence of comments.

   □ Evaluate whether these exits are properly controlled.

   □ Determine that exit usage is well documented as to its purpose and its effect on the system.

6. **Sensitive privileges.** To ensure that security rules appropriately restrict sensitive privileges, data sets, and utility programs, the next audit procedures are suggested.

   □ Verify that sensitive privileges are given only to those who need them.

   □ Verify that only security administrators at both central and local computer centers have these privileges.

   □ Obtain the data set names for the two or three critical application system master files, and verify that these sensitive data sets are adequately protected.

   □ Verify that sensitive utility programs are appropriately restricted. These programs can bypass security validations. Determine whether these utility programs are specified as usable only out of a controlled library by a specific log-on ID.

7. **Protection over programs and libraries.** The next audit procedures are suggested to ensure important programs and libraries are secured.

   □ Determine who has bypass privileges.

   □ Determine if all sensitive programs and libraries are properly protected.

   □ Determine if there are any unprotected data sets.

8. **Access controls over production libraries.** In order to determine whether adequate protection exists for system and production libraries, the next audit procedures are suggested.

   □ Obtain a copy of the data set report. Determine if adequate protection exists for the critical application system production data sets.

   □ Run data set profile listings on all critical application system for data sets with high-level qualifiers. Determine if a generic code exists for the high-level qualifier to accommodate all data set names not otherwise covered under discretes or qualified generic profiles.

   □ Determine which disk data sets are defined to the security software. This is a critical audit procedures in the review of either an application or a data center.

   □ Determine which rights users are granted to data sets. For example, update or alter access to the production job control. Ensure that program libraries are limited to a few individuals.

   □ Determine what statistics are being kept for analyzing access practices.

   □ Determine what audit records are being logged to the system logging facility. Determine whether records are maintained for successes and failure access attempts, which can later be reported by either write or read accesses.

   □ Verify when the passwords were last changed and what the password change interval is for each user.

9. **System logging of events.** In order to ensure all required system records are being logged, the next audit procedures are suggested.

   □ Examine the system logging facility parameters to determine if a computer operator can turn off recording.

☐ Verify that the system logs these records:

- Unauthorized attempts to enter the system
- Authorized and unauthorized attempts to access system-protected resources.
- Authorized and unauthorized attempts to modify profiles on data sets or users
- Names of each security data set and the data set volume ID

CONTROL RISKS IN ACTIVITY LOGGING

- Security control procedures could be lax in terms of who can add or delete authorized libraries or who can add, delete, or modify programs in an authorized library.

- Vendor security software may not protect the operating system–based started tasks, system activity logging data sets, system volumes, generation data group records, deletion of user catalogs, and modification and deletion of master catalogs.

- The system logging journal contents may be partially or totally lost in a disk/system crash caused accidentally (e.g., by a power failure to a volatile storage device) or deliberately (e.g., by someone trying to avoid detection).

- Logging of important security violation records produced by the external security software may have been suppressed, allowing security breaches to go unnoticed.

☐ Ensure that changes to the security database file are captured in the recovery and logging file.

☐ Determine which reports are being generated from the security software. Inquire how many of these reports are reviewed by the security administrator.

10. **Operational procedures.** In order to ensure proper operational procedures are in place, working, and documented, the next audit procedures are suggested.

☐ Obtain a copy of security software recovery procedures and review them for adequacy. Inquire whether these recovery procedures were tested to make sure they would work if needed.

☐ Obtain a copy of procedures used to define security software exit specifications. Exit specifications should be developed by the data security function and actual program code developed by the technical services/support function. If no procedures exist, obtain a copy of exit specifications for the current exits and the test plan and sign-off by the data security function.

11. **Controls over security administration.** To ensure the security administration function is properly controlled, the next audit procedures are suggested.

☐ Determine whether documented procedures are available.

☐ Ensure that all terminated employees are no longer active in the security system.

☐ Obtain a listing from security software showing who has the ability to update the security database. Verify that proper request forms are in place to request addition, deletion, and change of users in the security system.

☐ Ensure the user verification process uniquely identifies each user to the system and the resources he can access.

12. **Administrative procedures.** In order to ensure proper administrative procedures are in place, working, and documented, the next audit procedures are suggested.

   ☐ Determine the adequacy of procedures for accessing the security database and application systems in production status during normal and emergency situations.

   ☐ Obtain a copy of procedures used to review security violation of protected production data sets. Verify that these procedures include a daily review of production data set violations.

   ☐ Obtain a copy of security violation follow-up procedures to ensure violations are properly handled once identified. These violations should include determination of type of violation, severity, and written response requirements based on type and security of violation.

   ☐ Test the security system's decentralization of administrative function for adequacy. Determine if the scope of authority for the decentralized administrative function includes only their data.

   ☐ Determine whether the security/console log is being printed, reviewed, and initialed on a daily basis.

   ☐ Evaluate whether an access control security package is implemented and operated properly to control access to data files, whether database or nondatabase.

13. **Audit trails and reports.** To ensure that all critical audit trail reports, utility programs, and security reports are defined and utilized, the next audit procedures are suggested.

   • Prepare a work paper schedule listing all critical reports and utility programs.

   • Compare the schedule to actual reports and utility programs used, noting any problems and exceptions.

   • Inquire whether data security staff and management review all major security violations and audit trail reports and that they follow up on major problems.

B. General audit procedures for security over systems software
Conduct these reviews and/or tests for security over systems software.

■ Determine whether management policies and procedures regarding the access to and use of computer programs have been disseminated.

■ Determine whether one or more of the following identification and authentication techniques (a type of combination controls) are used prior to accessing system resources and facilities:

   ☐ Hand-held password-generating devices

   ☐ Multiple-level passwords

   ☐ ID cards and badges (electronic or mechanical: smart cards or magnetic stripe cards)

   ☐ Reading of eyes

   ☐ Reading signature, thumbprint, or palmprint

   ☐ Voice recognition

   ☐ Other personal information not easily known to others, such as maiden name, mother-in-law's or father-in-law's name

   ☐ Data encryption and scrambling techniques

- Determine whether adequate and clear "electronic separation of duties" is maintained in the application system by establishing password–person–program–terminal–transaction activity matrix relationships. Some examples of transaction activity in computer programs are read only, add, delete, and modify.

- For installations using program library management systems software, ascertain whether data processing management has selected proper default options and indeed is making use of all appropriate control features included in the vendor software. Ascertain the reasons for nonselection of any control features. Ensure that the library management systems software updates and controls both source and object code program libraries; reports all changes, additions, and deletions; and saves prior versions.

- Determine the existence of (or need for) a separate control group to develop, maintain, and control manual procedures and standards required to integrate with library management system procedures. Ascertain whether all program changes are approved and monitored by this control group. Verify whether a program turnover checklist is prepared and followed effectively.

- Ascertain whether only authorized IT staff and IT audit staff are using sensitive utility programs only as required for approved/authorized functions. This is to eliminate the potential misuse of powerful utility programs (e.g., DITTO, SuperZap in the IBM mainframe environment) to bypass or override controls in the application or operating system.

AUDIT/CONTROL RISK IN UTILITY PROGRAMS

External security software may not protect powerful utility programs, such as the tape initialization program that can destroy tape labels and tape contents and the utility program that can modify the contents of an operating system or application program.

- Verify whether a manual log describing the reasons for and use of utility programs with control override features is maintained and reviewed by management.

- For installations using program library management systems software with multiple program libraries, obtain a printout of the VTOC for all volumes existing in the system.

- Ascertain whether library and program names and cataloging procedures conform to established standards. This is to ensure there are no duplicate program names between and within the libraries. Review program change procedures in effect for each type of library, and evaluate the controls practiced to prevent incorrect program versions from being placed into production status. Review the library problem and incident log and evaluate the corrective actions taken.

- For installations having no automated program library systems software, determine if there is a need for it to control updating of both source and object code program libraries, to report all program changes and program version numbers, and to archive prior versions.

AUDIT/CONTROL RISKS IN PROGRAMMING

- Application programmers may be given the ability to transfer programs between test and production libraries once the development or maintenance work has been completed. In fact, the operations staff or quality assurance staff should be performing such transfers.

- Unauthorized libraries could be present.

- Unauthorized personnel may purge security rule tables or change security options and parameters for their own benefit.

- Actions of systems programmers may not be auditable at all or may be difficult to audit.

- Enter a few innocent or null unauthorized processing jobs and determine whether they are purged from the system. Select a few authorized production jobs and determine whether job priority classes can be changed. Assess the appropriate risks and exposures.

- Review the adequacy of security features, such as backup, restart, rerun, and recovery procedures, for a few critical application systems.

C. General audit procedures for security over applications software

1. **General access controls.** Interview the data security officer or person in charge of the security administration function, assess the following issues, and note any exceptions for improvement:

   □ Access to all application programs in the production operations environment should be limited to only the programmers responsible for maintaining them, and access privilege rules should be defined in terms of who can read, write, copy, rename, allocate, execute, catalog, delete, and change.

   □ Sensitive and critical application programs have restricted rules, such as execute only. Read and copy commands should not be permitted by anyone except the authorized maintenance programmer. Access to such programs should be allowed only at certain times of day and certain days of the week.

   □ All versions of programs, whether new or renamed, should receive the same kind of access control protection at all times.

AUDIT/CONTROL RISKS IN INSIDERS AND OUTSIDERS

- A skilled penetrator could disable or bypass the audit and security mechanisms so his work is undetected.

- Insiders are the most risky when compared to outsiders from a security point of view. They are often shielded by the informal trust system.

- Data input and update areas are the most common places for conducting illegal activities such as fraud and theft.

   □ System and program documentation manuals should be reasonably protected from unauthorized use.

   □ For both database and nondatabase application systems, a log file should be maintained to post each transaction or, alternately, an image of the transaction record both before and after it is updated in the master file. The log file can be used to back-out transactions, back up transactions, and facilitate recovery and restart processing.

   □ For application systems involving input data collection or data entry activities through point-of-sale, automatic teller machines, or touch-tone telephone media, incoming data are recorded on mirrored disks (data stored simultaneously in at least two places and on two separate magnetic media).

2. **Access controls over production program changes.** Conduct the next audit procedures for assessing security controls over changes to production programs.

☐ Assess whether program change control procedures are in place. Inquire whether production operations or application system maintenance staff periodically calculate hash totals of characters or bit counts in production application programs to ensure that there are no unauthorized modifications that might represent computer-related fraud or some other types of abuse.

☐ Ask whether automated program library management software is in place or being contemplated. Verify whether password-type controls are used to access the library management software through which changes to applications software are made and logged. Determine the possibility of printing program changes (e.g., statement or code additions, deletions, or changes) as output from the library management software for programmer verification to ensure the accuracy of program changes.

3. **Audit testing of security controls.** Take a sample of application systems in production status. Interview the appropriate functional users and assess the next areas. Note any exceptions for improvements.

☐ An electronic separation of duties should be available using the access control security system and application system features. This includes restricting employees to functions such as add, change, delete, read, write, copy, rename, print, inquire, browse, and override errors. When such restrictions cannot be implemented, the transaction logging facility should be turned on.

☐ The access privileges granted to employees should be in line with their job descriptions, and all employees listed in the user profiles for an application system should be actively working for the organization.

☐ All sensitive blank input forms, such as purchase orders, invoices, blank checks, securities, and other negotiable documents, should be kept in a locked cabinet or similar storage to prevent unauthorized use.

☐ Employees should be encouraged to view reports via VDU/CRT terminals rather than automatically receiving hard-copy output. Not only does this approach save time and money involved in printing the report, but it also provides additional security because a password is required to print a computer report or to run a job.

☐ Sensitive computer and noncomputer reports should be marked or stamped as such and should receive appropriate protection when they are received from other departments or travel from one person to another within the company.

☐ All unused and expired reports, computer-generated and otherwise, should be destroyed by shredding, burning, or other means to protect data confidentiality and sensitivity.

☐ All required source documents, input forms, tax records, property records, contracts, and government-related documents should be retained according to the established guidelines. These should be cross-referenced to the department of origination, transaction activity period, and retention date. These records should be retrievable easily and rapidly. When a sample is taken from paper media, electronic media, or mechanical media, it should be possible to retrieve the required records by using an inventory list.

D. General audit procedures for security over data communications software
Conduct the next reviews and/or tests for security over data communications software.

■ To ensure the cryptographic device has not been corrupted or replaced with a bogus service, determine whether the host computer is required to authenticate itself to the cryptographic device (and vice versa). Similarly, determine whether a cryptographic device is required to authenticate itself to the user (and vice versa). This would amount to four separate authentication procedures that would have to be performed in order to implicitly authenticate the user to the host and vice versa.

■ When the data communication network allows incoming dial-up connection, determine whether telephone numbers are changed regularly, kept confidential, and not posted in the computer room.

■ Take an inventory of data communications network nodes, lines, and equipment and compare to inventory records. Note any exceptions.

AUDIT/CONTROL RISKS IN DATA COMMUNICATIONS

■ In a dial-up environment, the length of the access code may be too short (e.g., two or three characters) or the code may be one that is easily guessed.

■ A special prefix telephone number may not be used for dial-up lines. Sequential numbers help individuals guess other network access phone numbers.

■ The "help" function on a sign-on screen could be helping both authorized (legitimate) and unauthorized individuals.

■ The modem might have been set to activate after one or two rings so that hackers trying to guess at the phone number would succeed. Try five or six rings so that hackers will go to other target locations.

■ Each node may not be carefully protected to prevent access to another network node.

■ Network users may not be informed of the status of network resources.

■ Network component problems including application-related problems are not reported properly, correctly, and timely.

■ Unauthorized users and operators may have access to network software distribution and updating and network resources.

■ Ascertain whether the network hardware and software were changed to take advantage of price reductions and technical improvements.

■ Identify any physical security controls, such as locks and keys over the data communications hardware and related equipment.

E. General audit procedures for security over computer terminals
Conduct the next reviews and/or tests for security over computer terminals.

■ Determine whether management policies and procedures regarding the access to and use of terminals have been disseminated.

■ Ascertain whether written procedures are available for data entry, update, print, and inquiry activities performed through the use of terminals. Test their adequacy and currency.

■ Verify whether there is a dedicated printer or terminal assigned to receive all terminal security and access control violation messages. Review these messages for a selected time period and determine whether appropriate corrective actions were taken.

- Ascertain the frequency of password changes. Review the procedures and methods for assigning, scheduling, recording, and communicating password changes. Ensure that the password algorithm is sufficiently complex that it is not too obvious.

- Ascertain whether terminals have a nonprinting (display) feature when entering user or operator passwords to prevent observation of passwords by others.

- Conduct tests to determine whether terminals become inactive or inoperative after some (three) unsuccessful attempts to sign-on or some time (three minutes), whichever comes first.

- Verify whether each terminal user's identity and authorization levels are established in accordance with the data available from the terminal. Take an inventory of terminals with number of users with access levels. Identify the sensitivity and volume of data being handled and importance to the organization. Inquire whether these terminals are limited to certain hours per day, by the type of transaction entered, or by the location of the terminal.

- Ascertain whether terminals or other devices are authenticated to the computer system through some kind of identification code.

- Evaluate the overall procedures followed in controlling the physical access to computer terminals. Determine whether they are adequate.

Data Security Controls Review: Audit Objectives and Procedures

Audit Objectives

- To ensure user profiles established for the IT staff and functional users for accessing data files are relevant and current.

- To determine the adequacy of audit trails and reports, access controls over production libraries, system logging procedures, and granting of sensitive privileges, and to ensure data integrity.

Audit Procedures

1. **General procedures.** Conduct the next audit steps for obtaining a general understanding of controls and procedures that would affect data security.

   ☐ Determine whether management policies and procedures regarding the access to and use of computer data files have been disseminated.

   ☐ Inquire whether the owner of data is identified and who decides who, when, and for what purposes access is permitted to the owner's production data sets or files and programs. Inquire whether data are classified as highly critical, critical, noncritical, or by some other method.

   ☐ Take an inventory of critical data files. For each, identify:

      - Owner of the file, and criticality of the file.

      - The name of the application system that accepts this file as input or output.

      - Reasons for creating and maintaining the data file.

      - Security and backup requirements for this file.

      - Who can use and modify the file and any limits placed on the total space that can be dynamically allocated to a user so an equitable space allocation service can be provided to all users.

☐ Ascertain whether a tape librarian function monitors: issuances, returns, and storage of computer data files (backup tapes, magnetic disks, and optical disks); computer programs (applications and systems software); and documentation (system, program, computer operations, and user) manuals. Reconcile actual computer data files, computer program files, and documentation manuals to the inventory records or logs maintained by the tape librarian. Determine their accuracy, completeness, and currency.

☐ Verify whether maintenance procedures call for a regular cleaning and certification of magnetic tape files. Similarly, ensure disk files are tested periodically. Ascertain whether tape files are scratched or erased before cleaning and recertification. Magnetic tape files can be degaussed before disposition or cleaned by overwriting one time with any one character. Similarly, magnetic disk files can be cleaned by overwriting three times with numbers 1, 0, and any special character in that order.

☐ Where applicable, select a random sample of tape files to verify they contain **external labels**. Conduct tests to determine whether label contents are accurate.

CONTENTS OF AN EXTERNAL LABEL

External labels for tape files contain information such as job identification, file names as used by the program, tape density, creating program identification number, creation date, scratch date, or just reel numbers.

☐ Ascertain that internal file header and trailer records are verified by either operating system or application system.

☐ Verify whether computer data file retention periods agree with the requirements of government laws and regulations, other regulatory agencies, and established management policies and procedures. Ascertain that job accounting data or system logging data are retained at least six months at a detailed level and in a summary form after that time.

☐ Verify whether multiple users are sharing the database. Identify the primary and secondary users. Ascertain whether user conflicts exist regarding the use of data. Verify whether user conflicts are resolved properly and in a timely manner by the database administrator (DBA).

☐ For database systems, evaluate the adequacy of edit and validation rules applied to critical and sensitive data elements in the data dictionary (DD).

☐ For critical and sensitive data elements in database systems, trace key data elements through the application system by reviewing programs, data files, and reports. Determine their accuracy and consistency.

☐ Review issue and change practices for password and other system identification codes. Verify that passwords are issued on an individual employee basis, that their length is between 6 and 10 characters randomly generated in an alpha/numeric combination, that they would be difficult to guess, and that they do not contain obvious words, such as nicknames, pet names, or date of birth. Determine whether there is a combination of identification codes available (e.g., user ID and password, password and access card) instead of a single type of identification. Review password tables and determine whether they contain passwords for terminated employees.

☐ Determine whether adequate and clear electronic separation of duties is maintained in the application system by establishing password–person–data–terminal–transaction activity matrix relationships. A typical transaction activity could be to add, change, delete, update, inquire, and retrieve data from computer files. Verify with users whether these matrix relationships are actually followed. Identify any inadequacies and inconsistencies to ensure no single person has complete control and access over entire transaction processing activities. Determine the need for additional or compensating controls if existing controls are not adequate and effective.

☐ For installations having no automated file management systems software, determine if there is a need for access to computer data files to be controlled and to provide management, audit, processing, transaction, or information trails.

☐ Ensure that live data are not used for the testing of application systems.

☐ Determine whether production data are identified and either physically or logically segregated from designated test data by placing them in separate data libraries.

☐ Verify whether the backup procedures manual contains:

- Data set name, its owner, and the device name.

- Frequency of backup (daily, weekly, monthly), person responsible for backup, rotation scheme (grandfather–father–son or generation levels), and retention periods (six months, year).

- Backup media issue, return, and scratch procedures.

- Tape certification and cleaning procedures.

☐ Evaluate the overall procedures followed in controlling access to computer data files. Determine whether they are adequate.

2. **Data classification.** Conduct the next audit steps to evaluate the data classification system in place.

☐ Verify that policy and the procedures manual call for identification of sensitivity and criticality levels of data and protection of sensitive data from beginning to end.

☐ Determine whether users have classified data according to sensitivity and criticality levels (e.g., sensitive, confidential) and protect data according to classification scheme at various phases of the data life cycle. Identify whether document/file security protection levels match with the sensitivity and criticality levels.

☐ Where necessary, ensure data are classified as confidential, secret, top secret, sensitive, and so on; that those data files are internally or externally marked as such; and that access restrictions to those files are closely controlled and monitored.

3. **Database user profiles.** If there is a database function, interview the DBA to assess security-related controls over the use of database files.

☐ Ascertain whether user profiles or user views (subschemas of the database) are created for each user according to his or her job description.

☐ Determine whether an individual is given access privileges to data, such as the ability to add, change, delete, inquire, or browse, in a file according to his or her specific job functions.

☐ When a DD or directory is used, verify that access to it is restricted with passwords or by some other means.

☐ Determine whether before-and-after image reporting is available when functional users perform maintenance on database files.

4. **Data file maintenance reports.** Perform the next audit procedures for assessing the control procedures over data file maintenance activity.

☐ Take a sample of application systems that are subject to heavy file maintenance activity.

☐ Ask application system functional users whether, for changed data, they receive reports from the IT department showing old data values ("from") and new data values ("to") for each change to a data fields or data element, so they can verify the accuracy and completeness of manual and automated file maintenance procedures. Inquire whether users follow up on discrepancies.

☐ Look for the evidence of supervisory or employee review of file maintenance reports.

5. **Handling confidential data.** Conduct the next audit procedures to determine whether confidential data are handled properly.

☐ Check that during nonworking hours, sensitive information is locked in drawers, file cabinets, or vaults. Confidential information should be hand-delivered by messengers to addressees or to their designates. If the receiver is not present, it should be taken back to the sender or secured by the messenger. Color-coded envelopes can be used to signify the confidentiality of information. Confidential information should be controlled by encryption during transmission over telecommunication lines. Assess the adequacy of practices in these areas.

☐ Inquire how hard-copy computer reports, sensitive and confidential documents, and negotiable documents are protected during use and whether they are disposed of by shredding or other means so data cannot be retrieved by unauthorized persons. Ensure that paper is not simply put in trash cans, which would allow for possible misuse. Evaluate security controls over disposition of magnetic media (e.g., tape, cartridge, and disk) by making sure that old media are degaussed prior to being discarded.

6. **Statistical and exception reports.** Conduct the next audit procedures to analyze statistical data.

☐ Take a sample of audit tests using the system logging facility records to search for several occurrences of a record type, in a short period of time, with each occurrence using a different password or pattern of passwords. This could indicate attempted unauthorized access by a person trying to guess a password or trying to generate a string of passwords.

☐ With the help of report-writing facilities offered in the security systems software or other report writer, these **statistical reports** can be listed.

- Frequency of invalid password attempts by user ID

- Number and the type of warning indicators

- Activities of selected and high-risk users

- Persistent unauthorized use of system commands

- Number of times a password changed in a given time period

- Data files not protected by security access rules

Take a sample and ascertain whether these security violations are properly investigated and resolved in a timely manner.

☐ Ascertain whether resource access analysis reports are available to data security administration showing who is accessing what resources (e.g., data, programs, and printers). Categories of **security violations** include violations:

- This period
- By resource type
- By event type
- By event type for specific resources
- For top 10 or 15 users

☐ Determine whether data set access analysis reports are available to data security administration showing who is accessing which data sets. Categories of **security violations** include:

- Data set logging by reason
- Data set violation and logging for top 10 or 15 users based on number of violations
- Data set logging analysis showing logging patterns
- Data set event type analysis showing different accesses

☐ Develop **exception reports** indicating:

- The number of individuals having update access to production programs and data files.
- When security alarm messages are sent to terminals that have been enabled as security officer or operators.
- When security/audit journal logging took place due to occurrence of predefined audit events.

CONTROL/AUDIT RISKS IN DATA SECURITY

- Appropriate action may not be pursued when a security variance is reported to the system officer or to the perpetrating individual's supervisor. In fact, procedures addressing such occurrences may not exist.

- Management may rely on variance detection as the only safeguard. The objective of variance detection is to allow management to detect and react to departures from established rules and procedures it has determined may constitute hazards. Nevertheless, variance detection can be a very useful technique to encourage a general awareness of security and to discourage dishonest employee behavior. A combination of controls, such as variance detection combined with effective policies and procedures, could be useful.

Firewalls Review

Audit Objective   To determine whether firewalls are properly configured and placed in the organization at strategic locations.

Audit Procedures

☐ Review firewall configuration reports, and make sure that firewalls are properly placed in the organization.

- Understand the types of firewalls used, and ensure that they meet the business purpose.

- Understand the advantage and disadvantages of each firewall that is installed. Ensure that advantages outweigh the disadvantages. Assess any potential risks and exposures resulting from the review.

Physical Access Security and Environmental Controls Review

Similar to logical access controls, physical access security and environmental controls are important to ensure overall security in the data center.

Audit Objectives

- To determine the adequacy of physical access controls; housekeeping controls; and fire prevention, detection, and suppression procedures.

- To ensure that adequate physical security over the data processing installation, facilities, and computer center exists.

- To assess the protective procedures covering water damage, electricity, air conditioning, natural disasters, and other emergency situations.

Audit Procedures

1. **Physical access controls.** Tour the computer center, observe the area, and make notes and drawings (sketches) of the physical layout of the area under consideration. Conduct the next audit procedures to evaluate the adequacy of physical access security controls.

   - Verify whether entrance points are adequately controlled to prevent unauthorized access.

   - Identify whether a receptionist controls entrance to the computer center and if a positive identification, such as a photo badge, is required prior to being allowed inside.

   - If no receptionist is available, find out whether keys, cipher locks, combination locks, badge readers, or other mechanical or electronic security devices are used to control access to the computer center.

   - If access to the computer center is electrically controlled, ascertain whether a standby battery or generator is available during power failure. Make sure electronic access codes are changed periodically and that one or two people maintain them in confidence.

   - Look for security guards stationed at all major entrances to the computer center. Find out whether security guard services extend to 24 hours.

   - Understand the procedures required for allowing visitors into the computer center, and determine whether a log is maintained with vital information, such as name of the visitor, the organization the visitor is representing, purpose of the visit, the person to see, date and time of the arrival and departure, and whether the visitor is a citizen or not.

   - Inquire whether receptionists or security guards are trained to challenge improperly identified visitors.

   - Find out whether the location of the computer center is obvious through the building lobby entrance index board or signs that enable vandals to target it.

   - Inquire whether doors, locks, bolts, hinges, frames, and other building materials are constructed in such a way as to reduce the probability of unauthorized entry.

☐ Determine whether VDU/CRT terminal controllers in the computer room are adequately protected to prevent use of all terminals in the event of a disaster of any nature. A concentration of all terminal controllers in one area is **not** advised because of the adverse effect a disaster would have on all terminals connected to these controllers. Usually terminal controllers are placed in areas where they serve a group of terminals.

2. **Housekeeping controls.** Tour inside the computer center, observe the area, and make notes of impressions about housekeeping practices. The next audit procedures are suggested to assess housekeeping controls.

☐ Look for signs stating "no smoking," "no eating," and "no drinking," and find out whether they are conspicuously displayed so anybody would notice them.

☐ Observe whether tile floors are clean and are washed regularly to prevent accumulation of dust and dirt.

☐ Inquire whether carpeting cleaners and floor waxes are of antistatic nature to prevent static electricity from being generated.

☐ Ascertain whether trash and debris are accumulated in low-fire-hazard waste containers and that these containers are emptied outside the computer center to reduce dust discharge.

☐ Look for plastic sheets to cover the computer equipment in case of water discharge from the ceiling either due to normal water leakage or water sprinkler activation.

☐ Touch and feel the equipment and work surfaces to determine their degree of cleanliness. Small particles of dust can go into the equipment, which could damage electrical circuits and other internal parts. Similarly, examine reel tapes and unsealed disks.

☐ Inquire how often the surfaces beneath the raised floors are cleaned.

☐ Assess whether tile pullers are visible and available to computer operations, cleaning people, and others as needed.

☐ Inquire whether computer waste (forms, carbons, reports) are disposed of properly by burning, shredding, or other means to make them unreadable and unusable.

☐ Verify that all magnetic media storage (tapes, cassettes, diskettes) cabinets in the tape library are kept at a distance of 20 to 30 inches from an exterior wall to protect against the potential effects of magnetic fields or radiation.

3. **Fire prevention, detection, and suppression procedures.** Interview the computer center manager, building maintenance engineer, and others as required to understand fire prevention, detection, and suppression techniques available. Conduct the next audit procedures to evaluate fire prevention, detection, and suppression procedures and controls.

☐ Inquire whether the computer room is separated from adjacent areas by noncombustible or fire-resistant partitions, walls, floors, and doors.

☐ Ascertain that raised floors, suspended ceilings, carpets, furniture, and window coverings are made of noncombustible materials.

☐ Look for paper stock and combustible supplies, such as toners, cleaners, and other chemicals, and observe whether they are stored outside the computer room area.

☐ Determine whether computer operations staff is trained in firefighting techniques and assigned individual responsibilities in case of fire.

☐ Determine the type of **fire, smoke detection, and extinguishing devices** used, and procedures in place to protect the data center from accidental or deliberate damage due to physical or natural hazards. Verify that carbon dioxide or halon fire extinguishers of proper capacity are available for use on electrical fires and that water-type fire extinguishers are available for use on nonelectrical fires. Inquire whether the data center is protected by automatic fire extinguishing systems. If so, conduct these audit steps:

- If water sprinklers are used, find out whether their activation will sound an alarm and if there is a delay in the release of water in order to prepare for the emergency incident.

- If a halon sprinkler is used, inquire how long it takes to evacuate the area.

- If a carbon dioxide sprinkler is used, inquire whether required people were given proper safety precautions to address carbon dioxide discharge.

☐ Assess whether portable fire extinguishers are placed strategically around the data center with location markers visible, that they are tested periodically, and that people are trained in using them.

☐ Inquire whether a **shutdown checklist** is available. Find out how easy it is to access emergency power shutdown control switches. Verify shutdown control switches shut off heating, ventilation, and air conditioning as well as computer and support equipment. Assess whether smoke/ionization detection equipment automatically activates the emergency power shutoff.

☐ Inquire whether smoke and ionization detection devices are installed in ceilings, raised floors, return air ducts, and other important zones. Find out how often these detectors are tested.

☐ Inquire how often **fire drills** are conducted and ensure that an adequate supply of fire-fighting water and other chemicals are available to combat fire.

☐ Verify whether periodic fire or evacuation drills are conducted in the computer center and in the entire building where the computer center is located to handle the emergency situations.

☐ Assess whether fire exit doors are protected by exit alarms.

☐ Determine the adequacy of the number of fire alarm boxes throughout the data center and that these alarms sound in the local area, such as building maintenance and computer center area, security guard location, help desk, central fire alarm station, and local fire department.

☐ Ascertain the frequency of fire system testing and certification by the local fire department. Inquire about the rating given to the local firefighting force by the American Insurance Association's Standards Fire Defense Rating Schedule or other.

4. **Water damage.** Damage due to water leakage in computer data centers is excessive and a common occurrence. The next audit procedures are suggested to assess management preparedness and controls to protect equipment from water damage.

☐ Inquire of the building maintenance engineer whether overhead water and steam pipes, except water sprinklers, are excluded from the computer room. A dry pipe system helps prevent water leaks.

☐ Ascertain whether adequate drainage is provided under raised floors, on the floor above, and other adjacent areas of the data center.

☐ Inquire whether electrical junction boxes under raised floors are kept away from the slab to prevent water damage.

☐ Assess whether exterior doors and windows are watertight to prevent water passage.

☐ Determine whether there is adequate protection provided against accumulated rainwater or leaks in the roof and rooftop cooling systems.

☐ For computer rooms not meeting the defined water damage standards, inquire whether floor drains use a sump pump connected to the uninterruptible power supply (UPS) system.

5. **Electricity.** Damage due to power failures in computer data centers is excessive and a common occurrence. Conduct the next audit procedures to assess management preparedness and controls to prevent power-related problems such as spikes and outages.

☐ Inquire how reliable the local power supply is and how many times there have been power failures or power spikes, surges, outages, brownouts. Understand whether alternative measures have been investigated.

☐ Determine the need to use a UPS system to provide smooth flow of electricity from power spikes, surges, outages, brownouts, and blackouts. There should be enough auxiliary power generators to generate electricity as needed for the computer and support equipment. There should be enough fuel (gas or propane) for alternate power generators for at least one week.

BUSINESS RISKS IN ELECTRICAL POWER

- A voltage spike is a sharp but brief increase in voltage, commonly caused by the turning off of heavy loads, such as air conditioners and copiers.

- A voltage surge is similar to a spike, but it is an increase in voltage of longer duration, commonly caused by the removal of heavy loads or equipment shutdown. It is an overvoltage condition.

- A voltage sag is an undervoltage condition, commonly caused by the addition of large loads to a power line within a building, such as turning on a copier or starting an elevator.

- A brownout condition is longer-term sag. It is a deliberate reduction of voltage output at a power-generating station to respond to high demand and thus avoid an outage. Computers cannot work during a brownout.

- A blackout is a total loss of power, lasting several hours, commonly caused by weather conditions or damage to power lines and equipment.

☐ Make sure the power supply to the air conditioning, heating, and other source of electricity is leading from a separate power supply. This source should not share with other power sources within the building.

☐ Make sure that the wiring in the computer room conforms to accepted local and state government electrical codes.

6. **Air conditioning.** Both computer equipment and magnetic storage media (e.g., data and program files on tapes and disks) are susceptible to changes in temperature and humidity levels. In order to minimize the impact from possible adverse effects, the next audit procedures are suggested.

☐ Inquire whether the air-conditioning system is used exclusively for the data center and is not being shared with other parts of the building.

☐ Ascertain whether air duct linings and filters are made of noncombustible materials.

☐ Observe whether the air compressor is located outside the data center.

☐ Inspect the cooling system for adequate protection against adverse weather conditions.

☐ Assess the need for a backup air-conditioning system.

☐ Inquire whether fire dampers are provided in the air-conditioning system. The air-conditioning unit must be shut down automatically when the halon unit is activated.

☐ Verify that air intakes are:

  • Covered with protective screening.

  • Located above street level.

  • Located to prevent intake of pollutants or other debris.

☐ Verify the existence of separate air-conditioning equipment and electrical power fluctuation control devices to ensure a constant power supply to the computer room.

7. **Natural disaster preparedness.** Natural disasters, such as tornados, earthquakes, hurricanes, and floods, are unpredictable. However, organizations exposed to such disasters should prepare themselves for the inevitable. In order to help minimize the impact from possible adverse effects, the next audit procedures are suggested.

☐ Interview the building architect or maintenance engineer to find out whether the computer center is structurally sound and protected against:

  • Hurricanes, tornados, and winds

  • Flood damage

  • Earthquakes

  • Winter storms and freezing

☐ Ascertain whether the building and computer equipment are properly grounded for lightning protection.

8. **Documented emergency procedures.** Written emergency procedures are very important for referencing, testing, and training purposes. In order to minimize the impact from possible adverse effects, the next audit procedures are suggested.

☐ Ascertain whether an emergency lighting system is in place to provide the required illumination automatically in case of interruption of normal lighting for any reason.

☐ Verify that there is a written emergency procedures manual covering the following items of concern:

  • CPU and air-conditioning power cutoff

  • Bomb threats, vandalism, and employee strikes

  • Fire evacuation, fighting, and testing instructions

  • Security of data and program files

  • Restart and recovery procedures due to equipment failures

  • Natural disasters

☐ Inquire when fire drills, first aid training, and cardiopulmonary resuscitation (CPR) classes were last performed.

☐ Review the test plans and documents for adequacy and relevancy.

9. **Environmental controls.** Large computers need a clean and controlled environment to operate properly. Conduct the next audit procedures to ensure that environmental controls exist in the computer room and tape library rooms.

☐ Ensure that fire extinguishers, heat and humidity control devices, alarm panels, pressure on halon tanks, and water detectors are tested periodically.

☐ Ensure that high-speed printers and other equipment that produce paper dust, such as report decollators and bursters, are placed outside of the computer room. This is to prevent dust coming in contact with the computer hardware.

☐ Determine how often the fire and water detection system is tested.

☐ Determine the need for a UPS machine and standby power generator to accommodate power surges and power losses respectively.

☐ Test temperature and humidity recordings on a surprise audit basis. Ensure that such measurements are recorded in a timely manner and that proper actions are taken when such measurements go out of the prescribed limits.

☐ Determine whether monitoring of physical security, environmental controls, and house-keeping activities is adequate.

(T) Contingency Planning

Auditing the contingency plan or disaster recovery plan is an important audit function since auditors have the professional and ethical responsibility to the organization for which they work, or to the clients they serve, to ensure continuity of business functions and operations. To discharge this responsibility, auditors must be actively involved in the disaster recovery plan development, testing, and maintenance processes as observers, reviewers, and reporters of actions or lack of actions of IT and end user staff and management. Another responsibility of auditors is to monitor the continual maintenance and periodic testing of the plan to reflect changes in the organization. Auditors should inform senior management if the plan is not updated and tested when needed.

Another major area for auditors to review is to determine the adequacy of insurance coverage on IT resources, such as property, software, and data and to determine the protection against human errors and omissions, fraud, theft, and embezzlement.

Auditors are interested in both vital records retention and records disposition practices as they affect both the security and confidentiality of records and the ability to resume business operations when interrupted due to a disaster (e.g., fire, flood), either in the computer center or in the functional user area.

Auditor's Role

The auditor's important role in developing and testing the disaster recovery plan may need clarification for other team participants. Many people participate in the planning and testing efforts, and misunderstandings and misinterpretations can easily develop among team members if they are not properly informed. The auditor should inform all team members of his or her role in the development and testing of the disaster recovery or contingency plan. Although the auditor does not actually prepare the planning document, he or she should advise the team members about its contents. The auditor, as a member of the testing team, reviews test results along with functional users to make sure those critical application system results are correct. The auditor does not make decisions or supervise the team members, which is the management's responsibility.

The auditor's role in the disaster recovery/contingency plan development and testing is clearly a consulting and participative role, where the auditor is a member of the disaster recovery/contingency planning team. The auditor is more of an observer, reviewer, and reporter of disaster planning, testing, and recovery-related actions. Some specific role-related activities in which the auditor participates are listed next.

- Attends meetings where issues are raised, problems are discussed, and solutions are suggested in areas related to computer contingency plans

- Reviews planning documents and backup and recovery site vendor's proposals for rendering such services for adequacy and suggests improvements as needed

- Participates in testing of the plan at the backup and recovery vendor's site along with functional users and IT staff, observes the testing process, and suggests cost-effective improvements to the plan based on feedback from the testing experience

- Ensures that functional users review the application test results by comparing them with known values or other means to ensure that the data files are up to date and that application programs and operating system are the correct version at the primary and backup computer centers

- Where needed, simulates a disaster with the help of senior management to test the recovery and resumption procedures

Audit Objectives and Procedures

General Audit Objectives

- To determine the adequacy of risk analysis.

- To evaluate the adequacy and effectiveness of off-site storage facilities.

- To determine whether the disaster recovery planning document is complete, clear, and understandable.

- To determine the adequacy of management's preparedness to address emergency situations.

- To ensure that disaster recovery plans are tested periodically and that those functional users review such test results for accuracy and completeness.

- To determine the adequacy of plan maintenance procedures.

- To identify concerns, problems, and issues and make cost-effective recommendations for improvements to be included in the disaster recovery plan.

- To ensure that disaster recovery planning, testing, and recovery activities in the computer center and user area are carried out according to: the established data processing policies, procedures, standards, and guidelines; good business and management practices; industry standards; and tax, accounting, government, legal, and regulatory requirements.

□ To identify overcontrolled (oversecured) and undercontrolled (undersecured) activities in the disaster recovery planning and testing areas. To ensure that weak controls in the disaster recovery planning and testing areas are balanced by strong controls in the end user and other computer center areas.

Audit Procedures

The audit procedures for reviewing the continuity of operations include:

1. **Information gathering.** Obtain relevant information by interviewing personnel and reading documents.

   □ Review the risk analysis document indicating possible threats and vulnerabilities and suggested controls to reduce such threats and vulnerabilities.

   □ Interview disaster recovery planning committee members, including their commitment, objectives, and responsibilities.

   □ Assess critical application systems with their priority levels.

   □ Review the disaster recovery requirements document indicating what is needed and where and when it is needed.

   □ Review the disaster recovery training document indicating who will be trained, when, and how.

   □ Review the disaster recovery plan testing document describing test scenarios and schedules.

   □ Review the disaster recovery plan maintenance procedures describing how the planning document will be updated and under what conditions.

   □ Review the preaudit survey notes taken during the preliminary information-gathering process.

   □ Review the audit notification letter with audit scope and specific objectives.

   □ Review copies of relevant IT management, backup computer facility vendor, and end user correspondence.

   □ Assess the third-party audit report issued as a result of the review of operations at the backup computer facility.

   □ Review the alternative processing contracts with backup facilities.

2. **Risk analysis.** Only critical application systems need to be processed during a disaster. To support this objective, only critical programs and data/records should be stored at an off site storage location. The next audit procedures are suggested to determine the adequacy of risk analysis.

   □ Identify critical application systems with inputs (source paper documents, machine-readable documents, data files) and outputs (reports, data files).

   □ Identify minimum hardware configuration needed during a major disaster including CPU terminals, network controllers, concentrators, printers, and data transmission lines, modems, and so on.

   □ Classify critical data according to whether they reside on magnetic/electronic, paper, or microfiche/microfilm media.

□ Review existing file backup procedures.

□ Formalize data/record retention and rotation schedules between onsite and offsite storage locations.

3. **offsite storage facilities.** Inquire whether commercial or private offsite storage facilities are used to store magnetic/electronic records, paper records, and microfiche/microfilm records. If a commercial offsite storage facility (e.g., banks, and nonbanks) is used, discover whether the vendor's financial background and reputation have been investigated. Visit the storage facilities, and contact other organizations that are using similar services.

   Also, assess the vendor's compliance with storage standards established by the National Institute of Standards and Technology (NIST), Underwriters Laboratory (UL), American National Standards Institute (ANSI), National Fire Protection Association (NFPA), and state and local governments. In addition, the next audit procedures are suggested to evaluate the adequacy and effectiveness of off-site storage vendors.

□ Ask about hours of operation and access privileges during evenings, weekends, and holidays.

□ Inquire how one client's media is separated from other clients' media.

□ Inquire how the media is transported (i.e., using plastic containers, cardboard boxes, or metal boxes with or without the use of seals transported in unmarked vehicles), security in vehicles, or employee monitoring with antitheft devices controlled by two-way radios for transmission of messages.

□ Review media rotation cycles to monitor the flow of media in and out of the facility (whether it is daily, weekly, monthly, or permanent storage).

□ Observe how visitors' access is restricted: whether they are required to sign in and out and are escorted at all times.

□ Inquire how the confidentiality of data stored on the media is maintained to prevent disclosure or unauthorized use of valuable data either internally or externally.

□ Inquire whether the vendor has media replacement insurance to protect clients from loss, misplacement, or damage of the media due to vendor negligence.

□ Understand whether a contract is required to do business with the commercial off-site storage vendor and know its terms and conditions, including media pickup and delivery fee, tape handling and storage fee, and emergency delivery fee.

□ Assess whether the traffic at the storage facility is videotaped with concealed cameras or other monitoring devices.

□ Understand the procedures to handle emergency or normal requests for media removal and delivery, including authorizations required and contact names and phone numbers.

□ Understand employee hiring and termination procedures, and inquire whether employees are bonded.

□ Ascertain whether a periodic inventory of media is performed and whether the results are compared to the official list of media.

□ Inquire what capabilities are installed to prevent, detect, and correct sonar, vibration, heat, smoke, fire, water, and burglar activities, including alarm systems tied to fire and police departments. Look for automatic halon fire extinguishers.

- Inquire how temperature, heat, humidity, power supply, and contamination are controlled, including backup systems and central station monitoring 24 hours a day.

- Understand the overall vendor's liabilities for media in its possession and penalties for loss or damage of media including deductibles, if any.

- Examine what precautions have been taken in terms of electrical interferences, static electricity, and magnetism.

- Check the facility for extraneous chemical or other pungent odors.

- Ensure that physical security controls are constantly and consistently applied.

Verify that the offsite storage location maintains not only blank checks and other negotiable instruments but also the registers and logs that are used to keep track of the usage of such checks. Ensure that a large enough supply of checks is available from offsite storage or from vendors in case of a disaster. Read letters of understanding negotiated with vendors.

Determine whether onsite or offsite storage rooms used for magnetic or paper records have adequate environmental controls, such as physical security, fire protection, humidity controls, temperature control, static grounding, and water detection devices.

Ascertain that an inventory list of computer hardware and peripheral equipment is available with manufacturer name, model, and serial number of each unit. Verify the physical existence of each unit.

Ensure that there is only one authorized main entrance to and exit from the data center. Where possible, this main entrance is to be manned by a receptionist or a security guard, preferably with closed-circuit television monitors. Review the training received, performance levels expected, and responsibilities assumed by security guards to handle security violations and emergencies.

Verify whether the offsite storage place has fire-resistant floor-to-ceiling doors or fire-resistant vaults that separate the contents from their surroundings. Ensure that doors have a dead-bolt lock to prevent break-ins.

Obtain a copy of the log maintained to record the movement of media on- and offsite. Ensure that a copy of the log is maintained offsite at all times. Examine the log for arrival and departure time of the vendor couriers, and check that the log indicates clearly what was picked up or delivered. Ensure that the logged information is detailed enough to track down media or records that are misplaced at the off-site storage facility or needed on an emergency basis. Take a month of logs and compare them to the vendor invoice to determine the accuracy of volume and the rate used, and compare that to the contract. Note any exceptions.

4. **Planning document.** Obtain a copy of the disaster recovery planning document. Examine it for details. To ensure that the disaster recovery planning document is complete, clear, and understandable, determine whether the document addresses the next items.

- There is a balance between the number of subscribers to an alternate backup hot site and the capacity of the computer.

- The vendor's willingness to offer presubscription testing in its facilities prior to signing a contract for backup processing services.

- A clear definition and indication of different types of fee charged by the backup vendor. Some examples of types of fee are: subscription fee, annual test times and corresponding fee, disaster notification fee, daily facility usage fee during a disaster, and extra equipment fee for tape and disk drives used over the base number.

☐ Whether the backup processing and recovery site vendor also provides off-site storage facilities for storing magnetic media backup, paper records, and supplies.

☐ Backup and recovery site vendor's liabilities for any loss or damage to media and data during storage and processing at its facilities, including maintaining client confidentiality.

☐ A temporary and emergency location for employees to work during a disaster, whether it is a warehouse, conference center, hotel/motel, or other prearranged office space.

☐ Names, phone numbers, and addresses of recovery team members, including their managers, to notify in case of a disaster and to inform where to report for work during a disaster.

☐ Transportation arrangements, including ground transportation such as special bus or private air transportation (i.e., a charter plane).

☐ Redirection of telecommunications traffic so business users are connected to remote hot-site processing and recovery facilities.

☐ Computer-related equipment and supplies, including personal computers, printers, facsimile machines, computer paper, and ink toners have two or more suppliers identified with their phone numbers and addresses.

☐ Names, phone numbers, and addresses of hotels or motels nearby the backup processing and recovery site for stay during recovery from a disaster.

☐ Consolidation of PC-based critical application systems on a compatible mainframe computer to be used during a disaster at the PC work area.

☐ Network configuration diagram and documentation describing network operations, network topologies and protocol architectures, traffic loads and patterns, and transmission rates and speeds.

☐ Availability of UPS, proper climate control, suitable fire prevention, detection, or suppression capabilities for both primary and secondary private branch exchange (PBX) installations.

☐ Migration of LAN-based critical application systems and data to central mainframe computers so that users can use these systems through dial-up mode from a backup and recovery site.

☐ Rerouting of incoming long-distance telephone traffic to the backup processing and recovery site so that user–mainframe connection is made.

☐ Location of alternate telephone traffic switching equipment offices locally, in case the primary local telephone company fails. The alternate telephone office can be used as a gateway to long-distance networks. Another alternative could be the installation of a company-owned microwave satellite link. Still another alternative could be use of independent cable, radio, or microwave links to private-access networks, including privately operated network gateways.

☐ Emergency team instructions are available for evacuation and recovery during a disaster. This may include procedures for reporting a fire, detecting a water leakage, powering down the electrical equipment, conducting fire drills, retrieving critical data and program files from offsite storage, testing systems software and application systems at the recovery site, operating from the recovery site, reestablishing the network, transporting users to recovery site, reconstructing the databases, transition procedures from emergency to normal service levels, and salvaging of records (paper and microfiche).

☐ Primary and emergency telephone numbers of vendors of peripheral equipment, hardware, and software, supply, and backup facilities.

☐ Trouble reporting and response escalation procedures to local telephone company during an outage.

☐ Documentation of contact persons at local, state, and federal governments and for understanding of emergency plan and protection procedures in the event of floods, earthquakes, hurricanes, or other nature-made disasters.

☐ Procedures to handle bomb threats or arson investigations prepared in conjunction with local police and fire department officials.

☐ Plan testing procedures at backup vendor site as well as at primary computer site.

5. **Functional user procedures.** Conduct the next audit steps to ensure that functional users themselves are prepared to address a disaster.

☐ Inquire whether fallback plans or alternate manual procedures and forms are developed by functional users to continue critical business operations, such as preparing payroll and invoices. These fallback procedures need to be tested and ready to function in the event of prolonged and delayed attempts to recover from a major disaster in the computer center. A reasonable approach would be to address two major situations separately: data center malfunction and natural disaster.

☐ In the case of a data center malfunction, functional user management needs to identify plans and procedures to continue critical business operations during the time until the backup computer takes over the critical application system operations and to continue noncritical business operations that are dependent on computer for a period of, say, 10 days until the entire data center's normal operations are restored.

☐ In the case of natural disasters (e.g., fire, flood, water damage), functional user management needs to identify alternate plans, procedures, equipment, facilities, and people required to operate critical job functions until the original facilities are restored or alternate facilities are located.

For example, if important application software is not working properly, contingencies may include reverting to manual processing for some operations, routing information to alternate systems or locations, correcting the software, or doing nothing until the problem is corrected.

6. **Emergency preparedness.** To ensure that management is doing all it can to prepare for unexpected disasters, conduct the next audit procedures.

☐ Determine whether instructions are available for emergency shutdown of the computer system.

☐ Ascertain whether the location of emergency exits, fire extinguishers, plastic coverings for equipment, power switches, and light switches are visible, and ensure that instructions are clear about operating them during an emergency.

☐ Examine the building evacuation procedures for reasonableness and applicability, and ask when they were tested last.

☐ Inquire about the availability of emergency telephone numbers for local police, ambulance, and fire departments, help desk, or building maintenance desk, and primary and backup recovery people.

☐ Inquire whether computer floor tile maintenance work, such as adding or changing tiles, is done outside of the computer room instead of inside. This is to prevent fiber and aluminum contaminants getting into the air. The preferred method is to perform all tile maintenance work outside the raised-floor room.

☐ Ascertain whether filters used in equipment such as humidifiers, air conditioning, and air purifiers are vendor recommended, not generic ones. This is to prevent larger particulates from getting into tape and disk drives and electrical switches. Determine the frequency of maintenance of such equipment and compare that to the manufacturer recommended schedule.

☐ Verify that the data center manager has conducted proper background investigation on the computer room–cleaning contractor prior to contracting out the services. Some areas of investigation include experience in cleaning business, user references, insurance coverage, fidelity bond coverage, and the type of cleaning equipment used.

☐ Inquire whether the computer room–cleaning contractor uses Occupational Safety and Health Agency (OSHA)–approved nonionic solution and lint-free towels to clean computer room tiles. Similarly, ensure that all equipment exteriors are cleaned with silicone-treated cloths.

☐ Inquire whether the UPS are online or off-line to the power company source. Online UPS is better than off-line UPS because online UPS remains in the line between the critical load and the power company at all times. Usually it takes longer for off-line UPS to activate and replace failed commercial power than an online model. Also, off-line models may not protect line voltage drops.

☐ Since the life of UPS is short (15 to 30 minutes), inquire whether private power generators are available to meet prolonged power supply problems. The power generator supplies alternate current to the UPS before the UPS power is exhausted. During this time, the UPS batteries get recharged. Ascertain whether there is adequate supply of backup fuel for the power generator. Confirm that power company representatives and building maintenance engineers were consulted prior to acquiring the UPS model and the private power generator.

7. **Testing and recovery procedures.** The real test of the plan is during the recovery from a disaster. The closest thing to a real recovery is a simulated disaster. The next audit procedures are suggested for determining the adequacy of testing and recovery procedures.

☐ Participate in the periodic test plans and programs.

☐ Observe the project team in action during testing and make notes of concerns.

☐ Prepare or obtain a checklist of time-driven actions and plans.

☐ Ensure that functional users have reviewed the test results for critical application systems when they are processed at backup computer facility.

☐ Ensure that someone in the recovery team is taking notes on the basis of time and action. These notes should include both positive and negative results, which later become part of the test report.

☐ Inquire who has access to information about master keys, combination numbers, special codes, or other physical security devices. Ensure that the security administrator has access to this information to facilitate efforts during recovery from a local disaster.

8. **Plan maintenance procedures.** Disaster recovery plan maintenance procedures are more important than plan development. A plan that is out of date is no use when needed. Conduct the next audit procedures to determine the adequacy of plan maintenance procedures.

☐ Understand how the plan should be updated, and under what conditions and criteria.

☐ Determine the adequacy of plan update frequency. Ideally, the plan should be updated prior to the next testing.

☐ Inquire how plan changes should be communicated, to whom and where.

☐ Ensure that there is one central location or person assigned the responsibility to update the planning document. In many cases, fragmented responsibility does not work.

☐ Determine the frequency of updating the hardware and software inventory list with input from all end users and computer centers. A periodic questionnaire should be sent to survey the additions and changes to original inventory list.

9. **Vital records retention program.** Conduct the next audit procedures to assess controls over a records retention program.

☐ Read the organization's published vital records retention guidelines to understand specific requirements. Obtain a copy of government and regulatory agency records retention requirements and guidelines in order to understand specific requirements.

☐ Ensure that hard-copy reports are not saved when the same records are microfilmed or microfiched. This is to minimize duplication of records in handling, storing, and retrieving.

☐ Inquire whether the legal staff has reviewed and updated the record retention schedule to ensure compliance with government and nongovernment records retention requirements.

☐ Ensure that a manual log for paper-based and magnetic media is maintained that shows the retention label number, the name of the section/department and contact person name, a description of the records, form or record number, the date sent to storage, and the date to be destroyed. Take a sample of record entries from the log, trace them to the storage place indicated, and confirm their existence.

☐ Ensure that an automated log for electronic (magnetic) media is maintained that shows file name and number, file owner name and department, a business description of the records, transaction types and codes, transaction beginning and ending dates, and expiration date. Ensure that an external label on the tape contains the same information. Take a sample of record entries from the log, trace them to the storage place indicated, and confirm their existence.

☐ Take a sample of expired records for three types of records (paper, mechanical, and electronic media) from the log. Confirm that after the expiration date, all paper materials were destroyed or recycled and sensitive magnetic materials (e.g., tapes) were degaussed. Where applicable, it is preferable to receive a new copy or replacement copy of the backup material before the old copy is destroyed.

☐ Observe/inquire whether these methods were used to dispose of sensitive documents:

- Paper-based reports, documents, letters, and memoranda are fed into a paper shredder by cutting them down the page instead of across to avoid reading the data or letters in the lines. Alternately, paper media can be burned or recycled.

- When turning in disks for reuse or replacement, format them first to prevent people from reading the file contents since the ERASE command does not really erase file contents and material can be recovered with utility programs.

- Disks are cut into two or more pieces before putting them in the trash can so that they will be useless to anybody.

10. **Insurance.** Perform the next audit procedures to evaluate the adequacy of insurance coverage to minimize potential business, legal, or financial losses.

☐ Obtain a copy of risk management reports or industry-specific studies or research reports for better understanding of potential risks and exposures, actual losses, insurance coverage allowed, deductible amounts allowed for each type of coverage, and the type of exclusions practiced. This understanding is required to properly assess the adequacy of insurance programs that are in effect.

☐ Where needed, coordinate with the risk management analyst to minimize duplication of efforts, to share the analyst's work results, and to exchange ideas, approaches, and audit work programs. However, the auditor's conclusions are his or her own and not those of the analyst. In other words, the auditor can share and use the work results of the analyst, but the auditor has to reach his or her own conclusions based on the auditor's own reviews and test results.

☐ Verify whether risk management has identified and quantified the possible risks and exposures and associated costs and benefits. Obtain a copy of the inventory of all property and insurable items available in the organization from the risk manager.

☐ Inquire whether the organization's risk management department and legal department's management participated in establishing the dollar limits on insurance policies and policy exclusions, including the amount for coinsurance provisions and liabilities.

☐ Review the insurance policy for adequate coverage in the areas of business interruption due to computer (hardware and software) failures, physical property (computer and its related equipment) damage, magnetic media (e.g., tapes, cassettes, disks, flash drives, thumb drives, pen drives, USB drives) and file reconstruction costs, valuable records retention and damage, errors and omissions, computer crime and fraud insurance, computer viruses, and personal computers.

☐ Inquire whether fidelity insurance coverage involving computers is available to protect against dishonest employees. Usually fidelity insurance covers the risk of loss due to a dishonest employee committing a fraud, theft, or embezzlement.

☐ Ascertain whether third-party fraud insurance coverage has been obtained to protect against computer fraud perpetrated by a third party. For example, fraud insurance in a banking environment covers electronic funds transfer (EFT), automated teller machine systems (ATMs), and the computer system, among other things. Some exclusions are extortion; loss of potential income; forged documents; war and nuclear risks; losses where the probable causes are errors, omissions, or mechanical failure; and others.

☐ Ascertain whether the insurance policy covers liability for bodily injury and property damage resulting from software/hardware vendor representatives and other outsiders (e.g., consultants/contractors). Inquire whether insurance is adequate to cover losses that may occur during the process of transporting computer tapes between on-site and off-site storage areas either done by own truck or by outside truck delivery services, and during on-site storage of program and data files by service bureau operations.

□ When an organization opts for self-insurance, understand the rationale for assuming such risk. Determine whether the reserves or contingency funds to cover possible losses are adequate by finding the industry's actual loss experience rate and past actual losses.

□ Verify whether risk management is sending copies of internal and external audit reports to the insurance carrier dealing with security control issues and problems in the coverage items with recommendations and corrective actions for those recommendations. Ascertain whether loss reports are sent to the insurance carrier explaining the circumstances leading to computer-related losses during the past five years. The insurance carrier is interested in knowing about the control environment in the client organization and wants to monitor that environment to minimize potential losses.

(U) Databases

Database Management Systems Software: Audit Objectives and Procedures

Audit Objectives

- To determine the adequacy of organizational structure and the reporting relationships.

- To determine whether the DBMS software was installed properly.

- To evaluate the security and integrity controls and procedures over the DBMS software for reasonableness and cost effectiveness.

- To assess the operational performance of the DBMS software.

Audit procedures

- Ensure that the data administrator (DA) reports directly to the data processing manager or executive to provide independence, authority, and responsibility.

- Ensure that the DA is responsible for data requirements, data description, and data standards as well as procedures regarding data storage, data retrieval, data and program file security, access controls, recovery, and backup.

CONTROL RISKS IN DATABASE SYSTEMS

- Production databases may not be separated from test databases, thus allowing unauthorized access to production databases.

- The data administration function may not be separated from application system development.

- The database administration group may move database changes between test and production libraries themselves without going through the designated program change control coordinator.

- Determine that the database administrator (DBA) is not allowed to operate the computer, write application programs, or perform systems programming functions.

- Determine that the DBA has established written procedures for the recovery of the database in the event of total or partial destruction of database files. Verify that the recovery procedures have been tested.

- Ensure that the DBA consults with users and systems analysts regarding data origination, data organization, and data storage and retrieval methods.

- Ensure that the DBA periodically reviews the DBMS software libraries to detect unauthorized libraries.

- Ensure that the DBA approves all modifications to the DBMS software. This includes both custom-developed and vendor-developed software. Determine whether the DBA approves changes to the DD.

- The auditor conducting a review of database structure, audit trails, controls, security, integrity, recovery and restart, and performance should be concerned with:

  □ Reviewing the schema to understand the physical design of records and segment layouts. Assess whether data are grouped efficiently by analyzing usage maps, query paths, entry points, and primary and secondary keys. The objective here is to have a shorter path.

  □ Reviewing the subschema to understand the user's view of the database. These "user views" present a logical database (schema) that is a subset of the physical database structure. Determine whether user views are defined for each transaction in terms of read-only, read and update, add, and delete and that they are in agreement with employee or department function.

  □ Determining whether the DBA has established and documented the audit trail along with its retention periods. Ensure that all transactions are time- and date-stamped so that they can be recorded in a proper accounting period.

  □ Identifying what resources need to be protected by passwords or other means. Determine whether violation criteria have been established.

  □ Determining the frequency of database backup. In general, the larger the database, the more frequent should be the backup. Inquire how database logs are stored and retained.

  □ Ascertaining who is responsible for database recovery. Ensure that written procedures for system recovery and restart are available for both online and batch portions of the system.

  □ Inquiring who is monitoring the performance and service levels of the database. Some common ways to improve the performance are by acquiring additional memory and data storage devices, by balancing the work load between peak and normal periods, and by reorganizing the database structure.

  □ Reviewing DBMS deadlock detection and resolution procedures for adequacy.

  □ Confirming whether user-defined tables (e.g., tax, department, account numbers, interest) are reviewed by functional users for completeness and accuracy.

- After the database is reorganized, ascertain whether the DBA reconciles the control totals before the reorganization with the control totals after the reorganization to ensure the integrity of the data file reorganization.

CONTROL/BUSINESS RISKS IN DATABASE SYSTEMS

- The database could be overstructured (i.e., too many files are defined to a logical model).

- The database may be reorganized too frequently, thus making it unavailable to users.

- The database may be reorganized infrequently, thus creating performance problems.   *(continued)*

CONTROL/BUSINESS RISKS IN DATABASE SYSTEMS *(Continued)*

- There may be too many physical I/O operations performed on the database, which degrades system performance due to its overhead.

- Physical databases are often created by rote, resulting in database performance problems. Physical database design should just be a normal extension of the logical database design in terms of conforming to the design rules.

- Confirm that logging and recovery provide transaction back-out initiated either by the application system or automatically for abended (abnormally ended) transactions, with automatic recovery at start-up. Dual logging facility provides continued operation, even in the event of a catastrophic error on the primary log file. Inquire whether a logical close processing facility is available for programs issuing multiple OPENs and CLOSEs while updating records. When a program abend occurs and transaction back-out is requested, this facility ensures that all updates accomplished since the beginning of the task are backed out. Without this facility, transaction back-out is applied only to updates made since the last close.

- Inquire that the DBMS maximizes transaction concurrency by supporting row-level locking so that multiple updates to the same block can be processed without delay. Users can also specify an automatic time-out limit to prevent unnecessary waiting.

- Ensure that the accounting facility is available to collect and report on a variety of access and resource utilization statistics and information.

- The security feature provides add, read, update, and delete protection for each table in the relational database. Review the access rules maintained in the database for accuracy and to ensure that only authorized users are defined to the system.

- Determine whether the database performance management software provides important statistics that can be used to fine-tune the database to achieve the desired performance goals. This, in turn, increases system throughput. Windowing facilities allow multiple logical screens to be viewed on one physical screen. Some of database performance statistics include:

  □ Number of transactions using the database

  □ Number of database calls by transaction type

  □ Number of physical I/Os

  □ Average time per request

  □ Number of system and transaction abends

- **Data compression software** is available to compress large volumes of database records. Compression saves disk space requirements, which, in turn, decreases cost and reduces backup/archival processing times.

Determine whether major features include:

- Compression specified at the schema level

- Compression statistics produced at the end of each compression run

- Reports showing summary information, such as:

  □ Percentage of each record type sampled that is compressible

  □ Expected compression percentage

  □ Expected percentage of compression due solely to the elimination of repeating strings

- For distributed database management software, determine whether multiple copies or replicas of a database can be created. Confirm that updates to a replicated database are automatically posted to all copies of the database, whether local or remote.

Data Dictionary Systems Software: Audit Objectives and Procedures

Audit Objectives

- To determine whether the DD is properly defined, controlled, and secured.
- To evaluate the integrity of DD systems.

Audit Procedures

The auditor concerned about the adequacy of controls over a DD system implementation and operation should conduct the next reviews and tests.

- Inquire whether the DD is active and interfaces with the DBMS. Ensure that the DD includes a data source for each data element, data validation, and data element location and its relationship to other data elements.

- Take a sample of critical and significant data items or elements and review them for adherence to established data standards.

- Ascertain whether passwords or some other security and access controls are defined and followed.

- Test the edit and validation criteria by entering valid and invalid data for critical data items or elements.

- Ensure that backup and recovery procedures are available and that they are followed.

- Determine whether DD system error rates are monitored by data processing staff and that timely corrective actions are taken.

- Interview functional users and others to assess if the DD system reports are clear, correct, and received in time to be useful. Inquire whether users have any problems or concerns in data entry and error correction procedures. In other words, determine whether the DD system is easy to use. Confirm that users have received adequate training in using a DD system.

- Inquire if the DD uses interactive fill-in-the-blank screens that eliminate the need to learn a complex data definition language.

- Understand whether users can perform multiple functions simultaneously.

- Determine whether a version management feature is available. This means version numbers are automatically assigned and maintained in test, quality assurance, training, history, or production status.

- Confirm that history versions can be deleted selectively.

> **CONTROL/AUDIT RISKS IN DATA SYSTEMS**
>
> - Passwords and other access codes may not be required to access, use, and update the DD.
>
> - Nondatabase applications may be loaded to the same DD as the database applications resulting in data corruption. The best procedure would be to use a separate DD for loading nondatabase applications and merge them after data cleanup.
>
> - The program record in the DD may not be used to document user-defined comments. If done regularly, program documentation would be current.
>
> - Multiple secondary dictionaries used for multiple system development/maintenance projects may not be in synchronization with the primary and production dictionary.

- Examine whether various security levels are provided. Some procedures might include:
  - Online user authorization
  - Record/row/file level locking
  - Passwords at the occurrence level
- Inquire whether user exits can be coded for specific attribute validation routines that provide for additional security and/or conform with standards.
- Confirm that relational tables can be dynamically defined and put into production status.
- Test and production entity occurrences can be renamed dynamically, permitting naming conventions to be applied incrementally.

Data Warehouse, Data Mart, and Data Mining: Audit Objectives and Procedures

Audit Objective

To ensure that organization is using data warehouse, data mart, and data mining techniques to achieve better quality of information and decision making.

Audit Procedures

- Review the current plans to implement data warehouse, data mart, and data mining techniques. Understand their business purpose, including cost/benefit analysis.
- If these techniques have already been implemented, determine whether they are achieving the business purpose (i.e., timely and quality of information and better decision making in the areas of marketing, fraud detection, and operations). Suggest ways to improve these techniques if they are not achieving their maximum potential.

(V) Functional Areas of Information Technology Operations: Audit Objectives and Procedures   Major concerns of auditors in reviewing functional areas of IT operations (i.e., data center operations) include how production jobs are scheduled, how storage media are used, how problems and changes are handled, how system backups are scheduled, and how the help desk is functioning.

The audit objectives of a data center operations management review are to ensure the proper implementation and verification of computer operational controls in the data center. This control assurance is needed to determine whether application systems are processed in a controlled and secured environment.

General Operating Practices Review

Audit Objective To ascertain whether job descriptions are complete and reflect actual job functions.

Audit Procedures

- Review organization charts and job descriptions. Ensure that segregation of duties among data entry, I/O control, systems development, systems maintenance, systems programming, computer operations, and user departments exists, where possible. Determine the need for compensating controls.

- Determine that job descriptions are current and distributed to employees and that they reflect actual conditions and practices.

Data Entry Function Review

Audit Objectives

- To determine the adequacy of batch data conversion and data entry activities.

- To determine the adequacy of online data conversion and data entry activities.

- To determine the adequacy of data editing and validation routines and procedures.

- To ensure that all data input errors are handled in a proper and timely manner.

Audit Procedures

1. **Batch data conversion and data entry procedures.** Conduct the next audit procedures to ensure that controls and procedures over batch data conversion and data entry activities are adequate.

   □ Determine if documented procedures exist that explain the manner in which data are converted and entered.

   □ Identify the persons performing work in the data input area. Ensure that no person performs more than one of these operations: origination, entering, processing, and distribution of data.

   □ Determine if there is a control group either in the functional user department or the IT department that independently controls the data to be entered. Identify control mechanisms used, such as: turnaround transmittal document, batching techniques, record counts, logging techniques, and predetermined control totals.

   □ Determine whether source documents used in data conversion or data entry are marked to prevent duplication or reentry into the system.

   □ Take a sample of critical business application systems. Ensure that a detailed data entry instruction manual is available, explaining how to enter and key verify the data fields. Assess whether the manual is complete and clear.

2. **Online data conversion and data entry procedures.** In order to ensure that controls and procedures over online data conversion and data entry activities are adequate, the next audit procedures are suggested.

   □ Confirm that data entry is performed at the point of source or close to the source to prevent delays and errors.

☐ Determine whether VDU/CRT terminals used for data entry work are protected from theft or preferably placed in a physically secured room.

☐ Determine if data entry can be made only from terminal devices with certain preassigned authority levels and that certain terminals are designated for specific application systems, at certain times of the day or certain days of the week.

☐ Ascertain if passwords are used to prevent unauthorized use of terminal devices.

☐ Determine if the user, through passwords or authorization codes, is allowed to enter only one or a limited number of transaction types.

3. **Online data editing and validation.** Conduct the next audit procedures to evaluate the adequacy of data editing and validation control routines and procedures.

☐ Determine if preprogrammed keying formats are used to ensure that data are entered in the proper field and format.

☐ Ascertain if a prompting technique is used to reduce the number of data entry errors.

☐ Determine the point at which input data are validated and edited. Confirm that incorrect data are rejected and not allowed to enter the system.

☐ Ascertain that data editing and validation procedures are performed on all data fields of an input record, even though an error may have been detected in an earlier data field of the same input record.

☐ Determine if data editing and validation procedures perform these checks: field sizes, date formats, check digit operations, limit/reasonableness tests, footing and cross-footing, sign tests, transaction code validations.

☐ Ensure that no one is allowed to override or bypass data editing and validation errors. If an override function is needed, limit use of this function to supervisory personnel only.

☐ Ascertain that the data I/O control group uses batch control totals to validate the completeness and accuracy of batches received as input data. Ensure that a reconciliation process is performed to ensure the completeness and accuracy of data input with system generated reports and manual totals.

CONTROL RISKS IN DATA ENTRY AND CONVERSION

- The data entry operator may be given access to production data master files and may perform maintenance to production data entry programs.

- Data conversion procedures may not have been documented or documented procedures may not be current.

- Keying errors during data conversion may not be detected or corrected.

- Incomplete or poorly formatted data records may be accepted and treated as if they were complete records.

- A data entry employee may fraudulently add, delete, or modify data records for self or interested parties.

---

4. **Data input error handling.** In order to ensure that all data input errors are handled properly and in a timely manner, the next audit procedures are suggested.

☐ Determine that procedures related to the identification, correction, and resubmission of rejected data have been established and documented.

□ Determine whether errors are displayed or printed immediately upon detection to facilitate prompt correction.

□ Ascertain that all rejected data are automatically written on to suspense files classified by the application system.

□ Review entries in the suspense files to establish whether they include information such as:

- Codes to indicate error types
- Date and time at which an entry is written to the suspense files
- Identification of user who originated the input

□ Inquire who is authorized to make corrections.

□ Ascertain if the suspense files produce follow-up messages and report the status of uncorrected transactions or errors on a regular basis.

□ Determine the need for aging the suspense file transactions and errors.

□ Determine that, before reentry, all corrections are reviewed and approved by supervisors.

□ Ascertain if user department management reviews reports from suspense files to analyze the level of transaction errors and status of uncorrected transactions.

Report Balancing and Reconciliation Procedures

Audit Objectives

- To ensure that clear responsibilities are assigned for report balancing and reconciliation activities.
- To examine the accuracy of report balancing procedures.

Audit Procedures

1. **Responsibility for balancing and reconciliation.** Conduct the next audit procedures to assess the adequacy of report balancing and reconciliation procedures.

□ Determine whether the data Input/Output (I/O) control group in the data processing department is responsible for reconciling the transactions processed with input batch totals to ensure that no data were added or lost during processing.

□ Determine if a log is kept, by application, to provide an audit trail of transactions processed.

□ Ascertain if the user department has a control group responsible for reviewing all reports.

□ Determine if the user department's control group reconciles report control totals with input batch totals before reports are released.

2. **Report balancing procedures.** In order to ensure that report balancing procedures are performed accurately and according to the application system/user documentation, conduct the next audit procedures.

□ Select five major and critical application systems that require report balancing by data control staff.

□ Obtain written balancing procedures and the last system run reports. Test that:

- Balancing was done correctly.

- All the key report fields are balanced.
- All control totals developed by users and data control staff are cross-compared.
- Procedures are up to date and accurately reflect the balancing process.
- All rejected items together with accepted items are balanced.

□ Interview end users to determine whether they:

- Find the data presented on reports accurate, reliable, and useful.
- Should be removed from or added to any report distribution lists.
- Have suggestions concerning the format, content, frequency, and timeliness of reports they receive.

Report Handling and Distribution Procedures

Audit Objectives

- To evaluate the adequacy of security access controls.
- To assess controls over online viewing of reports.
- To determine the adequacy of report distribution procedures.

Audit Procedures

1. **Security access controls.** If an automated report distribution system is being used, conduct the next audit procedures to evaluate the adequacy of security access controls in place.

   □ Review the security access control software rules to determine if all report distribution system data sets, program libraries, and utility programs are adequately defined and restricted.

   □ Review the report distribution system security capabilities and determine if they are adequate and/or have been utilized effectively.

2. **Online viewing controls.** If an automated report distribution system is being used, conduct the next audit procedures to determine if controls over online viewing are adequate.

   □ Review use of the distribution control database and surrounding procedures.

   □ Review security capabilities of the system and ensure that users who were defined to the system have a business need to view the reports.

   □ Determine if the online archival feature is effectively utilized.

3. **Report distribution controls.** If a manual report distribution system is being used, conduct the next audit procedures to determine if the report distribution list is up to date and that reports are distributed or available to end users in a timely manner.

   □ Review report distribution instructions for completeness and accuracy. Examine them for name of the recipient, department, location, phone number, number of copies, and so forth.

☐ Determine if there is a report distribution list for each application system.

☐ Verify that reports for all applications are included on the relevant report distribution list(s).

☐ Find out if report distribution lists are updated whenever any change is made in distribution requirements.

☐ Determine if report distribution lists include:

- Report frequency.
- Disposition of all copies of each report.
- Time schedules for the distribution of each report.
- Special instructions on any given report.

☐ Observe the actual distribution of reports to determine the flow of documents.

☐ Inspect the report delivery area or boxes and check dates of reports to determine any time lag between report production and delivery. Compare this any time lag against standards.

☐ Determine that reports are reviewed by data control staff for quality, such as incomplete report contents or missing pages, prior to distribution to end users.

☐ Understand the procedures used to deliver the reports. Ensure that a systematic and orderly distribution or pickup of reports exists. Assess the method of correcting report distribution errors.

☐ Determine the need for a report distribution log to indicate the person responsible for report distribution.

☐ Discuss with report distribution staff and end users their opinions of the current system and their suggestions to improve the system.

Output Error Handling Review

Audit Objectives

- To ensure that clear responsibilities are assigned for correcting output report errors.
- To determine whether all errors are handled properly and in a timely manner.

Audit Procedures

In order to ensure that all data output errors are handled properly and in a timely manner, the next audit procedures are suggested.

- Determine if output error reporting and control procedures have been established and documented.
- Ascertain if the end user is immediately notified of problems in output reports.
- Determine if the user department control group keeps a log of all reports containing errors.
- Establish that reports from rerun jobs are subjected to the same quality control review as the erroneous original reports.

Report Retention and Security Measures

Audit Objectives

- To determine whether retention periods for paper, electronic, and magnetic records have been established.
- To ensure that record retention periods are complied with.

Audit Procedures

- Determine if retention periods for paper/electronic/magnetic records have been established.
- Assess whether the retention period is reasonable for system backup and recovery, legal, tax, regulatory, management, and audit purposes.
- Determine if appropriate security methods (e.g., degaussing tapes or cartridges, shredding paper documents) have been used to dispose of unneeded records.
- Determine whether written procedures provide listings of reports classified as critical.
- Evaluate risks associated with critical reports and test procedures used to protect these reports.
- Understand the procedures in place for protecting confidential and critical reports from unauthorized pickup and viewing.
- Assess whether security provisions concerning the protection of critical reports awaiting distribution are adequate and are being followed.
- Assess whether end users receiving critical reports are aware of the criticality status and are taking proper actions to protect their confidentiality.

Controls over Microfiche and Microfilm Records

Audit Objectives

- To determine the adequacy of microfiche/microfilm processing procedures.
- To ensure that retention periods are adequate.
- To determine the adequacy of storage, distribution, and retrieval procedures.

Audit Procedures

1. **Accuracy of microfiche/microfilm processing.** Understand how microfiche or microfilm records are generated. Identify the associated end users for each type of microfiche and microfilm record. Conduct the following audit procedures to determine the accuracy of microfiche/microfilm records:

   □ Inquire whether the microfiche records are generated through off-line or online to the host computer.

   □ If offline, understand how data control management and user management ensures that all records that were supposed to be microfiched were indeed microfiched. Understand the relation between microfiche frames (number of records a frame can hold) and computer records.

   □ If online, inquire whether automated record counts are available to ensure that there is a match between computer-generated records and microfiche-generated records.

2. **Microfiche/microfilm record retention periods.** Select ten critical microfiche or microfilm records judgmentally. In order to determine the adequacy of record retention practices, conduct these audit procedures.

☐ Ask end users about microfiche and microfilm record retention periods.

☐ Verify that the retention periods documented in the data control are in agreement with the end user guidelines. Note any exceptions.

☐ Confirm that the retention periods are in agreement with the organization's records retention policies. Note any exceptions.

3. **Storage, distribution, and retrieval procedures.** Conduct the next audit procedures to ensure that controls and procedures over microfiche output distribution, storage, and retrieval are adequate.

☐ Obtain the microfiche distribution list and determine if it is current and complete and that it is utilized.

☐ Identify and inspect microfiche storage areas for adequacy and security.

☐ Request the data control staff to retrieve certain critical and old microfiche and microfilm records. Assess whether the retrieval process is timely and readily available. Suggest any improvements on manual procedures or need for automated record retrieval system.

Job Scheduling Review

Audit Objectives

- To evaluate the adequacy of job setup procedures.
- To evaluate the adequacy of security access controls.
- To assess the adequacy of operating controls.
- To determine the adequacy of job schedules.
- To evaluate the handling of special processing of jobs.

Audit Procedures

1. **Job setup procedures.** These following audit procedures are suggested to assess the accuracy and completeness of job setups:

☐ Review operating procedures to obtain familiarity with production job setups, job run sheets, and application program documentation.

☐ Judgmentally select five major and important application systems and obtain job run sheets for each.

☐ Using the job run sheet, make sure that each job and step procedures were set up in the job control library according to instructions.

☐ Using the job run sheet, make sure that the sequence of jobs was set up correctly considering job dependencies (e.g., predecessors and successors; accounts receivable job is a predecessor to a general ledger job while financial statement job is a successor to the general ledger job).

CONTROL RISK IN JOB DOCUMENTATION

The job documentation specialist may be given access to production job documentation, job control, and report distribution files and libraries, thus causing unnecessary exposure to unauthorized acts.

2. **Security access controls.** These audit procedures are suggested to assess the adequacy of logical security and access controls.

   ☐ For terminal/operator security level, ensure that the terminals defined to the system are in the authorized work area and that all operators defined to the system are using only the terminals they were authorized to use.

   ☐ For the operator/application security level, ensure that operators defined to the application have a business need to access the system.

   ☐ For application/commands security level, ensure that operators defined to the application have access to system commands based on their job needs.

   ☐ For command/function security level, ensure that people defined to the system need a second level of security in addition to application/command security level in order to use certain online screens, commands, functions, and terminals.

   ☐ For user ID/ownership security level, ensure that users defined to the system have access to certain data sets based on business need.

CONTROL RISK IN JOB DOCUMENTATION

The job control analyst may be given access to production data files and may perform maintenance to production application programs and job control files.

3. **Operational controls.** In order to assess operational controls over the job scheduling activities, the next audit procedures are suggested.

   ☐ Review all written procedures and forms for completeness, applicability, and adequacy.

   ☐ Verify whether all jobs are defined to the job scheduling system. If not, find out the reasons for omitting such jobs. Assess the applicability of reasons given.

   ☐ Determine if schedules are defined for each operating shift and that schedules are established at least a week in advance.

   ☐ Select the job schedule for a shift, analyze the job priorities and dependencies; ensure that all job predecessors and successors were properly taken into account when finalizing the job schedule.

   ☐ Draw a sample of application system jobs. Discuss with end users and confirm that they agree with the job priorities and job predecessors and successors.

   ☐ Make sure that all job scheduling data sets are backed up regularly both on-site and off-site for disaster recovery purposes. Ensure that backups are retained for at least one week.

   ☐ Determine whether procedures exist to ensure that scheduled jobs were actually executed. Inquire whether job schedules are reconciled with actual execution.

   ☐ Interview computer operations staff and management to find out the adequacy of job mix, availability of job initiators and hardware devices (e.g., tape/disk drives), job timing, and quality of job documentation. Solicit their comments and concerns for possible improvement.

4. **Special jobs.** This section applies to manual handling and scheduling of special jobs. In order to determine whether requests for special jobs are handled properly and in a timely manner and that the scheduling of special jobs does not conflict with regular production jobs, the following audit procedures are suggested.

☐ Examine several special job request forms and determine whether the form is complete with job name, date of request, originating department, job due date, location, telephone extension, return to, charge to, and special instructions.

☐ For each of the special request jobs received, determine whether data control completed the job ID, account number, due date, priority code, and date and initial prior to submission to computer operations.

☐ Confirm that these special jobs were run by noting dates and initials of computer operations staff.

☐ Calculate the time lag between date submitted by an end user to date completed by data processing. Assess whether the actual time lag is reasonable and falls within the standards established.

CONTROL RISK IN PRODUCTION SCHEDULE

The production scheduler may be given access to production data files and may perform maintenance to production application programs and job control files.

Production Job Turnover

Audit Objective To determine the adequacy and appropriateness of software configuration management and production job turnover procedures.

Audit Procedures

■ Understand the software configuration management and production turnover procedures available to move application system development and maintenance jobs into production. Inquire whether job turnover procedures are manual or automated. Manual procedures are difficult to control and error-prone and may not be suitable for a complex software environment.

■ Sometimes the software may be migrated within one CPU, across several CPUs as in a distributed environment, or across a network with increasing order of difficulty. Conduct the next audit procedures.

☐ Ascertain whether computer operations and production control staff conduct production acceptance testing of new or modified software prior to production turnover. If this practice is informal and uses manual procedures, there is a likelihood of greater frequency of production failures and an increase in the number of production-related problems. These problems, in turn, can cause downtime, shut down the system, reduce service levels, corrupt data, increase rerun time, cause overrun of scheduled batch jobs, disrupt business operations, and cause loss of data processing credibility in the end user community.

☐ Inquire whether the application system approval process is paper-based or online. Paper processes can cause problems because required information may be omitted or bypassed. If properly implemented, online approvals by managers are relatively more reliable.

- ☐ If the problems are excessive, determine the need to automate the production turnover process. Identify its associated benefits.

- ☐ Ensure that system implementation checklists or production job turnover procedures include items such as database, production control, technical services/support, network control, security, operations, application, change management, quality assurance, and end user areas.

CONTROL RISKS IN PRODUCTION OPERATIONS

The operations analyst may be given access to production data files and may perform maintenance to production application programs. Programmers may be given access to production data files.

Computer Operations

Audit Objectives

- To evaluate the controls and procedures over execution of production jobs and programs.

- To determine whether run instructions for critical jobs are complete.

- To ensure that job setup procedures are clearly documented and that job rerun/restart procedures are clear.

- To determine whether monitoring of system resources is adequate.

- To ensure that computer operations management reviews console/system logs for operator interventions during program/job execution, label overrides, and equipment checks and to ensure that the log is complete by capturing all activities.

- To ensure that file backup schedules and procedures are adequate.

- To determine whether the options and parameters selected in the system logging facility are relevant and useful.

- To ascertain whether production and operations problems are logged and followed up for corrective action.

- To ensure that good housekeeping practices are followed.

- To ensure that basic emergency procedures are followed and tested.

- To evaluate the adequacy of hardware preventive maintenance practices.

Audit Procedures

1. **Production job processing.** Conduct the next audit procedures to ensure that all scheduled production jobs are processed in a timely manner.

   - ☐ Obtain a list of all regularly scheduled application program and system backup jobs for a few days of audit time.

   - ☐ Ensure that all production jobs are completed per schedule. If not, ascertain the reasons for noncompliance. Determine the job backlog.

2. **Production job abends (abnormal ends).** In order to determine the causes of production job abends and to see how they were disposed, the next audit procedures are suggested.

☐ Using system logging facility records, extract a list of production job abends for a selected month.

☐ Trace these abends to the logs for documentary evidence to determine that:

- Abnormal ends (Abends) are properly reported.

- Causes for abends are determined.

- Abends are disposed of.

- The abend logs are reviewed by the computer operations supervisor(s) to prevent their recurrence.

3. **Production job reruns.** In order to determine the causes of production job reruns and to see how they were disposed, the next audit procedures are suggested.

☐ Using system logging facility records, extract a list of production job reruns for a selected month.

☐ Trace these reruns to the logs for documentary evidence to determine that:

- Reruns are properly reported.

- Causes for reruns are determined.

- Correct job control information was entered for the next time.

- The rerun logs are reviewed by the computer operations supervisor(s) to prevent their recurrence.

4. **System console logs.** Some key commands and information captured by operating system console logs are listed next.

☐ Operator commands and operator responses to system commands

☐ Equipment problems and failures (tape or disk failures)

☐ Equipment status

☐ Frequency of operator commands by command type or code

☐ Tape BLP overrides

☐ Abnormal job terminations

☐ How long a job was executed with start and stop times

☐ Terminal communication problems such as messages held

☐ Operating system abends

☐ Database dumps start and completion times

☐ Database recovery and startup messages

☐ Print files in queue

☐ Transactions up (available) or down (not available) requests from users

☐ Communication management system starts and finish times that are needed to back up databases

☐ Job reruns and their times

In order to verify that computer operations management does a review of the system console logs to detect operator interventions during program/job execution, label override, and equipment checks, the next audit procedures are suggested.

☐ Inquire how long console logs are retained. If the retention period is too short, say one week, suggest saving logs as microfiche records for longer periods, if desired.

☐ Manually scan console logs for powerful commands and codes for selected operating days or shifts.

☐ Using automated audit software tool, create reports showing the use of powerful commands and codes.

☐ Inquire how often the operations supervisors review the console logs.

CONTROL RISKS IN COMPUTER OPERATIONS

- Computer operators may turn off logging of system activity records, thus losing audit trails.

- The system activity records could be lost due to lack of space on the storage media (overflow).

- Computer console logs may not be retained long enough to facilitate follow-up work.

---

5. **Backup schedules.** Conduct the next audit procedures to evaluate the adequacy and completeness of backup schedules.

☐ Obtain documentation that describes system backups. This should indicate what programs and data files should be backed up and their frequency. For example, a database may be backed up several times a day.

☐ Interview computer operators and obtain their assessment of the system backup situation. Determine whether there is enough time in an operating shift to make system backups.

☐ Determine the need to do incremental system backups instead of full system backups. Only changes since the last backup are backed up in the incremental system backup, which saves time, whereas the entire system is backed up each time a backup is done in the full backup system approach. Full system backups take more time than incremental system backups.

6. **Backup procedures.** In order to ensure that operators follow prescribed backup procedures, the next audit procedures are suggested.

☐ Select a sample of operating days or shifts.

☐ Compare actual system backups against schedules.

☐ Note any deviations.

7. **Housekeeping activities.** In order to assess the housekeeping activities in a computer room, the next audit procedures are suggested.

☐ Tour the computer room. Assess whether it is free from dust and waste materials and that it is neatly organized.

☐ Ensure that flammable materials are not placed around the computer room to prevent a potential fire hazard.

☐ Inquire how often the area under the raised floor is cleaned.

8. **Computer operator practices.** Interview the shift supervisor for understanding of security control practices in the computer room, ask the following questions, and note any exceptions for improvement:

□ Do computer operators who are required to initiate production jobs have a unique password, not a group password, in order to validate their identify and to exact accountability?

CONTROLS OVER COMPUTER OPERATORS

- Separation of duties
- Mandatory vacations
- Activity logging
- Limited access to system documentation

□ Are computer operators prohibited from initiating, entering, updating, and correcting a record in the transaction or master file of an application system, and are they prohibited from making any significant decisions involved in the running of an application system and its logic?

□ Is computer operator decision making kept to a minimum and confined to activities/areas such as system and job start-up, file backups, system shutdown, equipment reconfiguration, emergency message broadcasting, job rerun, tape mounting and demounting, and file recovery/restart?

□ Are all actions taken by computer operators through console terminal commands recorded in a log, and is an exception report available for review by operations supervisors in order to detect any abnormal acts that could lead to computer-related fraudulent activities? Are console logs backed up on a magnetic tape for future retrieval?

□ Do computer operators take mandatory vacations with a minimum block of one week at one time, and where practical are operators given a chance to enlarge/enrich their jobs by rotating between operating shifts or other duties within the computer operations department? It is generally agreed that mandatory and long periods of vacation will help in detecting or surfacing any fraudulent activities.

□ Are computer operators aware of the importance of monitoring that temperature and humidity levels are within the manufacturer's suggested tolerance limits? Are they monitoring those levels?

□ When was the last time sprinklers or halon were tested by building maintenance and/or other professionals? Was it a successful exercise? Are the locations for the shut-off valves easily accessible and clearly labeled?

□ Are there training programs and career development plans for the entire computer operations staff? If so, assess their relevancy and reasonableness. Verify whether employees are allowed to attend professional seminars and conferences and to become members of professional organizations in order to increase their knowledge and to strengthen their career advancement.

□ Are computer reports decollated, bursted, and distributed according to the established guidelines, and are computer reports disposed of securely by burning or shredding to prevent them from being used by unauthorized people?

□ Are computer operators given only the operations documentation needed to do their job? Is system/program and user documentation restricted from their use?

□ Is the read-after-write option being practiced when online? Are real-time database updates made to magnetic disks?

□ How often are the computer room and the area under the raised floors vacuum cleaned to remove paper dust and other debris that could support a fire in the computer room?

□ Are excessive computer paper and supplies stored in the computer print room? Excessive storage could support a fire.

CONTROL RISK IN COMPUTER OPERATIONS

The computer operator may be given access to production data files and may perform maintenance to production application programs and job control files.

---

9. **Preventive maintenance.** Scheduled preventive maintenance is a good practice to keep hardware in good working condition. Conduct the next audit procedures to evaluate the adequacy and timeliness of preventive maintenance activities.

□ Understand the frequency of scheduled preventive maintenance work performed on hardware by vendors and/or in-house personnel.

□ Compare this frequency to hardware maintenance contracts. Note any exceptions.

□ Determine compliance with maintenance contractual agreements by examining maintenance log. Note any deviations.

□ Ascertain whether scheduled maintenance has had any adverse effect on normal production schedule or critical business season.

□ Determine whether preventive maintenance logs are retained. Identify abnormal hardware and software problems.

□ Ensure that the hardware and peripheral equipment maintenance period commences on the same day that the warranty or guarantee period expires. This is to prevent paying additional maintenance charges for services that should be received under warranty or to eliminate the time gap between the maintenance and warranty periods. Here the objective is to obtain a continuity of maintenance service and protection of the hardware and peripheral equipment.

□ Verify whether the hardware and peripheral equipment maintenance agreement includes a standard for maintenance call response time (8 to 12 hours is common or within 24 hours) that is defined as the maximum time allowed to elapse between the data processing staff notification of a problem to the vendor and the vendor's maintenance staff arrival on the vendee's premises.

Tape and Disk Management Systems

Audit Objectives

■ To determine whether tape/cartridge and disk management system functions are used to their fullest extent.

■ To evaluate the adequacy of review and use of system-generated reports for day-to-day management of operations.

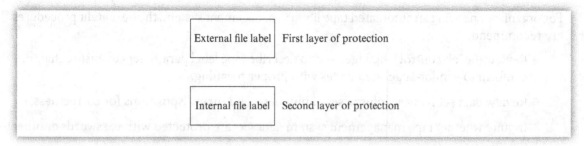

| External file label | First layer of protection |
| Internal file label | Second layer of protection |

EXHIBIT 1.10 External and Internal File Labels

Audit Procedures for Tape Management System The auditor performing a review of magnetic tape files to assure proper usage and control of tapes should:

- Inquire whether data in the tapes were classified as highly critical, critical, noncritical, or other.

- Confirm that the number of tape files maintained in the data center agrees with the physical inventory of tapes.

- Take a sample of tapes and confirm that external label descriptions match official descriptions to prevent possible use of incorrect file. External labels can be read by the operator. Computer programs read internal labels only. Internal file labels are better in minimizing the possibility of data or program file destruction than external file labels. Another way of looking at this issue is to treat external file labels as a first layer of protection and internal file labels as a secondary layer of protection, as shown in Exhibit 1.10.

The **Header (first) record** in an internal label usually contains this information:

- File name, reel number
- File ID number
- Volume serial number
- Sequence number
- File creation date
- File expiration date
- Blocking factor
- Record length in bytes
- Record type (i.e., fixed, variable)

The **Trailer (last) record** in an internal label usually contains this information

- End of file indicator
- Number of records
- Control totals such as batch totals
- Inquire whether tapes are degaussed before being sent out for cleaning, certification, or for other purposes.
- Review tape retention tables and confirm that tape retention periods in the tables are in agreement with management policies and regulatory agency guidelines.
- Test whether environmental controls (e.g., heat, humidity) in the tape library area are in compliance with the manufacturer's (vendor) recommended guidelines.

For organizations using an automated tape library management system, the next audit procedures are recommended.

- Review the job control language used to describe tape label parameters to ensure that they conform to vendor-suggested codes with proper meaning.

- Review data set names, volume serial numbers, and their dispositions for correctness.

- Inquire whether tape management system data sets are protected with passwords or other means.

- With the use of a batch utility program, print the audit records from the audit backup file (disk or tape) to identify audit exception records and I/O activity records.

- Inquire whether computer operations management is using a tape management system copy utility to back up the tape management catalog data sets and audit data sets and to restore the cataloged data sets if they are destroyed.

- Review security table for proper options such as tape inquiry and update capabilities on the cataloged data sets.

CONTROL RISK IN TAPE LIBRARY

The tape librarian may be given access to production data files and may perform maintenance to production application programs and job control files.

- Confirm that passwords to tape management system data sets are changed periodically and that passwords for terminated employees are not included.

- Ascertain that the tape management data set used to activate or deactivate the entire tape management systems is password protected, especially for the deactivation task.

- Ascertain whether the tape BLP option in the tape management system is controlled by restricting its use to limited individuals in the computer operations area.

Audit Procedures for Disk Management System

The auditor performing a review of magnetic disk files to ensure proper usage and control of disk resources should:

- Verify that access to disk media management systems is restricted through the use of passwords and based on the need-to-know philosophy.

- Determine whether disk media are most frequently used for day-to-day processing and storage and that tape/cartridge media are used for backup purposes only.

- Confirm that computer operations management receives periodic reports on disk media performance.

AUDIT/CONTROL RISKS IN COMPUTER STORAGE MEDIA

- Data sets may be erased by mistake.

- Data sets may be allowed to expire before their useful life has ended.

- Reel tapes, cartridges, disks, flash drives, thumb drives, pen drives, and USB drives. could be lost or misplaced.

- Disk drives or tape drives could malfunction, thereby not completing the system backups.
- Software, processing, or operator errors could compromise the integrity of original as well as backup data sets.

System Logs

Audit Objectives

- To determine whether appropriate system logs are produced.
- To ascertain whether system logs are secured.

Audit Procedures

1. **System logging facility event recording.** To ensure that the system logging facility routines select all system events for recording, the next audit procedures are suggested.

   □ Identify any selection criteria in effect that will exclude system logging facility records from being logged.

   □ Ensure that all selected events are written to permanent files to facilitate historical reviews of system activity by identifying the means used to write logging records to permanent files.

   □ Assess the steps taken by operators to prevent the system logging facility from stopping writing records when the operator forgets to dump records from disk to tape. Ensure that a file dump is taken at the beginning and at the end of every operating shift. Review the storage security and retention controls over system logging facility tape files. Determine their adequacy; usually data are saved for 30 to 40 days.

2. **System logging facility access controls.** To ensure that users or their programs can make no modifications to the system logging facility event records at any time, the next audit procedures are suggested.

   □ Ensure that parameter library data set is write-protected.

   □ Determine the access authority given to the log files.

   □ Determine that no unauthorized supervisor routines exist.

   □ Determine that the number of users with special access authority is limited.

   □ Determine the adequacy of audit trails.

   □ Review the jobs that dump system logging facility data sets. Determine that their execution is in a controlled environment through tests of production library execution and access controls.

3. **System logging facility reporting.** With the use of audit software or other report writing program, produce the following information from system logging facilities for further analysis:

   □ Number of occurrences of an initial program load

   □ Number of jobs or steps that were terminated abnormally

☐ Number of times critical data sets are opened, deleted, or renamed

☐ Number of records lost in any interruption in system logging facility recording

☐ Names of data sets scratched, lost, or renamed

☐ Number of occurrences of password invalidity

Help Desk Function Review

Audit Objectives

- To determine whether documentation describing problem isolation and determination is clear and complete.

- To evaluate the procedures for problem logging, tracking, resolution, and escalation.

- To ensure that help desk staff is properly trained in their job.

Audit Procedures

In order to assure the adequacy and reasonability of the help desk function and hot-line services, conduct the following audit procedures:

- Determine whether predefined problem isolation and determination procedures are available and that they are documented.

- Ascertain whether problem logging, tracking, and resolution procedures are available and that they are clearly documented. Inquire whether standard time guidelines are defined for problem resolution.

- Assess whether procedures are clearly established and reported as to the location of problem sources (i.e., problems resulting from a terminal, host computer, operating system, terminal controller, telecommunications circuits, third-party system, in-house application program, remote/local printer).

- Verify that contact names and phone numbers in the data processing department are available for problem reporting and routing.

- Find out if procedures are clear and complete in terms of handling a user problem, such as a user forgot a password, a password has expired, the system denies access although the password is correct, or a user cannot get through an application system because the system requires a multiple-level password.

- Assess whether a call list is available showing whom and how to contact people within the organization, such as data security, technical support, application support, end users, and third-party system support outside the organization.

- Determine the availability of problem escalation procedures for end users and help desk function for reporting to second-level people when problems are not resolved timely and/or first-level people are not available.

- If a voice response system is used either to supplement or to substitute for a human-based help desk function, test it by placing some problem calls through the system to ensure that the call routing is properly done and that the response on the receiving end is timely, competent, and adequate.

> **AUDIT RISKS IN HELP DESK OPERATION**
>
> The auditor may fail to recognize that:
>
> - Users like to know before the system goes down.
>
> - Help desk staff may not answer the phone quickly or keep the user on hold for long time.
>
> - The help received through the help desk staff is no help at all.
>
> - Weekend, evening, or night shift problems are not resolved properly due to inadequate help desk staff.
>
> - Help desk operators are not courteous and friendly.
>
> - Help desk staff may not return user calls.
>
> - Help desk staff is not knowledgeable in solving problems related to business application systems.

(W) Web Infrastructure: Audit Objectives and Procedures

Audit Objective

To ensure that Web management issues are properly addressed and controlled to reduce potential risks and exposures to the organization.

Audit Procedures

- Determine how performance issues, such as response time and service bottlenecks, are handled. Suggest using bigger-capacity routers, installing faster modems, and upgrading backbone links to speed Internet access.

- Determine how cookies are used or blocked.

- Determine whether Internet firewalls, encryption, and digital signatures are implemented to protect Web resources from unauthorized access and use.

(X) Software Licensing: Audit Objectives and Procedures

Audit Objectives

- To ensure that risks and exposures are minimized or eliminated with software licensing practices

- To determine whether software piracy polices are distributed and implemented throughout the organization.

- To ensure that IS contracts are properly administered and complied with.

Audit Procedures

- **Software licensing practices.** Review software licensing agreements in terms of site license, per-server license, or floating license. Understand how they are used in practice.

- **Software piracy policies.** Review the software piracy policies to protect the organization from legal suits by software owners. Test a sample of users for adhering to the software piracy policies.

- **Information systems contracts.** Review the contracts for terms and condition, penalties for nonperformance by vendors or consultants, and software development and maintenance work.

(Y) Electronic Funds Transfer/Electronic Data Interchange

Electronic Funds Transfer Systems A full scope review of an EFT system should include ATM systems, automated clearinghouse (ACH) systems, and wire transfer systems.[8] This review is more applicable to bank auditors.

ATM Systems An ATM should have controls similar to a human teller, including frequent reconcilement to the general ledger. Handling of deposits made through ATMs should be under joint custody until the amounts and items have been verified. Remaining procedures for ATM systems deal with controls over plastic cards and PINs. The use of PINs to ensure customer account protection is a critical control. Bank employees should not have access to customer PINs. Some banks have been known to retain reports that contain customer PINs. This practice greatly reduces the strength of the control over direct access to customer funds through an ATM. Computer programs used to generate PINs and the encryption key (base algorithm for generating PINs) should be generally restricted from most employees. Procedures to monitor the use of these programs should be in place.

Strict controls over access to unused plastic cards and to the facilities to emboss and encode information is required. This requirement closely relates to the procedure for controlling cards that have been retained at the ATM. Additionally, a common control practice is to ensure that cards and PIN mailers are not mailed simultaneously to the customer. Returned mail due to wrong address or other invalid information needs to be controlled so a bank employee cannot obtain a customer card and PIN for unauthorized access.

Some ATM systems allow online account maintenance that can associate any account with a specific ATM card. The card could then be used to withdraw funds from an account not owned by that customer or employee. Activity reports should be printed and reviewed to ensure proper use of these transactions. The auditor should test card and account relationships to ensure the integrity of the ATM process.

Audit Objective To determine the adequacy of controls over ATM systems.

Audit Procedures

- Review procedures related to ATM servicing and balancing functions, including:
  - ATM service team members are not employees with incompatible duties.
  - Separation of duties between balancing and servicing is maintained.
  - Control of cash and deposit envelopes to ensure proper posting and handling.
  - Control of "hot cards" retained at ATM to ensure proper distribution and/or destruction.
  - Control of off-line machine transaction cassettes or disks to ensure proper posting.

---

[8] *Understanding and Auditing EDI and Open Network Controls* (Chicago: Bank Administration Institute, 1991).

- Observe the servicing and balancing of selected ATM sites to ensure procedures are being followed.

- Determine that there are adequate controls over issuance, maintenance, and customer usage of PINs.

- Ensure that adequate controls exist over any encryption keys and PIN calculation programs.

- Determine that dual control procedures are in effect for accessing, processing, issuing, delivering, and destroying plastic cards.

ACH Systems Several problems with processing ACH items have been observed over the past few years. Some banks have problems with processing the same ACH items more than once because of poor balancing controls. ACH items may be sent to the bank several days in advance. In these cases, the bank should not give available credit to the customer until the proper date because the bank does not have the funds. Memo postings of ACH items to the online systems for same-day withdrawal is another concern for customer satisfaction.

More banks are beginning to originate ACH items for their corporate customers. Many of these systems are PC-based and use dial-up facilities between the customer and the bank. The auditor should carefully review controls over this process to ensure proper accountability for all transactions. Agreements between the bank and the customer should clarify requirements for both parties.

An area where ACH systems most likely will play a major role is in eliminating the paper documents involved in various transactions, such as purchasing using EDI systems and just-in-time inventories. Banks are becoming involved as the third party in the payment side of many of these transactions.

Audit Objective To determine the adequacy of controls over ACH systems.

Audit Procedure Review procedures for processing ACH transactions to ensure reconcilement to Federal Reserve Bank (Fed) totals and the proper handling of rejected items.

Wire Transfer Systems Wire transfer systems, including manual-based systems, are very high-risk areas for banks of all sizes. Transactions for wire transfer can involve significant cost. Fraud is a major concern. These fraud problems tend to involve insiders, simple schemes, poor security, and inadequate control procedures. If one employee has complete control over executing wire transfers and reconciling due-to, due-from, and Fed accounts, exposures to fraud potential is very high.

Audit Objective To ascertain whether controls over wire transfer systems are adequate.

Audit Procedures

- Determine that appropriate wire transfer controls are in place, including:
  - Callback procedures or use of authorization codes.
  - Authentication for nonrepeating wires.
  - Documentation of all wire transfers.
  - Approvals for unusual wires (e.g., over a certain amount).

- ☐ Recording phone calls relating to wires.

- ☐ Access control over authorization codes.

- ☐ Separation of duties between reconciling due-to, due-from, and Fed accounts and executing wire transfers.

- For PC-based wire transfer systems, ensure that proper physical and data security controls are in place.

Electronic Data Interchange Systems Documenting the EDI system provides the foundation and scope of the audit program.[9] This helps the auditor understand the EDI environment prior to performing the audit fieldwork, setting the budget, determining the technical resources required, and assessing the overall control evaluation.

Audit Objective To review, evaluate, and test the EDI information system in order to determine that controls exist and perform as expected according to standards and policies concerning the management and administration of EDI.

Audit Procedures The next audit procedures are suggested to ensure that properly authorized transactions are processed.

- Test EDI report distribution. Ensure that it is adequately controlled.

- Verify reject transaction processing. Ensure that all rejected transactions are flagged and reported as rejects and further processing of such transactions ceases.

- Confirm advice notification process. Ensure that input transactions generate advices that are returned to the transaction originator. Find out if transactions initiated by EDI trading partners are advised by the receivers and that these advices are properly reviewed.

- Determine that maintenance forms exist; note date of approval. Maintenance forms must be properly approved prior to input.

- Verify that dollar or specific transaction edits perform as expected. Confirm that EDI applications will prevent transactions other than a trading partner above specified dollar limit from processing or beyond a specific type of transaction. Ensure that the computer program will edit mandatory fields on all incoming transactions.

To determine whether EDI controls ensure that all received transactions are entered into the system, the next audit procedures are recommended.

- Examine EDI sequence control process. Ensure that there is computer sequence checking of the control numbers with out-of-sequence numbers getting flagged on the reports.

- Test batch total processing. Ensure that the system uses batch totals and performs reconciliations.

- Sample error processing and advice reconciliation. Ensure that errors and/or rejects are logged in a queue file and an appropriate advice is returned to the sender. Ensure that all transactions received are acknowledged by the system.

- Design and test for duplicate transaction entries. Ensure that duplication transactions are controlled and reviewed. Confirm that the EDI network edits and holds duplicate records.

---

[9] *EDP Auditing Guide* (Chicago: Bank Administration Institute, 1991).

The next audit procedures are advised to ensure that the EDI application controls the accuracy of information that is entered into the system.

- Confirm that there is adequate segregation of duties between the EDI users and the EDI security administrator.

- Identify and test any management overrides. Ensure that the EDI system will prevent the overriding or bypassing of data editing. Inquire if EDI has an automatic interface with the payment system to ensure that customers have the necessary funds to perform the required transactions, that the error message clearly indicates corrective action, and that there is a means of preventing duplicate or reentry of transactions.

- Evaluate exception report use, items reported, and actual use. Understand whether the exception report provides relevant, reliable, and useful information.

- Identify supervisor approval of transactions and test controls. Ensure that supervisors will review sensitive transactions after they are initiated. Ensure that there are controls over job scheduling to prevent unauthorized jobs getting processed.

AUDIT/CONTROL RISKS IN EDI APPLICATIONS

- For applications involving EDI, proper controls, such as dial-up and dial-back for connecting computers and networks, access security controls, such as positive identification of all users, and audit/information trails may not be established.

- EDI transactions and networks may not be backed up, and files/records may not be stored both on-site and off-site.

AU: update

To ensure that EDI file update processing occurs in a complete manner, the next audit procedures are suggested.

- Verify control over total processing. Confirm that there is an automated check of control totals generated by EDI to final file output.

- Determine the incoming file check to final outbound file. Confirm that there is an automated check of inbound file detail to final outbound file output.

- Validate that rejected and partially processed entries are identified and resolved. Ensure that the EDI application will flag and store rejected and partially processed entries.

- Determine the process to sequence and control outbound transactions. Confirm that the EDI application will assign record sequence control numbers for all outbound transmissions. Ensure that there are standardized default options assigned by users and that there is an error recovery mechanism that includes identification and correction procedures. Find out if reports are delivered to appropriate areas for reconciliation purposes. Confirm that invalid transactions are rejected before corrupting files.

The next audit procedures are suggested to ensure that the EDI application design provides auditable information.

- Verify cross-references that track source to output to provide an auditable link.

- Determine that input process places time and date stamps on all inbound transactions.

- Review report identification controls. Ensure that the reports include title, processing date, program name, and an identifying number.

- Review error prevention and detection procedures for adequacy.

- Test EDI audit trail procedures for logging, updating, and monitoring activities. Determine whether the EDI application produces an audit trail of before and after images for all updated files and a transaction log showing time, date, and operator. Ensure that there is logging and reporting of EDI application–generated activities, including the origination of the inbound transaction and destination of the outbound transaction.

To ensure that EDI application's data files, messages, programs, translators, utility programs, databases, and program libraries are secure, the next audit procedures are recommended.

- Confirm that passwords are stored in encrypted format and that users can dynamically change their passwords.

- Examine VAN security procedures and controls for adequacy. Make sure that if a security violation occurs, the VAN will log the violation and cease processing.

- Ensure that EDI system activity is logged to allow end-to-end tracing of transmissions.

- Ensure that EDI database resources are adequately protected and access authority is assigned strictly on a need-to-know basis. Verify whether access to the database is protected by security software.

- Ensure that utility programs are protected from unauthorized access and that audit trails show the changes made when utility programs are run.

- Ensure that EDI translator programs perform message acknowledgment and that these programs verify messages and identify the trading partner. Note that unacknowledged messages require special handling.

- Review to determine if development (test) libraries, production libraries, system software libraries, and data file libraries are separate from each other and that they are adequately protected with access appropriately assigned to specific individuals.

- Ensure that source program versions are adequately secured and controlled to facilitate concurrent development of multiple versions.

- Find out if there is an effective mechanism to escalate, report, and follow up on access violation.

The next audit procedures are suggested to ensure that EDI backup and recovery procedures are tested for disaster recovery.

- Review the EDI contingency backup plan. Verify that all data and program libraries are systematically backed up.

- Verify that functional users are familiar with the contingency plan procedures and that they participate in the contingency testing process.

- Ensure that all test events and problems are logged and distributed to all affected parties so that corrective action is taken.

(Z) Electronic Commerce: Audit Objectives and Procedures

Audit Objectives

- To ensure that e-commerce software is used for its intended purposes.

- To ensure that the e-commerce infrastructure is stable and secure to meet the business needs.

Audit Procedures

- Review whether the e-commerce software is facilitating product or service sales, shopping cart facilities are adequate, transaction processing is timely, and Web site traffic data analysis is performed periodically to meet the business needs.

- Review the e-commerce infrastructure for stability and security in terms of hardware, server operating system, server software, virtual private network, and value-added network. Determine whether the Web site is attractive to potential customers and suppliers.

(AA) Information Protection: Audit Objectives and Procedures

Computer Viruses

Audit Objective   To ensure that the organization is not severely exposed to computer viruses and that adequate controls are in place to prevent, detect, and correct the effect of viruses.

Audit Procedures   Review the controls in place to prevent, detect, and correct the computer viruses. Suggested controls to prevent or detect computer viruses follow.

- Computer security education should be a prerequisite to any computer use.

- All system users should be made aware of how to prevent and detect computer viruses.

- All executable program files should be compared daily by system users. Any unexplained change indicates a possible risk of a virus.

- All unlicensed programs should be deleted from PCs and network files by users or data security/LAN administrator. These programs could be a possible source for viruses.

- All inactive user accounts should be purged from the network files and directories by LAN/ data security administrator.

- Policies should address whether public domain and shareware software can be used or downloaded.

- An isolated system or test system concept should be implemented to test internally developed software and vendor-developed software and updates to vendor software prior to use. This is to test the software for a possible virus. The test system should not be used by other users, should not connect to networks, and should not contain any valuable data.

- Technical controls should be implemented to minimize the risk of virus. These controls include user authentication mechanisms (e.g., passwords), providing selective levels of access to files and directories (read-only, no access, access to certain users), and including write-protection mechanisms on tapes and diskettes.

- Antiviral software should be acquired and used to indicate "typical" malicious software. However, do not download or use pirated copies of antiviral software because they could be infected too.

- System-sweep programs should be acquired and used to automatically check files for changes in size, date, and content.

- When vendor software is purchased, the vendor should be asked what dependencies the product has: what other programs it was developed with or that it depends on to function. This information can be used to gauge the riskiness of using a product in terms of spreading the virus. In general, the fewer software dependencies a network has, the lower the virus risk.

- The number of software products of the same kind should be limited to prevent the spreading of virus. This means it is good to have only one version or copy of spreadsheet, word processing, or desktop publishing software on the network.

- Contingency procedures should be developed for restoring backups after a virus attack.

- Passwords should be sent over the wire in an encrypted manner to prevent tapping into the wire for disclosure of the password.

- Dial-back modems should be established for dial-in access through telephones.

- PC-based software diskettes should be screened for the presence of a virus prior to their use.

- Centralized purchase of PC-based software and hardware should be established.

- PC-based software and hardware should be acquired from reliable and reputable vendors only.

Electronic Mail

Audit Objective   To evaluate the adequacy of policies, procedures, and controls over the electronic mail system.

Audit Procedures   Electronic mail (e-mail) is a substitute for sending critical, time-bound, and time-sensitive short documents and messages in person, by phone, or by postal mail. E-mail arose from the needs of employees at all levels to receive and send documents and messages sooner and faster. The next audit procedures are suggested.

- Understand who is authorized to receive and send documents and messages through the use of the e-mail system. Determine whether the use of e-mail is required to do the job.

- Ascertain whether a policy is established defining e-mail usage so only employees at certain job levels, grades, and titles can use the e-mail system.

BUSINESS/CONTROL RISKS IN ELECTRONIC MAIL

- The privacy policy governing the use of e-mail may not be available to protect the company from legal suits when an employee reads other employee messages.

- A seamless (boundaryless), full-function e-mail system may not be available to key locations throughout the organization regardless of hardware and software vendor platforms.

- Inquire whether the e-mail system allocates default passwords to new users based on their initials. This practice should be discouraged. Alternately, the e-mail system should allow default passwords to new users on their first session, which should be followed by requesting the user to select a new password for second time and for subsequent use.

- Ascertain that the same terminal sign-on procedures used for accessing business systems are used to access the e-mail system.

- Find out whether the e-mail system requires both user ID and password to access, and use it.

- Determine whether the users of the e-mail system periodically change passwords (e.g., monthly).

- Inquire whether e-mail documents and messages can be printed at authorized and limited printers only.

- Verify if messages can be risk ranked and that high-risk messages cannot be printed at all or printed only at authorized and limited printers.

- Determine how long e-mail documents and messages stay on the system and understand the purging criteria. See that it is not too long. Two weeks is a common practice.

- Ensure that the security system prevents an employee from getting into others' e-mail message boxes.

- By taking a sample of receiving and sending messages, verify that employees are not using the e-mail machines for personal use.

- Inquire whether critical messages and documents can be encrypted.

- Test that employees who are authorized to sign-on to the e-mail system cannot automatically get into business applications and database systems. This means access to e-mail should be separate from access to other systems.

- Evaluate whether networks used for e-mail are vulnerable to computer viruses, worms, or other kind of security threats.

(BB) Encryption: Audit Objectives and Procedures

Audit Objective To determine whether the organization is using encryption methods to protect the confidentiality and privacy of corporate or personal data and information.

Audit Procedures

- Review the encryption methods for their strength, the length of the key (the longer the key, the stronger the protection), and the appropriateness of the encryption key system selected (symmetric or asymmetric key system).

- Ensure that digital signatures and digital certificates are properly issued, controlled, and distributed throughout the organization.

(CC) Enterprise-Wide Resource Planning Software: Audit Objectives and Procedures

Audit Objective To ensure that acquisition and implementation of enterprise-wide resource planning (ERP) system meets the strategic and operational objectives.

Audit Procedures

- Review management justification analysis document for acquiring and implementing the ERP system throughout the organization.

- Determine whether implementation of ERP system has improved the value chain.

- Determine whether implementation of ERP system has improved internal work flow and processes, decreased costs, increased revenues, and integrated well with other application systems. Identify problems in relying solely on one vendor for the ERP system.

(DD) Operational Applications Systems: Audit Objectives and Procedures

Data Origination and Preparation Controls Review

Audit Objective To evaluate controls and procedures over data origination and preparation activities.

Audit Procedures

- Review written procedures for originating, authorizing, collecting, preparing, and approving input transactions. Ascertain whether users understand and follow these procedures.

- Review source documents or other input forms to determine whether they are prenumbered. Also, review transaction identification codes and other frequently used constant data fields to determine whether they are precoded to minimize errors in data preparation, data entry, and data conversion.

- Where applicable, verify that all input for a batch system is sent through a data control section for scanning, reviewing, and logging prior to data entry.

- Determine whether users prepare input-control totals for batch systems and for online systems using a terminal entry and batch-updating method of processing. Verify whether users reconcile input-control totals to output-control totals.

- Ascertain whether the data control section has a cut-off schedule indicating when input data are due from user departments and when reports are due from the data control section.

- Ascertain whether the data control section reconciles input-control totals received from users to totals generated by computer.

- Determine whether filing and retention of source documents and other input forms are logical; documents are easily retrievable; and the retention practices meet the legal, tax, government, and regulatory agency requirements and the established management policies and procedures.

- Review the adequacy and currency of error correction and resubmission procedures, including whether users perform periodic review of the cumulative error listings. Evaluate the error logging and tracking methods used to ensure that errors are corrected and reentered properly and in a timely manner.

Data Input Controls Review

Audit Objective To evaluate controls and procedures over data input activities.

Audit Procedures

- For batch systems, ascertain whether data conversion or the keypunch instruction manual includes samples of source documents and identification of data fields to be entered and verified.

- For online systems, verify the use of methods to prevent data entry errors, such as self-help features, preselected formats or menu selection, and operator prompting. Evaluate video display units or computer terminal user procedures for data entry and inquiry activities.

- For transactions entered through online terminals, determine whether all input transactions are automatically logged with date and time of transmission, and determine whether user department, terminal, and user identification are included as part of the input transaction record.

- Review transaction logs for online input terminals to detect any unauthorized access and entry of data. Review the computer programs to learn whether they include automated internal program processing controls in the form of data-input edit and validation routines (i.e., check digits, reasonableness tests, batch totals, and record counts). Evaluate their accuracy and relevancy.

DATA FIELD VALIDATION CONTROLS

- Check digit calculations
- Consistency checks
- Range checks
- Reasonableness checks
- Limit checks
- Completeness checks

- Compare, validate, foot, and recompute selected critical data fields or elements with the use of manual and/or automated testing tools. Evaluate the accuracy and relevancy of test results.

- For online terminals, determine whether input data are validated and errors are corrected as data are entered into the computer system.

- Ascertain whether users review internal tables periodically to ensure the accuracy of their values.

- Review and evaluate the significance of default options or forced value coding features in critical application programs.

INPUT CONTROLS

- Batch/hash control totals
- Data editing and validation routines, such as transaction limit tests, cross-checks between data fields, sequence checks, completeness tests, logic tests, check-digit tests, anticipation controls, cross-footing or related data fields, test for invalid numeric and sign, date checks, test for valid codes, reasonableness tests

---

- Review and evaluate the rounding and truncating features in mathematical and financial calculations to determine the potential impact of rounding errors.

- Determine whether adequate audit trails are included in the DD. Check to see whether data-input edit and validation routines are described in the DD, and verify whether these data-input edit and validation tests are performed on data before a database master record is updated. Identify program and data interrelationships. This should allow for tracing a data path through the program and the system as a whole.

- Ascertain whether the computer programs have a procedure to use look-up tables for verification of codes (i.e., state, transaction, and account numbers) rather than being hard-coded in the program. (Hard-coded information is difficult to maintain and requires more programmer time and effort than do table-updating methods.)

- Review input error correction and resubmission procedures. When a correction is reentered into the system, ascertain whether it is subject to the same program edit and validation controls as the original transaction. Determine whether users perform periodic reviews of the entire error suspense file contents. Evaluate the error logging and tracking methods.

- Identify, with users, any critical error codes or messages that should have been active but have never appeared on error reports. Determine whether error message routines have been deactivated by reviewing computer program source listings. Evaluate the reasons for any deactivation noted and ascertain whether users are aware of such error code deactivation. (This is to determine whether error codes were deactivated with the knowledge of and/ or at the written request of users or whether error codes were simply no longer required because of changes that occurred after the original system design.) Note that the last three audit procedures are also applicable to the area of data processing and update controls.

Data Processing Controls Review

Audit Objective To evaluate controls and procedures over data processing activities.

Audit Procedures

- Review input control totals that facilitate the balancing of processing controls to determine whether all authorized transactions are processed accurately and properly.

- Ascertain whether there are automated run-to-run control totals so that data will not be lost between processing jobs, cycles, or programs.

PROCESSING CONTROLS

- Data editing and validation routines (explained in input controls)
- Restart/recovery procedures
- Run-to-run control totals

- Check to see whether the data control section reconciles manual batch control totals with automated batch-control totals; verify run-to-run control totals from one processing job to another before distribution of reports to users.

- Review the movement and control of data from one computer-processing job to another and between or within user departments. Determine whether existing controls are adequate and effective.

- Ascertain whether job-accounting reports are reviewed by computer operations supervisors for detection of unauthorized accesses and acts by users, computer operator, and others.

- Review the computer programs to determine whether they include automated program controls in the form of data-processing edit and validation routines (i.e., record counts, line counts, and reasonableness and relational tests). Evaluate their accuracy and relevancy.

- When data are moved or passed from one processing job or step to another, check to see that control totals are generated by the program and verified and that data are not merely moved or transferred from one job or step to another without such control.

- Review the default options and forced value coding features included either in vendor-supplied or in-house–developed applications software. Determine whether they work properly, and assess the possible consequences of their failure.

- Determine whether control totals are printed at the end of reports to provide adequate management, audit, transaction, information, or processing trails.

- Ascertain whether users review internal tables (used in master file updating) periodically to ensure the accuracy of their values.

- Ascertain whether before/after image reporting is available for all transaction, reference, or master-file updating activities.

- Compare, validate, foot, and recompute selected critical data fields or elements with the use of manual and/or automated testing and audit software tools. Evaluate the accuracy and relevancy of test results.

System-Related File Maintenance Controls Review

Audit Objective   To evaluate controls over system-related data and program files and libraries.

Audit Procedures

- For each application system in production status, ascertain whether backup and recovery procedures for data and program files are documented and tested prior to having moved the system from test to production status. Determine backup and recovery procedure adequacy and currency.

- Review written procedures for movement of backup materials and documents between the mainframe computer facility to the off-site storage facility. Determine whether these procedures are being followed actively and effectively.

- Verify whether critical computer program files, computer data files, DD, documentation, source documents and input forms, and supplies are stored both at on-site and off-site facilities. Compare actual existence of these materials to a log or book maintained by a tape librarian or similar function. Reconcile any differences and suggest corrective actions, if appropriate.

CONTROLS OVER DATA FILES

- Batch totals
- Hash totals
- File label checking
- File cross-footing checks
- Checksums
- File locking controls
- File compression and archiving procedures
- File backup and recovery procedures
- Designating file owners, sponsors, custodians, and users

- Verify the existence of a contingency plan and that critical application systems and data files are properly identified in the contingency plan.

- Review the contingency plan and backup arrangement contracts to determine whether they are complete and current. Identify and document any potential risks or exposures that would render the contract inoperative.

- Ascertain whether critical application systems have been tested on the backup computer using only program files, DD, data files, documentation, source documents and input forms, supplies, and contingency plan procedures taken from the off-site storage facility. This is to ensure the accuracy and currency of the contingency plan. Verify whether users have reviewed and reconciled the processing results produced by the backup computer with those produced by the primary computer.

Data Output Controls Review

Audit Objective To evaluate controls and procedures over system-output activities.

Audit Procedures

- Determine whether users reconcile input control totals to output control totals via processing control totals. This is to ensure the accuracy of computer program processing. System-generated reports can be used to perform this reconciliation.

- Determine whether data control personnel scan output reports to detect obvious errors, such as missing data fields, unreasonable values, and incorrect report format, before distributing to users.

- Verify that adequate identification is made of all reports and items on the reports, such as report name and number, date produced, accounting month-end or other effective date, company and department name and number, page number, program number (if necessary), end-of-report messages, subtotals, and report totals.

OUTPUT CONTROLS

- Output distribution procedures
- Security access controls for data viewing, file copying
- Output storage procedures
- Output disposal techniques
- I/O reconciliation procedures
- Limiting access to spooled data sets
- End-of-report markings

- Compare output report distribution lists with users actually receiving the reports and to find out whether unauthorized users are receiving the reports or authorized users are not receiving the reports.

- Determine whether outdated and unneeded output reports are destroyed by shredding instead of placing them in a waste container.

- Determine whether there is a continuing need for generated output report.

- Review output report retention periods. Determine their adequacy.

- Determine whether header and trailer record counts printed out at the end of each output report. If not, ascertain how data file integrity is maintained.

- Review output error correction and resubmission procedures. Determine their adequacy and relevancy. Evaluate the error logging and tracking methods.

- Ascertain whether users review the report balancing rules and reconciliation procedures periodically for accuracy and appropriateness.

Application System Documentation Controls Review

Audit Objective To determine the adequacy of application system documentation.

Audit Procedures

- Ascertain whether documentation of system, program, computer operations, help desk, network control, and system user functions and procedures are produced as part of system development and maintenance activities.

- Find out whether someone is held responsible and accountable for making various types of documentation available and keeping them current.

- Verify whether documentation problems such as lack of adequate documentation or difficulty in understanding are reported to IS management for timely and proper corrective action.

- Ascertain whether users and computer operations staff accept new application systems without proper documentation.

- Ascertain whether appropriate documentation is updated to reflect program changes and modifications.

- Determine the need for the use of automated software documentation aids.

- Verify whether a documentation librarian maintains a log of people who received various types of documentation.

- Verify whether system, program, computer operations, help desk, network control, and system user documentation manuals are available for each application system in production status (see Exhibit 1.11). Evaluate the contents for consistency and relevancy of documentation. Determine whether the documentation is adequate, complete, and current.

Data Integrity Controls Review

Audit Objective To evaluate the adequacy of data integrity controls.

Audit Procedures

- Identify and select critical data files for audit review and testing purposes. Obtain and review record layouts and program narratives to understand how certain data fields are updated and the processing logic associated with it.

     Using generalized or customized audit software or utility programs, accumulate total records in a file and/or total dollar value of critical data fields or other control totals.

Documentation type	Documentation contents
Systems manual	System flowchart, system requirements, system functions, design specifications, screen layouts, sample reports
Program manual	Program flowcharts, program functions, file layouts, program specifications
Computer operations manual	Job setup procedures, job narratives, job rerun and restart procedures, file backup procedures, report distribution procedures
User manual	System functions, sample screen and report layouts, report balancing procedures, file maintenance procedures, error correction
Help-desk manual	Contact names and phone numbers of users and IS staff; problem diagnostic and reporting procedures; problem escalation procedures; problem logging, tracking, and closing procedures
Network control manual	Information about circuits, nodes, lines, modems; problem diagnostic procedures; problem reporting and resolution procedures; network backup and contingency procedures

EXHIBIT 1.11 Application System Documentation Types and Contents

Then compare them to independently available control totals maintained by users. Develop a test plan, test cases, test data, and expected test results for comparison with actual test results. Evaluate the accuracy and relevancy of the test results.

- Evaluate the adequacy of data input and processing edit and validation rules applicable to critical and sensitive data elements contained in the DD. Trace the paths of data elements through the application system by reviewing programs, data files, and reports. Assess their accuracy and consistency.

- Evaluate whether automated program controls, such as data input and data processing edit and validation routines, are logical and appropriate to the application system.

- Verify that computer programs compare transaction dates on input transactions to parameter-controlled month-end cutoff dates to ensure consistency and that transactions entering after the cutoff date are included in the following month.

- Evaluate the adequacy of management, transaction, audit, information, or processing trails. Is an audit trail of changes to the database, in the form of a log, produced? If it is not, find out how the database is controlled.

- For online systems, test to see whether data fields are being updated when inquiry requests are being processed.

- For online systems using destructive (buried, in place) updating of random (direct) access files, ensure that there is a log of the status of a master-file record prior to and after the updating. Verify whether the log indicates the source of data.

User Satisfaction Review Assessment of system user satisfaction is a very important part of the audit of an application system. This is because it is the system user who paid for, owns, and uses the system. In fact, the system is not successful and useful if its user is not satisfied with system functions and results. One way to assess user satisfaction is to conduct user surveys periodically. System usability should be a major concern for the user and the auditor.

Audit Objective To assess user satisfaction with the results of the system.

Audit Procedures

- Determine whether management policies and procedures are available regarding access to and use of information. Assess their adequacy and relevancy.

- Ascertain whether the application system produces accurate, complete, timely, and reliable results.

CONTROLS TO ENSURE USER SATISFACTION

- User involvement in system development and maintenance projects
- User surveys
- Service-level agreements
- Performance standards
- TQM programs
- Threshold limits
- Problem management techniques

- Evaluate whether users are able to use the information produced by the application system in their decision-making process.

- Ascertain whether users are able to understand the reports and information produced by the application system.

- Verify whether users are satisfied with the information produced by the application system.

- Review user controls practiced in receiving, storing, securing, and retrieving information available on computer output reports, microfilm, microfiche, optical disk, and other output media. Determine their adequacy and relevancy.

- Ascertain whether users actively participate in developing user requirements, and design and program specifications, and review system test and acceptance test results for new or revised application systems.

- Review user controls practiced in transferring information through the exchange of memos, letters, and computer reports to and from the employees/departments. Determine their adequacy and relevancy.

- Where control weaknesses are identified in the data processing department, ascertain whether users have established compensating controls in their department. Determine whether the compensating controls are duplicated between and within user or data processing departments.

- Find out whether users work well with data processing employees in resolving problems, issues, concerns, errors, irregularities, and omissions resulting from various data processing activities.

- Ascertain whether user management periodically reviews and identifies the work areas requiring improvement either by automation or by improved manual procedures and methods. This is to increase employee and management efficiency, effectiveness, productivity, and performance.

(x) Compliance Audit Engagements

The section on compliance auditing first provides a general audit direction to conduct a compliance audit. This includes planning, risk assessment, and testing internal controls. Next, guidelines for conducting **specific** audits of compliance are provided. These include environmental auditing and human resource (personnel) policy auditing.

(A) General Audits of Compliance

Planning

In planning the audit, auditors should obtain an understanding of laws and regulations that are relevant to the audit. When laws and regulations are significant to audit objectives, auditors should design the audit to provide reasonable assurance of compliance with them. In all audits, auditors should be alert to situations or transactions that could be indicative of illegal acts or abuse. Auditors should exercise due professional care and caution in pursuing indications of possible fraud or other illegal acts that could result in criminal prosecution so as not to interfere with potential future investigations and/or legal proceedings.[10]

DEFINITIONS OF KEY TERMS: GENERAL COMPLIANCE

Noncompliance is a failure to follow requirements, or a violation of prohibitions, contained in laws, regulations, contracts, governmental grants, or an organization's policies and procedures.

Illegal acts are a type of noncompliance; specifically, they are violations of laws or regulations. They are failures to follow requirements of laws or implementing regulations, including intentional and unintentional noncompliance and criminal acts.

Criminal acts are illegal acts for which incarceration, as well as other penalties, is available if the organization obtains a guilty verdict.

Civil acts are illegal acts for which penalties that do not include incarceration are available for a statutory violation. Penalties may include monetary payments and corrective actions.

Fraud is the obtaining of something of value, illegally, through willful misrepresentation. Thus, fraud is a type of illegal act.

Abuse occurs when the conduct of an activity or function falls short of expectations for prudent behavior. Abuse is distinguished from noncompliance in that abusive conditions may not directly violate laws or regulations. Abusive activities may be within the letter of the laws and regulations but violate either their spirit or the more general standards of impartial and ethical behavior.

Errors are unintentional noncompliance with applicable laws and regulations and/or misstatements or omissions of amounts or disclosures in financial statements.

Irregularities are intentional noncompliance with applicable laws and regulations and/or misstatements or omissions of amounts or disclosures in financial statements.

Understanding Relevant Laws and Regulations

Auditors may obtain an understanding of laws and regulations through review of relevant documents and inquiry of attorneys. Generally more audits of compliance with laws and regulations take place in the public sector than in the private sector. For example, understanding relevant

---

[10] *Assessing Compliance with Applicable Laws and Regulations* (Washington, DC: U.S. Government Accountability Office, 1989).

laws and regulations can be important to planning a performance audit because government programs are usually created by law and are subject to more specific rules and regulations than the private sector. What is to be done, who is to do it, the goals and objectives to be achieved, the population to be served, and how much can be spent on what are usually set forth in laws and regulations. Thus, understanding the laws establishing a program can be essential to understanding the program itself. Obtaining that understanding may also be a necessary step in identifying laws and regulations that are significant to audit objectives.

Testing Compliance with Laws and Regulations

Auditors should design the audit to provide reasonable assurance about compliance with laws and regulations that are significant to audit objectives. Doing this requires determining if laws and regulations are significant to the audit objectives and, if they are, assessing the risk that significant illegal acts could occur. Based on that risk assessment, the auditors design and perform procedures to provide reasonable assurance of detecting significant illegal acts.

Risk Assessment

Vulnerability assessment. The probability of risk that noncompliance may occur and be material is the key factor in deciding how much compliance testing is required. A vulnerability assessment is the preferred technique of assessing the probability that applicable laws and regulations may not have been followed, and the internal controls assessment shows the likelihood of such noncompliance being detected or prevented.

A vulnerability assessment determines the probability that noncompliance and abuse, which is individually or in the aggregate material, could occur and not be prevented or detected in a timely manner by internal controls.

The vulnerability assessment evaluates the inherent risk of a law or regulation to noncompliance and abuse before considering internal controls and whether internal controls will prevent or detect noncompliance and abuse.

$$\text{Inherent risk} \times \text{Internal controls} = \text{Vulnerability or testing extent}$$

The extent of compliance testing is directly related to an activity's degree of vulnerability. The higher the vulnerability, the more extensive the compliance testing needs to be and vice versa. Thus, even though an activity may be generally risky to noncompliance and abuse, strong internal controls can reduce vulnerability to a relatively low level, thereby reducing necessary compliance testing to a relatively low level.

The rationale for performing a vulnerability assessment is that auditors can limit testing and focus on those areas most vulnerable to noncompliance and abuse if internal controls are found to be reliable. This produces a more cost-effective and timely audit.

Inherent risk. Inherent risk is the probability that a law or regulation related to audit objectives will not be complied with or that the area being reviewed is highly susceptible to noncompliance (e.g., pilferage of cash). Inherent risk is assessed before considering whether the internal controls would prevent or detect such noncompliance or abuse. Assessing inherent risk involves:

- Considering the requirements of applicable laws and regulations.
- Establishing susceptibility to noncompliance.

- Assessing management's commitment to reduce and control noncompliance.
- Determining whether previously identified noncompliance problems have been corrected.
- Testing transactions.

Auditors should consider the requirements of applicable laws and regulations. Some questions related to identifying the laws and regulations applicable to an audit include:

- Are the laws and regulations readily identifiable, vague, complex, or contradictory? Laws and regulations that are clear, understandable, and consistent with other laws and regulations are easier to adhere to and to check for compliance than laws and regulations lacking these characteristics.
- Do the laws and regulations relate to a new program, or have they undergone recent or frequent major changes? Laws and regulations that have recently been implemented or changed may be more likely to be violated because people are less familiar with them.

Auditors should identify the characteristics that increase the susceptibility to noncompliance. Some questions that should be considered include:

- Do incentives of noncompliance outweigh the potential penalties? If the law or regulation provides a benefit based on need, individuals will have an incentive to overstate their need in order to qualify or to get a larger benefit.
- Is it practicable or reasonable to expect compliance, or are the laws and regulations so burdensome or onerous that noncompliance could reasonably be expected?
- Does the activity have numerous transactions? The more transactions there are, the greater the chances that noncompliance could occur due to errors, irregularities, and abuse. Also, a large number of transactions increase the difficulty of detecting noncompliance.

KEY CONCEPTS TO REMEMBER: Indicators of Susceptibility to Noncompliance (Red Flags)

- Poor records or documentation
- Complex transactions
- Activities that are dominated and controlled by a single person or small group
- Unreasonable explanations to inquiries by auditors
- Auditee annoyance at reasonable questions by auditors
- Employees' refusal to give others custody of records
- Employees' refusal to take vacations and/or accept promotions
- Extravagant lifestyle of employees
- A pattern of certain contractors bidding against each other or, conversely, certain contractors not bidding against each other
- Use of materials on commercial contracts that were intended for use on government contracts
- A high default rate on government-backed loans

- Have important activities or programs been contracted out or delegated to those outside the organization without ensuring that adequate internal control systems and active monitoring oversight are in place?

- Does the activity have a significant amount of assets that are readily marketable (i.e., cash, securities) or that could be used for personal purposes (i.e., tools, cars, auto repair parts, or computers)? Such assets are very susceptible to improper use or theft.

Auditors should consider management's commitment to reduce and control noncompliance. A strong commitment by management to comply is a positive factor in reducing the risk of noncompliance. Some questions that should be considered include:

- Have problems been repeatedly disclosed in prior audits?

- Does management promptly respond when problems are first identified?

- Are recurring complaints received through hotline allegations?

- Is management willing to discuss its approach toward compliance?

- Is management knowledgeable of the subject area and potential problems?

- Does management have a constructive attitude, including a willingness to consider innovative approaches?

- Is there a stable management team with continuity and a good reputation, or is there high turnover and/or a poor management reputation?

The final step of assessing inherent risk involves testing a limited number of transactions. This testing usually occurs during the survey phase of an audit and is not intended to be a representative sample of transactions. The purpose of this testing is to gain a better understanding of the processes an organization follows and to confirm other observations made about the inherent risk of noncompliance.

Internal controls. Internal controls consist of policies and procedures used to provide reasonable assurance that goals and objectives are met; resources are adequately safeguarded, efficiently utilized, and reliably accounted for; and laws and regulations are complied with. Evaluating internal controls involves:

- Identifying internal control objectives (policies) that management has designed to ensure that laws and regulations are complied with and the control environment.

- Identifying key internal control techniques (procedures) that management has established to achieve objectives.

- Testing control procedures.

- Identifying needed follow-up actions.

Auditors should determine what control objectives related to audit objective management have been established. A control objective is a positive thing that management tries to attain or an adverse condition or negative effect that management is seeking to avoid.

The control environment reflects the overall attitude toward and awareness of management regarding the importance of controls. A good control environment is a positive factor in establishing and enhancing the effectiveness of specific policies and procedures, while a poor control environment has the opposite effect. Factors affecting the control environment include:

- Management's philosophy and operating style (tone at the top).

- The entity's organizational structure.

- Methods of delegating authority and responsibility.
- Management's methods for monitoring and following up on performance, including corrective action taken on audit recommendations.
- Personnel policies and practices.

Control objectives and control environment represent those goals and actions management wished to achieve, while control procedures are the specific steps designed and prescribed by management to provide reasonable assurance that its control objectives will be achieved.

EXAMPLES OF INHERENT LIMITATIONS IN INTERNAL CONTROL SYSTEMS

- Costs and benefits
- Employee collusion
- Management override
- Incorrect application of control procedures by employees

The auditor can obtain information on the control environment, objectives, and procedures by reading policy and procedure manuals, reviewing past audit reports, interviewing management and employees, and making observations.

Because of inherent limitations in the design and operation of any internal control system, auditors should **not** expect internal controls to prevent or detect all instances of noncompliance or abuse. The most pervasive limitation is that the cost of internal controls should not exceed their benefits. In deciding how extensive the system of internal controls should be, management compares the costs of more controls with the benefits to be gained.

Other limitations include the possibility that management may override the internal control system; employees may secretly be working together (collusion) to avoid or circumvent the controls; and employees may not be correctly applying the control techniques due to fatigue, boredom, inattention, lack of knowledge, or misunderstanding. As a result, auditors should always test actual transactions to have a reasonable basis for evaluating internal controls.

The auditors' understanding of the internal control system should be documented in the working papers. This can be done through flowcharts; narratives; questionnaire responses; records of interviews; and copies of policies and procedures, documents, and records.

For internal control procedures to be effective, they must be designed to achieve the intended objective(s) and must be correctly and consistently applied by the authorized employee(s). The best-designed internal controls are of little value if the procedures are not correctly followed. For example, if the entity has a procedure requiring the manager's approval for all purchases over $25,000 but the manager does not review the purchase orders, this procedure will not be very effective in preventing or detecting unnecessary purchases.

Testing internal controls. Testing internal controls consists of five steps.

Step 1. Defining what constitutes effective internal controls

Step 2. Selecting a small sample of transactions, either randomly or nonrandomly

Step 3. Evaluating whether the sample transactions were executed in accordance with the laws and regulations and internal controls

Step 4. Documenting the evaluation results

Step 5. Determining the probability that noncompliance will not be detected or prevented by the internal controls

If testing reveals material noncompliance or abuse, the auditor should determine what internal controls were intended to prevent or detect the noncompliance or abuse and ascertain the reasons they did not. If internal controls are weak or nonexistent, many more transactions may be in noncompliance. Auditors should consider expanding tests to determine the impact of weaknesses on audit objectives and of doing follow-up work later.

(B) Specific Audits of Compliance Two areas are addressed in this section: environmental auditing and human resource policy auditing.

Environmental Auditing The 1993 IIA study on environmental auditing defined seven categories under the title of environmental audits.[11] Internal environmental auditing is considered to be the self-evaluation process whereby an organization determines whether it is meeting its legal and internal environmental objectives or not.

DEFINITION OF KEY TERMS: ENVIRONMENTAL AUDITING

- An **environmental management system** is an organization's structure of responsibilities and policies, practices, procedures, processes, and resources for protecting the environment and managing environmental issues.

- **Environmental auditing** is an integral part of the environmental management system whereby management determines whether the organization's environmental control systems are adequate to ensure compliance with regulatory requirements and internal policies.

The seven environmental audit categories include: (1) compliance audits, (2) environmental management system audits, (3) transactional audits, (4) treatment, storage, and disposal facility audits, (5) pollution prevention audits, (6) environmental liability accrual audits, and (7) product audits.

1. **Compliance audits** are detailed, site-specific assessments of current, past, and planned operations. They assess whether activities and operations are within the legal constraints imposed by regulations. Compliance audits, which are the most common type of environmental audit, may be categorized according to the level of detail and effort they require.

   Preliminary assessment, sometimes called a document review or desktop audit, is used to provide insight into potential problem areas, especially those where projections regarding future conditions may warrant more intensive review.

   An environmental audit is a more detailed audit focusing on operations. This audit includes verification of compliance with permits and consent orders. The auditor typically traces the compliance process through to the reporting requirements to ensure regulatory compliance.

---

[11] Rebecca Thomson, Thomas Simpson, and Charles Le Grand, "Environmental Auditing," *Internal Auditor* (April 1993): 19–21.

Environmental investigations or site assessments are time- and labor-intensive assessments, conducted when the preceding phases indicate the potential risk of contamination or other noncompliance. The audit report includes interpretation of technical analyses, such as laboratory reports.

2. **Environmental management system audits** focus on the systems in place to ensure that they are operating properly to manage future environmental risks. These audits are conducted internally when the environmental auditing process matures and organizations become confident in their compliance with regulations.

3. **Transactional audits,** also called acquisition and divestiture audits, property transfer site assessments, property transfer evaluations, and due diligence audits, are environmental risk management tools for banks, land buyers, lending agencies, charitable organizations, investors, and any organization purchasing land for a facility site. Buyers, lenders, and others need to understand the environmental risks associated with the property they are purchasing, lending on, or accepting as a gift, because the environmental liability can easily exceed the market value of the asset.

4. **Treatment, storage, and disposal facility audits** involve the tracking of hazardous substances throughout their existence. Under U.S. environmental regulations, all hazardous materials are tracked from creation to destruction (cradle to grave), and all "owners" of these materials have liability for them as long as the owners exist.

5. **Pollution prevention audits** are operational appraisals that serve to identify opportunities where waste can be minimized and pollution can be eliminated at the source rather than controlled at the end of the pipe. Pollution prevention primarily involves manufacturing facilities. Manufacturing is likely to create pollution within multiple media (air, water, and solid waste) at several operational stages, including raw materials handling and storage, process chemical use, maintenance, finished materials handling, and disposal.

6. **Environmental liability accrual audits** are technical accounting and legal reviews involved with recognizing, quantifying, and reporting liability accruals for known environmental issues. The responsibility for assessing the reasonableness of cost estimates for environmental remediation falls to the internal audit function.

7. **Product audits** are appraisals within the production processes of a facility. Their objective is to provide assurance that the product is in compliance with chemical restrictions and with environmentally sensitive interests. Product auditing is resulting in the development of fully recyclable products.

An Approach to Conducting an Environmental Audit Gerald Vinten recommended four audit steps in conducting an environmental audit. The audit will address the operating environment, health and safety management, product safety and quality, loss prevention, minimizing resource use, and adverse effects on the environment.[12] The scope of the audit can be comprehensive or limited to a single topic, which can include organization strategy, functional areas of business, operational factors, and reporting and follow-up.

1. Organization strategy

   A. **Overall environmental policy.** These questions should be addressed: Is there an overall environmental policy? Has it the support of the board of directors, top management, and workforce? Is it communicated with shareholders, employees, customers, suppliers,

---

[12] Gerald Vinten, "The Greening of Audit," *Internal Auditor* (October 1991): 34–35.

local politicians, neighbors, and control authorities (e.g., the Environmental Protection Agency)? Is there a consistent ecological strategy for the organization? Are the organization's objectives set with due regard for ecological factors?

B. **Staff training and participation.** These questions should be addressed: Is there a system for informing staff about ways to improve environmental performance? Are there training programs, suggestion schemes, quality circles, performance targets, and operational and maintenance schedules? What motivation and training methods should be employed, and how are they evaluated? Are environmental matters raised as part of a social occasion to show what the organization is doing? Is there a recognition system for staff? Are staff encouraged to become involved in environmental projects? It has been found that "firms that were relatively more prosperous tended more often to pollute illegally."

   With reference to accident and emergency procedures: Are there adequate contingency plans for dealing with accidents and emergencies? Is the public relations department ready to communicate with employees, neighbors, the press, and others? Are there controls to ensure that only public relations statements that will stand up to independent scrutiny are permitted to be issued?

2. **Functional areas of business**

   A. **Marketing function.** These questions should be addressed: Do marketing initiatives create or reinforce the organization's image and reputation for its concern with environmental issues? Are products marked to draw attention to their environmentally positive features? Is the packaging made from environmentally acceptable materials? Are marketing channels set up by agreement between manufacturers and distributors to make recycling systems possible? If higher prices are attributable to ecological factors, are the price differentials due to the ecological factors highlighted?

   B. **Finance function.** These questions should be addressed: Is environmental impact taken into account in all investment decisions? Are ethical and green investments chosen wherever feasible? If an investment is likely to increase pollution, has a lower-pollution alternative been investigated, and have the likely costs been included in the project costing? Is a short-term outlook avoided where a longer-term perspective will lead to higher environmental dividends?

   C. **Production function.** These questions should be addressed: Has the earlier replacement of an existing production plant, and the acquisition of new, nonpolluting machinery, been considered? Are ecological materials and processes in use? Are clean technologies, with better input-output ratios, in use? Are useful materials and heat recovered? Are emissions minimized by postproduction environmental protection measures? Can raw materials specifications be altered without unduly affecting product quality and to improve environmental aspects?

   D. **Insurance function.** These questions should be addressed: Has a check been made regarding intrinsic damage that could ensue from environmental risks? Have checks been made of the possible risks to third parties caused by damage to the environment?

   Has the risk management strategy been checked to ensure that there is a suitable mix of assumption of risk, transfer of risk, and insurance cover?

   E. **International business divisions.** These questions should be addressed: Are exports, imports, and foreign production environment oriented? Is pressure being brought to achieve change?

F. Legal department. These questions should be addressed: Are all steps taken to comply with official regulations? Are environmental damage and liability risks kept to a minimum?

3. **Operational factors**

   A. Discharges. This question should be addressed: Are process controls and management systems adequate to ensure compliance with legislation and future objectives, as well as to avoid complaints? The scope of discharge includes air, water, and noise.

   B. Site tidiness. These questions should be addressed: Are measures taken to eliminate litter and sources of untidiness inside buildings, outside and in the immediate surroundings? Has suitable landscaping been considered to improve the appearance of the site?

   C. Transport. These questions should be addressed: Are staff encouraged to use public transport, and could the availability of public transport be increased by providing additional company-funded services? Is the organization using the most efficient and environmentally sound systems for transporting goods, people, and materials? Are only low-pollution vehicles purchased? Are existing vehicles reequipped and serviced with environmental considerations in mind?

   D. Water use. These questions should be addressed: Is water used efficiently? Can consumption be reduced by using another cooling method or controlling leakages more effectively?

   E. Recycling. These questions should be addressed: Are all opportunities considered for recycling? Could redundant, used products be recycled?

   F. Wastes. These questions should be addressed: Are steps taken to minimize, eliminate, or recycle waste? Are recycling opportunities being lost by failure to segregate different types of waste? Is waste disposed of responsibly?

   G. Energy use. These questions should be addressed: Are electricity, steam, water, and gas meters at the major points of use, and are targets set to reduce their usage? Is full use made of alternative energy sources, such as landfill gas, waste-derived fuel, solar and wind energy, and combined heat and power? Are energy-conservative schemes in existence and adequate? Are buildings and plants properly insulated? Can savings be made in heating and lighting costs?

   H. Canteen food. These questions should be addressed: Is healthy eating encouraged and health education provided? Is nutritional information provided? Is an improved range of healthy dishes and drinks provided? Are there safeguards to ensure food hygiene?

   I. Occupational health and safety. These questions should be addressed: Is there an occupational health department? Does it provide advice on practical accident and injury prevention? Does it look after employees' psychological needs? Does it advise on health education in home and family? Does it advise on stress reduction and time management?

   J. Data processing. These issues should be addressed: The data collected needs to be analyzed and then presented in a form that is easily understood and from which clear conclusions may be drawn. Wherever possible, conclusions should be discussed with the staff directly involved.

4. Reporting and follow-up

As soon as they are identified, significant defects need to be reported immediately to the chief executive officer for quick action. More routine findings should be presented to the board of directors as an executive summary and with clear recommendations for action. These should include an estimate of cost, resource needs, optimum time for introduction, and when the next review should take place. The board should be invited to approve the recommendations and authorized implementation. The implementation plan should include deadlines for action.

A periodic check will be made that the board decisions have been fully implemented, with any noncompliance reported back to the board. A quality assurance review of the audit process itself is also recommended.

An Approach to Audit Hazardous Waste Management Program Authors Jerry Kreuze, Gale Newell, and Stephen Newell recommended an audit program entitled "Internal Auditors' Guide to a Comprehensive Hazardous Waste Management Program."[13]

A. When acquiring new properties

1. Investigate previous owners and uses of properties.

2. Perform an environmental audit, to provide assurance that contaminants are not present on the properties.

B. Be familiar with hazardous waste creation, hauling, and disposal to:

1. Identify the products and by-products that are considered hazardous.

2. Investigate ways to minimize the amount of hazardous waste being created.

3. Confirm that existing hauling and disposal procedures are in conformity with applicable federal, state, and local ordinances, acts, and standards.

4. Verify company compliance with the numerous federal and state acts dealing with clean air and water, solid waste disposal, and toxic substance abuse.

5. Respond to new research findings on toxicity, new regulations, or newly imposed environmental standards.

6. Continuously monitor hazardous waste disposal sites to determine that the disposal methods are adequate and cost effective.

7. Ensure the availability of insurance, promote favorable rates, and alleviate potential liabilities in excess of insurance limits.

C. Perform an overall environmental risk assessment to:

1. Identify all environmental concerns faced by the company.

2. Categorize these concerns into three groups: high, moderate, or low risk.

3. Direct financial resources to those concerns that pose the greatest potential threat to the company's long-term existence.

4. Audit the above expenditures to determine if they are effectively reducing the company's overall environmental risk.

---

[13] Jerry Kreuze, Gale Newell, and Stephen Newell, "Liability for Hazardous Waste and the Internal Auditor," *Internal Auditor* (June 1990): 53.

Another Approach to Environmental Auditing Another approach to environmental auditing is presented by Wayne Socha and Sally Harvey.[14] The authors offered a list of areas for investigation that includes:

- Test toxic emissions compliance at all facilities. Smokestacks are not the only sign of potential pollution.

- Test pollution levels within the office environment. Tests by U.S. universities have shown that standard office equipment, such as laser printers and copiers, can violate federal ozone standards if air filters become clogged with dust.

- Review health and welfare protection for workers using PCs and workstations. Regulations protecting computer users are fairly routine for workers in Europe and South America. In North America, landmark legislation by the City of San Francisco signals that American workers may soon be protected. Look for these clues in spotting a concerned employer: polarized lighting, antiglare monitor screens, low-frequency electrical emission blockage on PCs, adjustable desks and chairs, and wrist rest pads, software that forces PC users to take rest breaks, and physical training to relieve stress.

- Review corporate transportation solutions. Is the employer taking an active role in reducing air, traffic, and noise pollution? Subsidized parking increases pollution from cars. Subsidized bus passes and car pools reduce pollution. For an even greater effect, pay people to car pool rather than trying to discourage driving by imposing higher parking rates. If car-pooling is already encouraged, do corollary policies support the practice? For example, if the driver in a car pool becomes sick in the middle of the day, do the policies allow everyone to go home early? Does the policy provide some other way for the rider employees to get home?

- Perform environmental audits on new products. Does the proposed product increase the depletion of resources? Is this a throwaway product?

> **AUDIT CONCERNS DURING ENVIRONMENTAL AUDITING**
>
> During an audit of environmental protection devices at a hazardous materials research center, the auditor has reviewed the architect's alarm device specifications, examined invoices for the devices, and interviewed the plant safety officer responsible for installation. The main concern of these procedures is assurance that the specified alarm system was purchased and installed and that it is working properly.

- Review packaging for saving potential. The packaging industry is being generally indicted for increasing the pollution load. While image-enhancing publicity is now being used to reverse the perception, could the company package more responsibly, thereby responding to the concern and saving money? One computer software manufacturer looked at the problem and found that 100% of the product could be produced using recycled products, except for the disks, with large savings in packaging production costs.

- Consider the impact of product content decisions. Environmental organizations may target anything containing tropical or temperate rain forest products.

- Conduct energy audits and encourage efficient building designs.

---

[14] Wayne Socha and Sally Harvey, "Mini-Green Audits," *Internal Auditor* (October 1991): 42–43.

- Compare corporate mission statements to reality. Most mission statements contain a generic clause professing concern with the community. Is this concern evidenced by action? Are resources allocated to building more responsible products or to fighting regulations designed to correct wasteful industries?

- Investigate the potential for recycling in the company. Recycling is another form of source reduction; in this case, do not buy products that cannot be recycled unless no other substitute exists. The company could use 50% recycled paper for internal reports rather than the same expensive paper used for customer correspondence. Internal publications made from expensive four-color, high-gloss production techniques are not easily recycled and sometimes are printed with inks containing heavy metals. Instead, use low-tech newsprint or even high-tech digital transmission or recyclable videotapes.

- Review hazardous waste exposure on property the firm controls or finances. U.S. banks and insurance firms have been sued for cleanup costs on property they neither controlled nor used. Some courts have held that financing a company that creates hazardous waste, such as gasoline service stations, passes the cleanup liability along to the capital provider.

Human Resource Policy Auditing This section discusses compliance with safety, hazard communication, security, benefits continuation, bulletin boards, exit interview, I-9 employment eligibility, independent contractors, telephone usage, smoking policy, drug testing, substance abuse policy, accommodating disabilities, and sexual harassment.[15]

Safety Firms that have successful safety programs typically share three characteristics: (1) a management commitment to safety, (2) active employee participation in safety activities, and (3) thorough investigation of accidents. Successful safety programs reduce accidents. Fewer accidents mean less work interruptions, fewer worker's compensation claims, and lower insurance costs.

OSHA is the federal government agency responsible for defining and enforcing job standards. The OSHA law covers all employers engaged in a business affecting commerce but excludes self-employed individuals, family firms, and workplaces covered by other federal safety laws. Employers covered by OSHA have a general duty to maintain a safe and healthful workplace. The general duty requirements mean that the employer must become familiar with safety standards that affect the workplace, educate employees on safety, and promote safe practices in the daily operation of the business.

AUDIT CONCERNS IN EMPLOYEE SAFETY REVIEW

In a manufacturing operations audit, the audit objective was to determine whether all legal and regulatory requirements concerning employee safety are being properly implemented. The audit procedure would be to examine documentation concerning the design and operation of the relevant systems and to observe operations for compliance.

Safety Responsibility

A safety responsibility policy serves as the framework for additional policy guidelines that direct safety activities. Typical safety activities include safety orientation, safety training, safety committee, workplace inspections, and accident investigations. Also effective in promoting safe work practices are safe operating procedures, job safety analysis, and publishing of safety rules. In order

---

[15] William Hubbartt, *Personnel Policy Handbook* (New York: McGraw-Hill, 1993), pp. 427–500.

to implement this policy, a safety manager should be designated to coordinate day-to-day safety activities and should be supported by higher-level management for having ultimate responsibility for directing workplace safety.

Safety policy guidelines provide a basis for promoting employee participation in safety activities. Active participation in safety is one important way to keep safety in everyone's mind. A safety mind-set helps to prevent accidents.

Some risks that could result from noncompliance, or pitfalls to avoid, include not holding supervisors and managers accountable for safety in their respective work areas, not including safety results on a supervisor's performance evaluation, and the tendency to publish a few safety rules and then let things slide. Under the law, an employer will be held liable for failing to enforce safety rules. If a company publishes a safety rule but neglects to require employees to comply with the rule, the firm may be subject to a citation.

Accident Investigation The purpose of accident investigation is to identify the accident's cause so that future accidents can be avoided. In addition to prevention of accidents, accident investigations serve several other important functions, such as: eliminating unsafe conditions, identifying training needs, redesigning jobs, preventing or combating fraud related to unethical worker's compensation claims, analyzing accident data, and reporting to government.

Hazard Communication Millions of workers are exposed to one or more chemical hazards on the job. Improper use of chemicals on the job can cause fire, explosion, contamination of water or sewer systems, and other serious accidents. Further, employees who fail to follow proper chemical-handling procedures may be subject to serious health problems, such as heart conditions, kidney and lung damage, sterility, cancer, burns, and rashes.

OSHA has issued Hazard Communication Standards to help prevent employee illness or injury from chemical products. The standards require chemical manufacturers and distributors to identify chemical hazards and communicate this information to employers using the products. Employers, in turn, are responsible for educating employees about workplace hazards.

The Hazard Communication Standards have six main requirements.

1. Determine what chemical hazards are in the workplace.

2. Establish a written Hazard Communication Program.

3. Develop and/or use warning labels on containers of hazardous chemicals.

4. Maintain a file of Material Safety Data Sheets (MSDS) that describe properties and precautions of each chemical used in the workplace.

5. Train employees to recognize chemical hazards and follow safety precautions.

6. Provide disclosure of limited trade secret information when requested by health care professionals dealing with employee chemical exposures.

Some risks that could result from noncompliance, or pitfalls to avoid, include: (1) failing to handle MSDS forms properly, resulting in lost forms, incomplete files, and inadequate information for responding to an emergency; (2) failure to develop a Hazard Communication Plan could result in an OSHA citation; and (3) not discussing chemical hazard issues with employees for fear of generating employee concerns about job safety, when in fact employees will be pleased to see that management is willing to deal with job safety issues. After hazard communication training, employees tend to be cautious and more likely to use personal protective equipment. An employer's failure to address chemical safety issues on their job, however, is more likely to prompt employee concerns and fears.

Security Management in every organization is concerned about protecting company assets from loss and protecting employees from harm. Security issues can range from protecting the premises from unauthorized entry, guarding against unauthorized release of business records, protecting the safety of employees or customers, and preventing theft.

A security policy assigns responsibilities and defines plans to help the firm prevent and control losses. Firms that fail to define certain security guidelines generally incur greater losses than organizations with comprehensive security practices.

Security issues are a matter of great concern in certain industries. Banks define stringent procedures for the handling and storage of cash. Health care facilities and drugstores follow rigid procedures in the handling of drugs. Certain government defense contractors are required to establish sophisticated systems and controls to protect confidentiality of classified defense projects.

Some areas that require security focus include: security services, such as guard services, installation of alarms, and video monitoring systems. These services should be connected to offsite monitoring of alarm and video systems for a timely response, locks and key control, locked files and administrative controls, documented asset and inventory control, visitor control, computer security requiring codes to access confidential data, personnel safety for employees entering or leaving the premises or parking areas. An employee identification system (a badge with picture) may be part of this process, as may background checks, reference checks, and surety bonds. Employers are no longer permitted to use polygraph (lie detector) machines in the employee selection process. The Employee Polygraph Protection Act of 1988 prohibits the use of lie detectors to test an employee or prospective employee. The law also prohibits discipline, discharge, or other discrimination against an employee based on polygraph tests or refusal to take a test. Private security firms, drug companies, and government units are exempted from the law.

A major risk that could result from noncompliance, or pitfalls to avoid, is that workplace security measures have the potential for conflict with individual privacy concerns or rights.

Benefits Continuation Employers with 20 or more employees are subject to the Consolidated Omnibus Budget Reconciliation Act (COBRA) of 1986. COBRA defines requirements for employers to offer continued health insurance coverage for employees or covered dependents who become ineligible for benefits.

When certain qualifying events occur under COBRA, the individual must be offered the opportunity to continue group health insurance. Qualifying events include termination of employment, reduction of hours, layoff, divorce, death, or losing dependent status due to age. The law specifies time limits for the period of continued coverage. Also, there are notification responsibilities and limits. Upon expiration of the benefit continuation period, the employee may exercise conversion rights. This means that the employee's coverage is converted to an individual policy with a higher premium rate.

Bulletin Boards Many organizations have a bulletin board to communicate information to employees. In addition, various states and federal labor laws require an employer to post notices about certain employee rights under the law. A bulletin board is company property, so the employer has full authority to regulate what items are posted. Bulletin boards may be used to post information on holidays, benefits, company policies, advancement opportunities, company rules, or other company news. Federal labor law posters that must be displayed in the workplace include: equal employment, minimum wage, overtime, child labor, federally financed construction, federal government contracts, OSHA poster "job safety and health protection," polygraph, and family and medical leave.

Exit Interview An exit interview is an important human resource tool for controlling unwanted turnover. An exit interview also promotes compliance with COBRA insurance continuation requirements. In an exit interview, the human resource specialist interviews a separating employee to discuss reasons for separation, explain benefits entitlement, and secure return of company property.

When an unusually large number of employees quit, the exit interview can help identify causes, such as poor supervisory relations, poor employee selection decisions, pay concerns, working conditions, or other problems. The first policy concern is to assign responsibility for exit interviews preferably to an independent third party, such as a human resource specialist. The second policy concern is to act on the information received from the exit interview.

I-9 Employment Eligibility The I-9 Employment Verification Form or other related forms must be completed by all employees after November 6, 1986, per the Immigration Reform and Control Act of 1986. The purpose of the law is to eliminate employment opportunities that attract illegal aliens to the United States. The law makes it the employer's responsibility to verify that the employee is a U.S. citizen or an alien authorized to work in the United States.

An employer may refuse to hire an individual who fails to provide appropriate I-9 documents. However, it is illegal to discriminate against an individual because of national origin or citizenship status.

Independent Contractors Independent contractors are self-employed individuals who contract with firms to provide a particular service. Some employers treat certain employees as independent contractors. A number of states and federal laws define and regulate the employment relationship.

The U.S. Internal Revenue Service defines employee status and requires income tax withholding from employees. State and federal unemployment insurance laws require employer contributions for employees. Workers' compensation laws require insurance coverage for employees. Wage hour laws stipulate minimum wage and overtime pay requirements for covered employees. Clearly, the determination of whether an individual is an employee or independent contractor has a significant effect on business costs and legal liability.

Unfortunately, there is no single definition for *independent contractor*. Each government agency that enforces laws relating to the employer–employee relationship has its own definitions and tests to determine whether a covered employment relationship exists. There are some common trends to aid in defining employment relationships.

These factors are typical of independent contractor status:

- Individual operates a separate business on a profit and loss basis.
- Individual performs services for other businesses.

- Individual exercises initiative and judgment in how work is performed.
- Individual maintains own tools, equipment, and separate office or facility.
- Individual is paid on a per-job basis.

These factors are typical of an employer-employee relationship:

- Employer exercises direction and control over employee, work methods, and hours of work.
- Employee generally performs tasks at employer's facility.
- Employee works only for employer.
- Employee is compensated on an hourly or weekly salary basis.

Telephone Usage Three common policy concerns about office employee telephone use include: (1) pleasant telephone manner, (2) use of proper telephone procedures, and (3) controlling abuse of telephones. With regard to abuse of office telephones, the major concern is unauthorized use of company telephones for local and long-distance personal calls.

Several telephone use guidelines include:

- Limit outgoing personal calls to nonworking time, such as lunch and breaks.
- Limit incoming personal calls to employees, particularly those in public contact jobs.
- Route incoming personal calls to voice mail, message center, or supervisor.
- Not allowing employees in production, service, or public contact jobs to be interrupted from work tasks by personal phone calls.
- Limit outgoing calls to a pay telephone in the plant or work area or use of cell phones during work.

Smoking Policy Employee attitudes about smoking have changed significantly over the past 20 years. Along with the changes of public attitudes about smoking, growing numbers of governmental units have defined laws or regulations restricting smoking. A number of these actions are listed next.

- OSHA regulations prohibit use of smoking materials when working near flammable substances.
- The federal government and the military adopted policies limiting use of smoking materials in government buildings.
- The Federal Aeronautics Administration now prohibits use of smoking materials on all domestic commercial airplane flights.
- Many cities have passed ordinances restricting smoking in public areas.

Advance notice to employees about the new smoking policy is essential. The scope of the smoking policy is a major issue to consider. The policy can range from a total ban on smoking in the workplace to limited restrictions. Incentives to promote employee interest in stopping smoking should be considered. This includes offering smoking clinics, either on-site or off-site.

Some common risks resulting from noncompliance or pitfalls to avoid include: smokers' rights versus nonsmokers' rights, impact of smoking or nonsmoking on work tasks not getting done, and impact of new privacy laws. These laws make it illegal for an employer to discipline or otherwise discriminate against an employee for legal off-duty activities. The intent of these laws is to prevent an employer from taking action against an employee for smoking off the job and may serve to bar broad policy criteria, such as hiring only nonsmokers or banning employees from smoking on and off the job.

Drug Testing A number of legal issues should be considered when implementing a drug-testing program. Constitutional issues, federal laws, state laws, and various regulations must be considered when defining drug-testing programs. The U.S. Constitution restricts governmental interference with individual rights. This means that public sector employees have been accorded privacy rights from the unreasonable search and seizures of drug tests. Private sector employees, however, have not been accorded the same protection from their employers. Some state constitutions contain privacy protection applicable to both private and public sector's conduct.

Drug testing has grown as a means to combat drug abuse on the job. Firms have used drug testing in a variety of ways, as described next.

- **New-hire testing.** A positive test result showing presence of drugs in the body is considered grounds to deny or withdraw a job offer.

- **Reasonable cause testing.** Nuclear plant workers, truck drivers, and railway engineers are subject to drug testing requirements.

- **Random testing.** The unscheduled or surprise testing of an employee or group of employees for the presence of drugs is intended to catch drug-using individuals who may be able to remain drug-free in anticipation of a scheduled drug test in order to pass the test.

- **Universal testing.** Universal testing involves the scheduled or unscheduled drug testing of all employees.

A major risk resulting from noncompliance with policies, or pitfalls to avoid, is sensitivity to an individual's right to privacy. An employer's insensitivity to employee privacy concerns or failure to adequately implement a testing program can cause serious morale problems and costly litigation.

Substance Abuse Policy *Substance abuse* can be defined as inappropriate or excessive use of alcoholic beverages, over-the-counter drugs, prescription drugs, or any use of illegal drugs. Substance abuse by employees is a contributing factor to workplace accidents, poor productivity, increased errors, and absenteeism.

A substance abuse policy typically defines specific prohibitions against possession or use of drugs or alcoholic beverages on company time or premises. A substance abuse policy identifies specific action steps that a supervisor can take rather than covering for the employee and enabling the substance abuser to continue.

Several state and federal labor laws may impact on a substance abuse policy. Government contractors are subject to the Drug-Free Workplace Act of 1988. This law requires employers receiving a government contract of $25,000 or more to certify that they maintain a drug-free workplace with a written plan to comply with the law. The employers' drug-free workplace program should include:

- A written policy distributed to employees regarding illegal drugs.

- A drug awareness program that includes information about hazards of drug use on the job, penalties for violating the policy, and education about available counseling or rehabilitation programs.

- Employee compliance with the policy, including the reporting of an employee conviction of a drug offense in the workplace.

- Corrective action that the employer will take against an employee for policy violation or drug conviction.

- The employer's good-faith effort to comply with the law.

The Drug-Free Workplace Act does not require drug testing. Also, the law does not require sanctions for job use or possession of alcoholic beverages. Both of these issues, however, may be included in a substance abuse policy if elected by the employer. The Americans with Disabilities Act (discussed in the next section) specifically defines recovered alcoholics and recovered former drug users as individuals with a disability subject to the law's protection.

Other potential liabilities could result from a substance abuse policy if the employer discharged an employee in a manner contrary to procedures published in a policy manual or employee handbook. Also, careless release of confidential facts or release of false information about an employee in the course of employment or reference check could result in litigation.

Accommodating Disabilities The Americans with Disabilities Act (ADA) of 1990 prohibits discrimination against individuals with disabilities. This far-reaching law deals with discrimination issues in employment, among other things. A policy providing guidance to supervisors on accommodating disabilities will help an organization to comply with the law. The policy can focus on those employment practices that involve supervisor decisions affecting disabled persons. The most likely areas for supervisor guidance are hiring processes, reemployment following medical leave or job accident, and other job changes, such as promotions or transfers. Important policy points are listed next.

- The firm's employment application should be revised to eliminate inquiries about prior illnesses, physical limitations, or prior workers' compensation claims. These inquiries are improper inquiries under ADA.

- The ADA specifically recognizes job descriptions prepared before advertising and interviewing candidates as evidence of essential job functions. Old job descriptions need updating to reflect actual job tasks performed on the job. New job descriptions should be prepared where no descriptions currently exist.

- All interview questions, hiring criteria, exams, and tests must be based on job-related standards consistent with business necessity in order to comply with ADA.

- Preemployment medical exams to determine the nature or severity of a disability are prohibited by ADA. A medical examination evaluating the individual's ability to perform job-related functions may be conducted after making an offer of employment but before the applicant begins performing job duties. Any medical exam should be administered to all entering employees in the same job category. An individual's employment may be conditioned on the results of the medical examination.

Enforcement of the employment sections of the ADA rests with the Equal Employment Opportunity Commission (EEOC). Enforcement can include an informal investigation questionnaire, fact-finding conference, conciliation, settlement, dismissal, or federal court enforcement action. Remedies can include reinstatement, back pay, or other actions.

To minimize claims and avoid discrimination findings, here are some pitfalls to avoid.

- Carefully define a disability. ADA defines a disability as a physical or mental impairment that substantially limits one or more of the major life activities of such individual having a record of such impairment and being regarded as having such impairment.

- Make sure that job descriptions are accurate and current.

- Document reasonable accommodation efforts. When a qualified individual with a disability has requested a reasonable accommodation to assist in the performance of a job, the employer should try to accommodate the request.

- Build a file of resource information where trained specialists can assist in identifying effective accommodations for disabled individuals.

Sexual Harassment With the enactment of the Civil Rights Act of 1991, companies may now be held liable for the acts of their employees and supervisors who engage in on-the-job sexual harassment, even if management is not aware of the problem. The U.S. Supreme Court ruled that workers who have suffered harassment do not have to prove psychological damage or the inability to do their jobs to recover significant damages. This ruling makes it easier for claimants to win lawsuits in this area.

Three examples of sexual harassment in nontraditional areas are discussed next. If a person is passed over for a promotion or denied benefits in favor of an individual who submitted to a sexual advance, the passed-over person is considered to be a victim of sexual harassment under federal and state guidelines. If a worker initially participates in social or sexual contact but then rejects continued unwelcome advances, that constitutes sexual harassment. If the harassment involved unwanted touching, it could result in wrongful discharge, fraud, intentional infliction of emotional distress for outrageous conduct, invasion of privacy, assault, and civil battery.

The EEOC guidelines specify preventive affirmative steps that may create immunity from liability for employers. In determining whether an employer is liable, some courts look to see if a comprehensive policy against sexual harassment was in place at the time the incident(s) occurred and whether the employer acted promptly and properly.

Penalties include as much as $300,000 in punitive and compensatory damages (i.e., pain and suffering) in a jury trial for charges of sexual harassment. Previously, monetary damages under federal law were limited to back pay and other forms of equitable relief.

Consulting Engagements Consulting engagements solve problems and make recommendations to improve a client's operations and processes by making changes. The scope of work includes internal control training, business process reviews, benchmarking studies, IT consulting, and design of performance measurements systems. The engagement steps consist of defining problems, developing alternatives, selecting the best alternative, and implementing the best alternative.

Internal Control Training Internal auditors, other employees of the organization, and management at all levels need an understanding of internal control concepts. This is because internal control affects every employee of the organization in terms of policies, work rules, and procedures.

Internal control training should integrate individual and organizational goals because internal control focuses on people, processes, and objectives. Internal auditors can play both student and teacher roles in that they become students to satisfy the continuing education requirement and they become teachers in educating and training other employees in the internal control concepts.

The internal control training syllabus should include:

- Reviewing recommendations of the Treadway Commission regarding internal control framework.

- Understanding control objectives and control procedures in various functional areas of business.

- Explaining employee's duties and responsibilities in promoting internal control in the organization.

- Discussing limitations of internal controls (what internal control can do and what it cannot do).

Business Process Reviews

Business process reengineering (BPR). In an effort to increase revenues and market growth, organizations are conducting business process reviews. The idea behind business process reviews, whether for a production process or a service process, is to streamline operations and to eliminate waste. The result is increased efficiencies, which can lead to greater effectiveness. A proven technique is BPR, which requires big thinking and making major, radical changes in the business processes. Work flow analysis is a part of BPR.

BPR is one approach for redesigning the way work is done to support the organization's mission and reduce costs. BPR starts with a high-level assessment of the organization's mission, strategic goals, and customer needs. Basic questions are asked, such as: Does our mission need to be redefined? Are our strategic goals aligned with our mission? Who are our customers? An organization may find that it is operating on questionable assumptions, particularly in terms of the wants and needs of its customers. Only after the organization rethinks **what** it should be doing does it go on to decide **how** best to do it.

Within the framework of this basic assessment of mission and goals, reengineering focuses on the organization's business processes: the steps and procedures that govern how resources are used to create products and services that meet the needs of particular customers or markets. As a structured ordering of work steps across time and place, a business process can be decomposed into specific activities, measured, modeled, and improved. It can also be completely redesigned or eliminated altogether. Reengineering identifies, analyzes, and redesigns an organization's core business processes with the aim of achieving dramatic improvements in critical performance measures, such as cost, quality, service, and speed.

Reengineering recognizes that an organization's business processes are usually fragmented into subprocesses and tasks that are carried out by several specialized functional areas within the organization. Often no one is responsible for the overall performance of the entire process. Reengineering maintains that optimizing the performance of subprocesses can result in some benefits, but cannot yield dramatic improvements if the process itself is fundamentally inefficient and outmoded. For that reason, reengineering focuses on redesigning the process as a whole in order to achieve the greatest possible benefits to the organization and their customers. This drive for realizing dramatic improvements by fundamentally rethinking how the organization's work should be done distinguishes reengineering from business process improvement (BPI) efforts that focus on functional or incremental improvement.

Reengineering is not a panacea. There are occasions when functional or incremental improvements are the method of choice, as when a process is basically sound or when the organization is not prepared to undergo dramatic change. When there is a need to achieve order-of-magnitude improvements, reengineering is the method of choice.

Business process improvement. BPI should be continuous, not discrete, and it tends to be more of an incremental change than BPR that may affect only a single task or segment of the organization. The concept of fundamental or radical change is the basis of the major difference between BPR and BPI. Quite often BPI initiatives limit their focus to a single existing organizational unit. This in itself breaks one of the tenets of BPR, which is that BPR must focus on redesigning a fundamental business process, not on existing departments or organizational units. While BPR seeks to define what the processes should be, BPI focuses more on how to improve an existing process or service.

Through BPI, organizations can achieve significant incremental improvements in service delivery and other business factors (e.g., increase in employee's productivity). The expected outcomes of BPI are not as dramatic as those associated with BPR initiatives, but the process is also not as traumatic as in achieving the radical changes seen with BPR. In many cases, incremental changes may be achieved in situations lacking the support necessary for more radical changes. Exhibit 1.12 shows the key differences between BPR and BPI.

Business process reengineering versus business process improvement

- BPR focuses on achieving dramatic improvements.
- BPI focuses on achieving incremental improvements.

Benchmarking Studies

Benchmarking defined. *Benchmarking* is the selection of best practices implemented by other organizations. Best practices are the best ways to perform a business process. Organizational change and improvement are the major elements of benchmarking. Benchmarks are the result of a study of organizational processes. Several Best Practices reports identified these first-level, basic processes that define a company's operations:

- Understanding markets and customers
- Designing products and services

Element	BPR	BPI
Degree of change	Radical (e.g., 80%)	Incremental (e.g., 10–30%)
Scope	Entire process	Single area, function/unit
Time	Years	Months
Driver	Business	Technology
Focus	Redefine process	Automate/eliminate the function
Work structure	Unified	Fragmented
Orientation	Outcome	Function

EXHIBIT 1.12 BPR versus BPI

- Marketing and selling those products and services
- Producing what customers need and want
- Delivering products and services
- Providing service to customers

Supporting these basic operations, management and support processes maximize the value with the use of human resources, IT, and financial/physical resources.

The best way to practice benchmarking is to:

- Analyze business processes (inventory major business processes, conduct documentary research, and attend conferences to understand new developments).
- Plan the benchmark study (define scope, request site visits, and develop a methodology for capturing the new data).
- Conduct the benchmark study (analyze best practices and identify performance gaps).
- Implement the benchmark results (incorporate best practices into business processes and reevaluate the business processes).

Types of benchmarking. Two types of benchmarking exist: business process benchmarking and computer system benchmarking. Business process benchmarking deals with BPI and BPR to reduce costs and to improve quality and customer service. Computer system benchmarking focuses on computer hardware/software acquisition, computer system design, computer capacity planning, and system performance. Each has its own place and time.

Business benchmarking is an external focus on internal activities, functions, or operations in order to achieve continuous improvement.[16] The objective is to understand existing processes and activities and then to identify an external point of reference, or standards, by which that activity can be measured or judged. A benchmark can be established at any level of the organization in any functional area, whether manufacturing or service industries. The ultimate goal is to attain a competitive edge by being better than the best.

Value creation is the heart of organizational activity, whether in a profit or a nonprofit entity. Benchmarking provides the metrics by which to understand and judge the value provided by the organization and its resources. Benchmarking focuses on continuous improvements and value creation for stakeholders (i.e., owners, customers, employees, and suppliers), utilizing the best practices to focus improvement efforts.

Benchmarking targets the critical success factors for a specific organization. It considers the mission of an organization, its resources, products, markets, management skills, and others. It requires an identification of customer(s), whether internal or external to the organization. Benchmarking is an early warning system of impending problems and is not a onetime measurement. Benchmarking can focus on improving organization structures, analyzing managerial roles, improving production processes, and developing strategic issues.

What are the sources of information for benchmarking? Benchmarking can be done by using published materials, insights gained at trade association meetings, and conversations with industry experts, customers, suppliers, academics, and others.

---

[16] C. J. McNair and Kathleen Leibfried, *Benchmarking* (New York: Harper Business, 1992).

When is the right time for business process benchmarking? Benchmarking should be undertaken when triggers are present. These triggers can arise internally or externally in response to information needs from some other major project or issue or problem in the company. Examples of these triggers include quality programs, cost reduction programs, new management, new ventures, and competitive moves. Benchmarking should be done as needed, without any preconceived notions.

Reasons for business process benchmarking. A company should benchmark for three reasons: (1) It wants to attain world-class competitive capability, (2) it wants to prosper in a global economy, and (3) it simply wishes to survive (desperation). A company can benchmark in six distinct ways: (1) internal benchmarking, (2) competitive benchmarking, (3) industry benchmarking, (4) best-in-class benchmarking, (5) process benchmarking, and (6) strategic benchmarking (see Exhibit 1.13).

Internal benchmarking is the analysis of existing practices within various departments or divisions of the organization, looking for best performance as well as identifying baseline activities and drivers. Drivers are the causes of work: the trigger that sets in motion a series of actions, or activities that will respond to the requests or demands by the stockholders.

In doing internal benchmarking, management is looking downward, examining itself first before looking for outside information. Significant improvements are often made during the internal analysis stage of the benchmarking process. Value-added activities are identified and non-value-adding steps are removed from the process. Internal benchmarking is the first step because it provides the framework for comparing existing internal practices to external benchmark data. *Internal benchmarking focuses on specific value chains or sequences of driver-activity combinations.*

> **BPR AND BPI**
>
> Techniques such as BPR and BPI are used to improve efficiency, reduce costs, and improve customer service. IT is an enabler of BPR and BPI, not a substitute for them.

Competitive benchmarking looks outward to identify how other direct competitors are performing. Knowing the strengths and weaknesses of the competitors provides good input for strategic and corrective actions.

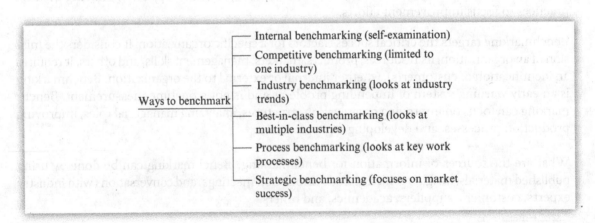

EXHIBIT 1.13 Ways to Benchmark

Industry benchmarking extends beyond the one-to-one comparison of competitive benchmarking to look for trends. It is still limited in the number of innovations and new ideas it can uncover because every company is following every other company in the industry. At best, it can help establish the performance baseline or can give an incremental gain. It gives a short-run solution and a quick fix to an existing problem. However, it does not support quantum leaps or breakthroughs in performance since the comparison is limited to one industry.

Best-in-class benchmarking looks across multiple industries in search of new, innovative practices, no matter what their source. Best-in-class benchmarking is the ultimate goal of the benchmarking process. It supports quantum leaps in performance and gives a long-run competitive advantage.

Process benchmarking centers on key work processes, such as distribution, order entry, or employee training. This type of benchmarking identifies the most effective practices in companies that perform similar functions, no matter in what industry.

Strategic benchmarking examines how companies compete and seeks the winning strategies that have led to competitive advantage and market success.

WHICH BENCHMARKING DOES WHAT?

- Internal benchmarking looks downward and inward.
- Competitive benchmarking looks outward.
- Industry benchmarking looks for trends. It provides a short-run solution and a quick fix to a problem.
- Best-in-class benchmarking looks for the best all around. It provides a quantum jump in improvement.
- Process benchmarking is specific.
- Strategic benchmarking is broad with big impact.

Information Technology Consulting IT consulting engagements can vary from organization to organization and may include IT strategic planning, computer capacity planning, business and IT continuity planning, customer service, and system development.

Regarding system development, the internal auditor should find out first whether a system development methodology is in place. A methodology can improve the quality of systems, decrease system development and maintenance costs, and increase user service levels and satisfaction. Once a methodology is in place, the internal auditor must ensure the proper application of such methodology. Another area of focus for the auditor is project control to reduce time delays and cost overruns.

During a system development consulting engagement, the internal auditor should:

- Determine whether the IT steering committee approves major system development and maintenance projects as part of its charter.

- Review the user's system service request to determine the need for a new system development or maintenance project. Understand the business need for the project.

- Review the feasibility study report for understanding of technical, functional, and economic requirements. Determine whether time and budget estimates are achievable.

- Review general system design to ensure complete coverage of user business needs. Determine whether design of controls is adequate.

- Review detailed system design for inputs (transactions with volumes, input screen formats), process (logic and flow), and outputs (report layouts, output screen formats, and file contents).

- Review system conversion and test plans to determine their adequacy and timing.

- Review system training plans to determine whether appropriate user parties will be trained to do their job properly with the new system.

- Review system implementation plans to determine whether the new system will be implemented all at once or with a phased approach.

Design of Performance Measurement Systems Performance measures should be accurately defined, analyzed, and documented so that all interested parties are informed about them. Performance standards should bring meaning to measurements. Employees who are being measured should feel that standards and specific performance measures are fair and achievable. Self-measurement may create confidence and trust and permit fast feedback and correction from employees. But it can also lead to distortions, concealment, and delays in reporting.

One of the design objectives should be that the performance standards must be simple, meaningful, comparable, reproducible, and traceable given similar business conditions. Care should be taken to compare items that are alike in terms of units of measurements (pounds, grams, liters, or gallons), time frames (hours or days), quantity (volume in units or tons), and quality (meeting the requirements).

During the design of performance measurements, the design team should take both human factors and technical factors into account. From a human factor viewpoint, ensure that the performance measures are not so loose that they present no challenge or so tight that they cannot be attainable. Ideally, both subordinates and superiors must participate in identifying and developing the performance metrics. From a technical factor viewpoint, employees should be given proper tools, training, and equipment to do their job. Otherwise frustration will result. Above all, the performance measures should be based on objective measurement instead of subjective measurement to minimize human bias and suspicion of the reported measurements.

Periodically, the performance measurements should be reviewed and updated to ensure their continued applicability to the situations at hand. Evaluations of performance measures should concentrate on the significant exceptions or deviations from the standards. Therefore, exception reporting is preferred. Significant variances (deviations) require analysis and correction of standards or procedures.

The standards should match the objectives of the operation or function being reviewed. In developing standards, it is better for the auditor to work with the client than alone, with standards later validated by subject matter experts or industry experts for authentication. Usually the standards can be found in standard operating procedures, job descriptions, organizational policies and directives, product design specifications, operating budgets, trade sources, organization's contracts, applicable laws and regulations, generally accepted business practices, GAAP, and GAAS.

IIA Standards Applicable to Operational Role of Internal Audit

2130—Control

The internal audit activity must assist the organization in maintaining effective controls by evaluating their effectiveness and efficiency and by promoting continuous improvement.

> **2130.A1** – The internal audit activity must evaluate the adequacy and effectiveness of controls in responding to risks within the organization's governance, operations, and IS regarding the:
>
> - Reliability and integrity of financial and operational information.
> - Effectiveness and efficiency of operations and programs.
> - Safeguarding of assets.
> - Compliance with laws, regulations, policies, procedures, and contracts.
>
> **2130.C1**—Internal auditors must incorporate knowledge of controls gained from consulting engagements into evaluation of the organization's control processes.

Practice Advisory 2130-1: Assessing the Adequacy of Control Processes

1. An organization establishes and maintains effective risk management and control processes. The purpose of control processes is to support the organization in the management of risks and the achievement of its established and communicated objectives. The control processes are expected to ensure, among other things, that:

- Financial and operational information is reliable and possesses integrity.
- Operations are performed efficiently and achieve established objectives.
- Assets are safeguarded.
- Actions and decisions of the organization are in compliance with laws, regulations, and contracts.

2. Senior management's role is to oversee the establishment, administration, and assessment of the system of risk management and control processes. Among the responsibilities of the organization's line managers is the assessment of the control processes in their respective areas. Internal auditors provide varying degrees of assurance about the effectiveness of the risk management and control processes in select activities and functions of the organization.

3. The CAE forms an overall opinion about the adequacy and effectiveness of the control processes. The expression of such an opinion by the CAE will be based on sufficient audit evidence obtained through the completion of audits and, where appropriate, reliance on the work of other assurance providers. The CAE communicates the opinion to senior management and the board.

4. The CAE develops a proposed internal audit plan to obtain sufficient evidence to evaluate the effectiveness of the control processes. The plan includes audit engagements and/or other procedures to obtain sufficient, appropriate audit evidence about all major operating units and business functions to be assessed, as well as a review of the major control processes operating across the organization. The plan should be flexible so that adjustments may be made during

the year as a result of changes in management strategies, external conditions, major risk areas, or revised expectations about achieving the organization's objectives.

5. The audit plan gives special consideration to those operations most affected by recent or unexpected changes. Changes in circumstances can result, for example, from marketplace or investment conditions, acquisitions and divestitures, organizational restructuring, new systems, and new ventures.

6. In determining the expected audit coverage for the proposed audit plan, the CAE considers relevant work performed by others who provide assurances to senior management (e.g., reliance by the CAE on the work of corporate compliance officers). The CAE's audit plan also considers audit work completed by the external auditor and management's own assessments of its risk management process, controls, and quality improvement processes.

7. The CAE should evaluate the breadth of coverage of the proposed audit plan to determine whether the scope is sufficient to enable the expression of an opinion about the organization's risk management and control processes. The CAE should inform senior management and the board of any gaps in audit coverage that would prevent the expression of an opinion on all aspects of these processes.

8. A key challenge for the internal audit activity is to evaluate the effectiveness of the organization's control processes based on the aggregation of many individual assessments. Those assessments are largely gained from internal audit engagements, reviews of management's self-assessments, and other assurance providers' work. As the engagements progress, internal auditors communicate, on a timely basis, the findings to the appropriate levels of management so prompt action can be taken to correct or mitigate the consequences of discovered control discrepancies or weaknesses.

9. In evaluating the overall effectiveness of the organization's control processes, the CAE considers whether:

- Significant discrepancies or weaknesses were discovered.

- Corrections or improvements were made after the discoveries.

- The discoveries and their potential consequences lead to a conclusion that a pervasive condition exists resulting in an unacceptable level of risk.

10. The existence of a significant discrepancy or weakness does not necessarily lead to the judgment that it is pervasive and poses an unacceptable risk. The internal auditor considers the nature and extent of risk exposure as well as the level of potential consequences in determining whether the effectiveness of the control processes are jeopardized and unacceptable risks exist.

11. The CAE's report on the organization's control processes is normally presented **once a year** to senior management and the board. The report states the critical role played by the control processes in the achievement of the organization's objectives. The report also describes the nature and extent of the work performed by the internal audit activity and the nature and extent of reliance on other assurance providers in formulating the opinion.

Practice Advisory 2130.A1-1: Information Reliability and Integrity

1. Internal auditors determine whether senior management and the board have a clear understanding that information reliability and integrity is a management responsibility. This responsibility includes all critical information of the organization regardless of how the information is stored. Information reliability and integrity includes accuracy, completeness, and security.

2. The CAE determines whether the internal audit activity possesses, or has access to, competent audit resources to evaluate information reliability and integrity and associated risk exposures. This includes both internal and external risk exposures and exposures relating to the organization's relationships with outside entities.

3. The CAE determines whether information reliability and integrity breaches and conditions that might represent a threat to the organization will promptly be made known to senior management, the board, and the internal audit activity.

4. Internal auditors assess the effectiveness of preventive, detective, and mitigation measures against past attacks, as appropriate, and future attempts or incidents deemed likely to occur. Internal auditors determine whether the board has been appropriately informed of threats, incidents, vulnerabilities exploited, and corrective measures.

5. Internal auditors periodically assess the organization's information reliability and integrity practices and recommend, as appropriate, enhancements to, or implementation of, new controls and safeguards. Such assessments can either be conducted as separate stand-alone engagements or integrated into other audits or engagements conducted as part of the internal audit plan. The nature of the engagement will determine the most appropriate reporting process to senior management and the board.

Practice Advisory 2130-A1-2: Evaluating an Organization's Privacy Framework

1. The failure to protect personal information with appropriate controls can have significant consequences for an organization. The failure could damage the reputation of individuals and/or the organization and expose an organization to risks that include legal liability and diminished consumer and/or employee trust.

2. Privacy definitions vary widely depending on the culture, political environment, and legislative framework of the countries in which the organization operates. Risks associated with the privacy of information encompass personal privacy (physical and psychological); privacy of space (freedom from surveillance); privacy of communication (freedom from monitoring); and privacy of information (collection, use, and disclosure of personal information by others). Personal information generally refers to information associated with a specific individual or that has identifying characteristics that, when combined with other information, can then be associated with a specific individual. It can include any factual or subjective information—recorded or not —in any form of media. Personal information could include:

- Name, address, identification numbers, family relationships.
- Employee files, evaluations, comments, social status, or disciplinary actions.
- Credit records, income, financial status.
- Medical status.

3. Effective control over the protection of personal information is an essential component of the governance, risk management, and control processes of an organization. The board is ultimately accountable for identifying the principal risks to the organization and implementing appropriate control processes to mitigate those risks. This includes establishing the necessary privacy framework for the organization and monitoring its implementation.

4. The internal audit activity can contribute to good governance and risk management by assessing the adequacy of management's identification of risks related to its privacy objectives and the adequacy of the controls established to mitigate those risks to an acceptable level. The internal auditor is well positioned to evaluate the privacy framework in their organization and identify the significant risks as well as the appropriate recommendations for mitigation.

5. The internal audit activity identifies the types and appropriateness of information gathered by the organization that is deemed personal or private, the collection methodology used, and whether the organization's use of that information is in accordance with its intended use and applicable legislation.

6. Given the highly technical and legal nature of privacy issues, the internal audit activity needs appropriate knowledge and competence to conduct an assessment of the risks and controls of the organization's privacy framework.

7. In conducting such an evaluation of the management of the organization's privacy framework, the internal auditor:

- Considers the laws, regulations, and policies relating to privacy in the jurisdictions where the organization operates.

- Liaisons with in-house legal counsel to determine the exact nature of laws, regulations, and other standards and practices applicable to the organization and the country/countries in which it operates.

- Liaisons with IT specialists to determine that information security and data protection controls are in place and regularly reviewed and assessed for appropriateness.

- Considers the level or maturity of the organization's privacy practices. Depending on the level, the internal auditor may have differing roles. The auditor may facilitate the development and implementation of the privacy program, evaluate management's privacy risk assessment to determine the needs and risk exposures of the organization, or provide assurance on the effectiveness of the privacy policies, practices, and controls across the organization. If the internal auditor assumes any responsibility for developing and implementing a privacy program, his or her independence will be impaired.

1300—Quality Assurance and Improvement Program

The CAE must develop and maintain a QAIP that covers all aspects of the internal audit activity.

Interpretation: *A QAIP is designed to enable an evaluation of the internal audit activity's conformance with the definition of internal auditing and the* Standards *and an evaluation of whether internal auditors apply the Code of Ethics. The program also assesses the efficiency and effectiveness of the internal audit activity and identifies opportunities for improvement.*

Practice Advisory 1300-1: Quality Assurance and Improvement Program

1. The CAE is responsible for establishing an internal audit activity whose scope of work includes the activities in the *Standards* and in the definition of internal auditing. To ensure that this occurs, Standard 1300 requires that the CAE develop and maintain a QAIP.

2. The CAE is accountable for implementing processes designed to provide reasonable assurance to the various stakeholders that the internal audit activity:

- Performs in accordance with the internal audit charter, which is consistent with the definition of internal auditing, the Code of Ethics, and the *Standards*.

- Operates in an effective and efficient manner.

- Is perceived by those stakeholders as adding value and improving the organization's operations.

These processes include appropriate supervision, periodic internal assessments and ongoing monitoring of quality assurance, and periodic external assessments.

3. The QAIP needs to be sufficiently comprehensive to encompass all aspects of operation and management of an internal audit activity, as found in the definition of internal auditing, the Code of Ethics, the *Standards*, and best practices of the profession. The QAIP process is performed by or under direct supervision of the CAE. Except in small internal audit activities, the CAE would usually delegate most QAIP responsibilities to subordinates. In large or complex environments (e.g., numerous business units and/or locations), the CAE establishes a formal QAIP function—headed by an internal audit executive—independent of the audit and consulting segments of the internal audit activity. This executive (and limited staff) administers and monitors the activities needed for a successful QAIP.

1310—Requirements of the Quality Assurance and Improvement Program

The QAIP must include both internal and external assessments.

Practice Advisory 1310-1: Requirements of the Quality Assurance and Improvement Program

1. A QAIP is an ongoing and periodic assessment of the entire spectrum of audit and consulting work performed by the internal audit activity. These ongoing and periodic assessments are composed of rigorous, comprehensive processes; continuous supervision and testing of internal audit and consulting work; and periodic validations of conformance with the definition of internal auditing, the Code of Ethics, and the *Standards*. This also includes ongoing measurements and analyses of performance metrics (e.g., internal audit plan accomplishment, cycle time, recommendations accepted, and customer satisfaction). If the assessments' results indicate areas for improvement by the internal audit activity, the CAE will implement the improvements through the QAIP.

2. Assessments evaluate and conclude on the quality of the internal audit activity and lead to recommendations for appropriate improvements. QAIPs include an evaluation of:

- Conformance with the definition of internal auditing, the Code of Ethics, and the *Standards*, including timely corrective actions to remedy any significant instances of nonconformance.

- Adequacy of the internal audit activity's charter, goals, objectives, policies, and procedures.

- Contribution to the organization's governance, risk management, and control processes.

- Compliance with applicable laws, regulations, and government or industry standards.

- Effectiveness of continuous improvement activities and adoption of best practices.

- The extent to which the internal audit activity adds value and improves the organization's operations.

3. The QAIP efforts also include follow-up on recommendations involving appropriate and timely modification of resources, technology, processes, and procedures.

4. To provide accountability and transparency, the CAE communicates the results of external and, as appropriate, internal quality program assessments to the various stakeholders of the activity (such as senior management, the board, and external auditors). At least annually, the CAE reports to senior management and the board on the quality program efforts and results.

1311—Internal Assessments

Internal assessments must include:

- Ongoing monitoring of the performance of the internal audit activity.

- Periodic reviews performed through self-assessment or by other persons within the organization with sufficient knowledge of internal audit practices.

Interpretation: *Ongoing monitoring is an integral part of the day-to-day supervision, review, and measurement of the internal audit activity. Ongoing monitoring is incorporated into the routine policies and practices used to manage the internal audit activity and uses processes, tools, and information considered necessary to evaluate conformance with the definition of internal auditing, the Code of Ethics, and the Standards.*

Periodic reviews are assessments conducted to evaluate conformance with the definition of internal auditing, the Code of Ethics, and the Standards.

Sufficient knowledge of internal audit practices requires at least an understanding of all elements of the International Professional Practices Framework.

Practice Advisory 1311-1: Internal Assessments

1. The processes and tools used in ongoing internal assessments include:

- Engagement supervision,

- Checklists and procedures (e.g., in an audit and procedures manual) are being followed,

- Feedback from audit customers and other stakeholders,

- Selective peer reviews of working papers by staff not involved in the respective audits,

- Project budgets, timekeeping systems, audit plan completion, and cost recoveries, and/or

- Analyses of other performance metrics (such as cycle time and recommendations accepted).

2. Conclusions are developed as to the quality of ongoing performance and follow-up action taken to ensure appropriate improvements are implemented.

3. The IIA's *Quality Assessment Manual*, or a comparable set of guidance and tools, should serve as the basis for periodic internal assessments.

4. Periodic internal assessments may:

- Include more in-depth interviews and surveys of stakeholder groups.

- Be performed by members of the internal audit activity (self-assessment).

- Be performed by Certified Internal Auditors (CIAs) or other competent audit professionals, currently assigned elsewhere in the organization.

- Encompass a combination of self-assessment and preparation of materials subsequently reviewed by CIAs or other competent audit professionals.

- Include benchmarking of the internal audit activity's practices and performance metrics against relevant best practices of the internal audit profession.

5. A periodic internal assessment performed within a short time before an external assessment can serve to facilitate and reduce the cost of the external assessment. If the periodic internal assessment is performed by a qualified, independent external reviewer or review team,

the assessment results should not communicate any assurances on the outcome of the subsequent external quality assessment. The report may offer suggestions and recommendations to enhance the practices of internal audit activities. If the external assessment takes the form of a self-assessment with independent validation, the periodic internal assessment can serve as the self-assessment portion of this process.

6. Conclusions are developed as to quality of performance and appropriate action initiated to achieve improvements and conformity to the *Standards*, as necessary.

7. The CAE establishes a structure for reporting results of internal assessments that maintains appropriate credibility and objectivity. Generally, those assigned responsibility for conducting ongoing and periodic reviews report to the CAE while performing the reviews and communicate results directly to the CAE.

8. At least annually, the CAE reports the results of internal assessments, necessary action plans, and their successful implementation to senior management and the board.

1312—External Assessments

External assessments must be conducted at least once every **five years** by a qualified, independent reviewer or review team from outside the organization. The CAE must discuss with the board:

- The need for more frequent external assessments.

- The qualifications and independence of the external reviewer or review team, including any potential conflict of interest.

Interpretation: *A qualified reviewer or review team demonstrates competence in two areas: the professional practice of internal auditing and the external assessment process. Competence can be demonstrated through a mixture of experience and theoretical learning. Experience gained in organizations of similar size, complexity, sector or industry, and technical issues is more valuable than less relevant experience. In the case of a review team, not all members of the team need to have all the competencies; it is the team as a whole that is qualified. The CAE uses professional judgment when assessing whether a reviewer or review team demonstrates sufficient competence to be qualified.*

An "independent reviewer or review team" means not having either a real or an apparent conflict of interest and not being a part of, or under the control of, the organization to which the internal audit activity belongs.

Practice Advisory 1312-1: External Assessments

1. External assessments cover the entire spectrum of audit and consulting work performed by the internal audit activity and should not be limited to assessing its QAIP. To achieve optimum benefits from an external assessment, the scope of work should include benchmarking, identification, and reporting of leading practices that could assist the internal audit activity in becoming more efficient and/or effective. This can be accomplished through either a full external assessment by a qualified, independent external reviewer or review team or a comprehensive internal self-assessment with independent validation by a qualified, independent external reviewer or review team. Nonetheless, the CAE is to ensure the scope clearly states the expected deliverables of the external assessment in each case.

2. External assessments of an internal audit activity contain an expressed opinion as to the entire spectrum of assurance and consulting work performed (or that should have been performed based on the internal audit charter) by the internal audit activity, including its conformance with the definition of internal auditing, the Code of Ethics, and the *Standards* and, as appropriate,

includes recommendations for improvement. Apart from conformance with the definition of internal auditing, the Code of Ethics, and the *Standards*, the scope of the assessment is adjusted at the discretion of the CAE, senior management, or the board. These assessments can have considerable value to the CAE and other members of the internal audit activity, especially when benchmarking and best practices are shared.

3. On completion of the review, a formal communication is to be given to senior management and the board.

4. There are two approaches to external assessments. The first approach is a full external assessment conducted by a qualified, independent external reviewer or review team. This approach involves an outside team of competent professionals under the leadership of an experienced and professional project manager. The second approach involves the use of a qualified, independent external reviewer or review team to conduct an independent validation of the internal self-assessment and a report completed by the internal audit activity. Independent external reviewers should be well versed in leading internal audit practices.

5. Individuals who perform the external assessment are free from any obligation to, or interest in, the organization whose internal audit activity is the subject of the external assessment or the personnel of such organization. Particular matters relating to independence, which are to be considered by the CAE in consultation with the board, in selecting a qualified, independent external reviewer or review team include:

- Any real or apparent conflict of interest of firms that provide:

  □ The external audit of financial statements.

  □ Significant consulting services in the areas of governance, risk management, financial reporting, internal control, and other related areas.

  □ Assistance to the internal audit activity. The significance and amount of work performed by the professional service provider is to be considered in the deliberation.

- Any real or apparent conflict of interest of former employees of the organization who would perform the assessment. Consideration should be given to the length of time the individual has been independent of the organization.

- Individuals who perform the assessment are independent of the organization whose internal audit activity is the subject of the assessment and do not have any real or apparent conflict of interest. "Independent of the organization" means not a part of, or under the control of, the organization to which the internal audit activity belongs. In the selection of a qualified, independent external reviewer or review team, consideration is to be given to any real or apparent conflict of interest the reviewer may have due to present or past relationships with the organization or its internal audit activity, including the reviewer's participation in internal quality assessments.

- Individuals in another department of the subject organization or in a related organization, although organizationally separate from the internal audit activity, are not considered independent for purposes of conducting an external assessment. A "related organization" may be a parent organization; an affiliate in the same group of entities; or an entity with regular oversight, supervision, or quality assurance responsibilities with respect to the subject organization.

- Real or apparent conflict involving peer review arrangements. Peer review arrangements between three or more organizations (e.g., within an industry or other affinity group, regional association, or other group of organizations—except as precluded by the "related organization" definition in the previous point) may be structured in a manner that alleviates independence concerns, but care is taken to ensure that the issue of independence does not arise. Peer reviews between two organizations would not pass the independence test.

- To overcome concerns of the appearance or reality of impairment of independence in instances such as those discussed in this section, one or more independent individuals could be part of the external assessment team to independently validate the work of that external assessment team.

6. Integrity requires reviewer(s) to be honest and candid within the constraints of confidentiality. Service and the public trust should not be subordinated to personal gain and advantage. Objectivity is a state of mind and a quality that lends value to a reviewer(s) services. The principle of objectivity imposes the obligation to be impartial, intellectually honest, and free of conflict of interest.

7. Performing and communicating the results of an external assessment require the exercise of professional judgment. Accordingly, an individual serving as an external reviewer should:

- Be a competent, CIA professional who possesses current, in-depth knowledge of the *Standards*.

- Be well versed in the best practices of the profession.

- Have at least three years of recent experience in the practice of internal auditing or related consulting at a management level.

Leaders of independent review teams and external reviewers who independently validate the results of the self-assessment should have an additional level of competence and experience gained from working previously as a team member on an external quality assessment, successful completion of the IIA's quality assessment training course or similar training, and CAE or comparable senior internal audit management experience.

8. The reviewer(s) should possess relevant technical expertise and industry experience. Individuals with expertise in other specialized areas may assist the team. For example, specialists in enterprise risk management (ERM), IT auditing, statistical sampling, operations monitoring systems, or control self-assessment may participate in certain segments of the assessment.

9. The CAE involves senior management and the board in determining the approach and selection of an external quality assessment provider.

10. The external assessment consists of a broad scope of coverage that includes the following elements of the internal audit activity:

- Conformance with the definition of internal auditing, the Code of Ethics, and the *Standards*; and the internal audit activity's charter, plans, policies, procedures, practices, and applicable legislative and regulatory requirements

- Expectations of the internal audit activity expressed by the board, senior management, and operational managers

- Integration of the internal audit activity into the organization's governance process, including the relationships between and among the key groups involved in the process

- Tools and techniques employed by the internal audit activity

- Mix of knowledge, experience, and disciplines within the staff, including staff focus on process improvement

- Determination as to whether the internal audit activity adds value and improves the organization's operations.

11. The preliminary results of the review are discussed with the CAE during and at the conclusion of the assessment process. Final results are communicated to the CAE or other official who authorized the review for the organization, preferably with copies sent directly to appropriate members of senior management and the board.

12. The communication includes:

- An opinion on the internal audit activity's conformance with the definition of internal auditing, the Code of Ethics, and the *Standards* based on a structured rating process. The term "conformance" means the practices of the internal audit activity, taken as a whole, satisfy the requirements of the definition of internal auditing, the Code of Ethics, and the *Standards*. Similarly, "nonconformance" means the impact and severity of the deficiencies in the practices of the internal audit activity are so significant they impair the internal audit activity's ability to discharge its responsibilities. The degree of "partial conformance" with the definition of internal auditing, the Code of Ethics, and/or individual *Standards*, if relevant to the overall opinion, should also be expressed in the report on the independent assessment. The expression of an opinion on the results of the external assessment requires the application of sound business judgment, integrity, and due professional care.

- An assessment and evaluation of the use of best practices, both those observed during the assessment and others potentially applicable to the activity.

- Recommendations for improvement, where appropriate.

- Responses from the CAE that include an action plan and implementation dates.

13. To provide accountability and transparency, the CAE communicates the results of external quality assessments, including specifics of planned remedial actions for significant issues and subsequent information as to accomplishment of those planned actions, with the various stakeholders of the activity, such as senior management, the board, and external auditors.

Practice Advisory 1312-2: External Assessments: Self-Assessment with Independent Validation

1. An external assessment by a qualified, independent reviewer or review team may be troublesome for smaller internal audit activities, or there may be circumstances in other organizations where a full external assessment by an independent team is not deemed appropriate or necessary. For example, the internal audit activity may (a) be in an industry subject to extensive regulation and/or supervision, (b) be otherwise subject to extensive external oversight and direction relating to governance and internal controls, (c) have been recently subjected to external review(s) and/or consulting services in which there was extensive benchmarking with best practices, or (d) in the judgment of the CAE, the benefits of self-assessment for staff development and the strength of the internal QAIP currently outweigh the benefits of a quality assessment by an external team.

2. A self-assessment with independent (external) validation includes:

- A comprehensive and fully documented self-assessment process, which emulates the external assessment process, at least with respect to evaluation of conformance with the definition of internal auditing, the Code of Ethics, and the *Standards*.

- An independent, on-site validation by a qualified, independent reviewer.

- Economical time and resource requirements—for example, the primary focus would be on conformance with the *Standards*.

- Limited attention to other areas—such as benchmarking, review and consultation as to employment of leading practices, and interviews with senior and operating management—may be reduced. However, the information produced by these parts of the assessment is one of the benefits of an external assessment.

3. The same guidance and criteria as set forth in Practice Advisory 1312-1 would apply for a self-assessment with independent validation.

4. A team under the direction of the CAE performs and fully documents the self-assessment process. A draft report, similar to that for an external assessment, is prepared including the CAE's judgment on conformance with the *Standards*.

5. A qualified, independent reviewer or review team performs sufficient tests of the self-assessment so as to validate the results and express the indicated level of the activity's conformance with the definition of internal auditing, the Code of Ethics, and the *Standards*. The independent validation follows the process outlined in The IIA's *Quality Assessment Manual* or a similar comprehensive process.

6. As part of the independent validation, the independent external reviewer —upon completion of a rigorous review of the self-assessment team's evaluation of conformance with the definition of internal auditing, the Code of Ethics, and the *Standards*:

- Reviews the draft report and attempts to reconcile unresolved issues (if any).

- If in agreement with the opinion of conformance with the definition of internal auditing, the Code of Ethics, and the *Standards*, adds wording (as needed) to the report, concurring with the self-assessment process and opinion and—to the extent deemed appropriate—in the report's findings, conclusions, and recommendations.

- If not in agreement with the evaluation, adds dissenting wording to the report, specifying the points of disagreement with it and—to the extent deemed appropriate—with the significant findings, conclusions, recommendations, and opinions in the report.

- Alternatively, may prepare a separate independent validation report—concurring or expressing disagreement as outlined above—to accompany the report of the self-assessment.

7. The final report(s) of the self-assessment with independent validation is signed by the self-assessment team and the qualified, independent external reviewer(s) and issued by the CAE to senior management and the board.

8. To provide accountability and transparency, the CAE communicates the results of external quality assessments—including specifics of planned remedial actions for significant issues and subsequent information as to accomplishment of those planned actions—with the various stakeholders of the activity, such as senior management, the board, and external auditors.

1320—Reporting on the Quality Assurance and Improvement Program

The CAE must communicate the results of the QAIP to senior management and the board.

Interpretation: *The form, content, and frequency of communicating the results of the QAIP is established through discussions with senior management and the board and considers the responsibilities of the internal audit activity and CAE as contained in the internal audit charter. To demonstrate conformance with the definition of internal auditing, the Code of Ethics, and the* Standards, *the results of external and periodic internal assessments are communicated upon completion of such assessments and the results of ongoing monitoring are communicated at least annually. The results include the reviewer's or review team's assessment with respect to the degree of conformance.*

No Practice Advisory for Standard 1320

2070—External Service Provider and Organizational Responsibility for Internal Auditing

When an external service provider serves as the internal audit activity, the provider must make the organization aware that the organization has the responsibility for maintaining an effective internal audit activity.

Interpretation: *This responsibility is demonstrated through the QAIP which assesses conformance with the definition of internal auditing, the Code of Ethics, and the* Standards.

No Practice Advisory for Standard 2070

1.3 Risk-Based Internal Audit Plan

Detailed risk assessments, which include identifying audit risk factors and developing approaches to risk assessment, are discussed in this section.

Audit resources are limited and expensive; hence they should be properly allocated and scheduled for maximum utilization. Risk models or risk analysis is often used in conjunction with development of long-range audit schedules. Performing risk analysis and risk assessment is a major step in audit planning work. A **risk** is defined as the probability that an unfavorable event occurs that could lead to a financial or other form of loss. The potential occurrence of such an event is called **exposure**. Risks are caused by exposures. Controls can reduce or eliminate risks and exposures.

STEPS INVOLVED IN A RISK ASSESSMENT MODEL

- Identifying risk factors
- Judging the relative importance of the risk factors
- Measuring the extent to which each risk factor is present in an audit unit
- Quantifying and evaluating the risk level
- Allocating the audit resources according to the risk level

Risks are inherent when business activities and transactions are processed in either a manual or an automated manner. Intentional or unintentional errors, omissions, and irregularities (e.g., theft and fraud) do occur when people handle transactions during analyzing, recording, approving, classifying, computing, processing, summarizing, posting, and reporting activities. These risks represent potentially damaging events that can produce losses.

(a) Audit Risk Factors

High-risk areas should receive high priority and low-risk areas should be given low priority. A systematic risk assessment approach is better than a haphazard, trial-and-error, approach. An IIA survey identified 19 potentially important audit risk factors. Each factor might be related to the risk or to the allocation of internal audit resources when the objective is to minimize losses to the firm.

1. **Quality of internal control system (most important factor).** The design and past performance of an internal control system is important in judging the probability of errors in the system. Audit units with a weak system of internal controls pose a higher risk of loss. Consequently, units with weak internal control should receive a larger share of audit resources.

2. **Competence of management.** Although difficult to measure objectively, the competence of a unit's management influences the confidence that the internal auditor has in the operations of the unit. The less competent the management, the higher the risk of losses to the firm.

3. **Integrity of management.** Even more difficult to assess or measure, the integrity of management bears an obvious relationship to the probability of losses to the firm through overrides of the control system.

4. **Size of unit.** The size of a unit will normally affect the magnitude of its potential losses. Thus, the larger an audit unit (in terms of total assets, revenue, cash flow, etc.), the larger the demand for audit resources.

5. **Recent change in accounting system.** A recent change in systems may invalidate past performance as a measure of control strength and usually increases the probability of errors during its break-in period.

6. **Complexity of operations.** As the operating complexity of an audit unit increases, the information and control system will also become more complex. This complexity can increase both the probability of error and the effort required to monitor the system.

7. **Liquidity of assets.** Highly liquid assets normally receive more audit attention than their asset size alone would indicate. Liquid assets are active, mobile resources that are an attractive target for defalcations. Thus, the more liquid the resources of an audit unit, the greater the level of internal auditing.

AUDIT RISK FACTORS

IIA Professional *Standards*—Planning suggests these risk factors be considered during the risk assessment process:

- Ethical climate and pressure on management to meet objectives
- Competence, adequacy, and integrity of personnel
- Asset size, liquidity, or transaction volume
- Financial and economic conditions
- Competitive conditions
- Complexity or volatility of activities
- Impact of customers, supplier, and government regulations
- Degree of computerized IS
- Geographical dispersion of operations
- Adequacy and effectiveness of the system of internal control

(continued)

AUDIT RISK FACTORS (*Continued*)

- Organizational, operational, technological, or economic changes
- Management judgments and accounting estimates
- Acceptance of audit findings and corrective action taken
- Date and results of previous audits

---

8. **Recent change in key personnel.** Control systems depend on competent judgments by key personnel. A lack of continuity in personnel may mean the control system is less effective than in previous periods.

9. **Economic condition of unit.** Because of pressure on management to produce improved economic results, the risk of control breakdowns is often greater in units with poor economic performance. In addition, poor economic performance may be a signal of such breakdowns. Thus, units with poor economic conditions are likely to pose more risk for the firm.

RISK FACTORS

Factors to be used in risk analysis include (1) financial exposure and potential loss, (2) results of prior audits, and (3) major operating changes. Skills available on the audit staff is not a risk factor since missing skills can be obtained from elsewhere unless too costly that risk may be accepted.

Factors that should be considered when evaluating audit risk in a functional area include: (1) volume of transactions, (2) dollar value of "assets at risk," and (3) average value per transaction.

---

10. **Rapid growth.** Rapid growth stretches the personnel and the management control system of an operation. While growth provides significant opportunities for profit, it also provides the opportunity for control problems to emerge.

11. **Extent of computerized data processing.** Computer processing provides a central hub through which much essential management information passes. In some cases, this hub is viewed as a black box; and great potential exists for the loss of asset control as well as the loss of significant information.

12. **Time since last audit.** Because the internal audit detects and deters inappropriate activity, the effects of internal auditing will likely be greatest just before and just after an audit. As the time since the last audit increases, the risk of loss of internal control increases.

13. **Pressure on management to meet objectives.** For the same reasons discussed in item 9, increased performance pressure increases the pressure to circumvent controls.

14. **Extent of government regulation.** This factor reflects the fact that the firm may be subject to some unpredictable forces, which may serve to increase risk.

15. **Level of employees' morale.** This factor may be important because low morale may indicate significant differences between the objectives of the top management and those of individuals at lower levels. Such differences can lead to increased risk.

16. **Audit plans of independent auditors.** Although internal and external auditors have differing concerns and objectives in auditing, their activities do overlap. The plans of external auditors can influence individuals in units, which might be subject to external and internal auditing.

17. **Political exposure.** Risk comes in many forms. The cost of events can be direct (i.e., lost profits and fraud losses) or indirect (i.e., reputation)

18. **Need to maintain appearance of independence by internal auditor.** This factor was included to see if the internal auditor's resource allocation would be significantly affected by the need to maintain the appearance (in addition to the substance) of independence within the firm. Given its low rating, this factor apparently is not a significant influence.

19. **Distance of unit from home office (least important factor).** This factor was included to determine if the out-of-sight, out-of-mind approach applied to internal audit risk. It may also reflect the foreign versus domestic aspects of relative risk.

(b) Approaches to Risk Assessment

The purposes of risk analysis and assessment are to identify risk and exposures, calculate the damage or loss, and make cost-effective control recommendations. Several risk assessment techniques and approaches are available to quantify risks. Some of them, used in combination, are listed next.

- Judgment and intuition
- Scoring approach
- Delphi technique
- Quantitative methods

Judgment and intuition always play an important role in risk assessment. The auditor calls on personal and professional experience and education. This is often called a gut-feel approach. Under this approach, risks may be labeled as high, medium, or low.

The **scoring approach** assigns a weight factor and a risk level to each characteristic. The product of these two numbers is the weighted risk score of the characteristic, and the sum over the risk scores of an area yields the area risk score. These areas can be ranked according to the weighted risk score. For example, a simplistic, five-factor scoring approach is shown in Exhibit 1.14.

The weight factors can be derived from using the **Delphi technique**. The audit department can use the Delphi technique to get the weights from the audit staff using their expertise in operational audits, financial audits, compliance audits, program audits, and computer system audits.

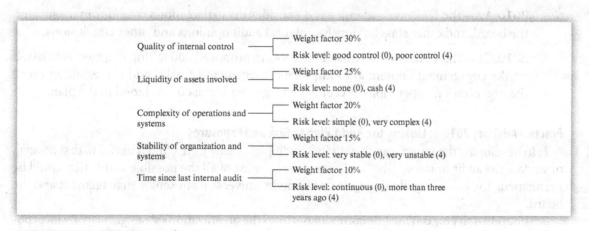

Quality of internal control	Weight factor 30%
	Risk level: good control (0), poor control (4)
Liquidity of assets involved	Weight factor 25%
	Risk level: none (0), cash (4)
Complexity of operations and systems	Weight factor 20%
	Risk level: simple (0), very complex (4)
Stability of organization and systems	Weight factor 15%
	Risk level: very stable (0), very unstable (4)
Time since last internal audit	Weight factor 10%
	Risk level: continuous (0), more than three years ago (4)

EXHIBIT 1.14 Risk-Scoring Approach

The rationale for using the Delphi technique is that it is sometimes difficult to get a consensus on the cost or loss value and the probabilities of occurrence.

An example of a **quantitative method** involves calculating an annual loss exposure value based on estimated costs and potential losses. The annual loss exposure values are considered in the cost-effective selection of controls and safeguards. The essential elements of risk analysis are an assessment of the damage, which can be caused by an unfavorable event, and an estimate of how often such an event may happen in a period of time. Quantitative means of expressing both potential impact and estimated frequency of occurrence are necessary in performing a quantitative risk analysis. The annual loss exposure is calculated as

$$ALE = I \times F$$

where

ALE = annual loss exposure
$I = s$ estimated impact in dollars
F = estimated frequency of occurrence per year

IIA *Standards* Applicable to Risk-Based Internal Audit Plan

2010—Planning

The CAE must establish risk-based plans to determine the priorities of the internal audit activity, consistent with the organization's goals.

Interpretation: *The CAE is responsible for developing a risk-based plan. The CAE takes into account the organization's risk management framework, including using* **risk appetite** *levels set by management for the different activities or parts of the organization. If a framework does not exist, the CAE uses his or her own judgment of risks after consultation with senior management and the board.*

2010.A1—The internal audit activity's plan of engagements must be based on a documented risk assessment, undertaken at least annually. The input of senior management and the board must be considered in this process.

2010.A2—The CAE must identify and consider the expectations of senior management, the board, and other stakeholders for internal audit opinions and other conclusions.

2010.C1—The CAE should consider accepting proposed consulting engagements based on the engagement's potential to improve management of risks, add value, and improve the organization's operations. Accepted engagements must be included in the plan.

Practice Advisory 2010-1: Linking the Audit Plan to Risk and Exposures

1. In developing the internal audit activity's audit plan, many CAEs find it useful to first develop or update the audit universe. The "audit universe" is a list of all the possible audits that could be performed. The CAE may obtain input on the audit universe from senior management and the board.

2. The audit universe can include components from the organization's strategic plan. By incorporating components of the organization's strategic plan, the audit universe will consider and reflect

the overall objectives of the business. Strategic plans also likely reflect the organization's attitude toward risk and the degree of difficulty to achieving planned objectives. The audit universe will normally be influenced by the results of the risk management process. The organization's strategic plan considers the environment in which the organization operates. These same environmental factors would likely impact the audit universe and assessment of relative risk.

3. The CAE prepares the internal audit activity's audit plan based on the audit universe, input from senior management and the board, and an assessment of risk and exposures affecting the organization. Key audit objectives are usually to provide senior management and the board with assurance and information to help them accomplish the organization's objectives, including an assessment of the effectiveness of management's risk management activities.

4. The audit universe and related audit plan are updated to reflect changes in management direction, objectives, emphasis, and focus. It is advisable to assess the audit universe on at least an annual basis to reflect the most current strategies and direction of the organization. In some situations, audit plans may need to be updated more frequently (e.g., quarterly) in response to changes in the organization's business, operations, programs, systems, and controls.

5. Audit work schedules are based on, among other factors, an assessment of risk and exposures. Prioritizing is needed to make decisions for applying resources. A variety of risk models exist to assist the CAE. Most risk models use risk factors such as impact, likelihood, materiality, asset liquidity, management competence, quality of and adherence to internal controls, degree of change or stability, timing and results of last audit engagement, complexity, and employee and government relations.

Practice Advisory 2010-2: Using the Risk Management Process in Internal Audit Planning

1. Risk management is a critical part of providing sound governance that touches all the organization's activities. Many organizations are moving to adopt consistent and holistic risk management approaches that should, ideally, be fully integrated into the management of the organization. It applies at all levels—enterprise, function, and business unit—of the organization. Management typically uses a risk management framework to conduct the assessment and document the assessment results.

2. An effective risk management process can assist in identifying key controls related to significant inherent risks. ERM is a term in common use. COSO of the Treadway Commission defines "ERM" as "a process, effected by an entity's board of directors, management, and other personnel, applied in strategy setting and across the enterprise, designed to identify potential events that may affect the entity, and manage risk to be within its risk appetite, to provide reasonable assurance regarding the achievement of entity objectives." Implementation of controls is one common method management can use to manage risk within its risk appetite. Internal auditors audit the key controls and provide assurance on the management of significant risks.

3. The IIA's *Standards* define "control" as "any action taken by management, the board, and other parties to manage risk and increase the likelihood that established objectives and goals will be achieved. Management plans, organizes, and directs the performance of sufficient actions to provide reasonable assurance that objectives and goals will be achieved."

4. Two fundamental risk concepts are inherent risk and residual risk (also known as current risk). Financial/external auditors have long had a concept of inherent risk that can be summarized as the susceptibility of information or data to a material misstatement, assuming that there are no related mitigating controls. The *Standards* define "residual risk" as "the risk remaining after management takes action to reduce the impact and likelihood of an adverse event, including control activities in responding to a risk." "Current risk" is often defined as the risk managed within existing controls or control systems.

5. "Key controls" can be defined as controls or groups of controls that help to reduce an otherwise unacceptable risk to a tolerable level. Controls can be most readily conceived as

organizational processes that exist to address risks. In an effective risk management process (with adequate documentation), the key controls can be readily identified from the difference between inherent and residual risk across all affected systems that are relied upon to reduce the rating of significant risks. If a rating has not been given to inherent risk, the internal auditor estimates the inherent risk rating. When identifying key controls (and assuming the internal auditor has concluded that the risk management process is mature and reliable), the internal auditor would look for:

- Individual risk factors where there is a significant reduction from inherent to residual risk (particularly if the inherent risk was very high). This highlights controls that are important to the organization.

- Controls that serve to mitigate a large number of risks.

6. Internal audit planning needs to make use of the organizational risk management process, where one has been developed. In planning an engagement, the internal auditor considers the significant risks of the activity and the means by which management mitigates the risk to an acceptable level. The internal auditor uses risk assessment techniques in developing the internal audit activity's plan and in determining priorities for allocating internal audit resources. Risk assessment is used to examine auditable units and select areas for review to include in the internal audit activity's plan that have the greatest risk exposure.

7. Internal auditors may not be qualified to review every risk category and the ERM process in the organization (e.g., internal audits of workplace health and safety, environmental auditing, or complex financial instruments). The CAE ensures that internal auditors with specialized expertise or external service providers are used appropriately.

8. Risk management processes and systems are set up differently throughout the world. The maturity level of the organization related to risk management varies among organizations. Where organizations have a centralized risk management activity, the role of this activity includes coordinating with management regarding its continuous review of the internal control structure and updating the structure according to evolving risk appetites. The risk management processes in use in different parts of the world might have different logic, structures, and terminology. Internal auditors therefore make an assessment of the organization's risk management process and determine what parts can be used in developing the internal audit activity's plan and what parts can be used for planning individual internal audit assignments.

9. Factors the internal auditor considers when developing the internal audit plan include:

- Inherent risks. Are they identified and assessed?

- Residual risks. Are they identified and assessed?

- Mitigating controls, contingency plans, and monitoring activities. Are they linked to the individual events and/or risks?

- Risk registers. Are they systematic, completed, and accurate?

- Documentation. Are the risks and activities documented?

In addition, the internal auditor coordinates with other assurance providers and considers planned reliance on their work. Refer to The IIA's Practice Advisory 2050-2: *Assurance Maps*.

10. The internal audit charter normally requires the internal audit activity to focus on areas of high risk, including both inherent and residual risk. The internal audit activity needs to identify areas of high inherent risk, high residual risks, and the key control systems on which the organization is most reliant. If the internal audit activity identifies areas of unacceptable residual risk, management needs to be notified so that the risk can be addressed. The internal auditor will, as

a result of conducting a strategic audit planning process, be able to identify different kinds of activities to include in the internal audit activity's plan, including:

- Control reviews/assurance activities—where the internal auditor reviews the adequacy and efficiency of the control systems and provides assurance that the controls are working and the risks are effectively managed.

- Inquiry activities—where organizational management has an unacceptable level of uncertainty about the controls related to a business activity or identified risk area and the internal auditor performs procedures to gain a better understanding of the residual risk.

- Consulting activities—where the internal auditor advises organizational management in the development of the control systems to mitigate unacceptable current risks.

Internal auditors also try to identify unnecessary, redundant, excessive, or complex controls that inefficiently reduce risk. In these cases, the cost of the control may be greater than the benefit realized. Therefore, there is an opportunity for efficiency gains in the design of the control.

11. To ensure relevant risks are identified, the approach to risk identification is systematic and clearly documented. Documentation can range from the use of a spreadsheet in small organizations to vendor-supplied software in more sophisticated organizations. The crucial element is that the risk management framework is documented in its entirety.

12. The documentation of risk management in an organization can be at various levels below the strategic level of the risk management process. Many organizations have developed **risk registers** that document risks below the strategic level, providing documentation of significant risks in an area and related inherent and residual risk ratings, key controls, and mitigating factors. An alignment exercise can then be undertaken to identify more direct links between risk "categories" and "aspects" described in the risk registers and, where applicable, the items already included in the audit universe documented by the internal audit activity.

13. Some organizations may identify several areas of high (or higher) inherent risk. While these risks may warrant the internal audit activity's attention, it is not always possible to review all of them. Where the risk register shows a high, or above, ranking for inherent risk in a particular area, and the residual risk remains largely unchanged and no action by management or the internal audit activity is planned, the CAE reports those areas separately to the board with details of the risk analysis and reasons for the lack of, or ineffectiveness of, internal controls.

14. A selection of lower-risk-level business unit or branch-type audits need to be included in the internal audit activity's plan periodically to give them coverage and confirm that their risks have not changed. Also, the internal audit activity establishes a method for prioritizing outstanding risks not yet subject to an internal audit.

15. An internal audit activity's plan will normally focus on:

- Unacceptable current risks where management action is required. These are areas with minimal key controls or mitigating factors that senior management wants audited immediately.

- Control systems on which the organization is most reliant.

- Areas where the differential is great between inherent risk and residual risk.

- Areas where the inherent risk is very high.

16. When planning individual internal audits, the internal auditor identifies and assesses risks relevant to the area under review.

2120—Risk Management

The internal audit activity must evaluate the effectiveness and contribute to the improvement of risk management processes.

Interpretation: *Determining whether risk management processes are effective is a judgment resulting from the internal auditor's assessment that:*

- *Organizational objectives support and align with the organization's mission.*
- *Significant risks are identified and assessed.*
- *Appropriate risk responses are selected that align risks with the organization's risk appetite.*
- *Relevant risk information is captured and communicated in a timely manner across the organization, enabling staff, management, and the board to carry out their responsibilities.*

The internal audit activity may gather the information to support this assessment during multiple engagements. The results of these engagements, when viewed together, provide an understanding of the organization's risk management processes and their effectiveness.

Risk management processes are monitored through ongoing management activities, separate evaluations, or both.

2120. A1—The internal audit activity must evaluate risk exposures relating to the organization's governance, operations, and IS regarding the:

- Reliability and integrity of financial and operational information.
- Effectiveness and efficiency of operations and programs.
- Safeguarding of assets.
- Compliance with laws, regulations, policies, procedures, and contracts.

2120. A2—The internal audit activity must evaluate the potential for the occurrence of fraud and how the organization manages fraud risk.

2120. C1—During consulting engagements, internal auditors must address risk consistent with the engagement's objectives and be alert to the existence of other significant risks.

2120. C2—Internal auditors must incorporate knowledge of risks gained from consulting engagements into their evaluation of the organization's risk management processes.

2120. C3—When assisting management in establishing or improving risk management processes, internal auditors must refrain from assuming any management responsibility by actually managing risks.

Practice Advisory 2120-1: Assessing the Adequacy of Risk Management Processes

1. Risk management is a key responsibility of senior management and the board. To achieve its business objectives, management ensures that sound risk management processes are in place and functioning. Boards have an oversight role to determine that appropriate risk management processes are in place and that these processes are adequate and effective. In this role, they may direct the internal audit activity to assist them by examining, evaluating, reporting, and/or recommending improvements to the adequacy and effectiveness of management's risk processes.

2. Management and the board are responsible for their organization's risk management and control processes. However, internal auditors acting in a consulting role can assist the organization in identifying, evaluating, and implementing risk management methodologies and controls to address those risks.

3. In situations where the organization does not have formal risk management processes, the CAE formally discusses with management and the board their obligations to understand, manage, and monitor risks within the organization and the need to satisfy themselves that there are processes operating within the organization, even if informal, that provide the appropriate level of visibility into the key risks and how they are being managed and monitored.

4. The CAE is to obtain an understanding of senior management's and the board's expectations of the internal audit activity in the organization's risk management process. This understanding is then codified in the charters of the internal audit activity and the board. Internal auditing's responsibilities are to be coordinated between all groups and individuals within the organization's risk management process. The internal audit activity's role in the risk management process of an organization can change over time and may encompass:

- No role.

- Auditing the risk management process as part of the internal audit plan.

- Active, continuous support and involvement in the risk management process such as participation on oversight committees, monitoring activities, and status reporting.

- Managing and coordinating the risk management process.

5. Ultimately, it is the role of senior management and the board to determine the role of internal auditing in the risk management process. Their view on internal auditing's role is likely to be determined by factors such as the culture of the organization, ability of the internal audit staff, and local conditions and customs of the country. However, taking on management's responsibility regarding the risk management process and the potential threat to the internal audit activity's independence requires a full discussion and board approval.

6. The techniques used by various organizations for their risk management practices can vary significantly. Depending on the size and complexity of the organization's business activities, risk management processes can be:

- Formal or informal.

- Quantitative or subjective.

- Embedded in the business units or centralized at a corporate level.

7. The organization designs processes based on its culture, management style, and business objectives. For example, the use of derivatives or other sophisticated capital markets products by the organization could require the use of quantitative risk management tools. Smaller, less complex organizations could use an informal risk committee to discuss the organization's risk profile and to initiate periodic actions. The internal auditor determines that the methodology chosen is sufficiently comprehensive and appropriate for the nature of the organization's activities.

8. Internal auditors need to obtain sufficient and appropriate evidence to determine that the key objectives of the risk management processes are being met to form an opinion on the adequacy of risk management processes. In gathering such evidence, the internal auditor might consider the following audit procedures.

- Research and review current developments, trends, industry information related to the business conducted by the organization, and other appropriate sources of information to determine risks and exposures that may affect the organization and related control procedures used to address, monitor, and reassess those risks.

- Review corporate policies and board minutes to determine the organization's business strategies, risk management philosophy and methodology, appetite for risk, and acceptance of risks.

- Review previous risk evaluation reports issued by management, internal auditors, external auditors, and any other sources.

- Conduct interviews with line and senior management to determine business unit objectives, related risks, and management's risk mitigation and control monitoring activities.

- Assimilate information to independently evaluate the effectiveness of risk mitigation, monitoring, and communication of risks and associated control activities.

- Assess the appropriateness of reporting lines for risk monitoring activities.

- Review the adequacy and timeliness of reporting on risk management results.

- Review the completeness of management's risk analysis and actions taken to remedy issues raised by risk management processes, and suggest improvements.

- Determine the effectiveness of management's self-assessment processes through observations, direct tests of control and monitoring procedures, testing the accuracy of information used in monitoring activities, and other appropriate techniques.

- Review risk-related issues that may indicate weakness in risk management practices and, as appropriate, discuss with senior management and the board. If the auditor believes that management has accepted a level of risk that is inconsistent with the organization's risk management strategy and policies or that is deemed unacceptable to the organization, the auditor should refer to Standard 2600 and related guidance for additional direction.

Practice Advisory 2120-2: Managing the Risk of the Internal Audit Activity

1. The role and importance of internal auditing has grown tremendously, and the expectations of key stakeholders (e.g., board, executive management) continue to expand. Internal audit activities have broad mandates to cover financial, operational, IT, legal/regulatory, and strategic risks. At the same time, many internal audit activities face challenges related to the availability of qualified personnel in the global labor markets, increased compensation costs, and high demand for specialized resources (e.g., IS, fraud, derivatives, and taxes). The combination of these factors results in a high level of risk for an internal audit activity. As a result, CAEs need to consider the risks related to their internal audit activities and the achievement of their objectives.

2. The internal audit activity is not immune to risks. It needs to take the necessary steps to ensure that it is managing its own risks.

3. Risks to internal audit activities fall into three broad categories: audit failure, false assurance, and reputation risks. The following discussion highlights the key attributes related to these risks and some steps an internal audit activity may consider to better manage them.

4. Every organization will experience control breakdowns. Often when controls fail or frauds occur, someone will ask: "Where were the internal auditors?" The internal audit activity could be a contributing factor due to:

- Not following the *International Standards for the Professional Practice of Internal Auditing*.

- An inappropriate QAIP (Standard 1300), including procedures to monitor auditor independence and objectivity.

- Lack of an effective risk assessment process to identify key audit areas during the strategic risk assessment as well as areas of high risk during the planning of individual audits—as a result, failure to do the right audits and/or time wasted on the wrong audits.

- Failure to design effective internal audit procedures to test the "real" risks and the right controls.

- Failure to evaluate both the design adequacy and the control effectiveness as part of internal audit procedures.

- Use of audit teams that do not have the appropriate level of competence based on experience or knowledge of high-risk areas.

- Failure to exercise heightened professional skepticism and extended internal audit procedures related to findings or control deficiencies.

- Failure of adequate internal audit supervision.

- Making the wrong decision when there was some evidence of fraud—for example, deciding "It's probably not material" or "We don't have the time or resources to deal with this issue."

- Failure to communicate suspicions to the right people.

- Failure to report adequately.

5. Internal audit failures may not only be embarrassing for internal audit activities; they also can expose an organization to significant risk. While there is no absolute assurance that audit failures will not occur, an internal audit activity can implement the following practices to mitigate such risk.:

- **QAIP.** It is critical for every internal audit activity to implement an effective QAIP.

- **Periodic review of the audit universe.** Review the methodology to determine the completeness of the audit universe by routinely evaluating the organization's dynamic risk profile.

- **Periodic review of the audit plan.** Review the current audit plan to assess which assignments may be of higher risk. By flagging the higher-risk assignments, management of the internal audit activity has better visibility and may spend more time understanding the approach to the critical assignments.

- **Effective planning.** There is no substitute for effective audit planning. A thorough planning process that includes updating relevant facts about the client and the performance of an effective risk assessment can significantly reduce the risks of audit failure. In addition, understanding the scope of the assignment and the internal audit procedures to be performed are important elements of the planning process that will reduce the risks of audit failure. Building internal audit activity management checkpoints into the process and obtaining approval of any deviation from the agreed-on plan is also key.

- **Effective audit design.** In most cases, a fair amount of time is spent prior to the start of testing for effectiveness in understanding and analyzing the design of the system of internal controls to determine whether it provides adequate control. Doing this provides a firm basis for internal audit comments that address root causes, which sometimes are the result of poor control design, rather than addressing symptoms. It will also reduce the chance for audit failure by identifying missing controls.

- **Effective management review and escalation procedures.** Internal audit management's involvement in the internal audit process (i.e., before the report draft) plays an important part in mitigating the risk of audit failure. This involvement might include work paper reviews, real-time discussions related to findings, or a closing meeting. By including management of the internal audit activity in the internal audit process, potential issues may be identified and assessed earlier in the assignment. In addition, an internal audit activity may have guidance procedures outlining when and what types of issues to escalate to which level of internal auditing management.

■ **Proper resource allocation.** It is important to assign the right staff to each internal audit engagement. It is especially important when planning a higher-risk or a very technical engagement. Making sure the appropriate competencies are available on the team can play a significant role in reducing the risk of audit failure. In addition to the right competencies, it is important to ensure the appropriate level of experience is on the team, including strong project management skills for those leading an internal audit engagement.

6. An internal audit activity may unknowingly provide some level of false assurance. "False assurance" is a level of confidence or assurance based on perceptions or assumptions rather than fact. In many cases, the mere fact that the internal audit activity is involved in a matter may create some level of false assurance.

7. The use of internal audit resources in assisting the organization to identify and evaluate significant exposures to risk needs to be clearly defined for projects other than internal audits. For example, an internal audit activity was asked by a business unit to provide some "resources" to assist with the implementation of a new enterprise-wide computer system. The business unit deployed these resources to support some of the testing of the new system. Subsequent to the deployment, an error in the design of the system resulted in a restatement of the financial statements. When asked how this happened, the business unit responded by saying that the internal audit activity had been involved in the process and had not identified the matter. Internal audit's involvement created a level of false assurance that was not consistent with its actual role in the project.

8. While there is no way to mitigate all of the risk of false assurance, an internal audit activity can proactively manage its risk in this area. Frequent and clear communication is a key strategy to manage false assurance. Other leading practices are listed next.

■ Proactively communicate the role and the mandate of the internal audit activity to the audit committee, senior management, and other key stakeholders.

■ Clearly communicate what is covered in the risk assessment, internal audit plan and internal audit engagement. Also explicitly communicate what is not in the scope of the risk assessment and internal audit plan.

■ Have a "project acceptance" process to assess the level of risk related to each project and internal audit's role in the project. The assessment may consider the: scope of the project, role of the internal audit activity, reporting expectations, competencies required, and independence of internal auditors.

9. If internal auditors are used to augment the staffing of a project or initiative, document their role and scope of their involvement as well as future objectivity and independence issues rather than using internal auditors as "loaned" resources, which may create false assurance. The credible reputation of an internal audit activity is an essential part of its effectiveness. Internal audit activities that are viewed with high regard are able to attract talented professionals and are highly valued by their organizations. Maintaining a strong "brand" is paramount to the internal audit activities' success and ability to contribute to the organization. In most cases, the internal audit activity's brand has been built over several years through consistent, high-quality work. Unfortunately, this brand can be destroyed instantly by one high-profile adverse event.

10. For example, an internal audit activity could be highly regarded with several of the key financial executives having had rotational assignments as internal auditors, which was viewed as a training ground for future executives. A string of significant restatements and regulatory investigations, however, would impact the reputation of the internal audit activity. The audit committee and the board might ask if the internal audit activity has the right talent and QAIP to support the organization.

11. In another example, during an audit of the human resource function, the internal auditors may discover that background checks were not being reviewed appropriately. The discovery that newly hired internal auditors did not have the appropriate education background, while others had been involved in criminal activity, could seriously impact the credibility of the internal audit activity.

12. Situations like these are not only embarrassing, but they also damage the efficacy of the internal audit activity. Protecting the reputation and the "brand" of the internal audit activity is important not only to the internal audit activity but to the entire organization. It is important that internal audit activities consider what types of risks they face that could impact their reputation and develop mitigation strategies to address these risks.

13. Some practices to protect the reputation include:

- Implement a strong QAIP over all processes in the internal audit activity, including human resources and hiring.

- Periodically perform a risk assessment for the internal audit activity to identify potential risks that might impact its brand.

- Reinforce code of conduct and ethical behavior standards, including The IIA's Code of Ethics, to internal auditors.

- Ensure that the internal audit activity is in compliance with all applicable company policies and practices.

14. To the extent that an internal audit activity experiences an event outlined above, the CAE needs to review the nature of the event and gain an understanding of the root causes. This analysis provides insight into the potential changes to be considered in the internal audit process or control environment to mitigate future occurrences.

1.4 Sample Practice Questions

As mentioned in the Preface of this book, a small batch of sample practice questions is included here to show the flavor of questions and to create a quiz-like environment. The answers and explanations for these questions are shown in a separate section at the end of this book just before the Glossary. If there is a need to practice more questions to obtain a greater confidence, refer to the section "CIA Exam Study Preparation Resources" presented in the front matter of this book.

1. The proper organizational role of internal auditing is to:
   a. Assist the external auditor in order to reduce external audit fees.
   b. Perform studies to assist in the attainment of more efficient operations.
   c. Serve as the investigative arm of the audit committee of the board of directors.
   d. Serve as an appraisal function to examine and evaluate activities as a service to the organization.

2. In some organizations, consideration is being given to the possibility of outsourcing internal audit functions. Management in a large organization should recognize that the external auditor might have an advantage, compared to the internal auditor, because of the external auditor's:
   a. Familiarity with the organization. Its annual audits provide an in-depth knowledge of the organization.
   b. Size. It can hire experienced, knowledgeable, and certified staff.
   c. Size. It is able to offer continuous availability of staff unaffected by other priorities.
   d. Structure. It may more easily accommodate audit requirements in distant locations.

3. The status of the internal auditing function should be free from the impact of irresponsible policy changes by management. The most effective way to ensure that freedom is to:
   a. Have the internal auditing charter approved by both management and the board of directors.
   b. Adopt policies for the functioning of the auditing department.
   c. Establish an audit committee within the board of directors.
   d. Develop written policies and procedures to serve as standards of performance for the department.

4. The consultative approach to auditing emphasizes:
   a. Imposition of corrective measures.
   b. Participation with auditees to improve methods.
   c. Fraud investigation.
   d. Implementation of policies and procedures.

5. In some cultures and organizations, managers insist that the internal auditing function is not needed to provide a critical assessment of the organization's operations. A management attitude such as this will most probably have an adverse effect on the internal auditing function's:
   a. Operating budget variance.
   b. Effectiveness.
   c. Performance appraisals.
   d. Policies and procedures.

6. As part of the process to improve auditor–auditee relations, it is very important to deal with how internal auditing is perceived. Certain types of attitudes in the work performed will help create these perceptions. From a management perspective, which attitude is likely to be the **most** conducive to a positive perception?
   a. Objective.
   b. Investigative.
   c. Interrogatory.
   d. Consultative.

7. In planning a system of internal operating controls, the role of the internal auditor is to:
   a. Design the controls.
   b. Appraise the effectiveness of the controls.
   c. Establish the policies for controls.
   d. Create the procedures for the planning process.

8. An audit committee should be designed to enhance the independence of both internal and external audit functions and to insulate the audit functions from undue management pressures. Using these criteria, audit committees should be composed of:
   a. A rotating subcommittee of the board of directors or its equivalent.
   b. Only members from the relevant outside regulatory agencies.
   c. Members from all important constituencies, specifically including representatives from banking, labor, regulatory agencies, shareholders, and officers.
   d. Only external members of the board of directors or its equivalent.

9. Accepting the concept that internal auditing should be an integral part of an organization can involve a major change of attitude on the part of top management. Which of the following would be the **best** way for internal auditors to convince management regarding the need for and benefits of internal auditing?

   a. Persuading top managers to accept the idea of internal audits by contacting company shareholders and regulatory agencies.

   b. Educating top managers about the benefits and communicating with them on a regular basis.

   c. Negotiating with top management to provide them with rewards, such as favorable audits.

   d. Involving top management in deciding which audit findings will be reported.

10. Which of the following features of a large manufacturing company's organization structure would be a control weakness?

   a. The IT department is headed by a vice president who reports directly to the president.

   b. The chief financial officer is a vice president who reports to the chief executive officer.

   c. The audit committee of the board consists of the chief executive officer, the chief financial officer, and a major stockholder.

   d. The controller and treasurer report to the chief financial officer.

11. Audit committees have been identified as a major factor in promoting independence of both the internal and external auditor. Which of the following is the **most** important limitation on the effectiveness of audit committees?

   a. Audit committees may be composed of independent directors. However, those directors may have close personal and professional friendships with management.

   b. Audit committee members are compensated by the organization and thus favor a stockholder's view.

   c. Audit committees devote most of their efforts to external audit concerns and do not pay much attention to internal auditing and the overall control environment.

   d. Audit committee members do not normally have degrees in the accounting or auditing fields.

12. Purchases from two new vendors increased dramatically after a new buyer was hired. The buyer was obtaining kickbacks from the two vendors based on sales volume. A possible means of detection is:

   a. Periodic vendor surveys regarding potential buyer conflict-of-interest or ethics violations.

   b. The receipt of an invoice to put new vendors on the master file.

   c. The use of purchase orders for all purchases.

   d. The use of change analysis and trend analysis of buyer or vendor activity.

13. Due to the small staff, one remote unit's petty cash custodian also had responsibility for the imprest fund checking account reconciliation. The cashier concealed a diversion of funds by altering the beginning balance on the monthly reconciliations sent to the group office. A possible audit test to detect this would be to:

   a. Compare monthly balances and use change and trend analysis.

   b. Require additional monitoring by headquarters whenever improper segregation of duties exists at remote units.

   c. Determine if any employees have high personal debt.

   d. Determine if any employees are leading expensive lifestyles.

14. In an organization that has a separate division that is primarily responsible for fraud deterrence, the internal auditing department is responsible for:

   a. Examining and evaluating the adequacy and effectiveness of that division's actions taken to deter fraud.

   b. Establishing and maintaining that division's system of internal controls.

   c. Planning that division's fraud deterrence activities.

   d. Controlling that division's fraud deterrence activities.

15. During the audit of payments under a construction contract with a local firm, the auditor finds a $900 recurring monthly reimbursement for rent at a local apartment complex. Each reimbursement is authorized by the same project engineer. The auditor finds no provision for payment of temporary living expenses in the construction contract. Discussion with the project engineer could not resolve the matter. The auditor should:

a. Inform the audit director.

b. Call the engineer into a private meeting to confront the situation.

c. Complete the audit as scheduled, noting the $900 recurring reimbursement in the working papers.

d. Wait until the engineer is surrounded by plenty of witnesses and then inquire about the payments.

16. In the course of performing an audit, an internal auditor becomes aware of illegal acts being performed by several of the highest-ranking officers of the company. To whom should the findings of the audit report be addressed?

a. Line-level supervision.

b. Members of the news media.

c. The officers involved in the illegal acts.

d. The audit committee of the board of directors.

17. Which of the following ensures that all inventory shipments are billed to customers?

a. Shipping documents are prenumbered and are independently accounted for and matched to sales invoices.

b. Sales invoices are prenumbered and are independently accounted for and traced to the sales journal.

c. Duties for recording sales transactions and maintaining customer account balances are separated.

d. Customer billing complaints are investigated by the controller's office.

18. An auditor for a large service company is performing an audit of the company's cash balance. The auditor is considering the most appropriate audit procedure to use to ensure that the amount of cash is accurately recorded on the company's financial statements. The most appropriate audit procedures for the objective are:

a. Review collection procedures and perform an analytical review of accounts receivable; confirm balances of accounts receivable; and verify the existence of appropriate procedures and facilities.

b. Compare cash receipt lists to the receipts journal and bank deposit slips; review the segregation of duties; observe and test cash receipts.

c. Review the organizational structure and functional responsibilities; and verify the existence and describe protection procedures for unused checks, including security measures.

d. Examine bank statement reconciliations, confirm bank balances, and verify cutoff of receipts and disbursements; foot totals of reconciliations and compare to cash account balances.

19. An internal auditor found that the supervisor does not properly approve employee time cards in one department. Which of the following could result?

a. Duplicate paychecks might be issued.

b. The wrong hourly rate could be used to calculate gross pay.

c. Employees might be paid for hours they did not work.

d. Payroll checks might not be distributed to the appropriate payees.

20. Which of the following controls would **most** likely minimize defects in finished goods due to poor-quality raw materials?

a. Proper handling of work-in-process inventory to prevent damage.

b. Implementation of specifications for purchases.

c. Timely follow-up on unfavorable usage variances.

d. Determination of spoilage at the end of the manufacturing process.

21. Which of the following is an appropriate audit procedure when testing payroll in a company with a satisfactory internal control environment?

a. Selectively interviewing a sample of employees.

b. Examining time cards or time sheets for proper approval.

c. Sending confirmation letters to government authorities.

d. Verifying all payroll calculations for one pay cycle.

22. Which of the following means would be the **most** appropriate to minimize the risk of a company's buyer purchasing from a vendor who is a relative?

a. Establish a purchasing economic order quantity.

b. Establish a predetermined reorder point for purchases.

c. Maintain an approved-vendor file for purchases.

d. Perform a risk analysis for the purchasing function.

23. The president wants to know whether the purchasing function is properly meeting its charge to purchase the right material at the right time in the right quantities. Which of the following types of audits addresses the president's request?

a. A financial audit of the purchasing department.

b. An operational audit of the purchasing function.

c. A compliance audit of the purchasing function.

d. A full-scope audit of the manufacturing operation.

24. Which account balance is **most** likely to be misstated if an aging of accounts receivable is not performed?

a. Sales revenue.

b. Sales returns and allowances.

c. Accounts receivable.

d. Allowance for bad debts.

25. An internal audit of payroll would **least** likely include:

a. Tests of computations for gross and net wages.

b. Comparison of payroll costs to budget.

c. Tracing a sample of employee names to employment records in the personnel department.

d. Observing the physical distribution of paychecks.

26. In response to a confirmation of the June 30 accounts receivable balances, a customer reported that the balance confirmed had been paid by a check dated and mailed June 20. The auditor reviewed the postings of cash receipts in July and found the payment had been recorded on July 13. Given this information, the next audit action should be to:

a. Require an adjusting entry to the payment to June.

b. Compare deposit slips to posting records.

c. Trace the billing invoice to the related shipping documents and inventory records, comparing dates "shipped" to "billed" to determine proper period.

d. Request a bank cutoff statement for July and reconcile the June deposits in transit and outstanding checks by examining supporting documentation.

27. The scope of work in developing and maintaining a quality assurance and improvement program (QAIP) includes which of the following processes?

I. Supervision.

II. Internal assessment.

III. Ongoing monitoring.

IV. External assessment.

a. I only.

b. I and II.

c. I, II, and III.

d. I, II, III, and IV.

28. Which of the following is **not** included in the ongoing and periodic assessment containing measurements and analyses of performance metrics with respect to internal audit's quality assurance and improvement program (QAIP)?

a. Money saved from the audit work.

b. Number of recommendations accepted.

c. Customer satisfaction.

d. Audit cycle time.

29. If the results of the assessment of the internal audit's quality assurance and improvement program (QAIP) indicate areas for improvement, which of the following will implement such improvements?
    a. Audit committee of the board.
    b. Chief audit executive.
    c. Chief executive officer.
    d. External auditor.

30. All of the following stakeholders receive the results of internal and external quality program assessment of internal audit's activity from the chief audit executive (CAE) **except**:
    a. Functional managers.
    b. Senior managers.
    c. Board of directors.
    d. External auditor.

31. Which of the following is unique to the external assessment of an internal audit's activity when compared to internal assessment?
    a. Findings.
    b. Conclusions.
    c. Recommendations.
    d. Overall opinion.

32. Which of the following is unique to the external assessment of an internal audit's activity when compared to internal assessment?
    a. Follow-up.
    b. Findings.
    c. Responses from the chief audit executive.
    d. Recommendations.

33. Which of the following facilitates and reduces the cost of the external assessment of an internal audit's activity?
    a. A periodic internal assessment performed within a short time before an external assessment.
    b. A periodic internal assessment performed in parallel with an external assessment.
    c. A periodic internal assessment performed within a long time before an external assessment.
    d. A periodic internal assessment performed within a short time after an external assessment.

34. Which of the following is unique to ongoing internal assessment of an internal audit's activity?
    a. Best practices.
    b. Cost recoveries.
    c. Benchmarking.
    d. Expected deliverables.

35. Which of the following is unique to external assessment of an internal audit's activity?
    a. Best practices.
    b. Cost recoveries.
    c. Benchmarking.
    d. Expected deliverables.

36. Which of the following is common between internal assessment and external assessment of an internal audit's activity?
    a. Audit *Standards*.
    b. Audit charter.
    c. Code of Ethics.
    d. Definition of internal auditing.

37. The scope of external assessment of an internal audit's activity should not be limited to which of the following?
    a. Assurance services.
    b. Consulting services.
    c. Leading practices.
    d. Quality assurance and improvement program.

38. Which of the following can be used by an independent external reviewer when establishing the scope of the external assessment of an internal audit's activity?
    a. Percentage of audit plan completed in a year by the internal audit.
    b. Number of findings reported in a year by the internal audit.
    c. Percentage of quality assurance and improvement program (QAIP) implemented by the internal audit.
    d. Number of audit recommendations accepted in a year by the auditees.

39. What should the audit strategy be?

a. It should be knowledge based.

b. It should be cycle based.

c. It should be request based.

d. It should be risk based.

40. Which one of the following items includes the other three items?

a. Inherent risk.

b. Control risk.

c. Audit risk.

d. Detection risk.

41. Which of the following would **not** be considered in performing a risk analysis exercise?

a. System complexity.

b. Results of prior audits.

c. Auditor skills.

d. System changes.

42. Management is concerned with a recent increase in expenditures and lower profits at a division and has asked the internal audit department to perform an operational audit of the division. Management would like to have the audit completed as quickly as possible and has asked the internal audit department to allocate all possible resources to the task. The director of internal audit is concerned with the time pressure since the internal audit department is heavily involved in a major legal compliance audit that had been requested by the audit committee. Which of the following comments are correct regarding the assessment of risk associated with the two projects?

I. Activities requested by the audit committee should always be considered higher risk than those requested by management.

II. Activities with higher dollar budgets should always be considered higher risk than those with lower dollar budgets.

III. Risk should always be measured by the potential dollar or adverse exposure to the organization.

a. I only.

b. II only.

c. III only.

d. I and III.

43. Risk models or risk analysis is often used in conjunction with development of long-range audit schedules. The key input in the evaluation of risk is:

a. Previous audit results.

b. Management concerns and preferences.

c. Specific requirements of the *Standards*.

d. Judgment of the internal auditor.

44. Directors may use a tool called risk analysis in preparing work schedules. Which of the following would **not** be considered in performing a risk analysis?

a. Financial exposure and potential loss.

b. Skills available on the audit staff.

c. Results of prior audits.

d. Major operating changes.

45. Factors that should be considered when evaluating audit risk in a functional area include:

1. Volume of transactions.

2. Degree of system integration.

3. Years since last audit.

4. Significant management turnover.

5. (Dollar) value of "assets at risk."

6. Average value per transaction.

7. Results of last audit.

Factors that **best** define materiality of audit risk are:

a. 1 through 7.

b. 2, 4, and 7.

c. 1, 5, and 6.

d. 3, 4, and 6.

46. In an audit of a purchasing department, which of the following generally would be considered a risk factor?

a. Purchase specifications are developed by the department requesting the material.

b. Purchases are made against blanket or open purchase orders for certain types of items.

c. Purchases are made from parties related to buyers or other company officials.

d. There is a failure to rotate purchases among suppliers included on an approved vendor list.

Managing Individual Engagements (40–50%)

2.1 Plan Engagements   323

2.2 Supervise Engagements   347

2.3 Communicate Engagement Results   361

2.4 Monitor Engagement Outcomes   382

2.5 Sample Practice Questions   385

2.1 Plan Engagements

In this section, topics such as audit process, audit planning, analytical reviews, planning materiality, determining audit objectives and scope, audit work program, and planning the audit work are discussed.

(a) Audit Process

The process of conducting an audit consists of the review of a series of activities and the following of a series of procedures. A structured methodology, consisting of audit phases or stages, can be used during the audit process to ensure quality and to ensure that all required activities are accomplished—starting from the beginning of an audit to the completion of the audit. Each phase has defined tasks to be completed. Five such phases include (1) preliminary survey, (2) audit program, (3) fieldwork, (4) reporting, and (5) monitoring and follow-up. The audit report is the end product of the audit process. The audit process described is linked to three overall audit areas: preaudit, during the audit, and postaudit (see Exhibit 2.1).

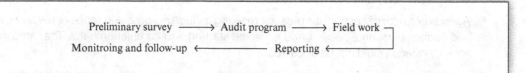

EXHIBIT 2.1 Sequence of Audit Phases

(i) Preliminary Survey

The preliminary survey is the first step in the audit process, and its purpose is familiarization, which is essential to a well-balanced and well-conducted audit. The survey activities include touring of facilities and operations, conducting audit inquiries, and performing analytical review. The audit scope and audit objectives are developed. Potential risks and exposures, goals, and standards for the audited area are identified and gathered.

Controls related to the activity being examined are identified. Questionnaires for mail survey and for personal interview are prepared to obtain background information and to understand auditees' control-related problems and issues. The audit program is not developed in this phase.

KEY CONCEPTS TO REMEMBER: Preliminary Survey

- Personal observation, physical inspection of equipment, review of documents, inquiries, flowcharts, analytical reviews, and walkthroughs are the major tools used in the preliminary survey phase.

- A flowcharting approach used in evaluating internal controls during the preliminary review provides the auditor with the best visual grasp of a system and a means for analyzing complex operations. Other approaches that do not provide such visual grasp include a questionnaire approach, a matrix approach, and a detailed narrative approach.

- Activities typically performed in the preliminary survey phase include: interviewing operating personnel, identifying the auditee's objectives, identifying standards used to evaluate performance, and assessing the risks inherent in the auditee's operations. Time budgeted for the audit should be determined after completion of the preliminary survey.

- When audit resources are limited and results of the preliminary survey and limited audit testing conducted reveal that an operating function is working as intended and no major deficiencies are noted, the auditor should send a memo to all interested parties summarizing the preliminary survey results and indicating that the audit has been canceled.

- During the preliminary survey phase of an audit of production cycle, management stated that the sale of scrap was well controlled. The best evidence to verify that assertion can be obtained by comparing the quantities of scrap expected from the production process with the quantities sold.

- During a preliminary survey, an auditor notes that several accounts payable vouchers for major suppliers show adjustments for duplicate payments of prior invoices. This would indicate a need for additional testing to determine related controls and the current exposure to duplicate payments made to suppliers.

- An example of preaudit work is conducting an entrance conference with the auditee.

- Agenda items for discussion at a preaudit meeting include purpose and scope of the audit, records and auditee personnel needed, and expected starting and completion dates. The sampling plan and key criteria would not be discussed.

- The auditor in charge has just been informed of the next audit assignment, and the audit team has been assigned. The audit budget will be finalized after the preliminary survey.

(ii) Audit Program

In the second phase of the audit process, audit procedures are developed to accomplish audit objectives. The audit procedures describe which activities to review and which transactions to examine. Writing an audit program is a documentation of audit planning. More is said about the audit program later in this section.

(iii) Fieldwork

The audit procedures included in the audit program are carried out in the third phase of the audit process. Fieldwork is examining records and evaluating information.

Evidence is collected in this phase to draw audit conclusions. The effectiveness of controls is evaluated here also. Working papers are prepared to document the results of the audit work.

KEY CONCEPTS TO REMEMBER: Fieldwork

- "Fieldwork" has been defined as "a systematic process of objectively gathering evidence about an entity's operations, evaluating it, and determining if those operations meet acceptable standards." Tasks in fieldwork include expanding or altering audit procedures if circumstances warrant, applying the audit program to accomplish audit objectives, and creating working papers that document the audit.

- If an auditor used an internal control questionnaire during the survey phase and received positive responses, he or she will confirm these responses in the fieldwork phase.

- The preliminary audit survey discloses a prior audit deficiency was never corrected. Subsequent fieldwork confirms that the deficiency still exists. The auditor should discuss the issue with the person(s) responsible for the problem, who should know how to solve it.

CONTROL STATUS DURING THE SURVEY AND THE FIELDWORK PHASES

- In the preliminary survey phase, the existence of controls is determined.
- In the fieldwork phase, the effectiveness of controls is tested.
- In the fieldwork phase, the adequacy of controls is evaluated.

(iv) Reporting

In the fourth phase of the audit process, audit results are communicated to the auditee both orally and in writing with a clear and professional opinion rendered. An exit conference is conducted to review the audit reports with auditees.

(v) Monitoring and Follow-Up

Monitoring and follow-up, the last phase, can be sophisticated or simple depending on a number of factors, including the size and complexity of the audit organization. Regardless of the type of audit chosen, each audit should include a firm basis for monitoring and follow-up actions, active status monitoring, and a determination of the results of actions taken on recommendations. The director of internal auditing should ensure follow-up of prior audit findings and recommendations to determine if corrective action was taken and is achieving the desired results.

Auditee responses to the audit report are reviewed to assess their adequacy and timeliness and the appropriateness of proposed corrective actions. Auditee responses and their corrective actions are monitored to ensure their timely completion. Effective follow-up is essential to get the full benefits of audit work. If monitoring and follow-up disclose that action on major recommendations is not progressing, additional steps should be considered promptly. Follow-up should be elevated to progressively higher levels of management of the organization to obtain prompt action. Continued attention is required until expected results are achieved. At this point, audit recommendations are closed.

Audit recommendations should be closed for only one of four reasons:

1. The recommendation was effectively implemented.
2. An alternative action was taken that achieved the intended results.
3. Circumstances have so changed that the recommendation is no longer valid.
4. The recommendation was not implemented despite the use of all feasible strategies.

When a recommendation is closed for the last reason, a judgment is made on whether the objectives are significant enough to be pursued at a later date in another assignment.

Auditing is a process similar to a manufacturing process. The audit process has a clear beginning and ending point with activities falling in between. The process accepts inputs (e.g., auditor time and effort, management input) and transforms them into meaningful outputs (e.g., audit reports, audit working papers). The audit process can be further explained in terms of "what happens when" and "who does what."

Exhibit 2.2 presents "what happens when"—that is, activities conducted in three overall audit areas, such as preaudit, during the audit, and postaudit, and ties the audit process to three such areas.

A description of "who does what" in the audit process follows. Different players (auditors) have different roles to fulfill in the process. Some common audit titles, in the order of hierarchy, include audit director, audit manager/supervisor, team leader/auditor in charge, and staff/senior auditor.

EXHIBIT 2.2 Audit Activities

Activities During Preaudit	Activities During Audit	Activities During Postaudit
Opening the audit project, short-term audit planning (scope, objectives, resources, and time frames), entrance conference, preliminary survey, audit program development, application of computer-assisted audit techniques, working paper preparation	Fieldwork, observations, testing, examinations, control evaluations, interim written reports, interim oral reports, working paper preparation, application of computer-assisted audit techniques, final audit report, correction of major findings	Exit conference, management (auditee) responses, correction of audit findings, monitoring of corrective actions, closing the audit project, auditor performance evaluation, customer satisfaction survey (i.e., obtaining feedback from auditees), project quality review (e.g., lessons learned), follow-up audit

Job duties or responsibilities of an audit director in a specific audit project include:

- Selecting or approving project team members.
- Approving project resources.
- Attending entrance and exit conferences as needed.
- Determining the need for expanded testing.
- Reviewing the summary audit findings.
- Monitoring the corrective action taken on reported audit findings.
- Conducting auditor performance appraisals.
- Obtaining feedback from audit customers.
- Closing the audit.

Job duties or responsibilities of an audit manager/supervisor in a specific audit project include:

- Opening an audit by approving the project budget.
- Attending entrance and exit conferences.
- Approving the audit program.
- Providing instructions to auditors.
- Reviewing the audit working papers.
- Ensuring that audit objectives are achieved.
- Reviewing the draft audit report.
- Developing follow-up audit plans.
- Conducting auditor performance appraisals.
- Closing the audit.

Job duties or responsibilities of an audit team leader/auditor-in-charge in a specific audit project include:

- Allocating the budgeted audit hours among assigned staff.
- Attending entrance and exit conferences.
- Preparing a preliminary audit program.
- Reviewing the audit working papers and preparing a review point sheet from a quality control viewpoint.
- Organizing and drafting the audit report.
- Conducting auditor performance appraisals.

Job duties or responsibilities of a staff/senior auditor in a specific audit project include:

- Conducting a preliminary survey.
- Developing an audit program.

- Attending entrance and exit conferences.
- Executing the audit program.
- Collecting audit evidence.
- Preparing the working papers.
- Updating the permanent audit files.
- Providing input to the draft audit report.

(b) Audit Planning

Two kinds of audit plans exist: staff plans and audit plans.

(i) Staff Plans

Staff planning should include assigning staff with the appropriate skills and knowledge for the job, assigning an adequate number of experienced staff and supervisors to the audit (consultants should be used when necessary), and providing for on-the-job training of staff.

The availability of staff and other resources is an important consideration in establishing the objectives, scope, and methodology of an audit. For example, limitations on travel funds may preclude auditors from visiting certain locations, or lack of an expertise in a particular methodology may preclude auditors from undertaking certain objectives. Auditors may be able to overcome such limitations by use of staff from local offices or by engaging consultants with the necessary knowledge, skills, and expertise.

(ii) Audit Plans

A written audit plan should be prepared for each audit and is essential to conducting audits efficiently and effectively. The form and content of the written audit plan will vary among audits. The plan generally should include an audit program and a memorandum or other appropriate documentation of key decisions about the objectives, scope, and methodology of the audit and of the auditors' basis for those decisions.

Documenting the audit plan is an opportunity for the auditors to review the work done in planning the audit to determine whether the proposed audit objectives are likely to result in a useful report, the proposed audit scope and methodology are adequate to satisfy the audit objectives promptly, and sufficient staff and other resources have been made available to perform the audit.

Written audit plans should generally include this information:

- **Introduction and background.** To the extent necessary, information should be provided about the legal authority for the audited organization, program, activity, operation, or function; its history and current objectives; its principal locations; and similar information needed by auditors to understand and carry out the audit plan.

- **Scope and objectives.** A clearly described scope and clearly stated objectives should indicate what the audit is to accomplish.

- **Audit methods.** The audit methodology should be clearly described and should present suggested steps, procedures, and sampling plans, which should be included in the audit program. For coordinated audits, the audit organization planning the work should ensure that comparable audit methods and procedures are followed to ensure that the data obtained from participating locations will be complete. Auditors should design the methodology to provide sufficient, competent, and relevant evidence to achieve the objectives of the audit. Methodology includes not only the nature of the auditors' procedures but also their extent (e.g., sample size).

- **Special instructions.** The auditors should clearly understand and reach early agreement on the responsibilities in each audit. This agreement is especially important when the work is to be directed by a central audit organization with work to be conducted at several different locations. This section of the plan may be used to list the responsibilities of each audit organization, such as preparing audit programs, conducting audit work, supervising audit work, drafting reports, handling auditee comments and questions, and processing the final report.

- **Report.** To the extent possible, the audit plan should set forth the general format of the audit report, cite the types of information to be included, and list the recipients of the report.

KEY CONCEPTS TO REMEMBER: Planning an Audit Assignment

- Documentation required to plan an internal auditing project should include evidence that the resources needed to perform the audit have been considered. The requirements for staffing levels, education and training, and audit research, along with others, should be included in the annual audit plan.

- In audit planning, internal auditors should review all relevant information. Audit planning should be documented, and the planning process should include obtaining background information about the activities to be audited; establishing audit objectives and scope of work; and determining how, when, and to whom the audit results will be communicated. Audit planning should not include collecting audit evidence on all matters related to the audit objectives—this is done in fieldwork after the audit program is written.

- The audit plan should include a detailed schedule of areas to be audited during the coming year; an estimate of the time required for each audit; risk, exposure, and potential loss to the organization; and the approximate starting date for each audit.

- When assigning individual staff members to actual audits, internal auditing managers are faced with a number of important considerations related to needs, abilities, and skills. The most important criteria are the complexity of the audit, the experience level of the auditor, and special skills possessed by the staff auditor. The least important are the staff auditor's desire for training in the audit area or the fact that the audit topic is the same as the auditor's major subject in college.

- The audit department of a large corporation has established its operating plan and budget for the coming year. The operating plan should include a prioritized listing of all audits, staffing, a detailed expense budget, and the targeted start date and completion date of each audit along with measurability criteria.

- An internal auditor judged an item to be immaterial when planning an audit. However, the auditor may still include the item if it is subsequently determined that adverse effects related to the item are likely to occur.

- When auditors are transferred from an operating department of the company, they should not be assigned to an audit of their previous department.

(continued)

KEY CONCEPTS TO REMEMBER (*Continued*)

- The audit department can engage an engineering consulting firm to perform the work when an internal auditing department has scheduled an audit of a construction contract. The audit work involves comparing materials purchased to those specified in the engineering drawings. The audit department does not have anyone on staff with sufficient expertise to complete this audit work.

- Audit objectives, an element in the audit planning process, typically take a long-term perspective, while audit staffing, audit programs, and audit procedures are short term.

- The long-range schedule as an audit-planning tool is general in nature and is used to ensure adequate audit coverage over time.

- A strategic audit plan covers audits identified to be performed over the next three to five years.

(c) Analytical Reviews

As a part of fieldwork, the internal auditor should perform analytical reviews to understand the relationships between various data. The focus is on determining the reasonableness of data. Techniques such as regression analysis, simple ratio analysis, and trend analysis can be used to provide insights into the financial and operational data. The outcome of the review is to provide a red flag to the auditor so that he or she can adjust the audit scope and the audit procedures accordingly. For example, analytical reviews can be used to indicate the possible existence of fraud.

The key is not to view the data and their relations individually but to integrate that information with other related data to provide greater insights into the dynamics of the data. Some examples of application of analytical reviews follow.

- Inventory turnover rates are compared with established industry standards to assess the performance of a business unit or division.

- Regular analytical review of operating divisions includes analysis of sales, cash flow, and profit statistics. Specifically, use of accelerated depreciation methods and sale of capital assets to obtain larger performance bonuses should be looked at in detail.

- The most persuasive means of assessing production quality control is to evaluate the number and reasons for sales adjustments and to perform trend analysis.

- Change analysis and trend analysis of buyer or vendor activity are analytical techniques to detect irregularities in purchasing. Purchases from two new vendors are increased dramatically after a new buyer was hired. Based on sales volume, it can be concluded that the buyer was obtaining kickbacks from the two new vendors.

- Analytical procedures in which current financial statements are compared with budgets or previous statements are intended primarily to determine overall reasonableness of statement contents.

- An unexpected decrease in total asset turnover ratio could indicate that fictitious inventory has been recorded.

- Accounts payable schedule verification may include the use of analytical evidence. An example is comparing the balance on the schedule with the balances of prior years.

- Workers' compensation claims can be analyzed for injuries by type of personal computer equipment and extensiveness of use of computers by individual employees.

- Analysis of loan default ratios by a loan officer in a bank should provide good trend analysis of that officer's loan activities and intentions.

- Analytical procedures revealed an extraordinary increase in account balances in maintenance supplies during the past year. These data need to be analyzed further before reaching conclusions. The increase could be a common indicator of fraud.

- A decrease in the accounts receivable turnover rate indicates a more liberal credit policy; an increase in the accounts receivable turnover rate indicates a conservative (tight) credit policy.

- During an operational audit, an auditor compares the inventory turnover rate of a subsidiary with established industry standards to assess the performance of the subsidiary and to indicate where additional audit work may be needed.

- A regression analysis technique is used to find a correlation between the operating conditions and age of water meters for a municipality.

- An aging analysis is prepared to evaluate the adequacy of the company's allowance for doubtful accounts.

- A comparison of cost data with current market quotations would be a reliable test of the valuation of marketable equity securities.

(d) Planning Materiality

Material errors, irregularities, and illegal acts will have a direct and material effect on financial statement amounts. "Materiality" is defined as the magnitude of a misstatement that would influence the judgment of a reasonable user of financial statements. Audit procedures must be designed to provide reasonable assurance of detecting material financial statement misstatements (i.e., material errors and irregularities). Thus, materiality refers to the level of precision (or accuracy) of the financial statements; the lower the materiality, the greater the precision and vice versa.

From an internal audit viewpoint, materiality refers not only to the financial statements but also to the business operations and computer systems. Consider these facts:

- From a financial statement standpoint, materiality is to be evaluated in relation to the financial statements as a whole.

- From an operations standpoint, materiality is to be evaluated in relation to a specific operation under consideration as well as all other operations affected by it.

- From a computer system standpoint, materiality is to be evaluated in relation to a specific information system under consideration as well as all other interfacing systems affected by it.

- Material weaknesses in either business operations or computer systems may or may not directly affect the financial statements.

For example, heavy use of pirated software may become a sensitive and material issue if it was known to software vendors or other interested third parties that existed to monitor software piracy situations in companies. Subsequent fines and penalties imposed could be high and the acquisition of software through official sources would cost money. In addition, loss of image and bad reputation is a major factor to think about.

FACTORS AFFECTING THE EXTENT OF AUDIT TESTING

- Materiality
- Audit risk
- Business risk
- Cost and time

Similarly, unauthorized dissemination of product formulas, process knowledge, and secret recipes to competitors would have a material effect when the competitor decides to take advantage of the newfound information. Another example is the impact of poor-quality products and possible violations related to environmental control by the organization.

Material weaknesses in business operations and computer systems have a business risk. The risk of adverse publicity and injury to the organization's reputation is of concern here. Business risk (exposure risk) is different from audit risk. From an internal auditor's perspective, "audit risk" is best defined as "the risk that the auditor may fail to detect a significant error or weakness during an examination and performance of an audit." Statement of Accounting Standards 47, *Audit Risk and Materiality in Conducting an Audit*, of the *American Institute of Certified Public Accountants* (*AICPA*), defines "audit risk" as "the probability that an auditor will issue an unqualified (clean) opinion on financial statements that actually contain material misstatements." Audit risk is therefore the complement of the level of assurance; *the lower the audit risk, the greater the assurance and vice versa*. Since audits are performed on a test or sampling basis, audit risk cannot be reduced to zero except at prohibitive cost. The concepts of materiality and audit risk suggest that the financial statements are accurate only within reasonable and practical limits.

In practice, decisions relating to materiality and the extent of audit testing are left to the professional judgment of the individual auditor. Increased audit testing would reduce both the business risk and the audit risk (and possibly the level of materiality) and at the same time would increase the cost of conducting the audit. This is because even small reductions in materiality and/or audit risk can result in disproportionately large increases in sample sizes and hence audit costs. *Short of 100% verification, audit risk cannot be reduced to zero.*

About 53% of respondents in a survey of government auditors indicated that they ordinarily attempt to quantify audit risk in determining the extent of audit testing.[1] Audit risk and materiality are important considerations in planning an audit and evaluating its results. Materiality plays a major role in planning the scope of an audit, the extent of audit testing, and in evaluating the sufficiency of audit evidence. As a practical matter, the materiality

---

[1] K. K. Raman and Relmond P. Van Daniker, *Materiality and Audit Risk in Governmental Auditing, A Research Monograph* (Alexandria, VA: Association of Government Accountants, 1990).

threshold is a gray area that separates what is very likely material from what is very likely not material.

(i) Types of Errors

Three types of errors can exist: known errors, likely errors, and possible errors (see Exhibit 2.3). "Errors" are defined as "financial statement misstatements that are either intentional or unintentional." Since audits are performed on a test or sampling basis, it is helpful to distinguish among the three types of errors.

Known errors are errors that have actually been detected by the auditor during substantive testing. **Likely errors** are estimated errors obtained by projecting to the population the same proportion of known errors observed in representative samples. Likely errors include known errors. **Possible errors** represent the amount of error at the upper limit of the confidence interval obtained in projecting sample results to the population. Possible errors are implicit in both statistical and nonstatistical sampling, although they can be quantified using only statistical sampling. Possible errors include both likely and known errors.

AUDIT PLANNING AND EVALUATION

In planning the audit, the scope of the audit should be large enough so that possible errors will not exceed the materiality threshold at a reasonable level of assurance.

In forming the audit opinion at the evaluation stage of the audit, if possible errors exceed the materiality threshold, the auditor must either issue an adverse opinion or collect more evidence to reduce uncertainty.

Many auditors use their estimated (planning) materiality to evaluate only known errors. These auditors may be underestimating the amount of error in financial statements since possible errors exceed known errors.

Auditors need to identify the potential users of the financial statements or audit reports before determining the appropriate level of assurance or materiality. This is because the user is the one being affected by the auditors' work.

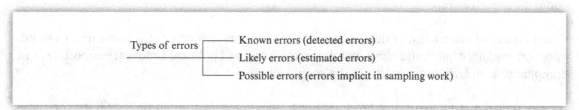

Types of errors ——— Known errors (detected errors)
——— Likely errors (estimated errors)
——— Possible errors (errors implicit in sampling work)

EXHIBIT 2.3 Types of Errors

Although there are no authoritative guidelines on what should be the maximum acceptable level of audit risk, usually a 95% assurance level (i.e., a 5% level of audit risk) would be reasonable. *Assurance level is the complement of audit risk.*

More auditors base their decisions on known and likely errors; fewer auditors base their decision on possible errors. The information about errors helps to evaluate the sufficiency of audit evidence and to decide whether additional audit testing is needed before issuing an opinion.

In determining the materiality of errors, most auditors take into consideration the combined effect of diverse errors not judged to be material individually, net out material and immaterial errors that have opposite effects, and take into account unadjusted errors from prior periods.

(ii) Who Should Set the Materiality Level?
Auditor and auditee should arrive at an understanding about the levels of materiality and the assurance level to be applied in an audit. This understanding should be based on cost/benefit considerations.

A structured audit approach will be more effective in controlling audit risk and audit costs than an unstructured one. A structured approach is one that relies on statistical sampling and/or formal decision aids for integrating audit evidence.

Auditor judgment plays an important role in determining materiality, in determining the amount of audit work to be performed, and in evaluating the evidence that is collected. Providing formal guidance to auditors may increase judgment consensus.

(iii) What Is Material and Immaterial?
Due professional care requires that the auditor consider the relative materiality or significance of matters to which audit procedures are applied. Various studies suggest that the magnitude of an error as a percentage of income is the most important factor in determining its materiality; items that have a more than 10% effect on income normally would be considered material, while items constituting less than 5% of income normally would be considered immaterial.

An auditor would most likely judge an error in an account balance to be material if the error involves a large percentage of net income. Least likely to be material are clerical mistakes that are unlikely to occur again, unverified routine transactions, and unusual transactions for the company. When a related party is involved, such as a major stockholder, an error would be considered material when the stockholder's receivables balance accounts for less than 1% of the company's receivables.

Other factors of materiality, besides income effect of the error, include effect on earnings trend, effect on working capital, and effect on total assets. Legal and political factors are important, and compliance with laws and regulations is also crucial.

As a practical matter, assurance level cannot be separated from materiality. Given the same sample size, an auditor with a lower materiality level will have a higher level of audit risk; for audit risk to be comparable across auditors, the assurance level must be related to a materiality level.

(iv) Qualitative versus Quantitative Materiality

Sometimes the nature of disclosure (sensitive or not) and the evidence of a desire to mislead (accidental or deliberate) are more important than quantitative factors. The auditor should weigh more toward human behavior.

(A) Quantitative and Qualitative Materiality Quantitative materiality is applicable during the planning stage of an audit. Qualitative materiality is applicable during the evaluation stage of an audit since it is not practical to plan the audit to detect qualitative misstatements.

In addition to quantitative materiality, the auditor should consider qualitative materiality. Qualitative materiality may include the cumulative effect of immaterial items or the needs of users. The materiality threshold should vary for each audit project and for each audit type (i.e., operational audit, financial audit, compliance audit, information technology [IT] audit).

Legal and political factors and environmental factors may affect the determination of qualitative materiality. Irregularities, fraud, illegal acts, legal covenants, and account misclassifications likely would be considered qualitatively material.

The auditor needs to strike a balance between cost effectiveness and preferences of user groups for financial statements completely free of errors.

(v) How to Compute Materiality

Materiality is computed by taking a base and multiplying that by a percentage. The base, in declining order of importance, includes total revenues, total expenditures, total assets, retained earnings, and income. The percentage used can be a flat percentage or one obtained from a sliding scale. A flat percentage is based on the notion that materiality is completely relative; a sliding scale is based on the notion that some amounts are large enough to be always material.

In the government auditors' survey, it was noted that a majority (65%) of the respondents use a flat percentage while 35% use a sliding scale to compute materiality.

(e) Determining Audit Objectives and Scope

(i) Audit Objectives

Audit objectives are what the audit project is going to accomplish. Clearly defining the audit assignment objective(s) is a must at the beginning of each audit since this definition guides the extensiveness of internal control assessment as well as the scope and methodology of the audit work. Audit assignments with broad objectives generally are more difficult to accomplish and require more staff resources and time than do assignments with specific objectives. Therefore, to the extent possible, audit objective(s) should be defined as precisely as possible to preclude unnecessary work while also meeting the assignment's purpose.

For example, this audit objective might require extensive data gathering based on a random statistical sample: Determine what percentage of program recipients are ineligible for benefits. In this case, one needs to find out the total recipients, eligible recipients, and ineligible recipients. Statistical projections are required based on the sample results.

In contrast, this audit objective might be accomplished with less extensive statistical sampling: Determine if the agency consistently uses reasonable controls to ensure that only eligible recipients receive benefits. In this case, one needs to assess the controls using different methods (e.g., review of controls over beneficiary enrollment), in which a sampling procedure is a part of the audit procedures.

At the beginning of an audit, there should be a meeting of the minds as to objectives between auditor and auditee in order to have useful results from the audit at the end. In all cases, the objectives, scope, and methodology section of the audit report should clearly describe the audit objectives, scope, and assumptions and basis for auditor conclusions.

(ii) Audit Scope

The scope of an internal audit is initially defined by the audit objectives. Preliminary survey, audit programs, audit project scheduling, and time estimates are driven by audit objectives. An example of an audit objective is evaluating whether cash receipts are adequately safeguarded.

AUDIT SCOPE

The scope of the internal audit function should not include reviewing the strategic management process, assessing management decision making both quantitatively and qualitatively, and reporting the results to the audit committee. Other than that, the scope can include anything from the mailroom to the shipping room. The reason is that strategic planning and decision making are the core duties of senior management. The internal auditor should not second-guess senior management; the auditor may not be qualified to perform such reviews.

Scope is the boundary of the audit. Determining the scope of the audit is part of audit planning. It addresses such things as the period and number of locations to be covered. The audit scope should include financial, operational, and compliance audits. The eight steps in determining the scope of the audit include:

1. Considering the significance and the needs of potential users of the audit report.

2. Obtaining an understanding of the area to be audited.

3. Considering legal and regulatory requirements.

4. Considering internal control structure.

5. Identifying criteria needed to evaluate matters of subject to the audit.

6. Identifying significant findings and recommendations from previous audits that could affect the current audit objectives. Auditors should determine if management has corrected the conditions causing those findings and implemented those recommendations.

7. Identifying potential sources of data that could be used as audit evidence and the reliability of these data, including data collected by the audited entity, data generated by the auditors, or data provided by third parties.

8. Considering whether the work of other auditors or of experts may be used to satisfy some of the auditors' objectives.

Neither audit objectives and audit scope nor audit methodology is determined in isolation. Auditors determine these three elements of the audit plan together, as the considerations in determining each often overlap.

(iii) Considerations for Audit Scope

Determining the audit scope normally involves matters such as the number of locations to be visited, time frames to be covered, and the type and depth of work needed to ensure that assignment objectives are accomplished and that all applicable audit standards are met. In establishing an audit scope, the audit team or the supervisor should consider questions such as:

- What elements of a finding are required? Is disclosing a particular condition enough, or is it necessary to establish cause and effect? Will it be necessary to evaluate the condition against criteria?

- Will assignment findings relate only to the samples or cases reviewed, or will it be necessary to generalize them to a larger universe?

- What are the relevant sources of data? Who/what holds the data (people, data tapes, and files)?

- Will the data be available? Are they likely to be reliable?

- What kind of information will be required? For example, will a judgmental sample be acceptable, or will a statistically projectable random sample be required?

- When are audit work results (i.e., audit reports) required?

Determining scope may require trade-offs. For example, a more narrow scope may result in a less powerful message. But it may be the best that can be done considering available resources and time. Is the more narrow scope acceptable?

(iv) Audit Scope Impairments

During the audit engagement, auditors may find scope impairments. When factors external to the audit organization and the auditor restrict the audit scope or interfere with the auditor's ability to form objective opinions and conclusions, the auditor should attempt to remove the limitation or, failing that, report the limitation. For example, under the next conditions, an audit will be adversely affected and the auditor will not have complete freedom to make an objective judgment.

- Interference or influence that improperly or imprudently limits or modifies the scope or type of an audit

- Interference with the selection or application of audit procedures or the selection of transactions to be examined

- Denial of access to sources of information, such as books, records, computer files and supporting documents, or denial of opportunity to obtain explanations by officials and employees of the organization, or activity under audit

- Unreasonable restrictions on the time allowed to complete an audit competently

338 Wiley CIAexcel Exam Review: Part 2, Internal Audit Practice

KEY CONCEPTS TO REMEMBER: Audit Scope

- When faced with an imposed scope limitation, the director of internal auditing should communicate the potential effects of the scope limitation to the audit committee of the board of directors.

- When an internal auditor is auditing the financial operations of an organization, the audit scope does not include a review of the financial decision-making process. The scope includes reviewing the reliability and integrity of financial information; reviewing systems established to ensure compliance with applicable policy, plans, procedures, and other types of authority; and appraising economy, efficiency, and effectiveness of the employment of resources.

- Internal auditors should review the means of safeguarding assets from losses arising from exposure to the elements.

(f) Audit Work Program

Preparing an audit program is the next step after completing the preliminary survey work. An audit program serves as a road map for the auditor. The audit program provides the auditor the necessary guidance to proceed with the detailed audit work in terms of audit procedures to be conducted and required audit evidence to be collected during the audit. The audit program should focus on major activities and key controls within and around such activities.

The audit program development should take a structured approach where the audit project is broken down into phases, tasks, and steps. Audit programs provide a description of the methodology and suggested steps and procedures to accomplish the audit objectives, a systematic basis for assigning work to audit supervisors and staff, and the basis for a summary record of work.

Audit procedures are the detailed steps, instructions, or guidelines provided for the auditor for the collection and accumulation of a particular type of audit evidence during the audit. Audit procedures can be verbal or written; the latter are preferred and are developed by auditors and approved by audit supervisors. They should be clear to enable auditors to understand what is to be accomplished.

An example of an audit procedure might be "obtain physical inventory sheets, verify the accuracy of inventory extension by multiplying the quantity with cost/price figures. Note any exceptions." Audit procedures usually begin with action words, such as these: review, verify, look, observe, analyze, confirm, interrelate, construct, reconstruct, prove, read, identify, inquire, determine, reconcile, ascertain, examine, scan, foot, cross-foot, compute, recompute, compare, count, trace, and retrace.

Written audit programs should not be used merely as checklists of steps to be conducted. Effective work on operational or performance audits require that the staff understand the objectives of the audit and use initiative and creativity in applying the audit program and in assessing the results of the work.

Two types of audit programs exist: standard audit programs and customized audit programs. Exhibit 2.4 compares each of these programs.

EXHIBIT 2.4 Standardized versus Customized Audit Programs

Standardized Audit Programs	Customized Audit Programs
Inexperienced auditors can execute the programs	Experienced auditors required to execute the programs
Do not require a great knowledge of the operating environment to develop the programs	Require lots of knowledge of the operating environment to develop good programs
Not much work is required to develop the programs	Significant amount of time and effort are required to develop the programs
Would be appropriate for use in a minimally changing operating environment	Would be appropriate for a complex or changing operating environment
Would be appropriate for use in multiple locations with similar operations	Cannot be used in multiple locations with dissimilar operations
Useful in conducting repeat, routine audits	Useful in conducting unique, nonroutine audits
Would **not** be appropriate for a complex or changing operating environment	Would **not** be appropriate for a simple or unchanging operating environment

KEY CONCEPTS TO REMEMBER: Audit Programs

- The primary role of an audit program is to serve as a tool for planning, directing, and controlling audit work.

- The primary purpose of developing a written audit program is to help ensure that the audit work is properly planned and documented.

- An audit program should be designed for each individual audit and should include audit steps and procedures to provide assurances that the objectives of the audit are met. To achieve established objectives of the audit department, the best criterion with respect to audit programs is to tailor each audit program to meet the needs of the specific audit assignment.

- Three criteria should be considered essential for developing audit programs: description of the objectives of the auditee operations as agreed to by the auditee, specificity as to the controls to be tested, and specificity as to audit work steps to be followed. The methodology to be used for the audit work steps is not a consideration.

- In the preparation of an audit program, three items are essential: the performance of a preliminary survey, a review of materials from prior audit reports, and a review of performance standards set by management. Preparation of a budget identifying the costs of resources needed is not essential during the audit program phase. It is essential during the planning stage of the audit.

- Upon discovering that an audit area was omitted from the audit program, the auditor should evaluate whether completion of the audit as planned will be adequate.

- Audit programs that test internal controls should be tailored for the audit of each operation.

- The audit program focuses on audit objectives and related audit procedures required to achieve those objectives.

- An example of an audit objective is to ensure that an update of a master file is performed accurately. An example of a related audit procedure is to reconcile computer-generated totals with totals on the updating reports.

(continued)

KEY CONCEPTS TO REMEMBER (*Continued*)

- An example of an audit objective is to determine whether inventory stocks are sufficient to meet projected sales.An example of an audit objective is to determine whether current company policies and procedures are sufficient to provide adequate control over employee additions and deletions to the payroll master file.

- An example of an audit procedure is to observe the procedures used to identify defective units produced.

- Due professional care standards require that the auditor consider the relative materiality or significance of matters to which audit procedures are applied.

(g) Planning the Audit Work

Planning and managing an audit assignment starts from developing work plans to completing the audit engagement. The majority of the audit work takes place during the fieldwork phase. In planning, auditors define the audit's objectives, scope, and methodology. Planning continues throughout the audit, and auditors should document their plan and changes to it. The most important task is to make sure that sufficient staff and other resources are available to do the audit work. Audit work can be done either at headquarters (home office) and/or at field offices. Exhibit 2.5 summarizes the advantages and disadvantages of headquarters and field office work.

IIA *Standards* Applicable to Plan Engagements

2200—Engagement Planning

Internal auditors must develop and document a plan for each engagement, including the engagement's objectives, scope, timing, and resource allocations.

EXHIBIT 2.5 Audit Work at Headquarters and Field Offices

At Headquarters	At Field Offices
Advantages	**Advantages**
More avenues to recruit new auditors	Reduction of travel time and expenses
Availability of qualified auditors due to location and ability to recruit auditors due to corporate name	Auditors will be familiar with local operations and people
Auditors with special skills can be hired	
Disadvantages	**Disadvantages**
Headquarters and auditors are not familiar with field office operations and people	More expensive to operate a separate office
Requires more travel time and expenses Auditors will be away from home and family	Lack of qualified auditors due to location
Auditors will feel burned out	Lack of specific skills among the audit staff Auditors will not be familiar with the corporate culture
	Auditors will not have management insight due to lack of ongoing contact

Practice Advisory 2200-1: Engagement Planning

1. The internal auditor plans and conducts the engagement, with supervisory review and approval. Prior to the engagement's commencement, the internal auditor prepares an engagement program that:

- States the objectives of the engagement.

- Identifies technical requirements, objectives, risks, processes, and transactions that are to be examined.

- States the nature and extent of testing required.

- Documents the internal auditor's procedures for collecting, analyzing, interpreting, and documenting information during the engagement.

- Is modified, as appropriate, during the engagement with the approval of the chief audit executive (CAE), or his or her designee.

2. The CAE should require a level of formality and documentation (e.g., of the results of planning meetings, risk assessment procedures, level of detail in the work program, etc.) that is appropriate to the organization. Factors to consider include:

- Whether the work performed and/or the results of the engagement will be relied upon by others (e.g., external auditors, regulators, or management).

- Whether the work relates to matters that may be involved in potential or current litigation.

- The experience level of the internal audit staff and the level of direct supervision required.

- Whether the project is staffed internally, by guest auditors, or by external service providers.

- The project's complexity and scope.

- The size of the internal audit activity.

- The value of documentation (e.g., whether it will be used in subsequent years).

3. The internal auditor determines the other engagement requirements, such as the period covered and estimated completion dates. The internal auditor also considers the final engagement communication format. Planning at this stage facilitates the communication process at the engagement's completion.

4. The internal auditor informs those in management who need to know about the engagement, conducts meetings with management responsible for the activity under review, summarizes and distributes the discussions and any conclusions reached from the meetings, and retains the documentation in the engagement working papers. Topics of discussion may include:

- Planned engagement objectives and scope of work.

- The resources and timing of engagement work.

- Key factors affecting business conditions and operations of the areas being reviewed, including recent changes in internal and external environment.

- Concerns or requests from management.

5. The CAE determines how, when, and to whom engagement results will be communicated. The internal auditor documents this and communicates it to management, to the extent deemed appropriate, during the planning phase of the engagement. The internal auditor communicates to management subsequent changes that affect the timing or reporting of engagement results.

Practice Advisory 2200-2: Using a Top-Down, Risk-Based Approach to Identify the Controls to Be Assessed in an Internal Audit Engagement

1. This Practice Advisory should be read in conjunction with Practice Advisories 2010-2: *Using the Risk Management Process in Internal Audit Planning*, 2210-1: *Engagement Objectives* and 2210.A1-1: *Risk Assessment in Engagement Planning* and the Practice Guide *GAIT for Business and IT Risk (GAIT-R)*.

2. This practice advisory assumes that the objectives for the internal audit engagement have been determined and the risks to be addressed have been identified in the internal audit planning process. It provides guidance on the use of a top-down, risk-based approach to identify and include in the internal audit scope (per Standard 2220) the key controls relied on to manage the risks.

3. "Top-down" refers to basing the scope definition on the more significant risks to the organization. This is in contrast to developing the scope based on the risks at a specific location, which may not be significant to the organization as a whole. A top-down approach ensures that internal auditing is focused, as noted in Practice Advisory 2010-2, on "providing assurance on the management of significant risks."

4. A system of internal control typically includes both manual and automated controls. (Note that this applies to controls at every level—entity, business process, and IT general controls—and in every layer of the control framework; e.g., activities in the control environment, monitoring, or risk assessment layers may also be automated.) Both types of controls need to be assessed to determine whether business risks are managed effectively. In particular, the internal auditor needs to assess whether there is an appropriate combination of controls, including those related to IT, to mitigate business risks within organizational tolerances. The internal auditor needs to consider including procedures to assess and confirm that risk tolerances are current and appropriate.

5. The internal audit scope needs to include all the controls required to provide reasonable assurance that the risks are effectively managed (subject to the comments in paragraph 9). These controls are referred to as key controls—those necessary to manage risk associated with a critical business objective. Only key controls need to be assessed, although the internal auditor can choose to include an assessment of non-key controls (e.g., redundant, duplicative controls) if there is value to the business in providing such assurance. The internal auditor may also discuss with management whether the non-key controls are required.

6. When the organization has a mature and effective risk management program, the key controls relied on to manage each risk will have been identified. In these cases, the internal auditor needs to assess whether management's identification and assessment of the key controls is adequate.

7. The key controls can be in the form of:

- Entity-level controls (e.g., employees are trained and take a test to confirm their understanding of the code of conduct). Entity-level controls may be manual, fully automated, or partly automated.

- Manual controls within a business process (e.g., the performance of a physical inventory).

- Fully automated controls within a business process (e.g., matching or updating accounts in the general ledger).

- Partly automated controls within a business process (also called hybrid or IT-dependent controls), where an otherwise manual control relies on application functionality, such as an exception report. If an error in that functionality would not be detected, the entire control could be ineffective. For example, a key control to detect duplicate payments might include the review of a system-generated report. The manual part of the control would not ensure the report is complete. Therefore, the application functionality that generated the report should be in scope.

The internal auditor may use other methods or frameworks, as long as all the key controls relied on to manage the risks are identified and assessed, including manual controls, automated controls, and controls within IT general control processes.

8. Fully and partly automated controls—whether at the entity level or within a business process—generally rely on the proper design and effective operation of IT general controls. *GAIT-R* discusses the recommended process for identifying key IT general controls.

9. The assessment of key controls may be performed in a single, integrated internal audit engagement or in a combination of internal audit engagements. For example, one internal audit engagement may address the key controls performed by business process users, while another covers the key IT general controls, and a third assesses related controls that operate at the entity level. This is common where the same controls (especially those at the entity level or within IT general controls) are relied on for more than one risk area.

10. As noted in paragraph 5, before providing an opinion on the effective management of the risks covered by the internal audit scope, it is necessary to assess the combination of all key controls. Even if multiple internal audit engagements are performed, each addressing some key controls, the internal auditor needs to include in the scope of at least one internal audit engagement an assessment of the design of the key controls as a whole (i.e., across all the related internal audit engagements) and whether it is sufficient to manage risks within organizational tolerances.

11. If the internal audit scope (considering other internal audit engagements as discussed in paragraph 9) includes some, but not all, key controls required to manage the targeted risks, a scope limitation should be considered and clearly communicated in the internal audit notification and final report.

2201—Planning Considerations

In planning the engagement, internal auditors must consider:

- The objectives of the activity being reviewed and the means by which the activity controls its performance.

- The significant risks to the activity, its objectives, resources, and operations and the means by which the potential impact of risk is kept to an acceptable level.

- The adequacy and effectiveness of the activity's risk management and control processes compared to a relevant control framework or model.

- The opportunities for making significant improvements to the activity's risk management and control processes.

2201.A1—When planning an engagement for parties outside the organization, internal auditors must establish a written understanding with them about objectives, scope, respective responsibilities, and other expectations, including restrictions on distribution of the results of the engagement and access to engagement records.

2201.C1—Internal auditors must establish an understanding with consulting engagement clients about objectives, scope, respective responsibilities, and other client expectations. For significant engagements, this understanding must be documented.

No Practice Advisory for Standard 2201

2210—Engagement Objectives

Objectives must be established for each engagement.

2210.A1—Internal auditors must conduct a preliminary assessment of the risks relevant to the activity under review. Engagement objectives must reflect the results of this assessment.

2210.A2—Internal auditors must consider the probability of significant errors, fraud, noncompliance, and other exposures when developing the engagement objectives.

2210.A3—Adequate criteria are needed to evaluate controls. Internal auditors must ascertain the extent to which management has established adequate criteria to determine whether objectives and goals have been accomplished. If adequate, internal auditors must use such criteria in their evaluation. If inadequate, internal auditors must work with management to develop appropriate evaluation criteria.

2210.C1—Consulting engagement objectives must address governance, risk management, and control processes to the extent agreed on with the client.

2210.C2—Consulting engagement objectives must be consistent with the organization's values, strategies, and objectives.

Practice Advisory 2210-1: Engagement Objectives

1. Internal auditors establish engagement objectives to address the risks associated with the activity under review. For planned engagements, the objectives proceed and align to those initially identified during the risk assessment process from which the internal audit plan is derived. For unplanned engagements, the objectives are established prior to the start of the engagement and are designed to address the specific issue that prompted the engagement.

2. The risk assessment during the engagement's planning phase is used to further define the initial objectives and identify other significant areas of concern.

3. After identifying the risks, the auditor determines the procedures to be performed and the scope (nature, timing, and extent) of those procedures. Engagement procedures performed in appropriate scope are the means to derive conclusions related to the engagement objectives.

Practice Advisory 2210.A1-1: Risk Assessment in Engagement Planning

1. Internal auditors consider management's assessment of risks relevant to the activity under review. The internal auditor also considers:

- The reliability of management's assessment of risk.
- Management's process for monitoring, reporting, and resolving risk and control issues.
- Management's reporting of events that exceeded the limits of the organization's risk appetite and management's response to those reports.
- Risks in related activities relevant to the activity under review.

2. Internal auditors obtain or update background information about the activities to be reviewed to determine the impact on the engagement objectives and scope.

3. If appropriate, internal auditors conduct a survey to become familiar with the activities, risks, and controls to identify areas for engagement emphasis, and to invite comments and suggestions from engagement clients.

4. Internal auditors summarize the results from the reviews of management's assessment of risk, the background information, and any survey work. The summary includes:

- Significant engagement issues and reasons for pursuing them in more depth.

- Engagement objectives and procedures.

- Methodologies to be used, such as technology-based audit and sampling techniques.

- Potential critical control points, control deficiencies, and/or excess controls.

- When applicable, reasons for not continuing the engagement or for significantly modifying engagement objectives.

2220—Engagement Scope

The established scope must be sufficient to satisfy the objectives of the engagement.

> **2220.A1**—The scope of the engagement must include consideration of relevant systems, records, personnel, and physical properties, including those under the control of third parties.
>
> **2220.A2**—If significant consulting opportunities arise during an assurance engagement, a specific written understanding as to the objectives, scope, respective responsibilities, and other expectations should be reached and the results of the consulting engagement communicated in accordance with consulting standards.
>
> **2220.C1**—In performing consulting engagements, internal auditors must ensure that the scope of the engagement is sufficient to address the agreed-on objectives. If internal auditors develop reservations about the scope during the engagement, these reservations must be discussed with the client to determine whether to continue with the engagement.
>
> **2220.C2**—During consulting engagements, internal auditors must address controls consistent with the engagement's objectives and be alert to significant control issues.

No Practice Advisory for Standard 2220

2030—Resource Management

The CAE must ensure that internal audit resources are appropriate, sufficient, and effectively deployed to achieve the approved plan.

Interpretation: *"Appropriate" refers to the mix of knowledge, skills, and other competencies needed to perform the plan. "Sufficient" refers to the quantity of resources needed to accomplish the plan. Resources are effectively deployed when they are used in a way that optimizes the achievement of the approved plan.*

Practice Advisory 2030-1: Resource Management

1. The CAE is primarily responsible for the sufficiency and management of internal audit resources in a manner that ensures the fulfillment of internal audit's responsibilities, as detailed in the internal audit charter. This includes effective communication of resource needs and reporting of status to senior management and the board. Internal audit resources may include employees, external service providers, financial support, and technology-based audit techniques. Ensuring the adequacy of internal audit resources is ultimately a responsibility of the organization's senior management and board; the CAE should assist them in discharging this responsibility.

2. The skills, capabilities, and technical knowledge of the internal audit staff are to be appropriate for the planned activities. The CAE will conduct a periodic skills assessment or inventory to determine the specific skills required to perform the internal audit activities. The skills assessment is based on and considers the various needs identified in the risk assessment and audit plan. This includes assessments of technical knowledge, language skills, business acumen, fraud detection and prevention competency, and accounting and audit expertise.

3. Internal audit resources need to be sufficient to execute the audit activities in the breadth, depth, and timeliness expected by senior management and the board, as stated in the internal audit charter. Resource planning considerations include the audit universe, relevant risk levels, the internal audit plan, coverage expectations, and an estimate of unanticipated activities.

4. The CAE also ensures that resources are deployed effectively. This includes assigning auditors who are competent and qualified for specific assignments. It also includes developing a resourcing approach and organizational structure appropriate for the business structure, risk profile, and geographical dispersion of the organization.

5. From an overall resource management standpoint, the CAE considers succession planning, staff evaluation and development programs, and other human resource disciplines. The CAE also addresses the resourcing needs of the internal audit activity, whether those skills are present or not within the internal audit activity itself. Other approaches to addressing resource needs include external service providers, employees from other departments within the organization, or specialized consultants.

6. Because of the critical nature of resources, the CAE maintains ongoing communications and dialog with senior management and the board on the adequacy of resources for the internal audit activity. The CAE periodically presents a summary of status and adequacy of resources to senior management and the board. To that end, the CAE develops appropriate metrics, goals, and objectives to monitor the overall adequacy of resources. This can include comparisons of resources to the internal audit plan, the impact of temporary shortages or vacancies, educational and training activities, and changes to specific skill needs based on changes in the organization's business, operations, programs, systems, and controls.

2230—Engagement Resource Allocation

Internal auditors must determine appropriate and sufficient resources to achieve engagement objectives based on an evaluation of the nature and complexity of each engagement, time constraints, and available resources.

Practice Advisory 2230-1: Engagement Resource Allocation

1. Internal auditors consider the following when determining the appropriateness and sufficiency of resources:

- The number and experience level of the internal audit staff

- Knowledge, skills, and other competencies of the internal audit staff when selecting internal auditors for the engagement

- Availability of external resources where additional knowledge and competencies are required

- Training needs of internal auditors, as each engagement assignment serves as a basis for meeting the internal audit activity's developmental needs

2240—Engagement Work Program

Internal auditors must develop and document work programs that achieve the engagement objectives.

2240.A1 – Work programs must include the procedures for identifying, analyzing, evaluating, and documenting information during the engagement. The work program must be approved prior to its implementation, and any adjustments must be approved promptly.

2240.C1 – Work programs for consulting engagements may vary in form and content depending on the nature of the engagement.

Practice Advisory 2240-1: Engagement Work Program

1. Internal auditors develop and obtain documented approval of work programs before commencing the internal audit engagement. The work program includes methodologies to be used, such as technology-based audit and sampling techniques.

2. The process of collecting, analyzing, interpreting, and documenting information is to be supervised to provide reasonable assurance that engagement objectives are met and that the internal auditor's objectivity is maintained.

2.2 Supervise Engagements

Topics such as audit scheduling, audit supervision, collecting data and information, and developing and reviewing audit working papers are discussed in this section.

(a) Audit Scheduling

An audit schedule is an essential part of planning internal auditing department activities. Since audit resources, in terms of available time and the number of auditors, are limited, the audit manager needs to balance the needs of the audit plan and the availability of resources. It is prudent to hire auditors with different skill and experience levels so that all required skills are available among the audit staff even though each auditor may not have all the required skills.

It is the audit manager's responsibility to match the available audit resources to the audit requirements. If the required resources are not available, the audit manager should try to acquire them from either internal or external sources.

The audit manager will notice that there are constraints on the conduct of the audit that may affect the completion of the audits as planned. Some examples of such constraints are: staff unavailability due to illness or termination; auditee not ready for the audit due to some business considerations, such as mergers, demergers, and other extraordinary events; and time constraints, such as accounting month closing work, quarter-end work, or year-end work. The audit manager needs to consider all these constraints with alternative plans in place.

When it comes to assigning the audit staff to particular audit responsibilities, the two approaches most often taken are the team concept and the pool concept. Under the team concept, individuals are given responsibility only for certain segments of the organization.

Under the pool concept, individuals are made available for assignment to any audit. What works best is determined by the needs of individual organizations, but both approaches have their advantages and drawbacks.

The team approach offers the opportunity for the individual staff members to become proficient in given areas quickly. Experienced audit staff members are more likely to work in specialized team–type areas. The pool approach allows the individual staff member to gain experience in a broader sense in many areas of the organization. What usually works in practice is a blending of the two approaches, with new staff auditors being available under the pool concept and more experienced auditors developing supervisory skills as well as expertise in more specialized areas.

During the planning of the audit, the audit manager needs to break down the audit project into small and manageable tasks, which can be assigned to audit staff to facilitate monitoring the audit results and progress. Project management tools and techniques, such as program evaluation and review techniques, critical path methods, and periodic progress reports, might help the audit manager to plan and control major and complex audit projects.

KEY CONCEPTS TO REMEMBER: Managing an Audit Assignment

- An audit department can use the pool concept to assign all staff and most senior auditors to engagements. Monthly audit work schedules would most likely ensure effective staff utilization.

- The effectiveness of an audit assignment is related to the findings and the action taken on those findings. Conducting an exit interview with auditees would contribute to assignment effectiveness.

- The internal audit department time budgets normally should be prepared in terms of hours or days.

- A primary purpose of an exit conference is to ensure the accuracy of the information used by an internal auditor. A secondary benefit of an exit conference is to improve relations with auditees. Another purpose of the exit conference is for the internal auditor to review and verify the appropriateness of the audit report based on auditee input.

- The primary reason that the auditor should document a closing conference is that information may be needed if a dispute arises.

- A purpose of an audit closing conference is to generate commitment for appropriate managerial action.

- A primary purpose of the audit closing conference is to resolve remaining issues.

- The best purpose of an exit conference is to ensure that there have been no misunderstandings or misinterpretation of fact. Auditors are required to discuss conclusions and recommendations at appropriate levels of management before issuing final written reports. The purpose of the exit conference is not whether the objectives of the audit and the scope of the audit work are known by the auditee, the auditee understands the audit program, or the list of persons who are to receive the final report are identified.

- The primary purpose of conducting a closing conference with the manager of an organizational unit audited should be to confirm the soundness of audit results and make such modifications as seem justified.

- During an exit conference, an auditor and an auditee disagreed about a well-documented audit finding. Assuming that the disagreement cannot be resolved prior to issuing the audit report, it should be handled by presenting both the audit finding and the auditee's position on the finding. Reasons for disagreement should be stated.

- Audit objectives of the audit closing or exit conference are to discuss the findings, resolve conflicts, and identify management's actions and responses to the findings.

- Recommendations in audit reports may or may not actually be implemented.

- Working papers should identify concerns for future audits, but such concerns are not an objective of the audit closing conference.

- Interim reports are issued during an audit to communicate information requiring immediate action.

- An oral report is appropriate when significant problems are discovered during the audit.

- If an audit is done in a sales department, a copy of the audit report should be sent to the sales director and vice president of marketing.

- Participants who would be appropriate to attend an exit conference include the responsible internal auditor, representatives from management who are knowledgeable of detailed operations, and those who can authorize implementation of corrective action.

- After an audit report with adverse findings has been communicated to appropriate auditee personnel, proper action is to schedule a follow-up review.

- Due professional care calls for consideration of the possibility of material irregularities during every audit assignment.

- Due care in the conduct of an audit implies the conduct of examinations and verifications to a reasonable extent.

- When written performance standards established by management are vague and have to be interpreted by the auditor, the auditor should establish agreement with the auditee as to the standards needed to measure performance.

- An auditor begins an audit with a preliminary evaluation of internal controls, the purpose of which is to decide on the extent of future auditing activities. If the auditor's preliminary evaluation of internal controls results in a finding that controls may be inadequate, the next step would be an expansion of audit work prior to the preparation of an audit report.

- The performance appraisal system for evaluating an auditor should include specific accomplishments directly related to the performance of the audit program (i.e., based on task outcomes).

(b) Audit Supervision

The most effective way to ensure the quality and expedite the progress of an audit assignment is by exercising proper supervision from the start of the planning process to the completion of audit work and reporting. Supervision adds seasoned judgment to the work performed by less experienced staff and provides necessary on-the-job training for them.

Assigning and using staff is important to satisfying audit objectives. Since skills and knowledge vary among auditors, work assignments must be commensurate with skills and abilities.

Supervisors should satisfy themselves that staff members clearly understand their assigned tasks before starting the work. Staff members should be informed not only of what work they are to do and how they are to proceed but also why the work is to be conducted and what it is expected to accomplish. With experienced staff, the supervisors' role may be more general. They may outline the scope of the work and leave details to assistants. With a less experienced staff, a supervisor may have to specify not only how to gather data but also techniques for analyzing them.

Effective supervision ensures that audit assignments are properly planned and produce a high-quality and consistent product. A competent supervisor can help in preparing audit plans, developing and controlling budgets and schedules, improving auditor and auditee relationships, ensuring the preparation of consistent and quality working papers, and reviewing audit reports.

Supervision is a continuing process, beginning with audit planning and ending with the conclusion of audit assignments and distribution of the final audit report. Supervisors should attend the initial and final meetings with the auditee, when possible. Supervisors should approve both the initial audit work program and any revisions to the audit work program. Nonconformance to the approved audit work program should be recorded in the working papers, giving adequate reasons. Supervisors should review the working papers and monitor and control audit budgets and schedules through observation and periodic progress and time reports. When supervisors review the audit report, they should refer to the working papers to ensure that all evidence and findings are adequately supported and that the deficiency audit findings are objective, fair, significant, and factual.

KEY CONCEPTS TO REMEMBER: Audit Supervision

- "The proficiency of the internal auditors and the difficulty of the audit assignment" best describes what should determine the extent of supervision required for a particular internal audit assignment. The extent of supervision is not determined by whether the audit involves possible fraud on the part of management, whether the audit involves possible violations of laws or government regulations, or the audit organization's prior experience in dealing with the particular auditee.

- Time budgets, weekly status reports, and time reports are of most assistance in the supervision of a specific audit assignment. An assignment board is of least assistance.

- Using only daily, close supervision and written memoranda is an acceptable approach for managing a small department but is not appropriate for use with a large audit department.

- Supervising an audit engagement properly includes ensuring that the approved audit program is carried out.

- Audits should be properly supervised to produce professional audits of consistently high quality. This requires review of all audit programs, working papers, and draft audit reports.

- Best control over the work on which audit opinions are based is a supervisory review of all audit work. An audit opinion is the auditor's professional judgment of the situation, which was reviewed by an audit supervisor.

- When reviewing the audit working papers, the audit supervisor is to determine whether working papers adequately support the audit findings, conclusions, and audit reports.

- An audit finding recorded in the working papers and report draft that omits the criteria used for evaluation should be a deficiency found by an audit supervisor when reviewing a set of working papers.

- An audit supervisor should evaluate the evidence collected by the auditor during the review of the audit working papers. Substantive testing supports the sufficient evidence; tests of control support competent evidence. The relationship of the sample to the audit objectives supports relevant evidence. An example of relevant evidence is selecting a stratified sample of billings by an agency specializing in newspaper advertising when the company is requesting artwork for a magazine advertising. Insufficient evidence is when an auditor interviews the firm's advertising manager, products marketing director, and major customers to determine the adequacy of contract and compliance with fair trade regulations. The auditor should have talked to legal counsel also.

(c) Collecting Data and Information

Information is the heart of the problem-solving process. Decisions are made using the information to solve existing problems and to make decisions. For the information to be useful in so many ways, it has to meet certain quality attributes, such as availability, timeliness, accuracy, and relevancy.

Knowledge is power. Knowledge is the result of information. The amount and the right kind of information a person has can make the difference between an informed decision and a guess, between success and failure. Knowledge is a synthesis of information. In this information age, knowing means winning. The more one knows about something, the more control one has over one's own destiny. *Relevant information enables one not only to avoid current failures but also to maximize future opportunities and minimize potential future problems.*

As changes create a need for more information, the value of information begins to increase significantly. The successful executives and professionals (e.g., auditors) will be those who have mastered the art of being information conscious. Information consists of facts, figures, rules, news, statistics, data, values, impressions—pieces of intelligence that singly or jointly increase awareness of the subject matter.

Information should be differentiated from assumptions. An assumption is a conclusion based on noninformation, which can be true or false. It has no evidence. Assumptions are made all the time. We make false assumptions, such as certain data are: easy to find when in fact they are difficult to find, difficult to find when in fact they are easy, inexpensive to buy when in fact they are expensive, and expensive to buy when in fact they are inexpensive.

Information is obtained only by asking questions or searching for it. Information is an outcome of a process that involves fact gathering, data collection, measurement, interpretation, analysis, and forecasting.

Information can be said to be the result of data. Data consist of raw numbers and facts. Information consists of meaningful numbers and facts. Information involves the addition of a certain value to data through some level of selection, interpretation, or rearrangement.

Since management makes decisions and auditors use information, the auditors need to know how and where the information is coming from. At least four sources of information are available: primary and secondary information and internal and external sources (see Exhibit 2.6).

Primary information is firsthand information from an original source. **Secondary information** is secondhand. Primary information is usually expensive to gather while secondary information is inexpensive to gather.

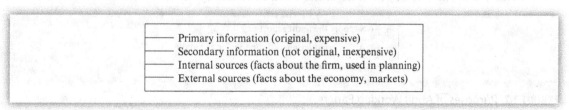

EXHIBIT 2.6 Sources of Information

Internal sources involve facts about an organization (sales data, customer data, financial data, and product data). Internal sources are used in planning and performance measurement.

External sources are facts about the world outside the organization. This information involves facts about competitors, markets, demographics, the environment, and the economy. Managers often make decisions without external sources. External sources are not usually perceived as being that important; they are more difficult to obtain and often are neglected, resulting in bad consequences. The goal should be to combine external sources with internal sources.

Managers should think of problems and opportunities as information needs, as a series of questions that need to be answered. *Information consciousness means to think information when thinking about problems.*

(d) Develop and Review Audit Working Papers

Working papers document the basis for findings, conclusions, and auditors' recommendations and should contain sufficient information to enable an experienced auditor previously not connected with the audit to ascertain from them what work the auditors performed to support the findings, conclusions, or recommendations.[2] This is the ultimate objective of the audit working papers. Working papers not only document the auditors' work but also allow for the review of audit quality.

Working papers are the link between fieldwork and the audit report. The requirements to prepare working papers may be satisfied with documentation maintained on disks or USB drives. Working papers serve three purposes: (1) They provide the principal support for the auditors' report, (2) aid the auditors in conducting and supervising the audit, and (3) allow others to review the audit's quality (see Exhibit 2.7).

Audit organizations should establish policies and procedures to ensure the safe custody and retention of working papers for a time sufficient to satisfy legal and administrative requirements. These policies should also cover the need to make the working papers available for others to review audit quality. Quality reviewers need a written explanation of the basis for the auditor's significant judgments. Arrangements need to be made to ensure that the director of internal audit will make working papers available to others after approval.

Working papers should contain:

- The objective, scope, and methodology, including any sampling criteria used, and results of the audit.
- Evidence of the work performed to support findings, judgments, and conclusions.
- Evidence of supervisory reviews of the work conducted.

Support the audit report
Aid in conducting and supervising the audit
Allow others to review the audit's quality

EXHIBIT 2.7 Purposes of Audit Working Papers

[2] Ibid.

EXHIBIT 2.8 Advantages and Disadvantages of Manually and Electronically Prepared Working Papers

Manually Prepared Working Papers	Electronically Prepared Working Papers
Advantages	**Advantages**
Can feel and touch the paper	Do not take valuable space to file and store
Can make notes and comments easily	Easy to transport among auditors
Approved by tax authorities	Cross-referencing is easy to do
Easy to work with due to familiar media	Changes can be made quickly and easily
	Save time overall
	Quick sharing of information among audit staff when used through a computer network
	Approved by tax authorities
Disadvantages	**Disadvantages**
Materials are bulky to handle	Require specific technical training
Take value space for filing and storage	Cannot attach normal signature
Difficult to make changes; take more time	Require elaborate access controls
Difficult to transport especially when there are multiple volumes	Cannot feel and touch like the paper Not easy to work with compared to paper
Paper can easily be destroyed by fire, flood	Require access to a computer
Cross-referencing is difficult and time consuming to do	Cross-referencing is difficult to verify

Working papers can be prepared electronically. The contents of the working papers will be the same whether they are paper or electronic. However, electronic media requires additional considerations due to technological factors. These considerations include generating backup copies of working papers, security and control procedures to access working papers, and data file retention procedures. Exhibit 2.8 presents major advantages and disadvantages for both manually and electronically prepared working papers.

KEY CONCEPTS TO REMEMBER: Audit Working Papers

- The functions of audit working papers are to: (1) facilitate third-party reviews; (2) aid in the planning, performance, and review of audits; (3) provide the principal evidential support for the auditor's report; (4) explain all audit verification symbols properly; and (5) make cross-references between the working papers and the audit report. However, the working papers are not to aid in the professional development of the operating staff or teach auditing skills to nonauditors.

- The purpose of summaries in working papers is to distill the most useful information from several working papers into a more usable form.

- A working paper is complete when it satisfies the audit objectives for which it is developed.

(continued)

KEY CONCEPTS TO REMEMBER (*Continued***)**

- Working papers document the auditing procedures performed, the information obtained, and the conclusions reached. Each individual working paper should, at a minimum, contain a descriptive heading.

- When determining the retention period for the working papers of a contract audit, it is best to seek the assistance of the legal department to ensure compliance with contract provisions.

- Working papers provide the principal evidential support for the internal auditor's report and are the principal purpose for retaining the working papers.

- Working papers should include documentation of the examination and evaluation of the adequacy and effectiveness of the system of internal control.

- When reviewing the audit working papers, the audit supervisor must determine that working papers adequately support audit findings, conclusions, and audit reports.

- To properly control working papers, the auditor should not make them available to people who have no authority to use them. With working papers, the auditor can share the results of an audit with the auditee, permit access to external auditors, and permit access to government auditors.

- Audit working papers should be reviewed to ensure that no issues are open at the conclusion of the fieldwork.

- The director of internal auditing should establish policies for indexing and the type of working papers files maintained.

- An adequately documented working paper should be concise but complete.

- Working papers are the property of the auditor. Good control of working papers requires that only the auditor who created a working paper can change an electronic working paper.

- When audit conclusions are challenged, the auditor's factual rebuttal is best facilitated by cross-referencing the working papers.

- Working papers should be disposed of when they are of no further use and in accordance with departmental policy. Retention and destruction policies should be approved by legal counsel.

- A primary purpose of an auditor's working papers is to provide evidence of the planning and execution of audit procedures performed.

- Working papers on fraud audits should not be retained indefinitely. Some guidelines are: (1) working papers should be disposed of when they have no further use; (2) working paper retention schedules should be approved by legal counsel; and (3) working paper retention schedules should consider legal and contractual requirements. Working papers should not be retained indefinitely.

- Audit working papers should not be overdocumented by including unnecessary forms, reports, and documents.

- Statistical summaries of working papers are used to consolidate numeric data scattered among several schedules.

- An auditor's working papers should support the findings and recommendations to be reported and should facilitate peer reviews.

- The primary purpose for indexing working papers is to permit cross-referencing and simplify supervisory review.

- The supervisory review of working papers determines that working papers adequately support findings, conclusions, recommendations, and audit reports.

- The primary objective of maintaining security over working papers is to prohibit unauthorized changes or removal of information.

- An internal auditor's working papers should be reviewed by the management of the internal auditing department and should contain certain standard information, such as heading, date work sheet completed, auditor's initials, and index number. Including all forms and directives used by the auditee department in the working papers would constitute inappropriate working paper preparation.

A working paper can include flowcharts, findings cross-referenced to supporting documentation, and tick marks explained in footnotes. The question of whether a working paper is complete or not is determined by whether the audit objective has been met and supported. Working papers should describe objectives, procedures, facts, conclusions, and recommendations. Working paper summaries can be used to promote efficient working paper review by supervisors. Working paper control is best described as restricting access to only those who have a legitimate need to know.

IIA *Standards* Applicable to Supervise Engagements

2300—Performing the Engagement

Internal auditors must identify, analyze, evaluate, and document sufficient information to achieve the engagement's objectives.

Practice Advisory 2300-1: Use of Personal Information in Conducting Engagements

1. Internal auditors need to consider concerns relating to the protection of personally identifiable information gathered during audit engagements as advances in IT and communications continue to present privacy risks and threats. Privacy controls are legal requirements in many jurisdictions.

2. "Personal information" generally refers to data associated with a specific individual or data that has identifying characteristics that may be combined with other information. It includes any factual or subjective information, recorded or not, in any form or media. Personal information includes:

- Name, address, identification numbers, income, blood type.

- Evaluations, social status, disciplinary actions.

- Employee files and credit and loan records.

- Employee health and medical data.

3. In many jurisdictions, laws require organizations to identify the purposes for which personal information is collected at or before the time of collection. These laws also prohibit using and disclosing personal information for purposes other than those for which it was collected except with the individual's consent or as required by law.

4. It is important that internal auditors understand and comply with all laws regarding the use of personal information in their jurisdiction and in those jurisdictions where their organizations conduct business.

5. It may be inappropriate, and in some cases illegal, to access, retrieve, review, manipulate, or use personal information in conducting certain internal audit engagements. If the internal auditor accesses personal information, it may be necessary to develop procedures to safeguard this information. For example, the internal auditor may decide not to record personal information in engagement records in some situations.

6. The internal auditor may seek advice from legal counsel before beginning audit work if there are questions or concerns about access to personal information.

2310—Identifying Information

Internal auditors must identify sufficient, reliable, relevant, and useful information to achieve the engagement's objectives.

Interpretation: *Sufficient information is factual, adequate, and convincing so that a prudent, informed person would reach the same conclusions as the auditor. Reliable information is the best attainable information through the use of appropriate engagement techniques. Relevant information supports engagement observations and recommendations and is consistent with the objectives for the engagement. Useful information helps the organization meet its goals.*

No Practice Advisory for Standard 2310

2320—Analysis and Evaluation

Internal auditors must base conclusions and engagement results on appropriate analyses and evaluations.

Practice Advisory 2320-1: Analytical Procedures

1. Internal auditors may use analytical procedures to obtain audit evidence. Analytical procedures involve studying and comparing relationships among both financial and nonfinancial information. The application of analytical procedures is based on the premise that, in the absence of known conditions to the contrary, relationships among information may reasonably be expected to exist and continue. Examples of contrary conditions include: unusual or nonrecurring transactions or events; accounting, organizational, operational, environmental, and technological changes; inefficiencies; ineffectiveness; errors; fraud; or illegal acts.

2. Analytical procedures often provide the internal auditor with an efficient and effective means of obtaining evidence. The assessment results from comparing information with expectations identified or developed by the internal auditor. Analytical procedures are useful in identifying:

- Unexpected differences.

- The absence of differences when they are expected.

- Potential errors.

- Potential fraud or illegal acts.

- Other unusual or nonrecurring transactions or events.

3. Analytical audit procedures include:

- Comparing current period information with expectations based on similar information for prior periods as well as budgets or forecasts.

- Studying relationships between financial and appropriate nonfinancial information (e.g., recorded payroll expense compared to changes in average number of employees).

- Studying relationships among elements of information (e.g., fluctuation in recorded interest expense compared to changes in related debt balances).

- Comparing information with expectations based on similar information for other organizational units as well as for the industry in which the organization operates.

4. Internal auditors may perform analytical procedures using monetary amounts, physical quantities, ratios, or percentages. Specific analytical procedures include ratio, trend, and regression analysis; reasonableness tests; period-to-period comparisons; comparisons with budgets; forecasts; and external economic information. Analytical procedures assist internal auditors in identifying conditions that may require additional audit procedures. An internal auditor uses analytical procedures in planning the engagement in accordance with the guidelines contained in Standard 2200.

5. Internal auditors may use analytical procedures to generate evidence during the audit engagement. When determining the extent of analytical procedures, the internal auditor considers the:

- Significance of the area being audited.

- Assessment of risk management in the area being audited.

- Adequacy of the internal control system.

- Availability and reliability of financial and nonfinancial information.

- Precision with which the results of analytical audit procedures can be predicted.

- Availability and comparability of information regarding the industry in which the organization operates.

- Extent to which other procedures provide evidence.

6. When analytical audit procedures identify unexpected results or relationships, the internal auditor evaluates such results or relationships. This evaluation includes determining whether the difference from expectations could be a result of fraud, error, or a change in conditions. The auditor may ask management about the reasons for the difference and would corroborate management's explanation, for example, by modifying expectations and recalculating the difference or by applying other audit procedures. In particular, the internal auditor needs to be satisfied that the explanation considers both the direction of the change (e.g., sales decreased) and the amount of the difference (e.g., sales decreased by 10%). Unexplained results or relationships from applying analytical procedures may be indicative of a significant problem (e.g., a potential error, fraud, or illegal act). Results or relationships that are not adequately explained may indicate a situation to be communicated to senior management and the board in accordance with Standard 2060. Depending on the circumstances, the internal auditor may recommend appropriate action.

2330—Documenting Information

Internal auditors must document relevant information to support the conclusions and engagement results.

> **2330.A1**—The CAE must control access to engagement records. The CAE must obtain the approval of senior management and/or legal counsel prior to releasing such records to external parties, as appropriate.

2330.A2—The CAE must develop retention requirements for engagement records, regardless of the medium in which each record is stored. These retention requirements must be consistent with the organization's guidelines and any pertinent regulatory or other requirements.

2330.C1—The CAE must develop policies governing the custody and retention of consulting engagement records as well as their release to internal and external parties. These policies must be consistent with the organization's guidelines and any pertinent regulatory or other requirements.

Practice Advisory 2330-1: Documenting Information

1. Internal auditors prepare working papers. Working papers document the information obtained, the analyses made, and the support for the conclusions and engagement results. Internal audit management reviews the prepared working papers.

2. Engagement working papers generally:

- Aid in the planning, performance, and review of engagements.
- Provide the principal support for engagement results.
- Document whether engagement objectives were achieved.
- Support the accuracy and completeness of the work performed.
- Provide a basis for the internal audit activity's quality assurance and improvement program.
- Facilitate third-party reviews.

3. The organization, design, and content of engagement working papers depend on the engagement's nature and objectives and the organization's needs. Engagement working papers document all aspects of the engagement process from planning to communicating results. The internal audit activity determines the media used to document and store working papers.

4. The CAE establishes working paper policies for the various types of engagements performed. Standardized engagement working papers, such as questionnaires and audit programs, may improve the engagement's efficiency and facilitate the delegation of engagement work. Engagement working papers may be categorized as permanent or carry-forward engagement files that contain information of continuing importance.

Practice Advisory 2330.A1-1: Control of Engagement Records

1. Internal audit engagement records include reports, supporting documentation, review notes, and correspondence, regardless of storage media. Engagement records or working papers are the property of the organization. The internal audit activity controls engagement working papers and provides access to authorized personnel only.

2. Internal auditors may educate management and the board about access to engagement records by external parties. Policies relating to access to engagement records, handling of access requests, and procedures to be followed when an engagement warrants an investigation need to be reviewed by the board.

3. Internal audit policies explain who in the organization is responsible for ensuring the control and security of the activity's records, which internal or external parties can be granted access to engagement records, and how requests for access to those records need to be handled. These policies will vary depending on the nature of the organization, practices followed in the industry, and access privileges established by law.

4. Management and other members of the organization may request access to all or specific engagement working papers. Such access may be necessary to substantiate or explain

engagement observations and recommendations or for other business purposes. The CAE approves these requests.

5. The CAE approves access to engagement working papers by external auditors.

6. There are circumstances where parties outside the organization, other than external auditors, request access to engagement working papers and reports. Prior to releasing the documentation, the CAE obtains the approval of senior management and/or legal counsel, as appropriate.

7. Potentially, internal audit records that are not specifically protected may be accessed in legal proceedings. Legal requirements vary significantly in different jurisdictions. When there is a specific request for engagement records in relation to a legal proceeding, the CAE works closely with legal counsel in deciding what to provide.

Practice Advisory 2330.A1-2: Granting Access to Engagement Records

Caution: Internal auditors are encouraged to consult legal counsel in matters involving legal issues as requirements may vary significantly in different jurisdictions. The guidance contained in this Practice Advisory is based primarily on the legal systems that protect information and work performed for, or communicated to, an engaged attorney (i.e., attorney–client privilege), such as the legal system in the United States. Practice Advisory 2400-1 discusses attorney–client privilege.

1. Internal audit engagement records include reports, supporting documentation, review notes, and correspondence, regardless of storage media. Engagement records generally are produced under the presumption that their contents are confidential and may contain a mix of facts and opinions. However, those who are not familiar with the organization or its internal audit process may misunderstand those facts and opinions. Outside parties may seek access to engagement records in different types of proceedings, including criminal prosecutions, civil litigation, tax audits, regulatory reviews, government contract reviews, and reviews by self-regulatory organizations. Most of an organization's records that are not protected by the attorney–client privilege may be accessible in criminal proceedings. In noncriminal proceedings, the issue of access is less clear and may vary according to the jurisdiction of the organization.

2. Explicit practices of the internal audit activity may increase the control of access to engagement records.

3. The internal audit activity may address access to, and control of, internal audit records regardless of the media used for storage.

4. The internal audit activity's policies should cover what to include in engagement records and specify the content and format of the engagement records and how internal auditors handle resolved review notes. The policies also should specify how long internal audit records are to be retained. The CAE, when specifying the length of retention for engagement records, should consider the organization's needs as well as legal requirements.

5. The internal audit activity's policies may document who in the organization is responsible for the control and security of internal audit records, who can be granted access to engagement records, and how requests for access to those records are to be handled. These policies depend on the practices followed in the organization's industry or legal jurisdiction. The CAE should be aware of changing practices in the industry and changing legal precedents. When developing policies, the CAE should consider who may seek access to internal audit records.

6. The policy granting access to engagement records may also address processes:

- For resolving access issues.

- For educating the internal audit staff concerning the risks and issues regarding access to their work products.

- To determine who may seek access to the work product in the future.

7. The CAE also may educate senior management and the board about the risks of access to engagement records. The board may review policies relating to who can be granted access to engagement records and how those requests are to be handled. The specific policies will vary depending on the nature of the organization and the access privileges that have been established by law.

8. When furnishing engagement records, the CAE usually:

- Provides only the specific documents as directed by legal counsel or policies. These usually exclude documents covered by attorney–client privilege. Documents that reveal attorneys' thought processes or strategies usually are privileged and not subject to forced disclosure.

- Releases documents in a form where they cannot be changed (e.g., as an image rather than in word processing format). For paper documents, the CAE releases copies and keeps the originals.

- Labels each document as confidential and places a notation that secondary distribution is not permitted without permission.

Practice Advisory 2330.A2-1: Retention of Records

1. Engagement record retention requirements vary among jurisdictions and legal environments.

2. The CAE develops a written retention policy that meets the organizational needs and legal requirements of the jurisdictions within which the organization operates.

3. The record retention policy needs to include appropriate arrangements for the retention of records related to engagements performed by external service providers.

2340—Engagement Supervision

Engagements must be properly supervised to ensure objectives are achieved, quality is assured, and staff is developed.

Interpretation: *The extent of supervision required will depend on the proficiency and experience of internal auditors and the complexity of the engagement. The CAE has overall responsibility for supervising the engagement, whether performed by or for the internal audit activity, but may designate appropriately experienced members of the internal audit activity to perform the review. Appropriate evidence of supervision is documented and retained.*

Practice Advisory 2340-1: Engagement Supervision

1. The CAE or designee provides appropriate engagement supervision. Supervision is a process that begins with planning and continues throughout the engagement. The process includes:

- Ensuring designated auditors collectively possess the required knowledge, skills, and other competencies to perform the engagement.

- Providing appropriate instructions during the planning of the engagement and approving the engagement program.

- Ensuring the approved engagement program is completed unless changes are justified and authorized.

- Determining engagement working papers adequately support engagement observations, conclusions, and recommendations.

- Ensuring engagement communications are accurate, objective, clear, concise, constructive, and timely.

- Ensuring engagement objectives are met.

- Providing opportunities for developing internal auditors' knowledge, skills, and other competencies.

2. The CAE is responsible for all internal audit engagements, whether performed by or for the internal audit activity, and all significant professional judgments made throughout the engagement. The CAE also adopts suitable means to ensure this responsibility is met. Suitable means include policies and procedures are designed to:

- Minimize the risk that internal auditors or others performing work for the internal audit activity make professional judgments or take other actions that are inconsistent with the CAE's professional judgment such that the engagement is impacted adversely.

- Resolve differences in professional judgment between the CAE and internal audit staff over significant issues relating to the engagement. Such means may include discussion of pertinent facts, further inquiry or research, and documentation and disposition of the differing viewpoints in engagement working papers. In instances of a difference in professional judgment over an ethical issue, suitable means may include referral of the issue to those individuals in the organization having responsibility over ethical matters.

3. All engagement working papers are reviewed to ensure they support engagement communications and necessary audit procedures are performed. Evidence of supervisory review consists of the reviewer initialing and dating each working paper after it is reviewed. Other techniques that provide evidence of supervisory review include: completing an engagement working paper review checklist; preparing a memorandum specifying the nature, extent, and results of the review; or evaluating and accepting reviews within the working paper software.

4. Reviewers can make a written record (i.e., review notes) of questions arising from the review process. When clearing review notes, care needs to be taken to ensure working papers provide adequate evidence that questions raised during the review are resolved. Alternatives with respect to disposition of review notes are to:

- Retain the review notes as a record of the reviewer's questions raised, the steps taken in their resolution, and the results of those steps.

- Discard the review notes after the questions raised are resolved and the appropriate engagement working papers are amended to provide the information requested.

5. Engagement supervision also allows for training and development of staff and performance evaluation.

2.3 Communicate Engagement Results

Topics such as audit reporting, including audit report purpose, audit report timeliness, audit report contents, report presentation, report distribution, oral reports, and summary reports are presented in this section.

(a) Audit Report Purpose

Written audit reports serve multiple purposes. They communicate the results of the audit work to auditees and others, make the results less susceptible to misunderstanding, and facilitate follow-up reviews to determine whether appropriate corrective actions have been taken.[3]

---

[3] Ibid.

(b) Audit Report Timeliness

To be of maximum use, the audit report must be timely. A carefully prepared report may be of little value to decision makers if it arrives too late. Therefore, the audit organization should plan for the prompt issuance of the audit report and conduct the audit with this goal in mind.

The auditors should consider interim reporting, during the audit, of significant matters to appropriate auditees. Such communication, which may be oral or written, is not a substitute for a final written report, but it does alert auditees to matters needing immediate attention and permits them to correct the problems before the final report is completed.

ADVANTAGES AND DISADVANTAGES OF INTERIM REPORTS

Advantages
- ☐ Final report-writing time can be minimized.
- ☐ Communication of critical information requiring immediate attention is facilitated.
- ☐ Informal and verbal communication can take place.

Disadvantages
- ☐ A formal, written interim report may negate the need for a final report in certain circumstances.
- ☐ It puts more demand on auditors to make sure the evidence is solid and complete.

Summary reports highlighting audit results may be appropriate for levels of management above the auditee. They may be issued separately from or in conjunction with the final report.

(c) Audit Report Contents

The contents of the audit report should include:

- Objectives, scope, and methodology.
- Audit findings, conclusions, and recommendations.
- Compliance with standards, regulations, and laws.
- Management (auditee's) responses.
- Noteworthy accomplishments (see Exhibit 2.9).

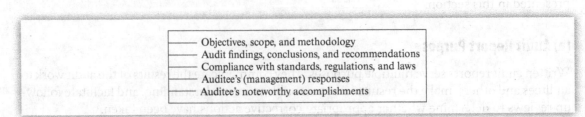

	Objectives, scope, and methodology
	Audit findings, conclusions, and recommendations
	Compliance with standards, regulations, and laws
	Auditee's (management) responses
	Auditee's noteworthy accomplishments

EXHIBIT 2.9 Components of Report Contents

(i) Objectives, Scope, and Methodology

Readers need knowledge of the objectives of the audit, as well as the audit scope and methodology for achieving the objectives, to understand the purpose of audit, judge the merits of the audit work and what is reported, and understand any significant limitations.

The statement of objectives being reported on should explain why the audit was made and state what the report is to accomplish. Articulating what the report is to accomplish normally involves identifying the audit subject and the aspect of performance examined. Because what is reported depends on the objectives, the statement should also communicate what finding elements are discussed and whether conclusions and recommendations are given.

EFFECTIVE COMMUNICATION

Effective communication (written and oral) skills are crucial for advancement in today's team-oriented workplace. Such skills are more important than technical skills and are greatly needed to solve problems.

The statement of objectives tells the reader the boundaries of the audit. To preclude misunderstanding in cases where the objectives are particularly limited and broader objectives can be inferred, it may be necessary to clearly define the audit boundaries by stating objectives that were **not** pursued.

The statement of scope should describe the depth and coverage of the audit work conducted to accomplish the audit's objectives. As applicable, it should explain the relationship between the universe and what was audited, identify organizations and geographic locations at which audit work was conducted and the period covered, cite the kinds and sources of evidence used and the techniques used to verify it, and explain any quality or other problems with the evidence. Significant constraints imposed on the audit approach by data limitations or scope impairments must be disclosed.

The statement on methodology should clearly explain the evidence-gathering and analysis techniques used to accomplish the audit's objectives. The explanation should identify any assumptions. It should describe any comparative techniques applied and measures and criteria used to assess performance in conducting the audit. If sampling is involved, the statement should describe the sample design and state why it was chosen.

Every effort should be made to avoid any misunderstanding on the part of the reader concerning work that was and was not done to achieve the audit objectives, particularly when the work was limited because of constraints on time or resources.

DETERMINING THE SIGNIFICANCE OF AUDIT FINDINGS

Audit findings and recommendations have a direct link in that recommendations should address or correct the findings. The benefit from audit work is not in the recommendations made but in their effective implementation. Important measures of audit organization's effectiveness are the type of issues it tackles and the changes or improvements it is able to effect.

Audit findings need to be significant to be of any use to the audited organization. This is because correcting a deficient audit finding requires resources. The significance of audit findings can be assessed from two aspects: the nature of the finding itself and the quality of the recommendations.

(continued)

With respect to the nature of the finding itself, both quantitative and qualitative aspects of a finding should be considered when determining its significance. Examples of quantitative aspects include: revenues increased, costs decreased, and number of defects reduced. Examples of qualitative aspects include: customer satisfaction increased, employee morale improved, and compliance to laws and regulations is achieved.

With respect to quality, recommendations should be action oriented and effective. To achieve the desired action, action-oriented recommendations must be properly directed, hard-hitting, specific, convincing, and significant.

To be effective, recommendations must identify a course of action that will correct identified problem or cause significant improvements. Effective recommendations:

- Deal with underlying causes.

- Are feasible.

- Are cost effective.

- Consider alternatives.

The significance of a recommendation depends on the subject matter and the specific situation. Frequently, significance can be assessed in terms of dollars. For example, assume that implementation of an audit recommendation would correct inadequate internal controls in an area where very significant amounts of money are subject to theft or manipulation. The inadequate controls are readily recognizable as a significant deficiency. A recommendation to strengthen the internal controls in an area of such significance and susceptibility would be key and worthy of special emphasis.

However, dollars are only one measure of significance, not necessarily the most important one. For example, the need to ensure implementation of recommendations to provide safe operations of a manufacturing or nuclear plant can hardly be overemphasized. Implementing such recommendations could prevent the loss of life, substantial bodily injury, or environmental contamination.

There is a vast difference between recommendations dealing with conditions that are imminently life threatening and those that are just significant enough to be reportable.

The significance of a finding and a recommendation should be known to the auditor and communicated to the auditee early during an assignment. The fact that a recommendation is considered to be a key one should not come as a surprise to the auditee being audited. It should have been made apparent during early discussions with the auditee and certainly at the exit conference.

Emphasis on key recommendations should be continued as the findings and recommendations are reported. Key recommendations should be identified and highlighted in reports in a context that makes their significance apparent. Executive summaries and transmittal memorandums can be used to further establish and emphasize the significance of key recommendations.

(ii) Audit Findings, Conclusions, and Recommendations

The report should include a full discussion of the significant audit findings and, where applicable, auditors' conclusions.

The report should present the significant findings developed in response to each audit objective. Any audit finding not included in the audit report because of insignificance should be separately communicated to management, preferably in writing. The audit report should reference findings communicated in a management letter.

All communications should be documented in the working papers. Sufficient, competent, and relevant information about findings should be included to promote adequate understanding of the matters reported and to provide convincing but fair presentations in proper perspective. Appropriate background information that readers need to understand the findings should also be included.

Audit findings have often been regarded as containing the elements of criteria, condition, and effect, plus causes when problems are found. However, the elements needed for a finding depend entirely on the objectives of the audit. Thus, a finding or set of findings is complete to the extent that the audit objectives are satisfied and the report clearly relates those objectives to the finding's elements.

DESIRABLE ATTRIBUTES OF A DEFICIENCY AUDIT FINDING

Audit findings have often been regarded as containing the elements of criteria, condition, and effect, plus cause when problems are found.[a] However, the elements needed for a finding depend entirely on the objectives of the audit. This means the element's "cause" and "effect" may be optional for a compliance audit, but they are musts for an operational audit. Thus, a finding or set of findings is complete to the extent that the audit objectives are satisfied and the report clearly relates those objectives to the finding's elements. A deficiency audit finding should have four elements or attributes; a recommendation is optional (see Exhibit A).

EXHIBIT A Elements of a Deficiency Audit Finding

- Criteria (what should be)
- Condition (what is)
- Cause (why condition occurred)
- Effect (what is the consequence)
- Recommendations (what is to be done)

Criteria

Criteria are the standards used to determine whether an operation, function, or program meets or exceeds expectations. Criteria provide a context for understanding the results of the audit. Where possible, the audit plan, should state the criteria to be used. In selecting criteria, auditors have a responsibility to use only criteria that are reasonable, attainable, and relevant to the matters being audited. Some examples of different types of criteria are listed next.

- Targets or goals set by management or prescribed by law or regulation
- Technically developed standards or norms
- Expert opinions
- Prior years' performance
- Performance of similar entities
- Expected direction of change in outcomes

When the criteria are vague, auditors should seek interpretation. If interpretation is not available, auditors should strive to agree on the appropriateness of these measures with the interested parties or, if applicable, indicate that they were unable to report on performance because of the lack of definite criteria. It represents "what should be" at the time of the audit.

Condition

Condition is a situation that exists. It has been observed and documented during the audit. It represents "what is" at the time of the audit.

(continued)

Cause

The term "cause" has two meanings, which depend on the audit objectives. When the auditors' objective is to explain why the poor (or good) performance observed in the audit happened, the reasons for the observed performance are referred to as cause. Identifying the cause of problems is necessary before making constructive recommendations for correction. Because problems can result from a number of plausible factors, auditors need to clearly demonstrate and explain with evidence and reasoning the link between the problems and the factor(s) they identified as the cause. When the auditors' objective includes estimating the impact of a program on changes in physical, social, or economic conditions, they seek evidence of the extent to which the program itself is the cause of those changes.

Effect

Like cause, the term "effect" also has two meanings, which depend on the audit objectives. When the auditors' objectives include identifying the actual or potential consequences of a condition that varies (either positively or negatively) from the criteria identified in the audit, effect is a measure of those consequences. Auditors often use the word "effect" in this sense to demonstrate the need for corrective action in response to identified problems. When the auditors' objectives include estimating the effectiveness of an operation or a program in causing changes in physical, social, or economic conditions, effect is a measure of the impact achieved by the operation or program. Here, effect is the extent to which positive or negative changes in actual physical, social, or economic conditions can be identified and attributed to program or operations.

Recommendations

Recommendations state what an audit organization believes should be done to accomplish beneficial results. They do not direct what must be done but seek to convince others (e.g., the auditee) of what needs to be done.

Recommendations should be action-oriented, convincing, well supported, and effective. When appropriately implemented, they should get the desired beneficial results.

[a] K. K. Raman and Relmond P. Van Daniker, *Materiality and Audit Risk in Governmental Auditing, A Research Monograph* (Alexandria, VA: Association of Government Accountants, 1990).

The audit report should contain conclusions when called for by the audit objectives. Conclusions are logical inferences about the function or operation based on the auditors' findings. Conclusions should be specified and not left to be inferred by readers. The report should not be written on the basis that a bare recital of facts makes the conclusions inescapable. The strength of the auditors' conclusions depends on the persuasiveness of the evidence supporting the findings.

The audit report should contain recommendations when the potential for significant improvement in operations and performance is substantiated by the reported findings. Recommendations to effect compliance with laws and regulations and improve management controls should also be made when significant instances of noncompliance are noted or significant weaknesses in controls are found. The audit report should also disclose the status of known uncorrected significant findings and recommendations from prior audits that affect the objectives and findings of the current audit.

Reports containing constructive recommendations can encourage improvements in the conduct of audited activities. Recommendations are most constructive when: they are directed at resolving the cause of identified problems; are action oriented and specific; are addressed to parties that have the authority to act; and are feasible and, to the extent practical, cost effective.

(iii) Compliance with Standards, Regulations, and Laws

The statement of conformity refers to the applicable standards that the auditors should have followed during the audit. The statement need not be qualified when standards that were not applicable were not followed. When applicable standards were not followed, auditors should modify the statement to disclose in the scope section of their report the required standard that was not followed, why, and the known effect that not following the standard had on the results of the audit.

The auditors' report should include all instances of noncompliance that auditors determine are significant. All instances of fraud or other illegal acts that could result in the entity, or manager or employee of the entity, being subject to criminal prosecution should also be reported.

In reporting significant instances of noncompliance identified in response to the audit objectives, the auditors should place their findings in proper perspective. To give the reader a basis for judging the prevalence and consequences of noncompliance, the instances of noncompliance should be related to the universe or the number of cases examined and quantified in terms of dollar value, if appropriate.

(iv) Management Responses

One of the most effective ways to ensure that a report is fair, complete, and objective is to obtain advance review and comments by responsible auditee (management) and others, as appropriate. Including the views of the auditee produces a report that shows not only what was found and what the auditors think about it but also what the responsible persons think and plan to do about it.

Auditors should normally request that the responsible auditees' views on significant findings, conclusions, and recommendations adversely affecting the audited entity be submitted in writing. When written comments are not obtained, oral comments should be requested.

Advance comments should be objectively evaluated and recognized, as appropriate, in the report. A promise or plan for corrective action should be noted but should not be accepted as justification for dropping a significant finding or a related recommendation.

When the comments oppose the report's findings, conclusions, or recommendations and are not, in the auditors' opinion, valid, the auditors may choose to state their reasons for rejecting them. Conversely, the auditors should modify their report if they find the comments valid.

(v) Noteworthy Accomplishments

Significant management accomplishments identified during the audit that were within the scope of the audit should be included in the audit report, along with deficiencies. Such information is necessary to fairly present the situation the auditors found and to provide appropriate balance to the report. In addition, inclusion of such accomplishments may lead to improved performance by other department heads or managers who read the report.

(d) Report Presentation

The audit report should be complete, accurate, objective, convincing, and as clear and concise as the subject permits (see Exhibit 2.10).

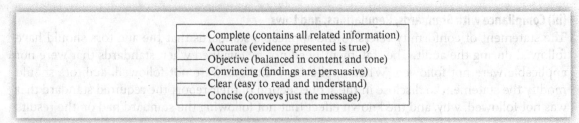

```
——— Complete (contains all related information)
——— Accurate (evidence presented is true)
——— Objective (balanced in content and tone)
——— Convincing (findings are persuasive)
——— Clear (easy to read and understand)
——— Concise (conveys just the message)
```

EXHIBIT 2.10 Characteristics of Report Presentation

(i) Complete

Being complete requires that the report contain all information needed to satisfy the audit objectives, promote an adequate and correct understanding of the matters reported, and meet the applicable report content requirements. It also means including appropriate background information.

Giving readers an adequate and correct understanding means providing perspective on the extent and significance of reported findings, such as frequency of occurrence relative to the number of cases or transactions tested and the relationship of the findings to the entity's operations.

Except as necessary to make convincing presentations, detailed supporting data need not be included. In most cases, a single example of a deficiency is not sufficient to support a broad conclusion or a related recommendation. All that it supports is that there was a deviation, an error, or a control weakness.

HOW TO GET ACTION ON AUDIT RECOMMENDATIONS

Four basic principles to ensure the benefits of the audit work include (1) quality recommendations, (2) commitment, (3) monitoring and follow-up system, and (4) special attention to key recommendations.

1. **Quality recommendations.** Whether audit results are achieved depends on the quality of the recommendation. A recommendation that is not convincing will not be implemented. A recommendation that does not correct the basic cause of a deficiency may not achieve the intended result.

   Basic to effective audit work are recommendations that, when adequately implemented, accomplish a defined and worthwhile result. They must state a clear, convincing, and workable basis for implementation. Their utility and continued relevance should be reevaluated as follow-up action progress.

2. **Commitment.** When the auditor is committed to the need for action on a recommendation, he or she will do what needs to be done to get it implemented. Without that commitment, a recommendation may not achieve the desired action.

   Auditors and audit organizations must be committed to identifying and bringing about needed change. The auditor's commitment should be personal and professional. The audit organization should be supportive and reinforce the commitment to its staff.

3. **Aggressive monitoring and follow-up.** Acceptance of a recommendation does not ensure results; effective implementation does. Continued attention is required until results are achieved.

   The audit organization should have a system that provides the structure and discipline needed to promote action on audit recommendations. It should ensure that recommendations are aggressively pursued until they have been resolved and successfully implemented. Also, auditors should assess whether the audited organizations have a follow-up system internally that adequately meets their basic responsibility for resolving and implementing audit recommendations.

> 4. **Special attention to key recommendations.** While all recommendations require follow-up, some deal with particularly serious or flagrant matters. They should receive special attention.
>
>   Auditors should ensure that key recommendations are fairly considered when effective use of the first three principles has not done so. They should reassess strategies to get positive action on those recommendations. Outside intervention (e.g., senior management, audit committee) should be considered when it would help to get necessary action on key recommendations of great significance.
>
> *Source: How to Get Action on Audit Recommendations* (Washington, DC: U.S. General Accounting Office, 1991).

(ii) Accurate

Accuracy requires that the evidence presented be true and that findings be correctly portrayed. The need for accuracy is based on the need to assure readers that what it reported is credible and reliable. One inaccuracy in a report can cast doubt on the validity of an entire report and can divert attention from its substance. Also, inaccurate reports can damage the credibility of the issuing audit organization and reduce the effectiveness of reports it issues.

The report should include only information, findings, and conclusions that are supported by competent and relevant evidence in the auditors' working papers. That evidence should demonstrate the correctness and reasonableness of the matters reported. The term "correct portrayal" means describing accurately the audit scope and methodology and presenting findings and conclusions in a manner consistent with the scope of audit work.

(iii) Objective

Objectivity requires that the presentation of the entire report be balanced in content and tone. A report's credibility is significantly enhanced when it presents evidence in an unbiased manner so that readers can be persuaded by the facts.

The audit report should be fair and not be misleading, and it should place the audit results in proper perspective. This means presenting the audit results impartially and guarding against the tendency to exaggerate or overemphasize deficient performance. In describing shortcomings in performance, auditors should present the explanation of responsible auditees, including the consideration of any unusual difficulties or circumstances they faced.

The tone of reports should encourage favorable reaction to findings and recommendations. Titles, captions, and the text of reports should be stated constructively. Although findings should be presented clearly and forthrightly, auditors should keep in mind that one of their objectives is to persuade and that this can best be done by avoiding language that generates defensiveness and opposition. Although criticism of past performance is often necessary, the report should emphasize needed improvements.

(iv) Convincing

Being convincing requires that the audit results are responsive to the audit objectives, the findings are presented persuasively, and the conclusions and recommendations follow logically from the facts presented. The information presented should be sufficient to enable the readers of the validity of the findings, the reasonableness of the conclusions, and the desirability of implementing the recommendations. Reports designed in this way can help focus the attention of management on the matters that warrant attention and can help stimulate correction.

(v) Clear

Clarity requires that the report be easy to read and understand. Reports should be written in language as clear and simple as the subject permits. Use of straightforward, nontechnical language is essential to simplicity of presentation. If technical terms and unfamiliar abbreviations and acronyms are used, they should be clearly defined. Acronyms should be used sparingly.

Both logical organization of material and accuracy and precision in stating facts and in drawing conclusions are essential to clarity and understanding. Effective use of titles and captions and topic sentences make the report easier to read and understand. Visual aids (i.e., pictures, charts, graphs, and diagrams) should be used when appropriate to clarify and summarize complex material.

(vi) Concise

Being concise requires that the report be no longer than necessary to convey the message. Too much detail detracts from a report, may even conceal the real message, and may confuse or discourage readers. Also, needless repetition should be avoided. Although room exists for considerable judgment in determining the content of reports, those that are complete but still concise are likely to receive greater attention.

(e) Report Distribution

The final report should be distributed to auditees directly interested in the audit work results and those responsible for acting on the findings and recommendations. Higher-level members in the organization may receive only a summary report. Reports may also be distributed to other interested or affected parties, such as external auditors and the board of directors.

Certain information may not be appropriate for disclosure to all report recipients because it is privileged, proprietary, or related to improper or illegal acts. Such information, however, may be disclosed in a separate report. If the conditions being reported involve senior management, report distribution should be to the board of the organization.

(f) Oral Reports

In some circumstances, it might be appropriate for auditors to issue oral reports. If they issue an oral report, auditors should keep a written record of what they communicated and the basis for not issuing a written report. An oral report may be most appropriate when emergency action is needed. Before issuing an oral report, auditors should determine that both of these conditions exist:

1. An oral report would effectively meet decision makers' needs for information about the results of the audit.

2. It is unlikely that parties other than those who would receive the oral report would have a significant interest in the results of the audit.

(g) Summary Reports

Summary written audit reports are generally intended for high-level management and/or the audit committee. However, a detailed audit report dealing with payroll department with significant control weaknesses should be most useful to the payroll department manager.

KEY CONCEPTS TO REMEMBER: Audit Reports

- The first-line supervisor is the lowest organizational level to receive the final report of the operational audit of the production department.

- The scope statement of an audit report should identify the audited activities and describe the nature and extent of the auditing performed.

- Interim reports are issued during an audit to communicate information requiring immediate attention.

- An audit report recommendation should address the cause of an audit finding.

- "Significance of deficiencies" is a proper element in an audit results section of a report.

- After an audit report with adverse findings has been communicated to appropriate auditee personnel, proper action is to schedule a follow-up review.

- An oral report to auditee management would be appropriate when an internal auditor observed that assembly-line workers without protective clothing were being exposed to dangerous chemicals.

- An oral report is appropriate when significant problems are discovered during the audit.

- The auditor can use oral reports to give immediate information to management and to exchange thoughts more accurately with a face-to-face discussion.

- The director of internal auditing or designee is responsible for the distribution of an audit report.

- If an audit is done in the sales department, a copy of the audit report should be sent to the sales director and vice president of marketing.

- An audit report should never be viewed as providing an infallible truth about a subject under the due professional care standard.

- An auditor found that employees in the plant maintenance department were not signing their time cards. This situation also existed during the last audit. The auditor should include this finding in the current audit report.

- An evaluation of the impact (effect) of the findings on the activities reviewed is not always required in an audit report. The audit report should include a statement that describes the audit objectives and identifies the audited activities, conducted, and presents pertinent statements of facts.

- When there is a disagreement between the auditor and the auditee concerning audit findings and recommendations, the most appropriate method of reporting would be to state both positions and identify the reasons for the disagreement.

- An audit report with routine findings in the accounts payable department should be distributed to the accounts payable supervisor, the department manager, division general manager, external auditor, and the corporate controller, not to the board of directors or audit committee.

- The reason for requiring auditees to reply promptly and outline the corrective action that has been implemented on reported deficiencies is to effect savings or to institute compliance as early as possible.

- A report issued by an internal auditor should contain an expression of opinion when an opinion will improve communications with the reader of the report. An audit opinion is the auditor's professional judgment of the situation that was reviewed. Due professional care requires that the auditor's opinions be based on sufficient factual evidence that warrants the expression of the opinions. Due care does not require the performance of extensive audit examinations. It requires

(continued)

the conduct of examination and verifications to a reasonable extent, the reasonable assurance that compliance does exist, and consideration of the possibility of material irregularities.

- Certain information may not be appropriate for disclosure to all report recipients because it is privileged, proprietary, or related to improper or illegal acts. If conditions being reported involve improper acts of a senior manager, the audit report should be distributed to the board of directors.

- Internal audit reports should contain the purpose, scope, and results. The audit results should contain the criteria, condition, effect, and cause of the finding. The cause is the reason for the difference between the expected and actual conditions.

- Internal auditing reports should be distributed to those members of the organization who are able to ensure that audit results are given due consideration. For higher-level members of the organization, that requirement can be satisfied with summary reports.

- The final audit report should be reviewed, approved, and signed by the internal auditing director or designee.

- The chair of the board of directors would normally not receive an internal auditing report related to a review of the purchasing cycle. Others who would receive such a report include the director of purchasing, the external auditor, and the general auditor.

- When a member of senior management commits illegal acts, such information may be disclosed in a separate audit report and distributed to the company's audit committee of the board of directors.

- The summary audit report for an accounts payable audit should be issued to the audit committee of the board of directors, not to the accounts payable manager, external auditor, or controller.

- Issuing an audit report eight weeks after the audit was concluded is not timely—two or three weeks is timely.

- An audit report containing significant internal control weaknesses in the accounts payable system of a company whose securities are publicly traded should be distributed to the audit committee and the external auditor due to potential for misstated financial statements.

- The findings in the audit report should include pertinent factual statements concerning the control weaknesses that were uncovered during the course of the audit.

- An audit policy should state that final audit reports will not be issued without a management response. An audit report with significant findings is completed except for management response. The best alternative is to issue an interim report regarding the important issues noted.

- Audit findings often emerge by a process of comparing what should be with what is. Findings are based on the attributes of criteria, condition, cause, and effect. The effect of the audit finding is risk or exposure encountered because of the condition.

- An objective audit report is one that is described as factual, unbiased, and free from distortion.

- It is important to develop a distribution list for each audit report, because the list specifies those individuals who have responsibilities with regard to the report.

- The most appropriate use of an oral audit report is to communicate conditions that demand immediate action.

- When an auditor has agreed to keep the marketing department vice president informed of the marketing audit progress on a regular basis, oral or written interim reports should be used for those progress reports.

- To enhance communications with senior management, auditors include a summary report with each written audit report. The summary report should contain highlights of the audit results.

- The primary reason for issuing a written audit report is to achieve precision by pinpointing problems and to achieve permanence. Oral reports do not have these attributes.

- The primary audience for the written report issued by the internal auditing department at the completion of an audit should be those managers inside or outside the audited area who can take corrective action.

- A concise statement of audit findings would be most appropriate for inclusion in the management summary section of a final internal auditing report.

- The final operational audit report regarding supply activities of a division would be circulated to the lowest level of management with sufficient authority to take action on audit recommendations, as it is their responsibility.

- A reason to use interim audit reports is to communicate a change in audit scope.

- The "Purpose" section of the final audit report includes a discussion of audit objectives.

- When illegal acts are being performed by several of the highest-ranking officers of the company, the audit report should be addressed to the audit committee of the board of directors.

- Opinions in the audit reports are the auditor's evaluations of the effects of the findings on the activities reviewed.

- In a review of warranty programs for new products introduced by a company with low and declining profits, an auditor has determined, and management has acknowledged, that the company will be unable to fulfill promised warranty coverage. The auditor should inform the audit committee.

- During an audit of a joint venture, the auditor discovered numerous audit exceptions where some credits would be due to each party. The audit report should contain all material audit exceptions and provide each partner with a net amount due.

- IIA *Standards* require auditors to follow up to see that the corrective action satisfies the audit recommendations.

IIA *Standards* Applicable to Communicate Engagement Results

2400—Communicating Results

Internal auditors must communicate the results of engagements.

Practice Advisory 2400-1: Legal Considerations in Communicating Results
Caution: Internal auditors are encouraged to consult legal counsel in matters involving legal issues as requirements may vary significantly in different jurisdictions. The guidance contained in this Practice Advisory is based primarily on the legal systems that protect information and work performed for, or communicated to, an engaged attorney (i.e., attorney–client privilege), such as the legal system in the United States.

Practice Advisory 2400-1 discusses attorney–client privilege.

1. The internal auditor needs to exercise caution when communicating noncompliance with laws, regulations, and other legal issues. Developing policies and procedures regarding the handling of those matters as well as a close working relationship with other appropriate areas (e.g., legal counsel and compliance) is strongly encouraged.

2. The internal auditor gathers evidence, makes analytical judgments, reports results, and determines whether management has taken appropriate corrective action. The internal auditor's need to prepare engagement records may conflict with legal counsel's desire to not leave discoverable evidence that could harm the organization's position in legal matters. For example, even if an internal auditor gathers and evaluates information properly, the facts and analyses disclosed may negatively impact the organization from a legal perspective. Proper planning and policy making—including role definition and methods of communication—are essential so that a sudden revelation does not place the internal auditor and legal counsel at odds with one another. Both parties need to foster an ethical and preventive perspective throughout the organization by sensitizing and educating management about the established policies.

3. A communication made between "privileged persons"—in confidence and for the purpose of seeking, obtaining, or providing legal assistance for the client—is necessary to protect the attorney–client privilege. This privilege, which is used primarily to protect communications with attorneys, can also apply to communications with third parties working with an attorney.

4. Some courts have recognized a privilege of critical self-analysis that shields self-critical materials (e.g., audit work products) from discovery. In general, the recognition of this privilege is premised on the belief that the confidentiality of the self-analysis in these instances outweighs the valued public interest.

5. Privilege usually applies when:

- The information results from a self-critical analysis undertaken by the party asserting the privilege.

- The public has a strong interest in preserving the free flow of the information contained in the critical analysis.

- The information is of the type whose flow would be curtailed if discovery were allowed.

6. Self-evaluative privileges are less likely to be available when a government agency—rather than a party involved in a private legal matter—seeks out the documents. Presumably, this reluctance results from recognition of the government's stronger interest in enforcing the law.

7. Documents intended to be protected under the work-product doctrine usually need to be:

- Some type of work product (e.g., memo, computer program).

- Prepared in anticipation of litigation.

- Completed by someone working at the direction of an attorney.

8. Documents prepared and delivered to the attorney before the attorney–client relationship is established are not generally protected by the attorney–client privilege.

2410—Criteria for Communicating

Communications must include the engagement's objectives and scope as well as applicable conclusions, recommendations, and action plans.

2410.A1—Final communication of engagement results must, where appropriate, contain the internal auditors' opinion and/or conclusions. When issued, an opinion or conclusion must take account of the expectations of senior management, the board, and other stakeholders and must be supported by sufficient, reliable, relevant, and useful information.

Interpretation: *Opinions at the engagement level may be ratings, conclusions, or other descriptions of the results. Such an engagement may be in relation to controls around a specific process, risk, or business unit. The formulation of such opinions requires consideration of the engagement results and their significance.*

> **2410.A2**—Internal auditors are encouraged to acknowledge satisfactory performance in engagement communications.
>
> **2410.A3**—When releasing engagement results to parties outside the organization, the communication must include limitations on distribution and use of the results.
>
> **2410.C1**—Communication of the progress and results of consulting engagements will vary in form and content, depending on the nature of the engagement and the needs of the client.

Practice Advisory 2410-1: Communication Criteria

1. Although the format and content of the final engagement communications varies by organization or type of engagement, they are to contain, at a minimum, the purpose, scope, and results of the engagement.

2. Final engagement communications may include background information and summaries. Background information may identify the organizational units and activities reviewed and provide explanatory information. It may also include the status of observations, conclusions, and recommendations from prior reports and an indication of whether the report covers a scheduled engagement or is responding to a request. Summaries are balanced representations of the communication's content.

3. Purpose statements describe the engagement objectives and may inform the reader why the engagement was conducted and what it was expected to achieve.

4. Scope statements identify the audited activities and may include supportive information, such as time period reviewed and related activities not reviewed to delineate the boundaries of the engagement. They may describe the nature and extent of engagement work performed.

5. Results include observations, conclusions, opinions, recommendations, and action plans.

6. Observations are pertinent statements of fact. The internal auditor communicates those observations necessary to support or prevent misunderstanding of the internal auditor's conclusions and recommendations. The internal auditor may communicate less significant observations or recommendations informally.

7. Engagement observations and recommendations emerge by a process of comparing criteria (the correct state) with condition (the current state). Whether there is a difference or not, the internal auditor has a foundation on which to build the report. When conditions meet the criteria, communication of satisfactory performance may be appropriate. Observations and recommendations are based on the following attributes:

- **Criteria.** The standards, measures, or expectations used in making an evaluation and/or verification (the correct state).

- **Condition/** The factual evidence that the internal auditor found in the course of the examination (the current state).

- **Cause.** The reason for the difference between expected and actual conditions.

■ **Effect.** The risk or exposure the organization and/or others encounter because the condition is not consistent with the criteria (the impact of the difference). In determining the degree of risk or exposure, internal auditors consider the effect their engagement observations and recommendations may have on the organization's operations and financial statements.

Observations and recommendations can include engagement client accomplishments, related issues, and supportive information.

8. Conclusions and opinions are the internal auditor's evaluations of the effects of the observations and recommendations on the activities reviewed. They usually put the observations and recommendations in perspective based on their overall implications. Any engagement conclusions should be clearly identified in the engagement report. Conclusions may encompass the entire scope of an engagement or specific aspects. They may cover, but are not limited to, whether operating or program objectives and goals conform to those of the organization, whether the organization's objectives and goals are being met, and whether the activity under review is functioning as intended. An opinion may include an overall assessment of controls or may be limited to specific controls or aspects of the engagement.

9. The internal auditor may communicate recommendations for improvements, acknowledgments of satisfactory performance, and corrective actions. Recommendations are based on the internal auditor's observations and conclusions. They call for action to correct existing conditions or improve operations and may suggest approaches to correcting or enhancing performance as a guide for management in achieving desired results. Recommendations can be general or specific. For example, under some circumstances, the internal auditor may recommend a general course of action and specific suggestions for implementation. In other circumstances, the internal auditor may suggest further investigation or study.

10. The internal auditor may communicate engagement client accomplishments, in terms of improvements since the last engagement or the establishment of a well-controlled operation. This information may be necessary to fairly present the existing conditions and to provide perspective and balance to the engagement final communications.

11. The internal auditor may communicate the engagement client's views about the internal auditor's conclusions, opinions, or recommendations.

12. As part of the internal auditor's discussions with the engagement client, the internal auditor obtains agreement on the results of the engagement and on any necessary plan of action to improve operations. If the internal auditor and engagement client disagree about the engagement results, the engagement communications state both positions and the reasons for the disagreement. The engagement client's written comments may be included as an appendix to the engagement report, in the body of the report, or in a cover letter.

13. Certain information is not appropriate for disclosure to all report recipients because it is privileged, proprietary, or related to improper or illegal acts. Such information should be disclosed in a separate report. The report should be distributed to the board if the conditions being reported involve senior management.

14. Interim reports are written or oral and may be transmitted formally or informally. Interim reports are used to communicate information that requires immediate attention, to communicate a change in engagement scope for the activity under review, or to keep management informed of engagement progress when engagements extend over a long period. The use of interim reports does not diminish or eliminate the need for a final report.

15. A signed report is issued after the engagement's completion. Summary reports highlighting engagement results are appropriate for levels of management above the engagement client and can be issued separately from or in conjunction with the final report. The term "signed" means the authorized internal auditor's name is manually or electronically signed in the report or on

a cover letter. The CAE determines which internal auditor is authorized to sign the report. If engagement reports are distributed by electronic means, a signed version of the report is kept on file by the internal audit activity.

2420—Quality of Communications

Communications must be accurate, objective, clear, concise, constructive, complete, and timely.

Interpretation: *Accurate communications are free from errors and distortions and are faithful to the underlying facts. Objective communications are fair, impartial, and unbiased and are the result of a fair-minded and balanced assessment of all relevant facts and circumstances. Clear communications are easily understood and logical, avoiding unnecessary technical language and providing all significant and relevant information. Concise communications are to the point and avoid unnecessary elaboration, superfluous detail, redundancy, and wordiness. Constructive communications are helpful to the engagement client and the organization and lead to improvements where needed. Complete communications lack nothing that is essential to the target audience and include all significant and relevant information and observations to support recommendations and conclusions. Timely communications are opportune and expedient, depending on the significance of the issue, allowing management to take appropriate corrective action.*

Practice Advisory 2420-1: Quality of Communications

1. Data and evidence should be gathered, evaluated, and summarized with care and precision.
2. Observations, conclusions, and recommendations should be derived and expressed without prejudice, partisanship, personal interests, and the undue influence of others.
3. Clarity can be improved by avoiding unnecessary technical language and providing all significant and relevant information in context.
4. Communications should be developed with the objective of making each element meaningful but succinct.
5. A useful, positive, and well-meaning content and tone focuses on the organization's objectives.
6. Communication should be consistent with the organization's style and culture.
7. The presentation of engagement results should occur without undue delay.

2421—Errors and Omissions

If a final communication contains a significant error or omission, the CAE must communicate corrected information to all parties who received the original communication.

> No Practice Advisory for Standard 2421

2430—Use of "Conducted in Conformance with the *International Standards for the Professional Practice of Internal Auditing*"

Internal auditors may report that their engagements are "conducted in conformance with the *International Standards for the Professional Practice of Internal Auditing*" only if the results of the quality assurance and improvement program support the statement.

> No Practice Advisory for Standard 2430

2431—Engagement Disclosure of Nonconformance

When nonconformance with the definition of internal auditing, the Code of Ethics, or the *Standards* impacts a specific engagement, communication of the results must disclose the:

- Principle or rule of conduct of the Code of Ethics or *Standard(s)* with which full conformance was not achieved.

- Reason(s) for nonconformance.

- Impact of nonconformance on the engagement and the communicated engagement results.

> No Practice Advisory for Standard 2431

2440—Disseminating Results

The CAE must communicate results to the appropriate parties.

Interpretation: *The CAE or designee reviews and approves the final engagement communication before issuance and decides to whom and how it will be disseminated.*

> **2440.A1**—The CAE is responsible for communicating the final results to parties who can ensure that the results are given due consideration.
>
> **2440.A2**—If not otherwise mandated by legal, statutory, or regulatory requirements, prior to releasing results to parties outside the organization, the CAE must:

- Assess the potential risk to the organization.

- Consult with senior management and/or legal counsel as appropriate.

- Control dissemination by restricting the use of the results.

> **2440.C1**—The CAE is responsible for communicating the final results of consulting engagements to clients.
>
> **2440.C2**—During consulting engagements, governance, risk management, and control issues may be identified. Whenever these issues are significant to the organization, they must be communicated to senior management and the board.

Practice Advisory 2440-1: Disseminating Results

1. Internal auditors discuss conclusions and recommendations with appropriate levels of management before the CAE issues the final engagement communications. This is usually accomplished during the course of the engagement and/or at postengagement meetings (i.e., exit meetings).

2. Another technique is for the management of the audited activity to review draft engagement issues, observations, and recommendations. These discussions and reviews help avoid misunderstandings or misinterpretations of fact by providing the opportunity for the engagement client to clarify specific items and express views about the observations, conclusions, and recommendations.

3. The level of participants in the discussions and reviews vary by organization and nature of the report; they generally include those individuals who are knowledgeable regarding detailed operations and those who can authorize the implementation of corrective action.

4. The CAE distributes the final engagement communication to the management of the audited activity and to those members of the organization who can ensure engagement results are given due consideration and take corrective action or ensure that corrective action is taken. Where appropriate, the CAE may send a summary communication to higher-level members in the organization. Where required by the internal audit charter or organizational policy, the CAE also communicates to other interested or affected parties, such as external auditors and the board.

Practice Advisory 2440-2: Communicating Sensitive Information Within and Outside the Chain of Command

1. Internal auditors often come into possession of critically sensitive information that is substantial to the organization and poses significant potential consequences. This information may relate to exposures, threats, uncertainties, fraud, waste and mismanagement, illegal activities, abuse of power, misconduct that endangers public health or safety, or other wrongdoings. Furthermore, these matters may adversely impact the organization's reputation, image, competitiveness, success, viability, market values, investments and intangible assets, or earnings.

2. Once the internal auditor has deemed the new information substantial and credible, he or she would normally communicate the information—in a timely manner—to senior management and the board in accordance with Standard 2060 and Practice Advisory 2060-1. This communication would typically follow the normal chain of command for the internal auditor.

3. If the CAE, after those discussions, concludes that senior management is exposing the organization to an unacceptable risk and is not taking appropriate action, he or she needs to present the information and the differences of opinion to the board in accordance with Standard 2600.

4. The typical chain-of-command communication scenario may be accelerated for certain types of sensitive occurrences because of laws, regulations, or common practices. For example, in the case of evidence of fraudulent financial reporting by an organization with publicly traded securities, local regulations may prescribe that the board be immediately informed of the circumstances surrounding the possibility of misleading financial reports even though senior management and the CAE may agree on which actions need to be taken. Laws and regulations in some jurisdictions specify that the board should be informed of discoveries of criminal, securities, food, drugs, or pollution laws violations as well as other illegal acts such as bribery or improper payments to government officials or to suppliers or customers.

5. In some situations, an internal auditor may face the dilemma of considering whether to communicate the information to persons outside the normal chain of command or even outside the organization. This communication is commonly referred to as whistle-blowing. The act of disclosing adverse information to someone within the organization but outside the internal auditor's normal chain of command is considered internal whistle-blowing, while disclosing adverse information to a government agency or other authority outside the organization is considered external whistle-blowing.

6. Most whistle-blowers disclose sensitive information internally, even if outside the normal chain of command, if they trust the organization's policies and mechanisms to investigate allegations of illegal or other improper activity and to take appropriate action. However, some persons possessing sensitive information may decide to take the information outside the organization if they: fear retribution from their employer or fellow employees; doubt that the issue will be properly investigated; believe that it will be concealed; or possess evidence about an illegal or improper activity that jeopardizes the health, safety, or well-being of people in the organization or community.

7. In a case where internal whistle-blowing is chosen, an internal auditor must evaluate alternative ways of communicating the risk he or she sees to persons or groups outside the normal chain of command. Because of risks and ramifications associated with these approaches, the internal auditor needs to proceed with caution in evaluating the evidence and reasonableness of his or her conclusions as well as examining the merits and disadvantages of each potential

action. Taking this action may be appropriate if it will result in responsible action by persons in senior management or the board.

8. Many jurisdictions have laws or regulations requiring public servants with knowledge of illegal or unethical acts to inform an inspector general, other public official, or ombudsman. Some laws pertaining to whistle-blowing actions protect citizens if they come forward to disclose specific types of improper activities. The activities listed in these laws and regulations include:

- Criminal offenses and other failures to comply with legal obligations.

- Acts that are considered miscarriages of justice.

- Acts that endanger the health, safety, or well-being of individuals.

- Acts that damage the environment.

- Activities that conceal or cover up any of the above activities.

Some jurisdictions offer no guidance or protection or offer protection only to public (i.e., government) employees.

9. The internal auditor should be aware of the laws and regulations of the various jurisdictions in which the organization operates. Legal counsel familiar with the legal aspects of whistle-blowing can assist internal auditors confronted with this issue. The internal auditor should always obtain legal advice if he or she is uncertain of the legal requirements or consequences of engaging in internal or external whistle-blowing.

10. Many professional associations hold their members accountable for disclosing illegal or unethical activities. A distinguishing mark of a profession is its acceptance of broad responsibilities to the public and its protection of the general welfare. In addition to examining the legal requirements, IIA members and all certified internal auditors must follow the requirements presented in the IIA Code of Ethics.

11. An internal auditor has a professional duty and an ethical responsibility to carefully evaluate all evidence and the reasonableness of his or her conclusions and decide whether further actions are needed to protect the organization's interests and stakeholders, the outside community, or the institutions of society. Also, the auditor will need to consider the duty of confidentiality imposed by the IIA Code of Ethics to respect the value and ownership of information and avoid disclosing it without appropriate authority unless there is a legal or professional obligation to do so. During this evaluation process, the auditor may seek the advice of legal counsel and, if appropriate, other experts. Those discussions may be helpful in providing a different perspective on the circumstances as well as offering opinions about the potential impact and consequences of possible actions. The manner in which the internal auditor seeks to resolve this type of complex and sensitive situation may create reprisals and potential liability.

12. Ultimately, the internal auditor makes a professional decision about his or her obligations to the employer. The decision to communicate outside the normal chain of command needs to be based on a well-informed opinion that the wrongdoing is supported by substantial, credible evidence and that a legal or regulatory imperative, or a professional or ethical obligation, requires further action.

Practice Advisory 2440.A2-1: Communications Outside the Organization

1. The internal audit activity's charter, the board's charter, organizational policies, or the engagement agreement may contain guidance related to reporting information outside the organization. If such guidance does not exist, the CAE may facilitate adoption of appropriate policies that may include:

- Authorization required for reporting information outside the organization.

- Process for seeking approval to report information outside the organization.

- Guidelines for permissible and nonpermissible information that may be reported.

- Outside persons authorized to receive information and the types of information they may receive.

- Related privacy regulations, regulatory requirements, and legal considerations for reporting information outside the organization.

- Nature of assurances, advice, recommendations, opinions, guidance, and other information that may be included in communicating information outside the organization.

2. Requests can relate to information that already exists (e.g., a previously issued internal audit report) as well as to information to be created or determined, which results in a new internal audit engagement or report. If the request relates to information or a report that already exists, the internal auditor needs to determine whether it is suitable for dissemination outside the organization.

3. In certain situations, it may be possible to create a special-purpose report based on an existing report or information to make the report suitable for dissemination outside the organization.

4. Some matters to consider when reporting information outside the organization include:

- Usefulness of a written agreement with the intended recipient concerning the information to be reported and the internal auditor's responsibilities.

- Identification of information providers, sources, report signers, recipients, and related persons to the disseminated report or information.

- Identification of objectives, scope, and procedures to be performed in generating applicable information.

- Nature of report or other communication including opinions, inclusion or exclusion of recommendations, disclaimers, limitations, and type of assurance or assertions to be provided.

- Copyright issues, intended use of the information, and limitations on further distribution or sharing of the information.

5. If the internal auditor discovers information reportable to senior management or the board while conducting engagements that require dissemination of information outside the organization, the CAE needs to provide suitable communication to the board.

2450—Overall Opinions

When an overall opinion is issued, it must take into account the expectations of senior management, the board, and other stakeholders and must be supported by sufficient, reliable, relevant, and useful information.

Interpretation: *The communication will identify:*

- *The scope, including the time period to which the opinion pertains.*

- *Scope limitations.*

- *Consideration of all related projects including the reliance on other assurance providers.*

- *The risk or control framework or other criteria used as a basis for the overall opinion.*

- *The overall opinion, judgment, or conclusion reached.*

The reasons for an unfavorable overall opinion must be stated.

> No Practice Advisory for Standard 2450

2.4 Monitor Engagement Outcomes

In this section, topics such as audit monitoring and follow-up and resolution of senior management's acceptance of risks are discussed.

Audit monitoring and follow-up can be sophisticated or simple, depending on a number of factors, including the size and complexity of the audit organization. Regardless of the type chosen, each audit should include: a firm basis for monitoring and follow-up actions, active status monitoring, and a determination of the results of actions taken on recommendations.

> **AUDIT FOLLOW-UP**
>
> The director of internal auditing should ensure follow-up of prior audit findings and recommendations to determine if corrective action was taken and is achieving the desired results.

Auditee responses to the audit report are reviewed to assess their adequacy and timeliness and appropriateness of proposed corrective actions. Auditee responses and their corrective actions are monitored to ensure their timely completion. Effective follow-up is essential to get the full benefits of audit work. If monitoring and follow-up disclose that action on major recommendations is not progressing, additional steps should be promptly considered. Follow-up should be elevated to progressively higher levels of management of the organization to obtain prompt action. Continued attention is required until expected results are achieved. At this point, audit recommendations are closed.

Reasons for closing audit recommendations include only one of these:

- The recommendation was effectively implemented.
- An alternative action was taken that achieved the intended results.
- Circumstances have so changed that the recommendation is no longer valid.
- The recommendation was not implemented despite the use of all feasible strategies.

When a recommendation is closed for the last reason, a judgment is made on whether the objectives are significant enough to be pursued at a later date in another assignment.

IIA *Standards* Applicable to Monitor Engagement Outcomes

2500—Monitoring Progress

The CAE must establish and maintain a system to monitor the disposition of results communicated to management.

2500.A1—The CAE must establish a follow-up process to monitor and ensure that management actions have been effectively implemented or that senior management has accepted the risk of not taking action.

2500.C1—The internal audit activity must monitor the disposition of results of consulting engagements to the extent agreed upon with the client.

Practice Advisory 2500-1: Monitoring Progress

1. To effectively monitor the disposition of results, the CAE establishes procedures to include:

- The time frame within which management's response to the engagement observations and recommendations is required.

- Evaluation of management's response.

- Verification of the response (if appropriate).

- Performance of a follow-up engagement (if appropriate).

- A communications process that escalates unsatisfactory responses/actions, including the assumption of risk, to the appropriate levels of senior management or the board.

2. If certain reported observations and recommendations are significant enough to require immediate action by management or the board, the internal audit activity monitors actions taken until the observation is corrected or the recommendation implemented.

3. The internal audit activity may effectively monitor progress by:

- Addressing engagement observations and recommendations to appropriate levels of management responsible for taking action.

- Receiving and evaluating management responses and proposed action plan to engagement observations and recommendations during the engagement or within a reasonable time period after the engagement results are communicated. Responses are more useful if they include sufficient information for the CAE to evaluate the adequacy and timeliness of proposed actions.

- Receiving periodic updates from management to evaluate the status of its efforts to correct observations and/or implement recommendations.

- Receiving and evaluating information from other organizational units assigned responsibility for follow-up or corrective actions.

- Reporting to senior management and/or the board on the status of responses to engagement observations and recommendations.

Practice Advisory 2500.A1-1: Follow-Up Process

1. Internal auditors determine whether management has taken action or implemented the recommendation. The internal auditor determines whether the desired results were achieved or if senior management or the board has assumed the risk of not taking action or implementing the recommendation.

2. Follow-up is a process by which internal auditors evaluate the adequacy, effectiveness, and timeliness of actions taken by management on reported observations and recommendations, including those made by external auditors and others. This process also includes determining whether senior management and/or the board have assumed the risk of not taking corrective action on reported observations.

3. The internal audit activity's charter should define the responsibility for follow-up. The CAE determines the nature, timing, and extent of follow-up, considering these factors:

- Significance of the reported observation or recommendation
- Degree of effort and cost needed to correct the reported condition
- Impact that may result should the corrective action fail
- Complexity of the corrective action
- Time period involved

4. The CAE is responsible for scheduling follow-up activities as part of developing engagement work schedules. Scheduling of follow-up is based on the risk and exposure involved as well as the degree of difficulty and the significance of timing in implementing corrective action.

5. Where the CAE judges that management's oral or written response indicates that action taken is sufficient when weighed against the relative importance of the observation or recommendation, internal auditors may follow up as part of the next engagement.

6. Internal auditors ascertain whether actions taken on observations and recommendations remedy the underlying conditions. Follow-up activities should be appropriately documented.

2600—Resolution of Senior Management's Acceptance of Risks

When the CAE believes that senior management has accepted a level of residual risk that may be unacceptable to the organization, the CAE must discuss the matter with senior management. If the decision regarding residual risk is not resolved, the CAE must report the matter to the board for resolution.

No Practice Advisory for Standard 2600

2.5 Sample Practice Questions

As mentioned in the Preface of this book, a small batch of sample practice questions is included here to show the flavor of questions and to create a quiz-like environment. The answers and explanations for these questions are shown in a separate section at the end of this book just before the Glossary. If there is a need to practice more questions to obtain a greater confidence, refer to the section "CIA Exam Study Preparation Resources" presented in the front matter of this book.

1. During a preliminary survey, an auditor notes that several accounts payable vouchers for major suppliers show adjustments for duplicate payment of prior invoices. This would indicate:

a. A need for additional testing to determine related controls and the current exposure to duplicate payments made to suppliers.

b. An unrecorded liability for the amount of purchases that are not processed while awaiting supplier master file address maintenance.

c. A lack of control in the receiving area that prevents timely notice to the accounts payable area that goods have been received and inspected.

d. The existence of a sophisticated accounts payable system that correlates overpayments to open invoices and therefore requires no further audit concern.

2. Writing an audit program occurs at which stage of the audit process?

a. During the planning stage.

b. Subsequent to testing internal controls to determine whether to rely on the controls or audit around them.

c. As the audit is performed.

d. At the end of each audit, the standard audit program should be revised for the next audit to ensure coverage of noted problem areas.

3. In planning an audit, an on-site survey could assist with all of the following **except:**

a. Obtaining auditee comments and suggestions on control problems.

b. Obtaining preliminary information on internal controls.

c. Identifying areas for audit emphasis.

d. Evaluating the effectiveness of the system of internal controls.

4. Which of the following is a proper step in an audit program?

a. Notification of the audit.

b. Observation of procedures.

c. Definition of audit objectives.

d. Planning for audit reporting.

5. "Fieldwork" has been defined as "a systematic process of objectively gathering evidence about an entity's operations, evaluating it, and determining if those operations meet acceptable standards." Which of the following is **not** part of the work performed during fieldwork?

a. Expanding or altering audit procedures if circumstances warrant.

b. Applying the audit program to accomplish audit objectives.

c. Creating working papers that document the audit.

d. Developing a written audit program.

6. IIA *Standards* require auditors to discuss conclusions and recommendations at appropriate levels of management before issuing final written reports. Auditors usually accomplish this by conducting exit conferences. Which of the following **best** describes the purpose of exit conferences?

a. To allow auditees to get started implementing recommendations as soon as possible.

b. To allow auditors to explain complicated findings before a written report is issued.

c. To allow auditors to "sell" findings and recommendations to management.

d. To ensure that there have been no misunderstandings or misinterpretations of facts.

7. In the preparation of an audit program, which of the following items is **not** essential?

a. Performance of a preliminary survey.

b. Review of material from prior audit reports.

c. Preparation of a budget identifying the costs of resources needed.

d. Review of performance standards set by management.

8. What action should an internal auditor take on discovering that an audit area was omitted from the audit program?

   a. Document the problem in the working papers and take no further action until instructed to do so.

   b. Perform the additional work needed without regard to the added time required to complete the audit.

   c. Continue the audit as planned and include the unforeseen problem in a subsequent audit.

   d. Evaluate whether completion of the audit as planned will be adequate.

9. In order to determine the extent of audit tests to be performed during fieldwork, preparing the audit program should be the next step after completing the:

   a. Preliminary survey.

   b. Survey of company policies.

   c. Assignment of audit staff.

   d. Time budgets for specific audit tasks.

10. Which of the following is a step in an audit program?

    a. The audit will commence in six weeks and include tests of compliance.

    b. Determine whether the manufacturing operations are effective and efficient.

    c. Auditors may not reveal findings to nonsupervisory, operational personnel during the course of this audit.

    d. Observe the procedures used to identify defective units produced.

11. Audit programs testing internal controls should:

    a. Be tailored for the audit of each operation.

    b. Be generalized to fit all situations without regard to departmental lines.

    c. Be generalized so as to be usable at all locations of a particular department.

    d. Reduce costly duplication of effort by ensuring that every aspect of an operation is examined.

12. An auditor begins an audit with a preliminary evaluation of internal control, the purpose of which is to decide on the extent of future auditing activities. If the auditor's preliminary evaluation of internal control results in a finding that controls may be inadequate, the next step would be:

    a. An expansion of audit work prior to the preparation of an audit report.

    b. The preparation of a flowchart depicting the internal control system.

    c. An exception noted in the audit report if losses have occurred.

    d. To implement the desired controls.

13. An internal auditor has just completed an on-site survey in order to become familiar with the company's payroll operations. Which of the following should be performed next?

    a. Assign audit personnel.

    b. Establish initial audit objectives.

    c. Write the audit program.

    d. Conduct fieldwork.

14. Interviewing operating personnel, identifying the objectives of the auditee, identifying standards used to evaluate performance, and assessing the risks inherent in the auditee's operations are activities typically performed in which phase of an internal audit?

    a. The fieldwork phase.

    b. The preliminary survey phase.

    c. The audit programming phase.

    d. The reporting phase.

15. The auditor in charge has just been informed of the next audit assignment and the assigned audit team. Select the appropriate phase for finalizing the audit time budget.

    a. During formulation of the long-range plan.

    b. After the preliminary survey.

    c. During the initial planning meeting.

    d. After the completion of all fieldwork.

16. Which of the following activities does **not** constitute audit supervision?

a. Preparing a preliminary audit program.

b. Providing appropriate instructions to the auditors.

c. Reviewing audit working papers.

d. Seeing that audit objectives are achieved.

17. When reviewing audit working papers, the **primary** responsibility of an audit supervisor is to determine that:

a. Each worksheet is properly identified with a descriptive heading.

b. Working papers are properly referenced and kept in logical groupings.

c. Standard departmental procedures are adhered to with regard to working paper preparation and technique.

d. Working papers adequately support the audit findings, conclusions, and reports.

18. When hiring entry-level internal audit staff, which of the following will **most** likely predict the applicant's success as an auditor?

a. Grade point average on college accounting courses.

b. Ability to fit well socially into a group.

c. Ability to organize and express thoughts well.

d. Level of detailed knowledge of the company.

19. An internal auditing supervisor, when reviewing a staff member's working papers, identified an unsupported statement that the auditee's unit was operating inefficiently. What action should the supervisor direct the auditor to take?

a. Remove the comment from the working paper file.

b. Obtain the auditee's concurrence with the statement.

c. Research and identify criteria to measure operating efficiency.

d. Explain that it is the opinion of the staff member.

20. Internal auditors often include summaries within their working papers. Which of the following **best** describes the purpose of such summaries?

a. Summaries are prepared to conform to IIA *Standards*.

b. Summaries are usually required for the completion of each section of an audit program.

c. Summaries distill the most useful information from several working papers into a more usable form.

d. Summaries are used to document the fact that the auditor has considered all relevant evidence.

21. A working paper is complete when it:

a. Complies with the auditing department's format requirements.

b. Contains all of the elements of a finding.

c. Is clear, concise, and accurate.

d. Satisfies the audit objective for which it is developed.

22. Working papers have the following characteristic:

a. They are the property of the organization and are available to all company employees.

b. They document the auditing procedures performed, the information obtained, and the conclusions reached.

c. They become the property of the independent outside auditors when completed.

d. They should be retained permanently in the organization's records.

23. Which of the following should be identified as a deficiency by an audit supervisor when reviewing a set of working papers?

a. A memorandum explaining why the time budget for a part of the audit was exceeded.

b. An audit finding recorded in the working papers and report draft that omits the criteria used for evaluation.

c. A memorandum explaining why an audit program step was omitted.

d. A letter to the auditee outlining the scope of the audit.

24. Which of the following techniques is **best** for emphasizing a point in a written communication?

   a. Place the point in the middle rather than at the beginning or end of the paragraph.

   b. Use passive rather than active voice.

   c. Highlight the point through the use of nonparallel structure.

   d. Use a short sentence with one idea rather than a longer sentence with several ideas.

25. Which of the following statements conveys negative information in such a way that a favorable response from the auditee may still be achieved?

   a. Your bookkeeper has failed to reconcile the bank statement each month.

   b. The bank statements have not been reconciled each month.

   c. Unfortunately, your bookkeeper has not taken the time to reconcile the bank statement each month.

   d. You have apparently failed to inform your bookkeeper that the bank statements should be reconciled on a timely basis.

26. An internal audit director has noticed that staff auditors are presenting more oral reports to supplement written reports. The best reason for the increased use of oral reports by the auditors is that such reports:

   a. Reduce the amount of testing required to support audit findings.

   b. Can be delivered in an informal manner without preparation.

   c. Can be prepared using a flexible format, thereby increasing overall audit efficiency.

   d. Permit auditors to counter arguments and provide additional information that the audience may require.

27. An internal auditor has completed an audit of an organization's activities and is ready to issue a report. However, the auditee disagrees with the internal auditor's conclusions. The auditor should:

   a. Withhold the issuance of the audit report until agreement on the issues is obtained.

   b. Perform more work, with the auditee's concurrence, to resolve areas of disagreement. Delay the issuance of the report until agreement is reached.

   c. Issue the audit report and indicate that the auditee has provided a scope limitation that has led to a difference as to the conclusions.

   d. Issue the audit report and state both the auditor and auditee positions and the reasons for the disagreement.

28. According to IIA *Standards*, reported audit findings emerge by a process of comparing what should be with what is. In determining what should be during an audit of a company's treasury function, which of the following would be the **least** desirable criteria against which to judge current operations?

   a. The operations of the treasury function as documented during the last audit.

   b. Company policies and procedures delegating authority and assigning responsibilities.

   c. Finance textbook illustrations of generally accepted good treasury function practices.

   d. Codification of best practices of the treasury function in relevant industries.

29. Which of the following is **not** a major purpose of an audit report?

   a. Inform.

   b. Get results.

   c. Assign responsibility.

   d. Persuade.

30. Which of the following would **not** be included in the statement of scope in an audit report?

   a. Period covered by the audit.

   b. Audit objectives.

   c. Activities not audited.

   d. Nature and extent of the auditing performed.

31. Providing useful and timely information and promoting improvements in operations are goals of internal auditors. To accomplish this in their reports, auditors should provide:

a. Top management with reports that emphasize the operational details of defective conditions.

b. Operating management with reports that emphasize general concerns and risks.

c. Information in written form before it is discussed with the auditee.

d. Reports that meet the expectations and perceptions of both operational and top management.

32. Auditors realize that at times corrective action is not taken even when agreed to by the appropriate parties. This should lead an internal auditor to:

a. Decide the extent of necessary follow-up work.

b. Allow management to decide when to follow up, since it is management's ultimate responsibility.

c. Decide to conduct follow-up work only if management requests the auditor's assistance.

d. Write a follow-up audit report with all findings and their significance to the operations.

33. Follow-up activity may be required to ensure that corrective action has taken place for certain findings. The internal audit department's responsibility to perform follow-up activities as required should be defined in the:

a. Internal auditing department's written charter.

b. Mission statement of the audit committee.

c. Engagement memo issued prior to each audit assignment.

d. Purpose statement within applicable audit reports.

34. Given the acceptance of the cost savings audits and the scarcity of internal audit resources, the audit manager also decided that follow-up action was not needed. The manager reasoned that cost savings should be sufficient to motivate the auditee to implement the auditor's recommendations. Therefore, follow-up was not scheduled as a regular part of the audit plan. Does the audit manager's decision violate IIA *Standards*?

a. No. The *Standards* do not specify whether follow-up is needed.

b. Yes. The *Standards* require the auditors to determine whether the auditee has appropriately implemented all of the auditor's recommendations.

c. Yes. Scarcity of resources is not a sufficient reason to omit follow-up action.

d. No. When there is evidence of sufficient motivation by the auditee, there is no need for follow-up action.

35. Reporting to senior management and the board is an important part of the auditor's obligation. Which of the following items is **not** required to be reported to senior management and/or the board?

a. Subsequent to the completion of an audit, but prior to the issuance of an audit report, the audit senior in charge of the audit was offered a permanent position in the auditee's department.

b. An annual report summary of the department's audit work schedule and financial budget.

c. Significant interim changes to the approved audit work schedule and financial budget.

d. An audit plan was approved by senior management and the board. Subsequent to the approval, senior management informed the audit director not to perform an audit of a division because the division's activities were very sensitive.

36. During an audit of purchasing, internal auditors found several violations of company policy concerning competitive bidding. The same condition that had been reported in an audit report last year, and corrective action had not been taken. Which of the following **best** describes the appropriate action concerning this repeat finding?

   a. The audit report should note that this same condition had been reported in the prior audit.

   b. During the exit interview, management should be made aware that a finding from the prior report had not been corrected.

   c. The director of internal auditing should determine whether management or the board has assumed the risk of not taking corrective action.

   d. The director of internal auditing should determine whether this condition should be reported to the independent auditor and any regulatory agency.

37. Which of the following audit committee activities would be of the **greatest** benefit to the internal auditing department?

   a. Review and approval of audit programs.

   b. Assurance that the external auditor will rely on the work of the internal auditing department whenever possible.

   c. Review and endorsement of all internal audit reports prior to their release.

   d. Support for appropriate follow-up of recommendations made by the internal auditing department.

38. An internal auditor reported a suspected fraud to the director of internal auditing. The director turned the entire case over to the security department. Security failed to investigate (employee) or report the case to management. The perpetrator continued to defraud the organization until being accidentally discovered by a line manager two years later. Select the **most** appropriate action for the audit director.

   a. The director's actions were correct.

   b. The director should have periodically checked the status of the case with security.

   c. The director should have conducted the investigation.

   d. The director should have discharged the perpetrator.

39. If an internal auditor finds that no corrective action has been taken on a prior audit finding that is still valid, IIA *Standards* state that the internal auditor should:

   a. Restate the prior finding along with the findings of the current audit.

   b. Determine whether management or the board has assumed the risk of not taking corrective action.

   c. Seek the board's approval to initiate corrective action.

   d. Schedule a future audit of the specific area involved.

40. Internal auditing is responsible for reporting fraud to senior management or the board when:

   a. The incidence of fraud of a material amount has been established to a reasonable certainty.

   b. Suspicious activities have been reported to internal auditing.

   c. Irregular transactions have been identified and are under investigation.

   d. The review of all suspected fraud-related transactions is complete.

41. Why should organizations require auditees to promptly reply and outline the corrective action that has been implemented on reported deficiencies?

   a. To close the open audit issues as soon as possible.

   b. To effect savings as early as possible.

   c. To indicate concurrence with the audit findings.

   d. To ensure that the auditor performance is evaluated.

Fraud Risks and Controls (5–15%)

3.1 Types of Fraud   391

3.2 Controls to Prevent or Detect Fraud   394

3.3 Audit Tests to Detect Fraud   396

3.4 Integrating Analytical Relationships to Detect Fraud   405

3.5 Interrogation or Investigative Techniques   415

3.6 Forensic Auditing   423

3.7 Use of Computers in Analyzing Data for Fraud and Crime   427

3.8 Sample Practice Questions   436

3.1 Types of Fraud

In this section, topics such as types of fraud, theft of assets, fraud by frequency, fraud involving conspiracy, and varieties of fraud are discussed.

(a) Overview of Fraud

What is fraud? Here is the legal definition of fraud by most statutes:

> Fraud is a generic term and embraces all the multifarious means that human ingenuity can devise, which are resorted to by one individual, to get an advantage over another by false representations. It includes all surprise, trick, cunning, and unfair ways by which another is cheated. Fraud is a term of law, applied to certain facts as a conclusion from them, but is not in itself a fact. It has been defined as any cunning deception or artifice used to cheat or deceive another.

Cheat and defraud means every kind of trick and deception, from false representation and intimidation to suppression and concealment of any fact and information by which a party is induced to part with property for less than its value or to give more than it is worth for the property of another. The terms **fraud** and **bad faith** are synonymous when applied to the conduct of public offenders.

(b) Types of Fraud

There are many varieties of frauds, limited only by the ingenuity of the perpetrators. Fraud can be classified in a number of ways from a discovery point of view. The reason for this classification is that different approaches and procedures are required to discover each type of fraud and to control each type's occurrence.

Howard Davia and his coauthors present four types of fraud: theft of assets, fraud by frequency, fraud by conspiracy, and varieties of fraud (see Exhibit 3.1).[1]

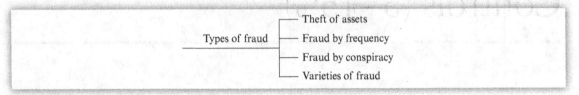

```
                                    ┌─── Theft of assets
                                    │
                Types of fraud  ────┤─── Fraud by frequency
                                    │
                                    ├─── Fraud by conspiracy
                                    │
                                    └─── Varieties of fraud
```

EXHIBIT 3.1 Types of Fraud

(i) Theft of Assets
Theft of assets is classified into three categories.

1. Theft of assets that appears openly on the books as distinct accounting entries (fraud open on the books are the least difficult to discover)

2. Theft of assets that appears on the books but is hidden as a part of other larger otherwise legitimate accounting entries (fraud hidden on the books)

3. Theft of assets is not on the books and could never be detected by an examination of "booked" accounting transactions (fraud off the books, most difficult to discover)

Fraud open on the books includes criminal acts that involve discrete entries in the accounting records. Here the term "discrete entry" means that the fraud involves the entire transaction; if that transaction is selected by an auditor for examination, this type of fraud offers the best chance for discovery (e.g., a fraudulent duplicate payment that stands by it).

Fraud hidden on the books involves acts of fraud that are included in accounting entries that appear on the books, but are not discrete entries. That is, the amount of the fraud is always buried in a larger, legitimate accounting entry, never appearing as a discrete amount (e.g., kickbacks).

In **fraud off the books,** the amount of the fraud is neither a discrete accounting entry nor a hidden part of an accounting entry. It is the loss of a valuable asset for the victim. Examples include diverting vending machine sales money and conversion of payment on accounts receivable that have been written off.

(ii) Fraud by Frequency
Another way of classifying fraud is by its frequency of occurrence: nonrepeating or repeating. In nonrepeating fraud, a fraudulent act, even though repeated many times, is singular in nature in that it must be triggered by the perpetrator each time (e.g., a weekly payroll check requires a time card every week in order to generate the fraudulent paycheck).

---

[1] Howard R. Davia, Patrick C. Coggins, John C. Wideman, and Joseph T. Kastantin, *Management Accountant's Guide to Fraud Discovery and Control* (New York: John Wiley & Sons, 1992).

In repeating fraud, a defrauding act may occur many times; however, it needs to be initiated only once. It then keeps running until it is stopped. It could possibly recur in perpetuity (e.g., a salaried payroll check that does not require input each time in order to generate the paycheck. It continues until a stop order is issued).

THREE ELEMENTS OF FRAUD

1. Intent to defraud
2. Commission of a fraudulent act
3. Accomplishment of the fraud

For the auditor, the significance of whether a fraud is nonrepeating or repeating lies in where to look for the evidence. For example, the auditor would have to review a computer application program to obtain evidence of a repeating fraud involving skimming of a few cents off every bank customer's account service charge.

(iii) Fraud Involving Conspiracy

Fraud can be classified as that involving conspiracy, that which does not involve conspiracy, and that involving partial (pseudo-) conspiracy. Here the word "conspiracy" is synonymous with "collusion." It has been proven that most frauds involve conspiracy, either bona fide or pseudo. In the bona fide conspiracy, all parties involved are fully aware of the fraudulent intent; in the pseudoconspiracy, one or more of the parties to the fraud is innocent of fraudulent intent.

(iv) Varieties of Fraud

The varieties of fraud can be grouped in two categories: "specialized" fraud, which is unique to people working in certain kinds of business operations, and the "garden varieties" of fraud, which all people are likely to encounter in general business operations.

Examples of specialized fraud include: embezzlement of assets entrusted by depositors to financial institutions such as banks, savings and loans, credit unions, and pension funds (called "custodial" fraud); and false insurance claims for life, health, auto, and property coverage.

Examples of garden varieties of fraud include kickbacks, defective pricing, unbalanced contracts or purchase orders, reopening completed contracts, duplicate payments, double payments, shell payments, and defective delivery. These eight types of fraud are the more common frauds occurring today.

According to Jack Bologna, corporate fraud can be generated internally (perpetrated by directors, officers, employees, or agents of a corporation for or against it or against others) and externally (perpetrated by others—suppliers, vendors, customers, hackers) against the corporation.[2] Bologna includes management fraud as a part of corporate fraud as the intentional overstatements of corporate or division profits. It is inspired, perpetrated, or induced by managers who seek to benefit in terms of promotions, job stability, larger bonuses, and status symbols.

---

[2] Jack Bologna, *Handbook on Corporate Fraud* (Stoneham, MA: Butterworth-Heinemann, 1993).

3.2 Controls to Prevent or Detect Fraud

Fraud prevention results in big savings because when fraud is prevented, there are no detection or investigation costs. This means a dollar spent in preventing fraud saves many more dollars later on. Therefore, greater attention should be paid to preventive controls rather than detective controls and recovery controls.

(a) Preventive Controls in General

Some examples of preventive controls are listed next.

- Sharing the company vision with all employees
- Distributing fraud policies and programs
- Conducting proactive audits using discovery sampling techniques
- Database query facilities and data mining tools
- Providing a hotline for fraud reporting by employees and others
- Monitoring employee performance
- Enforcing employee vacation privileges
- Discouraging collusion between employees, customers, or vendors with policies clearly explained to them
- Establishing a sound system of internal controls (both formal and informal)
- Providing fraud awareness training programs
- Providing employee assistance programs to deal with personal and work-related pressures
- Establishing physical security and information systems security controls
- Enforcing existing internal controls and fraud policies with the understanding that dishonesty will be punished
- Establishing separation of duties, dual custody, and dual controls
- Establishing total quality management programs
- Creating a positive work environment with open-door policy to facilitate open communications
- Creating teamwork with self-directed teams or quality circles
- Assigning responsibility for fraud prevention programs
- Hiring honest employees
- Publishing a code of ethics
- Establishing a system of authorizations and independent checks and balances
- Encouraging employee empowerment

(b) Detective Controls in General

Here are some examples of detective controls.

- Building audit trails in business transactions (whether automated or not)

- Testing controls
- Conducting regular internal audits
- Conducting surprise internal audits
- Conducting employee performance evaluations
- Watching employee lifestyle changes
- Observing employee behavior toward work, the organization, and other employees
- Periodically taking physical inventory of assets, financial securities, and other valuable items

(c) Computer Fraud–Related Controls

Management (directive) controls, such as performing preemployment screening procedures, requiring employees to sign a code of conduct, and conducting periodic training programs in computer security and privacy policies and procedures are good business practices. System-based preventive, detective, and recovery controls are also needed to effectively combat computer crime and fraud in the electronic age.

AUDITING FOR FRAUD GUIDELINES

- Good fraud auditors must be nosy.
- To catch a thief, auditors must learn to think like one.
- Detection of fraud takes a long time and hard work.
- Question the validity of any unusual transactions.

(d) Preventive Controls

Preventive controls can help in restricting the access of potential perpetrators to the computer facility, computer terminals, data files, programs, and system libraries. Separation of duties, rotation of duties, backup personnel, and a good system of internal controls are some examples of preventive controls.

(e) Detective Controls

Detective controls can help in discovering fraud in the event perpetrator slips past established prevention mechanisms. Some tips and procedures for fraud detection include: take a fresh approach to looking at the data (middle-of-the-month review instead of month-end), break the normal pattern of reporting (obtain early or late reports, ad hoc reports instead of scheduled), change review timing to throw things off their track (random times, not month-end, quarter-end, or year-end), and run normal reports at unusual times. Audit hooks can help in monitoring the computer fraud. Audit hooks are embedded in the application program and are flagged when incoming and processed transactions meet prescribed criteria. If the auditors requested and designed the audit hooks, they should provide the test data and assist in testing the computer system.

(f) Recovery Controls

Recovery controls can help in limiting losses (financial or other) resulting from a well-planned and well-executed computer fraud and crime.

Prior to auditing for fraud, the organization must answer these questions.

- What does the organization have that someone would want to steal?
- How would someone go about stealing from the organization?
- How vulnerable is the organization?
- How can the organization detect fraud and crime?

3.3 Audit Tests to Detect Fraud

It has been said that most frauds are detected by accident, not by planned effort. This should not stop auditors from planning to detect of fraud. Some known approaches to detect fraud include testing, statistical sampling, computer-assisted audit techniques, data query, and data mining tools.

(a) Tools and Techniques

Some examples of audit tests include analytical techniques, charting techniques, recalculations, confirmations, observations, physical examinations, inquiries, and document reviews.

Examples of statistical techniques include discovery sampling, a type of sampling procedure that has a specified probability of including at least one item that occurs very rarely in the population. Multiple regression analysis can be used to find relationships between two or more variables of interest.

Examples of computer-assisted audit techniques include finding exceptions in data through analysis of computer files. These files are searched for duplication of invoices or payments, or other anomalies.

Data query tools are used to search the database for known conditions of data sequencing and data dependencies. Auditors can query many points within a database. Data mining tools can be used to detect abnormal patterns in data.

(b) Steps to Take When Fraud Is Suspected

Handling suspected fraud is a difficult thing to do. It must be handled properly and with care. Amateurs in the personnel or audit department playing at the investigative business can cause many unforeseen problems and unpleasant surprises. If cases of suspected fraud are not handled properly, employee morale and trust can easily be shattered. Unsubstantiated charges can bring on lawsuits for defamation, illegal firing, false arrest, invasion of privacy, and stress. Confrontations with the suspected employee can be staged before the allegations are even documented or verified. Evidence that may support the charges can often go uncollected or be mishandled.

Jack Bologna provides these tips that could help in investigating internal corruption charges.

- Qualify the source of the allegation (i.e., check on the source's identity, credibility, knowledgeability, and reliability).
- Determine whether the source knows the information firsthand (personal knowledge) or whether it has been passed on by another (hearsay).
- Determine the motives of the source (revenge, spite, jealousy, pique, and money).

- If the source demands money before disclosing details, beware. Do not "front" money until verifiable information has been given and has been confirmed through independent means (other credible witnesses or documents).

- Qualify all further information about the alleged corruption; that is, verify and corroborate the charges through other independent sources and documents.

- Never take disciplinary action without a complete record of the corruption allegation, including the identity of the source of the allegations and his or her written account of the allegations (an oral account is not enough).

- Confirm the allegations through documents and the testimony (written and subscribed to) of other knowledgeable witnesses.

- Approach the vendors, suppliers, or others alleged to be involved; elicit their response and enlist their cooperation.

- Interview the suspected employee to seek his or her version of the situation (e.g., did the vendor make the offer or did the employee solicit the vendor?).[3]

Another related question that should be asked is: Should the investigation and audit proceed with inside resources (i.e., security department staff, legal department staff, or audit department staff, or a combination)? If the insiders are trained properly, work can proceed in house. If they are not properly trained, it is advisable to go outside to a reputable and experienced private detective, legal firm, consultant, public accounting firm, or other.

(i) Document Examination

Document examination is a part of gathering evidence for fraud. Document examination is a technique that uncovers perpetrators' efforts to conceal fraud by cover-up schemes involving documents. Documents can be altered, forged, created, changed, duplicated, or misplaced. According to Joseph Wells, most internal frauds are concealed by manipulating source documents, such as purchase orders, sales invoices, credit memorandums, and warehouse removal slips.[4] Investigators should be aware that missing documents, destroyed records, modified records, errors, or omissions can be attributed to human error, carelessness, or accident as well as deliberate action on the part of a suspect.

GUIDELINES FOR DOCUMENT EXAMINATION

- Always search for the strongest possible evidence.

- Investigate without delay.

- Do not ignore small clues or leads.

- Look for facts you can confirm or refute.

- Be persistent and creative.

- Concentrate on the weakest link in the fraud chain.

Source: Joseph Wells, (Austin, TX: Association of Certified Fraud Examiners, 1992).

---

[3] Ibid.
[4] Joseph T. Wells, *Fraud Examination: Investigative and Audit Procedures* (New York: Quorum Books, 1992).

(ii) Examining Accounting Records

According to Wells, one of the easiest ways to detect fraud in the accounting records is by looking for weaknesses in the various steps of the accounting transaction cycle. Legitimate transactions leave a trail that can be followed. Most transactions start with a source document, such as an invoice, a check, or a receiving report.

These source documents become the basis for journal entries, which are chronological listings of transactions with their debit and credit amounts. Journal entries are made in various accounting journals. The entries in the journals are then posted or entered into the accounts. The amounts in the accounts are summarized to become the financial statements for a period.

When fictitious entries are made to the accounting records, source documents are normally absent, fabricated, or altered. These documents, together with the journal entries, accounts, and financial statements, leave a trail that can reveal many frauds. The next guidelines help in searching for overstatement or understatement of amounts in financial statements.

- When searching for an understatement in the financial statements, one usually begins with the source documents and works forward to the financial statements. If the financial statements are understated, sometimes the information from the invoice will be deleted or altered.

- When searching for an overstatement in the financial statements, one starts with the financial statement and works backward to the source documents. Normally true overstatements will not have legitimate support documentation.

Analyzing past records can reveal some insights that can be used to establish the operating standards. These records should include the:

- Normal rate of loss per a specific time period.
- Number and nature of transactions processed per day.
- Number and nature of exceptional transactions handled.
- Number and nature of people movement in and out per day.

(iii) Documenting Fraud

Documenting fraud is as important as conducting the fraud investigation, if not more so. Documenting fraud is a continuous effort from inception to completion of the fraud investigation. During the documentation period, a great deal of evidence is in the form of documents. Wells states that many examiners (auditors) pay too much attention to documents. It is easy to get bogged down in details when examining records and lose sight of a simple fact: Documents do not make cases; witnesses do. The documents make or break the witness. So-called paper cases often confuse and bore juries. Only relevant documents should be collected. In order to guarantee document acceptance by the courts, one should provide:

- Proof that the evidence is relevant and material.
- Proper identification of the item.
- Proof of the chain of custody of the document.

Early in the case, the relevance of documents cannot be easily determined. For that reason, it is recommended that all documents possible be obtained; if they are not needed, they can always be returned or destroyed. General rules regarding the collection of documents include:

- Obtain original documents where feasible. Make working copies for review, and keep the original segregated.

- Do not touch originals any more than necessary; later they may be needed for forensic analysis.

- Maintain a good filing system for the documents. This is especially critical where large volumes of documents are obtained. Voluminous documents can be sequentially stamped for easy reference.[5]

(iv) Obtaining Documentary Evidence

Three principal methods exist for obtaining documentary evidence: subpoenas, search warrants, and voluntary consent[6] (see Exhibit 3.2).

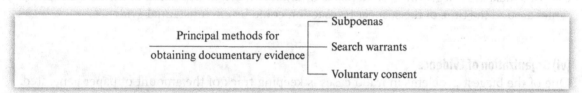

EXHIBIT 3.2 Principal Methods for Obtaining Documentary Evidence

Subpoenas are ordinarily issued by the court or grand jury and can take three forms. A subpoena *duces tectum* calls for the production of documents and records, whereas a regular subpoena is used for witnesses. If the examiner is not an agent of the grand jury or the court, obtaining documents by subpoena is not possible. Subpoenas can call for the production of documents at a grand jury or deposition at a specified time. A forthwith subpoena is usually served by surprise and reserved for those instances where it is thought the records will be secreted, altered, or destroyed.

Search warrants are issued by a judge upon presentation of probable cause to believe the records are being used or have been used in the commission of a crime. An affidavit is usually used to support the request for the search warrant. The affidavit must describe the reason(s) the warrant is requested, along with the place the evidence is thought to be kept.

Courts do not issue search warrants lightly, as the Constitution protects individuals against unreasonable searches and seizures. Search warrants are almost never used in civil cases. Although there are provisions in the law for warrantless search, examiners should avoid such searches at all costs. Searches can be conducted by voluntary consent.

Documents can be obtained by **voluntary consent,** and this is the preferred method. The consent can be oral or written. In the case of obtaining information from possible adverse witnesses or from the target of the examination, it is recommended that the consent be in writing.

---

[5] Ibid.
[6] Ibid.

(v) Types of Evidence

The examiner or auditor needs to be familiar with the types of evidence in order to obtain the right kind of evidence. Basically, evidence falls into one of two categories, either direct or circumstantial (see Exhibit 3.3).

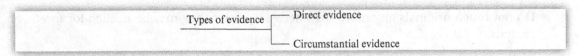

EXHIBIT 3.3 Types of Evidence

Direct evidence is that which shows *prima facie* the facts at issue. What constitutes direct evidence depends on the factors involved. For example, in the case of kickbacks, direct evidence might be a check from the person making the kickback directly to the target.

Circumstantial evidence is that which would indirectly show culpability. For example, in the case of a kickback allegation, cash deposits of unknown origin deposited to the account of the target around the time of the suspect transaction could be circumstantial evidence.

(vi) Organization of Evidence

One of the biggest problems in fraud cases is keeping track of the amount of paper generated. Good organization of documents in complex cases usually includes these guidelines.

- Segregate documents by either witness or transaction. Chronological organization is the least preferable method. The idea is to have the witness introduce the document, not the examiner or auditor.

- Make a "key document" file for easy access to the most relevant documents. Purge this file periodically of less important documents.

- Establish a database early on in the case of volumes of information, preferably a computerized database. The database should include, at a minimum, date of the document, individual from whom the document was obtained, date the document was obtained, brief description of the document, and subject to whom the document pertains.

LEGAL RULES OF EVIDENCE

There are strict legal rules regarding the handling of evidence and the chain of custody thereof. If the examiner is operating under a lawful order of the courts that compels a custodian of records to furnish original documents, they should be copied, preferably in the presence of the custodian, before being removed from the premises. If not operating under a court directive and the records are being provided voluntarily by the custodian, the examiner may retain copies instead of originals.

- Maintain a control log of events and documents in the case of voluminous evidence and complex cases. The purpose of maintaining a brief chronology of events is to establish the chain of events leading to the proof. The chronology may or may not be made a part of the formal report. At a minimum, it can be used for analysis of the case and kept in a working paper binder.

(vii) Charting Techniques

Three types of charting techniques for documenting fraud are link network diagrams, time flow diagrams, and matrices[7] (see Exhibit 3.4).

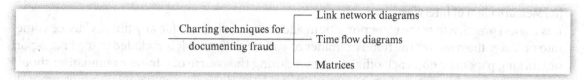

EXHIBIT 3.4 Charting Techniques for Documentary Fraud

Link network diagrams show the relationships among persons, organizations, and events. Different symbols can be used consistently to represent different entities (e.g., a square for an organization, a circle for a person, and a triangle for an event). A solid line can represent connection between entities and broken lines can show presumed relationships. The diagram should be clear and simple to understand.

Time flow diagrams show the relationships of significant events, in the order they occurred. A **matrix** is a grid that shows the relationship or points of contact between a number of entities. Known contact can be differentiated from presumed contact by use of different marks, such as a solid dot or an open dot. In complex cases, a matrix is a useful preliminary step to identify the relative status of the parties by showing the number of contacts of each. Later the matrix can be converted into a table or a chart. For example, a matrix can be used to identify the direction and frequency of telephone traffic between suspect parties.

(viii) Business and Individual Records

Original documents are preferred and should be obtained wherever possible. If necessary, the examiner should furnish the record custodian a receipt for the property. If the originals cannot be obtained, the examiner can settle for copies. The exact records obtained will vary from case to case, but basic business records often include:

- Organization of the business such as article of incorporation
- Financial statements and tax returns
- Customer lists
- Business diaries, address, and telephone and facsimile records
- Personnel records, including employment application
- Bank account records, deposit slips, and canceled checks
- Relevant contracts or agreements
- Computer programs and data file disks

Originals of individual records are usually easier to obtain than originals of business records. Some of the more relevant individual records include:

- Bank account records, deposit slips, and canceled checks
- Financial statements and tax returns

---

[7] Ibid.

- Credit card statements and payment records
- Telephone and facsimile toll records

(ix) Memorandum of Interview

It is a good practice to write a memorandum addressed to the case file any time evidence comes into or leaves the hands of the fraud examiner or auditor. Whether it is included in the final report or working papers or not, each official contact during the course of a fraud examination should be recorded on a "memorandum of interview" on a timely basis. Some guidelines for properly handling the memorandum of interview follow.

- Include all facts of possible evidence on the memorandum of interview.
- Reconfirm dates and supporting information with the interviewee to ensure their accuracy. Reconfirmation acts as a precautionary measure to make certain all facts are accurate before the report is written, not after.
- Include the quotations of the interviewee in the memorandum of interview.
- Transcribe all interviews in writing as soon as practicable following the interview. The main reason timeliness is so important is to ensure the accuracy of witness testimony. The longer the examiner waits to record the interview, the more will be forgotten.
- Record each witness interviewed on a separate memorandum of interview. Recordings of witnesses should not be mixed, since a request by the courts or others for a particular witness's statement can then be fulfilled without providing the entire report.

The contents of a memorandum of interview for a witness should contain these details:

- The nature of the inquiry
- The nature of the interview (e.g., voluntary or not)
- The date the interview was conducted
- The method of conducting the interview (i.e., in person or on the telephone)
- The identity of the interviewer (i.e., fraud examiner, auditor, detective)

Each source or informant contact should be documented on a memorandum of interview, but always referring to the source or informant by a symbol number (S-2, I-2). State the reliability of the individual source (e.g., job title, expertise). When a source or informant is paid money for information, ensure that the payment is noted in the body of the memorandum of interview. Do not pay an informant or source without obtaining a receipt of payment.

The identities of informants or sources should be fully documented and retained in a secure file, available only on a need-to-know basis. The symbol number used in the memorandum of interview should be cross-referenced to the secure file.

(x) Writing Fraud Reports

Writing reports of fraud investigation is one of the most demanding and important tasks of a fraud examiner or an auditor. Here are some reasons why a written report is so important:

- The report is an evidence of the work performed.
- The report conveys to the litigator all the evidence needed to evaluate the legal status of the case.

- The written report adds credibility to the examination and to the examiner.

- The report forces the fraud examiner to consider his or her actions before and during the interview, so that the objectives of the investigation can be best accomplished.

- The report omits immaterial information so that the facts of the case can be clearly and completely understood.

(xi) Characteristics of Fraud Reports

Important characteristics of good report writing include accuracy, clarity, impartiality, relevance, and timeliness (see Exhibit 3.5)

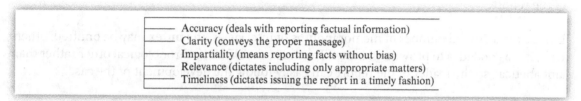

```
———— Accuracy (deals with reporting factual information)
———— Clarity (conveys the proper massage)
———— Impartiality (means reporting facts without bias)
———— Relevance (dictates including only appropriate matters)
———— Timeliness (dictates issuing the report in a timely fashion)
```

EXHIBIT 3.5 Characteristics of Fraud Reports

Accuracy deals with reporting factual information that is correct and that can be verified. There is no room for error. **Clarity** means conveying the proper message in the clearest possible language. If necessary, the interviewed person can be quoted, provided the quotation does not distort the context of the memorandum of interview. Complex terms should be explained since persons who are not familiar with technical terminology might read the report. **Impartiality** means reporting facts without bias. **Relevance** dictates including only matters appropriate to the examination. Irrelevant information confuses and complicates the written report and leaves the examiner open to criticism of his or her methodology. **Timeliness** dictates issuing the draft and the final reports in a timely manner so that they will accomplish their objective(s).

(xii) Written Report

In the absence of an established system of report writing, Wells recommends including five major sections: cover page, witness statements, cover letter, working papers, and index.[8] **The cover page** of a report typically includes all pertinent data gathered during the course of an examination. It includes file number, case description, perpetrator (employee) name, the lead investigator name, date of report, case status (pending, inactive, closed), report number, type of inquiry (civil, criminal, administrative), referrals, synopsis, financial data (all costs incurred, projected losses), final disposition, and predication (basis under which the investigation commenced to establish a reason for investigation).

> **DUE PROFESSIONAL CARE**
>
> The Institute of Internal Auditors Standard 1220—*Due Professional Care* requires that a written report be issued at the conclusion of the investigation phase. It should include all findings, conclusions, recommendations, and corrective action taken.

---

[8] Ibid.

The final report should include all relevant **witness statements**. Typically a **cover letter** to the requester of the investigation is included with the report. The purpose of the cover letter is to:

- Accompany the report.
- Set forth a succinct summary of witness testimony.
- Provide details on the location of potential witnesses.
- Set forth the apparent violation of law, if any, that the report addresses.

Summarized **working papers,** when necessary, should be enclosed as attachments to the report. If working papers are enclosed with the report, they should be so described in the cover letter of the report.

If there are a limited number of memorandums of interviews, the **index** may be omitted; otherwise, it is a good idea to provide an index. The index should be in chronological order rather than alphabetical, so the reader of the report can easily follow the development of the case.

(xiii) Privileged Reports

According to Wells, there is no privilege, per se, for investigative reports and notes, or for any fraud examination, forensic audit, or similar services. However, there are two exceptions.

1. If the examiner is conducting an investigation at the request of an attorney in anticipation of litigation, the report is considered in most courts as an attorney/client work product (i.e., privileged).
2. If a public authority, such as the police, federal agents, the courts or grand jury, or the like, is conducting the investigation, the report can be considered privileged.[9]

If the examination is being conducted under the authority of the lawyer-client-court privilege, each page of the report should be marked "Privileged and Confidential."

(xiv) Mistakes to Avoid in Writing Fraud Reports

Mistakes are costly, especially in fraud reports. Careless errors should be avoided and are inexcusable. Mistakes and errors can make a report useless. A brief description of areas to be careful about in writing fraud reports, based on Wells, follows.

- **Conclusions.** One of the most significant mistakes made by fraud examiners and auditors is the statement of conclusions in the written report. Under no circumstances should conclusions be made, as they may come back to haunt the examiner in litigation. The opposing counsel's main tactic is usually to try to impeach whatever testimony is given and to show that the examiner is biased. The conclusions of the investigations should be self-evident and able to stand alone. If not, the report has not been properly prepared.

- **Opinions.** Like conclusions, opinions have no place in the report. Under no circumstances should an opinion be written concerning the guilt or innocence of any person or party, as this is purview of the courts; it is up to the jury to decide guilt or innocence.

- **Informant and source information.** Under no circumstances whatsoever should the name of a confidential source or informant be disclosed in the report, nor anywhere else in writing. It is recommended that the source or informant be referred to by symbol number (e.g., S-1, I-1).[10]

---

[9] Ibid.
[10] Ibid.

3.4 Integrating Analytical Relationships to Detect Fraud

Topics such as the need to integrate analytical relationships, types of analytical procedures, and the need to prove illicit financial transactions in order to detect fraud are presented in this section.

(a) Major Impetus

The major impetus for the need to integrate analytical relationships in detecting fraud was the recommendation of the Treadway Commission that analytical procedures should be used more extensively to identify areas with a high risk of fraudulent financial reporting.

The results of a research study sponsored by the Institute of Management Accountants (IMA) titled *The Role of Analytical Procedures in Detecting Management Fraud* indicated that analytical procedures can be an effective supplement to an overall program to detect and prevent fraud.[11] However, the IMA study also says that a question remains unresolved as to exactly what types of errors (unintentional mistakes) or irregularities (fraudulent financial reporting or defalcation) are detected effectively through the use of analytical procedures.

The participants in the IMA study included internal auditors, controllers, and external auditors, and the findings showed that analytical procedures are not being used effectively to detect management fraud due to differing views concerning the participants' responsibility to use the procedures and lack of specific guidance and training in fraud detection methods. When fraud is detected, it is usually through other audit procedures, although commonly it is revealed by informal disclosures rather than detected.

TREADWAY COMMISSION: RECOMMENDATION ABOUT ANALYTICAL REVIEW PROCEDURES

Recommendation for the Independent Public Accountant

The Auditing Standards Board should establish standards that require independent public accountants to perform analytical review procedures in all audit engagements and which provide improved guidance on the appropriate use of these procedures.

The public accounting profession widely recognizes the usefulness of analytical review procedures, and auditors perform such procedures in many audits today. Analytical review procedures can encompass a broad range of audit steps. Usually involving comparisons of relationships among data, they range from relatively simple comparisons of ratios and trends to sophisticated statistical modeling techniques. Regardless of specific form, they focus on the overall reasonableness of a reported amount in relation to the surrounding circumstances.

The potential of analytical review procedures for detecting fraudulent financial reporting has not been fully realized. Unusual year-end transactions, deliberate manipulation of estimates or reserves, and misstatements of revenues and assets often introduce aberrations in otherwise predictable amounts, ratios, or trends that will stand out to a skeptical auditor. The Commission observed a number of cases where performing analytical review procedures would have increased the likelihood of the auditor's detecting fraudulent financial reporting.

Existing auditing standards allow, but do not require, analytical review procedures. The Commission recommends that auditing standards be revised to require the use of analytical review procedures on all audit engagements. The revised standards should require auditors to use analytical review procedures throughout the audit including at the planning phase.

Source: Report of the National Commission on Fraudulent Financial Reporting, October 1987, p. 52.

---

[11] Edward Blocher, *The Role of Analytical Procedures in Detecting Management Fraud* (Montvale, NJ: IMA 1993).

Further, the Commission recommends that the public accounting profession provide greater guidance on the application of analytical review procedures. Executive-level auditors should be required to participate in selecting the analytical review procedures to be performed and evaluating the results. Meaningful audit evidence from these procedures depends on the seasoned judgment of executive-level professionals, who should have a greater understanding than the nonexecutives of the company's industry as well as the environmental, institutional, and individual factors that increase the risk of fraudulent financial reporting.

The Treadway Commission defined fraudulent financial reporting as intentional or reckless conduct, whether by act or omission, that results in materially misleading financial statements. Fraudulent financial reporting can involve many factors and take many forms. It may entail gross and deliberate distortion of corporate records, such as inventory count tags, or falsified transactions, such as fictitious sales or orders. It may entail the misapplication of accounting principles. Company employees at any level may be involved, from top to middle management to lower-level personnel. If the conduct is intentional, or so reckless that it is the legal equivalent of intentional conduct, and results in fraudulent financial statements, it comes within the commission's operating definition of the term "fraudulent financial reporting."

Fraudulent financial reporting differs from other causes of materially misleading financial statements such as unintentional errors. The Commission also distinguished fraudulent financial reporting from other corporate improprieties, such as employee embezzlements, violation of environmental or product safety regulations, and tax fraud, which do not necessarily cause the financial statements to be materially inaccurate.

(b) Types of Analytical Procedures

The IMA research study investigated the use and effectiveness of analytical procedures in the possible link between different types of analytical procedures and the detection of management fraud.[12] The three principal types of analytical procedures are trend analysis, ratio analysis, and modeling techniques (see Exhibit 3.6).

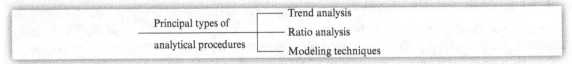

EXHIBIT 3.6 Principal Types of Analytical Procedures

Trend analysis examines the trend of the account balances as a basis for determining whether the current period data potentially are misstated (i.e., whether they depart significantly from the trend of the prior data). Trend analysis techniques vary from the simplest two-period comparisons to statistically based time-series models. Trend analysis is the most commonly employed analytical procedure.

Ratio analysis refers to procedures that involve the simultaneous analysis of two or more financial statement accounts. The value in using ratios is that often the relationship between the two (or more) accounts in the ratio is relatively stable over time, so that a variation in a ratio is a direct and clear signal of an underlying unusual condition: It can be a fraud, a simple error, or simply an unusual combination of environmental events. Ratio analysis is potentially a far more useful method for detecting error and fraud than trend analysis because ratio analysis uses the assumed stable relationship between accounts, while trend analysis looks at the behavior of only a single

---

[12] Ibid.

account. The behavior of a ratio is expected to be stable, while a single account balance can change for a number of reasons related to normal operating factors that do not reflect error or fraud.

A third type of analytical procedure, based on **modeling techniques**, can be more effective than either ratio analysis or trend analysis. The modeling approach is distinguished by the attempt to identify meaningful, stable relationships between financial and operating data.

A common type of modeling approach is the reasonableness test. This procedure involves the use of selected operating data, associated financial data, and external data to predict an account balance.

Reasonableness tests of the expense accounts are common. Two examples are: (1) the auditor or analyst estimates a value for utilities expense based on average temperature and hours of operation, and (2) payroll expense is estimated from operating data on the number of employees, the average pay rates, and the number of days of applicable operations.

The reasonableness test can be particularly effective because it links the financial data directly to relevant operating data. When, as is often the case, variations in operations are the principal cause for variations in the related accounts (especially the expense accounts), reasonableness tests provide a relatively precise means of detecting errors and frauds affecting these accounts; when a fraud is committed, it is likely that the reported financial and operating facts will not agree. That is, the perpetrator will find it difficult to disguise both the financial data and the related operating data.

For example, a reasonableness test of payroll expense can be an effective means of detecting fraud if there are phony employees or excess time is charged, because personnel records also must be manipulated fraudulently in the same pattern to prevent detection. Because these methods effectively model the relationships between the financial data and the operating transactions that are the basis for the recorded financial data, reasonableness tests are potentially the most effective of the analytical procedures.

(i) Use of Analytical Procedures in Practice

Analytical procedures are a substantive audit procedure and oriented to detecting rather than preventing management fraud. Participants in the IMA research study had a different perspective about their role in management fraud.

IMA RESEARCH FINDINGS

- Internal auditors saw their role as preventing fraud or investigating a fraud that had already been revealed. They tended not to use analytical procedures.

- External auditors saw their role as detecting fraud within the context of developing an opinion on the financial statements. They tended to use analytical procedures extensively.

- Controllers saw their role similar to internal auditors in both preventing and detecting fraud. They were found to be the best-trained and most extensive users of analytical procedures.

According to the IMA research study, internal auditors should take a more proactive role in the detection of management fraud.[13] The current guidance in IIA *Standards* provides necessary guidance in this area. The key point is that internal auditors should take greater responsibility in the detection of management fraud.

---

[13] Ibid.

(ii) Implications for Internal Auditors

A pervasive finding in the IMA research study is that there are significant differences among the three participant groups. Internal auditors took a prevention-oriented and control-based approach to fraud. External auditors and controllers tended to take a detection-oriented and analytical approach to fraud. The respective approaches were found to be effective.

In view of the Treadway Commission's recommendation for greater use of analytical procedures by external auditors, the IMA research study findings suggest

- Controllers, internal auditors, and others might employ analytical procedures more effectively as well.

- The analytical procedures now being done by the controllers to explain changes in account balances need to be redirected in part to looking for potential management fraud.

- As directed in IIA *Standards,* the control-based approach of the internal auditors needs to be augmented by analytical procedures to improve the overall effectiveness of the auditors in detecting fraud

(iii) More Examples of Analytical Procedures

Joseph Wells recommends financial statement analysis (ratio analysis, trend analysis, net worth method), statistical sampling, and flowcharting techniques to detect fraud[14] (see Exhibit 3.7). Each of these techniques is explained in text.

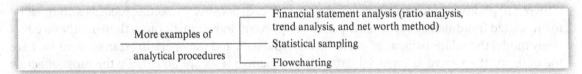

EXHIBIT 3.7 Examples of Analytical Procedures

(iv) Financial Statement Analysis

If financial statements are prepared with integrity, changes in account balances from one period to another should have logical explanations. Manipulating financial statements to hide missing assets or other problems sometimes hides frauds. Using ratios and trend analysis, fraud examiners or auditors can identify unusual relationships suggesting errors or irregularities. The discussion of financial statement analysis includes two elements: analysis of the balance sheet and income statement using ratios and trends and analysis of changes in cash balances from period to period using a statement of cash flows.

(A) Analyzing the Balance Sheet and Income Statement

The balance sheet and income statement can be analyzed three ways to reveal fraud and other types of errors.

1. Financial statement data from the current period can be compared with results from prior periods to look for unusual relationships.

---

[14] Ibid.

2. Financial statement data can be compared with similar information from other companies, or with industry statistics to look for unusual relationships. Because comparisons between similar companies are so valuable, industry-wide financial statements are distributed widely by several publishing companies.

3. Financial statements data can be associated with nonfinancial data to see if the numbers on the statements make sense. When searching for fraud, examiners should be inquisitive and challenge things that appear out of order or out of sequence. There should always be analytical relationships between representation in financial statements and physical goods or movements of assets.

KEY CONCEPTS TO REMEMBER: Plausible Relationships

- If sales are increasing, examiners would see:
    □ Buildup of inventory.
    □ Accounts receivable increasing.
    □ The cost of outbound freight increasing.
- If purchases are increasing, examiners would see the cost of inbound freight increasing.
- If inventory is increasing, examiners would see increases in the costs of warehousing, storage, and handling activities.
- If manufacturing volume is increasing, examiners would:
    □ Expect the per-unit cost of labor and material to be decreasing.
    □ See increases in the dollar amount of scrap sales and discounts on purchases.
- If profits are increasing, examiners would see increases in cash flows from operations.

Examining financial statement data to see if they make sense with respect to nonfinancial statement data is one of the best ways to detect fraud. Examiners who ask themselves if reported amounts are too small, too large, too early, too late, too often, and too rare or who look for things that are reported at odd times, by odd people, and using odd procedures are much more likely to detect fraud than those who view the financial statement without sufficient professional skepticism.

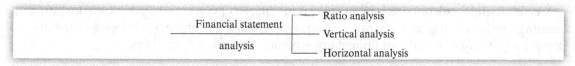

EXHIBIT 3.8 Financial Statement Analysis

Three techniques can be helpful in comparing financial statement data from period to period: ratio analysis, vertical analysis, and horizontal analysis (see Exhibit 3.8).

Ratio analysis involves computing key ratios to compare significant financial statement relationships from period to period. The most helpful ratios in detecting whether financial statements are reasonable include current ratio, quick ratio, and cash ratio.

> **SCOPE OF INTERNAL FRAUD**
>
> Much of internal fraud involves the theft of cash or inventory or the manipulation of receivables—major components of current assets.

These ratios only suggest potential problem areas. By themselves, they do not incriminate anyone or prove conclusively that fraud exists. When the current, quick, or cash ratios suggest a potential problem in either receivables or inventory, five additional ratios can be useful. These five ratios include:

1. Accounts receivable turnover
2. Days to collect receivables
3. Inventory turnover
4. Days to sell inventory
5. Days to convert inventory to cash

The examiner's responsibility is to use these ratios to identify significant, unexplained fluctuations and then determine if those fluctuations have logical explanations. If they do not, someone may be overstating or understating current assets or liabilities to conceal dishonest acts. Unexplained changes in the ratios can signal problems.

Vertical analysis is a technique for analyzing the relationships between line items on an income statement or balance sheet by expressing components as percentages. In vertical analysis of an income statement, net sales are assigned 100%. For a balance sheet, total assets are assigned 100%. All other items on the statements are then expressed as a percentage of these two numbers.

Horizontal analysis is a technique for analyzing the percentage change in individual income statements or balance sheet items from one year to the next. Horizontal analysis supplements ratio and vertical analysis and allows an examiner to determine whether any particular item has changed in an unusual way in relation to the change in net sales or total assets from one period to the next.

(B) Statement of Cash Flows

The statement of cash flows identifies sources and uses of cash during a period. The statement is extremely useful for identifying how an entity is funding its operation—whether from investments, earnings, or borrowing; and what it is doing with its money—whether it is being distributed to the principals, used to make additional investments, or used in operations.

Because cash is the asset most often misappropriated, the statement of cash flows is useful for identifying potential fraudulent acts.

The statement of cash flows can be very helpful when detecting fraud, especially for small businesses. In one fraud case, an accountant was stealing money instead of paying payroll taxes and other bills. The statement of cash flows highlighted the significant increase in payables. In another fraud case, cash receipts were stolen over a period of six years. The statement of cash flows showed significant increases in receivables. The discrepancies went unnoticed.

RED FLAGS TO WATCH IN FOR STATEMENT OF CASH FLOWS

- When sales are increasing, accounts receivable is decreasing.
- Inventory could be overstated to make net income look better.
- Cash could be stolen when accounts payable balance is increasing and delayed payment is occurring.
- Accounts payable balance increases when raw material inventory purchases are decreased.

The examiner or auditor should convert the traditional net income from operations reported in the income statement to obtain the net amount of cash from operation. This conversion helps in understanding the relationships of various components of cash flows.

FORMULA FOR DETERMINING NET AMOUNT OF CASH FROM OPERATIONS

Net income from operations	
plus	Depreciation
minus	Increase in accounts receivable
plus	Decrease in inventory
plus	Increase in accounts payable
equals	NET AMOUNT OF CASH FROM OPERATIONS

(v) Flowcharting Techniques.

Flowcharting techniques are useful in detecting fraud. The flowcharting method, despite its indirect approach, can prove money-laundering activities. Enterprises used to launder funds will generally have common ownership or other connections, usually under the control of the targets. Therefore, corporate and other business filings and records showing the principals in the suspect business should be obtained and patterns of ownership noted. Financial and bank records can then be subpoenaed to trace the flow of funds between the enterprises. Other charting techniques that were explained earlier include link network diagrams, time-flow diagrams, and matrices to show the relationships among persons, organizations, and events.

(c) Proving Illicit Financial Transactions.

This section describes various audit and examination techniques to identify and track the secret movement of funds in fraud, corruption, and money-laundering schemes. Joseph Wells collected many examples, of which a few are briefly presented here.[15] In all these cases, the illegal objectives may differ, but the means are the same, and the means are relatively limited in number.

- Company funds can be used to purchase expensive personal items as a form of embezzlement as well as for corrupt gifts.
- Money can be siphoned from a company account by cash or check for the benefit of the owners as well as to bribe another.

---

[15] Ibid.

■ Hidden interests can be taken in related transactions to earn fraudulent profits or can be given as a means of a payoff.

Typical schemes and devices that are utilized to conceal embezzlement, corrupt payments, and other illicit transfers fall into two categories: "on-book" and "off-book" schemes.

(i) On-Book and Off-Book Schemes

On-book schemes occur after the point of receipt of funds. Here illicit funds are drawn from the regular bank accounts and recorded on books, disguised as a legitimate trade payable, salary payment, or other business expense. Such payments are often made by regular business check, often payable to a sham business, through an intermediary. The payer may also cash the check, with the currency given to the recipient or used to create a slush fund for illegal purposes. Direct cash withdrawals are difficult to explain and deduce, if in significant amounts. Relatively small amounts of cash are often generated by fictitious charges to travel, entertainment, or miscellaneous accounts.

Off-book schemes refer to those schemes in which the funds used for illegal payments or transfers are not drawn from regular, known bank accounts. The payments do not appear anywhere on the books and records. In relatively small amounts, such payments may come directly from other ventures. In larger schemes, the funds are usually generated by unrecorded sales or by failing to record legitimate rebates from suppliers. Off-book schemes are often employed by businesses with significant cash sales (e.g., restaurants, bars, and retail shops).

The net worth method or comparative net worth analysis is used to prove illicit income circumstantially by showing that the suspect's assets or expenditures for a given period exceed that which can be accounted for from admitted sources of income. The technique is most useful when the recipient is taking currency or other payments that cannot be traced directly and when the amount of illicit income generally exceeds the recipient's legitimate income. Net worth evidence is also useful to corroborate testimony of hidden illicit payments.

(ii) Net Worth Computation Methods

According to Joseph Wells, there are two basic methods of net worth computation: the asset method and the expenditure method (sources and application of funds method)[16] (see Exhibit 3.9).

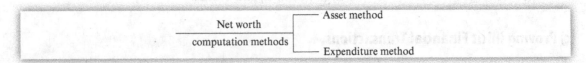

EXHIBIT 3.9 Net Worth Computation Methods

The **asset method** should be used when the suspect has invested illegal funds to accumulate wealth and acquire assets, causing net worth (value of assets over liabilities) to increase year to year. The **expenditure method** is best used when the suspect spends ill-gotten gains on lavish living, travel, and entertainment, which would not be reflected in an increase in net worth.

---

[16] Ibid.

ASSET METHOD FORMULA

	ASSETS
minus	liabilities
equals	NET WORTH
minus	prior year's net worth
equals	NET WORTH INCREASE
plus	living expenses
equals	INCOME (or EXPENDITURES)
minus	funds from known sources
equals	FUNDS FROM UNKNOWN SOURCES

Three steps should be undertaken when using the asset method.

1. All assets should be valued at cost, not fair market value. Subsequent appreciation or depreciation of assets is ignored.

2. The amount of funds available to the suspect from legitimate sources should be estimated or computed generously. Any doubts should be resolved in favor of the suspect.

3. Attempt to interview the suspect, in order to identify all alleged sources of funds and to negate defenses that he or she may raise later.

EXPENDITURES METHOD FORMULA

	EXPENDITURES (APPLICATION OF FUNDS)
minus	known sources of funds
equals	FUNDS FROM UNKNOWN SOURCES

Three steps should be undertaken for the expenditure method.

1. Establish the suspect's known expenditures for the relevant year. (Expenditures include the use or application of funds for any purpose, including deposits to bank accounts, purchase of major assets, travel and entertainment expenses, and payment of loan and credit card debts.)

2. Identify all sources of funds available to the suspect, including loans and gifts, as well as cash on hand from previous years.

3. The difference between the amount of the suspect's expenditures and known income is the amount attributed to unknown sources.

(iii) Money Laundering

An examiner tracing illicit funds may find an apparently legitimate source at the end of the trail: a prosperous cash retail business, a profitable real estate transaction, or offshore "loans" or investments. This is the realm of money laundering. Although money laundering is itself a crime (as a result of the Money Laundering Act of 1986), it is usually detected as a result of the investigation of the underlying offenses. Effective investigation measures include visual and electronic surveillance, sting and undercover operations.

Laundering schemes conducted through a front business are best proven through the cooperation of an insider, such as the business's accountant or tax preparer, or by infiltrating an agent.

Indirect methods of proving laundering activity include these two techniques:

1. **Ratio analysis and sampling techniques.** Overreporting revenues of a front business to launder funds may result in an imbalance of the normal ratio of costs to sales: Cost will appear unduly low compared to reported revenues. (This is why the ideal laundering operation has relatively low fixed costs against sales.) Surveillance of the suspect enterprise may provide additional evidence that revenues are being underreported, by showing low customer traffic. Surveillance may also permit sampling procedures wherein a count of the number of customers or sales during a given period is used to extrapolate total sales.

2. **Flowcharting technique.** A laundering operation may also be revealed by the flowcharting technique, which was presented earlier.

(iv) Federal Sentencing Guidelines for Organizational Defendants

Federal sentencing guidelines for organizational defendants became effective in November 1991. These guidelines provide judges with a compacted formula for sentencing business organizations for various white-collar crimes. Included are federal securities, employment and contract laws, as well as the crimes of mail and wire fraud, kickbacks and bribery, and money laundering.

These guidelines represent a unique carrot-and-stick approach calling for business organizations found guilty of crimes to face sanctions reaching potentially hundreds of millions of dollars (the stick). Organizations may be given offsetting credits against these penalties if they can demonstrate that: they exercised due diligence prior to the offense, the wrongdoing was investigated, and they cooperated with government investigators (the carrot).

An organization is well advised to be able to demonstrate, prior to the accusation of any offense, that it exercised due diligence in seeking to prevent and detect criminal conduct by its agents. Due diligence requires that the organization has taken, at a minimum, these seven steps.

1. Established compliance policies that define standards and procedures

2. Assigned specific high-level responsibility to ensure compliance with these standards and procedures

3. Used due care in not delegating substantial discretionary authority to individuals who could engage in illegal activities

4. Communicated standards and procedures to all employees (by requiring participation in training programs and disseminating publications)

5. Taken reasonable steps to achieve compliance with standards (by utilizing monitoring and auditing systems including a system for employees to report violations without fear of reprisal)

6. Consistently enforced standards through appropriate disciplinary mechanisms

7. Taken all reasonable steps to prevent future similar offenses

Internal auditors should play an active role in educating management about the importance of the federal sentencing guidelines and assist in the development of new or expanded programs to address their requirements.

3.5 Interrogation or Investigative Techniques

This section discusses topics such as interrogation techniques, including the verbal and nonverbal behavior, the role of interviewer and interrogator, the difference between interviewing and interrogation, and the difference between interview and investigation. In addition, investigative techniques, including processes and phases, team composition, target attacks such as objects and subjects, and search and seizure, are presented in this section.

(a) Interrogation Techniques

The objectives of fraud investigation are to determine who, why, and how. Possible approaches include:

- Testimonial evidence
- Documentary evidence
- Physical evidence (forensic analysis)
- Personal observation
- Theft act investigative methods, such as surveillance and covert operations and invigilation (close supervision of suspects)
- Concealment investigative methods, such as document examination, audits, computer searches, and physical asset counts
- Conversion investigative methods, such as public record searches and net worth analysis
- Inquiry investigative methods, such as interviewing and interrogating[17]

The latter approach is presented in detail.

(i) Interviewing and Interrogating in Fraud Investigations.
Auditors will encounter situations where they would be interviewing employees who were suspected of fraudulent activities. Handling a fraud situation is a very delicate matter with associated financial and legal risks. Knowing what questions to ask and how to ask them of suspects and knowing the difference between interviewing and interrogating would help auditors immensely from being exposed to legal and financial risks. These risks arise simply because of the auditors' lack of technical knowledge in the subject area.

Auditors meet many parties during the interviewing and interrogating process, including security staff, prosecutors, and other law enforcement officials. Auditors should clearly understand their own role and the role of others in this process.

During evidence collection activities, the investigative team interviews and interrogates many individuals. The interviewing and interrogation processes are quite different in terms of objectives, techniques, and timing. The goal of the interview is obtaining information about the incident. Here the intent is finding the answers to the five Ws: *who, what, when, where,* and *why.* Doing this requires talking to as many witnesses as possible. The goal of interrogation, however, is to establish enough evidence to consider the subject a suspect.

---

[17] W. Steve Albrecht, Gerald W. Wernz, and Timothy L. Williams, *Fraud: Bringing Light to the Dark Side of Business* (Burr Ridge, IL: Irwin Professional Publishing, 1995).

INTERVIEWING VERSUS INTERROGATION

- When gathering evidence, use the interview process: Individuals become witnesses.

- When an interviewee becomes a suspect, use the interrogation process: Witnesses become suspects.

Interrogation should be left to experienced investigators since they need to find a balance between the accused's privacy rights and their own job duties. Investigators must be soft-spoken with clear communications skills and must have incontrovertible facts. Making a false accusation that results in embarrassment or damage to the suspect can cost the organization significantly if the person wrongly accused decides to take legal action against the organization.

(ii) Interpretation of Behavior

Interviewers/interrogators should remember that extremes in a suspect's behavior often indicate deception.[18] At least, they should recognize that the stress of not telling the truth often causes changes in attitudes and verbal and nonverbal behavior. These changes should be compared with what is normal for the individual and the population in general. A profile of the truthful and untruthful suspect follows.

(iii) Verbal Behavior.

Truthful individuals are generally calm, relaxed, and cooperative while being interviewed. As suspects become more comfortable with the situation, they become more relaxed. Overall, truthful individuals are cordial, friendly, and relatively easy to handle.

The attitude displayed by untruthful suspects is usually impatience, in both word and action. They are tense and defensive while questioning, look at their watches, and suggest that they need to be somewhere else.

Truthful individuals generally respond to questions and make timely responses. Untruthful suspects are usually vague and stammering in their responses. There may be long pauses when speaking or answers that are too quick, too short, too long, or too elaborate. The guilty talk softly, mumble, and in many cases talk through their hand.

Guilty suspects often attempt to take an overly friendly, polite, or cooperative attitude toward the interviewers/interrogators. Guilty suspects use this tactic in an attempt to keep the interviewer as a friend rather than as an enemy. Guilty people hope this cooperative attitude will get them a break or even that they will be overlooked as a suspect. Excessive friendliness and politeness by a suspect should immediately alert the interviewer to the suspect's probable deception. This politeness often seems quite out of place.

VERBAL BEHAVIOR

The ultimate goal of verbal behavior is to elicit the truth from the reluctant suspect. The difficulty in assessing verbal behavior is that the words spoken to the interviewer may be exactly the same for both the truthful and the untruthful suspect. Only differences in the nonverbal behavior, tone of voice, loudness, and speed of delivery may differentiate truth from deception.

---

[18] David E. Zulawski and Douglas E. Wicklander, *Practical Aspects of Interview and Interrogation* (Boca Raton, FL: CRC Press, 1993).

A delay in response to an interviewer's question is a good indicator of a suspect's guilt. Innocent individuals rarely need to think about a response. They simply answer the question posed directly and promptly. The guilty, however, often pause or delay a response while they think. Inappropriate laughter by a suspect is an attempt to make the interviewer's question seem petty. The laughter can be used to cover the deceptive suspect's delay.

Truthful suspects respond directly and deny the allegation, saying, for example, "I did not steal any money." The guilty respond by denying specifically "I did not steal that $300." The qualified response is an indication of a deceptive individual.

Some guilty suspects will attempt to take the offensive using a surly, nasty, aggressive attitude toward interviewers. This attitude is designed to put interviewers on the defensive and cause them to back off from confronting suspects.

(iv) Nonverbal Behavior

Interviewers should remember that the entire body must be considered when observing nonverbal behavior. Also, both verbal and nonverbal behavior must be considered together.

- The guilty may perspire excessively, particularly on the trunk of the body. However, perspiration may not be a relevant clue if the suspect has engaged in strenuous activity or come from an extremely hot environment just prior to the meeting.

- The hands and the arms may provide the guilty with a barrier to protect the abdominal cavity and relieve the stress of sitting across from an interviewer/interrogator. The hands and the arms are used to perform created jobs or grooming gestures.

> **NONVERBAL BEHAVIOR**
>
> The interviewer should attempt to establish a behavioral norm for the suspect. Consideration should be given to the suspect's voice pattern, word choice, eye movement, attitude, and physical behavior.

- Scratching the nose, rubbing the brow, or adjusting the glasses could also be used as a ruse to cover the actual purpose of the hand movement.

- The drumming of fingers indicates a suspect's impatience. Clenched fists may show a suspect's frustration or a negative attitude toward the discussion or interviewer.

- Many guilty individuals begin to itch and scratch immediately after the introduction of a stressful topic.

- Suspects may use the thumbs to indicate a defensive or superior attitude. They will lean back in the chair, arms crossed and fingers tucked underneath the armpits with the thumbs extended upward.

- Crossed arms often indicate negative thoughts or displeasure with the conversation. They may also be used in situations where an individual feels uncertain or insecure. Individuals also cross their arms when they feel cold.

- Crossing the ankles or legs typically provides a defensive barrier against the interviewer. As a general rule, the more defensive an individual becomes, the higher the knee rise to protect the abdominal region.

- Truthful individuals generally have good eye contact with the interviewer. Often the deceptive individual's eyes will be cold and hostile. They have a flat look to them that does not allow the interviewer to look beneath the eye surface.

- In order to reduce the suspect's level of defensiveness, chairs should be positioned directly across from each other or slightly off to one side, which will lessen the confrontational feel of the meeting.

(v) Role of Interviewer/Interrogator

Interviewers blame denials only on the suspect's fear of consequences. Interviewers can also cause denials because of strategies or tactics employed during the interrogation. The suspect's perception of the interviewer and/or the interviewer's strategy often dictates whether the suspect will deny.

Interrogators who are overbearing, aggressive, or nonempathetic toward a suspect often increase the suspect's defensiveness, resulting in denial. When a suspect dislikes an interviewer, the dislike often turns into distrust and denial. Interrogators' attitudes should be that of mediators seeking the truth rather than that of dominant, authoritative figures. They should display professionalism.

When interviewers attempt to rush the suspect into a confession due to lack of time or other, the suspect may elect to deny simply because he or she believes the interviewers' hurried demeanor is a weakness to be exploited. By making denials and waiting interviewers out, the suspect believes that he or she can win the encounter.

The verbal and physical behavior displayed by interviewers/interrogators during the interrogation can also directly affect a suspect's decision to deny. If interviewers are perceived as unsure, inconsistent, or weak, the suspect will make a denial to test the interviewer's assertions.

If interviewers are uncertain of the case facts, misquote commonly known facts, or seem unprepared, suspects are encouraged to deny. The suspect's decision to deny is based on a belief that he or she has not been clearly identified with the case. The suspect is taking a chance that the interviewer's bumbling of the facts is directly related to the competency of the investigation. *Most suspects recognize that an incompetent investigation will be unlikely to result in their being proved guilty of the offense.*

Interrogators' word choices may cause denials, as might long pauses or silence. The use of silence by interviewers rarely enhances the likelihood of a confession. To the contrary, it allows the suspect an opportunity to think and assess other possibilities that might convince the interrogator of his or her innocence. In an interrogation, silence invites the suspect to join the conversation. Long pauses by the interrogator invite a denial from the suspect.

ROLE OF SILENCE IN INTERVIEWS AND INTERROGATIONS

- Silence is an effective strategy in an interview since it can be filled with more conversation. Remember that in an interview, the interviewee (suspect) does all the talking.

- Silence is not an effective strategy in an interrogation since the suspect can deny. Remember that in interrogation, the interviewer (auditor or investigator) does all the talking.

(vi) Interviewing versus Interrogation

An interview is a fact-gathering process that attempts to answer the six journalistic (investigative) questions: who, what, when, where, how, and why. The suspect who responds to questions posed by the interviewer dominates talking during the interview. During the interview, the interviewer may ask behavior-provoking questions to determine the suspect's truthfulness. The setting of an interview also tends to be much less formal than that of interrogation. In an interview, the interviewer often picks a time and location convenient for the person being interviewed. In the earliest stages of investigation, the interview is broad-based, with the interviewer attempting to give direction to the investigation.

An interview can turn into an investigation at any time. The change in the process from nonaccusatory to accusatory can be very direct or very subtle. In either case, the amount of talking done by the interviewee and suspect changes dramatically. During the interview process, the investigator has made the majority of questions broad and open-ended to elicit a narrative response from the suspect. To clarify specific points, the interviewer may have used closed-end questions. However, once the interviewer has elected to confront the suspect, the interviewer begins to do all the talking and offers face-saving rationalizations that minimize the seriousness of the suspect's involvement.

By contrast, an interrogation is designed to obtain information that might be incriminatory from a suspect who may be reluctant to give the information. The purpose of interrogation is to overcome the suspect's initial resistance and open a dialogue that will encourage the suspect to give information against his or her interests. An interrogator is still attempting to answer the six investigative questions (who, what, when, where, how, and why), but there are two basic differences between an interview and interrogation.

1. In interrogation, the suspect talks only when he or she is confessing.

2. The suspect resists telling the truth until he or she is convinced of the need to do otherwise.

Victims and witnesses typically are interviewed at a time and place convenient to them. If the interviewer/interrogator believes that the individual ultimately might be the suspect, an interrogation could follow. In such a case, the interviewer/interrogator should ask the suspect come to his or her office or at a location where a more formalized setting can be arranged. Regardless of whether the interviewer plans a nonaccusatory interview or an interrogation of a suspect, the interviewer's behavior should seem reasonable and fair.

There is never room for mistreatment of a witness or suspect by an interviewer. Yelling, screaming, or pounding fists on the table to obtain information from a reluctant witness have no place in either an interview or an interrogation.

> **INTERVIEW VERSUS INVESTIGATION**
>
> An interview is a noncustody and nonaccusatory situation. An investigation is quite the opposite.

In the interview, the interviewer should open the lines of communication so that the victim, witness, or suspect will begin to talk about the incident under investigation. It may be worthwhile to prepare specific written questions to ensure the accuracy of the way that they were asked. The key questions need to be camouflaged during the interview so that the interviewer does not highlight their importance. For example, when conducting a kickback investigation, an investigator may look at a buyer's phone records for investigative leads, but the interviewer does not request the buyer's phone number alone. To conceal the target of the investigation, the entire buying department's phone records may be requested. Although investigators may not be able to conceal the fact that they are looking at telephone records, at least they can conceal who they are looking at.

Rapport is needed both in normal interviewing and investigative situations. Rapport is more than just smiling. Even the most cooperative, agreeable witness can be turned off by an interviewer who fails to establish rapport. Interviewers who are too blunt and to the point, who attempt to obtain information without establishing rapport, are often faced with witness who are cold and uncooperative.

How is rapport established? The interviewer should attempt to establish rapport by finding some common ground or interest about which to speak to the individual. People tend to like people who have similar interests and personalities. The interrogator should avoid using words like "steal," "embezzle," or "fraud" when talking to the suspect. People who have a genuine smile are judged to be more honest and trustworthy than those who have cold, expressionless faces. *The kind of words used and the facial expressions displayed lead to good rapport.*

Words alone are not enough to build good rapport between the interviewer and the suspect. Interviewers should practice other techniques, such as mirroring. People who have a high level of rapport tend to mirror each other's behavior. **Mirroring** includes modeling the speech patterns, speed of delivery, breathing, posture, and gestures of the individual to whom the interviewer is speaking. This mirroring shows up as similar body positioning, physiology, tone of voice, and even choice of words used between the two parties. When interviewers mirror an individual's posture, gestures, and physiology, they can create within themselves the same emotions that the suspect is feeling.

TRUTH VERSUS UNTRUTH IN INTERVIEWS AND INTERROGATIONS

- Individuals who are telling the truth about the issue under investigation are more likely to give direct answers during the interview. In addition, they are often helpful and cooperative in their responses.

- Individuals who are not telling the truth are not as specific, direct, or helpful. In many cases, their responses are vague, too elaborate, short, or evasive.

AWARENESS OF COMMON LAW CAUSES OF ACTION

Employers or interviewers must be aware of three common law causes of action before conducting any interviews: false imprisonment; defamation; malicious prosecution, and assault and battery. Even though the employee has common law rights, the public or private employer has the right to investigate and to expect loyalty from the employee.

False imprisonment. This cause of action generally requires that an employee be detained without his or her consent or a legal justification to restrain the employee. A false imprisonment is a detention where no arrest warrant has been issued, or, if one has been issued, it is void. For an employee to prove a case of false imprisonment, he or she must prove that: (1) an arrest or forcible detention took place; (2) the arrest or imprisonment was caused by the company; (3) the detention was unlawful or made without a warrant; and (4) there was malice on the part of the company. An employer is entitled to interview an employee on company premises about violations of company policy without liability for false imprisonment. In a number of cases where false imprisonment was found to have occurred, the employee was physically restrained from leaving.

Defamation. After an incident of misconduct, suspects often allege defamation of character. The defamation of character may occur in the form of a slander or libelous statement. **Slander** is a false statement that was not written down but was spoken to one or more individuals. **Libel** is an untrue statement that was written down and was communicated to others.

In order for employees to establish that they have suffered a defamation of character, they must prove four things.

1. They must prove that particular words were actually spoken, including proving both the time and place that the activity took place.
2. They must also prove that these words were spoken or published to third persons.
3. They must show that the words written or spoken were actually false.
4. They must also show other facts that prove that the words are libelous or slanderous. This would include that there was malice on the part of the company or investigator and that the libel or slander was not privileged in any way.

An employer has a qualified privilege to communicate allegations during an investigation. However, this qualified privilege is lost if false communication were made out of spite or malice with knowledge that the statements were, in fact, false. In addition, these knowingly false statements must have been communicated to an excessive number of people. During the course of investigative interviews, interviewers should avoid repeating any information or allegations of which they are uncertain to third parties. *As a practical matter, the interview process is one of gathering information rather than giving information to the interviewee.*

An investigator should limit communicating allegations to those who have a need to know as part of the investigation or decision-making process relating to the consequences of the suspect's actions. An investigator can establish the qualified privilege by noting on investigative reports that the document is privileged for counsel. This establishes an attorney–client privilege and protects many documents during an investigation.

The interviewer/interrogator should understand that a qualified privilege exists to express oral charges to superiors, police, prosecutors, or other persons having a need to know within the company. Care should be taken that the report of what happened during the investigation, interview, or interrogation is fair and that statements made are fair and done without malice to the suspect.

1. **Malicious prosecution.** Companies investigating employee theft, illegal drug use, or other illegal activities within a company must decide whether it is in their best interest to contact a law enforcement agency. Certain businesses, such as financial institutions, are required to report thefts to the Federal Bureau of Investigation. Illegal activities, such as the theft of firearms or controlled substances, are also closely monitored by federal and state agencies. Since most companies do not have a requirement to notify public law enforcement of internal problems, they generally do not do so because of the cost of prosecution and the difficulty of proving circumstantial cases. A corporation's bonding company may also need to be made aware of loss to keep the insurance contract in force.

Once the company has decided to prosecute an employee, the company can be opening the door to potential liability for an allegation of malicious prosecution and false arrest. For an employee to establish a malicious prosecution claim against the company, the employee must prove that (1) the employer instituted or continued a criminal proceeding, (2) the proceeding was terminated in the employee's favor, (3) no probable cause existed for initiating a proceeding, and (4) the employer's motive in initiating the proceeding was malice or some purpose other than bringing the employee to justice.

Malice on the part of the company or an employer may be shown through personal animosity between the person making the accusation and the accused employee. It can also be inferred from the lack of a complete investigation on the part of the company. Furthermore, the company may show the element of malice if it conveys facts that are untrue or withholds facts that might mitigate the conclusion reached by police investigators.

(continued)

Private-sector investigators can limit their and the company's potential liability for a malicious prosecution allegation by allowing the prosecution or police officer to make the decision to prosecute.

Assault and battery. Although assault and battery are related, they are fundamentally different. Battery is bodily contact that either causes harm or is offensive to a reasonable person's sense of dignity; assault is words or actions that place the employee in fear of receiving a battery. Actual physical contact is not an element of assault; violence, either threatened or offered, is required. An assault can occur when the person uses threatening words or gestures and has the ability to commit the battery.

Source: David E. Zulawski and Douglas E. Wicklander, *Practical Aspects of Interview and Interrogation* (Boca Raton, FL: CRC Press, 1993).

(b) Investigative Techniques

(i) Investigative Process

The investigative process for a computer fraud incident can be divided into three phases.

> **Phase 1: Initiating the investigation.** This phase includes securing the crime scene, collecting evidence, developing incident hypothesis, and investigating alternative explanations.
>
> **Phase 2: Analyzing the incident.** This phase covers analysis of the evidence collected in the first phase along with alternative explanations to determine whether a crime has occurred.
>
> **Phase 3: Analyzing the evidence.** This phase involves preparing to present the incident with findings and recommendations to management or law enforcement authorities.

The *order* of investigation is:

1. Gather facts.
2. Interview witnesses.
3. Develop incident hypothesis.
4. Test the hypothesis.
5. Report to management and others.

(ii) Team Composition

Investigating a fraud or computer-related crime requires a team approach with many participants, where the talent and skills of each participant are required. Each participant has a specific task to complete, consistent with his or her skills and experience. These participants (specialists) can include representatives from corporate investigations, law enforcement officials, system auditors, corporate counsel, consultants, information technology (IT) security management, and functional user management. The objectives of the system auditor and the IT security management are similar during a computer crime investigation. The duties of the manager of the crime team are clear while the duties of team participants may not be clear due to overlapping functions and responsibilities.

(iii) Target

A victim organization should practice a delay technique when its computer system is attacked. If a system perpetrator can be delayed longer while attacking, investigative authorities can trace the perpetrator's origins and location.

It is important for the investigative team to know what the intruder is targeting for an attack. Although there are many targets, Peter Stephenson describes these targets as part of denial-of-service attacks.

- **Hard disks.** An attacker can fill up the hard disk to overload it in order to make it inoperable.

- **Bandwidth.** An attacker can fill up the bandwidth so that the network becomes useless.

- **Caches.** An attacker can block the cache or bypass it for further use.

- **Swap space.** An attacker can fill up the swap space so that it cannot be used.

- **Random access memory (RAM).** An attacker can allocate a large amount of RAM. Some system resources, such as mail servers, will become sensitive to too much RAM because they do not need much RAM to begin with. Users can notice that RAM is missing in a personal computer (PC) during a system BIOS boot-up.

- **Kernel tables.** Attackers try to overflow the kernel tables, causing serious problems on the system. Systems with write-through caches and small write buffers are sensitive to this type of attack.[19]

(iv) Objects/Subjects

An investigation revolves around two things: objects and subjects. Examples of **objects** include computers, networks, switches, processes, data, and programs. **Subjects** include employees (former and current) and outsiders (hackers, intruders, adversaries, crackers, virus writers, cloners, and phrackers).

(v) Search and Seizure

Ownership, occupancy, and possession are three influencing factors in a crime warrant search. A search warrant or court order is necessary to use the trap-and-trace technique, which involves the telephone company finding the intruder. Traps can be placed on in-circuit emulators, network protocol analyzers, and hardware analyzers.

If computer equipment involved in a computer crime is not covered by a search warrant, the investigator should leave it alone until a warrant can be obtained. A court order is also required to access the evidence and to conduct surveillance techniques. To get a court-ordered search, one has to show that there is probable cause to believe that the suspect is committing an offense and that normal procedures have failed or are unlikely to work or are dangerous to health and life. An independent judge must issue the court order, not a police officer, security investigator, law enforcement agent, or prosecutor.

3.6 Forensic Auditing

Auditing for fraud is called forensic auditing. The purpose of forensic examination (auditing) is to establish whether a fraud has occurred. One of the major purposes of financial auditing is to attest the financial statements of an organization. Unlike financial auditing, forensic auditing has no generally accepted auditing standards. In fact, most self-proclaimed forensic auditors are certified public accountants or internal auditors specializing in fraud detection.

---

[19] Peter Stephenson, *Investigating Computer-Related Crime* (Boca Raton, FL: CRC Press, Florida, 2000).

According to Joseph Wells, forensic auditing can be divided into four phases: (1) problem recognition and planning, (2) evidence collection, (3) evidence evaluation, and (4) communication of results[20] (see Exhibit 3.10).

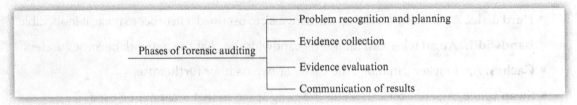

EXHIBIT 3.10 Phases of Forensic Auditing

(a) Phase 1: Problem Recognition and Planning

In the problem recognition and planning phase, the pertinent facts and circumstances regarding fraud are gathered. Here fraud examiners learn as much about the potential fraud as possible, without actually gathering evidence. There must be some indication of fraud for an examiner to become involved. The suspected fraud may have become known because of an anonymous tip, a fraud symptom such as a questionable document, suspicion on the part of an employee, or an unusual event or relationship.

The important point is that there must be a legitimate reason to believe that fraud exists. Background checks into the suspects, the environment, and other conditions are conducted. Possible explanations for the potential problem are explored. The problem could be a mistake or unintentional error rather than a fraud. At this stage, no one is convicted or incriminated. Indeed, evidence has not yet been gathered.

(b) Phase 2: Evidence Collection

The purpose of the evidence collection phase is twofold: to determine whether (1) the initial evidence of suspected fraud is misleading, and (2) if further action is recommended to gather sufficient, competent, and relevant evidence to resolve the fraud.

Several rules must be remembered in the evidence-gathering stage. To be effective in detecting fraud, the auditor or the examiner must attempt to identify the three elements of fraud—act, concealment, and conversion—and work on the easiest element first. Most frauds can be resolved by concentrating on the most obvious solutions and the weakest point in the fraud. If someone has an opportunity to commit fraud and/or appears suspicious, he or she probably is the perpetrator.

Another method of obtaining evidence is to search for fraud opportunities by using vulnerability charts and internal control critical combination charts. Fraud cannot occur unless there is an opportunity. The greater or more accessible the opportunity, the more often it is likely to be exploited. Vulnerability charts and critical combinations of controls help examiners arrange risks in the order of their probabilities.

TIMELY RESOLUTION OF A FRAUD

In determining when the examination will take place, it should always be remembered that delaying an investigation can lead to destroyed or lost evidence. Early resolution of a fraud case protects both the victim and the perpetrator.

---

[20] Wells, *Fraud Examination*.

These charts involve correlating stolen assets with potential thieves, possible methods of fraud, effectiveness of controls around the fraud, possible concealment courses, and possibilities of conversion. These charts are objective ways of focusing on the most likely fraud perpetrators. Document examination is another technique to uncover concealment efforts.

Sometimes the gathering of evidence involves using employee searches. This detection technique involves examining employees' desks, lockers, lunchboxes, and other personal effects. When searching, it is important not to violate personal rights. If a search is conducted in an improper way, it can lead to allegations of invasion of privacy, false imprisonment, defamation of character, or assault and/or battery against the examiner. Evidence can be declared inadmissible if obtained illegally.

A seldom-used but powerful method of obtaining evidence is invigilation. Invigilation is the close supervision of suspects during an examination period. It involves imposing such strict temporary controls that during the period of supervision, fraud is almost impossible to commit. Invigilation requires top management support, as it is expensive and time consuming. It should be applicable only in high-risk areas. Invigilation has been successfully used to catch fraud committed by suppliers, night watchmen, and warehouse employees.

(c) Phases 3 and 4: Evidence Evaluation and Communication of Results

After evidence for fraud is properly evaluated, the auditor or the examiner needs to communicate the results of the work to the interested parties. The written report is the only evidence of the work performed and is the best vehicle to communicate results of the examination work. Fraud cases frequently are won or lost on the strength of the report.

(d) Software Forensics

(i) Definition

The term "software forensics" means "using computer hardware and software to gather and analyze evidence." Use of sophisticated software forensics may identify authorship of various code modules. By routinely analyzing modules on protected systems, substitution of valid software by intruders can be detected. This esoteric approach theoretically offers protection against attacks that would not be detected by network perimeter defenses, such as those that use covert channels, or attacks by internal users where those users are knowledgeable and sophisticated enough to circumvent normal host security. The possible benefit of this method must be balanced against the normally low probability of such an attack and the complexity of the defense as well as its limits in detecting software modification, such as introducing Trojan horse programs.

Examples of forensic tools include virus detection software, audit software, password-cracking programs, disk imaging software, auditing tools, operating system file utility programs, file zip and unzip utility programs, cable testers, line monitors, alcohol cleaning kits, and antistatic sealing tapes.

In a computer crime—for that matter, in any crime—successful prosecution depends heavily on presenting good evidence to the court. Computer forensics is used to provide that good evidence. Computer forensics is the art of retrieving computer data in such a way that will make it admissible in court. Computer forensics can be used to convict a computer criminal.

SAFEGUARDS TO PROTECT EVIDENCE

- Regular backups
- Offsite storage of backups
- Transaction logging
- Data storage on a backup tape/CD-ROM, USB flash drives, and cloud storage
- Chain-of-custody rules

The victim organization should be able to know who used a computer system and why, trace the criminal's activity through transaction logs, and protect the evidence. From a court's viewpoint, the evidence needs to be: (1) understandable to a judge and jury, (2) credible, and (3) defensible. This requires the security manager to think like lawyers, police officers, and criminals.

(ii) Guidelines to a Successful Computer Forensics

This list provides guidelines to a successful computer forensics.

- If you suspect that a computer system has been used in a crime, cut off its links to the network immediately.
- Leave any evidence untouched. This requires freezing or taking a snapshot of the computer records and data.
- Don't create a "reasonable doubt" situation to a judge or jury.
- Prove when each transaction has occurred with time and date stamps.
- Protect the evidential matter (e.g., programs, data, and hardware) in such a way that it will not be modified, tainted, or fabricated. This is very important to the court.
- Store that evidential matter (e.g., data and programs) in an immutable form (e.g., backup tape or CD-ROM) so that it is defensible in a court; and easy to handle, present, and protect.

(iii) Use of Hash Algorithms in Computer Forensics

The U.S. National Institute of Standards and Technology has developed a national software reference library (NSRL) that includes known program executable files, library files, word processors, network browsers, accounting packages, compressed files used to install applications, operating system files, and the like. On a specific computer, these files can make up from 25% to 95% of the total number of files. Reviewing these files for evidence can take hundreds of staff hours. In most cases, these files do not contain evidence. Without some automated process, an investigator must review each file manually to determine whether it can be used in the evidence.

The idea is to collect as many different examples, versions, and updates of software as possible in order to generate file signatures for as many known files as possible. Each file within a package is "fingerprinted" by passing the file through a program that computes a hash code. The code is computed in such as a way that if one bit in the file is changed, a completely different hash code is produced. The primary hash value used here is the secure hash algorithm (SHA-1). Several other standard hash values also are computed for each file. These include message digest 4 (MD4), message digest 5 (MD5), and a 32-bit cyclic redundancy checksum (CRC32).

When a computer hard disk, CD, or other storage medium becomes part of an investigation, the files stored on it can be "fingerprinted" using SHA-1, MD4, MD5, or CRC32. These fingerprints can be compared to the known file fingerprints in the NSRL's reference data set (RDS) database. Those files that have matching hash values can be discarded from the investigation without further examination; those that do not match the RDS database should be examined further. If expected files do not show up in the known file list, they may be missing. This may indicate that files were deleted to cover up illegal activity and may prompt the investigator to pursue other means of investigating the file system.

The major benefit of this approach is savings in investigator's time because he or she does not have to review all the files on a computer involved in a computer crime. Only the files that changed the hash value need to be looked at.

3.7 Use of Computers in Analyzing Data for Fraud and Crime

Topics covered in this section include collection and preservation of computer evidence, chain of computer evidence, and computer fraud and crime examples.

(a) Collection and Preservation of Computer Evidence

(i) Guidelines for the Care and Handling of Computer Evidence

More often than not, investigation of computer-related crimes involves highly technical matters, making it imperative during a search that appropriate steps are taken to ensure both proper handling and preservation of evidence. There are seven recognized considerations involved in the care and handling of evidence:

1. Discovery and recognition

2. Protection

3. Recording

4. Collection

5. Identification

6. Preservation

7. Transportation

(A) Discovery and Recognition   The investigator's capability to discover and to recognize the potential source of evidence is vital. When a computer is involved, the evidence is probably not apparent or visible. Nevertheless, the investigator must recognize that computer storage devices are nothing more than electronic or magnetic file cabinets and should be searched if it would normally be reasonable to search a file cabinet.

(B) Protection   The physical condition of evidence collected and seized is a major concern. Care should be taken to protect the area where evidence is located. Documents should be handled

so as not to destroy latent prints or identifying characteristics. Computer-related evidence is sensitive to heat and humidity and should not be stored in the backseat or trunk of a car without special precautions.

(C) Recording The alleged crime scene should be properly recorded. The use of a video camera to videotape computer equipment, workstations, and so on, and related written documentation at the crime scene is highly encouraged. Examiners should remember to photograph the rear side of the computer (particularly the cable connections).

(D) Collection Collecting computer-related evidence is somewhat different from collecting other forms of evidence. When collecting evidence, examiners should take these precautions:

- Go after original books, records, magnetic storage media, or printouts where possible.

- Be aware of degaussing equipment. A degausser is an electronic appliance that creates a strong magnetic field used to effectively erase a magnetic tape or disk. When collecting this type of evidence, ensure that any degaussing equipment is secured or rendered inoperative.

- Documents and paper should be handled with cloth gloves, placed in an evidence container, and sealed.

- It is vital to seize all storage media, even ones that purportedly have been erased. Technical personnel may be able to capture data thought to have been erased or determine that erasures never occurred. ("Delete" commands do not actually erase disk sectors but merely make them available to magnetically write new information over existing information).

CARE AND HANDLING OF COMPUTER EVIDENCE

Considerations involved in the care and handling of computer evidence include discovery and recognition, protection, recording, collection, identification, preservation, and transportation.

(E) Identification It is usually more difficult to identify computer evidence than other forms of evidence; special knowledge of the item being marked is required. A list of things to look for during the gathering of computer evidence follows.

- Information on the evidence tag should include the hardware identification and operating system used to produce the tapes, disks, printouts, and so on.

- Do not write on a magnetic disk surface.

- USB drives should be marked only with a felt-tip pen or a label that has been filled out, then attached.

- Printouts should be marked with permanent marking pens.

(F) Preservation Computer evidence can be very volatile. For example, turning the computer's power off prematurely can cause a loss of evidence. A list of ways to preserve computer evidence follows.

- Remove evidence as soon as possible to prevent tampering. Tapes and disks can be erased or damaged quickly and easily.

- Write-protect magnetic media as soon as possible to prevent deliberate or inadvertent alteration of evidence.

- Store magnetic media in a proper temperature (40°–90°F) and humidity (20%–80%) in a dust-free environment. Tobacco smoke is also damaging. Avoid placing the media near strong magnetic fields (e.g., telephones, radio transmitters, photocopiers, or degaussers).

(G) Transportation Particular care should be taken in the handling of computer evidence while in transit. A list of things to do during transportation of computer evidence follows.

- Transport magnetic media at the proper temperature and humidity.

- Write-protect all magnetic media and label disks and USB drives.

- Label the wires connecting various devices at both ends to aid in system reassembly at a later time.

- Photograph the labeled equipment and wires before disconnecting.

- Disassemble, tag, and inventory the equipment.

- Carefully pack seized devices in suitable containers for transport.

- Transport magnetic media in dust-free, climate-controlled environments. Temperature extremes may render magnetically stored evidence unreadable, and various types of contamination can damage electronic equipment.

- Do not take magnetic media through metal detectors, conveyor belts, or X-ray machines. This equipment generates strong magnetic fields that could destroy computer evidence.

(ii) Guidelines for the Preservation and Submission of Computer Evidence

These guidelines are applicable to preservation and submission of computer evidence, specifically to hardware, magnetic media, and documentation.

I. Hardware

A. PC/central processing output (CPU)

1. Determine if the system has an internal hard drive. If possible, secure hard drive read/write heads with the appropriate software command. Do not remove the internal hard drive from the computer.

2. Label cables and ports.

3. Initial and date PC as required by the department's chain-of-custody procedures.

4. Wrap in plastic, and box for shipment to the laboratory.

B. Monitor and keyboard

1. Label cables.

2. Initial and date the monitor and keyboard as required by the department's chain-of-custody procedures.

3. Wrap in plastic, and box for shipment to the laboratory.

C. External/removable hard drives, external USB drives, external tape / hard drives, and printers/plotters

    1. Secure the hard drive read/write heads, if possible. Some are secured by software commands, and others are secured automatically.

    2. Remove USB drives from drive(s). Secure the disks, if possible.

    3. Note and record the switch setting for the external tape drive.

    4. Note and record the switch settings for printers and plotters.

    5. Initial and date each item as required by the department's chain-of-custody procedures.

    6. Wrap each item in plastic, and box for shipment to the laboratory.

D. Modems/acoustic couplers, and cables

    1. Disconnect the modem or acoustic coupler from the telephone.

    2. Label both ends of each cable, describing the connection to the PC, printer, and so on.

    3. Label all ports.

    4. Initial and date each item as required by the department's chain-of-custody procedures.

    5. Wrap each item in plastic, and box for shipment to the laboratory.

II. Magnetic media
A. Magnetic tapes and disks

    1. Keep them away from magnetic fields.

    2. Initial and date using felt-tip pen as required by the department's chain-of-custody procedures.

    3. Place them in appropriate evidence containers. Do not use plastic envelopes because of the risk of static electric discharge.

    4. Label the outside of shipment container "DO NOT X-RAY" to warn that evidence should be kept away from magnetic fields, and ship to the laboratory.

III. Documentation
A. Manuals/handwritten notes, printouts/listings

    1. Handle with gloves to preserve for latent fingerprint examination.

    2. Initial and date all loose sheets, note pads, manuals, and other paper documents as required by the department's chain-of-custody procedures.

    3. Place in appropriate evidence container.

    4. Ship to the laboratory.

(iii) Guidelines for the Examination of Computer Evidence
Guidelines for examination of computer evidence, specifically for receipt of evidence, examination of evidence, and reporting results follow.

I. Receipt of evidence

A. Log evidence into appropriate evidence control system and assign to an examiner.

    1. Record date and time received by some unique numbering system.

    2. Identify the examiner.

    3. Prepare documentation for chain of custody from evidence control to the examiner.

B. Transfer evidence to the examiner.

    1. Determine if other expert analyses, such as accounting and latent fingerprint examination, is necessary.

    2. Prepare chain-of-custody documentation for other experts as necessary for complete examination.

    3. Determine that all pieces of equipment listed as having been submitted are actually present.

    4. Mark and initial each piece of evidence as required by the laboratory system and prepare working papers for notes.

II. Examination of evidence

A. Determine if the submitted system is operational.

    1. Review submitting communication to determine if the system was operational at the time of seizure.

    2. Take logical steps to render the system operational.

B. USB drives and hard disk systems.

    1. Write-protect all disks/drives.

    2. Write-protect the hard disk using appropriate software.

    3. Identify the computer to be used for examination.

    4. Convert the operating system if necessary.

    5. Create directory/subdirectory listings.

    6. Check for hidden and deleted files using appropriate commercial or custom software.

    7. Display and print files.

III. Reporting results

A. Prepare reports, documenting what was done and the results.

B. Send printouts and report to the victim organization or subject matter expert for additional analysis.

C. Repack the computer and all disks.

D. Return the evidence to victim organization.

(iv) Using a Computer as an Investigative Tool

Computers can be used to collect and compile large amounts of data and provide statistics, reports, and graphs to assist the investigator in analysis and decision making. In deciding whether to employ computer resources to assist in an investigation, these requirement analysis factors should be carefully considered.

- Is automation necessary or appropriate?
- What output is desired?
- What software or hardware is available?
- What data elements are required based on output requirements?
- Who will do the data entry, how many records will have to be entered, how long will it take to enter all of the data, and what are the data characteristics (alpha, numeric, field size)?
- If there are calculated fields in the report, can the software create those fields?
- Who needs the report (agent or prosecutor)?
- Will the software or the hardware handle the number of records required?
- What is the security classification of the data to be entered?
- How much time is there for program development, and will an existing investigative tool suffice?
- Will the design of input/output screen layouts, report formats, sequence-of-data presentation, design of menus to drive the system, and design of a backup system is available?
- Will the development of a user's guide be available and training of prospective system users be provided?

(b) Chain of Computer Evidence

This section addresses various aspects of properly maintaining computer-related evidence. These procedures are important in avoiding problems of proof caused by improper care and handling of such evidence.

Maintaining evidence in the form of computer storage media presents problems that differ from handling other types of evidence. Because they are subject to erasure and easily damaged, magnetic or electronic storage devices must be carefully guarded and kept under controlled temperature and humidity to avoid deterioration.

In investigating and prosecuting a case involving such evidence, one of the early steps a prosecutor should take is to retain an appropriate computer expert or technical assistance. This can be critical in avoiding problems resulting from inept maintenance procedures or inadvertent loss of key information.

Sometimes the contents of dozens or even hundreds of computer tapes or disks must be copied to allow the business to continue operating while the case is being prosecuted. This must be done under the close supervision of an expert who can not only ensure that it is done right but also determine the least costly procedure.

Initials of the seizing agent and the date should be scratched on each storage media container, and a chain-of-custody sheet or log should be made for every container. The log should show, at a minimum, the date, place, and specific location of the seizure and the name of the agent making the seizure.

The agents investigating the case are likely to have considerable expertise in maintaining computer evidence, gained from training and experience. Their advice and assistance can be invaluable to the prosecutor in minimizing problems of proof inherent in computer-related crimes.

(c) Computer Fraud and Crime Examples

(i) Military and Intelligence Attacks

Espionage can take three forms: industrial espionage, economic espionage, and foreign government espionage. **Industrial espionage** is the act of gathering proprietary data from private companies or the government for the purpose of aiding another company. Industrial espionage can be perpetrated either by companies seeking to improve their competitive advantage or by governments seeking to aid their domestic industries. The three most damaging types of industrial espionage include pricing data, manufacturing process information, and product development/specification information (trade secrets).

Foreign industrial espionage carried out by a government is often referred to as **economic espionage**. Information related to technology, information on commodities, interest rates, and contract data are the targets of economic espionage. In addition to possible economic espionage, **foreign intelligence services** may target unclassified systems to further their intelligence acts. Some unclassified information that may be of interest includes: travel plans of senior officials; civil defense and emergency preparedness; satellite data; personnel and payroll data; and law enforcement, investigative, and security files. Countermeasures against intelligence attacks include implementing user awareness, education, and training programs.

Wiretapping (electronic eavesdropping) is listening in on another's communication during transmission of messages and information. It also occurs when data flowing over cables is intercepted. Countermeasures include: locking up the cable closet, using traffic padding technique to confuse the eavesdropper, and implementing voice encryption techniques with Secure Sockets Layer protocol.

Data leakage is removal of data from a computer system by covert means. It might be possible to examine computer operating system usage journals to determine if and when data files may have been accessed. Data leakage attacks might be conducted through the use of Trojan horse, logic bomb, or scavenging methods. Countermeasures include encryption, access controls, and cryptographic techniques.

(ii) Business Attacks

Employee sabotage is the most common business attack. The number of incidents of employee sabotage is much smaller than instances of employee theft, but the cost of such incidents can be quite high. Common examples of computer-related employee sabotage include: destroying hardware or facilities, planting logic bombs that destroy programs or data, "crashing" computer systems, and entering data incorrectly, deleting data, or changing data (data diddling).

Data diddling involves changing data before or during input to computers or during output from a computer system. The changes can be done by anyone associated with or having access to the process of creating, recording, transporting, encoding, examining, checking, converting, and transforming data that ultimately enter a computer. Examples include: forging or counterfeiting documents; exchanging valid computer magnetic media with prepared replacements; source document entry violations; and neutralizing, bypassing, or avoiding manual controls. *Manipulating input is the most common method of perpetrating fraud using a computer. Data diddling attacks can be prevented with access controls, program change controls, and integrity checking software.*

SuperZapping, an example of a business attack, involves unauthorized use of a computer utility program to modify, destroy, copy, disclose, insert, use, or deny use of data stored in a computer system or computer media. This powerful utility program bypasses operating system security controls and even the access control security software controls. By definition, superZapping is not a computer crime by itself. *A reliable way to detect superZapping work is by comparing current data files with previous data files.*

Simply **writing computer virus programs** is not a criminal activity. However, using, releasing, and spreading a virus with bad intentions of destroying computer resources are the basis for criminal activity.

(iii) Financial Attacks

The salami technique of financial attacks involves theft of small amounts of assets (primarily money) from a number of sources. For example, the perpetrator steals a few cents from each customer account on a large number of bank accounts, theft that is unnoticed by most customers. However, the account totals will be kept in balance with double-entry record-keeping system. The salami technique can also be affected by round-down fractions of money, which can be moved into the perpetrator's bank account.

Collecting customers' credit card information through Web sites and unauthorized access to **wire transfer fund** accounts in a financial institution are other examples of financial attacks. Transfer of money between two parties without a financial institution's involvement is another example of a financial attack.

Toll fraud through telephone cloning is another example of a financial attack; this type of fraud costs telephone companies significant amounts of money.

(iv) Terrorist Attacks

Terrorists can hold data hostage, or they can demand ransom money for data and programs stolen.

(v) Grudge Attacks

Employees who were fired may have a grudge against the organization where they have worked. The general public may have a grudge against an organization where they do not like what the organization is doing or has done.

(vi) "Fun" Attacks

People can target organizations for fun and challenge to get publicity and to satisfy their intellectual curiosity. Their goal is not to make money.

RELATED CONCEPTS IN COMPUTER CRIME

- A person must have a motive, the opportunity, and the means to commit a crime.

- Computer crime is possible when controls are predictable and avoidable (bypassable).

- System predictability (i.e., users and attackers know how the system reacts to a given condition) is a key to a successful computer crime.

- Computer crime can be minimized with dynamic controls and variable features.

- White-collar crimes tend to be situation oriented, meaning that a change in a person's lifestyle and job situations can make the person commit crime.

- Unknown misbehavior of unknown perpetrators is the major reason for the inability to calculate the risk resulting from computer crime.

3.8 Sample Practice Questions

As mentioned in the Preface of this book, a small batch of sample practice questions is included here to show the flavor of questions and to create a quiz-like environment. The answers and explanations for these questions are shown in a separate section at the end of this book just before the Glossary. If there is a need to practice more questions to obtain a greater confidence, refer to the section "CIA Exam Study Preparation Resources" presented in the front matter of this book.

1. What is a data diddling technique?
   a. Changing data before input to a computer system.
   b. Changing data during input to a computer system.
   c. Changing data during output from a computer system.
   d. All of the above.

2. What is a salami technique?
   a. Taking small amounts of assets.
   b. Using the rounding-down concept.
   c. Stealing small amounts of money from bank accounts.
   d. All of the above.

3. With respect to computer security and fraud, a legal liability exists to an organization under which of the following conditions?
   a. When estimated security costs are greater than estimated losses.
   b. When estimated security costs are equal to estimated losses.
   c. When estimated security costs are less than estimated losses.
   d. When actual security costs are equal to actual losses.

4. Are an investigator's handwritten notes considered valid evidence in court of law?
   a. No.
   b. Maybe.
   c. Yes.
   d. Depends.

5. Which of the following security techniques allow time for response by investigative authorities?
   a. Deter.
   b. Detect.
   c. Delay.
   d. Deny.

6. Most of the evidence submitted in a computer crime case is:
   a. Legal evidence.
   b. Documentary evidence.
   c. Secondary evidence.
   d. Admissible evidence.

7. When computers and peripheral equipment are seized in relation to a computer crime, it is an example of:
   a. Duplicate evidence.
   b. Physical evidence.
   c. Best evidence.
   d. Collateral evidence.

8. From a computer security viewpoint, courts expect what amount of care from organizations?
   a. Super care.
   b. Due care.
   c. Extraordinary care.
   d. Great care.

9. Which of the following is **not** a criminal activity in **most** jurisdictions?
   a. Writing a computer virus program.
   b. Using a computer virus program.
   c. Releasing a computer virus program.
   d. Spreading a computer virus program.

10. Once evidence is seized, a law enforcement officer should follow which of the following?
    a. Chain of logs.
    b. Chain of events.
    c. Chain of custody.
    d. Chain of computers.

11. The concept of admissibility of evidence does **not** include which of the following?
    a. Relevance.
    b. Competence.
    c. Materiality.
    d. Sufficiency.

12. Evidence is needed to do which of the following?
  a. Charge a case.
  b. Classify a case.
  c. Make a case.
  d. Prove a case.

13. What determines whether a computer crime has been committed?
  a. When the crime is reported.
  b. When a computer expert has completed his or her work.
  c. When the allegation has been substantiated.
  d. When the investigation is completed.

14. The correct sequence of preliminary investigation is:

  I. Consult with a computer expert.

  II. Prepare an investigative plan.

  III. Consult with a prosecutor.

  IV. Substantiate the allegation.
  a. IV, I, II, and III.
  b. III, I, II, and IV.
  c. IV, II, III, and I.
  d. I, IV, II, and III.

15. A search warrant is required:
  a. Before the allegation has been substantiated.
  b. After establishing the probable cause(s).
  c. Before identifying the number of investigators needed.
  d. After seizing the computer and related equipment.

16. If a computer or peripheral equipment involved in a computer crime is **not** covered by a search warrant, what should the investigator do?
  a. Seize it before someone takes it away.
  b. Leave it alone until a warrant can be obtained.
  c. Analyze the equipment or its contents, and record it.
  d. Store it in a locked cabinet in a secure warehouse.

17. Computer fraud is increased when:
  a. Employees are not trained.
  b. Documentation is not available.
  c. Audit trails are not available.
  d. Employee performance appraisals are not given.

Sample Practice Questions, Answers, and Explanations

Domain 1: Managing the Internal Audit Function (40–50%)

1. The proper organizational role of internal auditing is to:

   a. Assist the external auditor in order to reduce external audit fees.

   Incorrect. Reduction of external audit fees is a result of internal audit work but not a role.

   b. Perform studies to assist in the attainment of more efficient operations.

   Incorrect. This does not represent a complete description of the proper role.

   c. Serve as the investigative arm of the audit committee of the board of directors.

   Incorrect. This role is too limited for internal auditing. It also serves operations management and top management.

   d. Serve as an appraisal function to examine and evaluate activities as a service to the organization.

   Correct. This alternative describes the basic role concept of internal auditing.

2. In some organizations, consideration is being given to the possibility of outsourcing internal audit functions. Management in a large organization should recognize that the external auditor might have an advantage, compared to the internal auditor, because of the external auditor's:

   a. Familiarity with the organization. Its annual audits provide an in-depth knowledge of the organization.

   Incorrect. The internal audit staff, not the external auditor, through its continuous auditing, gains an in-depth knowledge of the organization.

   b. Size. It can hire experienced, knowledgeable, and certified staff.

   Incorrect. The internal audit staff is able to maintain an experienced knowledgeable and certified (CIA) staff, without the potential threat of staff reassignment.

   c. Size. It is able to offer continuous availability of staff unaffected by other priorities.

   Incorrect. The internal staff is continuously available and not subject to greater priority work with other clients.

   d. Structure. It may more easily accommodate audit requirements in distant locations.

   Correct. The external auditor can offer better service in other geographical areas because of its dispersion of offices.

3. The status of the internal auditing function should be free from the impact of irresponsible policy changes by management. The most effective way to ensure that freedom is to:

   a. **Have the internal auditing charter approved by both management and the board of directors.**

      Correct. Approval of the charter by the board of directors will protect the internal auditing function from management actions, which could weaken the status of the internal auditing department.

   b. Adopt policies for the functioning of the auditing department.

      Incorrect. While adoption of the *Standards* serves as a guide and a measure of internal auditing performance, it will not protect and preserve the department's status.

   c. Establish an audit committee within the board of directors.

      Incorrect. The establishment of an audit committee does not ensure the status of internal auditing without its involvement in areas such as approval of the charter.

   d. Develop written policies and procedures to serve as standards of performance for the department.

      Incorrect. Written policies and procedures serve to guide the audit staff but have little impact on management.

4. The consultative approach to auditing emphasizes:

   a. Imposition of corrective measures.

      Incorrect. The word "imposition" implies an adversarial relationship.

   b. **Participation with auditees to improve methods.**

      Correct. Since auditors alone cannot implement audit recommendations, auditee participation and involvement makes improvements better.

   c. Fraud investigation.

      Incorrect. Auditors, not consultants, investigate fraud.

   d. Implementation of policies and procedures.

      Incorrect. Due to the requirement for independence, auditors should never implement policies and procedures.

5. In some cultures and organizations, managers insist that the internal auditing function is not needed to provide a critical assessment of the organization's operations. A management attitude such as this will most probably have an adverse effect on the internal auditing function's:

   a. Operating budget variance.

      Incorrect. An operating budget variance report is a control device used to monitor actual performance versus budget. Management foot-dragging could cause unfavorable variances, but favorable variances could also occur if many audits were cut short due to scope impairments.

   b. **Effectiveness.**

      Correct. In this type of situation, management is highly averse to analysis or possible criticism of its actions and will inhibit the internal audit department's effectiveness.

   c. Performance appraisals.

      Incorrect. An unbiased evaluation of audit staff would not be affected by lack of cooperation on the part of non-audit management.

   d. Policies and procedures.

      Incorrect. Policies and procedures of the internal audit function are developed by the internal audit department and should not be affected by non-audit management.

6. As part of the process to improve auditor–auditee relations, it is very important to deal with how internal auditing is perceived. Certain types of attitudes in the work performed will help create these perceptions. From a management perspective, which attitude is likely to be the **most** conducive to a positive perception?

   a. Objective.

      Incorrect. An objective attitude is desirable but by itself will not lead to a more positive relationship.

   b. Investigative.

      Incorrect. An investigative attitude is not likely to enhance the relationship.

   c. Interrogatory.

      Incorrect. An interrogatory attitude is not likely to enhance the relationship.

   d. **Consultative.**

      Correct. A consultative attitude leads to two-way communication.

7. In planning a system of internal operating controls, the role of the internal auditor is to:

a. Design the controls.

Incorrect. This is a role of management.

b. Appraise the effectiveness of the controls.

Correct. This is the proper role of the internal auditor, which is to report the results to management.

c. Establish the policies for controls.

Incorrect. This is a role of management.

d. Create the procedures for the planning process.

Incorrect. This is a role of management.

8. An audit committee should be designed to enhance the independence of both internal and external audit functions and to insulate the audit functions from undue management pressures. Using these criteria, audit committees should be composed of:

a. A rotating subcommittee of the board of directors or its equivalent.

Incorrect. Rotating subcommittee members can be internal to a company and would not have independence.

b. Only members from the relevant outside regulatory agencies.

Incorrect. External members should represent different backgrounds, not just regulatory background.

c. Members from all important constituencies, specifically including representatives from banking, labor, regulatory agencies, shareholders, and officers.

Incorrect. The size of the audit committee is limited and cannot include too many people, such as representatives from shareholders and labor.

d. Only external members of the board of directors or its equivalent.

Correct. Audit committees should be made up of external members of the board of directors or other similar oversight committees.

9. Accepting the concept that internal auditing should be an integral part of an organization can involve a major change of attitude on the part of top management. Which of the following would be the **best** way for internal auditors to convince management regarding the need for and benefits of internal auditing?

a. Persuading top managers to accept the idea of internal audits by contacting company shareholders and regulatory agencies.

Incorrect. Manipulation is not an option since it can be done only if the party manipulating has power. Its effects are also short-lived and do not lead to long-term commitment.

b. Educating top managers about the benefits and communicating with them on a regular basis.

Correct. Education and communication, although lengthy and costly, are the only way to achieve long-term results.

c. Negotiating with top management to provide them with rewards, such as favorable audits.

Incorrect. Negotiation is not an alternative since the two parties do not have equal power. Furthermore, internal auditors often do not have immediate rewards available to them to offer management.

d. Involving top management in deciding which audit findings will be reported.

Incorrect. Involving top management in this manner is not appropriate.

10. Which of the following features of a large manufacturing company's organization structure would be a control weakness?

a. The IT department is headed by a vice president who reports directly to the president.

Incorrect. This is a strength since it prevents the information technology operation from being dominated by a user.

b. The chief financial officer is a vice president who reports to the chief executive officer.

Incorrect. This is a strength since it prevents the information technology operation from being dominated by a user.

c. The audit committee of the board consists of the chief executive officer, the chief financial officer, and a major stockholder.

Correct. The audit committee should be made up of independent directors.

d. The controller and treasurer report to the chief financial officer.

Incorrect. This is a strength since it prevents the information technology operation from being dominated by a user.

11. Audit committees have been identified as a major factor in promoting independence of both the internal and external auditor. Which of the following is the **most** important limitation on the effectiveness of audit committees?

a. **Audit committees may be composed of independent directors. However, those directors may have close personal and professional friendships with management.**

   Correct. This is a major limitation that has hampered the effective operation of audit committees.

b. Audit committee members are compensated by the organization and thus favor a stockholder's view.

   Incorrect. Audit committee members are usually outside directors. Many of these directors have a broad viewpoint and are not limited to a stockholder's view.

c. Audit committees devote most of their efforts to external audit concerns and do not pay much attention to internal auditing and the overall control environment.

   Incorrect. Audit committees devote considerable time to the external audit function, but the evidence is that they are increasingly devoting time to internal audit reports.

d. Audit committee members do not normally have degrees in the accounting or auditing fields.

   Incorrect. A committee member need not have an accounting degree to understand most reporting and control issues.

12. Purchases from two new vendors increased dramatically after a new buyer was hired. The buyer was obtaining kickbacks from the two vendors based on sales volume. A possible means of detection is:

a. Periodic vendor surveys regarding potential buyer conflict-of-interest or ethics violations.

   Incorrect. If the vendor was in collusion with the buyer, either no response or an incorrect response would be elicited.

b. The receipt of an invoice to put new vendors on the master file.

   Incorrect. If collusion exists, the purchasing agent can arrange for the invoice.

c. The use of purchase orders for all purchases.

   Incorrect. If collusion exists, the purchasing agent can arrange for the purchase order.

d. **The use of change analysis and trend analysis of buyer or vendor activity.**

   Correct. This is an example of analytical procedures to detect patterns and trends.

13. Due to the small staff, one remote unit's petty cash custodian also had responsibility for the imprest fund checking account reconciliation. The cashier concealed a diversion of funds by altering the beginning balance on the monthly reconciliations sent to the group office. A possible audit test to detect this would be to:

a. **Compare monthly balances and use change and trend analysis.**

   Correct. Verifying the beginning balance one month to the ending balance of the prior month is a good quick-change analysis that would catch this diversion.

b. Require additional monitoring by headquarters whenever improper segregation of duties exists at remote units.

   Incorrect. This is not always possible or desired and not necessarily cost justified.

c. Determine if any employees have high personal debt.

   Incorrect. Rumors as to personal finances may be unfounded, and they may be illegal to check out without the employee's knowledge.

d. Determine if any employees are leading expensive lifestyles.

   Incorrect. Rumors as to personal finances may be unfounded, and they may be illegal to check out without the employee's knowledge.

14. In an organization that has a separate division that is primarily responsible for fraud deterrence, the internal auditing department is responsible for:

a. **Examining and evaluating the adequacy and effectiveness of that division's actions taken to deter fraud.**

   Correct. Control is the principal mechanism for the deterrence of fraud. Management, in turn, is primarily responsible for the establishment and maintenance of control. Internal auditors are primarily responsible for the examination and evaluation of the adequacy and effectiveness of actions taken by management in the fulfillment of their obligation.

b. Establishing and maintaining that division's system of internal controls.

   Incorrect. Establishing the system of internal controls for an operating division is a management responsibility.

c. Planning that division's fraud deterrence activities.

   Incorrect. The planning and execution of an operating division's activities are the responsibility of management.

d. Controlling that division's fraud deterrence activities.

   Incorrect. Management is primarily responsible for the establishment and maintenance of control.

15. During the audit of payments under a construction contract with a local firm, the auditor finds a $900 recurring monthly reimbursement for rent at a local apartment complex. Each reimbursement is authorized by the same project engineer. The auditor finds no provision for payment of temporary living expenses in the construction contract. Discussion with the project engineer could not resolve the matter. The auditor should:

a. **Inform the audit director.**

   Correct. The audit director should be informed before pursuing potential fraud.

b. Call the engineer into a private meeting to confront the situation.

   Incorrect. The project engineer has already been asked about the facts and did not resolve the issue.

c. Complete the audit as scheduled, noting the $900 recurring reimbursement in the working papers.

   Incorrect. The unexplained payment may be an indicator of fraud.

d. Wait until the engineer is surrounded by plenty of witnesses and then inquire about the payments.

   Incorrect. Raising this issue in public may expose the auditor to liability for slander.

16. In the course of performing an audit, an internal auditor becomes aware of illegal acts being performed by several of the highest-ranking officers of the company. To whom should the findings of the audit report be addressed?

a. Line-level supervision.

   Incorrect. The auditees at the line level are not in a position to take corrective action. Disclosing sensitive information to this level also creates a situation where rumors can act to the detriment of the company.

b. Members of the news media.

   Incorrect. The internal auditor owes loyalty to the company that employs him or her. This obligation includes maintaining confidentiality of potentially damaging information that is under investigation.

c. The officers involved in the illegal acts.

   Incorrect. Confronting the implicated officers with the full findings only serves to give them time to hide their misdeeds while other responsibility levels are being notified.

d. **The audit committee of the board of directors.**

   Correct. The audit committee of the board of directors is independent of management and should be notified of the illegal acts of the senior management members.

17. Which of the following ensures that all inventory shipments are billed to customers?

a. **Shipping documents are prenumbered and are independently accounted for and matched to sales invoices.**

   Correct. This procedure will provide assurance that all shipments are invoiced.

b. Sales invoices are prenumbered and are independently accounted for and traced to the sales journal.

   Incorrect. This procedure ensures that sales invoices are recorded, not that those shipments are invoiced.

c. Duties for recording sales transactions and maintaining customer account balances are separated.

   Incorrect. This procedure provides no assurance that shipments are invoiced.

d. Customer billing complaints are investigated by the controller's office.

   Incorrect. Customers who are not billed for a delivery may not notify the company.

18. An auditor for a large service company is performing an audit of the company's cash balance. The auditor is considering the most appropriate audit procedure to use to ensure that the amount of cash is accurately recorded on the company's financial statements. The most appropriate audit procedures for the objective are:

a. Review collection procedures and perform an analytical review of accounts receivable; confirm balances of accounts receivable; and verify the existence of appropriate procedures and facilities.

Incorrect. Audit procedures consisting of reviewing collection procedures, performing an analytical review of accounts receivable, confirming balances of accounts receivable, and verifying the existence of appropriate procedures and facilities would be appropriate for the objective of ensuring that all cash due is received. However, these audit procedures would be inappropriate for ensuring that the amount of cash was accurately recorded on the company's financial statements.

b. Compare cash receipt lists to the receipts journal and bank deposit slips; review the segregation of duties; observe and test cash receipts.

Incorrect. Comparing cash receipt lists to the receipts journal and bank deposit slips, reviewing the segregation of duties, observing, and testing cash receipts would be appropriate audit procedures to satisfy the objective of safeguarding cash receipts. However, these audit procedures would be inappropriate for ensuring that the amount of cash was accurately recorded on the company's financial statements.

c. Review the organizational structure and functional responsibilities; and verify the existence and describe protection procedures for unused checks, including security measures.

Incorrect. Reviewing the organizational structure and functional responsibilities; and verifying the existence and describing protection procedures for unused checks, including security measures, would be appropriate audit procedures to achieve the objective of ensuring that appropriate safeguards are in place to protect cash. However, these audit procedures would be inappropriate for ensuring that the amount of cash was accurately recorded on the company's financial statements.

d. **Examine bank statement reconciliations, confirm bank balances, and verify cutoff of receipts and disbursements; foot totals of reconciliations and compare to cash account balances.**

Correct. Examining bank statement reconciliations, confirming bank balances, verifying cutoff of receipts and disbursements, footing totals, and comparing cash account balances would be appropriate audit procedures to achieve the objective of ensuring that the amount of cash was accurately recorded on the company's financial statements.

19. An internal auditor found that the supervisor does not properly approve employee time cards in one department. Which of the following could result?

a. Duplicate paychecks might be issued.

Incorrect. Failing to approve time cards would not result in duplicate paychecks

b. The wrong hourly rate could be used to calculate gross pay.

Incorrect. This may result if the hourly rates used to calculate pay are not matched to personnel records.

c. **Employees might be paid for hours they did not work.**

Correct. This would decrease the chances of discovering employees who entered hours they did not work on their time cards.

d. Payroll checks might not be distributed to the appropriate payees.

Incorrect. This could be prevented by positively identifying paycheck recipients.

20. Which of the following controls would **most** likely minimize defects in finished goods due to poor-quality raw materials?

a. Proper handling of work-in-process inventory to prevent damage.

Incorrect. This would not ensure that raw materials are of sufficient quality.

b. **Implementation of specifications for purchases.**

Correct. Specifications for materials purchased provide an objective means of determining that the materials meet the minimum quality level required for production.

c. Timely follow-up on unfavorable usage variances.

Incorrect. This would only help ensure that raw materials are used in the proper quantities

d. Determination of spoilage at the end of the manufacturing process.

Incorrect. This would only permit proper determination of spoilage after raw materials have been used in production.

21. Which of the following is an appropriate audit procedure when testing payroll in a company with a satisfactory internal control environment?

    a. Selectively interviewing a sample of employees.

       Incorrect. Employees normally have no direct knowledge of the payroll cycle or entries.

    b. **Examining time cards or time sheets for proper approval.**

       Correct. Supervisory review and approval of employees' time records is essential in a properly functioning internal control environment to provide assurance of employee time worked.

    c. Sending confirmation letters to government authorities.

       Incorrect. Government authorities will not normally provide such confirmation. It is the employers' responsibility to ensure accuracy.

    d. Verifying all payroll calculations for one pay cycle.

       Incorrect. If controls were to be relied on, it would be more appropriate to test to ensure supervisory initials as evidence of control rather than to recalculate.

22. Which of the following means would be the **most** appropriate to minimize the risk of a company's buyer purchasing from a vendor who is a relative?

    a. Establish a purchasing economic order quantity.

       Incorrect. This procedure will control the quantity ordered but will not control the vendor.

    b. Establish a predetermined reorder point for purchases.

       Incorrect. This procedure will help to ensure the maintenance of sufficient quantity on hand but will not control the vendor.

    c. **Maintain an approved-vendor file for purchases.**

       Correct. This procedure will help to ensure that purchases are made only from approved vendors.

    d. Perform a risk analysis for the purchasing function.

       Incorrect. This procedure will help to identify and evaluate the risks involved in the purchasing function but will not control the vendor.

23. The president wants to know whether the purchasing function is properly meeting its charge to purchase the right material at the right time in the right quantities. Which of the following types of audits addresses the president's request?

    a. A financial audit of the purchasing department.

       Incorrect. This type of audit deals almost exclusively with the financial and accounting aspects of operations.

    b. **An operational audit of the purchasing function.**

       Correct. An operational audit would address the effectiveness, efficiency, and economy of the entire purchasing operation. This is what the president has requested.

    c. A compliance audit of the purchasing function.

       Incorrect. This type of audit deals almost exclusively with compliance matters.

    d. A full-scope audit of the manufacturing operation.

       Incorrect. Such an audit would deal with financial, compliance, and operational aspects of the whole manufacturing operation. This goes beyond the president's request.

24. Which account balance is **most** likely to be misstated if an aging of accounts receivable is not performed?

    a. Sales revenue.

       Incorrect. Aging accounts receivable would provide no information on sales revenue.

    b. Sales returns and allowances.

       Incorrect. The balance of the sale returns and allowance account is determined by actual returns and allowance, not by the age of accounts receivable.

    c. Accounts receivable.

       Incorrect. The balance of the accounts receivable account is not affected by the age of accounts receivable.

    d. **Allowance for bad debts.**

       Correct. The allowance for bad debts is determined based on the probability of collecting accounts receivable. The age of an account is a major determinant of its collectibility.

25. An internal audit of payroll would **least** likely include:

a. Tests of computations for gross and net wages.

Incorrect. This choice is a routine procedure.

b. Comparison of payroll costs to budget.

Incorrect. This choice is a routine procedure.

c. Tracing a sample of employee names to employment records in the personnel department.

Incorrect. This choice is a routine procedure.

d. Observing the physical distribution of paychecks.

Correct. Most companies large enough to have internal auditing do not physically distribute paychecks on a regular basis. Moreover, this is generally regarded as an extended procedure most applicable to fraud audits.

26. In response to a confirmation of the June 30 accounts receivable balances, a customer reported that the balance confirmed had been paid by a check dated and mailed June 20. The auditor reviewed the postings of cash receipts in July and found the payment had been recorded on July 13. Given this information, the next audit action should be to:

a. Require an adjusting entry to the payment to June.

Incorrect. The issue concerns the late deposit, not adjusting the receipt.

b. Compare deposit slips to posting records.

Correct. Determine if the check was deposited but the posting was delayed. This is an indication of lapping.

c. Trace the billing invoice to the related shipping documents and inventory records, comparing dates "shipped" to "billed" to determine proper period.

Incorrect. This test deals with late billing, not late posting of receipts.

d. Request a bank cutoff statement for July and reconcile the June deposits in transit and outstanding checks by examining supporting documentation.

Incorrect. This procedure would reconcile bank and book records; the issue is the possible delay in posting the receipt.

27. The scope of work in developing and maintaining a quality assurance and improvement program (QAIP) includes which of the following processes?

I. Supervision.

II. Internal assessment.

III. Ongoing monitoring.

IV. External assessment.

a. I only.

Incorrect. This is not the most complete answer.

b. I and II.

Incorrect. This is not the most complete answer.

c. I, II, and III.

Incorrect. This is not the most complete answer.

d. I, II, III, and IV.

Correct. The chief audit executive is accountable for implementing processes and QAIP designed to provide reasonable assurance to the various stakeholders that the internal audit activity. These processes include appropriate supervision, periodic internal assessments and ongoing monitoring of quality assurance, and periodic external assessments.

28. Which of the following is **not** included in the ongoing and periodic assessment containing measurements and analyses of performance metrics with respect to internal audit's quality assurance and improvement program (QAIP)?

a. Money saved from the audit work.

Correct. A QAIP is an ongoing and periodic assessment of the entire spectrum of audit and consulting work performed by the internal audit activity. This periodic assessment includes ongoing measurements and analyses of performance metrics (e.g., internal audit plan accomplishment, cycle time, recommendations accepted, and customer satisfaction). Although an objective measure, money saved from the audit work is not useful due to difficulties in quantifying savings and problems in agreement with the auditees and organization's management.

b. Number of recommendations accepted.

Incorrect. See correct answer (a).

c. Customer satisfaction.

Incorrect. See correct answer (a).

d. Audit cycle time.

Incorrect. See correct answer (a).

29. If the results of the assessment of the internal audit's quality assurance and improvement program (QAIP) indicate areas for improvement, which of the following will implement such improvements?

a. Audit committee of the board.

Incorrect. See correct answer (b).

b. Chief audit executive.

Correct. A QAIP is an ongoing and periodic assessment of the entire spectrum of audit and consulting work performed by the internal audit activity. If results of the assessments indicate areas for improvement by the internal audit activity, the chief audit executive will implement the improvements through the QAIP.

c. Chief executive officer.

Incorrect. See correct answer (b).

d. External auditor.

Incorrect. See correct answer (b).

30. All of the following stakeholders receive the results of internal and external quality program assessment of internal audit's activity from the chief audit executive (CAE) **except**:

a. Functional managers.

Correct. Functional managers need not to know these results because there are too many of them to distribute material to and because the scope of the quality program affects the entire organization, not just their individual business function. To provide accountability and transparency, the CAE communicates the results of external and, as appropriate, internal quality program assessments to the various stakeholders of the activity (such as senior management, the board, and external auditors).

b. Senior managers.

Incorrect. At least annually, the CAE reports to senior management on the quality program efforts and results.

c. Board of directors.

Incorrect. At least annually, the CAE reports to the board of directors on the quality program efforts and results.

d. External auditor.

Incorrect. See correct answer (a).

31. Which of the following is unique to the external assessment of an internal audit's activity when compared to internal assessment?

a. Findings.

Incorrect. Findings are common with internal assessments.

b. Conclusions.

Incorrect. Conclusions are common with internal assessments.

c. Recommendations.

Incorrect. Recommendations are common with internal assessments.

d. Overall opinion.

Correct. External assessments of an internal audit activity contain an expressed opinion as to the entire spectrum of assurance and consulting work performed (or that should have been performed based on the internal audit charter) by the internal audit activity, including its conformance with the definition of internal auditing, the Code of Ethics, and the *Standards* and, as appropriate, includes recommendations for improvement.

32. Which of the following is unique to the external assessment of an internal audit's activity when compared to internal assessment?

a. Follow-up.

Incorrect. Follow-up is common with internal wassessments.

b. Findings.

Incorrect. Findings are common with internal assessments.

c. Responses from the chief audit executive.

Correct. Receiving written responses from the chief audit executive (CAE) that include an action plan and implementation dates is unique to the external assessments. Here the CAE assumes the auditee role and the external assessor assumes the auditor role.

d. Recommendations.

Incorrect. Recommendations are common with internal assessments.

33. Which of the following facilitates and reduces the cost of the external assessment of an internal audit's activity?

    a. A periodic internal assessment performed within a short time before an external assessment.

    Correct. A periodic internal assessment performed within a short time before an external assessment can serve to facilitate and reduce the cost of the external assessment.

    b. A periodic internal assessment performed in parallel with an external assessment.

    Incorrect. See correct answer (a).

    c. A periodic internal assessment performed within a long time before an external assessment.

    Incorrect. See correct answer (a).

    d. A periodic internal assessment performed within a short time after an external assessment.

    Incorrect. See correct answer (a).

34. Which of the following is unique to ongoing internal assessment of an internal audit's activity?

    a. Best practices.

    Incorrect. Best practices are common to both internal assessment and external assessments.

    b. Cost recoveries.

    Correct. The processes and tools used in ongoing internal assessments include project budgets, timekeeping systems, audit plan completion, and cost recoveries, among others.

    c. Benchmarking.

    Incorrect. Benchmarking is common to both internal assessment and external assessments.

    d. Expected deliverables.

    Incorrect. See correct answer (b).

35. Which of the following is unique to external assessment of an internal audit's activity?

    a. Best practices.

    Incorrect. Best practices are common to both internal assessment and external assessments.

    b. Cost recoveries.

    Incorrect. Cost recoveries are used in internal assessments.

    c. Benchmarking.

    Incorrect. Benchmarking is common to both internal assessment and external assessments.

    d. Expected deliverables.

    Correct. The chief audit executive is to ensure the scope clearly states the expected deliverables of the external assessment in each case.

36. Which of the following is common between internal assessment and external assessment of an internal audit's activity?

    a. Audit *Standards*.

    Correct. By definition, the scope of external assessment is broader than that of internal assessment. However, Audit *Standards* are common to both of them.

    b. Audit charter.

    Incorrect. Review of the audit charter is part of the external assessment, not part of the internal assessment.

    c. Code of Ethics.

    Incorrect. Review of the Code of Ethics is part of the external assessment, not part of the internal assessment.

    d. Definition of internal auditing.

    Incorrect. The definition of internal auditing is part of the external assessment, not part of the internal assessment.

37. The scope of external assessment of an internal audit's activity should not be limited to which of the following?

    a. Assurance services.

    Incorrect. See correct answer (d)

    b. Consulting services.

    Incorrect. See correct answer (d)

    c. Leading practices.

    Incorrect. See correct answer (d)

    d. Quality assurance and improvement program.

    Correct. External assessments cover the entire spectrum of audit and consulting work performed by the internal audit activity and should not be limited to assessing its quality assurance and improvement program. To achieve optimum benefits from an external assessment, the scope of work should include benchmarking, identification, and reporting of leading practices that could assist the internal audit activity in becoming more efficient and/or effective.

38. Which of the following can be used by an independent external reviewer when establishing the scope of the external assessment of an internal audit's activity?

a. Percentage of audit plan completed in a year by the internal audit.

Incorrect. This choice is targeted at auditees and internal audit management. It is a routine task but does not focus on the big picture of the assessment of the internal audit's activity.

b. Number of findings reported in a year by the internal audit.

Incorrect. This choice is targeted at auditees and internal audit management. It is a routine task but does not focus on the big picture of the assessment of the internal audit's activity.

c. Percentage of quality assurance and improvement program (QAIP) implemented by the internal audit.

Correct. Internal auditors are required to do a full self-assessment of QAIP. Failure of internal auditors to do this full assessment will send a red flag to the external assessors. Assessment of QAIP is common between internal assessments and external assessments. The QAIP assesses the efficiency and effectiveness of the internal audit's activity and identifies opportunities for improvement. Since the QAIP is a part of internal audit *Standards*, its conformity is very important which will decide the breadth and depth of the external assessment's scope of work.

d. Number of audit recommendations accepted in a year by the auditees.

Incorrect. This choice is targeted at auditees and internal audit management. It is a routine task but does not focus on the big picture of the assessment of the internal audit's activity.

39. What should the audit strategy be?

a. It should be knowledge based.

Incorrect. It does not consider risk as explicitly as the correct choice.

b. It should be cycle based.

Incorrect. It does not consider risk as explicitly as the correct choice.

c. It should be request based.

Incorrect. It does not consider risk as explicitly as the correct choice.

d. It should be risk based.

Correct. Audits should be planned and conducted according to the risk level; that is, high-risk auditable areas should be reviewed first, followed by medium-risk areas, which are followed by low-risk areas. The medium- and low-risk auditable areas should be reviewed only when audit resources are available.

40. Which one of the following items includes the other three items?

a. Inherent risk.

Incorrect. Inherent risk is the susceptibility of a management assertion to a material misstatement, assuming that there are no related internal control structure policies or procedures.

b. Control risk.

Incorrect. Control risk is the risk that a material misstatement in a management assertion will not be prevented or detected on a timely basis by the entity's internal control structure policies or procedures.

c. Audit risk.

Correct. Audit risk is the risk that the auditor may unknowingly fail to appropriately modify his or her opinion on financial statements that are materially misstated. It is the product of the other three risks: It is equal to inherent risk multiplied by control risk, which is multiplied by detection risk. "Audit risk" is an all-inclusive term here.

d. Detection risk.

Incorrect. Detection risk is the risk that the auditor will not detect a material misstatement present in a management assertion.

41. Which of the following would **not** be considered in performing a risk analysis exercise?

   a. System complexity.

   Incorrect. This is considered in performing a risk analysis exercise.

   b. Results of prior audits.

   Incorrect. These are considered in performing a risk analysis exercise.

   c. Auditor skills.

   Correct. Auditor skills become a consideration during audit scheduling. Risk analysis is done prior to the start of an audit, where factors such as system complexity, system changes, and results of prior audit are very important to consider. These factors determine whether an auditable area is high risk, medium risk, or low risk.

   d. System changes.

   Incorrect. These are considered in performing a risk analysis exercise.

42. Management is concerned with a recent increase in expenditures and lower profits at a division and has asked the internal audit department to perform an operational audit of the division. Management would like to have the audit completed as quickly as possible and has asked the internal audit department to allocate all possible resources to the task. The director of internal audit is concerned with the time pressure since the internal audit department is heavily involved in a major legal compliance audit that had been requested by the audit committee. Which of the following comments are correct regarding the assessment of risk associated with the two projects?

I. Activities requested by the audit committee should always be considered higher risk than those requested by management.

II. Activities with higher dollar budgets should always be considered higher risk than those with lower dollar budgets.

III. Risk should always be measured by the potential dollar or adverse exposure to the organization.

   a. I only.

   Incorrect. Requests from management and the audit committee should both be considered by the internal audit department. Although an audit committee request is important, it is not always more important, nor does it always imply higher risk (item I).

   b. II only.

   Incorrect. Risk is measured by the potential exposure to the organization. The size of the departmental budget is an important determinant, but is not a sufficient determinant (item II).

   c. III only.

   Correct. This is the basic definition of risk given in the IIA *Standards* (item III).

   d. I and III.

   Incorrect. It contains both correct and incorrect answers.

43. Risk models or risk analysis is often used in conjunction with development of long-range audit schedules. The key input in the evaluation of risk is:

a. Previous audit results.

Incorrect. The informed judgment of the internal auditor is still required to assess the magnitude of risk posed by previous audit results.

b. Management concerns and preferences.

Incorrect. To assess the risk posed by management concerns, informed judgment of the internal auditor is required.

c. Specific requirements of the *Standards*.

Incorrect. The *Standards* do not specify the basic input risk analyses.

d. Judgment of the internal auditor.

Correct. In assessing the magnitude of risk associated with any factor in a risk model, informed judgment by the auditor is required.

44. Directors may use a tool called risk analysis in preparing work schedules. Which of the following would **not** be considered in performing a risk analysis?

a. Financial exposure and potential loss.

Incorrect. These factors should definitely be considered in risk analysis.

b. Skills available on the audit staff.

Correct. This does not involve risk associated with potential auditees.

c. Results of prior audits.

Incorrect. These factors should definitely be considered in risk analysis.

d. Major operating changes.

Incorrect. These factors should definitely be considered in risk analysis.

45. Factors that should be considered when evaluating audit risk in a functional area include:

1. Volume of transactions.
2. Degree of system integration.
3. Years since last audit.
4. Significant management turnover.
5. (Dollar) value of "assets at risk."
6. Average value per transaction.
7. Results of last audit.

Factors that **best** define materiality of audit risk are:

a. 1 through 7.

Incorrect. Although all items are used to define audit risk, not all factors are used to define materiality of audit risk.

b. 2, 4, and 7.

Incorrect. Factors 2 and 4 cannot be quantified into materiality.

c. 1, 5, and 6.

Correct. Factors 1, 5, and 6 can all be quantified into values, which can be measured into materiality.

d. 3, 4, and 6.

Incorrect. Factors 3 and 4 cannot be quantified into materiality.

46. In an audit of a purchasing department, which of the following generally would be considered a risk factor?

a. Purchase specifications are developed by the department requesting the material.

Incorrect. It is a normal procedure; purchasing reviews the specifications only.

b. Purchases are made against blanket or open purchase orders for certain types of items.

Incorrect. It is normal procedure for high-use items.

c. Purchases are made from parties related to buyers or other company officials.

Correct. This invariably involves high risk.

d. There is a failure to rotate purchases among suppliers included on an approved vendor list.

Incorrect. An approved vendor list is often maintained as a control factor to help ensure that purchases are made only from reliable vendors. However, rotation is not usually appropriate.

Domain 2: Managing Individual Engagements (40–50%)

1. During a preliminary survey, an auditor notes that several accounts payable vouchers for major suppliers show adjustments for duplicate payment of prior invoices. This would indicate:

   a. **A need for additional testing to determine related controls and the current exposure to duplicate payments made to suppliers.**

      Correct. A preliminary survey is a process used to become familiar with activities and risks in order to identify areas for audit emphasis. This preliminary survey information should prompt the auditor to identify the magnitude of such duplicate payments.

   b. An unrecorded liability for the amount of purchases that are not processed while awaiting supplier master file address maintenance.

      Incorrect. This situation is not identified in the question.

   c. A lack of control in the receiving area that prevents timely notice to the accounts payable area that goods have been received and inspected.

      Incorrect. The existence of duplicate payments is not related to a problem in the receiving area.

   d. The existence of a sophisticated accounts payable system that correlates overpayments to open invoices and therefore requires no further audit concern.

      Incorrect. Duplicate payments are not overpayments; they are exceptions and should be handled as such.

2. Writing an audit program occurs at which stage of the audit process?

   a. **During the planning stage.**

      Correct. Planning should include writing the audit program.

   b. Subsequent to testing internal controls to determine whether to rely on the controls or audit around them.

      Incorrect. The external auditor may use this approach in designing substantive tests of balances. (AICPA SAS 55).

   c. As the audit is performed.

      Incorrect. The program is prepared in advance and modified, as appropriate, during the course of the audit.

   d. At the end of each audit, the standard audit program should be revised for the next audit to ensure coverage of noted problem areas.

      Incorrect. While this choice could be done, the program should be updated during the planning process.

3. In planning an audit, an on-site survey could assist with all of the following **except**:

   a. Obtaining auditee comments and suggestions on control problems.

      Incorrect. Survey would assist in obtaining auditee comments.

   b. Obtaining preliminary information on internal controls.

      Incorrect. Survey would assist in obtaining information on internal controls.

   c. Identifying areas for audit emphasis.

      Incorrect. Survey would assist in identifying areas for audit emphasis.

   d. **Evaluating the effectiveness of the system of internal controls.**

      Correct. Determining the effectiveness of internal controls would require testing.

4. Which of the following is a proper step in an audit program?

   a. Notification of the audit.

      Incorrect. This action is taken prior to the development of an audit program. It is done during audit planning.

   b. **Observation of procedures.**

      Correct. Techniques such as observation and inspection are part of an audit program, which describes specific actions (steps) to be taken by the auditor.

   c. Definition of audit objectives.

      Incorrect. This action is taken prior to the development of an audit program. It is done during audit planning.

   d. Planning for audit reporting.

      Incorrect. This action is taken prior to the development of an audit program. It is done during audit planning.

5. "Fieldwork" has been defined as "a systematic process of objectively gathering evidence about an entity's operations, evaluating it, and determining if those operations meet acceptable standards." Which of the following is **not** part of the work performed during fieldwork?

a. Expanding or altering audit procedures if circumstances warrant.

Incorrect. This is a requirement of the *Standards* that relates to fieldwork.

b. Applying the audit program to accomplish audit objectives.

Incorrect. This statement concerning fieldwork is true, and it is in harmony with the *Standards*.

c. Creating working papers that document the audit.

Incorrect. Working paper preparation is a requirement of IIA *Standards*, which should be met during fieldwork.

d. Developing a written audit program.

Correct. This is a requirement of the audit-planning *Standard*. The audit program should be developed before the fieldwork begins.

6. IIA *Standards* require auditors to discuss conclusions and recommendations at appropriate levels of management before issuing final written reports. Auditors usually accomplish this by conducting exit conferences. Which of the following **best** describes the purpose of exit conferences?

a. To allow auditees to get started implementing recommendations as soon as possible.

Incorrect. This is a secondary benefit of exit conferences.

b. To allow auditors to explain complicated findings before a written report is issued.

Incorrect. Complicated findings must be explained thoroughly in written reports.

c. To allow auditors to "sell" findings and recommendations to management.

Incorrect. This is a secondary benefit of exit conferences.

d. To ensure that there have been no misunderstandings or misinterpretations of facts.

Correct. The major purpose of an exit conference is to discuss problems, conclusions, and recommendations and to ensure that there have been no misunderstandings or misinterpretations of facts. This is the primary purpose of exit conferences.

7. In the preparation of an audit program, which of the following items is **not** essential?

a. Performance of a preliminary survey.

Incorrect. It is needed to determine audit objectives and controls in use.

b. Review of material from prior audit reports.

Incorrect. This is done to get background on the audit.

c. Preparation of a budget identifying the costs of resources needed.

Correct. Resources to be used is necessary. However, conversion to costs needed is not essential for the program.

d. Review of performance standards set by management.

Incorrect. This refers to obtaining information on the validity of criteria to be used or to be evaluated during the audit.

8. What action should an internal auditor take on discovering that an audit area was omitted from the audit program?

a. Document the problem in the working papers and take no further action until instructed to do so.

Incorrect. Although the finding should be documented, it should be determined whether any changes may need to be made to the audit plan.

b. Perform the additional work needed without regard to the added time required to complete the audit.

Incorrect. The budgeted hours should be reviewed and increases approved prior to undertaking any additional steps.

c. Continue the audit as planned and include the unforeseen problem in a subsequent audit.

Incorrect. The unforeseen area may have an impact on the planned audit and need to be incorporated into the plan.

d. Evaluate whether completion of the audit as planned will be adequate.

Correct. Changes are often needed in the audit plan as work progresses. The auditor should review the plan with his or her supervisor since revised budgets may be needed.

9. In order to determine the extent of audit tests to be performed during fieldwork, preparing the audit program should be the next step after completing the:

a. **Preliminary survey.**

Correct. During the preliminary survey, the internal auditor becomes acquainted with the auditee and decides how much reliance he can place on the internal control system. This allows the auditor to initially determine whether to extend or limit audit tests. The auditor then prepares the audit program.

b. Survey of company policies.

Incorrect. The survey of company policies may be a segment of the preliminary survey. However, completing the survey of company policies is not sufficient to begin preparing the audit program; the entire preliminary survey must be completed.

c. Assignment of audit staff.

Incorrect. Audit staff are usually assigned to specific assignments before completing either the preliminary survey or the audit program.

d. Time budgets for specific audit tasks.

Incorrect. Specific tasks to be performed are determined during the audit program preparation.

10. Which of the following is a step in an audit program?

a. The audit will commence in six weeks and include tests of compliance.

Incorrect. This is simply the proposed starting time and partial scope.

b. Determine whether the manufacturing operations are effective and efficient.

Incorrect. This is an audit objective.

c. Auditors may not reveal findings to nonsupervisory, operational personnel during the course of this audit.

Incorrect. This is a rule for the conduct of the audit personnel.

d. **Observe the procedures used to identify defective units produced.**

Correct. This is an audit step because it is a procedure to be followed to obtain necessary evidence.

11. Audit programs testing internal controls should:

a. **Be tailored for the audit of each operation.**

Correct. A tailor-made program will be more relevant to an operation than a generalized program.

b. Be generalized to fit all situations without regard to departmental lines.

Incorrect. A generalized program cannot take into account variations resulting from changing circumstances and varied conditions.

c. Be generalized so as to be usable at all locations of a particular department.

Incorrect. A generalized program cannot take into account variations resulting from changing circumstances and varied conditions.

d. Reduce costly duplication of effort by ensuring that every aspect of an operation is examined.

Incorrect. Every aspect of an operation need not be examined—only those likely to conceal problems and difficulties.

12. An auditor begins an audit with a preliminary evaluation of internal control, the purpose of which is to decide on the extent of future auditing activities. If the auditor's preliminary evaluation of internal control results in a finding that controls may be inadequate, the next step would be:

a. **An expansion of audit work prior to the preparation of an audit report.**

Correct. If the preliminary findings indicate control problems, the auditor usually decides to do some expanded testing.

b. The preparation of a flowchart depicting the internal control system.

Incorrect. If a flowchart were necessary, the auditor would have prepared one during the preliminary evaluation.

c. An exception noted in the audit report if losses have occurred.

Incorrect. The auditor is not ready to make a report until more work has been performed.

d. To implement the desired controls.

Incorrect. Auditors do not implement controls; that is a function of management.

13. An internal auditor has just completed an on-site survey in order to become familiar with the company's payroll operations. Which of the following should be performed next?

a. Assign audit personnel.

Incorrect. Audit personnel are normally assigned before the on-site survey takes place.

b. Establish initial audit objectives.

Incorrect. Initial audit objectives are established at the beginning of the planning process. They should be specified before the on-site survey takes place.

c. Write the audit program.

Correct. The audit program is normally prepared after the on-site survey. The on-site survey allows the auditor to become familiar with the auditee, and thus provides input to the audit program.

d. Conduct fieldwork.

Incorrect. Fieldwork can be performed only after the audit program has been written. Thus, fieldwork could not immediately follow the on-site survey.

14. Interviewing operating personnel, identifying the objectives of the auditee, identifying standards used to evaluate performance, and assessing the risks inherent in the auditee's operations are activities typically performed in which phase of an internal audit?

a. The fieldwork phase.

Incorrect. The activities described must be performed before the audit program can be developed, the fieldwork completed, or reporting can be undertaken.

b. The preliminary survey phase.

Correct. These activities are normally accomplished during the preliminary survey phase

c. The audit programming phase.

Incorrect. The activities described must be performed before the audit programming phase.

d. The reporting phase.

Incorrect. The reporting phase is the last phase of the four choices given, hence it comes after the preliminary survey phase.

15. The auditor in charge has just been informed of the next audit assignment and the assigned audit team. Select the appropriate phase for finalizing the audit time budget.

a. During formulation of the long-range plan.

Incorrect. An initial budget is determined at this time, but revisions, based on the preliminary survey, may be required.

b. After the preliminary survey.

Correct. The preliminary survey establishes the subject of the review, the theory of the audit approach, and the structure of the project. If the survey discloses significant differences from the project that was placed in the long-range plan, budget adjustments should be requested and authorized.

c. During the initial planning meeting.

Incorrect. The audit project is not sufficiently well defined at this point to complete the budget.

d. After the completion of all fieldwork.

Incorrect. At this point, the bulk of the audit hours have been expended and the usefulness of the budget as a control and evaluation tool would be negated.

16. Which of the following activities does **not** constitute audit supervision?

a. Preparing a preliminary audit program.

Correct. This choice is a planning task.

b. Providing appropriate instructions to the auditors.

Incorrect. This is a supervisory task.

c. Reviewing audit working papers.

Incorrect. This is a supervisory task.

d. Seeing that audit objectives are achieved.

Incorrect. This is a supervisory task.

17. When reviewing audit working papers, the **primary** responsibility of an audit supervisor is to determine that:

a. Each worksheet is properly identified with a descriptive heading.

   Incorrect. While it is true that a descriptive heading generally should be on each worksheet, it is not of primary importance.

b. Working papers are properly referenced and kept in logical groupings.

   Incorrect. While it is desirable that working papers be properly referenced, it is not of primary importance.

c. Standard departmental procedures are adhered to with regard to working paper preparation and technique.

   Incorrect. Although a supervisor would be concerned as to whether departmental procedures are followed, it is not of primary importance.

d. Working papers adequately support the audit findings, conclusions, and reports.

   Correct. IIA *Standards* require that appropriate audit supervision include the determination that working papers adequately support findings, conclusions, and reports. This is of primary importance because nothing reduces the credibility of an internal audit department as much as ineptly developed findings that can collapse under attack.

18. When hiring entry-level internal audit staff, which of the following will **most** likely predict the applicant's success as an auditor?

a. Grade point average on college accounting courses.

   Incorrect. Accounting educational performance is undoubtedly one criterion that must be examined. Reviewing the performance in only one subject area is much too limited a criterion when the broad scope of internal auditing work is considered.

b. Ability to fit well socially into a group.

   Incorrect. The ability to get along well socially is a benefit to any internal auditor but cannot be considered the most important characteristic of a good candidate.

c. Ability to organize and express thoughts well.

   No characteristic gets to the heart of an internal auditor's job more than the ability to gather, analyze, and draw conclusions from facts. The internal auditor's success in implementing well-founded recommendations is most closely tied to his or her ability to communicate.

d. Level of detailed knowledge of the company.

   Incorrect. Entry-level internal auditors typically would have relatively little detailed knowledge of the company. It is desirable for applicants to demonstrate a general knowledge of the company, but this is not the most reliable predictor of successful performance as an internal auditor.

19. An internal auditing supervisor, when reviewing a staff member's working papers, identified an unsupported statement that the auditee's unit was operating inefficiently. What action should the supervisor direct the auditor to take?

a. Remove the comment from the working paper file.

Incorrect. While this might become necessary, if the staff auditor has reason to believe inefficiency, an attempt to support that belief is the first priority.

b. Obtain the auditee's concurrence with the statement.

Incorrect. Without support, this statement does not have credibility. It is conjecture and violations of *Standards*.

c. Research and identify criteria to measure operating efficiency.

Correct. At a minimum, this would be needed to comply with IIA *Standards* as to having the working papers complete. A standard or norm for efficient operation has to be used to measure how inefficient an operation is before such an opinion can be rendered.

d. Explain that it is the opinion of the staff member.

Incorrect. Without support, this statement does not have credibility. It is conjecture and violations of *Standards*.

20. Internal auditors often include summaries within their working papers. Which of the following **best** describes the purpose of such summaries?

a. Summaries are prepared to conform to IIA *Standards*.

Incorrect. This choice is not required by IIA *Standards*.

b. Summaries are usually required for the completion of each section of an audit program.

Incorrect. Audit programs do not usually require it.

c. Summaries distill the most useful information from several working papers into a more usable form.

Correct. This is the primary reason for such summaries.

d. Summaries are used to document the fact that the auditor has considered all relevant evidence.

Incorrect. This choice is too comprehensive.

21. A working paper is complete when it:

a. Complies with the auditing department's format requirements.

Incorrect. Format requirements are superficial and indicate only that mechanical requirements have been met. They do not relate to content.

b. Contains all of the elements of a finding.

Incorrect. A working paper may relate to only a part of the finding—one element or several.

c. Is clear, concise, and accurate.

Incorrect. These items are characteristics of the working paper content. The qualities may be present without the working paper being complete.

d. Satisfies the audit objective for which it is developed.

Correct. This is the objective of each working paper: to support the particular purpose for which the working paper was generated.

22. Working papers have the following characteristic:

a. They are the property of the organization and are available to all company employees.

Incorrect. While working papers are the property of the organization, they should be made available only to authorized personnel.

b. They document the auditing procedures performed, the information obtained, and the conclusions reached.

Correct. Working papers do document auditing procedures, information obtained, and the conclusions reached.

c. They become the property of the independent outside auditors when completed.

Incorrect. Although it is common practice for internal auditors to grant access to working papers to the independent outside auditors, the internal audit working papers are the property of the organization.

d. They should be retained permanently in the organization's records.

Incorrect. Working paper retention should be consistent with the guidelines of the organization and should satisfy pertinent legal or regulatory requirements.

23. Which of the following should be identified as a deficiency by an audit supervisor when reviewing a set of working papers?

  a. A memorandum explaining why the time budget for a part of the audit was exceeded.

  Incorrect. This is appropriate to include in working papers.

  b. An audit finding recorded in the working papers and report draft that omits the criteria used for evaluation.

  Correct. This would indeed be a deficiency because the basis for comparing what was, with what should have been would be missing.

  c. A memorandum explaining why an audit program step was omitted.

  Incorrect. This is appropriate to include in working papers.

  d. A letter to the auditee outlining the scope of the audit.

  Incorrect. This is appropriate to include in working papers.

24. Which of the following techniques is **best** for emphasizing a point in a written communication?

  a. Place the point in the middle rather than at the beginning or end of the paragraph.

  Incorrect. Placing it at the beginning or end of the paragraph best emphasizes the point.

  b. Use passive rather than active voice.

  Incorrect. Use of the active voice best emphasizes the point.

  c. Highlight the point through the use of nonparallel structure.

  Incorrect. Parallel structure will emphasize the point better. Nonparallel structure usually detracts from the point.

  d. Use a short sentence with one idea rather than a longer sentence with several ideas.

  Correct. Long sentences with several ideas will create information overload and disguise the important point.

25. Which of the following statements conveys negative information in such a way that a favorable response from the auditee may still be achieved?

  a. Your bookkeeper has failed to reconcile the bank statement each month.

  Incorrect. Placing the blame and using words such as "failed" will make the individual react negatively.

  b. The bank statements have not been reconciled each month.

  Correct. Using the passive version without placing blame or making the statement personal is more likely to make the reader react positively.

  c. Unfortunately, your bookkeeper has not taken the time to reconcile the bank statement each month.

  Incorrect. Placing the blame in a manner that seems mean-spirited and using words such as "unfortunately" will make the reader react negatively.

  d. You have apparently failed to inform your bookkeeper that the bank statements should be reconciled on a timely basis.

  Incorrect. Placing the blame on the reader and using words such as "failed" will make the reader react negatively.

26. An internal audit director has noticed that staff auditors are presenting more oral reports to supplement written reports. The best reason for the increased use of oral reports by the auditors is that such reports:

a. Reduce the amount of testing required to support audit findings.

Incorrect. The amount of testing required to support audit findings is unrelated to the use of oral reports. Whether findings are reported through oral or written reports, they still must be adequately supported.

b. Can be delivered in an informal manner without preparation.

Incorrect. Even though audit reports are delivered orally, they still should be prepared carefully. Poorly planned and delivered oral reports will be difficult for the audience to follow and may create unnecessary misunderstandings.

c. Can be prepared using a flexible format, thereby increasing overall audit efficiency.

Incorrect. The format of the report will depend on the audience. Factors to consider in delivering reports may include the background and expectations of the audience as well as the time available. This applies to both written and oral reports. Since oral reports do not eliminate the need for a final report, overall audit efficiency is not affected.

d. **Permit auditors to counter arguments and provide additional information that the audience may require.**

Correct. Oral reports permit auditors to counter arguments and provide additional information that the audience may require. Since oral reports evoke face-to-face responses, auditors can provide an immediate response to any auditee objections or provide additional information as appropriate.

27. An internal auditor has completed an audit of an organization's activities and is ready to issue a report. However, the auditee disagrees with the internal auditor's conclusions. The auditor should:

a. Withhold the issuance of the audit report until agreement on the issues is obtained.

Incorrect. As long as the auditor is satisfied that the audit is completed, it would be inappropriate to delay the issuance of the audit report. Further, agreement may never be obtained.

b. Perform more work, with the auditee's concurrence, to resolve areas of disagreement. Delay the issuance of the report until agreement is reached.

Incorrect. The auditor is satisfied with the audit conclusions. There would be little justification for expanding the audit work.

c. Issue the audit report and indicate that the auditee has provided a scope limitation that has led to a difference as to the conclusions.

Incorrect. The disagreement is not caused by a scope limitation.

d. **Issue the audit report and state both the auditor and auditee positions and the reasons for the disagreement.**

Correct. This would be consistent with IIA *Standards*.

28. According to IIA *Standards*, reported audit findings emerge by a process of comparing what should be with what is. In determining what should be during an audit of a company's treasury function, which of the following would be the **least** desirable criteria against which to judge current operations?

a. The operations of the treasury function as documented during the last audit.

Correct. Past practices may or may not have been at the level of best practices or may not have been in compliance with company procedures. This would not be an appropriate criterion.

b. Company policies and procedures delegating authority and assigning responsibilities.

Incorrect. Company policies and procedures specify what should be a part of the treasury function's operations.

c. Finance textbook illustrations of generally accepted good treasury function practices.

Incorrect. Generally accepted good practices can usually be found in leading textbooks describing the field. The auditor should look to the finance discipline for a description of good practices.

d. Codification of best practices of the treasury function in relevant industries.

Incorrect. Industry identification of best practices can serve as relevant criteria for both the auditor and the organization.

29. Which of the following is **not** a major purpose of an audit report?

a. Inform.

Incorrect. This is a major purpose.

b. Get results.

Incorrect. This is a major purpose.

c. Assign responsibility.

Correct. Assigning responsibility is a function of management.

d. Persuade.

Incorrect. This is a major purpose.

30. Which of the following would **not** be included in the statement of scope in an audit report?

a. Period covered by the audit.

Incorrect. This should be included in the scope section.

b. Audit objectives.

Correct. This should be included in the purpose section.

c. Activities not audited.

Incorrect. This should be included in the scope section.

d. Nature and extent of the auditing performed.

Incorrect. This should be included in the scope section.

31. Providing useful and timely information and promoting improvements in operations are goals of internal auditors. To accomplish this in their reports, auditors should provide:

a. Top management with reports that emphasize the operational details of defective conditions.

Incorrect. Top management can best perceive general concepts.

b. Operating management with reports that emphasize general concerns and risks.

Incorrect. Operating management can best perceive details of operations.

c. Information in written form before it is discussed with the auditee.

Incorrect. Do not surprise auditees; discuss the matters with them before they are reported.

d. Reports that meet the expectations and perceptions of both operational and top management.

Correct. The audit report needs to address the expectations and perceptions both of the top management and the operating management. As a result, it needs general concepts as well as details of operations.

32. Auditors realize that at times corrective action is not taken even when agreed to by the appropriate parties. This should lead an internal auditor to:

a. Decide the extent of necessary follow-up work.

Correct. IIA *Standards* state that the director of internal auditing should determine the nature, timing, and extent of follow-up.

b. Allow management to decide when to followup, since it is management's ultimate responsibility.

Incorrect. IIA *Standards* state that follow-up work is not management's responsibility.

c. Decide to conduct follow-up work only if management requests the auditor's assistance.

Incorrect. IIA *Standards* state that follow-up work is not management's responsibility.

d. Write a follow-up audit report with all findings and their significance to the operations.

Incorrect. The auditor has to provide an opinion as to the decision made with regard to lack of action.

33. Follow-up activity may be required to ensure that corrective action has taken place for certain findings. The internal audit department's responsibility to perform follow-up activities as required should be defined in the:

a. Internal auditing department's written charter.

Correct. Responsibility for follow-up should be defined in the internal auditing department's written charter.

b. Mission statement of the audit committee.

Incorrect. Follow-up is not specified in the content of the audit committee's mission statement.

c. Engagement memo issued prior to each audit assignment.

Incorrect. This memo may contain a statement about responsibility for follow-up, but such a statement should be based on the wording and authority of the departmental charter.

d. Purpose statement within applicable audit reports.

Incorrect. Follow-up authority and responsibility may be cited in applicable audit reports, but first the definition should be contained in the departmental charter.

34. Given the acceptance of the cost savings audits and the scarcity of internal audit resources, the audit manager also decided that follow-up action was not needed. The manager reasoned that cost savings should be sufficient to motivate the auditee to implement the auditor's recommendations. Therefore, follow-up was not scheduled as a regular part of the audit plan. Does the audit manager's decision violate IIA *Standards*?

a. No. The *Standards* do not specify whether follow-up is needed.

Incorrect. Follow-up is required.

b. Yes. The *Standards* require the auditors to determine whether the auditee has appropriately implemented all of the auditor's recommendations.

Incorrect. The purpose of follow-up is to see that actions are taken, not just that the auditor's recommendations have been implemented.

c. Yes. Scarcity of resources is not a sufficient reason to omit follow-up action.

Correct. IIA *Standards* require follow-up action. Lack of resources is not a sufficient reason.

d. No. When there is evidence of sufficient motivation by the auditee, there is no need for follow-up action.

Incorrect. Follow-up is required.

35. Reporting to senior management and the board is an important part of the auditor's obligation. Which of the following items is **not** required to be reported to senior management and/or the board?

  a. Subsequent to the completion of an audit, but prior to the issuance of an audit report, the audit senior in charge of the audit was offered a permanent position in the auditee's department.

  Correct. This would not have to be communicated. The audit work was done. The director of internal auditing would have to determine that there was no impairment of the independence of the senior's work. If there was none, the report could be issued without reporting the personnel change.

  b. An annual report summary of the department's audit work schedule and financial budget.

  Incorrect. This is a standard part of the required reporting to senior management and the board.

  c. Significant interim changes to the approved audit work schedule and financial budget.

  Incorrect. This is a standard part of the required reporting to senior management and the board.

  d. An audit plan was approved by senior management and the board. Subsequent to the approval, senior management informed the audit director not to perform an audit of a division because the division's activities were very sensitive.

  Incorrect. Both senior management and the board had approved the audit plan. The change dictated by senior management should be reported to the board.

36. During an audit of purchasing, internal auditors found several violations of company policy concerning competitive bidding. The same condition that had been reported in an audit report last year, and corrective action had not been taken. Which of the following **best** describes the appropriate action concerning this repeat finding?

  a. The audit report should note that this same condition had been reported in the prior audit.

  Incorrect. This action is insufficient.

  b. During the exit interview, management should be made aware that a finding from the prior report had not been corrected.

  Incorrect. This action is insufficient.

  c. The director of internal auditing should determine whether management or the board has assumed the risk of not taking corrective action.

  Correct. This action meets the requirements of IIA *Standards*.

  d. The director of internal auditing should determine whether this condition should be reported to the independent auditor and any regulatory agency.

  Incorrect. This action would be inappropriate.

37. Which of the following audit committee activities would be of the **greatest** benefit to the internal auditing department?

  a. Review and approval of audit programs.

  Incorrect. Review and approval of audit programs is the responsibility of internal audit supervision.

  b. Assurance that the external auditor will rely on the work of the internal auditing department whenever possible.

  Incorrect. External audit's reliance on the work of internal auditing is the subject of an AICPA pronouncement.

  c. Review and endorsement of all internal audit reports prior to their release.

  Incorrect. Review and approval of internal audit reports is the responsibility of the director of internal auditing or designee.

  d. Support for appropriate follow-up of recommendations made by the internal auditing department.

  Correct. The audit committee can lend considerable weight to the recommendations of internal auditing.

38. An internal auditor reported a suspected fraud to the director of internal auditing. The director turned the entire case over to the security department. Security failed to investigate or report the case to management. The perpetrator (employee) continued to defraud the organization until being accidentally discovered by a line manager two years later. Select the **most** appropriate action for the audit director.

a. The director's actions were correct.

Incorrect. According to the *Standards*, the director should have ensured that the internal auditing department's responsibilities were met with timely follow-up.

b. The director should have periodically checked the status of the case with security.

Correct. The director should have periodically checked the status of the case with security. Follow-up is specified by IIA *Standards*.

c. The director should have conducted the investigation.

Incorrect. A security department would generally have more expertise in the investigation of a fraud.

d. The director should have discharged the perpetrator.

Incorrect. The fraud was only suspected when reported to the director. Immediate discharge would have violated the suspect's rights. In addition, the director would not normally have the authority to discharge an employee in an audited area.

39. If an internal auditor finds that no corrective action has been taken on a prior audit finding that is still valid, IIA *Standards* state that the internal auditor should:

a. Restate the prior finding along with the findings of the current audit.

Incorrect. By definition, this choice is Incorrect.

b. Determine whether management or the board has assumed the risk of not taking corrective action.

Correct. This is per IIA *Standards*.

c. Seek the board's approval to initiate corrective action.

Incorrect. By definition, this choice is Incorrect.

d. Schedule a future audit of the specific area involved.

Incorrect. By definition, this choice is Incorrect.

40. Internal auditing is responsible for reporting fraud to senior management or the board when:

a. The incidence of fraud of a material amount has been established to a reasonable certainty.

Correct. If the incidence of significant fraud has been established with reasonable certainty, the auditor is responsible for reporting such to senior management or the board.

b. Suspicious activities have been reported to internal auditing.

Incorrect. No reporting is required when suspicious acts are reported to the auditor.

c. Irregular transactions have been identified and are under investigation.

Incorrect. Irregular transactions under investigation would not require reporting until the investigation phase is completed.

d. The review of all suspected fraud-related transactions is complete.

Incorrect. Reporting should occur sooner as per the choice (a).

41. Why should organizations require auditees to promptly reply and outline the corrective action that has been implemented on reported deficiencies?

a. To close the open audit issues as soon as possible.

Incorrect. This is a mechanical aspect of the audit reporting process.

b. To effect savings as early as possible.

Correct. The objective of the audit is to effect savings resulting from the auditee's corrective action as early as possible so that the organization will benefit from the action taken.

c. To indicate concurrence with the audit findings.

Incorrect. The auditee may not always concur with the audit findings.

d. To ensure that the auditor performance is evaluated.

Incorrect. This is an administrative function of the audit department.

Domain 3: Fraud Risks and Controls (5–15%)

1. What is a data diddling technique?
   a. Changing data before input to a computer system.

      Incorrect. Although this is one data diddling technique, it is not the most complete answer.

   b. Changing data during input to a computer system.

      Incorrect. Although this is one data diddling technique, it is not the most complete answer.

   c. Changing data during output from a computer system.

      Incorrect. Although this is one data diddling technique, it is not the most complete answer.

   d. All of the above.

      Correct. The data diddling technique involves changing data before or during input to computers or during output from a computer system. Data diddling can be prevented by limiting access to data and programs and limiting the methods used to perform modification to such data and programs. Integrity checking also helps in prevention. Rapid detection is needed—the sooner the better—because correcting data diddling is expensive.

2. What is a salami technique?
   a. Taking small amounts of assets.

      Incorrect. Although this is one salami technique, it is not the most complete answer.

   b. Using the rounding-down concept.

      Incorrect. Although this is one salami technique, it is not the most complete answer.

   c. Stealing small amounts of money from bank accounts.

      Incorrect. Although this is one salami technique, it is not the most complete answer.

   d. All of the above.

      Correct. A salami technique is a theft of small amounts of assets and money from a number of sources (e.g., bank accounts, inventory accounts, and accounts payable and receivable accounts). It is also using the rounding-down concept, where a fraction of money is taken from bank accounts.

3. With respect to computer security and fraud, a legal liability exists to an organization under which of the following conditions?
   a. When estimated security costs are greater than estimated losses.

      Incorrect. This choice poses no legal liability because costs are greater than losses.

   b. When estimated security costs are equal to estimated losses.

      Incorrect. This choice requires judgment and qualitative considerations because costs are equal to losses.

   c. When estimated security costs are less than estimated losses.

      Correct. Courts do not expect organizations to spend more money than losses resulting from a security flaw, threat, risk, or vulnerability. Implementing countermeasures and safeguards to protect information system assets cost money. Losses can result from risks (i.e., exploitation of vulnerabilities). When estimated costs are less than estimated losses, then a legal liability exists. Courts can argue that the organization's management should have installed safeguards but did not and that management did not exercise due care and due diligence.

   d. When actual security costs are equal to actual losses.

      Incorrect. It is not applicable because actual costs and losses are not known at the time of implementing safeguards.

4. Are an investigator's handwritten notes considered valid evidence in court of law?
   a. No.

      Incorrect. See correct answer (c)

   b. Maybe.

      Incorrect. See correct answer (c)

   c. Yes.

      Correct. An investigator's handwritten notes are considered valid evidence as long as the affected parties can read and understand the notes. Handwritten notes are no different from typed or printed versions.

   d. Depends.

      Incorrect. See correct answer (c)

5. Which of the following security techniques allows time for response by investigative authorities?

   a. Deter.

      Incorrect. This choice would not allow such a trap.

   b. Detect.

      Incorrect. This choice would not allow such a trap.

   c. Delay.

      Correct. If a system perpetrator can be delayed longer while attacking a computer system, investigative authorities can trace his or her origins and location.

   d. Deny.

      Incorrect. This choice would not allow such a trap.

6. Most of the evidence submitted in a computer crime case is:

   a. Legal evidence.

      Incorrect. "Legal evidence" is a broad term and is not useful here.

   b. Documentary evidence.

      Correct. Documentary evidence is created information, such as letters, contracts, accounting records, invoices, and management information reports on performance and production.

   c. Secondary evidence.

      Incorrect. Secondary evidence is any evidence offered to prove the writing other than the writing itself and is a part of the best evidence rule. The best evidence is original.

   d. Admissible evidence.

      Incorrect. Admissible evidence is evidence that is revealed to the jury or other trier of fact with express or implied permission to use it in deciding disputed issues of fact.

7. When computers and peripheral equipment are seized in relation to a computer crime, it is an example of:

   a. Duplicate evidence.

      Incorrect. Duplicate evidence is a document produced by some mechanical process that makes it more reliable evidence of the contents of the original than other forms of secondary evidence (e.g., a photocopy of the original). Modern statutes make duplicates easily substitutable for originals. Duplicate evidence is a part of the best evidence rule.

   b. Physical evidence.

      Correct. Physical evidence is obtained via direct inspection or observation of people, property, or events.

   c. Best evidence.

      Incorrect. Best evidence is evidence that is the most natural and reliable. The best evidence is primary.

   d. Collateral evidence.

      Incorrect. Collateral evidence is evidence relevant only to some evidential fact and that is not by itself relevant to a consequential fact.

8. From a computer security viewpoint, courts expect what amount of care from organizations?

   a. Super care.

      Incorrect. See correct answer (b).

   b. Due care.

      Correct. Courts will find computer owners responsible for their insecure systems. Courts will not find liability every time a computer is hijacked. Rather, courts will expect organizations to become reasonably prudent computer owners taking due care (reasonable care) to ensure adequate security. The term "due care" means having the right policies and procedures, access controls, firewalls, and other reasonable security measures in place. Computer owners need not take super care, extraordinary care, or great care, just due care.

   c. Extraordinary care.

      Incorrect. See correct answer (b).

   d. Great care.

      Incorrect. See correct answer (b).

9. Which of the following is **not** a criminal activity in **most** jurisdictions?

   a. Writing a computer virus program.

   Correct. It is the intentions of the developer of a computer virus program that matter the most in deciding what is a criminal activity. Simply writing a virus program is not a criminal activity.

   b. Using a computer virus program.

   Incorrect. Using a virus with intentions of destroying computer resources is a criminal activity.

   c. Releasing a computer virus program.

   Incorrect. Releasing a virus with intentions of destroying computer resources is a criminal activity.

   d. Spreading a computer virus program.

   Incorrect. Spreading a virus with intentions of destroying computer resources is a criminal activity.

10. Once evidence is seized, a law enforcement officer should follow which of the following?

    a. Chain of logs.

    Incorrect. This choice is indirectly related to the chain of custody.

    b. Chain of events.

    Incorrect. This choice is indirectly related to the chain of custody.

    c. Chain of custody.

    Correct. The chain of custody or the chain of evidence is a method of authenticating an object by the testimony of witnesses who can trace possession of the object from hand to hand and from the beginning to the end. It is required when evidence is collected and handled so that there is no dispute about it. It deals with who collected, stored, and controlled the evidence and does not ask who damaged the evidence. It looks at the positive side of the evidence. If the evidence is damaged, there is nothing to show in the court.

    d. Chain of computers.

    Incorrect. This choice is indirectly related to the chain of custody.

11. The concept of admissibility of evidence does **not** include which of the following?

    a. Relevance.

    Incorrect. Relevant evidence is evidence that had some logical tendency to prove or disprove a disputed consequential fact.

    b. Competence.

    Incorrect. Competent evidence (i.e., admissible evidence) is evidence that satisfied all the rules of evidence except those dealing with relevance.

    c. Materiality.

    Incorrect. Materiality is the notion that evidence must be relevant to a fact that is in dispute between the parties

    d. Sufficiency.

    Correct. Laying a proper foundation for evidence is "the practice or requirement of introducing evidence of things necessary to make further evidence relevant, material, or competent." Sufficiency is not part of the concept of admissibility of evidence.

12. Evidence is needed to do which of the following?

    a. Charge a case.

    Incorrect. See correct answer (d).

    b. Classify a case.

    Incorrect. See correct answer (d).

    c. Make a case.

    Incorrect. See correct answer (d).

    d. Prove a case.

    Correct. Proper elements of proof and correct types of evidence are needed to prove a case. It is proper to maintain computer-related evidence. Special procedures are needed to avoid problems of proof caused by improper care and handling of such evidence.

13. What determines whether a computer crime has been committed?

a. When the crime is reported.

Incorrect. See correct answer (c).

b. When a computer expert has completed his or her work.

Incorrect. See correct answer (c).

c. When the allegation has been substantiated.

Correct. A computer crime is committed when the allegation is substantiated with proper evidence that is relevant, competent, and material.

d. When the investigation is completed.

Incorrect. See correct answer (c).

14. The correct sequence of preliminary investigation is:

I. Consult with a computer expert.

II. Prepare an investigative plan.

III. Consult with a prosecutor.

IV. Substantiate the allegation.

a. IV, I, II, and III.

Correct. Step 1 is substantiating the allegation. Step 2 is consulting with a computer expert, as appropriate. Step 3 is preparing an investigation plan that sets forth the scope of the investigation and serves as a guide in determining how much technical assistance will be needed. Step 4 is consulting with a prosecutor, depending on the nature of the allegation and scope of the investigation. Items to discuss with the prosecutor may include the elements of proof, evidence required, and parameters of a prospective search.

b. III, I, II, and IV.

Incorrect. See correct answer (a).

c. IV, II, III, and I.

Incorrect. See correct answer (a).

d. I, IV, II, and III.

Incorrect. See correct answer (a).

15. A search warrant is required:

a. Before the allegation has been substantiated.

Incorrect. See correct answer (b).

b. After establishing the probable cause(s).

Correct. Once the allegation has been substantiated, the prosecutor should be contacted to determine if there is probable cause for a search. Because of the technical nature of a computer-related crime investigation, presenting a proper technical perspective in establishing probable cause becomes crucial to securing a search warrant.

c. Before identifying the number of investigators needed.

Incorrect. See correct answer (b).

d. After seizing the computer and related equipment.

Incorrect. See correct answer (b).

16. If a computer or peripheral equipment involved in a computer crime is **not** covered by a search warrant, what should the investigator do?

a. Seize it before someone takes it away.

Incorrect. See correct answer (b).

b. Leave it alone until a warrant can be obtained.

Correct. If a computer or peripheral equipment involved in a computer crime is not covered by a search warrant, leave it alone until a warrant can be obtained. The investigator needs a warrant to collect anything.

c. Analyze the equipment or its contents, and record it.

Incorrect. See correct answer (b).

d. Store it in a locked cabinet in a secure warehouse.

Incorrect. See correct answer (b).

17. Computer fraud is increased when:

a. Employees are not trained.

Incorrect. There is no direct correlation between computer fraud and this choice.

b. Documentation is not available.

Incorrect. There is no direct correlation between computer fraud and this choice.

c. Audit trails are not available.

Correct. Audit trails indicate what actions are taken by the system. The fact that the system has adequate and clear audit trails will deter fraud perpetrators because they fear getting caught.

d. Employee performance appraisals are not given.

Incorrect. There is no direct correlation between computer fraud and this choice.

Glossary

This glossary contains key terms useful to CIA Exam candidates. Reading the glossary terms prior to studying the theoretical subject matter covered in the review books and prior to answering the online test bank's practice questions can help the candidate understand the domain contents better. In addition, this glossary is a good source for answering multiple-choice questions on the CIA Exam. Certain glossary terms are repeated in the Part 1, Part 2, and Part 3 glossary sections for students' convenience due to their common topics and the fact that each Part Exam must be passed separately.

Abuse

Abuse occurs when the conduct of an activity or function falls short of expectations for prudent behavior. Abuse is distinguished from noncompliance in that abusive conditions may not directly violate laws or regulations. Abusive activities may be within the letter of the laws and regulations but violate either their spirit or the more general standards of impartial and ethical behavior.

Activity reports

Activity reports of the internal auditing department highlight significant audit findings and recommendations and inform senior management and the board of any significant deviations from approved audit work schedules, staffing plans, and financial budgets, and the reasons for them.

Add value

The internal audit activity adds value to the organization (and its stakeholders) when it provides objective and relevant assurance, and contributes to the effectiveness and efficiency of governance, risk management, and control processes.

Adequate control

Adequate control is a level of control that is present if management has planned and organized in a manner that provides reasonable assurance that the organization's risks have been managed effectively and that the organization's goals and objectives will be achieved efficiently and economically.

Alternative risk-transfer tools

There are five alternative risk-transfer tools:

> **Captive insurance methods.** A noninsurance firm is created for the purpose of accepting the risk of the parent firm who owns an insurer. Here, a parent firm establishes a subsidiary (called captive insurance company) to finance its retained losses. Captives combine risk transfer and risk retention.

Financial insurance contracts. These contracts are based on spreading risk over time, as opposed to across a pool of similar exposures. These contracts usually involve a sharing of the investment returns between the insurer and the insured.

Multiline/multiyear insurance contracts. These contracts combine a broad array of risks (multiline) into a contract with a policy period that extends over multiple years (multiyear). For example, a pure risk may be combined with a financial risk.

Multiple-trigger policies. These policies reflect the source of the risk and are not as important as the impact of the risk on the earnings of the firm. A pure risk is combined with a financial risk. The policy is "triggered," and payment is made, only upon the occurrence of an adverse event.

Risk securitization. This method involves the creation of securities, such as bonds, or derivatives contracts, options, swaps, or futures, that have a payout or price movement linked to an insurance risk. Examples include catastrophe options, earthquake bonds, catastrophe bonds, and catastrophe equity puts.

Multiple-trigger policies and risk securitization tools are more commonly used.

Analytical procedures

Analytical auditing procedures are performed by studying and comparing relationships among both financial and nonfinancial information. The application of analytical auditing procedures is based on the premise that, in the absence of known conditions to the contrary, relationships among information may reasonably be expected to exist and continue. Examples of contrary conditions include unusual or nonrecurring transactions or events; accounting, organizational, operational, environmental, and technological changes; inefficiencies; ineffectiveness; errors; irregularities; or illegal acts.

Anecdotal records

Such records constitute a description or narrative of a specific situation or condition.

Appreciation

"Appreciation" means the ability to recognize the existence of problems or potential problems and to determine the further research to be undertaken or the assistance to be obtained.

Assurance maps

Assurance maps are organization-wide and coordinated exercises involving mapping assurance coverage provided by multiple parties against the key risks facing the organization so that duplicate efforts, missed risks, and potential gaps can be identified and monitored. The chief audit executive, senior management, and the board need assurance maps to ensure proper coordination among diverse risk activities.

Assurance services

These services are an objective examination of evidence for the purpose of providing an independent assessment on governance, risk management, and control processes for the organization. Examples may include financial, performance, compliance, system security, and due diligence engagements.

Attribute

An attribute is a characteristic that describes a person, thing, or event. It is an inherent quality that an item either has or does not have.

Attribute listing

An attribute listing emphasizes the detailed observation of each particular characteristic or quality of an item or situation. Attempts are then made to profitably change the characteristic or to relate it to a different item.

Attribute sampling

Attribute sampling is the measurement or evaluation of selected sampling units to determine whether they have the attribute of interest, and the computation of some statistical measure (statistic) from these measurements to estimate the proportion of the population that has the attribute.

Auditable activities

Auditable activities consist of those subjects, units, or systems that are capable of being defined and evaluated. Auditable activities may include (1) policies, procedures, and practices; (2) cost centers, profit centers, and investment centers; (3) general ledger account balances; (4) information systems (manual and computerized); (5) major contracts and programs, (6) organizational units such as product or service lines; (7) functions such as information technology, purchasing, marketing, production, finance, accounting, and human resources; (8) transaction systems for activities such as sales, collection, purchasing, disbursement, inventory and cost accounting, production, treasury, payroll, and capital assets; (9) financial statements; and (10) laws and regulations.

Auditee

The term "auditee" includes any individual, unit, or activity of the organization that is audited.

Audit objectives

Audit objectives are broad statements developed by internal auditors and define intended audit accomplishments.

Audit procedures

Audit procedures are the tasks the internal auditor undertakes for collecting, analyzing, interpreting, and documenting information during an audit. Audit procedures are the means to attain audit objectives.

Audit program

An audit program is a document that lists the audit procedures to be followed during an audit and states the objectives of the audit.

Audit report

An audit report is a signed, written document that presents the purpose, scope, and results of the audit. Results of the audit may include findings, conclusions (opinions), and recommendations.

Audit risk

Audit risk is the risk that the auditor may unknowingly fail to appropriately modify his or her opinion on financial statements that are materially misstated. It is also defined as the risk that an auditor may fail to detect a significant error or weakness during an examination.

Audit risk is equal to inherent risk multiplied by control risk and multiplied by detection risk. Inherent risk is the susceptibility of a management assertion to a material misstatement, assuming that there are no related internal control structure policies or procedures. Control risk is the risk that a material misstatement in a management assertion will not be prevented or detected on a timely basis by the entity's internal control structure policies or procedures. Detection risk is the risk that the auditor will not detect a material misstatement present in a management assertion.

Audit scope

"Audit scope" refers to the activities covered by an internal audit. Audit scope includes (a) audit objectives, (b) nature and extent of auditing procedures performed, (c) time period audited, and (d) related activities not audited in order to delineate the boundaries of the audit.

Audit working papers

Audit working papers record the information obtained, the analyses made, and the conclusions reached during an audit. Audit working papers support the bases for the findings and recommendations to be reported.

Audit work schedules

Audit work schedules include (a) what activities are to be audited; (b) when they will be audited; and (c) the estimated time required, taking into account the scope of the audit work planned and the nature and extent of audit work performed by others.

Authorization

Authorization implies that the authorizing authority has verified and validated that the activity or transaction conforms to established policies and procedures.

Authorizing

Authorizing includes initiating or granting permission to perform activities or transactions.

Bell curve

A bell curve is a distribution with roughly the shape of a bell. It often used in reference to the normal distribution, but other distributions, such as the t distribution, are also bell shape.

Bias

The word "bias" refers to the existence of a factor that causes an estimate made on the basis of a sample to differ systematically from the population parameter being estimated. Bias may originate from poor sample design, deficiencies in carrying out the sampling process, or an inherent characteristic of the measuring or estimating technique used.

Board

A board is an organization's governing body, such as a board of directors, supervisory board, head of an agency or legislative body, board of governors or trustees of a nonprofit organization, or any other designated body of the organization, including the audit committee, to which the chief audit executive functionally reports.

Cause

Cause is the reason for the difference between the expected and actual conditions (why the difference exists).

Central limit theorem

In its simplest form, the central limit theorem states that for sample data from a population with a finite variance, the sampling distribution of the sample means approaches the normal distribution as the sample size becomes larger and larger.

Central tendency

"Central tendency" is a general term for the midpoint or typical value of a distribution. Mean and median are examples of measures of central tendency.

Charter (internal audit)

The internal audit charter is a formal document that defines the internal audit activity's purpose, authority, and responsibility. The charter: establishes the internal audit activity's position within the organization; authorizes access to records, personnel, and physical properties relevant to the performance of engagements; and defines the scope of internal audit activities.

Checklists

Checklists focus one's attention on a logical list of diverse categories to which the problem could conceivably relate.

Chief audit executive (CAE)

CAE refers to a person in a senior position responsible for effectively managing the internal audit activity in accordance with the internal audit charter and the definition of internal auditing, the Code of Ethics, and the *Standards*. The CAE or others reporting to the CAE will have appropriate professional certifications and qualifications. The specific job title of the CAE may vary across organizations.

Civil acts

Civil acts are illegal acts for which penalties that do not include incarceration are available for a statutory violation. Penalties may include monetary payments and corrective actions.

Cluster sample

A cluster sample is a simple random sample in which each sampling unit is a collection of elements.

Code of Ethics

The Code of Ethics of The Institute of Internal Auditors are principles relevant to the profession and practice of internal auditing, and Rules of Conduct that describe behavior expected of internal auditors. The Code of Ethics applies to both parties and entities that provide internal audit services. The purpose of the Code of Ethics is to promote an ethical culture in the global profession of internal auditing.

Coefficient of variation

The coefficient of variation is the ratio produced by dividing the standard deviation by the mean value. It provides an indication of the consistency of the data.

Compliance

"Compliance" refers to the ability to reasonably ensure conformity and adherence to an organization's policies, plans, procedures, laws, regulations, contracts, and other requirements.

Compliance requirement

"Compliance requirement" refers to conditions established by management for the organization. The term also refers to conditions that may be imposed on the organization by law or regulation or agreed to by contractual agreement. These conditions affect the manner in which an organization's operations are conducted and objectives are achieved. Compliance requirements include those established, imposed, or agreed to for the purpose of safeguarding organization assets including prevention and/or detection of unauthorized acquisition, use, or disposition of resources.

Conclusions (opinions)

Conclusions (opinions) are the internal auditor's evaluations of the effects of the findings on the activities reviewed. Conclusions usually put the findings in perspective based on their overall implications.

Condition

A condition is the factual evidence that the internal auditor found in the course of the examination (what does exist).

Conditional distribution

A conditional distribution is the distribution of one or more variables given that one or more other variables have specified values.

Conditional probability

Conditional probability is the likelihood that an event will occur, given that some other event is already known.

Confidence coefficient

The confidence coefficient is a measure (usually expressed as a percentage) of the degree of assurance that the estimate obtained from a sample differs from the population parameter being estimated by less than the measure of precision (sampling error).

Confidence interval

A confidence interval is an estimate of a population parameter that consists of a range of values bounded by statistics called upper and lower confidence limits.

Confidence level

The confidence level is a number, stated as a percentage that expresses the degree of certainty associated with an interval estimate of a population parameter. It is the probability that an estimate based on a random sample falls within a specified range.

Confidence limits

Confidence limits are two statistics that form the upper and lower bounds of a confidence interval.

Conflict of interest

A conflict of interest is any relationship that is, or appears to be, not in the best interest of the organization. Such a relationship would prejudice an individual's ability to perform his or her duties and responsibilities objectively.

Consulting services

Consulting services are advisory and related client service activities, the nature and scope of which are agreed with the client, that are intended to add value and improve an organization's governance, risk management, and control processes without the internal auditor assuming management responsibility. Examples include counsel, advice, facilitation, and training.

Continuous variable

A continuous variable is a quantitative variable with an infinite number of attributes.

Control

Control is any action taken by management, the board, and other parties to manage risks and to increase the likelihood that established objectives and goals will be achieved. Management plans, organizes, and directs the performance of sufficient actions to provide reasonable assurance that objectives and goals will be achieved. Thus, control is the result of proper planning, organizing, and directing by management. The control environment includes six elements: (1) integrity and ethical values, (2) management's philosophy and operating style, (3) organizational structure, (4) assignment of authority and responsibility, (5) human resource policies and practices, and (6) competence of personnel.

Control environment

The control environment is the attitude and actions of the board and management regarding the importance of control within the organization. It provides the discipline and structure for the achievement of the primary objectives of the system of internal control. The control environment includes these elements: (1) integrity and ethical values; (2) management's philosophy and operating style; (3) organizational structure; (4) assignment of authority and responsibility; (5) human resource policies and practices; and (6) competence of personnel.

Control processes

Control processes are the policies, procedures, and activities that are part of a control framework, designed to ensure that risks are contained within the risk tolerances established by the risk management process.

Cost/benefit relationship

The term "cost/benefit relationship" means that the potential loss associated with any exposure or risk is weighed against the cost to control it.

Criminal acts

Criminal acts are illegal acts for which incarceration, as well as other penalties, is available if the organization obtains a guilty verdict.

Criteria

Criteria are the standards, measures, or expectations used in making an evaluation and/or verification (what should exist).

Degrees of freedom

A random sample of size n is said to have $n - 1$ degrees of freedom for estimating the population variance, in the sense that there are $n - 1$ independent deviations from the sample mean on which to base such an estimate.

Dependent event

Two events are dependent if the occurrence of one event influences the probability of the occurrence of the other event.

Descriptive statistic

A descriptive statistic is one used to describe a set of cases on which observations were made. It consists of techniques and measures that help managers describe data. Frequency distribution transforms ungrouped data into more meaningful forms.

Detective controls

Detective controls are actions taken to detect and correct undesirable events that have occurred.

Deviation

Deviation is the difference between the particular number and the average of the set of number under consideration.

Directing

Directing involves, in addition to accomplishing objectives and planned activities, authorizing and monitoring performance, periodically comparing actual with planned performance, and documenting these activities to provide additional assurance that systems operate as planned.

Directive controls

Directive controls are actions taken to cause or encourage a desirable event to occur.

Director of internal auditing

The term "director of internal auditing" is used for the top position in an internal auditing department. The term is also called general auditor, chief internal auditor, chief audit executive, and inspector general.

Discrete Variable

A discrete variable is a quantitative variable with a finite number of attributes.

Dispersion

Dispersion refers to the extent to which the elements of a sample or the elements of a population are not all alike in the measured characteristic, are spread out, or vary from one another. Items that measure dispersion include range, deviation, mean absolute deviation, variance, standard deviation, and coefficient of variation.

Dynamic risk

Dynamic risk, in contrast to static risk, is produced because of changes in society. Dynamic risks also can be either pure or speculative. Examples of sources of dynamic risk include urban unrest, increasingly complex technology, and changing attitude of legislatures and courts about a variety of issues.

Economical performance

Economical performance accomplishes objectives and goals at a cost commensurate with the risk.

Econometrics

Econometrics is the application of statistical methods to economic data.

Effect

Effect is the risk or exposure the auditee organization and/or others encounter because the condition is not the same as the criteria (the impact of the difference).

Effective control

Effective control is present when management directs systems in such a manner as to provide reasonable assurance that the organization's objectives and goals will be achieved.

Efficient performance

Efficient performance accomplishes objectives and goals in an accurate and timely fashion with minimal use of resources.

Engagement

The term "engagement" refers to a specific internal audit assignment, task, or review activity, such as an internal audit, control self-assessment review, fraud examination, or consultancy. An engagement may include multiple tasks or activities designed to accomplish a specific set of related objectives.

Engagement objectives

Engagement objectives are broad statements developed by internal auditors that define intended engagement accomplishments.

Engagement work program

An engagement work program is a document that lists the procedures to be followed during an engagement, designed to achieve the engagement plan.

Error

The term "error," as it relates to internal audit reports, is an unintentional misstatement or omission of significant information in a final audit report. Errors are unintentional noncompliance with applicable laws and regulations and/or misstatements or omissions of amounts or disclosures in financial statements.

Event

An event is a collection of all individual outcomes from an experiment or a study.

External auditors

The term "external auditors" refers to those audit professionals who perform independent annual audits of an organization's financial statements.

External reviews

External reviews of the internal auditing department are performed to appraise the quality of the department's operations. External reviews should be performed by qualified persons who are independent of the organization and who do not have either a real or apparent conflict of interest.

External service provider

An external service provider is a person or firm outside of the organization that has special knowledge, skill, and experience in a particular discipline.

Financial engineering

The goal of financial engineering is to reduce financial risks which, in part, are achieved through financial instruments such as derivative securities (e.g., hedging with forward contracts). Financial engineering can also be applied to insurance and reinsurance areas using alternate risk transfer methods (e.g., captive insurance), as part of a company's risk mitigation strategy. In a way, financial engineering is related to risk engineering in terms of sharing common goals such as risks, hedging, insurance, and captive insurance.

Financial risk

Financial risks are risks arising from volatility in foreign currencies, interest rates, and commodities. They include credit risk, liquidity risk (bankruptcy risk), interest rate risk, and market risk.

Findings

Findings are pertinent statements of fact. Audit findings emerge by a process of comparing what should be with what is.

Finite population correction (FPC) factor

The FPC factor is a multiplier that makes adjustments for the sampling efficiency gained when sampling is without replacement and when the sample size is large (greater than 5% or 10%) with respect to the population size. This multiplier reduces the sampling error for a given sample size or reduces the required sample size for a specified measure of precision (in this case, desired sampling error).

Flowchart

A flowchart is a representation, primarily through the use of symbols, of the sequence of activities in a system (process, operation, function, or activity).

Follow-up

Follow-up by internal auditors is defined as a process by which they determine the adequacy, effectiveness, and timeliness of actions taken by management on reported audit findings. Such findings also include relevant findings made by external auditors and others.

Formal internal reviews

Formal internal reviews are periodic self-assessments of the internal auditing department to appraise the quality of the audit work performed. These reviews generally are performed by a team or an individual selected by the director of internal auditing.

Fraud

Fraud encompasses an array of irregularities and illegal acts characterized by intentional deception. Fraud is the obtaining of something of value, illegally, through willful misrepresentation. Thus, fraud is a type of illegal act characterized by deceit, concealment, or violation of trust. Fraudulent acts are not dependent on the threat of violence or physical force. Frauds are perpetrated by parties and organizations to: obtain money, property, or services; avoid payment or loss of services; or secure personal or business advantage.

Frequency distribution

A frequency distribution is a distribution of the count of cases corresponding to the attributes of an observed variable. A table is used in which data are grouped into classes and the number of items that into each class is recorded.

General semantics

General semantics are approaches that help the individual to discover multiple meanings or relationships in words and expressions.

Goals

Goals are specific objectives of specific systems. They also may be referred to as operating or program objectives or goals, operating standards, performance levels, targets, or expected results.

Governance

The term "governance" refers to the combination of processes and structures implemented by the board to inform, direct, manage, and monitor the activities of the organization toward the achievement of its objectives.

Hazard

Hazard is a condition that creates or increases the probability of a loss. Three types of hazards exist: (1) physical hazard, (2) moral hazard, and (3) morale hazard. Physical hazard is a condition of the subject of insurance that creates or increases the chance of loss, such as structural defects, occupancy, or similar conditions. Moral hazard is a dishonest predisposition on the part of an insured that increases the chance of loss. Morale hazard is a careless attitude on the part of an insured that increases the chance of loss or causes losses to be greater than would otherwise be the case.

Hazard risk

Hazard risks are risks that are insurable, such as natural disasters, various insurable liabilities, impairment of physical assets and property, and terrorism.

Hedge or hedging

Hedge or hedging is taking a position opposite to the exposure or risk. This can be done with financial derivatives, such as futures contracts, forward contracts, options, and swaps. A perfect hedge is not possible because financial derivatives used to hedge do not move together, leaving some risk. The idea behind hedging is to minimize risk. Value is created for shareholders if corporate hedging does not duplicate the shareholders' "homemade" hedging.

Histogram

A histogram is a graphic representation of a frequency distribution—that is, of the distribution of a variable.

Illegal acts

The term "illegal acts" refers to violations of laws and governmental regulations. Illegal acts are a type of noncompliance; specifically, they are violations of laws or regulations. They are failures to follow requirements of laws or implementing regulations, including intentional and unintentional noncompliance and criminal acts.

Impairment

Impairment to organizational independence and individual objectivity may include personal conflict of interest, scope limitations, restrictions on access to records, personnel, and properties, and resource limitations (funding).

Independence

Independence refers to the freedom from conditions that threaten the ability of the internal audit activity to carry out internal audit responsibilities in an unbiased manner.

Independence allows internal auditors to carry out their work freely and objectively. This concept requires that internal auditors be independent of the activities they audit. Independence is achieved through organizational status and objectivity. It is the freedom from conditions that threaten the ability of the internal audit activity to carry out internal audit responsibilities in an unbiased manner.

Independent event

Two events are independent if the occurrence of one event in no way influences the probability of the occurrence of the other event.

Inferential statistic

An inferential statistic is a statistic used to describe a population using information from observations just on a probability sample of cases from the population. It draws conclusions about a large body of data by examining only a portion of that data.

Information

Information is data the internal auditor obtains during an audit to provide a sound basis for audit findings and recommendations. Information should be sufficient, competent, relevant, and useful.

Information technology (IT) controls

These are controls that support business management and governance as well as provide general and technical controls over IT infrastructures, such as applications, information, infrastructure, and people.

Information technology (IT) governance

IT governance consists of the leadership, organizational structures, and processes that ensure that the enterprise's IT supports the organization's strategies and objectives.

Insurance

Insurance is an economic device whereby an individual or a corporation substitutes a small certain cost (the premium) for a large uncertain financial loss (the claim, or contingency insured against) that would exist if it were not for the insurance policy (contract). Insurance is most appropriate for situations in where there is a low frequency and a high severity of occurrence. Insurance is a risk transfer mechanism.

Insurable interest

An insurable interest is an interest that might be damaged if the peril insured against occurs; the possibility of a financial loss to an individual or a corporation that can be protected against through insurance.

Internal audit activity

The term "internal audit activity" refers to a department, division, team of consultants, or other practitioner(s) that provides independent, objective assurance and consulting services designed to add value and improve an organization's operations. The internal audit activity helps an organization accomplish its objectives by bringing a systematic, disciplined approach to evaluate and improve the effectiveness of governance, risk management, and control processes.

Internal auditing

Internal auditing is an independent, objective assurance and consulting activity designed to add value and improve an organization's operations. It helps an organization accomplish its objectives by bringing a systematic disciplined approach to evaluate and improve the effectiveness of risk management, control, and governance processes.

Internal auditing department

Internal auditing department includes any unit or activity within an organization that performs internal auditing functions.

Internal auditor

An internal auditor is an individual within an organization's internal auditing department who is assigned the responsibility of performing internal auditing functions.

Internal control

Internal control is a process within an organization designed to provide reasonable assurance regarding the achievement of five primary objectives: (1) the reliability and integrity of information; (2) compliance with policies, plans, procedures, laws, regulations, and contracts; (3) the safeguarding of assets; (4) the economical and efficient use of resources; and (5) the accomplishment of established objectives and goals for operations or programs. The auditor verifies that these processes are established.

International Professional Practices Framework (IPPF)

The International Standards for the Professional Practice of Internal Auditing (Standards) is the conceptual framework that organizes the authoritative guidance promulgated by the IIA's internal auditing standards (IASB). These *Standards* include Attribute *Standards* and Performance *Standards* from the IPPF.

Interval data

Interval data arise when the data have ordinal properties, such as measuring the distance between two data items.

Interval estimate

"Interval estimate" is a general term for an estimate of a population parameter that is a range of numerical values. It is the estimation of a parameter in terms of an interval, called an interval estimate, for which one can assert with a given probability (or degree of confidence) that it contains the actual value of the parameter.

Interval variable

The interval variable is a quantitative variable the attributes of which are ordered and for which the numerical differences between adjacent attributes are interpreted as equal.

Investigative questions

The scope includes asking six investigative (journalism) questions—what, where, why, when, who, and how—to better understand the root causes of issues and problems.

Irregularities

Irregularities are intentional noncompliance with applicable laws and regulations and/or misstatements or omissions of amounts or disclosure in financial statements with significant information in accounting records, financial statements, other reports, documents or records. Irregularities include fraudulent financial reporting, which renders financial statements misleading, and misappropriation of assets. They involve: (1) falsification or alteration of accounting or other records and supporting documents; (2) intentional misapplication of accounting principles; and (3) misrepresentation or intentional omission of events, transactions, or other significant information.

Joint probability

Joint probability is the probability that two or more events will happen simultaneously or sequentially.

Judgment sample

Unlike a probability sample, a judgment sample is one in which personal judgment plays a significant part. Although judgment samples are sometimes required by practical considerations and may lead to satisfactory results, they do not lend themselves to analysis by standard statistical methods.

Kurtosis
Kurtosis is the relative peakedness or flatness of a distribution.

Legal concepts
Several legal concepts exist as they apply to managers, executives, officers, and board of directors in any organization. For example, officers and directors need to follow duty of due care, duty of loyalty, and duty of obedience, not duty of absolute care or duty of utmost care. Only reasonable and ordinary care is expected of the officers and the board of directors because no one can anticipate all problems or protect from all disasters or losses. Especially, officers and board of directors are expected to follow the highest levels of legal concepts due to their fiduciary and governance responsibilities (i.e., duty of loyalty and duty of obedience). Examples of legal concepts follow:

Due process means following rules and principles so that an individual is treated fairly and uniformly at all times with basic rights protected. It also means fair and equitable treatment to all concerned parties so that no person is deprived of life, liberty, or property without due process of the law, which is the right to notice and a hearing. Due process means each person is given an equal and a fair chance of being represented or heard and that everybody goes through the same process for consideration and approval. It means all people are equal in the eyes of the law. Due law covers due process and due care. Due process requires due care and due diligence.

Two types of due process exist: procedural due process and substantive due process. Procedural due process ensures that a formal proceeding is carried out regularly and in accordance with the established rules and principles. Substantive due process deals with a judicial requirement that enacted laws may not contain provisions that result in the unfair, arbitrary, or unreasonable treatment of an individual. It protects personal property from governmental interference or possession.

Due care means reasonable care in promoting the common good, maintaining the minimal and customary practices, and following the best practices. Due law covers due process and due care. For example, it is the responsibility that managers and their organizations have a duty to provide for information security to ensure that the type of control, the cost of control, and the deployment of control are appropriate for the system being managed. Another related concept of due care is good faith, which means showing "honesty in fact" and "honesty in intent." Both due care and due diligence are similar to the "prudent man" or "reasonable person" concept.

Due diligence reviews involve pre-assessment, examination, analysis, and reporting on major activities with due care before they are finalized or approved by management. Its purpose is to minimize potential risks from undertaking new businesses and ventures and involving in mergers, acquisitions, and divestitures. Due diligence requires organizations to develop and implement an effective system of controls, policies, and procedures to prevent and detect violation of policies and laws. It requires that the organization has taken minimum and necessary steps in its power and authority to prevent and detect violation of policies and laws. In other words, due diligence is the care that a reasonable person exercises under the circumstances to avoid harm to other persons or to their property. Due diligence is another way of saying due care. Both due care and due diligence are similar to the "prudent man" or "reasonable person" concept. A due diligence defense is available to a defendant in that it makes the defendant not liable if the defendant's actions are reasonable and they are proven.

Due professional care calls for the application of the care and skill expected of a reasonably prudent and competent person in the same or similar circumstances. For example, due professional care is exercised when internal audits are performed in accordance with the IIA Standards. The exercise of due professional care requires that: (1) internal auditors be independent of the activities they audit, (2) internal audits be performed by those persons who collectively possess the necessary knowledge, skills, and disciplines to conduct the audit properly, (3) audit work be planned and supervised, (4) audit reports be objective, clear, concise, constructive, and timely, and (5) internal auditors follow up on reported audit findings to ascertain that appropriate action was taken.

Duty of loyalty is applicable to the officers and the directors of a corporation not to act adversely to the interests of the corporation and not to subordinate their personal interests to those of the corporation and its shareholders.

Duty of care is the legal obligation that each person has to others not to cause any unreasonable harm or risk of harm resulting from careless acts. A breach of the duty of care is negligence. An example is that corporate directors and officers must use due care and due diligence when acting on behalf of a corporation. Duty of reasonable care is same as the duty of care.

Duty of obedience is expected of officers and directors of a corporation to act within the authority conferred upon them by the state corporation statute, the articles of incorporation, the corporate bylaws, and the resolutions adopted by the board of directors.

Management

The term "management" includes those individuals with responsibilities for setting and/or achieving the organization's objectives.

Marginal distribution

"Marginal distribution" refers to the distribution of a single variable based on an underlying distribution of two or more variables.

Marginal probability

Marginal probability is the sum of all relevant joint probabilities.

Mean

Mean is the sum of all the values in a set of observations divided by the number of observations. Mean is also known as "average" or "arithmetic mean," as it indicates the typical value for a set of observations. For example, if five students make the grades 15, 75, 80, 95, and 100, the mean is 73.

Mean absolute deviation (MAD)

MAD is a measure of the difference between the individual items in a population and the mean value. It is the average of the total unsigned differences. The average distance of each value in a distribution from the mean value of the distribution (sum of the differences divided by the number of items in the distribution).

Median

Median is the exact midpoint of a distribution, with an equal number of items below it and above it. For example, if five students make the grades 15, 75, 80, 95, and 100, the median is 80.

Mode

Mode is a measure of central tendency; a statistic used primarily with nominal variables. It is the number that occurs most frequently in a series. For example, if more students (of a given group) make 75 than any other one grade, 75 is the mode.

Monitoring

Monitoring encompasses supervising, observing, and testing activities and appropriately reporting to responsible individuals. Monitoring provides an ongoing verification of progress toward achievement of objectives and goals.

Multicollinearity

Multicollinearity is a condition of overlapping that occurs when highly correlated independent variables are included in the regression model.

Must

The IIA *Standards* use the word "must" to specify an unconditional requirement.

Mutually exclusive event

Two events are mutually exclusive if the occurrence of one event prevents the occurrences of the other. The joint probability of two events is zero.

Natural hedges

Natural hedges are created from the relationship between the revenues and costs of a business unit or a subsidiary. The more revenues over the cost, the better protection is. The key is the extent to which cash flows adjust naturally to currency changes due to exchange-rate fluctuations. One way to explore the likelihood of a natural hedge is to determine whether a subsidiary's revenue and cost functions are sensitive to domestic or global business conditions.

Nominal data

Nominal data arise when numbers or other symbols are used to describe an item, category, or attribute.

Nominal variable

A nominal variable is a quantitative variable the attributes of which have no inherent order.

Noncompliance

Noncompliance is a failure to follow requirements, or a violation of prohibitions, contained in laws, regulations, contracts, governmental grants, or organization's policies and procedures.

Normal distribution (curve)

A normal distribution is a theoretical distribution that is closely approximated by many actual distributions of variables.

Objective risk

Objective risk differs from subjective risk primarily in the sense that it is more precisely observable and therefore measurable. In general, objective risk is the probable variation of actual from expected experience.

Objectives

Objectives are the broadest statements of what the organization chooses to accomplish.

Objectivity

The term "objectivity" refers to an unbiased mental attitude that allows internal auditors to perform engagements in such a manner that they believe in their work product and that no quality compromises are made. Objectivity requires that internal auditors do not subordinate their judgment on audit matters to others.

Operational risk

Operational risk is a risk related to the organization's internal systems, products, services, processes, technology, and people.

Operations

The term "operations" refers to the recurring activities of an organization directed toward producing a product or rendering a service. Such activities may include, but are not limited to, marketing, sales, production, purchasing, human resources, finance and accounting, and governmental assistance.

Ordinal data

Ordinal data consists of data elements that can be rank-ordered on the basis of some relationship between them, such as strength.

Ordinal variable

An ordinal variable is a quantitative variable the attributes of which are ordered but for which the numerical difference between adjacent attributes is not necessarily interpreted as equal.

Outlier

An outlier is an extremely large or small observation; it applies to ordinal, interval, and ratio variables.

Outside service provider

The term "outside service provider" refers to a person or firm, independent of the organization, that has special knowledge, skill, and experience in a particular discipline. Outside service providers include, among others, actuaries, accountants, appraisers, environmental specialists, fraud investigators, lawyers, engineers, geologists, security specialists, statisticians, information technology specialists, the organization's external auditors, and other auditing organizations. An outside service provider may be engaged by the board, senior management, or the director of internal auditing.

Parameter

A parameter is a number that describes a population. It is a measure, such as mean, median, standard deviation, or proportion, that is calculated or defined by using every item in the population.

Peril

Peril is the cause of possible loss, the event insured against. "Open peril" is a term used to describe a broad form of property insurance in which coverage applies to loss arising from any fortuitous cause other than those perils or causes specifically excluded.

Point estimate

A point estimate is an estimate of a population parameter that is a single numerical value.

Population

A population is a set of persons, things, or events about which there are questions. It is all the numbers of a group to be studied as defined by the auditor; the total collection of individuals or items from which a sample is selected. Population is also called a universe.

Portfolio risk

Portfolio risk considers risk and return of a firm when it is investing in acquisition or expansion projects. Management needs to find the relationship between the net present values (NPVs) for new projects and the NPVs for existing projects. In a portfolio framework, the trade-off between risk and expected NPV for different combinations of investments can be analyzed.

Practice Advisories

Practice Advisories assist internal auditors in applying the definition of internal auditing, the Code of Ethics, and the *Standards* and promoting good practices. Practice Advisories address internal auditing's approach, methodologies, and consideration but not detail processes or procedures. They include: practices relating to international, country, or industry-specific issues; specific types of engagements; and legal or regulatory issues. These are IIA published documents.

Practice Guides

Practice Guides provide detailed guidance for conducting internal audit activities. They include detailed processes and procedures, such as tools and techniques, programs, and step-by-step approaches, as well as examples of deliverables. These are IIA published documents.

Precision

Each estimate generated from a probability sample has a measurable precision, or sampling error, that may be expressed as a plus or minus figure. A sampling error indicates how closely we can reproduce from a sample the results that we would obtain if we were to take a complete count of the population using the same measurement methods. Note that precision is the same as sampling error.

Preventive controls

Preventive controls are actions taken to deter undesirable events from occurring.

Probability

Probability is the ratio of the number of outcomes that will produce a specific event to the total number of possible outcomes, or the likelihood that specific events will occur, expressed as a proportion or percentage.

Probability distribution

A probability distribution is a distribution of a variable that expresses the probability that particular attributes or ranges of attributes will be, or have been, observed.

Probability sampling

Probability sampling involves the selection of a sample by some random method to obtain information or draw conclusions about a population. All possible samples, and thus each item in the population, have a known and specified (nonzero) probability of being drawn.

Proficiency

"Proficiency" means the ability to apply knowledge to situations likely to be encountered and to deal with them without extensive recourse to technical research and assistance.

Programs

Programs are special-purpose activities of an organization. Such activities include, but are not limited to, the raising of capital, sale of a facility, fund-raising campaigns, new product or service introduction campaigns, capital expenditures, and special-purpose government grants.

Pure risk

Risk is a possibility of loss. Many types of risks exist, including pure risk, speculative risk, static risk, dynamic risk, subjective risk, and objective risk. Pure risk is a condition in which there is the possibility of loss or no loss (e.g., default of a debtor or disability). Pure risks are of several types, including personal risks, property risks, liability risks, and performance risks. Risk management is a scientific approach to the problem of dealing with the pure risks facing an individual or an organization. Insurance is viewed as simply one of several approaches for dealing with such risks. The techniques of insurance and self-insurance are commonly limited to the treatment of pure risks, such as fire, product liability, and worker's compensation. Traditionally, risk management tools—avoidance, loss control, and transfer—have been applied primarily to the pure or hazard risks facing a firm.

Purpose statements

Purpose statements in audit reports describe the audit objectives and may, where necessary, inform the reader why the audit was conducted and what it was expected to achieve.

Quality assurance

Quality assurance is a program by which the director of internal auditing evaluates the operations of the internal auditing department. The purpose of the quality assurance program is to provide reasonable assurance that internal auditing work conforms to the IIA *Standards*, the internal auditing department's charter, and other applicable standards. The quality assurance program should include these elements: (1) supervision, (2) internal reviews, and (3) external reviews.

Random number sampling

Random number sampling is a sampling method in which combinations of random digits, within the range of the number of items in a population, are selected by using one of the random number generation methods until a given sample size is obtained. For example, if a sample of 60 items is required from a population numbered 1 through 2,000, then 60 random numbers between 1 and 2,000 are selected.

Random selection

Random selection is a selection method that uses an acceptable method of generating random numbers in a standard manner. The method minimizes the influence of nonchance factors in selecting the sample items.

Range

The term "range" refers to the distance (or difference) between the highest and lowest values. This is a quick measure of the dispersion (spread) of the distribution. It is a statistic used primarily with interval-ratio variables.

Ratio analysis

Ratio analysis is the study of financial condition and performance through ratios derived from items in the financial statements or from other financial or nonfinancial information.

Ratio data

Ratio data are the highest level of data measurements and the strongest data measurement technique.

Ratio estimate

A ratio estimate is an estimate of a population parameter that is obtained by multiplying the known population total for another variable by a ratio of appropriate sample values of the two variables.

Ratio variable

A ratio variable is a quantitative variable the attributes of which are ordered, spaced equally, and have a true zero point.

Reasonableness test

A reasonableness test is a comparison of an estimated amount, calculated by the use of relevant financial and nonfinancial information, with a recorded amount.

Recommendations

Recommendations are actions the internal auditor believes necessary to correct existing conditions or improve operations.

Regression analysis

Regression analysis is a mathematical procedure used to determine and measure the predictive relationship between one variable (dependent variable) and one or more other variables (independent variable).

Residual risk

Residual risk is the risk remaining after management takes action to reduce the impact and likelihood of an adverse event, including control activities in responding to a risk. Residual risk is

current risk, which, in turn, is called managed risk with existing control systems. Residual risk is calculated as potential risks minus covered risks, resulting in uncovered risk.
Several equations are available to express residual risks:

Residual risks = Total risks − Mitigated risks
Residual risks = Potential risks − Covered risks
Residual risks = Total risks − Control measures applied
Residual risks = Potential risks − Countermeasures applied
Residual risks = Uncovered or Unaddressed risks

Risk

The term "risk" means the possibility of an event occurring that will have an impact on the achievement of objectives. Risk is measured in terms of impact and likelihood. It is the probability that an event or action may adversely affect the organization or activity under audit. Risks can be classified or categorized into three types: static versus dynamic, subjective versus objective, and pure versus speculative. Risk is uncertainty about loss. Risks should be avoided where possible; if not, they should be managed well. There are at least six types of risks, including pure, strategic, operational, financial, hazard, and speculative.

Risk acceptance

The term "risk acceptance" means accepting a potential risk and continuing with operating a process or system. It is like accepting risks as part of doing business (a kind of self-insurance). Risk acceptance is also called risk tolerance and risk appetite in order to achieve a desired result.

Risk appetite

The risk appetite of an organization is the level of risk that it is willing to accept.

Risk assessment

Risk assessment includes identification, analysis, measurement, and prioritization of risks. Risk assessment (or risk analysis) is the process of identifying the risks and determining the probability of occurrence, the resulting impact, and additional safeguards that would mitigate this impact. Risk assessment is a systematic process for assessing and integrating professional judgments about probable adverse conditions and/or events. The risk assessment process should provide a means of organizing and integrating professional judgments for development of the audit work schedule.

Risk assignment

Risk assignment consists of transferring or assigning risk to a third party by using other options to compensate for the loss, such as an insurance company or outsourcing firm.

Risk avoidance

Risk avoidance eliminates the risk causes and/or consequences (e.g., add controls that prevent the risk from occurring, remove certain functions of the system, or shut down the system when risks are identified). It is like reducing, avoiding, or eliminating risks by implementing cost-effective safeguards and controls. Risk situations that have high severity and high frequency of loss should be either avoided or reduced. Risk reduction is appropriate when it is possible to reduce either risk severity or frequency. Otherwise, the risk should be avoided or transferred. Examples of risk avoidance controls include (1) separating threats from assets or assets from threats to minimize risks and (2) separating resource allocation from resource use to prevent resource misuse.

Risk control

Risk control identifies the presence or lack of effective controls in the form of prevention, detection, and correction of risks. Risk control focuses on minimizing the risk of loss to which an organization is exposed. The situation of high frequency and low severity should be managed with additional controls (loss control). Risk control includes risk avoidance and risk reduction.

Risk engineering

The goal of risk engineering is to reduce risks in traditional and non-traditional insurance activities which, in part, are achieved through risk financing to fund financial losses. Risk financing includes internal funds for risks (e.g., self insurance and residual risk) and external transfer of risks (e.g., insurance, hedging, and captive insurance). In a way, risk engineering is related to financial engineering in terms of sharing common goals such as risks, hedging, insurance, and captive insurance.

Risk factors

Risk factors are the criteria used to identify the relative significance of and likelihood that conditions and/or events may occur that could adversely affect the organization.

Risk financing

Risk financing concentrates on arranging the availability of internal funds to meet occurring financial losses. It also involves external transfer of risk. Risk financing includes risk retention and risk transfer, which is a tool used by captive insurers. Risk retention applies to risks that have a low expected frequency and a low potential severity. Risk transfer applies to risks that have a low expected frequency and a high potential severity (e.g., buying insurance). Insurance should be purchased for losses in excess of a firm's risk retention level.

When losses have both high expected frequency and high potential severity, it is likely that risk retention, risk transfer, and loss control all will need to be used in varying degrees. Common methods of loss control include reducing the probability of losses (i.e., frequency and severity reduction) and decreasing the cost of losses that do occur (i.e., cost reduction). Note that "high" and "low" loss frequency and severity rates are defined differently for different firms.

Risk financing includes internal funding for risks (self-insurance and residual risk) and external transfer of risks, such as insurance and hedging. It can be unfunded or funded retention of risks. The unfunded retention is treated as part of the overall cost of doing business. A firm may decide to practice funded retention by making various pre-loss arrangements to ensure that money is readily available to pay for losses that occur. Examples of funded retention include use of credit, reserve funds, self-insurance, and captive insurers.

Risk limitation

"Risk limitation" means limiting or containing risks by implementing controls that minimize the adverse impact of a threat's exercising a vulnerability (e.g., use of supporting, preventive, and detective controls) or by authorizing operation for a limited time during which additional risk mitigation efforts by other means is installed.

Risk management

Risk management is the total process of identifying, assessing, controlling, and mitigating risks as it deals with uncertainty. It includes risk assessment (risk analysis); cost/benefit analysis; the selection, implementation, testing, and evaluation of safeguards (risk mitigation); risk financing (risk funding); and risk monitoring (reporting, feedback, and evaluation). It is expressed as:

Risk management = Risk assessment + Risk mitigation + Risk financing + Risk monitoring

The ultimate goal of risk management is to minimize the adverse effects of losses and uncertainty connected with pure risks. Risk management is broken down into two major categories: risk control and risk financing.

Risk mapping

Risk mapping involves profiling risk events to their sources (i.e., threats and vulnerabilities), determining their impact levels (i.e., low, medium, or high), and evaluating the presence of or lack of effective controls to mitigate risks.

Risk mitigation

Risk mitigation involves implementation of preventive, detective, and corrective controls along with management, operational, and technical controls to reduce the effects of risks. Risk mitigation includes designing and implementing controls and control-related procedures to minimize risks.

Risk monitoring

Risk monitoring addresses internal and external reporting and provides feedback into the risk assessment process, continuing the loop.

Risk registers

Risk registers document the risks below the strategic level and include inherent risks (high or higher) and unchanged residual risks, lack of or ineffectiveness of key internal controls, and lack of mitigating factors (e.g., contingency plans and monitoring activities). Risk registers provide direct links among risk categories, risk aspects, audit universe, and internal controls.

Risk retention

Risk retention is retention of risk and is most appropriate for situations in which there is a low probability of occurrence (frequency) with a low potential severity. These are situations that seldom occur, and, when they do happen, the financial impact is small or negligible. Severity dictates whether a risk should be retained. If the potential severity is more than the organization can afford, retention is not recommended. Frequency determines whether the risk is economically insurable. The higher the probabilities of loss, the higher the expected value of loss and the higher the cost of transfer.

Risk spreading or sharing

Risk spreading or sharing involves spreading or sharing risks with other divisions or business units of the same organization. It is viewed as a special case of risk transfer, in which the risk is transferred from an individual to a group, from one division to another, or from one business unit to another. Risk sharing is a form of risk retention, depending on the success of the risk-sharing arrangement.

Risk transfer

Risk transfer involves payment by one party (the transferor) to another party (the transferee, or risk bearer). The five forms of risk transfer are: (1) hold-harmless agreements, (2) incorporation, (3) diversification, (4) hedging, and (5) insurance. Risk transfer is most likely ideal for a risk with a low expected frequency and a high potential severity.

Sample

The term "sample" refers to a portion of a population that is examined or tested in order to obtain information or draw conclusions about the entire population.

Sampling distribution

A sampling distribution is the distribution of a statistic.

Sampling error or precision

Each estimate generated from a probability sample has a measurable precision, or sampling error, that may be expressed as a plus or minus figure. A sampling error indicates how closely we can reproduce from a sample the results that we would obtain if we were to take a complete count of the population using the same measurement methods. By adding the sampling error to and subtracting it from the estimate, we can develop upper and lower bounds for each estimate. This range is called a confidence interval. Sampling errors and confidence intervals are stated at a certain confidence level. For example, a confidence interval at the 95% confidence level means that in 95 of 100 instances, the sampling procedure we used would produce a confidence interval containing the population value we are estimating.

Sampling frame

A sampling frame is a means of access to a population, usually a list of the sampling units contained in the population. The list may be printed on paper, on a magnetic tape/disk file, or in a physical file of such things as payroll records or accounts receivable.

Sampling with replacement

Sampling with replacement is a sampling method in which each item selected for a sample is returned to the population and can be selected again. In this method, the population can be regarded as infinite.

Sampling without replacement

Sampling without replacement is a sampling method in which an item selected for a sample is used up; it is not returned to the population and cannot be selected again. In this method, the population can be regarded as finite.

Scope limitation

Scope limitation is a restriction placed on the internal auditing department that precludes the department from accomplishing its objectives and plans. Among other things, a scope limitation may restrict the: (1) scope defined in the charter; (2) department's access to records, personnel, and physical properties relevant to the performance of audits; (3) approved audit work schedule; (4) performance of necessary auditing procedures; and (5) approved staffing plan and financial budget.

Self-insurance

Self-insurance is a risk-retention program that incorporates elements of the insurance mechanism where the self-insured organization pays the claims rather than an insurance company.

Senior management

"Senior management" refers to those individuals to whom the director of internal auditing is responsible.

Should

The IIA *Standards* use the word "should" where conformance is expected unless, when applying professional judgment, circumstances justify deviation.

Simple random sample

A probability sample in which each member of the population has an equal chance of being drawn to the sample.

Significance

The term "significance" refers to the relative importance of a matter within the context in which it is being considered, including quantitative and qualitative factors, such as magnitude, nature, effect, relevance, and impact. Professional judgment assists internal auditors when evaluating the significance of matters within the context of the relevant objectives.

Significant

The term "significant" refers to the level of importance or magnitude assigned to an item, event, information, or problem by the internal auditor.

Significant audit findings

Significant audit findings are those conditions that, in the judgment of the director of internal auditing, could adversely affect the organization. Such audit findings may include conditions dealing with irregularities, illegal acts, errors, inefficiency, waste, ineffectiveness, conflicts of interest, and control weaknesses.

Simple random sample

A simple random sample is a probability sample in which each member of the population has an equal chance of being drawn to the sample.

Skewed distribution

Skewed distribution is not a symmetrical distribution; hence it cannot be considered a normal distribution.

Speculative risk

Speculative risk exists when there is uncertainty about an event that could produce either a profit or a loss. It involves the chance of loss or gain (e.g., hedging, options, and derivatives).

Spread

"Spread" is a general term for the extent of variation among cases.

Standard

A standard is a criterion by which the operations of an internal auditing department are evaluated and measured. A standard is intended to represent the practice of internal auditing as it should be.

Standard deviation

Standard deviation is a numerical measure of the spread of a group of values about their mean. It is a statistic used with interval-ratio variables. It is also called root mean square deviation and is the square root of the variance. We take the square root to account for the fact that we squared the differences in computing the variance. It is the measure of variability of a statistical sample that serves as an estimate of the population variability. This is the most common and useful of the dispersion measures.

Standard error of the mean

The standard error of the mean is the standard deviation of the sampling distribution of a sample statistic. It is a measure of the variability within a sample.

Standards

Professional pronouncements promulgated by the IIA's Internal Auditing Standards Board (IASB) that delineates the requirements for performing a broad range of internal audit activities and for evaluating internal audit performance. They include Attribute *Standards* and Performance *Standards* from the International Professional Practice Framework (IPPF).

Static risk

Static risk, which can be either pure or speculative, stems from an unchanging society that is in stable equilibrium. Examples of pure static risk include the uncertainties due to such random events as lightning, windstorms, and death. Business undertakings in a stable economy illustrate the concept of speculative static risk.

Statistic
A statistic is a number computed from data on one or more variables.

Statistical estimate
A statistical estimate is a numerical value assigned to a population parameter on the basis of evidence from a sample.

Strata
The term "strata" refers to two or more mutually exclusive subdivisions of a population defined in such a way that each sampling unit can belong to only one subdivision or stratum.

Strategic risk
Strategic risk is a high-level and corporate-wide risk, which includes strategy risk, political risk, economic risk, regulatory risk, reputation risk, global risk, leadership risk, customer risk, and market brand management risk. It is also related to failure of strategy and changing customer needs and business conditions.

Stratified random sample
If the population to be sampled is first subclassified into several subpopulations called strata, the sample may be drawn by taking random samples from each stratum. The samples need not be proportional to the strata sizes.

Subjective risk
"Subjective risk" refers to the mental state of an individual who experiences doubt or worry as to the outcome of a given event. In addition to being subjective, a particular risk may be either pure or speculative and either static or dynamic.

Supervision
Supervision is a process that begins with planning and continues throughout the examination, evaluation, report, and follow-up phases of the audit assignment. Supervision includes: (1) ensuring that the auditors assigned possess the requisite knowledge and skills; (2) providing appropriate instructions during the planning of the audit and approving the audit program; (3) seeing that the approved audit program is carried out unless changes are both justified and authorized; (4) determining that audit working papers adequately support the audit findings, conclusions, and reports; (5) ensuring that audit reports are accurate, objective, clear, concise, constructive, and timely; (6) ensuring that audit objectives are met; and (7) providing opportunities for developing internal auditors' knowledge and skills.

Survey
A survey is a process for gathering information, without detailed verification, on the activity being examined. The main purposes of a survey are to: (1) understand the activity under review; (2) identify significant areas warranting special emphasis; (3) obtain information for use in performing the audit; and (4) determine whether further auditing is necessary.

Symmetric measure of association
A symmetric measure of association is measure of association of variables that do not make a distinction between independent and dependent variables.

System
A system (process, operation, function, or activity) is an arrangement, a set, or a collection of concepts, parts, activities, and/or people that are connected or interrelated to achieve objectives and goals. (This definition applies to both manual and automated systems.) A system may also be a collection of subsystems operating together for a common objective or goal.

Systematic selection with a random start

Systematic selection with a random start is a sampling method in which a given sample size is divided into the population size in order to obtain a sampling interval. A random starting point between 1 and the sampling interval is obtained. This item is selected first; then every item whose number or location is equal to the previously selected item plus the sampling interval is selected, until the population is used up.

Technology-based audit techniques

The term "technology-based audit techniques" refers to any automated audit tool, such as generalized audit software, test data generators, computerized audit programs, specialized audit utilities, and computer-assisted audit techniques.

Tolerable error

Tolerable error is the specified precision or the maximum sampling error that will still permit the results to be useful. It is also called bound on error.

Trend analysis

Trend analysis is the analysis of the changes in a given item of information over a period of time.

Understanding

"Understanding" means the ability to apply broad knowledge to situations likely to be encountered, to recognize significant deviations, and to be able to carry out the research necessary to arrive at reasonable solutions.

Unobtrusive measures

Unobtrusive measures are measures that are not readily noticeable to others.

Variable sampling

The term "variable sampling" refers to sampling in which the selected sampling units are measured or evaluated (in terms of dollars, pounds, days, etc.), and some statistical measure (statistic) is computed from these measurements to estimate the population parameter or measure.

Variance

Variance is sometimes called the average squared deviation. It is computed by taking the difference between individual value and the mean, squaring it, then adding all the squared differences and dividing by the number of items.

Work measurement

Work measurement is an industrial engineering program that applies some of the general principles of creative problem solving to the simplification of operations or procedures.

Index

A

ABC method of inventory, 53
Abuse, 266, 469
Access security controls, 149–50
Accident investigation, 278
Accomplishments, noteworthy, 367
Accounting records, examining, 398
Accounting system, recent change in, 303
Accounts payable, computer-assisted, 64
Accounts receivable, computer-assisted, 39
Accounts receivable turnover, 39
ACH. *See* automated clearinghouse (ACH) systems
Activity reports, defined, 469
Actual costs *vs.* standard costs, 108
Add value, defined, 469
Adequate control, defined, 469
Adverse opinion, 143
Agent of a third party, 10
AICPA. *See* American Institute of Certified Public Accountants (AICPA)
Air conditioning, 214–15
Alcoholic beverages, 283
Alternative risk-transfer tools, defined, 469
American Institute of Certified Public Accountants (AICPA), 332
American Insurance Association's Standards Fire Defense Rating Schedule, 213
Americans with Disabilities Act, 283
Analytical procedures
    defined, 470
    examples of, 408
    in practice, use of, 407
    principal types of, 406
    types of, 406
Analytical reviews, 330–31
Anecdotal records, defined, 470
Annual survey, 8
Antiboycott laws, 12
Antiretaliatory legislation, 8
Antitrust laws, 12, 51

Application controls, 150
    general controls *vs.*, 149
    relationship between general and, 150–51
Application system
    development and maintenance controls, 150
    documentation controls review, 263
    documentation types and contents, 264
    life cycle of, 158
Appreciation, defined, 470
Assault and battery, 422
Asset, liquidity of, 303
Asset method, 412
Asset method formula, 413
Assurance, false, 312, 314
Assurance audit engagements, 25–28
Assurance maps, defined, 470
Assurance services, defined, 470
ATMs. *See* automated teller machine systems (ATMs)
ATM systems, 250
Attribute, defined, 470
Attribute listing, defined, 470
Attribute sampling, defined, 471
Auditable activities, defined, 471
Audit approach in a transportation department, 91
Audit assignment, managing an, 348–49
Audit committee, 5–6, 8, 314–15
Audit concern of multinational corporation, 115
Audit/control risks
    in computer storage media, 246–47
    in data communications, 205
    in EDI applications, 253
    in insiders and outsiders, 203
    responsibilities, 173
Audit cycle/area
    expenditure: accounts payable, 61–64
    expenditure: payroll, 68–77
    expenditure: personnel administration, 64–68
    expenditure: purchasing, 48–55

    expenditure: quality assurance of materials, 59–60
    expenditure: receiving, 55–58
    financial reporting: consolidation and general ledger posting, 135–37
    financial reporting: financial report preparation and issuance, including records retention, 137–38
    financial reporting: journal entry preparation, 134–35
    financial reporting: tax accounting and reporting, 139–42
    production/conversion: cost accounting, 102–9
    production/conversion: fixed assets, 94–100
    production/conversion: inventory control, 77–83
    production/conversion: plant maintenance, 100–102
    production/conversion: production control, 83–86
    production/conversion: quality control, 91–94
    production/conversion: shipping, 86–88
    production/conversion: traffic, 88–91
    revenue: accounts receivable, 37–39
    revenue: advertising and sales promotion, 42–44
    revenue: billing, 36–37
    revenue: cash receipts, 39–41
    revenue: commissions, 41–42
    revenue: credit management, 35
    revenue: intercompany transfers, 47–48
    revenue: marketing administration, 44–46
    revenue: product distribution, 46–47
    revenue: warranty accounting, 41
    treasury: cash management, 112–15
    treasury: debt management, 109–12
    treasury: dividends management, 125–27
    treasury: equity management, 116–21

Audit cycle/area (*continued*)
  treasury: foreign currency exchange
    management, 130–32
  treasury: investment management, 122–25
  treasury: risk and insurance management,
    128–30
  treasury: write-off accounting, 132–33
Audit design, effective, 313
Auditee, defined, 471
Audit evidence-gathering sources, 162
Audit findings
  conclusions, and recommendations, 364–66
  desirable attributes of a deficiency, 365–66
  determining the significance of, 363–64
Auditing for fraud guidelines, 395
Auditing software development, acquisition,
    and maintenance, 168–70
Audit objectives, defined, 471
Audit objectives and scope
  audit objectives, determining, 335–36
  audit scope, 336–38
  audit scope considerations, 337
  audit scope impairments, 337–38
  methodology and, 363–64
Auditors, audit plans of independent, 304
Auditor's role in software development,
    acquisition, and maintenance: audit
    objectives and procedures, 170–86
  auditability, 173
  auditor's role, 170–71
  audit scope, 171–73
  controllability, 173
  maintainability, 172
  securability, 173
  usability, 172
Audit plan, periodic review of, 313
Audit planning, 328–30
  audit plans, 328–29
  planning an audit assignment, 329–30
  report, 329
  special instructions, 329
  staff plans, 328
Audit procedures, 338
  defined, 471
Audit process, 323–28
  audit activities, 326
  audit director, job duties or responsibilities
    of, 327
  audit fieldwork, 325
  audit manager/supervisor, job duties or
    responsibilities of, 327
  audit program, 325
  audit team leader/auditor-in-charge, job
    duties or responsibilities of, 327
  control status during survey and fieldwork
    phases, 325
  monitoring and follow-up, 325–26
  preliminary survey, 324
  reporting, 325
  staff/senior auditor, job duties or
    responsibilities of, 327–28
Audit program, defined, 471
Audit recommendations, how to get action on,
    368–69
Audit report, 371–73

contents, 362–67
  purpose, 361
  timeliness, 362
Audit report, defined, 471
Audit risk, defined, 471
*Audit Risk and Materiality in Conducting an
    Audit*, 332
Audit risk factors
  accounting system, recent change in, 303
  asset, liquidity of, 303
  auditors, audit plans of independent, 304
  computerized data processing, extent of, 304
  economic condition of unit, 304
  government regulation, extent of, 304
  home office, distance of unit from, 305
  internal auditor, maintaining appearance of
    independence by, 305
  internal control system, quality of, 303
  key personnel, recent change in, 304
  last audit, time since, 304
  management, competence of, 303
  management, integrity of, 303
  morale, level of employees', 304
  operations, complexity of, 303
  political exposure, 305
  pressure on management to meet
    objectives, 304
  rapid growth, 304
  risk factors, 304
  size of unit, 303
Audit risks in help desk operation, 249
Audit scheduling, 347–49
Audit scope, defined, 471
Audits of compliance, general, 266–71
  inherent limitations in internal control
    systems examples, 270
  Inherent risk, 267–69
  internal controls, 269–71
  key terms, definition of, 266
  laws and regulations, testing compliance
    with, 267
  laws and regulations, understanding
    relevant, 266–67
  noncompliance (red flags), indicators of
    susceptibility to, 268
  risk assessment, 267–71
  vulnerability assessment, 267
Audits of compliance, specific, 271–90
  accident investigation, 278
  benchmarking, best-in-class, 289
  benchmarking, business process, 288
  benchmarking, competitive, 288
  benchmarking, industry, 289
  benchmarking, internal, 288
  benchmarking, process, 289
  benchmarking, strategic, 289
  benchmarking, types of, 287
  benchmarking defined, 286–87
  benefits continuation, 279
  bulletin boards, 279–80
  business process benchmarking, 288
  business process improvement (BPI),
    285–86
  business process reviews business process
    reengineering (BPR), 285–86

canteen food, 274
competitive benchmarking, 288
compliance audits, 271–72
consulting engagements, 284
data processing, 274
disabilities accommodation, 283–84
discharges, 274
drug testing, 282
employee safety review, audit concerns
    in, 277
energy use, 274
environmental audit, approach to
    conducting an, 272–75
environmental auditing, 271–72
environmental auditing, approach to,
    276–77
environmental auditing, audit concerns
    during, 276
environmental liability accrual audits, 272
environmental management system
    audits, 272
environmental policy, overall, 272–73
exit interview, 280
finance function, 273
functional areas of business, 273–74
hazard communication, 278–79
hazardous waste management program,
    approach to audit of, 275
human resource policy auditing, 277
I-9 Employment Eligibility, 280
independent contractors, 280–81
industry benchmarking, 289
information technology consulting, 289–90
insurance function, 273
internal benchmarking, 288
internal control training, 284–85
international business divisions, 273
legal department, 274
marketing function, 273
operational factors, 274–75
organization strategy, 272–73
performance measurement systems, design
    of, 290
pollution prevention audits, 272
process benchmarking, 289
product audits, 272
production function, 273
recycling, 274
reporting and follow-up, 275
safety responsibility, 277–78
security, 279
sexual harassment, 284
site tidiness, 274
smoking policy, 281–82
staff training and participation, 273
strategic benchmarking, 289
substance abuse policy, 282–83
telephone usage, 281
transactional audits, 272
transport, 274
treatment, storage, and disposal facility
    audits, 272
wastes, 274
water use, 274
Audit supervision, 349–50

Audit trail
    computer controls and, 155–56
    hard-copy, 161
Audit universe, periodic review of, 313
Audit work, planning, 340
Audit working papers, 353–55
    advantages and disadvantages of manually
        and electronically prepared, 353
    defined, 472
    developing and reviewing, 352–55
Audit work program, 338–40
    about, 338
    audit programs, about, 339–40
    audit programs, standardized vs.
        customized, 339
Audit work schedules, defined, 472
Authorization, defined, 472
Authorizing, defined, 472
Automated clearinghouse (ACH) systems, 250
Automated teller machine systems (ATMs), 225

B
Balance sheet and income statement,
    analyzing, 408–11
Balancing and reconciliation,
    responsibility, 233
Bandwidth, 423
Bank reconciliations
    computer controls and, 157
Batch data conversion and data entry
    procedures, 231
Behavior
    interpretation of, 416
    nonverbal, 417–18
    verbal, 416–17
Bell curve, defined, 472
Benchmark, ways to, 305
Benchmarking
    best-in-class, 289
    business process, 288
    competitive, 288
    defined, 286–87
    industry, 289
    internal, 288
    process, 289
    strategic, 289
    types of, 287
Benefits continuation, 277, 279
Bias, defined, 472
BLP. See bypass label processing (BLP)
Board, defined, 472
Board of directors, 8, 109–10, 116–23, 126,
    130, 132–33, 272
BPI. See business process improvement (BPI)
BPR. See business process reviews business
    process reengineering (BPR)
Bulletin boards, 279–80
Burden efficiency variance, 108
Burden expenditure variance, 108
Burden volume variance, 108
Business attacks, 433
Business/control risks
    in electronic mail, 256
    in feasibility study phase, 174
    in local area networks, 193

    in postimplementation phase, 177
    in software development, 174–75, 177
    in system design phase, 175
Business courtesies, 9–10, 12
Business inducements, 11
Business process benchmarking, 288
Business process improvement (BPI), 285–86
Business process reengineering vs. business
    process improvement, 286
Business process reviews business process
    reengineering (BPR), 285–86
Business risks
    in detail requirements phase, 175
    in electrical power, 214
Bypass label processing (BLP), 197

C
CAATs. See computer-assisted audit
    techniques (CAATs)
Caches, 423
Canteen food, 274
Captive insurance methods, defined, 469
Cash receipts, computer-assisted, 40
Cause, defined, 472
Central limit theorem, defined, 472
Central tendency, defined, 472
CEO. See chief executive officer (CEO)
Certified Internal Auditors (CIAs), 296.
        See also sample practice questions,
        answers, and explanations
    exam content specifications, xv–xviii
    exam-taking tips and techniques, xiii
Chain-of-command communication, 379
Charter (internal audit), defined, 472
Charting techniques, 401
Checklists, defined, 472
Chief audit executive, defined, 473
Chief executive officer (CEO), 5–7, 275
CIAs. See Certified Internal Auditors (CIAs)
Circumstantial evidence, 400
Civil acts, 266
    defined, 473
Civil Rights Act, 284
Cluster sample, defined, 473
COBRA. See Consolidated Omnibus Budget
    Reconciliation Act (COBRA)
Code of conduct
    within an organization, 4–5
    content of a, 9–12
    corporate, 2, 7, 9
    disciplinary actions and, 8
    of the Institute of Internal Auditor (IIA), 1
    monitoring compliance with, 6, 8
    monitoring compliance with the, 6
    training, 6
Code of corporate conduct, 6–8
Code of ethics
    corporate, 4
    defined, 473
    role of corporate, 1–2
Coefficient of variation, defined, 473
Commissions, computer-assisted
    techniques for, 42
Common law causes of action, awareness
    of, 420

Communication, effective, 363
Compensation, competitive levels of, 7
Competitive benchmarking, 288
Compliance
    audits, 271–72
    audits of compliance, general, 266–71
    audits of compliance, specific, 271–90
    defined, 473
    requirement defined, 473
    with standards, regulations, and laws, 367
    tools to monitor, 8
Compliance audit engagements, 266–90
Computer
    as an investigative tool, 431–32
    crime, related concepts in, 435
    fraud and crime examples, 433–35
    hardware, 429–30
    simulation in purchasing, 54
    viruses, 255–56
    virus programs, 434
Computer-assisted audit techniques
    accounts payable, 64
    accounts receivable, 39
    cash receipts, 40
    commissions, 42
    cost accounting, 108
    credit management, 35
    debt management, 112
    dividends management, 127
    equity management, 121
    fixed assets, 100
    inventory control, 83
    investment management, 125
    payroll, 76
    personnel administration, 68
    production control, 86
    purchasing, 54
    sales/billing/invoicing, 37
    shipping, 88
    tax, 142
Computer-assisted audit techniques
    (CAATs), 162
Computer controls
    audit trails and, 155–56
    bank reconciliations and, 157
    classification of, 151–53
    compensating controls, 154–55
    compensating controls, review of, 155–58
    control, attributes of a, 153
    control assessment challenge, 152
    control grids/matrices, 156–57
    controls by action or objective, 152
    control total verifications, 156
    corrective controls, 152
    cost/benefit analysis of controls, 153–54
    costs vs. controls vs. convenience, 154
    detective controls, 152
    directive controls, 151
    error logs, 156
    exception and statistical reports, 157–58
    independent reviews, 157
    internal control questionnaires, 157
    interrelationships between controls, 158–59
    life cycle of a data item, 159
    life cycle of an application system, 158

Computer controls (*continued*)
 logical access security controls, 157
 manual/automated reconciliations, 158
 preventive controls, 151–52
 recovery controls, 152–53
 report balancing, 158
 transaction logs, 156
 use of controls, 159
Computer evidence
 care and handling of, 428
 chain of, 432–33
 collection of, 428
 guidelines for examination of, 430–31
 guidelines for preservation and submission of, 429–30
 guidelines for the care and handling of, 427
 identification of, 428
 preservation of, 428–29
 transportation of, 429
Computer forensics
 guidelines to a successful, 426
 use of hash algorithms in, 426
Computerized data processing, extent of, 304
Computer operations, 240–44
 audit objectives, 240
 audit procedures, 240–44
 backup procedures, 242
 backup schedules, 242
 computer operator practices, 243–44
 control risks in computer operations, 242, 244
 controls over computer operators, 243
 housekeeping activities, 242
 preventive maintenance, 244
 production job abends (abnormal ends), 240–41
 production job processing, 240
 production job reruns, 241
 system console logs, 241–42
Conclusions (opinions), defined, 473
Condition, defined, 473
Conditional distribution, defined, 473
Conditional probability, defined, 473
Conduct, activities to ensure a standing level of, 7
Confidence
 coefficient, defined, 474
 interval, defined, 474
 level, defined, 474
 limits, defined, 474
Confidential data, handling, 209
Confidentiality, 3, 9, 18, 31–32, 123, 197
Conflict-of-interest, 2–3, 297–99
 defined, 474
 policy, 4–5
 statements, 2, 66
Consolidated Omnibus Budget Reconciliation Act (COBRA), 279
Consulting engagements, 284
Consulting services, defined, 474
Contingency planning
 about, 216
 audit objectives, 217–18
 auditor's role, 216–17
 audit procedures, 218–26
 emergency preparedness, 222–23

information gathering, 218
 insurance, 225–26
 off-site storage facilities, 219–20
 plan maintenance procedures, 224
 planning document, 220–22
 risk analysis, 218–19
 testing and recovery procedures, 223–24
 user procedures, functional, 222
 vital records retention program, 224–25
Contingency planning documents, 189
Contingency plans, 308
Continuous variable, defined, 474
Contract auditing, 27–28
Contracts, comparison of, 28
Control, defined, 307, 474
Control/audit risks
 in data communications, 188
 in data security, 210
 in data systems, 230
 in end user computing, 184
 in network changes, 195
 in network configuration, 189
 in network management, 190
 in network performance management, 191
 in software prototyping, 181–82
Control/business risks
 in database systems, 227–28
Control environment, defined, 474
Control flowcharting method, 83
Control mechanisms, 7, 199, 231
Control processes, defined, 474
Control risks
 in computer operations, 242, 244
 in conversion and production support phases, 177
 in database systems, 226
 in data entry and conversion, 232
 in job documentation, 238
 in network administration, 189
 in network security, 190
 in production operations, 240
 in production schedule, 239
 in program development phase, 176
 in software acquisition, 178
 in tape library, 246
 in user acceptance phase, 177
Controls
 to ensure user satisfaction, 265
 key, 307–8
 mitigating, 308
 over computer operators, 243
Conversion plan, 177
Corporate code of ethics, 4. *See also* Code of ethics
Corporate culture *vs.* corporate ethics, 1
Corporate ethical climate, 6
Corporate policy for compliance with domestic and foreign laws, 8
Cost/benefit relationship, defined, 475
Cost-of-quality reports, 60
CRC32. *See* 32-bit cyclic redundancy checksum (CRC32)
Credit management, computer-assisted, 35
Credit memos *vs.* debit memos, 37, 64
Credit practices, unfair, 7

Criminal acts, 266
 defined, 475
Criteria, defined, 475
Cryptographic device, 205

D
DA. *See* data administrator (DA)
Data administrator (DA), 226
Data and information, collecting, 351–52
Data and network communications and connections
 audit objectives and procedures, 186–96
Database administrator (DBA), 207, 226–27
Database management systems (DBMSs), 149
Databases, 226–30
 audit objectives, 226
 audit procedures, 226–30
 control/business risks in database systems, 227–28
 control risks in database systems, 226
 data compression software, 228–29
Database user profiles, 208–9
Data center operations controls, 149
Data communications, 186–88
 audit objectives, 186
 audit procedures, 187–88
 control/audit risks in, 188
Data communications systems software, 187
Data dictionary (DD), 183
Data dictionary systems software, 229–30
 audit objectives, 229
 audit procedures, 229–30
 control/audit risks in data systems, 230
Data diddling, 433–34
Data editing and validation, online, 232
Data encryption, 192
Data entry function review, 231–33
Data field validation controls, 259
Data files, controls over, 261
Data input controls review, 258–60
Data input error handling, 232–33
Data integrity controls review, 263–64
Data integrity is maintained, 145
Data item, life cycle of a, 159
Data leakage, 433
Data origination and preparation controls review, 258
Data output controls, 262
Data output controls review, 262–63
Data processing, 274
Data processing controls, 260
Data processing controls review, 260–61
Data security controls review, 206–10
 audit objectives, 206
 audit procedures, 206–10
 confidential data, handling, 209
 database user profiles, 208–9
 data classification, 208
 data file maintenance reports, 209
 general procedures, 206–8
 statistical and exception reports, 209–10
Data warehouse, data mart, and data mining, 230
DBA. *See* database administrator (DBA)
DBMSs. *See* database management systems (DBMSs)

DD. *See* data dictionary (DD)
Debit balances, 64
Defamation, 421
Degrees of freedom, defined, 475
Delphi technique, 305–6
Dependent event, defined, 475
Descriptive statistic, defined, 475
Detective controls, 152, 475
Deviation, defined, 475
Direct evidence, 400
Directing, defined, 475
Directive controls, 151, 475
Director of internal auditing, defined, 475
Disabilities accommodation, 277, 283–84
Discharges, 274
Disclaimer of opinion, 143
Discrete Variable, defined, 475
Dispersion, defined, 475
Documentary evidence
    obtaining, 399
    principal methods for obtaining, 399
Document examination guidelines, 397
Drug-Free Workplace Act, 282–83
Drug testing, 277, 282
Due diligence, 414
Due diligence audit engagements, 30
Due professional care, 403
Dynamic risk, defined, 476

E
Econometrics, defined, 476
Economical performance, defined, 476
Economic condition of unit, 304
Economic espionage, 433
Economic order quantity (EOQ), 79
EDI. *See* electronic data interchange (EDI)
    systems
EEOC. *See* Equal Employment Opportunity
    Commission (EEOC)
Effect, defined, 476
Effective control, defined, 476
Efficient performance, defined, 476
EFT. *See* electronic funds transfer (EFT)
Electricity, 214
Electronic commerce, 254–55
Electronic data interchange (EDI) systems,
    252–55
Electronic funds transfer (EFT), 225
Electronic funds transfer (EFT)/electronic data
    interchange, 250–54
    ATM systems, 250
    audit/control risks in EDI applications, 253
    audit objective, 250
    audit procedures, 250–52
    EDI backup and recovery procedures, 254
    electronic data interchange (EDI) systems,
        252–55
    electronic funds transfer (EFT) systems,
        250–52
    VAN security procedures and controls, 254
    wire transfer systems, 251–52
Electronic mail (e-mail), 256–57
Emergency preparedness, 222–23
Emergency procedures, documented,
    215–16

Employee indoctrination, 8, 66
Employee Polygraph Protection Act, 279
Employee safety review, audit concerns
    in, 277
Encryption, 257
End user computing, 182–86
    audit challenges in, 183
    audit objectives, 182
    audit procedures, 182–86
    control/audit risks in, 184
Energy use, 274
Engagement, defined, 476
Engagement objectives, defined, 476
Engagement outcomes monitoring, 382–84
    about, 382
    audit follow-up, 382
    Standards Applicable to Monitor
        Engagement Outcomes, 382–84 (*See
        also under* Standards Applicable to
        Monitor Engagement Outcomes)
Engagement results communication, 361–82
    accomplishments, noteworthy, 367
    audit finding, desirable attributes of a
        deficiency, 365–66
    audit findings, conclusions, and
        recommendations, 364–66
    audit findings, determining the significance
        of, 363–64
    audit objectives, scope, and methodology,
        363–64
    audit recommendations, how to get action
        on, 368–69
    audit report contents, 362–67
    audit report purpose, 361
    audit reports, 371–73
    audit report timeliness, 362
    communication, effective, 363
    compliance with standards, regulations, and
        laws, 367
    interim reports, advantages and
        disadvantages of, 362
    management responses, 367
    oral reports, 370
    report distribution, 370
    report presentation, 367–70
    report presentation, characteristics of, 368
    Standards Applicable to Communicate
        Engagement Results, 373–82 (*See
        also under* Standards Applicable to
        Communicate Engagement Results)
    summary reports, 370
Engagements. *See also* assurance audit
        engagements; compliance audit
        engagements; consulting engagements;
        due diligence audit engagements;
        performance audit engagements;
        privacy audit engagements; quality
        audit engagements; security audit
        engagements; Standards Applicable
        to Plan Engagements; individual
        engagements management
    financial audit and, 143–45
    operational audits and, 32–34
Engagements plan, 323–47
    analytical reviews, 330–31

    audit objectives and scope, 335–38 (*See also*
        audit objectives and scope)
    audit planning, 328–30 (*See also* audit
        planning)
    audit process, 323–28 (*See also* audit
        process)
    audit work, planning the, 340
    audit work program, 338–40 (*See also* audit
        work program)
    planning materiality, 331–35 (*See also*
        planning materiality)
    Standards Applicable to Plan Engagements,
        340–55 (*See also* Standards Applicable
        to Plan Engagements)
Engagements supervision, 347–61
    audit assignment, managing an, 348–49
    audit scheduling, 347–49
    audit supervision, 349–50
    audit working papers, 353–55
    audit working papers, advantages and
        disadvantages of manually and
        electronically prepared, 353
    audit working papers, developing and
        reviewing, 352–55
    data and information, collecting, 351–52
    Standards Applicable to Supervise
        Engagements, 355–61 (*See also under*
        Standards Applicable to Supervise
        Engagements)
Engagement work program, defined, 476
Enterprise-wide resource planning software
    (ERP), 257
Environmental
    controls, 216
    liability accrual audits, 272
    management system, 271
    management system audits, 272
    policy, overall, 272–73
    regulations, 12
Environmental auditing, 271–72
    approach to, 276–77
    approach to conducting an, 272–75
    audit concerns during, 276
    defined, 271
EOQ. *See* economic order quantity (EOQ)
Equal employment opportunity, 11
Equal Employment Opportunity Commission
    (EEOC), 283–84
ERM, defined, 307–8
ERP. *See* enterprise-wide resource planning
    software (ERP)
Error, defined, 476
Errors, 266
Ethical
    behavior, 1, 3, 5–6, 13, 266, 315
    climate, 6, 9, 303
    dilemma, 6–8
Ethical standards, 1, 4, 6, 13
    in complex situations, 13
    factors influencing, 3–4
Ethics
    double standard for, 13
    implementation procedures, 11
    policy, 2
Event, defined, 476

Evidence
circumstantial, 400
collection, 424–25
collection and preservation of, 427–32
direct, 400
discovery and recognition of, 427
evaluation and communication of
results, 425
examination of, 431
14 traditional forms of, 159
legal rules on, 400
organization of, 400
protection of, 427–28
in purchasing and accounts payable, 54
receipt of, 431
recording, 428
safeguards to protect, 426
Exception reports, 210
Exit interview, 280
Expenditure cycle, 33, 48–76
accounts payable audit cycle/area, 61–64
payroll audit cycle/area, 68–77
personnel administration audit cycle/area,
64–68
purchasing audit cycle/area, 48–55
quality assurance of materials audit cycle/
area, 59–60
receiving audit cycle/area, 55–58
Expenditure method, 412
Expenditures method formula, 413
Exposure, 302
External auditors, defined, 476
External label, contents of, 207
External reviews, defined, 476
External service provider, defined, 477
External sources, 352
Extinguishing devices, 213

F
False assurance, 312, 314
Feasibility study report, 174
Federal Aeronautics Administration, 281
Federal sentencing guidelines for
organizational defendants, 414
File maintenance controls review, system-
related, 261–62
Finance function, 273
Financial attacks, 434
Financial audit, 144
engagements, 143–45
purpose and scope of, 143
Financial auditing, 144–45
Financial insurance contracts, defined, 470
Financial interest, 10
Financial reporting cycle, 33, 133–45
consolidation and general ledger posting,
135–37
financial report preparation and issuance,
including records retention, 137–38
fraud in, 6–9
journal entry preparation, 134–35
tax accounting and reporting, 139–42
Financial review, 144
Financial risk, defined, 477
Financial statement analysis, 408–9

Financial transactions, proving illicit, 411–14
Findings, defined, 477
Finite population correction (FPC) factor,
defined, 477
Fire, smoke detection, 213
Fire drills, 213
Fire extinguishers, 58
Fire prevention, detection, and suppression
procedures, 212–13
Firewalls review, 210–2112
Flowchart, defined, 477
Flowcharting techniques, 411, 414
Follow-up, defined, 477
Forecasting techniques, guidelines for, 82
Foreign Corrupt Practices Act, 11
Foreign intelligence services, 433
Forensic auditing, 423–27
computer forensics, guidelines to a
successful, 426
computer forensics, use of hash algorithms
in, 426
evidence collection, 424–25
evidence evaluation and communication of
results, 425
forensic auditing, phases of, 424
fraud, timely resolution of a, 424
problem recognition and planning, 424
safeguards to protect evidence, 426
software forensics, 425–27
Forensic auditing, phases of, 424
Forensics, software, 425–27
Formal internal reviews, defined, 477
Formulas in inventory, 82
Fraud, 266
defined, 477
in financial reporting, 6–9
investigations, interviewing and
interrogating in, 415–16
timely resolution of a, 424
Fraud, audit tests to detect, 396–404
accounting records, examining, 398
charting techniques, 401
documentary evidence, obtaining, 399
documentary evidence, principal methods
for obtaining, 399
document examination, 397
document examination, guidelines for, 397
due professional care, 403
evidence, legal rules of, 400
evidence, organization of, 400
evidence, types of, 400
fraud, documenting, 398–99
fraud reports, characteristics of, 403
fraud reports, mistakes to avoid in
writing, 404
fraud reports, writing, 402–3
memorandum of interview, 402
privileged reports, 404
records, business and individual, 401–2
search warrants, 399
steps to take when fraud is suspected,
396–400
subpoenas, 399
tools and techniques, 396
voluntary consent, 399

written report, 403–4
Fraud, controls to prevent or detect, 394–96
computer fraud–related controls, 395
detective controls, 395
detective controls in general, 394–95
fraud guidelines, auditing for, 395
preventive controls, 395
preventive controls in general, 394
recovery controls, 395–96
Fraud, integrating analytical relationships to
detect, 405–14
analytical procedures, more examples
of, 408
analytical procedures, principal types of, 406
analytical procedures, types of, 406
analytical procedures in practice, use of, 407
asset method formula, 413
balance sheet and income statement,
analyzing the, 408–11
expenditures method formula, 413
federal sentencing guidelines for
organizational defendants, 414
financial statement analysis, 408–9
financial transactions, proving illicit, 411–14
flowcharting techniques, 411
IMA research findings, 407
internal auditors, implications for, 408
internal fraud, scope of, 410
major impetus, 405–6
modeling techniques, 407
money laundering, 413–14
net amount of cash from operations,
formula for determining, 411
net worth computation methods, 412–13
on-book and off-book schemes, 412
plausible relationships, 409
ratio analysis, 406, 409
statement of cash flows, 410–11
statement of cash flows, red flags to watch
in the, 411
Treadway Commission: recommendation
about analytical review procedures, 405
trend analysis, 406
Fraud, types, 391–93
fraud, overview of, 391
fraud, three elements of, 393
fraud, types of, 392–93
fraud, varieties of, 393
fraud by frequency, 392–93
fraud involving conspiracy, 393
theft of assets, 392
Fraud and crime, use of computers in
analyzing data, 427–35
business attacks, 433
computer as an investigative tool, using a,
431–32
computer crime, related concepts in, 435
computer evidence, care and handling
of, 428
computer evidence, chain of, 432–33
computer evidence, collection of, 428
computer evidence, guidelines for care and
handling of, 427
computer evidence, guidelines for
examination of, 430–31

computer evidence, guidelines for preservation and submission of, 429–30
computer evidence, identification of, 428
computer evidence, preservation of, 428–29
computer evidence, transportation of, 429
computer fraud and crime examples, 433–35
  data diddling, 433–34
  data leakage, 433
  documentation, 430
  economic espionage, 433
  evidence, collection and preservation of, 427–32
  evidence, discovery and recognition of, 427
  evidence, examination of, 431
  evidence, protection of, 427–28
  evidence, receipt of, 431
  evidence, recording, 428
  financial attacks, 434
  foreign intelligence services, 433
  "fun" attacks, 434
  grudge attacks, 434
  hardware, 429–30
  magnetic media, 430
  military and intelligence attacks, 433
  reporting results, 431
  salami technique, 434
  SuperZapping, 434
  terrorist attacks, 434
  wiretapping, 433
Frequency distribution, defined, 477
"Fun" attacks, 434
Functional areas of business, 273–74

G
GAAS. *See* generally accepted auditing standards (GAAS)
GAGAS. *See* generally accepted government auditing standards (GAGAS)
GAIT-R. *See* Practice Guide GAIT for Business and IT Risk (GAIT-R)
Generally accepted auditing standards (GAAS), 173
Generally accepted government auditing standards (GAGAS), 173
General semantics, defined, 478
Gifts, 2–4, 9–10, 48, 51
Goals, defined, 478
Governance, defined, 478
Government business, 12
Government regulation, extent of, 304
Grace log-ins, 193
Gratuities, 4, 9
Greed, 4
Grudge attacks, 434

H
Hard disks, 423
Hardware, computer, 429–30
Hazard, defined, 478
Hazard communication, 277–79
Hazard Communication Plan, 278
Hazard Communication Standards (OSHA), 278

Hazardous waste management program, approach to audit of, 275
Hazard risk, defined, 478
Hedging, defined, 478
Hedonism, 4
Help desk function review, 248–49
Help desk operation, audit risks in, 249
Hiring practices, 7
Histogram, defined, 478
Home office, distance of unit from, 305
Honesty and objectivity, 3
Horizontal analysis, 410
Housekeeping controls, 212
Human resource policy auditing, 277

I
I-9 Employment Eligibility, 280
IIA. *See* Institute of Internal Auditors (IIA)
Illegal acts, 266, 478
IMA research findings, 407
Immigration Reform and Control Act, 280
Impairment, defined, 478
Independence, defined, 478–49
Independent contractors, 277, 280–81
Independent event, defined, 479
Individual engagements management
  engagement outcomes monitoring, 382–84 (*See also* engagement outcomes monitoring)
  engagement results communication, 361–82 (*See also* engagement results)
  engagements plan, 323–28 (*See also* engagements plan)
  engagements supervision, 347–61 (*See also* engagements supervision)
Industry benchmarking, 289
Inferential statistic, defined, 479
Information
  defined, 479
  inside, 10
  primary and secondary, 351
Information protection
  audit objectives and procedures, 255–57
  business/control risks in electronic mail, 256
  computer viruses, 255–56
  electronic mail, 256–57
Information systems
  audit and control procedures, 147–48
  audit objectives, 146
  audits, integrated, 145
  audit scope, 145
  contracts, 250
  control objectives, 145–46
  control types, 148–51
Information systems audit evidence, 159–62
  activity monitoring, 161
  audit evidence-gathering sources, 162
  bulk processing techniques, 162
  evidence types, 160
  file of documents, 161
  hard-copy audit trail, 161
  hard-copy input, 159
  hard-copy output, 161
  hard-copy processing, 160
  location of information, 160–61

  movement of documents, 160
  procedure manual, 161
  segregation of duties, 161–62
  simplified processing, 160
  transaction authorization, 160
  transaction initiation, 159
Information technology
  access security controls, 149–50
  application controls, 150
  application system development and maintenance controls, 150
  audit engagements, 145
  compliance and substantive reviews and/or tests, 148
  consulting, 289–90
  data center operations controls, 149
  general and application controls, relationship between, 150–51
  general controls, 149–50
  system software controls, 149
Information technology (IT) controls, defined, 479
Information technology (IT) governance, defined, 479
Information technology operations, 230–49
  audit procedures, 231–49
  batch data conversion and data entry procedures, 231
  computer operations, 240–44
  control risks in data entry and conversion, 232
  controls over microfiche and microfilm records, 236–37
  data editing and validation, online, 232
  data entry function review, 231–33
  data input error handling, 232–33
  general operating practices review, 231
  help desk function review, 248–49
  job scheduling review, 237–39
  online data conversion and data entry procedures, 231–32
  output error handling review, 235
  production job turnover, 239–40
  report balancing and reconciliation procedures, 233–34
  report handling and distribution procedures, 234–35
  report retention and security measures, 236
  system logs, 247–48
  tape and disk management systems, 244–47
Input controls, 259
Inside information, 10
Institute of Internal Auditors (IIA)
  Standards Applicable to Communicate Engagement Results, 373–82 (*See also under* Standards Applicable to Communicate Engagement Results)
  Standards Applicable to Monitor Engagement Outcomes, 382–84 (*See also under* Standards Applicable to Monitor Engagement Outcomes)
  Standards Applicable to Operational Role of Internal Audit, 291–95 (*See also under* Standards Applicable to Operational Role of Internal Audit)

Institute of Internal Auditors (IIA) (*continued*)
Standards Applicable to Plan Engagements, 340–55 (*See also under* Standards Applicable to Plan Engagements)
Standards Applicable to Risk-Based Internal Audit Plan, 306–15 (*See also under* Standards Applicable to Risk-Based Internal Audit Plan)
Standards Applicable to Strategic Role of Internal Audit, 13–306 (*See also* Standards)
Standards Applicable to Supervise Engagements, 355–61 (*See also under* Standards Applicable to Supervise Engagements)
Institute of Management Accountants (IMA)
The Role of Analytical Procedures in Detecting Management Fraud, 404
Insurable interest, defined, 479
Insurance, 225–26
defined, 479
function, 273
function, effectiveness of, 130
Internal audit activity, defined, 479
Internal audit charter, 308
Internal audit function
operational role of, 25–302
risk-based internal audit plan, 302–15
sample practice questions, 316–21
strategic role of internal audit, 1–25
TQM and, 29–30
Internal auditing, defined, 479
Internal auditing department, defined, 479
Internal auditor(s), 414
defined, 480
implications for, 408
need to maintain "appearance" of independence by, 305
"Internal Auditors' Guide to a Comprehensive Hazardous Waste Management Program," 275
Internal auditor's role in systems development, 167
Internal audit planning, 308–9
Internal benchmarking, 288
Internal control
defined, 480
questionnaires, 157
system, quality of, 303
training, 284–85
Internal fraud, scope of, 410
Internal sources, 352
International business divisions, 273
International Professional Practices Framework (IPPF), defined, viii, 480
Interrogation or investigative techniques, 405–14
behavior, interpretation of, 416
behavior, nonverbal, 417–18
behavior, verbal, 416–17
common law causes of action, awareness of, 420
fraud investigations, interviewing and interrogating in, 415–16
interrogation techniques, 415–22
interviewer/interrogator, role of, 418

interviewing *vs.* interrogation, 416, 418–22
interviews and interrogations, role of silence in, 418
interview *vs.* investigation, 419
investigative process, 422
investigative techniques, 422–23
objects/subjects, 423
search and seizure, 423
target, 422–23
team composition, 422
truth *vs.* untruth in interviews and interrogations, 420
Interval data, defined, 480
Interval estimate, defined, 480
Interval variable, defined, 480
Inventory
control, 82–83
formulas in, 82
Investigative questions, defined, 480
Irregularities, 266
Irregularities, defined, 480

J
JIT. *See* Just-in-Time (JIT)
Job scheduling review, 237–39
audit objectives, 237
control risk in job documentation, 238
control risk in production schedule, 239
job setup procedures, 237
operational controls, 238
security access controls, 238
special jobs, 239
Joint probability, defined, 480
Judgment and intuition, 305
Judgment sample, defined, 480
Jury duty, 68
Just-in-Time (JIT), 55, 59

K
Kernel tables, 423
Key outside role, 10
Key personnel, recent change in, 304
Kurtosis, defined, 481

L
LAN. *See* local area networks (LAN)
Landekich, Stephen, 1–2
Last audit, time since, 304
Legal department, 274
Libel, 421
Life cycle of a data item, 159
Life cycle of an application system, 158
Link network diagrams, 401
Local area networks (LAN), 191–94
audit objectives, 191
audit procedures, 192–94
business/control risks in local area networks, 193
Logical access security controls, 157
Lot size variance, 109
Loyalty, 3

M
Magnetic media, 430
Mainframe computer audit software, 76

Major impetus, 405–6
Malicious prosecution, 421
Management
competence of, 303
defined, 482
integrity of, 303
responses, 367
review and escalation procedures, effective, 313–14
Managers' bonuses, 13
Manager's performance, 13
Manual(s) development process, 176
Marginal distribution, defined, 482
Marginal probability, defined, 482
Marketing function, 273
Materiality, defined, 331
Material Safety Data Sheets (MSDS), 278
MD4. *See* message digest 4 (MD4)
MD5. *See* message digest 5 (MD5)
MDS. *See* Material Safety Data Sheets (MSDS)
Mean, defined, 482
Mean absolute deviation (MAD), defined, 482
Median, defined, 482
Message digest 4 (MD4), 426–27
Message digest 5 (MD5), 426–27
Microcomputer audit software, 76
Microfiche and microfilm records, controls over, 236–37
microfiche/microfilm processing, accuracy of, 236
microfiche/microfilm record retention periods, 237
storage, distribution, and retrieval procedures, 237
Military and intelligence attacks, 433
Mirroring, 420
Mode, defined, 482
Modeling techniques, 407
Money laundering, 413–14
Money Laundering Act, 413
Monitoring, defined, 482
Morale, level of employees', 304
Morality and dignity, high standards of, 3
MRP system, 78
Multicollinearity, defined, 483
Multiline/multiyear insurance contracts, defined, 470
Multinational corporation, audit concern of a, 115
Multiple-trigger policies, defined, 470
Must, defined, 483
Mutually exclusive event, defined, 483

N
National software reference library (NSRL), 426
Natural disaster preparedness, 215
Natural hedges, defined, 483
Net amount of cash from operations, formula for determining, 411
Net change, 82
Network balancing procedures, 189
Network changes, 195–96
control/audit risks in, 195
Network management systems, 188–91
administration, 188–89

audit objectives, 188
audit procedures, 188–89
control/audit risks in network configuration, 189
control/audit risks in network management, 190
control/audit risks in network performance management, 191
control risk in network administration, 189
control risks in network security, 190
network configuration management, 189–90
network security, 190
network terminal expansion system, 190–91
Network security, 190
Network terminal expansion system, 190–91
Net worth computation methods, 412–13
New-hire testing, 282
Nominal data, defined, 483
Nominal variable, defined, 483
Noncompliance, 266, 483
Normal distribution (curve), defined, 483
NSRL. *See* national software reference library (NSRL)
NSRL's reference data set (RDS) database, 427

O

Objective risk, defined, 483
Objectives, defined, 483
Objectivity, defined, 483
Objects/subjects, 423
Occupational Safety and Health Agency (OSHA), 223, 277
  Hazard Communication Standards, 278
  Poster, 280
  smoking, regulations on, 281
Off-site storage facilities, 219–20
Ombudsman function, 8
On-book and off-book schemes, 412
Online viewing controls, 234
Operating systems, 162–67
  audit objectives, 162–63
  audit procedures, 163
  control options, parameters, and system commands, 166
  risk in systems software administration, controlling, 164
  security over mainframes, workstations, and servers, 167
  software, 164–66
  systems software administration, 163–64
Operating systems software, 164–66
  access security features, 164
  buffer management, 165
  integrity analysis, 165
  performance measurement and accounting, 164–65
Operational
  factors, 274–75
  risk, defined, 482
  role of internal audit, 25–302
Operational applications systems, 258–66
  application system documentation controls review, 263
  application system documentation types and contents, 264

audit objective, 258
audit procedures, 258–66
controls to ensure user satisfaction, 265
data field validation controls, 259
data files, controls over, 261
data input controls review, 258–60
data integrity controls review, 263–64
data origination and preparation controls review, 258
data output controls, 262
data output controls review, 262–63
data processing controls, 260
data processing controls review, 260–61
file maintenance controls review, system-related, 261–62
input controls, 259
user satisfaction review, 264–65
Operational audits
  engagements, 32–34
  expenditure cycle, 33, 48–76 (*See also* expenditure cycle)
  financial reporting cycle, 33, 133–45 (*See also* financial reporting cycle)
  overview diagram for, 33
  overview of, 32–34
  production/conversion cycle, 33, 77–109
  revenue cycle, 33–48 (*See also* revenue cycle)
  treasury cycle, 33, 109–33, Se also under treasury cycle
Operations, complexity of, 303
Operations, defined, 483
Oral reports, 370
Ordinal data, defined, 483
Ordinal variable, defined, 483
Organization strategy, 272–73
Organization structure, 7, 34, 45, 287
OSHA. *See* Occupational Safety and Health Agency (OSHA)
Outlier, defined, 484
Output error handling review, 235
Outside employment, 2
Outside service provider, defined, 484
Ownership interests, 2

P

Parameter, defined, 484
Payroll
  compatible and incompatible functions in, 76
  computer-assisted audit techniques, 76
  sampling in, 76
Performance audit engagements, 32
Performance incentives, 7
Performance measurement
  for buyers, 55
  for suppliers, 55
Performance measurement systems, design of, 290
Peril, defined, 484
Personnel administration, computer-assisted, 68
Physical access controls, 211–12
Physical access security and environmental controls review, 211–16
  air conditioning, 214–15

audit objectives, 211
audit procedures, 211–16
business risks in electrical power, 214
electricity, 214
emergency procedures, documented, 215–16
environmental controls, 216
fire prevention, detection, and suppression procedures, 212–13
housekeeping controls, 212
natural disaster preparedness, 215
physical access controls, 211–12
water damage, 213–14
Plan maintenance procedures, 224
Planning, effective, 313
Planning document, 220–22
Planning materiality, 331–35
  audit planning and evaluation, 333
  audit testing, factors affecting the extent of, 332
  errors, known, 333
  errors, types of, 333
  materiality, how to compute, 335
  materiality, qualitative *vs.* quantitative, 335
  materiality, quantitative and qualitative, 335
  what is material and immaterial?, 334
  who should set the materiality level?, 334
Plausible relationships, 409
Point estimate, defined, 483
Policy of confidentiality, 8
Political
  activities, 12
  contributions, 11
  corruption, 4
  exposure, 305
Pollution prevention audits, 272
Population, defined, 484
Portfolio risk, defined, 484
Post implementation report, 177
Practice advisories, defined, 484
Practice Guide GAIT for Business and IT Risk (GAIT-R), 342
Practice guides, defined, 485
Practice questions. *See* sample practice questions
Precision, defined, 485
Pressure on management to meet objectives, 304
Preventive controls, 151–52, 485
Primary information, 351
Privacy audit engagements, 31–32
Privilege, 374
Privileged reports, 404
Probability, defined, 485
Probability distribution, defined, 485
Probability sampling, defined, 485
Problem recognition and planning, 424
Procedure manual, 161
Process benchmarking, 289
Product audits, 272
Product defects, 7
Production
  function, 273
  job turnover, 239–40
  trouble reports, 177

Production/conversion cycle, 33, 77–109
    cost accounting, 102–9
    fixed assets, 94–100
    introduction to, 77–109
    inventory control, 77–83
    plant maintenance, 100–102
    production control, 83–86
    quality control, 91–94
    shipping, 86–88
    traffic, 88–91
Professional competence, 3
Professionalism, 1, 4
Proficiency, defined, 485
Proficiency and effectiveness, 3
Profit participation in organizations, 2
Programs, defined, 485
Program(s) development process, 176
Program/unit test plan, 176
Proprietary information, 8, 10
Public disclosure, 3
Purchasing
    computer-assisted audit techniques, 54
    computer simulation in, 54
    systems, risks in, 54
    total quality management (TQM) and,
        54–55
Pure risk, defined, 485
Purpose statements, defined, 485

Q
Qualified opinion, 143
Quality assurance, defined, 486
Quality Assurance and Improvement Program
    (QAIP)
    Standard 1300, 294–95
        Practice Advisory 1300-1, 294–95
    Standard 1310, Requirements of, 295
        Practice Advisory 1310-1, 295
Quality audit engagements, 28–29
Quality audit of internal audit function, 29
Quantitative method, 306
Questions. *See* sample practice questions

R
RAM. *See* random access memory (RAM)
Random access memory (RAM), 423
Random number sampling, defined, 486
Random selection, defined, 486
Range, defined, 486
Rapid growth, 304
Rapport, 420
Ratio analysis, 406, 409, 414, 486
Ratio data, defined, 486
Ratio estimate, defined, 486
Ratio variable, defined, 486
Raw materials, 82
Reasonableness test, defined, 486
Receiving, 58
Recommendations, defined, 486
Reconciliations, manual/automated, 158
Record keeping and reporting, 10
Recovery controls, 152–53
Recycling, 274
Regeneration, 82
Regression analysis, defined, 486

Reorder point, 78
Report balancing and reconciliation
        procedures, 233–34
    audit objectives, 233
    balancing and reconciliation, responsibility
        for, 233
    report balancing procedures, 233–34
Report distribution, 370
Report distribution controls, 234–35
Report handling and distribution procedures,
        234–35
    audit objectives, 234
    online viewing controls, 234
    report distribution controls, 234–35
    security access controls, 234
Reporting and follow-up, 275
Reporting results, 431
Report of the National Commission on
    Fraudulent Financial Reporting
    (Treadway Commission), 6, 285,
    405–6, 408
Report presentation, 367–70
    characteristics of, 368
Report retention and security measures, 236
Reports, interim, 362
Reports, oral, 370
Reports, summary, 370
Reprisal against employees, 8
Residual risk, defined, 486
Resource allocation, proper, 314
Resource planning software,
    enterprise-wide, 257
Revenue cycle, 33–48
    accounts receivable audit cycle/area, 37–39
    advertising and sales promotion audit cycle/
        area, 42–44
    billing audit cycle/area, 36–37
    cash receipts audit cycle/area, 39–41
    commissions audit cycle/area, 41–42
    credit management audit cycle/area, 35
    intercompany transfers audit cycle/area,
        47–48
    introduction to, 34
    marketing administration audit cycle/area,
        44–46
    product distribution audit cycle/area, 46–47
    warranty accounting audit cycle/area, 41
Rework variance, 109
Risk(s), 302
    acceptance, defined, 487
    analysis, 218–19
    appetite, defined, 487
    assessment, approaches to, 305–6
    assessment model, steps involved in, 302
    assignment, defined, 487
    avoidance, defined, 487
    business, 175, 214
    control, defined, 487
    current, 307
    defined, 485–56
    factors, defined, 488
    factors, individual, 308
    financing, defined, 488–57
    inherent, 307–8
    limitation, defined, 488

    management, defined, 488
    management processes and systems, 308
    mapping, defined, 489
    mitigation, defined, 489
    monitoring, defined, 489
    in purchasing systems, 54
    registers, 308–9
    registers, defined, 489
    residual, 307–9
    retention, defined, 489
    in sampling, 64
    securitization, defined, 470
    spreading or sharing, defined, 489
    in systems software administration,
        controlling, 164
    transfer, defined, 489
Risk-based internal audit plan, 302–15. *See
    also* Standards Applicable to Risk-
    Based Internal Audit Plan
    about, 302
    audit risk factors, 302–5
    benchmark, ways to, 305
    risk assessment, approaches to, 305–6
    risk assessment model, steps involved
        in, 302
*The Role of Analytical Procedures in Detecting
    Management Fraud* (IMA), 404

S
Safeguards to protect evidence, 426
Safety, 277
Safety responsibility, 277–78
Salami technique, 434
Sales/billing/invoicing
    computer-assisted audit techniques, 37
Sample, defined, 489
Sample practice questions, answers, and
    explanations. *See also* certified Internal
    Auditors (CIAs)
    fraud risks and controls, 436–37, 489–91
    managing individual engagements, 385–90,
        476–87
    managing the internal audit function,
        316–21, 493–75
Sampling
    distribution, defined, 489
    frame, defined, 488
    with replacement, defined, 490
    techniques, 414
    without replacement, defined, 490
Scope limitation, defined, 489
Scoring approach, 305
Scrap variance, 109
Search and seizure, 423
Search warrants, 399
Secure hash algorithm (SHA-1), 426–27
Security, 279
    access controls, 234
    over mainframes, workstations, and
        servers, 167
    violations, 210
Security audit engagements, 30–31
Security violations, 189
Segregation of duties, 161–62
Self-evaluative privileges, 374

Self-insurance, defined, 490
Senior management, defined, 490
Service goals, 77
Sexual harassment, 12, 277, 284
SHA-1. *See* secure hash algorithm (SHA-1)
Should, defined, 490
Shutdown checklist, 213
Sick leave, 68
Significance, defined, 490
Significant audit findings, defined, 491
Simple random sample, defined, 491
Single-source strategies, 55
Site tidiness, 274
Skewed distribution, defined, 491
Slander, 421
Smoking policy, 277, 281–82
Social decay, 4
Software acquisition, 178
    audit objectives, 178
    audit procedures, 178
    control risks in, 178
Software development, 173–77
    audit objectives, 173–74
    audit procedures, 174
    business/control risks in feasibility study
        phase, 174
    business/control risks in
        postimplementation phase, 177
    business/control risks in system design
        phase, 175
    business risks in detail requirements
        phase, 175
    control risks in conversion and production
        support phases, 177
    control risks in program development
        phase, 176
    control risks in user acceptance phase, 177
Software forensics, 425–27
Software licensing
    audit objectives and procedures, 249–50
    information systems contracts, 250
    software licensing practices, 249
    software piracy policies, 249
Software maintenance or program change
    control
    audit objectives, 178
    audit objectives and procedures, 178–80
    audit procedures, 178–79
Software piracy policies, 249
Software prototyping, 180–82
    audit objectives, 180
    audit procedures, 180–82
    control/audit risks in, 181–82
Software security controls review
    access control security software review—
        audit objectives and procedures,
        196–206
    access controls over production libraries,
        199
    access controls over production program
        changes, 204
    access security rules, 198
    administrative procedures, 201
    audit/control risks in data
        communications, 205

audit/control risks in insiders and
    outsiders, 203
audit testing of security controls, 204
audit trails and reports, 201
control options and parameters, 197
controls over security administration, 200
data ownership and separation of storage
    resources, 198
interface validations, 197
logical access control security software,
    Implementation of, 197–201
operational procedures, 200
protection over programs and libraries, 199
security over applications software, general
    audit procedures for, 203–4
security over computer terminals, general
    audit procedures for, 205–6
security over data communications software,
    general audit procedures for, 205
security over systems software, general audit
    procedures for, 201–3
sensitive privileges, 198
system and user exits, 198
system logging of events, 199–200
Speculative risk, defined, 491
Spoilage variance, 109
Spread, defined, 491
Staff training and participation, 273
Standards. *See* Institute of Internal Auditors
    (IIA)
Standard(s)
    defined, 491
    deviation, defined, 491
    error of the mean, defined, 491
    revision variance, 109
Standards Applicable To Communicate
    Engagement Results, 373–82
Communicating Results (Standard
    2400), 373
    Legal Considerations in Communicating
        Results (Practice Advisory 2400-1),
        373–74
Criteria for Communicating (Standard
    2410), 374–75
    Communication Criteria (Practice
        Advisory 2410-1), 375–77
Disseminating Results (Standard 2470),
    378–81
    Communicating Sensitive Information
        Within and Outside the Chain of
        Command (Practice Advisory 2470-2),
        379–80
    Communications Outside the
        Organization (Practice Advisory 2470.
        A2-1), 380–81
    Disseminating Results (Practice Advisory
        2470-1), 378–79
Engagement Disclosure of Nonconformance
    (Standard 2431), 378
Errors and Omissions (Standard 2421), 377
Overall Opinions (Standard 2480), 381–82
Quality of Communications (Standard
    2420), 377
    Quality of Communications (Practice
        Advisory 2420-1), 377

Use of *"Conducted in Conformance with
    the International Standards for the
    Professional Practice of Internal
    Auditing"* (Standard 2430), 377
Standards Applicable to Monitor Engagement
    Outcomes, 382–84
    Monitoring Progress (Standard 2500),
        382–83
        Follow-up Process (Practice Advisory
            2500.A1-1), 383–84
        Monitoring Progress (Practice Advisory
            2500-1), 283
    Resolution of Senior Management's
        Acceptance of Risks (Standard 2600), 384
Standards Applicable to Operational Role of
    Internal Audit, 291–301
    Control (Standard 2130), 291
        Assessing the Adequacy of Control
            Processes (Practice Advisory 2130-1),
            291–92
        Evaluating an Organization's Privacy
            Framework (Practice Advisory 2130-
            A1-2), 293–94
        Information Reliability and Integrity
            (Practice Advisory 2130.A1-1), 292–93
    External Assessments (Standard 1312),
        297–301
        External Assessments (Practice Advisory
            1312-1), 297–300
        External Assessments: Self-Assessment
            with Independent Validation (Practice
            Advisory 1312-2), 300–301
    External Service Provider and
        Organizational Responsibility for
        Internal Auditing (Standard 2070), 302
    Internal Assessments (Standard 1311),
        296–97
        Internal Assessments (Practice Advisory
            1311-1), 296–97
    Quality Assurance and Improvement
        Program (QAIP) (Standard 1300),
        294–95
    QAIP Practice Advisory 1300-1, 294–95
    Reporting on the Quality Assurance and
        Improvement Program (Standard
        1320), 301
    Requirements of Quality Assurance and
        Improvement Program (QAIP)
        (Standard 1310), 295
    QAIP Practice Advisory 1310-1, 295
Standards Applicable to Plan Engagements,
    340–55
    Engagement Objectives (Standard
        2210), 344
        Engagement Objectives (Practice
            Advisory 2210-1), 344
        Risk Assessment in Engagement Planning
            (Practice Advisory 2210.A1-1), 344–45
    Engagement Planning (Standard 220), 340
    Audit Work at Headquarters and Field
        Offices, 340
    Controls to Be Assessed in an Internal
        Audit Engagement, Top-Down
        Risk-Based Approach to Identify the
        (Practice Advisory 2200-2), 342–43

Standards Applicable to Plan Engagements (*continued*)
Engagement Planning (Practice Advisory 2200-1), 341
Engagement Resource Allocation (Standard 2230), 346
Engagement Resource Allocation (Practice Advisory 2230-1), 346
Engagement Scope (Standard 2220), 345
Engagement Work Program (Standard 2240), 346–47
Engagement Work Program (Practice Advisory 2240-1), 347
Planning Considerations (Standard 2201), 343
Resource Management (Standard 2030), 345
Resource Management (Practice Advisory 2030-1), 345–46
Standards Applicable to Risk-Based Internal Audit Plan
Planning (Standard 2010), 306
Audit Plan Linked to Risk and Exposures (Practice Advisory 2010-1), 306–7
Risk Management Process used in Internal Audit Planning (Practice Advisory 2010-2), 307–9
Risk Management (Standard 2120), 310–15
Interpretation, 310
Risk Management Processes, Assessing the Adequacy of (Practice Advisory 2120-1), 310–12
Risk of the Internal Audit Activity, Managing the (Practice Advisory 2120-2), 312–15
Standards Applicable to Strategic Role of Internal Audit, 13–306
Communication and Approval (Standard 2020), 14
Communication and Approval (Practice Advisory 2020-1), 14
Control (Standard 2130), 24–25
Coordination (Standard 2050), 17–22
Assurance Maps (Practice Advisory 2050-2), 19–21
Coordination (Practice Advisory 2050-1), 18
Relying on the Work of Other Assurance Providers (Practice Advisory 2050-3), 21–22
Direct Interaction with the Board (Standard 1111), 13–44
Board Interaction (Practice Advisory 1111-1), 13–14
Governance (Standard 2110), 15–17
Governance: Assessments (Practice Advisory 2110-3), 17
Governance: Definition (Practice Advisory 2110-1), 15–16
Governance: Relationship with Risk and Control (Practice Advisory 2110-2), 16
Managing the Internal Audit Activity (Standard 2000), 14
Nature of Work (Standard 2100), 15
Policies and Procedures (Standard 2040), 14–15

Policies and Procedures (Practice Advisory 2040-1), 15
Reporting to Senior Management and the Board (Standard 2060), 23
Reporting to Senior Management and the Board (Practice Advisory 2060-1), 23
Risk Management (Standard 2120), 23–24
Standards Applicable to Supervise Engagements, 355–61
Analysis and Evaluation (Standard 2320), 356–57
Analytical Procedures (Practice Advisory 2320-1), 356–57
Documenting Information (Standard 2330), 357–60
Control of Engagement Records (Practice Advisory 2330.A1-1), 358–59
Documenting Information (Practice Advisory 2330-1), 358
Granting Access to Engagement Records (Practice Advisory 2330.A1-2), 359–60
Retention of Records (Practice Advisory 2330.A2-1), 360
Engagement Supervision (Standard 2340), 360–61
Engagement Supervision (Practice Advisory 2340-1), 360–61
Identifying Information (Standard 2310), 356
Performing the Engagement (Standard 2300), 355–56
Personal Information Use in Conducting Engagements (Practice Advisory 2300-1), 355–56
Statement of Accounting Standards 47, 332
Statement of cash flows, 410–11
Static risk, defined, 491
Statistic, defined, 492
Statistical estimate, defined, 492
Statistical reports, 209
Strata, defined, 492
Strategic benchmarking, 289
Strategic risk, defined, 492
Strategic role of internal audit, 1–25
code of conduct, monitoring compliance with the, 6
code of ethics, role of corporate, 1–2
conflicts of interest, 2–3
ethical behavior, options for facilitating, 5–6
ethical standards, factors influencing, 3–4
ethical standards in complex situations, integrating, 13
fraud in financial reporting, 6–9
Stratified random sample, defined, 490
Subjective risk, defined, 492
Subpoenas, 399
Substance abuse policy, 277, 282–83
Supervision, defined, 492
Supervisor calls (SVCs), 163
SuperZapping, 434
Survey, defined, 492
SVCs. *See* supervisor calls (SVCs)
Swap space, 423
Symmetric measure of association, defined, 492
System
aging analysis, 147

assets are safeguarded, 145
availability is ensured, 145
controllability is maintained, 145
defined, 492
economy and efficiency are maintained, 145
effectiveness is ensured, 145
interruption impact analysis, 147
logging of events, 199–200
maintainability is ensured, 145
outage analysis, 147
quality is maintained, 145
reliability is ensured, 145
resource utilization statistical analysis, 147
security is ensured, 145
software controls, 149
storage media analysis, 147
usability is ensured, 145
user exits and, 198
System application development, 167–70
audit approaches to, 168–70
auditing software development, acquisition, and maintenance, 168–70
auditor participation in system development process, 168
how much auditor participation is enough?, 168
internal auditor's role in systems development, 167
risk factors, 170
Systematic selection with a random start, defined, 493
System logs, 247–48
audit objectives, 247
system logging facility access controls, 247
system logging facility event recording, 247
system logging facility reporting, 247–48
Systems design reports, detail, 175
Systems design reports, general, 175
Systems development
internal auditor's role in, 167
what went wrong in, 186
System security, 196–216
about, 196
software security controls review: access control security software review—audit objectives and procedures, 196–206
Systems software administration, 163–64
Systems software changes, 166–67
emergency database systems software changes, 166–67
master catalogue changes, 167
systems software changes, 166
Systems test plan, 176
System utility programs, 191

T
Tape and disk management systems, 244–47
audit/control risks in computer storage media, 246–47
audit objectives, 244
audit procedures for disk management system, 246–47
audit procedures for tape management system, 245–46
control risk in tape library, 246

file labels, external and internal, 245
 header (first) record, 245
 trailer (last) record, 245
Target, 422–23
Team composition, 422
Technology-based audit techniques,
      defined, 493
Telecommunications and networks
   what went wrong in, 195–96
Telephone usage, 277, 281
Termination procedures, 66
Terrorist attacks, 434
Test data method, 64
Testing and recovery procedures, 223–24
Third parties
   and contract auditing, audits of, 25–27
   overview of, 25–27
32-bit cyclic redundancy checksum (CRC32),
      426–27
Time flow diagrams, 401
Time lag, 60
Tolerable error, defined, 493
Toll fraud, 434
Total quality management (TQM)
   JIT receiving and, 59
   purchasing and, 54–55
Training plan, 176
Transactional audits, 272
Transport, 274
Transportation department, audit approach
      in, 91
Travel and entertainment, 10
Treadway Commission. *See* Report of the
      National Commission on Fraudulent
      Financial Reporting (Treadway
      Commission)

Treasury cycle, 33, 109–33
   cash management, 112–15
   debt management, 109–12
   dividends management, 125–27
   equity management, 116–21
   foreign currency exchange management,
      130–32
   investment management, 122–25
   risk and insurance management, 128–30
   write-off accounting, 132–33
Treatment, storage, and disposal facility
      audits, 272
Trend analysis, 406, 493
Truth *vs.* untruth in interviews and
      interrogations, 420

U
Understanding, defined, 493
Unethical acts, 4
Uninterruptible power supply (UPS), 214,
      216, 221
Unobtrusive measures, defined, 493
Unqualified opinion, 143
UPS. *See* uninterruptible power supply (UPS)
User acceptance, 176
User procedures, functional, 222
User satisfaction review, 264–65
User service request report, 174
U.S. Internal Revenue Service, 280

V
Value-added network, 194
Value-added network (VAN), 190
VAN. *See* value-added network (VAN)
VAN security procedures and controls, 254
Variable sampling, defined, 493

Variance
   burden efficiency, 108
   burden expenditure, 108
   burden volume, 108
   calculations, 108
   defined, 492
   lot size, 109
   rework, 109
   scrap, 109
   spoilage, 109
   standard revision, 109
VDU/CRT. *See* video display unit
      (VDU/CRT)
Vendor certification, 55
Vertical analysis, 410
Video display unit (VDU/CRT), 172–73
Vital records retention program, 224–25
Voice communications, 196
Volume table of contents (VTOC), 163
Voluntary consent, 399

W
Water damage, 213–14
Water use, 274
Web-based online test bank software, xi
Web infrastructure, 249
Whistle-blowers/whistle-blowing, 379–80
White-collar crimes, 414
Wide area network, 195
WIP inventory, 82
Wiretapping, 433
Wire transfer systems, 251–52
Witness statements, 404
Workers' compensation laws, 280
Work measurement, defined, 493
Worship of the dollar, 4